9/4/01

BEACHAM'S GUIDE
to the
ENDANGERED SPECIES
of NORTH AMERICA

BEACHAM'S GUIDE
to the
ENDANGERED SPECIES
of NORTH AMERICA

Volume 2
Amphibians, Fishes, Snails, Mussels and Clams

Edited By
Walton Beacham
Frank V. Castronova
Suzanne Sessine

GALE GROUP

Detroit
New York
San Francisco
London
Boston
Woodbridge, CT

Frank V. Castronova, *Senior Editor*
Walton Beacham, *Editor*
Zoran Minderović, Suzanne Sessine, Ellen Thackery, *Associate Editors*
Stacey Blachford, Deirdre S. Blanchfield, Kelli M. Closner, Melissa C. McDade, *Assistant Editors*
Amy Loerch Strumolo, Christine B. Jeryan, *Contributing Editors*
Laura Bergheim, *Research Editor*

Victoria B. Cariappa, *Research Manager*
Tim Lehnerer, *Research Assistant*

Theresa Rocklin, *Director, Technical Support Services*
Richard Antonowicz, Nataliya Mikheyeva, *Programmer/Analysts*
Luann Brennan, Mary K. Fyke, Mark Springer, *Technical Training Specialists*

Ronald D. Montgomery, *Manager, Data Capture*
Gwendolyn S. Tucker, *Project Administrator, Data Capture*
Beverly Jendrowski, *Data Capture Specialist*
Civie A. Green, *Data Capture Associate*

Mary Beth Trimper, *Manager, Composition*
Evi Seoud, *Assistant Manager, Composition Purchasing and Electronic Prepress*
Dorothy Maki, *Manufacturing Manager*
Wendy Blurton, *Senior Buyer*

Maria Franklin, *Permissions Manager*
Sarah Tomasek, *Permissions Associate*

Cynthia Baldwin, *Senior Art Director*
Mike Logusz, *Graphic Artist*

Barbara Yarrow, *Manager, Imaging and Multimedia Content*
Randy Bassett, *Imaging Supervisor*
Robert Duncan, *Senior Imaging Specialist*
Dan Newell, *Imaging Specialist*
Leitha Etheridge-Sims, Mary Grimes, *Image Cataloguers*
Robyn V. Young, *Senior Editor, Image Acquisitions*
Deborah Beacham, *Photo Editor*

Library of Congress Cataloging-in-Publication Data

Beacham's guide to the endangered species of North America / edited by Walton Beacham, Frank V. Castronova, Suzanne Sessine.
    p. cm.
    Includes bibliographical references.
    ISBN 0-7876-5028-5 (set: hardcover)—ISBN 0-7876-5029-3 (vol. 1)—ISBN 0-7876-5030-7 (vol. 2)—ISBN 0-7876-5031-5 (vol. 3)—ISBN 0-7876-5032-3 (vol. 4) —ISBN 0-7876-5033-1 (vol. 5)—ISBN 0-7876-5034-X (vol. 6)
    1. Endangered species—North America. 2. Nature conservation—North America. I. Beacham, Walton, 1943- . II. Castronova, Frank V. (Frank Vincent), 1971- . III. Sessine, Suzanne, 1976- .
QH77.N56 B43 2000
578.68'0973—dc21   00-062297

10 9 8 7 6 5 4 3 2 1
Printed in Canada

Contents

Introduction vii

Mammals 1:1

Birds 1:247

Reptiles 1:533

Amphibians 2:677

Fishes 2:743

Snails 2:1093

Mussels and Clams 2:1169

Arachnids and Crustaceans 3:1357

Insects 3:1439

Lichens 3:1543

Fern Allies 3:1553

True Ferns 3:1569

Conifers 3:1619

Dicots 3:1633

Monocots 6:3157

Glossary 6:3343

Organizations 6:3369

Geographic Index 6:3373

Master Index 6:3407

Introduction

Scope

Beacham's Guide to the Endangered Species of North America describes more than 1,200 animals and plants that occur in North America both within and outside the boundaries of the United States of America. These volumes cover species that were identified before April 2000 by the U. S. Fish and Wildlife Service (FWS) as either Endangered or Threatened. This set of books supercedes and updates *The Official World Wildlife Fund Guide to the Endangered Species of North America*, which was published by Beacham Publishing, Inc., in 1990-94.

The species described herein have been identified as Endangered or Threatened by the FWS. Inclusion on the federal list prohibits any governmental agency from initiating or funding activities that might have adverse impacts on an endangered or threatened species (such as activities that cause habitat degradation). Also, the importation and sale of these endangered species or any derived products is restricted within the boundaries of the United States.

How to Use This Set of Books

The species are arranged taxonomically. Volume 1 includes mammals, birds, and reptiles; amphibians, fishes, snails, and mussels and clams are in volume 2; in volume 3 are arachnids and crustaceans, insects, lichens, fern allies, true ferns, and conifers; dicots can be found at the end of volume 3 and in volumes 4, 5, and 6; monocots are in volume 6. Each species account begins with the species' common and scientific names. Most entries will also include one or more full-color images of the species described. Following this, the user will find a **Summary** section, which outlines the key information found within the species account. Within this section is found: the species' status as determined by the FWS; the date listed by the FWS; the family to which the species belongs; and brief descriptions of the following (if applicable or known): physical description, habitat, food, reproduction, threats, and the range of states, countries, or geographical regions in which the species occurs.

The main body of each species account begins with the **Description** section, which provides a general description of the plant's or animal's physical characteristics.

Behavior describes reproductive information, social organization and behavior, and dietary preferences and requirements.

Habitat describes the species' preferred habitat.

Distribution describes where the species can be currently found and where the species may have been found in the past.

Threats describes the natural or human-made events which have led to the decline of the species' population, and potential threats.

Conservation and Recovery describes conservation efforts and the survival outlook for the species.

Contacts lists street addresses, telephone and facsimile numbers, and web addresses for organizations which can be of assistance to the researcher.

In the **References** section are sources that the user can use to gain more information on the species.

In volume 6 the following appendices and indexes are found:

The **Glossary** provides definitions of specialized terms used throughout the text of the book.

The **Organizations** appendix lists agencies that focus on environmental and wildlife issues.

The **Geographic Index** is organized by country, body of water, or other geographical area, and arranges species alphabetically within each geographical division.

The **Master Index** lists the species alphabetically by common name and by scientific name, with references to its nominal counterpart, and also includes variant common and scientific names.

Acknowledgment

Special thanks are due to Dr. Bill Freedman, Professor of Biology at Dalhousie University, Halifax, Nova Scotia, Canada, for his editorial and research efforts related to this project.

Comments and Suggestions are Welcome

The editors invite comments and suggestions from users of *Beacham's Guide to the Endangered Species of North America.* You may contact us by mail at: The Editors, *Beacham's Guide to the Endangered Species of North America,* Gale Group, Inc., 27500 Drake Rd., Farmington Hills, MI 48331-3535; by telephone at (248) 699-4253 or (800) 347-4253; or by facsimile at (248) 699-8065. Our web site is http://www.galegroup.com.

Photo Acknowledgments

These photos are on the covers of all six volumes of *Beacham's Guide to the Endangered Species of North America* (clockwise from upper left): Mitchell's Satyr Butterfly, Larry West, U. S. Fish and Wildlife Service; Cactus Ferruginous Pygmy-owl, George Andrejko; Pitkin Marsh Lily, Robert J. Gustafson; Louisiana Black Bear, Louisiana Department of Wildlife and Fish.

These photos appear on the spines of each volume: volume 1, Tipton Kangaroo Rat, B. "Moose" Peterson/WRP; volume 2, Puerto Rican Crested Toad, David M. Dennis; volume 3, Silvery Blue Butterfly *(Glaucopsyche lygdamus),* George Proctor; volume 4, Stebbins' Morning-glory, Rich York; volume 5, Hoffman's Slender-flowered Gilia, Steve Junak; volume 6, Thread-leaved Brodiaea, B. "Moose" Peterson/WRP.

Amphibians

Wyoming Toad

Bufo hemiophrys baxteri

Wyoming Toad, photograph. U. S. Fish and Wildlife Service. Reproduced by permission.

Status	Endangered
Listed	January 17, 1984
Family	Bufonidae (Toad)
Description	Small, crested toad.
Habitat	Marshy areas adjacent to the Laramie River in Wyoming.
Food	Insects and larvae.
Reproduction	Lays egg masses in standing pools.
Threats	Herbicides, predation, irrigation practices.
Range	Wyoming

Description

The Wyoming toad, the only toad in the Laramie Basin, is a small bufonid about 2 in (5 cm) long with crests on the head that form a humped ridge. Light brown with dark blotches, the body is covered with many warts.

The Canadian toad (*Bufo hemiophrys hemiophrys*), a closely related species, occurs in Manitoba, Alberta, Saskatchewan, Minnesota, Montana, and the Dakotas. Some scientists argue that the Wyoming toad is a full species, rather than a subspecies. Further research is needed to determine this toad's precise taxonomic classification.

Behavior

The tadpole of the Wyoming toad feeds primarily on plant matter, but the full-grown toad preys on insects, larvae, and any small organism that moves. Because of poor eyesight, the toad tends to miss motionless prey. The female discharges eggs in strips of jelly in standing pools. The male clings to her back and fertilizes the eggs as they reach the water. Tadpoles hatch between three and 20 days later, depending on the water temperature, and begin to metamorphose. The toad develops hind limbs first, then front limbs; as the lungs develop, its tail gets shorter and gradually disappears.

Habitat

This species is found in wetlands adjacent to the Laramie River in the Laramie Basin. It is strongly aquatic, spending most of its time in and around water.

Distribution

The Wyoming toad was once common in the Laramie River basin in southeastern Wyoming and probably inhabited similar marshy habitats in other parts of the state. Fossils found throughout the region suggest that the species was abundant thousands of years ago. Researchers from the University of Wyoming have monitored breeding sites annually since 1945 and became alarmed when their 1978 and 1979 surveys found very few toads.

In 1980 the University of Wyoming and the U.S. Fish and Wildlife Service (FWS) conducted an extensive survey of the Laramie Basin. A single population of the toad was located on private land in Albany County, where a number of males were heard calling, but no females, tadpoles, or eggs were found. The 40-acre (16-hectare) site was thought to support about 25 individuals. A survey of this site in 1983 revealed only two toads, and in the following year, none.

In 1987, a new population was discovered on private land in Albany County, which considerably brightens the Wyoming toad's chances for survival. The new site—about 10 mi (16 km) west of Laramie—is home to about 200 toads, which scientists consider a fairly good breeding population.

Threats

The reasons for the toad's basin-wide disappearance are not understood, but the leopard frog (*Rana pipiens*), once fairly common, has also disappeared from the Laramie Basin. Scientists believe that the decline of both toads may be linked with herbicide application. Herbicides have been used by the Wyoming Department of Agriculture for weed control in roadside ponds and along field edges typically used by the Wyoming toad. Regional aerial application of Baytex (Fenthion) with diesel fuel began in 1975 to kill mosquitoes. The combination of Baytex and diesel fuel is highly toxic to toads and frogs. Predation may also be a factor in the sudden decline of the Wyoming toad. The California gull has become more numerous in recent years. Local ranchers report that fields are sometimes "white with gulls" in early spring when toads are breeding. Other predators, such as raccoons, foxes, and skunks have all increased in number.

Conservation and Recovery

By 1994 the Wyoming Game and Fish Department had brought into captivity the last known wild Wyoming toad populations in an effort to prevent the species from becoming extinct. The Wyoming Game and Fish Department, along with the FWS,

started the Wyoming Toad Recovery program. Three zoos—Cheyenne Mountain Zoological Park, Omaha's Henry Doorly Zoo, and Toledo Zoological Gardens—received tadpoles and toads.

The recovery efforts have not always gone smoothly. There are a number of husbandry issues, including climate simulation and diet, that have to be resolved in order to prevent the loss of the captive populations. The toads also are very susceptible to "red leg", a bacterial infection, which has been one of the leading causes of death. Experts from zoos have been advising the various government agencies in their efforts to improve the husbandry techniques and discover the underlying factors involved with the high incidence of red leg. This husbandry advice from zoo professionals has led to a dramatic decrease in the mortality rate, dropping from around 50% to less than 10%.

Zoos have also had a great impact on the captive breeding of the Wyoming toad. They studied the breeding season of the toads and discovered several factors that need to be present in order to greatly increase the chances of successful breeding. They have worked with the government officials to determine the effects of male and female hibernation on reproduction. Zoos have also shown others involved in the recovery program how to use synthetic hormones to induce the toads to lay eggs.

As a result of the improved breeding and husbandry techniques, the captive population greatly increased in 1995, allowing many animals to be released back into the wild. To increase their chances for survival, the tadpoles were placed in head start tanks at the release sites. These are wading pools, covered with screen, that house tadpoles and toadlets. Tadpoles and toadlets have separate tanks, allowing for the different needs. The tanks are checked regularly to remove toadlets from the tadpole tank and to make sure that the toadlets are not able to escape through gaps between the screen and the pool wall. Measures have also been taken at the release sites to protect the tanks from grazing cattle and to biologically control the mosquito populations without pesticides. During the summer months, tadpoles and toadlets were released at three different lakes in the Laramie area: Lake George, Rush Lake, and Mortenson Lake. These sites will be monitored closely over the next few years to see if Wyoming toads are able to reestablish their place in the wild.

Contact

U.S. Fish and Wildlife Service
Regional Office, Division of Endangered Species
P.O. Box 25486
Denver Federal Center
Denver, Colorado 80225
http://www.r6.fws.gov/

References

Baxter, G. T., and M. Stone. 1980. "Amphibians and Reptiles of Wyoming." Wyoming Game and Fish Department Bulletin, Laramie.

Porter, K. P. 1968. "Evolutionary Status of a Relict Population of *Bufo hemiophrys* Cope." *Evolution* 22: 583-594.

Swaringen, Karen. March 1996. American Zoological Association. "AZA Conservation Spotlight."

Houston Toad

Bufo houstonensis

Status	Endangered
Listed	October 13, 1970
Family	Bufonidae (Toad)
Description	Brown, dark-spotted toad with a distinctive call.
Habitat	Permanent or seasonal wetlands.
Food	Insects.
Reproduction	Egg masses of between 500 and 6,000 eggs.
Threats	Loss of wetlands, urbanization.
Range	Texas

Description

The Houston toad is brown (occasionally reddish) with dark brown or black spots. Its back is covered with single or multiple fused warts. Females reach up to 3.2 in (8 cm) in length; males average slightly smaller. The Houston toad is similar to the dwarf American toad (*Bufo americanus charlesmithi*) but displays larger crests behind the eye sockets. The toad's mating call is described as similar to the tinkling of a small bell.

Behavior

The Houston toad uses rain pools, flooded fields, and natural or man-made ponds for breeding, which occurs at sporadic intervals. Females reach sexual maturity at about two years of age. Breeding begins in spring when the air temperature rises above 57°F (14°C). Masses of between 500 and 6,000 eggs are laid between mid-February and late June. For tadpoles to develop, pools must persist for at least 60 days. After breeding, the toad seeks refuge in leaf litter, under logs, or in burrows.

Habitat

Houston toads are found in seasonal or permanent ponds but are restricted to sandy loams that are suitable for burrowing. Surrounding vegetation varies from mixed deciduous forest to open coastal prairie grasslands. When spring rains are below normal, ponds dry up prematurely, killing tadpoles before they can metamorphose.

Distribution

Historically, the Houston toad ranged across the central coastal region of Texas. Population sites have been documented from Austin, Bastrop, Burleson, Colorado, Fort Bend, Harris, and Liberty counties.

The Houston toad is currently thought to survive near Austin in Bastrop County wetlands north of the Colorado River, in Burleson County south of Bryan (around Lake Woodrow), and in Harris County south of Hobby Airport. Several small, experimental populations were recently established in Colorado County.

The largest population is found in Bastrop County on state lands within Bastrop and Buescher state parks and an adjacent nature preserve. This population has increased in recent years and may number as many as 1,500 individuals. Low numbers of toads (probably under 50) still exist in Burleson County but often fail to breed because of insufficient water. The Houston toad has not been seen in Harris County since 1976 but may survive there. The toad's sporadic breeding pattern and secretive nature make it difficult to find new populations or even to relocate previously identified ones.

Houston Toad, photograph by C. Kenneth Dodd, Jr., USGS. Reproduced by permission.

Threats

Drought in the 1950s sharply curtailed Houston toad numbers, and the subsequent expansion of the Austin and Houston metropolitan areas has permanently reduced the toad's habitat. Wetlands have been replaced with residential suburbs and related developments. In the mid-1960s, large tracts of forest in Bastrop County along the Colorado River were cleared for residential development and for recreational sites. Road construction and the laying of sewage lines significantly altered drainage patterns in the region, drying out many seasonal ponds. The University of Texas Environmental Science Park (Buescher Division) was established in 1971, comprising 720 acres (291 hectares) adjacent to Buescher State Park in Bastrop County. Much of this area is now maintained as a nature preserve and is managed to enhance the habitat needs of the Houston toad. In 1979, 1,400 acres (570 hectares) were added to this preserve, including land previously designated as Critical Habitat for the toad.

Conservation and Recovery

In the early 1980s, biologists implemented a propagation program at the Houston Zoo and subsequently released captive-bred toads at the Bastrop County Preserve and at the Attwater Prairie Chicken National Wildlife Refuge in Colorado County. Egg masses were also moved from Bastrop County to ponds in Colorado County in an attempt to expand the toad's distribution.

Contact

U.S. Fish and Wildlife Service
Regional Office, Division of Endangered Species
P.O. Box 1306
Albuquerque, New Mexico 87103-1306
Telephone: (505) 248-6911
Fax: (505) 248-6915
http://southwest.fws.gov/

References

Hillis, D. M., et al. 1984. "Reproductive Ecology and Hybridization of the Endangered Houston Toad." *Journal of Herpetology* 18: 56-72.

U.S. Fish and Wildlife Service. 1984. "Houston Toad Recovery Plan." U.S. Fish and Wildlife Service, Albuquerque.

Arroyo Toad

Bufo microscaphus californicus

Arroyo Toad, photograph by B. "Moose" Peterson/WRP. Reproduced by permission.

Status	Endangered
Listed	December 16, 1994
Family	Bufonidae
Description	A small light greenish gray or tan toad with warty skin and dark spots.
Habitat	Rivers with shallow, gravelly pools adjacent to sandy terraces, and associated terrestrial habitat.
Food	Adults eat terrestrial invertebrates; larvae feed on algae and organic detritus.
Reproduction	Lays eggs in water, which hatch into aquatic larvae, which metamorphose into small toads.
Threats	Habitat destruction and degradation by riverine management and impoundment, predation, pollution, and other stressors.
Range	California

Description

The *Bufo microscaphus californicus* (arroyo toad) is a small toad in the family Bufonidae, measuring 2-3 in (5-8 cm). It is a light greenish gray or tan toad with warty skin and dark spots. Its underside is buff colored and often without spots. A light-colored stripe crosses the head and eyelids, and a light area usually occurs on each sacral hump and in the middle of the back.

This taxon was originally described as *B. cognatus californicus* from a specimen collected at Santa Paula, Ventura County in 1915. The specimen was later shown to differ in several respects from *B. cognatus* and was afforded specific status as *B. californicus*. In the following two decades, this toad was considered a subspecies of *B. compactilis* and of *B. woodhousei*. The currently accepted taxonomy of the arroyo toad as a subspecies of *B. microscaphus*, the southwestern toad, is based on morphological similarities. The arroyo toad is geographically isolated from the Arizona toad by the

Mojave and Colorado Deserts. Work is now in progress to determine if the arroyo toad is genetically distinct.

Behavior

The arroyo toad's movement consists of hopping rather than walking, and prefers shallow pools and open, sandy stream terraces. Its courtship vocalization is a high trill, usually lasting eight to 10 seconds and breeding occurs on large streams with persistent water from late March until mid-June. Eggs are deposited and larvae develop in shallow pools with minimal current and little or no emergent vegetation and with sand or pea gravel substrate overlain with flocculent silt. After metamorphosis, the juvenile toads remain on the bordering gravel bars until the pool dissipates. Adult toads excavate shallow burrows on the terraces where they shelter during the day when the surface is damp or during longer intervals in the dry season

Habitat

The arroyo toad is restricted to rivers that have shallow, gravelly pools adjacent to sandy terraces. Juveniles and adults forage for insects on sandy stream terraces that have nearly complete closure of cottonwoods, oaks, or willows, and almost no grass or herbaceous cover at ground level. It also uses upland habitats up to a half mile from the stream for feeding and overwintering.

Distribution

Arroyo toads were historically found along the length of drainages in southern California from San Luis Obispo County to San Diego County, but now they survive primarily in the headwaters as small isolated populations. Urbanization and dam construction beginning in the early 1900s in southern California caused most of the extensive habitat degradation. The species was formerly distributed southward along the northwestern coastal region of Baja California, Mexico, to the vicinity of San Quintin.

Most remaining populations in the United States occur on privately owned lands, primarily within or adjacent to the Cleveland National Forest. Less than 50% of the known extant populations of arroyo toad occur in areas owned or managed by the Forest Service. Due mostly to habitat destruction, only eight drainages remain where populations of this species may be viable. In 1990, only seven pairs of arroyo toads were known to have bred anywhere within the toad's range . Due to the isolation and the small sizes, almost all populations are at great risk of extinction.

Threats

Activities that could potentially result in the loss of the arroyo toad, include, but are not limited to, unauthorized collecting or capture of the species, except as noted above to momentarily move an individual out of harm's way; introduction of exotic species into occupied habitat; unauthorized destruction/alteration of the species' habitat; violation of a construction, discharge or withdrawal permit that affects occupied habitat; pesticide applications affecting occupied habitat in violation of label restrictions; or other illegal discharges or dumping of toxic chemicals, silt, or other pollutants into waters supporting the species.

Habitat destruction and alteration constitutes the most severe threat facing the arroyo toad. This toad is now confined to the headwaters of streams it occupied historically along their entire lengths. Formerly found on rivers with near-perennial flow throughout southern California from San Luis Obispo County to San Diego County, it is believed to be extirpated in San Luis Obispo County. Populations persist in Santa Barbara, Ventura, Los Angeles, Riverside, and San Diego Counties. Recent sightings of scattered individuals have been reported from Orange, San Bernardino, and southwest Imperial Counties.

The majority of the remaining populations in Santa Barbara and Ventura Counties are located on the Los Padres National Forest. This National Forest supports the majority of southern California's remaining intact large river systems and maintains five viable populations of arroyo toads. Sespe Creek in Ventura County has the largest known population. Other populations are found on the Sisquoc, Santa Ynez, and upper and lower Piru drainages.

Populations to the south are located primarily in San Diego and Riverside Counties and are predominantly found in the vicinity of the Cleveland National Forest and on private lands within or adjacent to national forest. In San Diego County, arroyo toads have been found on the Santa Margarita, Guejito, Sweetwater, Vallecito, San Luis Rey, Santa Ysabel, Witch, Cottonwood, Temescal, Agua Caliente, Santa Maria, Lusardi, Pine Valley, Noble, Kitchen, Long Potrero, Upper San Diego, San Vincente, and Morena drainages. Populations on Temescal, Agua Caliente, Pine Valley, and Cottonwood drainages may be considered viable. Recent surveys have located very small populations of arroyo toads in four creeks in southwestern Riverside County. The single recent occurrence of arroyo toads in San Bernardino County is on Deep Creek in the San Bernardino National Forest.

Several factors presently threaten the remaining 25% of the habitat of the arroyo toad including: (1) Short- and long-term changes in river hydrology, including construction of dams and water diversions; (2) alteration of riparian wetland habitats by agriculture and urbanization; (3) construction of roads; (4) site-specific damage by off-highway vehicle use; (5) development of campgrounds and other recreational activities; (6) over-grazing; and (7) mining activities.

Dam construction was responsible for the loss of approximately 40% of the estimated original range of the arroyo toad. Twenty-six large impoundments are currently located within the range of this species, inundating over 120 mi (190 km) of suitable habitat. Additional areas have been identified as potential dam sites and, if constructed, would destroy 25% of the current range of the arroyo toad.

In addition to habitat loss through direct inundation, dams can have significant effects on habitat quality downstream. Artificial flow regulation disrupts the natural processes that produce the terrace and pool habitats required by arroyo toads. Unseasonable water releases may prevent arroyo toads from breeding due to habitat changes.

Another consequence of sustained unnatural perennial flows below dams is an adverse effect on the habitat of this species by encouraging vegetative growth in a riparian corridor, which increases ground stability and hence confines and deepens the creek channel. Water temperatures are reduced below the temperatures needed or larval development.

The arroyo toad is also sensitive to stream diversions as they cause the riparian areas to dry. Water diversions that alter normal flows have degraded habitats and adversely affected arroyo toads by leading to: the early drying of breeding pools, causing breeding failures or loss of the larval population; restriction of the period essential for rapid growth when newly-metamorphosed toads can forage on damp gravel bars; and loss of damp subsurface soil, which may result in high adult mortality during late summer and early fall.

Development projects in riparian wetlands have caused permanent losses of riparian habitats and are the most conspicuous factor in the decline of the arroyo toad. Agriculture and urbanization have already destroyed much of the suitable arroyo toad habitat south of the Santa Clara River in Ventura County. Stream terraces have been converted to farming, road corridors, and residential and commercial uses, while the streams themselves have been channelized for flood control. Large stretches of riparian corridor habitat have also been degraded or destroyed by cattle and feral pigs.

Recreational activities in riparian wetlands have had substantial negative effects to arroyo toad habitat and individuals. Off-highway vehicles cause extensive damage to the shallow pools in which arroyo toads breed.

Streamside campgrounds in southern California national forests have frequently been located adjacent to arroyo toad habitat. In the Los Padres National Forest, each of the three campgrounds on Piru and Sespe Creeks were developed on terraces used by arroyo toads within 150-300 ft (45-60 m) of their breeding pools. On the upper Santa Ynez River, also in Los Padres National Forest, three of four campgrounds are also located in arroyo toad habitat. The placement of campgrounds is similar in the Cleveland National Forest in San Diego County; upper San Juan Creek, upper San Luis Rey River, and Cottonwood Creek all have campgrounds situated adjacent to arroyo toad breeding habitats.

The use of heavy equipment in yearly reconstruction of roads and stream crossings in the national forests has had significant and repeated impacts to arroyo toads and toad habitat.

Maintenance of the road to Ogilvy Ranch, a private inholding in the Los Padres National Forest, is likely responsible for a depressed population of arroyo toads in Mono Creek. The Ogilvy Ranch road makes 18 crossings of Mono Creek, many directly through or near arroyo toad breeding pools. In summer 1992, the Los Padres National Forest declined to open the Ogilvy Ranch road in order to protect populations of arroyo toads and other candidate amphibians and reptiles. However, the road was opened with a bulldozer in the fall. As juvenile arroyo toads were likely burrowed in the soft sand adjacent to the creek, grading the road up the creek destroyed habitat and probably killed individual toads. Regular maintenance of roads in the Los Padres National Forest negatively affects arroyo toad individuals and toad habitat on the Santa Ynez River and Piru and Sespe Creeks, as well.

Mining activities are an additional threat to this species. Recreational suction dredging for gold adversely affects toad habitat and individuals. Dredging destroys breeding pools used by arroyo toads and causes excessive siltation downstream, which asphyxiates eggs and small larvae. For example, during the Memorial Day weekend of 1991, four small dredges operating on Piru Creek produced sedimentation visible more than 0.6 mi (1 km) downstream and adversely affected 40,000-60,000 arroyo toad larvae. Subsequent surveys revealed nearly total destruction of the species in this stream section; less than 100 larvae survived, and only four juvenile toads were located.

Several rivers in the Los Padres National Forest were recently temporarily closed to gold mining, and it is uncertain whether the ban will be made permanent. In December 1992, a group of miners challenged the Forest Service's authority to close Piru Creek to mining. These individuals practiced various methods of gold exraction until cited by the Forest Service. It is probable that future challenges will occur and, if successful, will threaten the population of arroyo toads on Piru Creek.

Populations of the arroyo toad are becoming so small and confined that even limited taking by campers, recreationists, and scientific researchers could adversely affect this species' viability. These toads are threatened from collecting by children near the campgrounds. No data exists on the extent of such collection activities, but it is probable that it continues to occur.

Over the past 20 years, at least 60 species of fishes have been introduced to the western U. S. States, 59% of which are predatory. The introduction of exotic predators to southern California waters has been facilitated, in part, by the inter-basin transport of water. Introduced predators had substantial impacts on the sizes of extant populations of arroyo toads and may have contributed to regional extinctions.

Virtually all rivers that contain or once contained arroyo toads support populations of introduced predatory fish, such as green sunfish, largemouth bass, mosquitofish, black bullhead, arroyo chub, prickly sculpin, rainbow trout, oriental gobies, and red shiners. All of these introduced fish prey on tadpoles and have been observed inducing high arroyo toad larval mortality in breeding pools on the Piru, Sespe, and Santa Ynez drainages. It is probable that predation by introduced fish species occurs elsewhere.

Arroyo toads occur in streams with perennial or near perennial flow. Most streams with populations of arroyo toads also have populations of introduced bullfrogs. Adult bullfrogs are highly predatory and have been observed to prey on adult arroyo toads. Habitat for bullfrogs has been enhanced within the existing range of the arroyo toad via diversions and artificially maintained perennial flows below dams. Increased bullfrog populations in these permanent water areas threaten the survival of arroyo toad populations.

Alteration of the natural intermittent flow regmes by dams has had significant adverse impacts to arroyo toads. Prior to 1992, the California Department of Water Resources, which operates Pyramid Dam on Piru Creek in the Los Padres and An-

geles National Forests, frequently discharged excess flows from the reservoir resulting in the depressed population of arroyo toads on lower Piru Creek. Recent coordination among the Department of Water Resources, Forest Service, and Fish and Wildlife Service have resulted in releases from the dam that more closely mimic natural flows, benefitting the arroyo toad. Water releases of several million gallons per day from Barrett Dam on Cottonwood Creek during the period when larval arroyo toads were metamorphosing negatively affected the population in San Diego County in summer 1993.

Several other factors have also contributed to the decline of the species including drought, fire, and light and noise pollution. Additionally, there has been direct mortality of the toads due to road construction and maintenance, water inundation or drainage from dams and diversions, off-highway vehicle use, cattle and pig trampling, mining, and recreational activities.

By far, the most significant natural factor adversely affecting the arroyo toad is drought and resultant deterioration of riparian habitats. Southern California recently experienced five consecutive years of lower than average rainfall. These drought conditions, when combined with human-induced water reductions, have degraded riparian ecosystems and have created extremely stressful conditions for most aquatic species.

Drought also affects arroyo toads in another manner. Female arroyo toads must feed for at least two months in order to develop the fat reserves needed to produce a clutch of eggs. In drought years, females may find insufficient insect prey to produce eggs before males cease their courtship behavior of calling, resulting in no reproduction in that year. The extremely low reproduction of 1990 was likely due to four years of severe drought. Although rainfall patterns in 1992 and 1993 returned to near normal levels, drought is a naturally recurring phenomenon in southern California. There is no doubt that arroyo toads evolved with periodic, severe drought. However, the recurrence of this natural event combined with the many manmade factors negatively affecting arroyo toad survival remains a significant threat to the species persistence.

Periodic fires may adversely affect arroyo toads by causing direct mortality, destroying streamside vegetation, or eliminating vegetation that sustains the watershed. Recent natural and human-induced wildfires had devastating effects on populations of arroyo toads. The 1991 Lions Fire on upper Sespe Creek in the Los Padres National Forest destroyed habitat containing the largest known extant population of arroyo toads including 15 known breeding pools and over 50% of the known adult population on the Sespe drainage. Surveys in 1992 revealed that the effects of the fire and subsequent flooding, erosion, and siltation caused the death of not less than 50% of the resident adult population of arroyo toads.

The vocalizations of male toads are crucial to the breeding success of this species, as their calls are the key factor to finding mates. Light and noise pollution from adjacent developments or campgrounds may also reduce arroyo toad reproductive success by disrupting the vocalization behavior of males during the breeding season. Generally, the local population of arroyo toads declines as campground use increases.

Unseasonal water releases from dams may prevent arroyo toads from breeding altogether, as discussed in Factor A, or may wash away eggs and larvae if releases are made after breeding has occurred. For example, large unscheduled releases from Pyramid Lake in May 1991 virtually eliminated all reproduction by arroyo toads below the dam in Piru Creek in what would have been the best year for reproduction following five years of drought. A proposal to convey State Water Project water from Pyramid Lake to Piru Lake via Piru Creek would also threaten arroyo toad survival on Piru Creek, if releases substantially alter natural flow regimes.

Grazing brings another potential source of mortality to this species. Horses and cattle graze in riparian areas and may trample eggs and larvae of arroyo toads. Grazing also increases levels of sedimentation in streams that can smother eggs and larvae.

Off-highway vehicle use is believed to be the primary factor responsible for the decimation of the Mojave River population of the arroyo toad. On Memorial Day weekend in 1991, a fence protecting a breeding pool on Piru Creek was cut, and off-highway vehicles had access to the creek. The disturbance destroyed a small sand bar that maintained a shallow pool, resulting in the loss of 12,000-16,000 arroyo southwestern tadpoles.

Recreational use of campgrounds is heaviest in early summer, when arroyo toad larvae and juveniles are present and most vulnerable. As the young toads are diurnal, sedentary, and live on the sand bars, they are often crushed. Recreational use has

resulted in the alteration of stream and breeding pool morphology and trampling of juvenile toads. Adult arroyo toads, which forage in open areas in the campgrounds, are frequently killed on campground roads at night.

Habitat loss, high mortality, and low reproduction from all of the sources discussed above also result in the fragmentation of surviving populations into isolated subpopulations. While these subpopulations may continue to survive and reproduce over the short term, their long-term survival is not secure, because little opportunity exists for natural dispersal and recolonization following local extirpations. Habitat fragmentation increases the probability of local extirpation due to stochastic events and also likely results in reduction of genetic variability within the small, isolated subpopulations.

The recent years of extremely low reproductive success have likely been a bottleneck in the remaining populations of arroyo toads, in which few individuals will reach sexual maturity until 1995. As mature adults age and die, little recruitment into the breeding population is likely, and numerous local extinctions of already small populations are probable. As individuals may not survive and reproduce due to detrimental events such as drought or road maintenance, and, as the population numbers are low and the range is restricted, such events could cause the extinction of the species.

Conservation and Recovery

Until the Recovery Plan has been developed, recovery efforts will depend on the enforcement of regulations prohibiting the take (includes harass, harm, pursue, hunt, shoot, wound, kill, trap, capture, or collect; or attempt any such conduct), import or export, transport in interstate or foreign commerce in the course of commercial activity, or sell or offer for sale in interstate or foreign commerce any listed wildlife species. It is also illegal to possess, sell, deliver, carry, transport, or ship any such wildlife that has been taken illegally.

The arroyo toad has been extirpated from about 75% of its historical range and now survives in small, isolated, imperiled populations. Some critical habitat is in the Cleveland, Los Padres, and San Bernardino National Forests. This publicly owned habitat must be strictly protected from any threatening activities. Other habitat is on privately owned land and is potentially threatened by various activities. These critical habitats should also be protected. This could be done by acquiring the habitats and establishing ecological reserves, or by negotiating conservation easements with the landowners. Because of the imperilment of the remaining populations of the arroyo toad, an active program of habitat protection and improvement is required. Its populations should be monitored, and studies made of its habitat needs.

Contacts

U. S. Fish and Wildlife Service
Regional Office, Division of Endangered Species
Eastside Federal Building
911 N. E. 11th Ave.
Portland, Oregon 97232-4181
Telephone: (503) 231-6121
http://pacific.fws.gov/

U.S. Fish and Wildlife Service
Ventura Fish and Wildlife Office
2493 Portola Road, Suite B
Ventura, California 93003-7726
Telephone: (805) 644-1766

Reference

U.S. Fish and Wildlife Service. 16 December 1994. "Determination of Endangered Status for the Arroyo Southwestern Toad." *Federal Register* 59:64839-65229.

Puerto Rican Crested Toad

Peltophryne lemur

Puerto Rican Crested Toad, photograph by David M. Dennis. Reproduced by permission.

Status	Threatened
Listed	August 4, 1987
Family	Bufonidae (Toad)
Description	Medium-sized toad; yellow-olive to dark brown in color; distinctive long, upturned snout.
Habitat	Coastal plain on exposed limestone or porous soil.
Food	Insects.
Reproduction	Egg masses laid in freshwater ponds.
Threats	Loss of habitat.
Range	Puerto Rico

Description

The Puerto Rican crested toad is a medium-sized toad, 2.5-4.5 in (6.3-11.4 cm) in snout-vent length, yellowish-olive to blackish-brown in color, with prominent supraorbital crests and a distinctive long, upturned snout. Males are considerably smaller than females, and exhibit less prominent crests. No studies have been conducted on the Puerto Rican crested toad's feeding habits, but as a general rule toads are opportunistic feeders that primarily consume insects and other invertebrates.

Behavior

Although not completely understood, breeding appears to be sporadic and highly dependent upon occasional heavy rains. When rainfall and surface water are adequate, more than one breeding event may occur in a single season. Breeding is concentrated in a very short period, and within a few weeks the toadlets metamorphose and quickly disperse. There is a high fidelity in breeding sites that offer the right combination of elevation, topography, and ponded fresh water.

Habitat

The Puerto Rican crested toad occurs at low elevations (below 660 ft or 200 m) where there is exposed limestone or porous, well-drained soil offering an abundance of fissures and cavities. Adult toads are semifossorial and widely dispersed when not breeding. Because of this cryptic behavior, the location or even presence of adult toads when not breeding is difficult to detect.

Distribution

This toad is presently known to exist only on the main island of Puerto Rico. A single large population is known from the southwest coast in the Guánica Commonwealth Forest, and a small population is believed to survive on the north coast. It has also been collected on the southern coastal plain near Coamo. Northern coastal plain collections have been made near Isabela, Quebradillas, Arecibo, Barceloneta, Vega Baja, and Bayamón. The species has also been propagated in captivity and approximately 850 toadlets were released in Cambalache Commonwealth Forest on the north coast in 1984 and 1985. To date, more than 4,000 toadlets have been produced in captivity at the Metro Toronto Zoo and returned to Puerto Rico.

Historically, the Puerto Rican crested toad has been collected on the island of Virgin Gorda in the British Virgin Islands. The known historic distribution on Virgin Gorda is very limited and the species has not been observed there for at least two decades. It is assumed to have been extirpated from that island. Exact numbers are unknown. The Guánica Commonwealth Forest population is relatively stable and consists of approximately 1,500-2,000 individuals. The northern population consists of approximately 25 individuals. Nothing is known about population numbers in other localities, especially since the species is very difficult to encounter on a periodic basis.

Threats

Loss of habitat from filling and drainage of breeding sites, and direct loss of adults and their habitat during land development are considered the primary factors for the toad's present status. Although the Puerto Rican crested toad has historically been rare, the species has undoubtedly declined further as its coastal lowland habitat has been destroyed by agricultural and urban development. In particular, known breeding sites have been filled or drained for construction, cultivation, and mosquito control. Construction projects are currently proposed which could affect the toad's status in the Guánica Commonwealth Forest area; however, discussions are continuing in an effort to find alternatives that will avoid destruction of toad breeding habitat.

Secondary factors may also be affecting the species' status. Predation on dispersing toadlets may be heavy, particularly from wading birds, and could become a significant factor if populations are greatly reduced by other problems. Additionally, reproduction in this species appears to rely on climatic events, sometimes one or more years apart, that occur at irregular intervals. Such reliance may create natural fluctuations in population sizes that could, when compounded by a reduced availability

of breeding sites, increase the likelihood of whole subpopulations being eliminated. Extremes in sex ratios have also been reported; a low incidence of males in one area, and a low incidence of females at another locality However, the significance of these observations is difficult to assess without more information about the reproductive biology of this species.

Conservation and Recovery

Protection of habitat is considered the highest priority need. Limited numbers of breeding sites are apparently used by toads from a large surrounding area. In one case, a marked and recaptured female traveled 2.4 mi (3.8 km). The conservation of whole subpopulations may be dependent on the identification and protection of these sites. Additional surveys are needed to better determine the species' distributions and abundance. Should reintroduction be necessary, captive breeding has been successfully accomplished in the past and could be used again to provide individuals for this purpose.

Contacts

U.S. Fish and Wildlife Service
Regional Office, Division of Endangered Species
1875 Century Blvd., Suite 200
Atlanta, Georgia 30345
http://southeast.fws.gov/

Boquerón Ecological Services Field Office
U. S. Fish and Wildlife Service
P.O. Box 491
Boquerón, Puerto Rico 00622-0491
Telephone: (787) 851-7297
Fax: (787) 851-7440

References

Garcia Diaz, J. 1987. "Rediscovery of *Bufo lemur* Cope and Additional Records of Reptiles from Puerto Rico." *Stahlia* 10: 1-6.

Paine, F.L. 1985. "International Studbook of the Puerto Rican Crested Toad (*Peltophryne lemur*)." Buffalo Zoological Gardens, New York. 33 pp.

Pregill, G. 1981. "Cranial Morphology and the Evolution of West Indian toads (Salientia: Bufonidae): Resurrection of the Genus *Peltophryne* Fitzinger." *Copeia* 1981: 273-285.

Rivero, J.A., H. Mayorga, E. Estremera, and I. Izquierdo. 1980. "Sobre el *Bufo lemur* Cope (Amphibia, Bufonidae)." *Caribbean Journal of Science* 15: 33-40.

U.S. Fish and Wildlife Service. 4 August 1987. "Determination of Threatened Status for the Puerto Rican Crested Toad." *Federal Register* 52 (149): 28828-28831.

Guajón

Eleutherodactylus cooki

Status	Threatened
Listed	June 11, 1997
Family	Leptodactylidae
Description	Large solid brown frog, approximately 3.3 in (8.4 cm) long.
Habitat	Crevices and grottoes in and among boulders.
Food	Unknown.
Reproduction	Eggs laid on humid faces of boulders.
Threats	Habitat degradation and loss due to land conversion to agriculture, deforestation and earth movement for rural development, road construction, and dam construction for the formation of a reservoir.
Range	Puerto Rico

Description

Eleutherodactylus, the largest vertebrate genus with more than 400 described species, has northwestern South America and the West Indies as its two centers of species diversity. Almost all species share two characteristics: T-shaped terminal phalanges—probably an adaptation for climbing—and direct development, allowing for reproduction away from water. In the West Indies, *Eleutherodactylus* species are a dominant amphibian group. No single species is naturally found on more than one of the four Greater Antilles, and most are restricted to small areas within an island. Seventeen species of this genus are known from Puerto Rico, and collectively they are commonly known as *coquis.*

The guajón, *Eleutherodactylus cooki,* known commonly as *demonio de Puerto Rico* (demon of Puerto Rico) is a relatively large frog, approximately 3.3 in (8.4 cm) in length. It is solid brown in color, although attending and calling males may have a yellow throat. The guajón may be the only species of *Eleutherodactylus* in Puerto Rico that exhibits sexual dimorphism in color. Both sexes of these frogs have large white-rimmed eyes, giving the species a specter or phantomlike appearance. The species is characterized by having large truncate discs and a peculiar, low, and melodious voice which is completely different from any other species of *Eleutherodactylus* in Puerto Rico.

Behavior

The number of egg clutches and juveniles was observed to be greatest during the months of October and September. Eggs are laid on the humid faces of boulders in protected microhabitats within the grottoes and up to 59 eggs, which may actually be multiple clutches, are apparently guarded by the males. Diurnal activity of the guajón occurs only inside the caves. Many guajóns, however, have been observed leaving the caves at dusk, presumably to forage and rehydrate, and returning before dawn.

Habitat

The guajón lives in crevices and grottoes in and among boulders. Such grottoes are commonly referred to as guajónales. This species derives its name from the grottoes or guajónales where the frogs live. The species is apparently limited in distribution by where this rock formation occurs.

Distribution

The guajón, first collected by Chapman Grant in 1932, is a habitat specialist now only known from the municipalities of Yabucoa, San Lorenzo, Humacao, and Las Piedras in the Pandura range in the extreme southeastern corner of Puerto Rico. During surveys conducted in 1986, 1992, and 1996, the guajón was found at its historical localities, all of which occur within the municipalities of Yabucoa and San Lorenzo. Dr. Fernando Bird also reports the species from the municipalities of Las Piedras and Humacao. Little historical data is available on abundance; therefore, reductions in populations are difficult to document. The guajón is extremely restricted in geographical distribution and occurs only on privately owned lands. Scientists have documented population fluctuations, apparently related to precipitation and temperature. Numbers are lowest during the winter months, during the period of least rainfall and lowest temperatures.

Threats

The major threat to the species is habitat degradation and loss, most of which has been caused by land conversion to agriculture, deforestation and earth movement for rural development, road construction, and dam construction for the formation of a reservoir. Deforestation often leads to more frequent flash floods, resulting in the drowning of adult guajóns and the destruction of nests. The practice of planting crops right up to the entrance of the caves may eliminate nocturnal habitat of the species and increase the pesticide and fertilizer runoff into the water flowing under the caves. Caves are also often used as garbage dumps. The heavy cut and fill associated with road construction has eliminated habitat; a major four-line highway is currently proposed through the area, as is the construction of a major reservoir.

Disease has not been documented as a factor in the decline of this species. However, examination of both preserved and live specimens of the guajón have revealed that the species is parasitized by the tick *Ornithodoros talaje*. Nevertheless, the effect of this parasite on the guajón has yet to be studied. Nocturnally active introduced species such as cats, rats, and mongoose may adversely affect densities of this species by feeding on the frogs and their eggs. There is also the possibility that guajón individuals have been killed out of fear by local people;

at least one scientist has noted that many people seem to be afraid of the appearance of these frogs. The peculiar calling and phantomlike appearance of this frog made many local people fearful of the species, believing that the mere sight of one would be fatal.

Other threats are more generalized in nature, though none the less threatening for that. In recent years there has been a pronounced decline in global populations of amphibians. Factors that may be responsible for this worldwide decline of amphibians include habitat destruction and modification, acid rain, pesticide contamination, introduction of non-native predators and competitors, agriculture, mining and logging, increased levels of ultraviolet radiation, collection, and global climatic change.

Flash floods, droughts, and catastrophic storms—such as Hurricane Hugo in 1989—may have caused localized extirpations of other species of *Eleutherodactylus* in specific areas in Puerto Rico. Hurricane Hugo decreased the numbers of *E. portoricensis*, a species restricted in distribution which is not abundant.

Conservation and Recovery

Although not previously identified as a determinant factor in the decline of the guajón specifically, scientific collecting of related species of coqui in Puerto Rico may well have contributed to declines. In a survey of only seven museums in both Puerto Rico and the United States, numerous specimens of the web-footed coqui (*E. karlschmidti*) and the mottled coqui (*E. eneidae*) were located. The specimens totaled 473 preserved individuals of the former and 325 of the latter species. The status of both these related species are now being evaluated by the U.S. Fish and Wildlife Service because of their extreme rarity. Collection of other *Eleutherodactylus* species for use in local art has also been documented, and this activity is currently being evaluated by the Commonwealth government for possible regulation.

Contacts

U.S. Fish and Wildlife Service
Regional Office, Division of Endangered Species
1875 Century Blvd., Suite 200
Atlanta, Georgia 30345
http://southeast.fws.gov

Caribbean Field Office
U.S. Fish and Wildlife Service
P.O. Box 491
Boquerón, Puerto Rico 00622
Telephone: (809) 851-7297

References

Drewry, G. E. 1986. "Golden Coqui Recovery Survey and Brief Status Evaluation of Five Other Puerto Rican *Eleutherodactylus* Species." Caribbean Field Office: U.S. Fish and Wildlife Service.

Joglar, R. L. 1992. "Status Survey of Four Species of *Eleutherodactylus*: Final Report." Caribbean Field Office: U.S. Fish and Wildlife Service.

Powell, R., and R. W. Henderson, eds. 1996. "Biology of the Puerto Rican Cave-dwelling Frog, *Eleutherodactylus cooki*." *Contributions to West Indian Herpetology* 12: 251-258.

Powell, R., and R. W. Henderson, eds. 1996. "Declining Amphibian Populations in Puerto Rico." *Contributions to West Indian Herpetology* 12: 371-380.

U. S. Fish and Wildlife Service. 11 June 1997. "Threatened Status for the Guajón." *Federal Register* 62 (112): 31757-31762.

Wake, D. B., and H. J. Morowitz. 1991. "Declining Amphibian Populations—a Global Phenomenon Findings and Recommendations." *Alytes* 9 (2): 33-42.

Golden Coqui

Eleutherodactylus jasperi

Status	Threatened
Listed	November 11, 1977
Family	Leptodactylidae (Frog)
Description	Gold-colored frog with a rounded snout.
Habitat	Mountaintops in dense bromeliad thickets.
Food	Insects.
Reproduction	Live-bearer.
Threats	Loss of habitat, limited distribution.
Range	Puerto Rico

Golden Coqui, photograph. U. S. Fish and Wildlife Service. Reproduced by permission.

Description

The golden coqui (*Eleutherodactylus jasperi*) is a small frog attaining a maximum size (snout-vent length) of slightly less than 1 in (2.5 cm). It has an indistinct tympanum and lacks prevomerine teeth. The color is olive-gold to yellow-gold without pattern. Juveniles resemble the adults.

Behavior

Growth rates, longevity, and details of the fertilization process of the golden coqui are unknown. Gravid females have been collected from April to August. The number of mature eggs ranges from three to six. Based on a single laboratory experiment, about a month elapses between the time of fertilization and birth of the young. An observation of two size-classes of subadults in the same plant with a female suggests that a single female may reproduce more than one time per year. The golden coqui is the only frog species in the Western hemisphere family Leptodactylidae definitely known to give birth to live young.

Habitat

The habitat area is located within an elevational range of 2,297-2,789 ft (700-850 m). The species has been found only in water-containing bromeliads of the genera *Vriesia, Hoenbergia,* and *Guzmania.* A low incidence of golden coquis in isolated bromeliads suggests that dispersal distances are short. Colonization of bromeliad clusters seems to be independent of whether they occur on the ground, in trees, or on vertical surfaces of cliffs.

Distribution

The golden coqui is found only in Puerto Rico. All specimens to date have been collected from a small semicircular area of a 6-mi (9.7-m) radius south of Cayey, generally at elevations above 2,297 ft (700 m). Distribution of the golden coqui is restricted to areas of dense bromeliad growth (less than 3.3 ft [1 m] separating individual plants). Bromeliad growths are associated with rock faces, isolated trees, and the margins of forest in a mountainous area that receives a large amount of moisture in the form of dew. Heavy dew is apparently produced by the orographic uplift of air striking the mountain range. Studies carried out in 1976 indicated that it was normal to find two or more adults and two or more size-classes of juveniles per bromeliad. Population levels are not currently known and may be critical. Surveys carried out in 1986, 1987, and 1989 did not encounter any individuals.

Threats

The coqui's threatened status is based on the past and potential loss of habitat to development for homes, agriculture, and other purposes; on the potential for overcollecting; and on the fact that the species has a specialized, obligate bromeliad-dwelling mode of existence. This mode of existence—coupled with a low reproductive rate, inability to disperse, and a limited range—makes its existence naturally precarious. Recent studies indicate that acid rain may play a role in the decline of this and other species of *Eleutherodactylus* in Puerto Rico.

Conservation and Recovery

All currently known habitat is privately owned, and habitat protection through purchase, donation, lease, or easement should be the highest priority action. Additional surveys are urgently needed in order to determine the current status of the species. Critical habitat has been designated for portions of Cerro Avispa, Monte el Gato, and Sierra de Cayey at elevations above 2,296.6 ft (700 m).

Contacts

Regional Office of Endangered Species
U. S. Fish and Wildlife Service
1875 Century Blvd., Suite 200
Atlanta, Georgia 30345
http://southeast.fws.gov/

Boquerón Ecological Services Field Office
U. S. Fish and Wildlife Service
P.O. Box 491
Boquerón, Puerto Rico 00622-0491
Telephone: (787) 851-7297
Fax: (787) 851-7440

References

Drewry, G. E., and R. L. Jones. 1976. "A new ovoviviparous frog (*Eleutherodactylus jasperi*) from Puerto Rico." *Journal of Herpetology* 10 (3): 161-165.

U. S. Fish and Wildlife Service. 1984. "Recovery plan for the golden coqui (*Eleutherodactylus jasperi*)." U. S. Fish and Wildlife Service, Atlanta.

California Red-legged Frog

Rana aurora draytonii

Status	Threatened
Listed	May 23, 1996
Family	Ranidae
Description	Largest native frog in the western United States; has red abdomen and hind legs.
Habitat	Dense, shrubby or emergent riparian vegetation closely associated with deep, still or slow-moving water.
Food	Invertebrates and some vertebrates such as Pacific tree frogs and California mice.
Reproduction	Egg masses of 2,000-5,000 eggs; hatch in six to 14 days.
Threats	Loss and alteration of habitat.
Range	California, Mexico

Description

The California red-legged frog is one of two subspecies of the red-legged frog found on the Pacific coast. The California red-legged frog is the largest native frog in the western United States, ranging from 1.5-5.1 in (3.8-12.9 cm) in length. The abdomen and hind legs of adults are largely red; the back is characterized by small black flecks and larger irregular dark blotches with indistinct outlines on a brown, gray, olive, or reddish background color. Dorsal spots usually have light centers. Dorsolateral folds are prominent on the back. Tadpoles range from 0.6-3.1 in (1.5-7.9 cm) in length and the background color of the body is dark brown and yellow with darker spots.

Several morphological and behavioral characteristics differentiate California red-legged frogs from northern red-legged frogs. Adult California red-legged frogs are significantly larger than northern red-legged frogs by 1.4-1.6 in (3.6-4.0 cm). Dorsal spots of northern red-legged frogs usually lack light centers common to California red-legged frogs, but this is not a strong diagnostic characteristic. California red-legged frogs have paired vocal sacs and

call in air, whereas northern red-legged frogs lack vocal sacs and call underwater. Female California red-legged frogs deposit egg masses on emergent vegetation so that the egg mass floats on the surface of the water. Northern red-legged frogs also attach their egg masses to emergent vegetation, but the mass is submerged.

Behavior

California red-legged frogs breed from November through March with earlier breeding records occurring in southern localities. Northern red-legged frogs breed in January to March soon after the ice melts. California red-legged frogs found in coastal drainages are rarely inactive, whereas those found in interior sites may hibernate.

Egg masses that contain about 2,000-5,000 moderate-sized, dark reddish brown eggs are typically attached to vertical emergent vegetation, such as bulrushes or cattails. California red-legged frogs are often prolific breeders, laying their eggs during or shortly after large rainfall events in late winter and early spring. Eggs hatch in six to 14 days. In coastal

California Red-legged Frog, photograph by Mark Jenkins. U. S. Fish and Wildlife Service. Reproduced by permission.

lagoons, the most significant mortality factor in the pre-hatching stage is water salinity. One hundred percent mortality occurs in eggs exposed to salinity levels greater than 4.5 parts per thousand. Larvae die when exposed to salinities greater than 7.0 parts per thousand. Larvae undergo metamorphosis three and one-half to seven months after hatching. Of the various life stages, larvae probably experience the highest mortality rates, with less than 1% of eggs laid reaching metamorphosis. Sexual maturity normally is reached at three to four years of age, and California red-legged frogs may live eight to 10 years.

The diet of California red-legged frogs is highly variable. Larvae probably eat algae; adults consume invertebrates. Vertebrates, such as Pacific tree frogs and California mice, represented over half of the prey mass eaten by larger frogs. Juvenile frogs were found to be active diurnally and nocturnally, whereas adult frogs were largely nocturnal. Feeding activity likely occurs along the shoreline and on the surface of the water.

Habitat

The California red-legged frog occupies a fairly distinct habitat, combining both specific aquatic and riparian components. The adults require dense, shrubby, or emergent riparian vegetation closely associated with deep, still, or slow moving water. The largest densities of California red-legged frogs are associated with deep-water pools with dense stands of overhanging willows and an intermixed fringe of cattails. Well-vegetated terrestrial areas within the riparian corridor may provide important sheltering habitat during winter. California red-legged frogs estivate in small mammal burrows and moist leaf litter. California red-legged frogs have been found up to 98 ft (30 m) from water in adjacent dense riparian vegetation for up to 77 days.

California red-legged frogs disperse upstream and downstream of their breeding habitat to forage and seek estivation habitat.

Estivation habitat is essential for the survival of California red-legged frogs within a watershed.

Estivation habitat, and the ability to reach estivation habitat can be limiting factors in California red-legged frog population numbers and survival.

Estivation habitat for the California red-legged frog is potentially all aquatic and riparian areas within the range of the species. Such habitat includes any landscape features that provide cover and moisture during the dry season within 300 ft (91 m) of a riparian area. This could include boulders or rocks and organic debris such as downed trees or logs; industrial debris; and agricultural features, such as drains, watering troughs, spring boxes, abandoned sheds, or hayricks. Incised stream channels with portions narrower than 18 in (45.7 cm) and depths greater than 18 in (45.7 cm) may also provide estivation habitat.

Distribution

The historical range of the California red-legged frog extended along the coast from the vicinity of Point Reyes National Seashore, Marin County, California, and inland from the vicinity of Redding in California's Shasta County, to northwestern Baja California in Mexico.

California red-legged frogs are known to occur in 243 streams or drainages in 22 counties, primarily in the central coastal region of California. Monterey, San Luis Obispo, and Santa Barbara counties support the greatest number of currently occupied drainages. Historically the California red-legged frog was known from 46 counties, but the taxon is now extirpated from 24 of those counties. In seven of the 22 occupied counties, California red-legged frogs are known from a single occurrence. The most secure aggregations of California red-legged frogs are found in aquatic sites that support substantial riparian and aquatic vegetation and lack exotic predators, such as bullfrogs, bass, and sunfish. Only three areas within the entire historic range of the California red-legged frog may currently support more than 350 adults: Pescardero Marsh Nature Preserve, Point Reyes National Seashore, and Rancho San Carlos. The San Francisco Airport drain-age location, identified as containing over 350 individuals, is now thought to be nearly extirpated. Threats, such as expansion of exotic predators, proposed residential development, and water storage projects, occur in the majority of drainages known to support California red-legged frogs.

Threats

The California red-legged frog has sustained a 70% reduction in its geographic range in California as a result of several factors acting singly or in combination. Habitat loss and alteration, overexploitation, and introduction of exotic predators were significant factors in the California red-legged frog's decline in the early to mid-1900s. It is estimated that California red-legged frogs were extirpated from the Central Valley floor before 1960. Remaining aggregations of California red-legged frogs in the Sierra foothills became fragmented and were later eliminated by reservoir construction, continued expansion of exotic predators, grazing, and prolonged drought.

Habitat loss and alteration are the primary factors that have negatively affected the California red-legged frog throughout its range. For example, in the central valley of California, over 90% of historic wetlands have been diked, drained, or filled primarily for agricultural development and secondarily for urban development. Wetland alterations, clearing of vegetation, and water diversions that often accompany agricultural development make aquatic sites unsuitable for California red-legged frogs. Urbanization with its associated roadway, stream channelization, and large reservoir construction projects has significantly altered or eliminated California red-legged frog habitat, with the greatest impact occurring in southern California. The majority of extant localities are isolated and fragmented remnants of larger historical populations.

Current and future urbanization poses a significant threat to the California red-legged frog. Sixty-five drainages are associated with urbanization threats. Proposed urban developments include the East County Area Plan in Alameda County, which involves development of up to 52,000 acres (20,000 hectares), and projects currently proposed in the Ruby Hills/Arroyo Del Valle watershed and south Livermore valley; reservoir canyon ponds in Santa Clara County; Alamo, Shadow, and Brookside Creeks in Contra Costa County; the Carmel River in Monterey County; and the Santa Ynez River in Santa Barbara County. In Santa Cruz County, a proposed commuter rail project linking Santa Cruz to Watsonville could increase urban development in southern portions of the county.

Loss of habitat and decreases in habitat quality will occur as a result of on-site degradation of the stream environment and/or riparian corridor, or through modification of instream flow. Where streams or wetlands occur in urban areas, the quality of California red-legged frog habitat is degraded by a variety of factors. Among these factors are introduction of exotic predators, elimination of stream bank vegetation, collecting, and loss of upland habitat.

Water projects, which accompany urban and agricultural growth, have had a negative effect on California red-legged frogs and their habitat. The timing and duration of water releases from reservoirs, particularly on the central California coast, can render a stream unsuitable for California red-legged frog reproduction and maintain populations of exotic predators in downstream areas that would normally be dry in summer. Reservoirs are typically stocked with predatory species of fish and bullfrogs. These species often disperse into surrounding California red-legged frog habitat disrupting natural community dynamics. California red-legged frogs generally are extirpated from downstream portions of a drainage one to five years after filling of a reservoir. In some larger drainages, however, isolated California red-legged frog populations have persisted upstream.

Water diversions, groundwater well development, and stock pond or small reservoir construction projects degrade or eliminate habitat. Diverting water from natural habitats to these projects disrupts the natural hydrologic regime. During periods of drought, reduced availability of water within natural drainages combined with drawdown from the impoundments, disrupts reproduction, foraging, estivation, and dispersal.

Storm damage repair and flood control maintenance on streams are current threats to California red-legged frogs. Routine flood control maintenance includes vegetation removal, herbicide spraying, shaping of banks to control erosion, and de-silting of the creek, all of which degrade California red-legged frog habitat.

Routine road maintenance, trail development, and facilities construction activities associated with parks in or adjacent to California red-legged frog habitat can result in increased siltation in the stream. If this siltation occurs during the breeding season, asphyxiation of eggs and small California red-legged frog larvae can result.

Placer mining may threaten California red-legged frog habitat because of heavy siltation. The siltation resulted from upstream gold mining. Deep holes in streams created by instream placer mining also may provide habitat for exotic predatory fish. Creeks, streams and rivers are open to suction dredging throughout the year in 13 of 22 counties within the current range of the California red-legged frog.

Road-killed California red-legged frogs have been documented at several locations in San Mateo and Santa Cruz Counties. Road kills may deplete frog aggregations in borderline habitat and otherwise protected areas. Where roads cross or lie adjacent to California red-legged frog habitat, they may act as barriers to seasonal movement and dispersal.

Livestock grazing is another form of habitat alteration that is contributing to declines in the California red-legged frog. Cattle have an adverse affect on riparian and other wetland habitats because they tend to concentrate in these areas, particularly during dry seasons. Cattle trample and eat emergent and riparian vegetation, often eliminating or severely reducing plant cover. Loss of riparian vegetation results in increased water temperatures, which encourage bullfrog reproduction. Riparian vegetation loss due to cattle grazing includes the loss of willows, which are associated with the highest densities of California red-legged frogs. Cattle grazing also results in increased erosion in the watershed, which accelerates the sedimentation of deep pools used by California red-legged frogs and adversely affects aquatic invertebrates. Aquatic invertebrates are common prey items of California red-legged frogs.

Grazing effects are not limited to riparian areas. Improper grazing of upland vegetation can expose soils to erosive impacts of raindrops, reduce water infiltration, and accelerate runoff. This can erode topsoil and cut rills and gullies, concentrating runoff, deepening gullies, lowering water tables, and increasing sediment production. Sediment introduced into streams can alter primary productivity and food supply, and fill interstitial spaces in streambed material, thereby impeding water flow, reducing dissolved oxygen levels, and restricting waste removal. Suspended sediments reduce light penetration to plants and reduce oxygen-carrying capacity of the water. Reduction in photosynthesis and primary production decreases productivity of the entire ecosystem.

Livestock grazing can cause a nutrient loading problem in areas where cattle are concentrated near the water, but in other areas it can reduce nutrients through removal of riparian vegetation. Riparian vegetation provides organic material for approximately 50% of a stream's nutrient energy. Detritus from such plants is a principal source of food for aquatic invertebrates. Streamside vegetation also provides habitat for terrestrial insects, another important dietary component for other aquatic or riparian-associated species. Livestock grazing also has been implicated as a contributing factor in the decline and disappearance of California red-legged frogs from the lower Salinas River and the San Francisco peninsula.

In addition to cattle, feral pigs also disturb the riparian zone through their rooting, wallowing and foraging behavior in the shallow margins of water bodies. Feral pigs disturb and destroy vegetative cover, trample plants and seedlings, and cause erosion. At Pinnacles National Monument, soil compaction and possible disturbance of frog eggs caused by feral pigs have been noted in California red-legged frog habitat. Off-road vehicle use adversely affects California red-legged frogs in ways similar to livestock grazing and feral pig disturbance. Off-road vehicles damage riparian vegetation, increase siltation in pools, disturb the water in stream channels and crush eggs, larvae, juveniles, and adults. California red-legged frogs were eliminated in part by off-road vehicle activities at the Mojave River above Hesperia, at Rincon station on the west fork of the San Gabriel River, and in Piru Creek above Pyramid Lake.

Heavy recreational use of parks also can degrade habitat for the California red-legged frog. At Big Basin Redwood Park in Santa Cruz County, heavy recreational use may have contributed to the disappearance of California red-legged frogs from Opal Creek.

Timber harvest threatens California red-legged frogs through loss of riparian vegetation and increased erosion in the watershed, which fills pools with sediment and smothers egg masses. In Santa Cruz County, timber harvest is proposed adjacent to Adams Creek and Whitehouse Creek and occurs periodically on a tributary of Blooms Creek. The proposed timber harvests would occur in three of 18 streams in the county that support California red-legged frogs. In Pescadero Creek at Portola State Park, erosion and siltation caused by severe winter storms and upstream logging operations may have been the cause of the disappearance of California red-legged frogs from this portion of the stream.

Six consecutive years of drought in California severely affected remaining California red-legged frogs in the Sierra foothills. Many sites in intermittent streams that held California red-legged frogs before the drought were completely dry during field surveys conducted between 1985-1992. Sites still holding pools of water had water levels so low that access by predators was enhanced. Livestock grazing at many sites exacerbated effects of the drought by limiting or preventing riparian habitat regeneration. Long-term survival of California red-legged frogs may be compromised by the elimination of refuge areas during times of the year when the stream is dry. However, California red-legged frog populations are undoubtedly capable of recovering from drought, provided other factors have not irreparably degraded their habitat, and provided they have not been completely extirpated from the drainage.

Extensive flooding has been a significant contributing factor in the extirpation of the California red-legged frog from desert drainages of southern California.

A considerable amount of occupied California red-legged habitat exists in the form of isolated patches along stream courses. These patches of suitable habitat represent mere remnants of a much larger historical habitat that once covered whole drainages. Fragments of formerly extensive populations of California red-legged frogs are now isolated from other populations. Populations isolated in habitat fragments are vulnerable to extinction through random environmental events or anthropogenic catastrophes. With only three of 243 known creeks or drainages supporting populations of over 350 adults, all remaining occurrences are considered vulnerable to these threats. Once a local extinction event occurs in an isolated habitat fragment, the opportunity for recolonization from a source population is reduced. Thus, local extinctions via stochastic processes, coupled with habitat fragmentation may represent a substantial threat to the continued existence of the California red-legged frog over much of its range.

Conservation and Recovery

At several parks, the National Park Service has conducted or is planning to conduct status surveys for California red-legged frogs. The forest service has conducted and has ongoing amphibian surveys in many National Forests within the historic range of the California red-legged frog. In Los Padres National Forest, the forest service has altered flow regimes in Piru Creek between Pyramid Lake and Lake Piru to benefit the endangered arroyo southwestern toad. Although no specific studies have been done, these flow regime changes also may benefit the California red-legged frog. The forest service has also designated more than 31 mi (50 km) of Sespe Creek in Los Padres National Forest as "Wild and Scenic" under the National Wild and Scenic Rivers Act of 1968.

The Contra Costa Water District undertook construction of a large reservoir project on Kellogg Creek, Contra Costa County, with the Bureau of Reclamation involved to amend water service contracts and modify water rights to facilitate project construction. A mitigation and monitoring program was proposed to compensate for California red-legged frog habitat losses at Los Vaqueros. The mitigation plan included a bullfrog and exotic fish control program to be carried out for the life of the reservoir project. In addition, Bureau of Reclamation projects have guided water contract renewals as well as road maintenance activities and grazing leases, all of which may affect California red-legged frogs. U. S. Fish and Wildlife Service (FWS) is involved in the development of two Habitat Conservation Plans to potentially protect three localities of California red-legged frogs.

FWS has established five recovery areas within the historical range of the California red-legged frog: the western foothills and Sierran foothills to 5,000 ft (105 km) in elevation in the central valley hydrographic basin; the central coast ranges from San Mateo and Santa Clara counties south to Ventura and Los Angeles counties; the San Francisco Bay/Suisun Bay hydrologic basin; southern California, south of the Tehachapi Mountains; and the northern coastal range in Marin and Sonoma counties. These five units are essential to the survival and recovery of the California red-legged frog.

Contacts

U. S. Fish and Wildlife Service
Regional Office, Division of Endangered Species
Eastside Federal Complex
911 N. E. 11th Ave.
Portland, Oregon 97232-4181
Telephone: (503) 231-6121
http://pacific.fws.gov/

Sacramento Fish and Wildlife Office
U. S. Fish and Wildlife Service
Federal Building
2800 Cottage Way, Room W-2605
Sacramento, California 95825-1846
Telephone: (916) 414-6600
Fax: (916) 460-4619

Reference

U.S. Fish and Wildlife Service. 23 May 1996. "Determination of Threatened Status for the California Red-Legged Frog." *Federal Register* 61(101): 25813-25833.

Flatwoods Salamander

Ambystoma cingulatum

Status	Threatened
Listed	April 1, 1999
Family	Ambystomatidae
Description	Slender, small-headed mole salamander, black to chocolate-black in color dorsally.
Habitat	Open, mesic woodland of longleaf/slash pine flatwoods maintained by frequent fires.
Food	Invertebrates.
Reproduction	Larvae metamorphose in March or April.
Threats	Loss of habitat due to land conversion; forest management practices; predation from fish; pesticides; herbicides; droughts; floods.
Range	Alabama, Florida, Georgia, South Carolina

Description

The *Ambystoma cingulatum* (flatwoods salamander) is a slender, small-headed mole salamander that rarely exceeds 5 in (13 cm) in length when fully mature. Adult dorsal color ranges from black to chocolate-black with highly variable, fine, light gray lines forming a netlike or cross-banded pattern across the back. Undersurfaces are plain gray to black with a few creamy or pearl-gray blotches or spots. Sexual dimorphism (the existence of separable male and female forms) is only apparent in breeding males (swollen cloacal region) or in gravid (with fertilized eggs) females. Adults most closely resemble Mabee's salamander, *A. mabeei*, with which it shares part of its range in South Carolina. Mabee's salamanders are often more brownish; have light flecking concentrated on their sides rather than the overall pattern of the flatwoods salamander; and have a single row of jaw teeth as opposed to multiple rows in the flatwoods salamander. Although the flatwoods salamander closely resembles Mabee's salamander, it is most closely related to the ringed salamander (*A. annulatum*), which occurs in portions of Arkansas, Missouri, and Oklahoma.

Flatwoods salamander larvae are long and slender, broad-headed and bushy-gilled, with white bellies and striped sides. They have distinctive color patterns, typically a tan mid-dorsal (middle of upper surface) stripe followed by a grayish black dorsolateral (back and sides) stripe, a pale cream midlateral (side) stripe, a blue-black lower lateral stripe, and a pale yellow ventrolateral (belly) stripe. The head has a dark brown stripe passing through the eye from the nostril to the gills.

Behavior

Before the breeding sites become flooded, the males and females court. The females lay their eggs (singly or in clumps) beneath leaf litter, under logs and sphagnum moss (grows in wet acid areas) mats, or at bases of bushes, small trees, or clumps of grass. Egg masses have also been found at the entrances of and within crayfish burrows. Embryos begin development immediately, but the egg must be inundated before it will hatch. Depending on when eggs are inundated, the larvae usually metamorphose (change into adult form) in March or April; the length of the larval period varies from 11-18 weeks.

Flatwoods Salamander, photograph by John Jensen. Reproduced by permission.

The timing and frequency of rainfall are critical to the successful reproduction and recruitment of flatwoods salamanders. Fall rains are required to facilitate movements to the pond and winter rains are needed to ensure that ponds are filled sufficiently to allow hatching, development, and metamorphosis of larvae. In contrast, too much rainfall in the summer will keep pond levels from dropping below the grassy pond edge, as needed to provide dry substrate for egg deposition. This reliance on specific weather conditions results in unpredictable breeding events and reduces the likelihood that recruitment will occur every year.

Adult flatwoods salamanders leave the pond site after breeding. Studies have suggested a homing ability, based on data that salamanders exit the breeding pond near the point of their arrival; flatwoods salamanders were found more than 5,400 ft (1,645 m) from their breeding pond. Thus, a flatwoods salamander population has been defined as those salamanders using breeding sites within 2 mi (3 km) of each other, barring an impassable barrier

such as a perennial stream. This salamander feeds on invertebrates.

Habitat

Optimum habitat for the flatwoods salamander is an open, mesic (moderate moisture) woodland of longleaf/slash pine flatwoods maintained by frequent fires. Pine flatwoods are typically flat, low-lying open woodlands that lie between the drier sandhill community upslope and wetlands down slope. An organic hardpan, 1-2 ft (0.3-0.6 m) into the soil profile, inhibits subsurface water penetration and results in moist soils with water often at or near the surface. Historically, longleaf pine generally dominated the flatwoods with slash pine restricted to the wetter areas. Wiregrasses, especially *A. beyrichiana,* are often the dominant grasses in the herbaceous (non-woody) ground cover. The ground cover supports a rich herbivorous invertebrate community that serves as a food source for the flatwoods salamander.

Adult and subadult flatwoods salamanders are fossorial (adapted for living underground). They enlarge crayfish burrows or build their own. Captive flatwoods salamanders have been observed digging burrows and resting at night with just the tip of their heads exposed. Preliminary data indicate that flatwoods salamander males first breed at one year of age and females at two years of age. There are no data on survivorship by age class for the species. The longevity record for their close relative, *A. annulatum*, is four years, 11 months; however, many Ambystomatidae live 10 years or longer. An adult female flatwoods salamander has been maintained in captivity for four years, four months.

Adult flatwoods salamanders move to their wetland breeding sites during rainy weather, in association with cold fronts, from October to December. Breeding sites are isolated (not connected to any other water body) areas of pond cypress, blackgum, or slash pine dominated depressions which dry completely on a cyclical basis. They are generally shallow and relatively small, 3-4 acres (1.2-1.6 hectares) in area and 1-2 ft (0.3-0.6 m) in depth. These wetlands have a marsh-like appearance with sedges often growing throughout and wiregrasses, panic grasses, and other herbaceous species concentrated in the shallow water edges. Trees and shrubs grow both in and around the ponds. A relatively open canopy is necessary to maintain the herbaceous component, which serves as cover for flatwoods salamander larvae and their aquatic invertebrate prey. Ponds typically have a burrowing crayfish fauna and a diverse macroinvertebrate fauna, but lack large predatory fish, such as sunfish, bass, and bowfin.

Flatwoods salamanders need to maintain moist skin for respiration and osmoregulation (to control the amounts of water and salts in their bodies). Since they may disperse long distances from their breeding ponds to upland sites where they live as adults, desiccation (drying out) can be a limiting factor in their movements. Thus, it is important that areas connecting their wetland and terrestrial habitats are protected in order to provide cover and appropriate moisture regimes during their migration.

High quality habitat for the flatwoods salamander includes a number of isolated wetland breeding sites within a landscape of longleaf pine/slash pine flatwoods having an abundant herbaceous ground cover. Since temporary ponds are not likely permanent fixtures of the landscape due to succession, there will be inevitable extinctions of local populations. By maintaining a mosaic of ponds with varying hydrologies and by providing terrestrial habitats for use as colonization corridors, some protection against extinction can be achieved. A mosaic of ponds will ensure that appropriate breeding conditions will be achieved under different climatic regimes. Colonization corridors will allow movement of salamanders to new breeding sites or previously occupied ones.

Distribution

The historical range of the flatwoods salamander included parts of the States of Alabama, Florida, Georgia, and South Carolina that are in the lower Coastal Plain. It is possible that flatwoods salamanders once occurred in extreme southeastern Mississippi due to similarities in habitat to historical sites in adjacent Alabama. Surveys in 1995 did not report the occurrence of flatwoods salamanders in Mississippi.

The present distribution of the flatwoods salamander consists of isolated populations scattered across the remaining longleaf pine/slash pine flatwoods. Surveys indicate that the salamander survives in only 12% of its historical range.

Range-wide surveys of available habitat in Alabama, Florida, Georgia, and South Carolina have been ongoing since 1990 in an effort to locate new populations. More than 1,300 wetlands, which had a minimum of marginal suitability for the flatwoods salamander, were sampled, most of them multiple times. Of these, flatwoods salamanders were found at 110 sites (8% success rate).

In Alabama, there are five historical localities for the flatwoods salamander, all in the extreme southern portion of the State. Surveys conducted from 1992-1995 at the historical breeding ponds and from 1992-1998 at other potential breeding sites were unsuccessful at locating any flatwoods salamander populations. The salamander was last observed in Alabama in 1981.

In Georgia, 33 historical records in 19 counties have been reported for Georgia; however, flatwoods salamanders have not been relocated at any of these sites in recent years. Surveys over the last eight years of at least 478 wetlands with potential habitat for the flatwoods salamander have resulted in the location of 28 new breeding sites (6% success rate), comprising 11 populations. Most of these breeding sites occur on Fort Stewart Military Installation.

In South Carolina, there are 29 historical records for the flatwoods salamander. Despite annual surveys since 1990, flatwoods salamanders have been relocated at only three of these sites. One site is located on the Francis Marion National Forest and the other two are on private land. A new flatwoods salamander breeding site, representing a fourth population, was found in 1998 on the Francis Marion National Forest during state-wide surveys of approximately 118 wetlands considered to be potential habitat for this species.

In Florida, 39 of the 43 historical sites were relocated. Nine (23%) contained flatwoods salamanders. Additional survey work in 23 counties and at least 530 wetlands with potential habitat, resulted in the location of 81 new breeding sites (15% of total sites surveyed). Fifty-six (69%) of these new breeding sites occur in Liberty and Okaloosa counties. These sites were found due to extensive surveys of the Apalachicola National Forest and Eglin Air Force Base, both of which contain some of the best remaining pine flatwoods habitat in the Southeast. The total number of extant flatwoods salamander populations known to occur in Florida is 36 with 15 (42%) occurring on the Apalachicola National Forest and Eglin Air Force Base.

The combined State data from all survey work completed in the 1990s indicate that 51 populations of flatwoods salamanders are known from across the historical range. Most of these occur in Florida (36 populations or 71%).

Threats

The major threat to the flatwoods salamander is loss of both its longleaf pine/slash pine flatwoods terrestrial habitat and its isolated, seasonally ponded breeding habitat. The combined pine flatwoods (longleaf pine-wiregrass flatwoods and slash pine flatwoods) historical acreage was approximately 32 million acres (13 million hectares). Today, the combined flatwoods acreage has been reduced to 5.6 million (2.3 hectares) acres or approximately 18% of its original extent. These remaining pine flatwoods (non-plantation forests) are typically fragmented, degraded, second-growth forests.

Land use conversions, primarily urban development and conversion to agriculture and pine plantations, eliminated large acreages of pine flatwoods. Surveys of historical flatwoods salamander localities documented the destruction of nine sites from urban development or agriculture and loss of three additional sites due to their conversion to pine plantations. If present rates of loss continue, by 2025 nearly all natural pine flatwoods stands could be destroyed in Florida and Georgia.

Flatwoods salamander wetland breeding sites have also been degraded and destroyed. Alterations in hydrology, agricultural and urban development, silvicultural practices, dumping in or filling of ponds, conversion of wetlands to fish ponds, domestic animal grazing, and soil disturbance reduced the number and diversity of these small wetlands.

Forest management strategies commonly used on pine plantations contribute to degradation of flatwoods salamander forested and wetland habitat. These include soil-disturbing site preparation techniques, lowered fire frequencies and reductions in average area burned per fire event, high seedling stocking rates, and herbicide use, which may reduce plant diversity in the understory. The result of these strategies is a forest that approaches even-age structure, has a dense understory, and low herbaceous cover. Forestry practices that directly affect wetland breeding sites include ditching ponds or low areas to drain water from a site, converting second-growth pine forests to bedded pine plantations, harvesting cypress from the ponds, disposing of slash in wetlands during timber operations, using ponds as part of ditched fire breaks, using fertilizers near wetlands which can result in eutrophication (water enriched in nutrients), and disturbing the soil at a wetland.

Clear-cut harvesting of forested sites appears to be an additional threat. Amphibians, especially salamanders, are vulnerable to habitat drying and reduction of refugia because their moist permeable skin acts as a respiratory organ and must remain moist to function properly. Surveys show that salamanders are displaced from ponds in cut forests, and that there was lowered survivorship in individuals of the breeding population that immigrated to the breeding pond from the clear-cut.

Road construction plays a part in habitat degradation and destruction. At least one historical flatwoods breeding site has been filled in association with the construction of a road. Roads increase the accessibility of breeding ponds to off-road vehicle enthusiasts that use pond basins for "mud bogging," which disturbs the soil and vegetation and degrades the quality of a site for flatwoods salamander breeding. Roads may also alter the quality of isolated wetlands by draining, damming, or redirecting the water in a basin and contributing hydrocarbons and other chemical pollutants via runoff and sedimentation. Roads may also bisect corridors that the salamanders use for migration between ponds.

Exposure to increased predation from fish is a potential threat to the flatwoods salamander. When isolated, seasonally ponded breeding sites are often converted to more permanent wetlands inhabited by fish. Ponds may be modified specifically to serve as fish ponds or sites may be altered due to the construction of drainage ditches or firebreaks, which provide avenues for fish to enter the wetlands. Studies of other ambystomatid species have demonstrated a decline in larval survival in the presence of predatory fish. Fire ants may also pose a threat to the flatwoods salamander.

Habitat fragmentation of the longleaf pine ecosystem, resulting from habitat conversion, threatens the survival of the remaining flatwoods salamander populations Studies have shown that the loss of small fragmented populations is common, and re-colonization is critical for their regional survival. As patches of available habitat become separated beyond the dispersal range of a species, populations are more sensitive to genetic, demographic, and environmental variability and may be unable to recover. Roads contribute to habitat fragmentation by isolating blocks of remaining contiguous habitat. They may disrupt migration routes and dispersal of individuals to and from breeding sites.

Pesticides and herbicides may pose a threat to amphibians such as the flatwoods salamander, because their permeable eggs and skin readily absorb substances from the surrounding aquatic or terrestrial environment. In frogs, use of agricultural pesticides has resulted in lower survival rates, deformities, and lethal effects on tadpoles. Other negative effects of commonly used pesticides and herbicides on amphibians include delayed metamorphosis, paralysis, reduced growth rates, and mortality. Herbicides may also alter the density and species composition of vegetation surrounding a breeding site and reduce the number of potential sites for egg deposition, larval development, or shelter for migrating salamanders.

Long-lasting droughts or frequent floods may affect local flatwoods salamander populations. Although these are natural processes, other threats, such as habitat fragmentation and habitat degradation, may stress a population to the point that it cannot recover or re-colonize other sites.

Conservation and Recovery

The flatwoods salamander occurs on Federal lands administered by the Department of Defense, Fish and Wildlife Service, and U.S. Forest Service. These land management agencies are required to evaluate the potential adverse impacts to the flatwoods salamander from their activities. Federal activities that could affect the flatwoods salamander through destruction or modification of suitable habitat include forest management, military operations, and road construction.

Some populations on Federal lands have benefited where prescribed burning has been used as a regular management tool. However, multiple use priorities on public lands, such as timber production, and military and recreational use, make protection of the flatwoods salamander secondary. The National Environmental Policy Act requires an intensive environmental review of projects that may adversely affect a federally listed species.

At the State and local levels, regulatory mechanisms are also limited. The flatwoods salamander is listed as a rare protected species in Georgia. This designation protects the species by prohibiting actions that cause direct mortality or the destruction of its habitat on lands owned by the State of Georgia and by preventing its sale, purchase, or possession. At present, there is only one known flatwoods salamander population on lands owned by the State of Georgia. In South Carolina, the flatwoods salamander is listed as endangered. Prohibitions extend only to the direct take of the flatwoods salamander. These regulations offer no protection against the most significant threat to the flatwoods salamander, which is loss of its habitat. The flatwoods salamander is considered rare in Florida, but there are no protective regulations for this species or its habitat in the State.

Fire is needed to maintain the natural pine flatwoods community. Ecologists consider fire suppression the primary reason for the degradation of remaining longleaf pine forest acreage. Pine flatwoods naturally burn every three to four years, probably most commonly in the summer months. Sampling of longleaf pine flatwoods sites in Florida indicated that less than 30% of sites on private lands received prescribed burning to mimic the effects of natural fire. The disruption of the natural fire cycle has resulted in an increase in slash pine on sites formerly dominated by longleaf pine, an increase in hardwood understory, and a decrease in herbaceous ground cover. Ponds surrounded by pine plantations and protected from the natural fire regime become unsuitable flatwoods salamander breeding sites, due to canopy closure and the resultant reduction in emergent herbaceous vegetation needed for egg deposition and larval development sites. Current forest management is moving away from burning as a management tool due to liability considerations and concerns that fire will damage the quality of the timber.

Contacts

U. S. Fish and Wildlife Service
Jackson Ecological Services Field Office
6578 Dogwood View Parkway, Suite A
Jackson, Mississippi 39213-7856
Telephone: (601) 965-4900
Fax: (601) 965-4340

U. S. Fish and Wildlife Service
Regional Office, Division of Endangered Species
1875 Century Blvd., Suite 200
Atlanta, Georgia 30345
http://southeast.fws.gov/

Reference

U.S. Fish and Wildlife Service. 1 April 1999. "Final Rule To List the Flatwoods Salamander as a Threatened Species." *Federal Register* 64 (62): 15691-15704.

Santa Cruz Long-toed Salamander

Ambystoma macrodactylum croceum

Status	Endangered
Listed	March 11, 1967
Family	Ambystomidae (Salamander)
Description	Dark, stout-bodied salamander with a broad head and a blunt snout.
Habitat	Shallow, vegetated ponds for breeding; moist soils in chaparral or forested upland areas in the summer.
Food	Omnivorous.
Reproduction	200 eggs laid singly.
Threats	Loss of habitat.
Range	California

Description

The Santa Cruz long-toed salamander, *Ambystoma macrodactylum croceum*, a subspecies of the long-toed salamander, has a snout-to-vent (anal opening) length of up to 3.6 in (9 cm). The body is stout, the head broad, and the snout blunt. Long, slender toes (four on the front and five on the rear feet) appear splayed. Color is a shiny dark brown to black with lighter spotting.

Behavior

To avoid the drying effects of direct sunlight, the Santa Cruz salamander spends most of its life underground in animal burrows or in chambers dug along the root systems of shrubs and woody plants. Adult salamanders are omnivorous, feeding on insects, eggs, larvae, plant matter, and sometimes smaller salamanders.

When the rainy season begins in September or October, salamanders leave their summer feeding grounds and migrate to habitual breeding ponds. Moving only on wet or foggy nights, individuals gradually make their way to these ponds, where they pair and breed. Mating reaches its peak during January and February when heavy rains have filled the ponds. The female lays her eggs on the submerged stalks of spike rush or similar aquatic plants.

Each of about 200 eggs is laid singly and attached to the vegetation. Eggs hatch in about a week, and larvae begin to metamorphose, a process that takes 90-140 days, depending on temperature and weather conditions. In March, adult salamanders return to the summer feeding grounds, leaving the larvae to develop. When ponds begin to dry out toward the end of summer, juveniles seek shelter underground. During the next rainy season, these juveniles disperse and do not return to the breeding pond until sexually mature in three or four years.

Habitat

Summer habitat is typically moist soils in chaparral or more heavily forested upland areas along the coast. Shade and an abundance of soil humus are prime requirements. Breeding ponds are relatively shallow and support abundant submerged vegetation. They fill with rainwater in winter and spring and dry by late summer. Ponds must hold water for at least 90 days, long enough for larvae to develop into juveniles.

Distribution

The Santa Cruz long-toed salamander was discovered in 1954 at Valencia Lagoon in Santa Cruz County. A relict species, it was widely distributed

Santa Cruz Long-toed Salamander, photograph. U. S. Fish and Wildlife Service. Reproduced by permission.

throughout California more than 10,000 years ago, during and immediately after the last glaciation. As the climate became warmer and drier, several populations were isolated in the region between Santa Cruz and Monterey and developed into a distinct subspecies.

The Santa Cruz salamander is found only in Monterey and Santa Cruz Counties in four distinct populations near the towns of Bennett, Ellicott, Seascape, and Valencia.

Threats

Because breeding ponds are used year after year, their destruction or alteration poses a grave threat to this salamander's survival. The breeding pond at Valencia—Valencia Lagoon—was half-filled during highway construction in 1955, and in 1969 the remaining wetlands were drained and an artificial pond built at the site. The salamander survived but

did not flourish. Breeding ponds at Seascape and Bennett are threatened by agricultural and residential development.

Conservation and Recovery

In 1988 U. S. Fish and Wildlife Service personnel helped state agencies devise a management plan for the Valencia Lagoon. The plan includes a redesign of habitat ponds and provides piped-in water from a nearby well to maintain water levels in dry years. Ponds at Ellicott were purchased by the federal government and are now protected as a wildlife refuge. In addition to protecting the ponds, it is important to preserve upland woodlands, where the salamanders feed in the summer. The state of California owns the Santa Cruz Long-Toed Salamander Ecological Reserve and areas at Ellicott Station, which provide some protection for a portion of the salamander's habitat.

Contact

U. S. Fish and Wildlife Service
Regional Office, Division of Endangered Species
Eastside Federal Complex
911 N. E. 11th Ave.
Portland, Oregon 97232-4181
Telephone: (503) 231-6121
http://pacific.fws.gov/

Reference

U. S. Fish and Wildlife Service. 1976. "Santa Cruz Long-Toed Salamander Recovery Plan." U. S. Fish and Wildlife Service, Portland, Oregon.

Sonora Tiger Salamander

Ambystoma tigrinum stebbinsi

Status	Endangered
Listed	January 6, 1997
Family	Ambystomidae (Salamander)
Description	Large salamander with a dark venter and light colored blotches, bars, or reticulation on a dark background.
Habitat	Springs, cienegas, and possibly backwater pools where permanent or nearly permanent water allowed survival of mature branchiates.
Food	Invertebrates, minnows, larval amphibians.
Reproduction	Lays eggs in pond-like habitats, including cattle watering tanks. In permanent waterbodies the adults remain aquatic and retain certain larval characteristics. In waterbodies that are seasonally dry, there is complete metamorphosis into non-gilled adults.
Threats	Disease and predation by introduced non-native fishes and bullfrogs; loss of habitat; low genetic viability.
Range	Arizona

Description

The Sonora tiger salamander, *Ambystoma tigrinum stebbinsi*, is a large salamander with a dark venter and light colored blotches, bars, or reticulation on a dark background. Snout/vent lengths of metamorphosed individuals vary from approximately 2.6-4.9 in (6.5-12.2 cm) Larval salamanders are aquatic with plume-like gills and well-developed tail fins. Larvae hatched in the spring are large enough to metamorphose into terrestrial salamanders from late July to early September, but only an estimated 17-40% metamorphose annually. Remaining larvae mature into branchiates, aquatic and larval-like but sexually mature salamanders that remain in the breeding pond, or over-winter as larvae.

The Sonora tiger salamander was discovered in 1949 at the J. F. Jones Ranch stock tank in Parker Canyon, San Rafael Valley, Arizona. In 1954, based on color patterns of metamorphosed animals, the Sonora tiger salamander was described from southern Santa Cruz County, Arizona as the subspecies *stebbinsi* of the broad-ranging tiger salamander (*Ambystoma tigrinum*). Color patterns were again used to make the next taxonomical determination. In 1965 and 1967, *Ambystoma tigrinum stebbinsi* and *Ambystoma tigrinum tahense* were equated, from the Rocky Mountains region, with *Ambystoma tigrinum nebulosum*, from northern Arizona and New Mexico. Nevertheless, *Ambystoma tigrinum stebbinsi* continued to be recognized in the scientific literature.

Findings were published in 1988 that established the description of color patterns in *Ambystoma tigrinum stebbinsi* was only accurate for recently metamorphosed individuals. About 40% of

Sonoran Tiger Salamander, photograph. U. S. Fish and Wildlife Service. Reproduced by permission.

metamorphosed adults exhibit a unique reticulate pattern, while 60% are marked with light colored blotches, spots, or bars on a dark background that is indistinguishable from *Ambystoma tigrinum mavortium,* found in the central United States and adjacent portions of Mexico. Starch gel electrophoresis of 21 presumptive gene loci of Ambystoma tigrinum stebbinsi were compared with gene loci of Ambystoma rosaceum (from Sonora), Ambystoma tigrinum mavortium, and Ambystoma tigrinum nebulosum. Based on this analysis, distinctive reticulate color patterns, low heterozygosity, and apparent geographic isolation, subspecific designation of *Ambystoma tigrinum stebbinsi* was considered warranted. Further analysis of mitochondrial DNA the same year reaffirmed subspecific designation. Color pattern and allozyme data suggests that *Ambystoma tigrinum stebbinsi* is closely related to *Ambystoma tigrinum mavortium;* however, the *Ambystoma tigrinum stebbinsi* haplotype is derived from *Ambystoma tigrinum nebulosum.* The most likely explanation for these observations is that *Ambystoma tigrinum stebbinsi* arose from a hybridization between *Ambystoma tigrinum mavortium* and *Ambystoma tigrinum nebulosum.*

The grassland community of the San Rafael Valley and adjacent montane slopes, where all extant populations of *Ambystoma tigrinum stebbinsi* occur, may represent a relict grassland and therefore a refugium for grassland species. Tiger salamanders in this area became isolated and, over time, genetically distinct from ancestral *Ambystoma tigrinum mavortium* and *Ambystoma tigrinum nebulosum.*

Based on color patterns and electrophoretic analysis, *Ambystoma* collected in Mexico at one site in Sonora and 17 sites in Chihuahua were all *Ambystoma rosaceum,* not *Ambystoma tigrinum stebbinsi.* Reanalysis of reported *Ambystoma tigrinum stebbinsi* collected in Sonora and at Yepomera, Chihuahua revealed that these specimens were actually *Ambystoma tigrinum rosaceum.*

Behavior

Larval and adult Sonora tiger salamanders are predators that feed voraciously on aquatic invertebrates, minnows, larval amphibians, and other small animals. Terrestrial adults also feed on land invertebrates. Terrestrial adults migrate to breeding ponds in the springtime.

Habitat

All sites where Sonora tiger salamanders have been found are located in the Santa Cruz and San Pedro river drainages, including sites in the San Rafael Valley and adjacent portions of the Patagonia and Huachuca mountains in Santa Cruz and Cochise counties, Arizona. All confirmed historical and extant aquatic populations are found in cattle tanks or impounded cienegas within 19 mi (30.4 km) of Lochiel, Arizona. If the Los Fresnos population is the subspecies *stebbinsi*, it is the only population known to occur in a cienega. Historically, the Sonora tiger salamander probably inhabited springs, cienegas, and possibly backwater pools where permanent or nearly permanent water allowed survival of mature branchiates.

Distribution

Research through the end of the 1980s had documented 18 sites for the Sonora tiger salamander, and additional extensive survey work from 1993 through 1996 revealed another 18 sites, bringing the confirmed site-total to 36. Salamanders tentatively identified as the Sonora tiger subspecies have also been found at Portrero del Alamo at the Los Fresnos cienega in the headwaters of the San Pedro River, San Rafael Valley, Sonora, Mexico and at the lower Peterson Ranch Tank in Scotia Canyon, Cochise County, Arizona. No salamanders have been observed in recent visits to Scotia Canyon; thus, this population may be extirpated. A single terrestrial Sonora tiger salamander was found near Oak Spring in Copper Canyon of the Huachuca Mountains. This individual likely moved to this site from a population at the "Game and Fish Tank" located approximately 0.6 mi (960 m) to the southwest.

A total of 79 aquatic sites in the San Rafael Valley and adjacent slopes of the Huachuca and Patagonia mountains have been surveyed for salamanders. These include most potential aquatic habitats on public lands. However, private lands in the center of the San Rafael Valley have not been surveyed intensively.

Thirty sites in northeastern Sonora and 26 sites in northwestern Chihuahua, Mexico, were surveyed by Collins and Jones in 1987. No Sonora tiger salamanders were found at these sites. *Ambystoma rosaceum* and *Ambystoma tigrinum velasci* occur at localities in Sonora and Chihuahua to the south and east of the extant range of the Sonora tiger salamander. *Ambystoma tigrinum mavortium* occurs at scattered localities to the east in the San Pedro, Sulphur Springs, and San Simon valleys of Arizona, but at least some of these populations were introduced by anglers and bait collectors.

Populations of this salamander fluctuate greatly under the influence of drought and disease, which periodically extirpate or greatly reduce populations. Several tanks supporting aquatic populations went dry during drought in 1994 and again in 1996. As tanks dry out, some larval and branchiate salamanders metamorphose and leave the tanks; others desiccate and die. Disease killed all aquatic salamanders at least three sites in 1985, and also was evident in aquatic populations at seven tanks in 1995-1996. Tanks in which salamanders have been eliminated may be recolonized through reproduction by terrestrial metamorphs. Drying of tanks also may eliminate non-native predators and create sites suitable for salamander colonization.

Because populations are dynamic, the number and location of extant aquatic populations change over time, as exhibited by the differences between survey results in 1985 and 1993-1996. It can be very difficult to determine whether a population is extant or not. If salamander numbers are low, isolated individuals may not be detected during sampling; also, aquatic salamanders may have been recently eliminated due to drought or disease, but terrestrial salamanders may still be present in the area. Of the 36 sites where aquatic Sonora tiger salamanders were recorded since the mid or early 1980s, no salamanders have been found at four tanks during the last three visits from 1993 to 1996. Salamanders were probably extirpated from these locations. Salamanders also were found to be extirpated from the J.F. Jones Ranch Tank, the type locality. Salamanders have not been found during the last three visits from 1993 through 1996 at five other tanks, and they may well be extirpated from these sites. Another three sites where salamanders were found from 1980 to

1983 have not been surveyed since that time. The status of populations at these tanks is unknown. At the remaining 23 tanks, salamanders have been found during one or more of the last three visits from 1993 through 1996. These populations are probably extant.

Populations of aquatic salamanders include as many as several hundred individuals. However, 10 or more salamanders in any one visit were found at only 16 of 32 occupied sites examined by Collins from 1993 through 1996. Large, reproducing populations of Sonora tiger salamanders were more concentrated in the southeastern portion of the San Rafael Valley in the 1990s as compared to the 1980s. Sampling during 1993-1996 revealed few populations and low numbers of salamanders in the northern portion of the valley.

Threats

A variety of factors threaten the Sonora tiger salamander. Disease and predation by introduced non-native fishes and bullfrogs (*Rana catesbeiana*) are probably the most serious and immediate threats, both of which have been implicated in the elimination of aquatic populations. Tiger salamanders are also widely used in Arizona as fishing bait, and this collection of them for bait could extirpate or greatly reduce populations. Other subspecies of tiger salamander introduced into habitats of the Sonora tiger salamander for bait propagation or by anglers could, through interbreeding, genetically swamp distinct *Ambystoma tigrinum stebbinsi* populations. The possibility of the transmission of disease increases as salamanders are moved among tanks by anglers or bait collectors. Additional threats include habitat destruction, reduced fitness resulting from low genetic heterozygosity, and the increased probability of chance extirpation characteristic of small populations.

Stream headcutting threatens the presumed Sonora tiger salamander populations at Los Fresnos cienega in Sonora. Erosion is occurring in Arroyo Los Fresnos downstream from the cienega and the headcut is moving upstream. The causes of this erosion are uncertain, but are presumably livestock grazing and roads in this sparsely populated region. If the causes of this erosion are left unchecked and headcutting continues, it is likely that the cienega habitat will be lost within the foreseeable future. The loss of Los Fresnos cienega may extirpate this

tiger salamander population. If the salamanders at the Los Fresnos cienega are Sonora tiger salamanders, this would represent the only known natural cienega habitat occupied by an aquatic population of this species.

All confirmed Sonora tiger salamander populations have been found in stock tanks or impounded cienegas constructed to collect runoff for livestock. Many tanks probably date from the 1920s and 1930s when government subsidies were available to offset construction costs; however, some tanks were constructed as early as the 1820s and as late as the 1960s. These stock tanks have, to some degree, created and replaced permanent or semipermanent Sonora tiger salamander water sources. Although the tanks provide suitable aquatic habitats, current management and the dynamic nature of these artificial impoundments compromise their ability to support salamander populations in the long term. The tanks collect silt from upstream drainages and must be cleaned out periodically, typically with heavy equipment. This maintenance is done when stock tanks are dry or nearly dry, at an average interval of about 15 years. As the tanks dry out, a proportion of aquatic salamanders typically metamorphose and migrate from the pond. If, however, water is present during maintenance, eggs, branchiate, and larval salamanders may be present and would be lost as a result of the excavation of remaining aquatic habitat. Aquatic salamanders also may occur in the mud of dry or nearly dry tanks and would be affected. Any terrestrial metamorphs at the tank or in areas disturbed would be lost during maintenance activities.

Flooding and drought pose additional threats to stock tank populations of Sonora tiger salamanders. The tanks are simple earthen impoundments without water control structures. Flooding could erode and breach downstream berms or deposit silt, resulting in a loss of aquatic habitat. Long-term drought could dry up stock tanks, as happened in 1994 and 1996. Fires in watersheds above the tanks may lead to increased erosion and sedimentation following storms and exacerbate the effects of flooding.

Sonora tiger salamanders have persisted in stock tanks despite periodic maintenance, flooding, and drought. If the tanks refill soon after drought or other events that result in loss of aquatic habitat, they could presumably be recolonized through terrestrial metamorph reproduction. However, if a tank was dry for several years and isolated from other salamander localities, insufficient terrestrial salamanders may remain and immigration from other populations may be inadequate to recolonize the stock tank. Potential grazing practice changes also threaten aquatic Sonora tiger salamander populations. Stock tanks could be abandoned or replaced by other watering facilities, such as troughs supplied by windmills or pipelines. Troughs do not provide habitat for Sonora tiger salamanders.

Ambystoma tigrinum stebbinsi is considered a species of special concern by the State of Arizona, but this designation affords the species and its habitat no legal protection. Collecting the Sonora tiger salamander in the San Rafael Valley is prohibited, except under special permit. The transport and stocking of live bullfrogs, fishing with live bait fish, and fishing with *Ambystoma* within the range of this salamander in Arizona is also prohibited. Despite these prohibitions, some illegal collecting occurs. Bullfrogs and non-native fish are present at numerous extant and historical Sonora tiger salamander localities, suggesting continued illegal introductions. In 1987, it was reported that tiger salamanders were illegally collected from the San Rafael Valley and transported to at least two tanks in the northern Patagonia Mountains. This incident led them to suspect that bait collectors and anglers often move salamanders among stock tanks.

Furthermore, abandonment, modification, and breaching of stock tanks is allowed on private and public lands, and such actions could eliminate Sonora tiger salamander populations. The extent of these practices and their consequent threats to Ambystoma populations are not presently known. Since Sonora tiger salamander populations are relatively small, collection and associated activities may significantly reduce recruitment, the size of branchiate or larval populations, and genetic diversity within a tank. All these results would increase the likelihood of extirpations.

Arizona anglers and commercial bait dealers also often introduce larval tiger salamanders into ponds and tanks for future bait collecting. The very act of moving larval salamanders to different locations could eventually establish new populations. It was suggested that transport and introduction of salamanders within the San Rafael Valley may have greatly influenced their present distribution.

Moving salamanders could also transmit disease and cause unintentional introductions of fish or bullfrogs, which might reduce or extirpate populations.

The transportation and introduction of salamanders poses an additional threat. *Ambystoma tigrinum mavortium* is common in stock tanks and ponds to the east of the San Rafael Valley. Bait dealers and anglers probably introduced many of these populations. If *Ambystoma tigrinum mavortium* is introduced into Sonora tiger salamander localities, populations of the latter could be lost due to genetic swamping by interbreeding of the two subspecies. This is of particular concern for Sonora tiger salamander populations inhabiting stock tanks that could wash out during a storm or dry out during drought. Additionally, Sonora tiger salamander genetic heterozygosity is among the lowest reported for any salamander. Low heterozygosity indicates low genetic variation, which increases demographic variability and the chance of local extirpations.

Sonora tiger salamander populations are eliminated by non-native fish predation, particularly sunfish and catfish. In laboratory studies, bullhead, mosquito fish, and sunfish ate Sonora tiger salamander eggs, hatchlings, and small larvae. Introduced non-native fish are well-established in the San Rafael Valley and have been implicated in apparent Sonora tiger salamander extirpations from five stock tanks, including the type locality. Non-native fish are known to occur at only one of 23 sites where salamanders have been found during one or more of the last three visits from 1993 through 1996. However, non-native fish occur at seven of ten sites where the salamander is thought to be extirpated or where it has not been found during the last three visits. The effect of native fishes on salamander populations is unknown, although some native species have a potential to prey on Sonora tiger salamanders. No native fish are known to occur with aquatic populations of salamanders.

Bullfrogs occur with Sonora tiger salamanders at 16 of 23 sites at which salamanders have been found during one or more of the last three visits from 1993 through 1996. Adult bullfrogs are known to prey on salamanders; however, bullfrog tadpoles do not eat viable salamander eggs or hatchlings. Bullfrogs were found to be more widely distributed in the San Rafael Valley in the 1990s as compared to 1985. The effect of predation by bullfrogs on salamander populations is unknown, but increased mortality attributable to bullfrog predation would likely reduce population viability.

Virtually no recruitment was noted in recent surveys, as evidenced by a lack of surviving larvae in tanks where eggs were known to have been deposited. Lack of recruitment appeared to be a result of predation by overwintering branchiate and larval salamanders. This predation may occur because degraded habitat has lost the structural complexity of emergent and shoreline vegetation, logs, and rocks that would provide cover and protection from predation. Lack of shoreline and emergent vegetation is at least partially due to trampling and foraging by cattle.

A disease characterized by sloughing of skin and hemorrhaging killed all branchiate salamanders at Huachuca Tank, Parker Canyon Tank #1, and Inez Tank in 1985, and has been detected at seven tanks in 1995-1996. The disease may be caused by a combination of a virus and the Aeromonas bacterial infections. Parker Canyon Tank #1 and Inez Tank were recolonized by 1987, and salamanders were found once again at Huachuca Tank in 1994. These tanks were presumably recolonized by reproducing terrestrial metamorphs that survived the disease or that moved to these tanks from adjacent populations. At the seven tanks where the disease was found in 1995-1996, the effects on the populations will not be known until the disease runs its course. If the disease recurs with enough frequency, populations could be lost due to lack of recruitment of juveniles into the adult cohort. Genetic variability is already very low in this subspecies, and this disease has the potential to depress genetic variability even further, greatly increasing the chances of population extirpations. Bullfrogs, wading birds, waterfowl, and other animals that move among tanks may facilitate spread of the disease.

The ability of Sonora tiger salamanders to move between populations is unknown, but arid grassland, savanna, or pine-oak woodland separate all populations and movement through these relatively dry landscapes is probably limited. Movement would be most likely during storms or where wet drainages are available as movement corridors. The distance between aquatic populations of Sonora

tiger salamander is frequently more than 1 mi (1.6 km), and much greater distances separate several sites. Game and Fish Tank, for example, is 6.3 mi (10 km) from the nearest adjacent aquatic population. Even if these salamanders are capable of moving relatively long distances, some populations may be geographically isolated. Small, isolated populations have an increased probability of extirpation.

Disease, predation by non-native predators, and drying of tanks during drought further increase the chance of extirpation. Once populations are extirpated, natural recolonization of these isolated habitats may not occur.

Conservation and Recovery

The Coronado National Forest conferred with the Fish and Wildlife Service on the effects of issuance of grazing permits in the Duquesne, Campini, and San Rafael allotments within the range of the Sonora tiger salamander. The Service determined that issuance of the permits would not likely jeopardize the continued existence of the salamander provided that stock tank maintenance and management plans were promptly developed and implemented for the allotments. These plans would ensure the maintenance of quality aquatic habitat for the Sonora tiger salamander.

Contact

U. S. Fish and Wildlife Service
Division of Endangered Species and Habitat Conservation
2105 Osuna Road N.E.
Albuquerque, New Mexico 87103-1001
Telephone: (505) 346-2525
E-mail: r2esweb@fws.gov
http://ifwes.fws.gov/

Reference

U.S. Fish and Wildlife Service. 6 January 1997. "Endangered and Threatened Wildlife and Plants; Determination of Endangered Status for Three Wetland Species Found in Southern Arizona and Northern Sonora, Mexico." *Federal Register* 62 (3): 665-689.

Desert Slender Salamander

Batrachoseps aridus

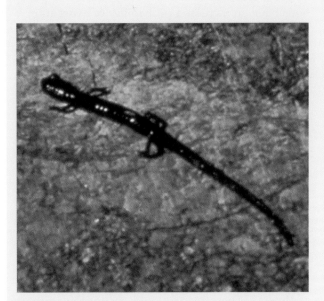

Status	Endangered
Listed	June 4, 1973
Family	Plethodontidae (Lungless Salamander)
Description	Reclusive, nocturnal salamander.
Habitat	Desert canyons; fractures in limestone walls.
Food	Insects.
Reproduction	Eggs laid between November and January.
Threats	Low numbers, limited distribution.
Range	California

Desert Slender Salamander, photograph by Larry D. Foreman. Bureau of Land Management. Reproduced by permission.

Description

The desert slender salamander is an anatomically primitive member of its genus, measuring less than 4 in (10.2 cm) from the snout to the tip of the tail. It has four toes on each foot and a large rounded head. It is dark maroon to deep chocolate with numerous tiny silvery blue spots and scattered large patches of gold. The belly is dark maroon, and the tail a contrasting flesh color. This salamander was discovered and described as a new species in 1970.

Behavior

The reclusive desert slender salamander spends most of its life within porous-soil, bedrock fractures, or limestone sheeting, where groundwater seepage provides moisture. Occasionally found under loose rocks by day, the salamander is most active at night. When disturbed, it winds itself up into a watch-spring-like coil.

This salamander stalks and eats small invertebrates, with flies and ants making up the bulk of its diet. The influence of season, temperature, moisture, food supply, predation, and breeding on the salamander's surface activity and population size are largely unknown. Little is known about the salamander's breeding habits. Females probably lay eggs between November and January soon after the first heavy rains of winter.

Habitat

This salamander lives in an arid region of low and erratic rainfall, high summer temperatures, and strong spring winds. Seasonal watercourses between steep canyon walls of igneous and metamorphic rock are found above and below the limestone strata inhabited by the salamander. Exposed bedrock, talus, and coarse-grained sand form surface material on surrounding slopes. The sparse plant community, typical of a desert oasis, consists of fen palm, narrow-leaved willow, squaw-waterweed, stream orchid, maidenhair fern, and sugarbush.

Distribution

Because it was so recently discovered, little information is available on the historical distribution of the desert slender salamander. It has been found only on the lower slopes of the Santa Rosa Mountains in Riverside County in southern California. Because of its isolation from other members of the genus and its primitive characteristics, scientists surmise that the slender desert salamander is a relict species that was more widespread during earlier, wetter geological epochs.

The desert slender salamander is known from two locations—Hidden Palms Canyon and Guadalupe Canyon. Hidden Palms Canyon is at the box end of Deep Canyon, a large gorge that drains the surrounding slopes of the Santa Rosa Mountains. The inhabited area is less than an acre and supports fewer than 500 individuals. The Guadalupe Canyon population appears much smaller in range and numbers, consisting of perhaps 100 individuals, but this site has not been closely studied.

Threats

The major threat to the survival of this salamander is its extremely restricted distribution. This makes the species particularly vulnerable to any natural catastrophe. For example, unusually severe rainfall and flooding associated with a tropical storm in 1976 caused the erosion and collapse of a limestone wall that made up as much as one-third of the salamander's habitat at Hidden Palms. At the other extreme, an extended drought could dry up groundwater seepage, rendering the species extinct. Human activity in the area is slight.

Conservation and Recovery

Land surrounding both populations, comprising about 138 acres (55 hectares), was acquired by the state of California in 1973. The following year, this tract was established as the Hidden Palms Ecological Reserve, managed by the California Fish and Game Commission. After the flooding of 1976, the rock wall of the Hidden Palms habitat was reinforced to prevent any further collapse. Boulder barricades were constructed to restrict unauthorized access to both canyons. The management plan for the reserve will consider other steps as needed to stabilize the habitat or to discourage human disturbance.

Contact

U. S. Fish and Wildlife Service
Regional Office, Division of Endangered Species
Eastside Federal Complex
911 N.E. 11th Ave.
Portland, Oregon 97232-4181
(503) 231-6121
http://pacific.fws.gov/

References

Brame, A. H. 1970. "A New Species of *Batrachoseps* (Slender Salamander) from the Desert of Southern California." *Los Angeles County Museum Contributions to Science* No. 200.

U. S. Fish and Wildlife Service. 1982. "Desert Slender Salamander Recovery Plan." U. S. Fish and Wildlife Service, Portland.

San Marcos Salamander

Eurycea nana

Status	Threatened
Listed	July 14, 1980
Family	Plethodontidae (Lungless Salamander)
Description	Long narrow body light brown above with a row of pale flecks and yellowish white below.
Habitat	Lakes and rivers.
Food	Amphipods, aquatic snails, and fly larvae.
Reproduction	Egg masses in standing pools.
Threats	Groundwater pumping.
Range	Texas

Description

The slender-bodied San Marcos salamander, *Eurycea nana*, is about 2.4 in (6 cm) long and displays a prominent gill fringe behind the head. It is light brown above with a row of pale flecks on either side of the midline and yellowish white below. The large eyes have a dark ring around the lens. Limbs are short and slender with four toes on the forefeet and five on the hind feet. At first glance, it is similar to a lizard but lacks scales and claws. The specific name *nana* is from the Greek *nanos*, meaning "dwarf." This voiceless salamander is also earless.

Prominent external features of the small, slender salamander are moderately large eyes with a dark ring around the lens, well-developed and highly pigmented gills, relatively short, slender limbs with four toes on the forefeet and five on the hind feet, and a slender tail with well-developed dorsal fin. Compared to other neotenic *Eurycea* from Texas, the San Marcos salamander is smaller and more slender, different in coloration, has larger eyes relative to the size of its head, a greater number of costal grooves, and fewer pterygoid and premaxillary teeth.

Behavior

Salamanders lay jelly-covered eggs from which tiny fishlike larvae emerge and develop in the manner of tadpoles. The San Marcos salamander breeds and lays eggs in standing pools amid thick mats of aquatic vegetation. Eggs hatch in about 24 days. This species is carnivorous and feeds on amphipods, midge fly larvae, and aquatic snails. It remains stationary until prey pass closely and then abruptly snaps its head, taking the prey.

Salamanders in laboratory aquaria feed on amphipods and young brine shrimp. Stomach content analyses of 80 preserved specimens revealed the salamander's diet in its natural habitat included amphipods and midge fly larvae and pupae; other small insect pupae and naiads and small aquatic snails were found in lesser numbers. Small amounts of *Lyngbya* sp. and grains of sand occasionally were present, apparently as incidental items ingested along with principal food items. Feeding behavior observed in the laboratory indicated that the salamanders did not actively pursue their prey. Salamanders remained stationary until the prey items were near their head, then abruptly snapped forward while opening their mouths to engulf food items. This information suggests they respond either to visual or vibrational cues from living prey.

Male *E. nana* reach sexual maturity (possess at least one full darkly-pigmented lobe in each testis) after attaining a snout-vent length of 0.7 in (1.9 cm) or 1.4 in (3.5 cm) total length. All males with snout-vent lengths greater than 0.9 in (2.3 cm) or 1.6-1.8 in (4-4.5 cm) total length were mature, possessing

San Marcos Salamander, photograph. U. S. Fish and Wildlife Service. Reproduced by permission.

darkly-pigmented testes with one to three lobes. Laboratory studies suggest that the salamanders breed in June and possibly again in the fall.

Salamanders had the following four classes of ova in the oviducts: very small clear ova, small opaque-white ova, small yellow ova, and large yellow ova. Females carrying large yellow ova are considered gravid and presumably ready for oviposition. Large yellow ova were present in females with snout-vent lengths greater than 0.8 in (2 cm) or 1.4 in (3.5 cm) total length. Females with a snout-vent length longer than 1 in (2.5 cm) carried one to 19 large yellow ova. Large yellow ova were present in some females in nearly every month of the year.

Courtship and egg deposition by *E. nana* has not been reported and no eggs have been collected from the habitat. However, courtship, oviposition, and hatching have been observed for the closely related Comal Springs salamander. Eggs of this species were deposited singly on plant material, stones, and the bottom of a glass bowl about 24 hours after courtship. The Comal Springs salamander has reproduced successfully several time in artificial spring upwellings at the Dallas Aquarium. Most, if not all, *Eurycea* breed in running water of brooks, caves, or springs. In most cases, adherent eggs are deposited singly on the bottom and sides of stones, or on aquatic vegetation.

The San Marcos salamander is capable of altering its dorsal coloration from light tan to dark brown in accord with the lightness or darkness of the substrate. This color change is accomplished by migration of pigment in melanophores, giving them these structures the appearance of expanding or shrinking.

The salamander's external gills expand and appear bright red from increased blood flow in cool water of low oxygen content. The bushy red gills are prominent on individuals when collected from the springs, but they show marked reduction, almost to the point of apparent resorption when specimens are kept in well-oxygenated aquaria.

Habitat

The San Marcos salamander is found in shallow alkaline springs carved out of limestone with sand and gravel substrates. Pools and streambeds are often punctuated with large limestone boulders. Aquatic vegetation is profuse, and the pool surfaces are covered with moss (*Leptodictyium riparium*) and thick mats of coarse, blue-green algae. In Spring Lake it occurs where rocks are associated with spring openings, and in rocky areas up to 492 ft (150 m) downstream of the dams at Spring Lake.

The salamander is also found in shallow spring areas on the uppermost (northernmost) portion of Spring Lake on a limestone shelf in an area immediately in front of Aquarena Springs Hotel. The substrate in this area is sand and gravel interspersed with large limestone boulders. Concrete banks in front of the hotel and boulders in shallow (3.3-6.6 ft, or 1-2 m deep) water support a lush growth of an attached aquatic moss. Interspersed with the moss and blanketing the shallow sandy substrate are thick filamentous mats of a coarse, filamentous blue-green alga, the dark reddish-brown color of which almost perfectly matches the dark dorsal coloration of the San Marcos salamander.

Spirogyra sp. and a few other larger filamentous green algae species, as well as the carnivorous angiosperm known as bladderwort (*Utricularia gibba*), are present in small amounts in the aquatic moss. A wide variety of rooted aquatic macrophytes occur on the periphery of the salamander habitat at 3-10-ft (0.9-3.1-m) depths. The macrophytes include arrowhead (*Sagittaria platyphylla*), parrot's feather (*Myriophyllum brasiliense*), water primrose (*Ludwigia reens*), and wild celery (*Vallisneria americana*). In deeper water, Carolina fanwort (*Cabomba caroliniana*), Hydrilla (*Hydrilla verticillata*), and elodea (*Egeria densa*) become the dominant macrophytes of the mud and detritus-laden benthic region.

The salamanders are abundant within the wiry mesh of the aquatic moss and the filamentous mats of *Lyngbya* sp. in the shallow headwaters area. Sandy substrates devoid of vegetation and muddy silt or detritus-laden substrates with or without vegetation are apparently unsuitable habitats for *E. nana*. Specimens occasionally are collected from beneath stones in predominantly sand and gravel areas. In view of the abundance of predators (primarily larger fish, but also crayfish, turtles, and aquatic birds) in the immediate vicinity of the springs, protective cover such as that afforded by the moss and cyanophycean bacteria (=blue-green algae) is essential to the survival of the salamander. This vegetation also supports a plentiful food supply for the salamander.

Flowing water is apparently a prerequisite for suitable *E. nana* habitat, as no specimens were found in still water areas of the lake or river. The flowing spring waters in the principal habitat are slightly alkaline, stenothermal (narrow range of temperatures) at 69.8-71.6°F (21-22°C), and clear.

In summary, the San Marcos salamander apparently requires: (1) thermally constant waters; (2) flowing water; (3) clean and clear water; (4) sand, gravel, and rock substrates with little mud or detritus; (5) vegetation for cover; and (6) an adequate food supply.

Distribution

The limited range of the San Marcos salamander comprises the San Marcos Springs, Spring Lake, and a few hundred feet (1 ft=0.3 m) of the San Marcos River in Hays County of Texas. In 1976, population numbers in the floating algal mats at the uppermost portion of Spring Lake to be between about 17,000 and 21,000 individuals. Following the same procedure, a survey published in 1993 estimated that the mats were inhabited by about 23,000 salamanders. Also published that year, an additional search of rocky susbtrates around the spring openings throughout Spring Lake located an estimated 25,000 salamanders. At the time, estimates of the population below Spring Lake associated with the rocky substrate were calculated to be approximately 5,000 individuals. The total population estimates from these combined studies stood at 53,200 for Spring Lake in 1993, and some of these estimates, notably the rocky substrate figures, were thought to be low.

Threats

Although the population appears relatively stable for the moment, the salamander is threatened by potential degradation or modification of its very limited habitat. This region, which is halfway between San Antonio and Austin, has experienced an upsurge in residential and agricultural development. The rising demand for water for human use and irrigation may well cause the spring sources to dry up in a very few years. The endangered Texas wild-rice (*Zizania texana*), found further downstream near the town of San Marcos, has suffered from generally lower water levels in recent years.

Conservation and Recovery

The owner of Spring Lake has taken care to safeguard the spring sources and has cooperated closely with biologists to ensure that wildlife populations are protected. The key to preserving the San Marcos salamander is controlling the amount of water that is pumped out of the ground—a divisive issue in semi-arid south-central Texas. Critical Habitat was designated for the salamander to include its entire known range in Hays County.

Experiments are underway at the Dallas Aquarium to develop captive breeding techniques for the salamander in the event that the natural population at San Marcos Spings is lost, using techniques patterned after those used for the breeding the Comal salamander. Efforts to induce propagation at another facility in simulated spring environments were unsuccessful.

The 1996 San Marcos/Comal (Revised) Recovery Plan, which covers the San Marcos salamander and four other listed species, notes that recovery goals for the habitat's species include the survival of these species in their native ecosystems; the development of an ecosystem approach using strategies to address both local, site-specific and broad regional issues related to recovery; and the conservation of the integrity and function of the aquifer and spring-fed ecosystems that these species inhabit.

Delisting is considered unattainable for all five species (including the San Marcos salamander) due to the potential for extinction from catastrophic events. Consequently, the revised Recovery Plan calls for the establishment and continued maintenance of refugia capability for all five species in case of a catastrophic event.

Contact

Regional Office of Endangered Species
U. S. Fish and Wildlife Service
P. O. Box 1306
Albuquerque, New Mexico 87103
http://southwest.fws.gov/

References

Bishop, S. C. 1943. *Handbook of Salamanders*. Comstock Publishing, Ithaca, New York.

Tupa, D. D., and W. K. Davis. 1976. "Population Dynamics of the San Marcos Salamander, *Eurycea nana* Bishop." *Texas Journal of Science* 32: 179-195.

U. S. Fish and Wildlife Service. 1980. "Determination of the San Marcos salamander (*Eurycea nana*) as Threatened." *Federal Register* 45: 47355-47364.

U. S. Fish and Wildlife Service. 1984. "San Marcos River Recovery Plan." U. S. Fish and Wildlife Service, Albuquerque.

U. S. Fish and Wildlife Service. 1987. "Endangered and Threatened Species of Texas and Oklahoma (with 1988 Addendum)." U. S. Fish and Wildlife Service, Albuquerque.

U. S. Fish and Wildlife Service. 1996. "San Marcos and Comal Springs and Associated Aquatic Ecosystems (Revised) Recovery Plan." U. S. Fish and Wildlife Service, Albuquerque.

Barton Springs Salamander

Eurycea sosorum

Status	Endangered
Listed	April 30, 1997
Family	Plethodontidae (Lungless Salamander)
Description	Slender salamander with slightly elongate limbs and reduced eyes; color varies from pale purplish-brown to gray or yellowish-cream.
Habitat	Barton Springs, Texas.
Food	Amphipods and other small invertebrates.
Reproduction	Breeds year-round; lays eggs underground.
Threats	Urbanization.
Range	Texas

Description

The *Eurycea sosorum* (Barton Springs salamander) was first collected from Barton Springs Pool in 1946, was recognized in 1978 as distinct from other central Texas *Eurycea* salamanders based on its restricted distribution and unique morphological and skeletal characteristics (such as its reduced eyes, elongate limbs, dorsal coloration, and reduced number of presacral vertebrae), and was given formal description based on genetic studies in June 1993. The Barton Springs salamander is entirely aquatic and neotenic (meaning it does not metamorphose into a terrestrial form and retains its bright red external gills throughout life) and depends on a constant supply of clean, flowing water from Barton Springs. Adults attain an average length of 2.5 in (6.35 cm). This species is slender, with slightly elongate limbs and reduced eyes. Dorsal coloration varies from pale purplish-brown or gray to yellowish-cream. Irregular spacing of dorsal pigments and pigment gaps results in a mottled, "salt and pepper" pattern.

Behavior

The Barton Springs salamander appears to be primarily a surface-dwelling species that retreats underground to lay eggs and to weather unfavorable conditions such as drought; its diet is believed to consist almost entirely of amphipods (*Hyallela azteca*) and other small invertebrates. Primary predators of the Barton Springs salamander are believed to be fish and crayfish. Observations of larvae and females with eggs indicate breeding occurs year-round. The Barton Springs salamander's eggs are white and have never been observed in the wild. The salamander is vulnerable to declining water quality and quantity and other forms of habitat modification.

Habitat

The Barton Springs salamander is known to only inhabit Barton Springs, the fourth largest spring in Texas. The water that discharges at Barton Springs originates from the Barton Springs segment of the Edwards aquifer. The Barton Springs segment covers roughly 155 sq mi (400 sq km) from southern Travis County to northern Hays County, Texas. The watersheds of the six creeks upstream (west) of the recharge zone span about 264 sq mi (680 sq km). This area is referred to as the contributing zone and includes portions of Travis, Hays, and Blanco Coun-

Barton Springs Salamander, photograph. U. S. Fish and Wildlife Service. Reproduced by permission.

ties. The recharge and contributing zones, known as the Barton Springs watershed, make up the total area that provides water to the aquifer, which equals about 354 sq mi (920 sq km).

The Barton Springs salamander is found near three of four hydrologically connected spring outlets that collectively make up Barton Springs. These three outlets are known as Parthenia, Eliza, and Sunken Garden, and they occur in Zilker Park, which is owned and operated by the City of Austin.

The area around Parthenis Springs, the main spring outlet, was impounded in the late 1920s to create Barton Springs Pool, while flows from Eliza and Sunken Garden springs are also retained by concrete structures and form small pools located on either side of Barton Springs Pool. The salamander has been observed at depths of about 0.3-16 ft (9-500 cm) of water under gravel and small rocks, submerged leaves, and algae; among aquatic vegetation; and buried in organic debris. It is generally not found on exposed limestone surfaces or in silted areas.

No other species of *Eurycea* is known to occur in this portion of the aquifer. Although the extent to which the Barton Springs salamander occurs in the aquifer is unknown, it is likely concentrated near the spring openings where food supplies are abundant, water chemistry and temperatures are relatively constant, and where the salamander has immediate access to both surface and subsurface habitats. Barton Springs is also the main discharge point for the entire Barton Springs segment, and is one of the few perennial springs in the area.

Distribution

No evidence exists that the range of the Barton Springs Salamander has ever extended beyond the immediate vicinity of Barton Springs in Zilker Park, Austin, Travis County, Texas. The species was reported to be abundant among the aquatic vegetation in the deep end of Barton Springs Pool during the later 1940s. The Barton Springs Salamander's numbers appear to have declined sharply in recent years. The first comprehensive surveys conducted in Barton Springs Pool a week apart in November 1992 counted 80 and 150 individuals. A comprehensive survey done immediately after an October 1994 flood reported a total of 16 salamanders, while only 10 were counted in March 1995. In June 1993, the City of Austin began monthly surveys that produced counts ranging from one to 27 individuals for the period between July 1993 to March 1995 and from three to 45 individuals between April 1995 to April 1996. Where "dozens or hundreds" of individuals were estimated to occur among sunken leaves in Eliza Pool during the 1970s, surveys in the late 1980s and mid-1990s variously reported zero to 28 living individuals. The salamander was first observed at Sunken Garden Springs in January 1993. Less than 20 individuals have been reported on any given visit to that outlet. Because it is part of the Barton Springs complex and is hydrologically connected to Parthenia Springs, biologists had speculated that the salamander occurred at Sunken Garden Springs, though it had not been observed in surveys conducted there between 1987-1992. Low water levels and the presence of large rocks and sediment make searching for salamanders difficult at Sunken Garden Springs.

Threats

The primary threat to the Barton Springs salamander is degradation through urban expansion of the quality and quantity of water that feeds Barton Springs. Urbanization dramatically increases stormwater runoff as natural ground cover is lost to impervious paved surfaces. Greater stormflow increases the frequency and severity of flooding, while simultaneoulsy making water resources more susceptible to severe dwindling during drought conditions. Sediment from soil erosion constitutes the largest volume of pollutants in surface waters and is itself the biggest carrier of additional pollutants found in water, including suspended solids, nutrients, petroleum hydrocarbons, bacteria, heavy metals, volatile organic compounds, commercial solvents, fertilizers, and pesticides.

Groundwater contamination is also caused by highway construction, leaking septic tanks and pipelines, and petroleum storage tank releases.

Karst aquifers characterized by porous limestone like the Barton springs segment transport pollutants rapidly once contaminated runoff enters creeks and other recharge features. The Edwards aquifer is

therefore one of the most sensitive in Texas to the groundwater pollution that very frequently accompanies rapid urban development. Because groundwater originating from Barton Creek remains in the aquifer for short periods before discharging at the springs, there is little time for attenuation of pollutants before discharging at Barton Springs. Amphibians are known to be very sensitive to environmental contaminants because of their semipermeable skin. The Barton Springs salamander lives at the main discharge point for the aquifer, is continuously exposed to the waters emanating from it, and its diminishing presence serves as an early warning sign of deteriorating water quality and quantity in the Barton Springs watershed, which is the primary source of drinking water for the city of Austin.

One of the most immediate threats to the Barton Springs salamander is siltation of its habitat, owing primarily to major highway and subdivision construction activities in the Barton Creek watershed. High levels of suspended solids, such as the ones that occurred for five months after the October 1994 flood, are very harmful to aquatic fauna; Barton Springs Pool had its lowest recorded population counts of the salamander during this period.

Sediments cover much of the bottom of Eliza Pool and Sunken Garden Springs, and the Barton Springs salamander is typically found in silt-free areas near the spring outlets.

Problems caused by increased habitat sediment loads for the salamander include loss of livable areas, asphyxiation through clogging of the gills, smothered eggs, reduced oxygen availability in the water, loss of spawning sites, and reduced light transmission for aquatic-plant photosynthesis that can damage the food chain.

Contaminants like petroleum hydrocarbons and heavy metals also bind readily to sediments, and they are especially toxic to *Hyallela azteca*, the primary food item of the Barton Springs salamander Chronic releases from underground storage tanks are a major source of ground-water pollution. Gasoline, diesel fuel, and other petroleum products are all toxic pollutants that can effect acquifiers very quickly, and lead is also a very dangerous component of petrochemical pollution. Sewage effluent may contain a host of dangerous chemicals, heavy metals, pesticides, fertilizers, nitrogen and phosphorus nutrients, inorganic acids, and microorganisms. Wastewater discharges have been identified as a primary cause of algal blooms, a recurring problem in both Barton Creek and at Barton Springs. Increased nutrients promote eutrophication of aquatic ecosystems, including the growth of bacteria, algae, and nuisance aquatic plants, and lowered oxygen levels. Leaking septic tanks and inadequate filtering in septic fields have also been identified as a major source of groundwater contamination.

An estimated 4,800 septic systems currently exist in the Barton Springs watershed and may contribute as much as 23% of the total nitrogen load to the aquifer. Because of the Barton Springs salamander's limited range, a single catastrophic spill has the potential to impact the entire species and its habitat. Catastrophic spills can result from major transportation accidents, underground storage tank leaks, pipeline ruptures, sewage spills, vandalism, and other sources.

Increased demands on water supplies from the aquifer reduce the quality and quantity of water in the Barton Springs segment and at Barton Springs. The volume of springflow is regulated by the level of water in the aquifer. Spring discharge decreases as water storage in the aquifer drops; when water storage drops, the potential for "bad water" intrusion to the aquifer increases markedly. In addition to contributing to declining groundwater supplies, water wells often are a major source of groundwater contamination because they provide pollutants direct access into the aquifer. Reduced groundwater levels exacerbate the problem through decreased dilution of pollutants.

Other potential impacts to the salamander's surface habitat may include the use of high pressure fire hoses in areas where the salamander occurs, hosing silt from the shallow end of Barton Springs Pool into the salamander's habitat, diverting water from Sunken Garden Springs into Barton Creek below Barton Springs, and runoff from the train station above Eliza Pool.

Conservation and Recovery

The long-term survival of the Barton Springs salamander can only be ensured by preserving the health of the Edwards aquifer and the Barton Springs complex. This can only be done through an organized, concerted, and disciplined effort by all affected Federal, State, and local governments and the private citizenry to protect the Barton Springs watershed. This united action is necessary because, aside from the potential for catastrophic spills, it is the accumulated burden of many smaller developmental activities and water withdrawals that threaten the habitat of the Barton Springs salamander. Conservation of this species entails removing threats to its survival. These include protecting the quality and quantity of springflow from Barton Springs by implementing comprehensive management programs to control and reduce point and nonpoint sources of pollution throughout the Barton Springs watershed; minimizing the risk and likelihood of pollution events that would affect water quality; strengthening efforts to protect groundwater and springflow quantity; continuing to examine and implement pool cleaning practices and other park operations that protect and perpetuate the salamander's surface habitat and population; and public outreach and education. It is also anticipated that listing will encourage continued research on the critical aspects of the Barton Springs salamander's biology such as longevity, natality, sources of mortality, feeding and breeding ecology, and sensitivity to water contaminants.

The Service's original intention to list the Barton springs salamander as Endangered in 1996 was put aside because of a Conservation Agreement with various Texas agencies and authorities that would have increased protection for the salamander's habitat. This action was disallowed by a Texas court, and Fish and Wildlife Service was required to make a listing determination within thirty days; the court's decision on what was allowable information to consider and the limited time frame meant the Service had to make its determination without being able to examine all the information potentially available. During the comment period, the Service received written and oral comments, a majority of which supported the proposed action.

Contacts

U. S. Fish and Wildlife Service
Ecological Services Field Office
10711 Burnet Road, Suite 200
Austin, Texas 78758-4460
Telephone: (512) 490-0057

U. S. Fish and Wildlife Service
Regional Office, Division of Endangered Species
P.O. Box 1306
Albuquerque, New Mexico 87103-1306
Telephone: (505) 248-6911
Fax: (505) 248-6915
http://southwest.fws.gov/

Reference

U. S. Fish and Wildlife Service. 30 April 1997. "Final Rule To List the Barton Springs Salamander as Endangered." *Federal Register* 62 (83): 23377-23392.

Red Hills Salamander

Phaeognathus hubrichti

Status	Threatened
Listed	December 3, 1976
Family	Plethodontidae (Lungless Salamander)
Description	Large dark brown to dark gray body with stubby limbs and a prehensile tail.
Habitat	Ravine slopes in mature hardwood forests.
Food	Insects.
Reproduction	Four to nine eggs.
Threats	Restricted habitat; intensive logging.
Range	Alabama

Description

Regarded as a relict from cooler, moister prehistoric times, the Red Hills salamander, *Phaeognathus hubrichti*, is considered large, attaining a maximum total length of 9 in (22.5 cm). The elongated body has 20-22 costal grooves, with 12 or more intercostal folds between adpressed limbs (front limbs bent backward, hindlimbs forward). The limbs are noticeably short. Adults lack gills. The color of the body and prehensile tail is uniform dark brown to dark gray, although irregular fading in preserved animals may produce a bi-colored effect.

Behavior

This highly specialized salamander is extremely sensitive to any alteration of its habitat. It rarely leaves its burrow (in hillsides where soils are suitable), and preys upon ground-dwelling arthropods located within burrows or outside burrows near the burrow entrance.

Based on observations of captive individuals, clutch size is probably four to nine eggs, which are deposited in cavities inside burrows. The overall reproductive rate of the species is low.

Habitat

Prime habitat for the Red Hills salamander is on moderately steep, forested ravines and bluffs with a northern exposure. Natural vegetation of these moist, steep, sheltered slopes and ravines consists of a beech-magnolia forest community. Characteristic woody species in the forest overstory include American beech (*Fagus grandifolia*), bigleaf magnolia (*Magnolia macrophylla*), southern magnolia (*M. grandiflora*), white oak (*Quercus alba*), and tulip tree (*Liriodendron tulipifera*).

The habitat is characterized by mature hardwoods in a loamy, friable topsoil. A layer of siltstone underlies many population sites, and salamander burrows almost invariably extend into cavities scooped out of this soft rock. Siltstone efficiently retains moisture, which is necessary for the salamander's survival. Individuals have been found nesting near groundwater seepages.

Distribution

This species is endemic to the Red Hills region of the Gulf coastal plain of southern Alabama.

Threats

The most important limiting factors for this species are its specific habitat requirements and its low rate of reproduction. In optimal habitat, the salamander is found in uniform densities, suggesting that such factors as predation, food supply, insecticide contamination, or competition are not important threats.

Red Hills Salamander, photograph by C. Kenneth Dodd, Jr., USGS. Reproduced by permission.

Logging operations in the region have been detrimental to the species. A large tract of habitat nearly 3,700 acres (1,500 hectares) was clear-cut and mechanically bedded in 1976. Much of the tract was then planted with pine, creating conditions that do not support the salamander. It is estimated that another 3,090 acres (1,250 hectares) have been rendered marginally habitable by intensive select-cutting. On the other hand, long-rotation, limited select-cutting does not appear to harm the salamander.

Paper companies own up to 44% of the remaining habitat and are currently using a variety of timber management techniques. The International Paper Company, which owned about 13% of the habitat in 1983, publicly announced that it would adjust its management practices to benefit the salamander. Other paper companies have avoided intensive cutting on the steep slopes and bluffs that were likely to support the salamander.

Conservation and Recovery

The recovery of the Red Hills salamander is being promoted through a Habitat Conservation Plan (HCP) developed by International Paper Timberlands Operating Company, Ltd. (International Paper) and the U.S. Fish and Wildlife Service. Under this plan, about 6,400 acres (2,590 hectares) that include the best salamander habitat on International Paper lands will be conserved. The recommended recovery goal is to acquire or otherwise protect a refuge of at least 40,000 acres (16,000 hectares) within the current range.

The Red Hills Salamander HCP provides for long-term conservation of the salamander on International Paper lands while permitting limited take of the species during otherwise legal activities. The incidental take permit, issued for a period of 30 years, applies to International Paper lands in Conecuh and Monroe Counties of south-central Alabama, where the company owns 29,463 acres (11,924 hectares) within the Red Hills salamander's historic range. Of this acreage, only around 6,400 acres (2,590 hectares) are currently occupied by the salamander, but this represents 12% of the species' total range.

The two best habitat classifications ("optimal" and "suitable but suboptimal") apply to 4,514 acres (1,827 hectares), or about 92% of the occupied Red Hills salamander sites observed on International Paper lands. To minimize and mitigate the take of Red Hills salamanders, these high quality habitats are designated as refugia under the HCP. They are surrounded by 50-ft (15.2-m) forested buffers, which total an additional 1,900 acres (769 hectares). Limited timber practices can continue in the buffers, but at least 50% canopy cover will be retained. The buffers should reduce soil disturbance and desiccation, and protect the habitat quality of the refuge. In addition, International Paper will train employees to identify salamander habitat, establish buffers, and conduct timber activities within buffer zones in compliance with the terms of the HCP. Normal forest management practices can proceed in the marginally suitable habitat, which represents the balance (8%) of occupied range on International Paper land. Incidental take of the salamander is permitted only in the marginally suitable habitat.

The success of the Red Hills salamander HCP has led International Paper to begin development of an HCP to promote the recovery of the gopher tortoise (*Gopherus polyphemus*), which is listed as Threatened west of the Mobile and Tombigbee Rivers. Companies, in cooperation with state and federal agencies to protect rare species and manage their habitats, are becoming an increasingly key element in the recovery process for a number of species, and the Red Hills Salamander HCP serves as a model for how such plans can work for the good of all.

Contact

U. S. Fish and Wildlife Service
Regional Office, Division of Endangered Species
1875 Century Blvd., Suite 200
Atlanta, Georgia 30345
http://southeast.fws.gov/

References

Brandon, R. A. 1965. "Morphological Variation and Ecology of the Salamander *Phaeognathus hubrichti.*" *Copeia* 1965: 67-71.

Highton, R. 1961. "A New Genus of Lungless Salamander from the Coastal Plain of Alabama." *Copeia* 1961: 65-68.

Jordan, J. R., Jr. 1975. "The Status of the Red Hills Salamander." *Journal of Herpetology* 9: 211-215.

U. S. Fish and Wildlife Service. 1983. "Red Hills Salamander Recovery Plan." U. S. Fish and Wildlife Service, Atlanta.

Cheat Mountain Salamander

Plethedon nettingi

Status	Threatened
Listed	August 18, 1989
Family	Plethodontidae (Lungless Salamander)
Description	Gray to black with silver or gold flecks on its back.
Habitat	Moist, highland woods.
Food	Insects.
Reproduction	Egg masses laid May to August.
Threats	Habitat alteration by timbering, mining, and recreational development.
Range	West Virginia

Description

The Cheat Mountain salamander is one of the lungless salamanders, also known as woodland salamanders. These salamanders lack lungs and must rely on respiratory exchange directly through their skin. This species, which grows to a length of about 4.6 in (12 cm), has a dark back, marked with silver or gold flecks, and a dark gray to black belly. It generally has 18 vertical grooves on its sides that show the position of the ribs. Once considered a subspecies of *Plethodon richmondi*, it was reclassified as a full species in 1971.

Behavior

This salamander generally spends the day under rocks and logs or in rock crevices. At night, particularly in wet weather, it forages on the forest floor for mites, springtails, beetles, flies, and other insects. Although mating has not been observed, it is assumed to be similar to other woodland salamanders. The eggs are fertilized internally and undergo complete development. Unlike most other salamanders there is no aquatic larval stage. Masses of from four to 17 eggs are deposited on logs or moss from May to June.

Habitat

The Cheat Mountain salamander is found in moist West Virginia forests at elevations above about 3,000 ft (915 m), typically where red spruce (*Picea rubens*) and yellow birch (*Betula alleghaniensis*) are the dominant species

Distribution

The precise historic range of the species is unknown because almost all of its preferred habitat was stripped of trees before the species was discovered. Researchers believe that the species was much more widespread in West Virginia prior to deforestation in the late nineteenth and early twentieth centuries.

Today the Cheat Mountain salamander survives in the Allegheny Mountains of eastern West Virginia in Pendleton, Pocahontas, Randolph, and Tucker counties. Its range consists of an area of approximately 700 sq mi (1,813 sq km), almost entirely within the Monongahela National Forest. A total of 68 populations are known; 60 are on Forest Service land, three are in West Virginia state parks, and five are on private land. Detailed population studies of the known sites are now in progress. During the

Cheat Mountain Salamander, photograph by Craig W. Stihler. Reproduced by permission.

initial surveys made during the 1980s fewer than 10 salamanders were observed at three-quarters of the sites.

Threats

The chief threat to the Cheat Mountain salamander is alteration of its habitat by logging and other activities that remove the forest canopy. Loss of forest cover exposes the salamander to hot, dry conditions in which it cannot survive. Between 1880 and 1920 virtually all of the old-growth timber in eastern West Virginia was cut. The Cheat Mountain salamander managed to survive in pockets of marginal high-elevation habitat. One of the healthiest populations is found near a 200-acre (81-hectare) tract of the only virgin red spruce remaining. In recent decades some forest regeneration has taken place. Today mixed spruce-hardwood forests cover an estimated 27,000-67,000 acres (10,927-27,114 hectares), and timber sales are again taking place. One population has been extirpated by clear-cutting

and seven others are likely to die out because of timbering activity.

In addition, some high-elevation forest is being cut for the construction of ski resorts. Within the species' range four resorts are operating and another is being developed.

High-elevation coal mining has also had a negative effect on the species. At least five salamander populations have been severely affected by mining activities.

Conservation and Recovery

The Fish and Wildlife Service published a Recovery Plan for the Cheat Mountain salamander in 1991. The key to the conservation of this rare amphibian is the protection of its habitat of older-growth forest. Sixty of the known critical habitats occur in the Monongohela National Forest, owned and managed by the U.S. Forest Service, while another three are in West Virginia state parks, and five are privately owned. The publicly owned habitats should be protected from threatening human influences, especially those associated with forestry. The critical habitats on private land could also be protected by acquiring the habitat and designating ecological reserves, or by negotiating conservation easements with the landowners. The populations of the Cheat Mountain salamander should be surveyed more extensively and monitored, and research undertaken into its biology, habitat needs, and beneficial management practices.

Contacts

U.S. Fish and Wildlife Service
Regional Office, Division of Endangered Species
One Gateway Center, Suite 700
Newton Corner, Massachusetts 02158
http://northeast.fws.gov

U.S. Fish and Wildlife Service
1825 Virginia Street
Annapolis, Maryland 21401

Reference

U.S. Fish and Wildlife Service. 1991. "Cheat Mountain Salamander *(Plethedon nettingi)* Recovery Plan." U.S. Fish and Wildlife Service, Newton Corner, Massachusetts.

Shenandoah Salamander

Plethedon shenandoah

Status	Endangered
Listed	August 18, 1989
Family	Plethodontidae (Lungless Salamander)
Description	Two color phases; dark-backed with a few gold flecks or with a narrow red stripe on the back.
Habitat	North-facing talus slopes.
Food	Insects.
Reproduction	Egg masses laid from May to August.
Threats	Competition from abundant salamander species.
Range	Virginia

Shenandoah Salamander, photograph by C. Kenneth Dodd, Jr. Reproduced by permission.

Description

The Shenandoah salamander is one of the lungless salamanders, also known as woodland salamanders. These salamanders lack lungs and must rely on respiratory exchange directly through their skin. Two color phases of this species are known. Individuals of the unstriped phase have dark backs, marked with a few gold or silver flecks, and dark gray to black bellies. Striped phase individuals have a narrow red stripe down their backs. This salamander grows to a length of about 4.6 in (12 cm). It generally has 18 vertical grooves on its sides that mark the position of the ribs.

This species was first described as a subspecies of *Plethodon richmondi* in 1967 and later considered a subspecies of the Cheat Mountain salamander (*P. nettingi*. It was recognized as a distinct species in 1979.

Behavior

The Shenandoah salamander generally spends the day under rocks and logs or in rock crevices. At night, particularly in wet weather, it forages for mites, springtails, beetles, flies, and other insects. Although mating has not been observed, it is assumed to be similar to other woodland salamanders. The eggs are fertilized internally and undergo complete development. Unlike most other salamanders there is no aquatic larval stage. Masses of from four to 17 eggs are deposited on logs or moss from May to August.

Habitat

The Shenandoah salamander is found on north-facing talus slopes at elevations above 3,000 ft (915 m). It is limited to areas where the moisture conditions are favorable, but can survive in drier areas than other *Plethodon* species.

Distribution

Because of its recent discovery and limited range, the actual historic range of the Shenandoah salamander is unknown. Because of the species' narrow ecological niche, it is surmised that it was never numerous.

Today the Shenadoah salamander survives on talus slopes on three mountains in Madison and Page counties, Virginia. All three sites are within the boundaries of Shenandoah National Park. There are no current population estimates.

Threats

The major threats to the Shenendoah salamander are thought to be habitat damage caused by the defoliation of trees by introduced insects, and perhaps by acidic precipitation. It may also be suffering from competition with the abundant red-backed salamander (*Plethodon cinereus*). The Shenandoah salamander can survive in dryer conditions than the red-backed salamander. However, as the talus slopes disintegrate and organic debris decomposes, moister conditions develop, which favors the red-backed salamander.

Conservation and Recovery

The Fish and Wildlife Service published a Recovery Plan for the Shenandoah salamander in 1994. All of its known critical habitats are protected within Shenandoah National Park. However, there is ongoing habitat damage by introduced pest insects that feed on dominant species of trees. The populations of the Shenandoah salamander should be surveyed more extensively and monitored, and research undertaken into its biology, habitat needs, and beneficial management practices (particularly the control of insect damage).

Contacts

U.S. Fish and Wildlife Service
Office of the Regional Director
Hadley, Massachusetts 01035-9589
Telephone: (413) 253-8308
Fax: (413) 253-8308
http://northeast.fws.gov/

U.S. Fish and Wildlife Service
Chesapeake Bay Ecological Services Field Office
177 Admiral Cochrane Drive
Annapolis, Maryland 21401-7307
Telephone: (410) 573-4500
Fax: (410) 263-2608
E-mail: Laurie_Hewitt@fws.gov
http://www.fws.gov/r5cbfo/index.html

References

Jaeger, R. G. 1970. "Potential Extinction through Competition Between Two Species of Terrestrial Salamanders." *Evolution* 24: 632-642.

Jaeger, R. G. 1974. "Competitive Exclusion: Comments on Survival and Extinction of Species." *Bioscience* 24: 33-39.

Jaeger, R. G. 1980. "Density-dependent and Density-independent Causes of Extinction of a Salamander Population." *Evolution* 34(4): 617-621.

U.S. Fish and Wildlife Service. 1994. "Shenandoah Salamander (*Plethodon shenandoah*) Recovery Plan." Hadley, Massachusetts.

Texas Blind Salamander

Typhlomolge rathbuni

Status	Endangered
Listed	March 11, 1967
Family	Plethodontidae (Lungless Salamander)
Description	Sightless, cave-dwelling amphibian; white or pinkish with a blood-red gill fringe.
Habitat	Underground water systems.
Food	Insects, other invertebrates.
Reproduction	Unknown.
Threats	Ground water pumping and pollution
Range	Texas

Description

The Texas blind salamander, *Typhlomolge rathbuni*, is a smooth, unpigmented, sightless, cave-dwelling salamander that reaches a mature length of about 5 in (13 cm). This slender, frail-legged amphibian is white or pinkish with a fringe of blood-red, external gills. The head is large and broad; eyes are reduced (visible as two small dark spots deep beneath the skin); limbs are slender and long; four toes occur on the fore legs and five on the hind legs; snout is flattened.

Behavior

Observations on captive individuals indicate that the Texas blind salamander feed indiscriminately on small aquatic organisms and do not appear to exhibit an appreciable degree of food selectivity. Young *T. rathbuni* feed well on copepods. Larger salamanders are documented to eat amphipods, blind shrimp (*Palaemonetes antrorum*), daphnia, small snails, and other invertebrates. Cannibalism has also been documented.

Due to the presence of juveniles throughout the year, the Texas blind salamander appears to be sexually active all year, which is expected since there is little seasonal change in the aquifer. Gravid females have been observed each month of the year. One gravid female contained 39 eggs. There appears to be a correlation between size (age class), number of testicular lobes, and number of times sperm has been produced.

The Texas blind salamander reproduced for the first time in captivity at the Cincinnati Zoo. Three different spawning events occurred between December 1979 and January 1980. Clutch size ranged from eight to 21 eggs per spawning. The eggs were unpigmented and were attached to pieces of gravel singly or in clusters of two or three eggs. Light intensity did not appear to affect embryonic development. However, relatively constant water temperature similar to that within the aquifer (69.8°F; 21°C) is necessary for normal egg development.

The Dallas Aquarium has also induced the Texas blind salamander to breed in captivity. Two individuals were apparently engaged in courtship behavior on May 11, 1994, and repeated this activity on May 15. The first clutch of 13 eggs was deposited singly on the limestone rocks in the aquarium on May 21 and 22. The eggs hatched within 12-16 days of oviposition, and the larvae began feeding within one month after hatching. Successful reproduction continues to occur at the Dallas Aquarium.

Habitat

The Texas blind salamander is an obligate troglobitic species that occupies the subterranean waters of the Edwards Aquifer in Hays County, Texas. It is neotenic (non-transforming) and aquatic through-

Texas Blind Salamander, photograph. U. S. Fish and Wildlife Service. Reproduced by permission.

out its life and lives in water-filled, cavernous areas in the San Marcos area of the Edwards Aquifer. Observations in caves with access to the water table indicate that this salamander moves through the aquifer by traveling along submerged ledges and may swim short distances before spreading its legs and settling to the bottom of the pool. Due to the relatively constant 69.8°F (21°C) temperature of subterranean waters in the Edwards Aquifer, the Texas blind salamander is believed to be adapted to this temperature regime and may be sensitive to changes in water temperatures. However, additional research is necessary to determine critical temperature minima and maxima for different life stages of this species.

Distribution

This species is endemic to the caverns of the Edwards Plateau in Hays County, Texas. All collections of sightings of the Texas blind salamander have occurred there. The species was previously known to occur in Wonder Cave but searches in 1977 did not locate any specimens. The total distribution for the salamander may be a small as 26 sq mi (67 sq km) in a portion of the Edwards Aquifer beneath and near the city of San Marcos.

Threats

The Edwards Plateau is located in the vicinity of San Marcos, halfway between Austin and San Antonio. For many years, water has been pumped from the aquifer to supply irrigation ponds and ditches. More recently, growth of the city of San Marcos and suburban development associated with Austin and San Antonio have placed heavier demands on the aquifer. Water levels have dropped appreciably and will probably continue to fall in the foreseeable future. Increasing development of the region threatens to pollute groundwater with sediments and sewage run-off.

Conservation and Recovery

Survival of this salamander and other endemic cave-dwelling creatures depends upon the stability and continued purity of the Edwards aquifer. The Nature Conservancy purchased Ezell's Cave in 1967. In 1972, Ezell's Cave was designated as a National Natural Landmark by the National Park Service, thus helping to preserve one of the species' historic habitats.

Personnel at the Cincinnati Zoo and the Dallas Aquarium have successfully propagated the species in captivity. The Dallas Aquarium is developing a captive breeding program for the species. The U. S. Fish and Wildlife Service (FWS) has recently provided funding for the collection and distribution to one or two additional facilities to increase the chances for successful captive propagation.

The 1996 San Marcos/Comal (Revised) Recovery Plan, which covers the Texas blind salamander and four other listed species, notes that recovery goals for the habitat's species include the survival of these species in their native ecosystems; the development of an ecosystem approach using strategies to address both local, site-specific and broad regional issues related to recovery; and the conservation of the integrity and function of the aquifer and spring-fed ecosystems that these species inhabit.

Delisting is considered unattainable for all five species (including the Texas blind salamander) due to the potential for extinction from catastrophic events. Consequently, the revised recovery plan calls for the establishment and continued maintenance of refugia capability for all five species in case of a catastrophic event.

Contact

U. S. Fish and Wildlife Service
Regional Office, Division of Endangered Species
P.O. Box 1306
Albuquerque, New Mexico 87103-1306
Telephone: (505) 248-6911
Fax: (505) 248-6915
http://southwest.fws.gov/

References

Longley, G. 1978. "Status of the Texas Blind Salamander." Report No. 2. U. S. Fish and Wildlife Service, Albuquerque.

U. S. Fish and Wildlife Service. 1987. "Endangered and Threatened Species of Texas and Oklahoma (with 1988 Addendum)." U. S. Fish and Wildlife Service, Albuquerque.

U. S. Fish and Wildlife Service. 1996. "San Marcos and Comal Springs and Associated Aquatic Ecosystems (Revised) Recovery Plan." U. S. Fish and Wildlife Service, Albuquerque.

Fishes

Shortnose Sturgeon

Acipenser brevirostrum

Status	Endangered
Listed	March 11, 1967
Family	Acipenseridae (Sturgeon)
Description	Yellowish brown body with a dark head and back.
Habitat	Estuaries, freshwater rivers and streams.
Food	Crustaceans, insects, mollusks, plant matter, detritus.
Reproduction	Spawns between February and May.
Threats	River damming, pollution.
Range	Georgia, Maine, New Jersey, New York, North Carolina, South Carolina; New Brunswick, Canada

Description

The shortnose sturgeon, *Acipenser brevirostrum*, is often confused with a young Atlantic sturgeon (*Acipenser oxyrhynchus*), but it differs by having a wider mouth and shorter snout. Its underhanging mouth is preceded by four barbels, which function as sensory organs similar to the "whiskers" of a catfish. The yellowish brown body of the shortnose sturgeon is contrasted by its dark head and back. The undersurface is light yellow or white. The skeleton is largely cartilaginous, and scales are bony plates. Its maximum size is about 3 ft (90 cm), which is considerably smaller than a full-grown Atlantic sturgeon.

Behavior

Primarily nocturnal, the shortnose sturgeon feeds on crustaceans, insects, and small mollusks. It also ingests quantities of sediment, plant matter, and detritus. It is extremely long-lived, particularly in northern waters, sometimes reaching 50 years old.

It is a bay or estuary fish for most of its life but returns to freshwater streams and rivers to spawn. Very few individuals have ever been caught in the open ocean. Peak spawning occurs between February and May but may begin as early as January in the south. Females probably spawn only once every three years, depositing as many as 200,000 eggs, most of which do not survive. Juveniles mature in three to six years.

Habitat

The shortnose sturgeon prefers deep pools with soft substrates and vegetated bottoms, and moves from shallow to deeper water in winter. It spawns in freshwater wetlands or stream areas with fast flow and a gravel-cobble bottom.

Distribution

This shortnose sturgeon is found along the Atlantic coast from the St. John River in Canada to the Indian River, Florida. It was common in the Hudson, Delaware, Potomac, Connecticut, and St. Johns rivers.

The largest concentrations of the shortnose sturgeon are found in the St. John River (New Brunswick), Kennebec River (Maine), Hudson River (New York), Delaware River (New Jersey), Winyah Bay, Pee Dee River, and Lake Marion (South Carolina), and the Altamaha River (Georgia). In the last decade, a population was discovered in the Cape Fear drainage in North Carolina.

USFWS, Ted Dingley

The most reliable population estimate for shortnose sturgeon in the Androscoggin and Kennebec Rivers DPS is the composite Schnabel estimate: An average of 7,222 with a 95% confidence interval of 5,046-10,765. This is considered to reflect a combined population of adult shortnose sturgeon that spawn throughout the Androscoggin/Kennebec Rivers DPS. Shortnose sturgeon are known to spawn in cycles, and estimates indicate that adults may spawn at intervals of three years.

In the Hudson River, a recent Cornell University study (1995-1997) sponsored by the National Marine Fisheries Service and the U. S. Army Corps of Engineers, used gill nets in high concentration areas of adult shortnose sturgeon and over large regions of the river to study the population numbers. The study, ongoing at the time of this publication, had so far tagged over 2,700 shortnose sturgeon; as part of the program, some 4,200 fish had been captured and measured since 1993. Using the 1995 data, researchers computed a preliminary mark-and-recapture estimate of 55,265 adults (with a standard error margin of 10,436), seeming proof of a solid population growth over a 1992 estimate of 13,000.

Threats

In this century both the range and population size of the shortnose sturgeon have decreased. Part of this decline was caused by the countless dams that have been built along the Atlantic Coast, which cut off the sturgeon from many of its upriver spawning grounds. Water pollution has also been a significant factor in the decline of this species in the major rivers and estuaries. Late maturation, slow growth, and periodic spawning make it difficult for the sturgeon to replenish its numbers.

When originally listed, shortnose sturgeon were considered endangered throughout their range in the eastern United States, though not all extant populations were identified at the time of their original listing. Today, at least 17 populations of shortnose sturgeon are known within the species' wide latitudinal range. Recognizing that the knowledge concerning shortnose sturgeon increased during the years following the species' Endangered Species Act (ESA) listing, the National Marine Fisheries Service (NMFS) began a status review in the late 1980s to assess whether individual shortnose sturgeon populations should be considered "distinct" for ESA purposes. In 1987, the NMFS announced a decision to combine the Androscoggin and Kennebec River populations as a single distinct unit, for ESA purposes

Although it is occasionally taken by sport fishermen who do not recognize it as distinct from the Atlantic sturgeon, the shortnose sturgeon is thought to be adequately protected by existing game fish regulations. It is unlawful under provisions of the Endangered Species Act to possess (alive or dead) or harass a shortnose sturgeon.

Conservation and Recovery

The NMFS' 1996 "Status Review of Shortnose Sturgeon in the Androscoggin and Kennebec Rivers" analyzed listing factors from the ESA and concluded that the sturgeon continued to be endangered due to substantial habitat and/or range threats resulting from hydroelectric facilities, channel dredging, and the introduction of pollutants via sewage treatment plants, paper mills, and other industrial facilities. It found, however, that overutilization of the fish for commercial, recreational, scientific, or commercial purposes was not a threat at the time, although pressure for commercial utilization could increase if the species were removed from protected status. It also found that existing regulatory mechanisms other than the ESA may limit the direct harvest of shortnose sturgeon but are inadequate to ensure the detailed review of potentially damaging construction activities closely scrutinized through the ESA Section 7 consultation process.

Documented recovery criteria for shortnose sturgeon populations do not currently exist, although the NMFS Shortnose Sturgeon Recovery Team, established in 1992, is presently drafting a "Shortnose Sturgeon Recovery Plan" that will include such criteria. Factors in developing the plan include the outcome of research to determine the extent of the spawning areas and to expand basic knowledge of the sturgeon's biology.

Contacts

U.S. Fish and Wildlife Service
Division of Endangered Species
1875 Century Blvd., Ste 200
Atlanta, Georgia 30345
http://southeast.fws.gov/

U.S. Fish and Wildlife Service
Division of Endangered Species
300 Westgate Center Dr
Hadley, Massachusetts 01035
http://northeast.fws.gov/

References

Dadswell, M. J., *et al.* 1984. "Synopsis of Biological Data on Shortnose Sturgeon, *Acipenser brevirostrum*." Report NMFS 14, National Marine Fisheries Service, Washington, D. C.

Ross, S. W., *et al. 1988. Endangered, Threatened, and Rare Fauna of North Carolina: A Re-evaluation of the Marine and Estuarine Fishes.* Occasional Papers of the North Carolina Biological Survey, Raleigh.

U.S. Fish and Wildlife Service. 1982. "Recovery Plan for the Shortnose Sturgeon." U.S. Fish and Wildlife Service, Hadley, MA.

Vladykov, V. D., and J. R. Greeley. 1963. "Order Acipenseroidei in Fishes of the Western North Atlantic." *Memoir Sears Foundation for Marine Research* 1(3), 1963:24-60.

Gulf Sturgeon

Acipenser oxyrinchus desotoi

Status	Threatened
Listed	September 30, 1991
Family	Acipenseridae
Description	A large, fusiform fish with an extended snout, ventral mouth, chin barbels, and the upper lobe of the tail longer than the lower.
Habitat	Large rivers and estuaries.
Food	Feeds on aquatic invertebrates and small fish.
Reproduction	Lays numerous eggs in a benthic nest.
Threats	Habitat destruction and degradation by dredging, pollution, and other stressors.
Range	Alabama, Florida, Georgia, Louisiana, Mississippi, Texas

Description

The *Acipenser oxyrinchus desotoi* (Gulf sturgeon) has a fusiform (or cylindrical) body with an extended snout, ventral mouth, chin barbels, and the upper lobe of the tail longer than the lower. Adults range from 6-8 ft (1.8-2.4 m) in length, with adult females larger than males. It is a subspecies of the Atlantic sturgeon (*Acipenser oxyrinchus*), and is distinguished from the East Coast subspecies (*A. o. oxyrinchus*) by its longer head, pectoral fins, and spleen.

Behavior

The Gulf sturgeon is an anadromous species that migrates between fresh and salt water. It feeds on or near the bottom on aquatic invertebrates and small fish.

Habitat

The Gulf sturgeon breeds in fresh water of large rivers, and may feed in fresh or salt water. During its annual migration, it requires nearshore (bays and estuaries) and offshore (Gulf of Mexico) feeding areas and freshwater rivers with adequate water qual-ity and quantity, hard bottoms for spawning, and spring flows and deep holes for thermal refugia.

Distribution

The Gulf sturgeon is restricted to the Gulf of Mexico and its drainages, primarily from the Mississippi River to the Suwannee River, including the States of Alabama, Florida, Georgia, Louisiana, and Mississippi. Sporadic occurrences are known as far west as Texas (Rio Grande), and marine waters in Florida south to Florida Bay.

Threats

The Gulf sturgeon has suffered from excessive direct fishing, by-catch in nets set for other species, and habitat destruction and degradation caused by dredging, hydrologic management, siltation, and pollution by sewage, nutrients, and pesticides.

Conservation and Recovery

The Gulf sturgeon is now protected from fishing throughout its range. An Interjurisdictional Fishery Management Plan has been prepared for the species by the Gulf States Marine Fisheries Commission. It

Gulf Sturgeon, photograph by John Moran/ The Gainesville (FL) Sun. Reproduced by permission.

is also covered by the draft Mobile River Basin Aquatic Ecosystem Recovery Plan prepared by the Fish and Wildlife Service, and by the Suwannee River Cooperative River Basin Study. The population status of the Gulf sturgeon is being monitored, and research has been undertaken to better understand its biology and ecological requirements. The Mobile District of the U.S. Army Corps of Engineers has worked with conservation agencies on projects to improve habitat for the Gulf sturgeon. This includes efforts to restore thermal refugia habitat and access into Battle Bend Cutoff and the Blue Spring Run in the Apalachicola River, and studies to monitor the Pearl River Gulf sturgeon populations.

Contact

U. S. Fish and Wildlife Service
Jacksonville Ecological Services Field Office
6620 Southpoint Drive South, Suite 310
Jacksonville, Florida 32216-0958
Telephone: (904) 232-2580

Reference

U.S. Fish and Wildlife Service. 23 Aug. 1995. "Endangered and Threatened Wildlife and Plants: Decision on Designation of Critical Habitat for the Gulf Sturgeon." *Federal Register* 60(163): 43721-43723.

White Sturgeon

Acipenser transmontanus

Status	Endangered
Listed	September 6, 1994
Family	Acipenseridae (Sturgeon)
Description	Large, slow-maturing, long-lived fresh-water fish with a flattened, shovel-like-head.
Habitat	Deep river holes and lakes at a depth of 20-300 ft (3-100 m).
Food	Chironomids, clams, snails, aquatic insects, and fish.
Reproduction	Spawn during the period of peak flows from April through July.
Threats	Reduced river flows, low reproduction, poor water quality.
Range	Idaho, Montana, British Columbia

Description

The white sturgeon is a large, slow-maturing, long-lived freshwater fish. It has a flattened, shovel-like head and a row of sensory barbels in front of its ventral, toothless mouth.

All sturgeon are distinguished from other fish in that they have a cartilaginous skeleton with a persistent notochord, and a protractile, tube-like mouth and sensory barbels ventrally on the snout. The white sturgeon is distinguished from other *Acipenser* by the specific arrangement and number of scutes (bony plates) along its body.

Behavior

For the white sturgeon in general, the size or age of first maturity in the wild is quite variable. Females normally require a longer period to mature than males, with females from most sturgeon species spawning between 15-25 years of age. Only a portion of adult white sturgeon are reproductive or spawn each year. The spawning frequency for females is estimated at two to 11 years.

Spawning occurs when the physical environment permits vitellogenesis (egg development) and cues ovulation. White sturgeon are broadcast spawners, releasing their eggs and sperm in fast water. In the lower Columbia River below McNary Dam, land-locked populations of white sturgeon normally spawn during the period of peak flows from April through July. Spawning at peak flows with high water velocities disperses and prevents clumping of the adhesive eggs. Following fertilization, eggs adhere to the river substrate and hatch after a relatively brief incubation period of eight to 15 days, depending on water temperature. Recently hatched yolk-sac larvae swim or drift in the current for a period of several hours and settle into interstitial spaces in the substrate. Larval white sturgeon require 20-30 days to metamorphose into juveniles with a full complement of fin rays and scutes.

Habitat

The Kootenai River population of white sturgeon is restricted to approximately 168 river mi (270 river km) in the Kootenai River basin. This reach extends from Kootenai Falls, Montana, located 31 river mi (50 river km) below Libby Dam, downstream through Kootenay Lake to Cora Linn Dam at the outflow from Kootenay Lake, British Columbia, Canada. Historically, Kootenai Falls represented an impassible natural barrier to the upstream migra-

White Sturgeon, photograph by Pat Marcuson. Reproduced by permission.

tion of the white sturgeon. A natural barrier at Bonnington Falls downstream of Kootenay Lake has isolated the Kootenai River white sturgeon from other white sturgeon populations in the Columbia River basin since the last glacial age (approximately 10,000 years).

Based on tagging studies, Kootenai River white sturgeon are relatively sedentary during the summer and inhabit the deepest holes of the Kootenai River and Kootenay Lake. Kootenai River locations used by white sturgeon were generally sites over 20 ft (6 m) deep with column velocities less than 0.77 fps (less than 0.24 mps) and water temperature of 57-68°F (14-20°C), while depths utilized in Kootenay Lake ranged from 30-300 ft (10-100.5 m). Compared with other waters containing white sturgeon, the Kootenai River is a relatively cool river with summer high temperatures of 68-72°F (20-22°C).

White sturgeon in the Kootenai River are considered opportunistic feeders, although white sturgeon more than 28 in (80 cm) in length may feed on a variety of prey items, including chironomids, clams, snails, aquatic insects, and fish. Kokanee salmon (*Oncorhynchus nerka*) in Kootenay Lake, prior to a dramatic population crash beginning in the mid 1970's, were once considered an important prey item for adult white sturgeon.

Distribution

White sturgeon historically occurred on the Pacific Coast from the Aleutian Islands to central California.

Little was known regarding the status and life history of the white sturgeon population in the Kootenai River basin prior to studies initiated during the late 1970s. The Kootenai River population of white sturgeon is one of 18 landlocked populations of white sturgeon known to occur in western North America. The Kootenai River originates in Kootenay National Park in British Columbia, Canada. The river flows south into Montana, turns northwest into Idaho, and north through the Kootenai Valley back into British Columbia, where it flows through Kootenay Lake and eventually joins the Columbia River at Castlegar, British Columbia.

Estimates show a decline in the white sturgeon population from an estimated 1,194 fish (range 907-1503) in 1982 to 880 (range 638-1,211) in 1990, although these are not directly comparable because the 1990 survey occurred in a river sampling reach almost 31 river mi (50 river km) longer. However, FWS believes recent population trends and population estimates accurately reflect the current status of the fish. Trends in population demographics reveal an aging population with no known recruitment of age one sturgeon since 1978. Additionally, although mark-recapture studies reveal that white sturgeon move freely between the Kootenai River and Kootenay Lake, there is no evidence that white sturgeon reside or spawn in other tributaries entering Kootenay Lake, British Columbia.

In general, individual white sturgeon in the Kootenai River are broadly distributed, migrating freely between the Kootenai River and the deep, oligotrophic Kootenay Lake. In 1980, it was thought that only one to five adult white sturgeon resided in Montana, found in the river reach immediately downstream of Kootenai Falls. Although white sturgeon use the main channel of the Kootenai River upstream to Kootenai Falls, few individuals have been reported from tributaries to the Kootenai River in Idaho and Montana.

Threats

Significant modifications to the natural hydrograph in the Kootenai River, caused by flow regulation at Libby Dam, is considered the primary reason for the Kootenai River white sturgeon's continuing lack of recruitment and declining numbers. Since 1972, when Libby Dam began regulating flows (though not fully operational until 1975), spring flows in the Kootenai River have been reduced an average 50%, and winter flows have increased by 300% over normal. As a consequence, natural high spring flows required by white sturgeon for reproduction rarely occur during the May to July spawning season when suitable temperature, water velocity, and photoperiod conditions exist.

Another contributing factor to the white sturgeon decline is the elimination of side channel slough habitat in the Kootenai River floodplain due to diking and bank stabilization to protect agricultural lands from flooding. Much of the Kootenai River has been channelized and stabilized from Bonners Ferry downstream to Kootenay Lake, resulting in reduced aquatic habitat diversity, altering flow conditions at potential remaining spawning and nursery areas, and altering remaining substrates and conditions necessary for survival.

Although not fully understood, there is evidence that the overall biological productivity of the Kootenai River downstream of Libby Dam has been altered, resulting in modifications to the quality of water now entering the lake by removing nutrients, by permitting the stripping of nutrients from the water in the river downstream from the dam, and altering the time at which the nutrients are supplied to the lake. Potential threats to the Kootenai River white sturgeon from declining biological productivity include: (1) decreased prey abundance and limited food availability for all life stages of sturgeon downstream of Libby Dam, (2) reduced condition factor in adult white sturgeon, possibly impacting fecundity and reproduction, and (3) a possible reduction in the overall capacity for the Kootenai River and Kootenay Lake systems to sustain substantial populations of white sturgeon and other native fishes.

Conservation and Recovery

Water flows in the river are the most significant factor affecting the survival of the sturgeon. The Army Corps of Engineers and BPA have committed to experimental flow releases from Libby Dam for Kootenai River white sturgeon in possibly three out of the next ten years. However, providing these flows is contingent upon meeting other project priority uses. The proposed action increases discharge and sustains flows in the Kootenai River at only 57% of the discharge the Service believes is necessary to maximize sturgeon spawning and maintain suitable larval rearing habitats. Existing regulatory mechanisms are not sufficient to ensure the survival and recovery of this species. The British Columbia Ministry of Environment, Lands and Parks, is currently experimenting with fertilization of Kootenay Lake to increase biological productivity and enhance native fisheries. Beginning in 1993, BPA funded IDFG and Idaho State University to study primary productivity, community respiration, and nutrient cycling in the Kootenai River from Libby Dam downstream to Kootenay Lake. It will be several years before results from these studies explain to what extent, if any, reduced biological productivity has been a contributing factor to the Kootenai River white sturgeon's population decline.

Contacts

U.S. Fish and Wildlife Service
Division of Endangered Species
Eastside Federal Complex
911 N.E. 11th Avenue
Portland, Oregon 97232
http://pacific.fws.gov/

U.S. Fish and Wildlife Service
Division of Endangered Species
Denver Federal Center
P.O. Box 25486
Denver, Colorado 80225
http://www.r6.fws.gov/

Reference

U.S. Fish and Wildlife Service. 6 September 1994. "Determination of Endangered Status for the Kootenai River Population of the White Sturgeon." *Federal Register* 59(171).

Pallid Sturgeon

Scaphirhynchus albus

Status	Endangered
Listed	September 6, 1990
Family	Acipenseridae (Sturgeon)
Description	Large, bony-plated fish with flattened head.
Habitat	Large, turbid, free-flowing rivers with rock or gravel bottoms.
Food	Crustaceans, worms, insect larvae, other fish.
Reproduction	Spawns in swift water over gravel or rocky bottoms.
Threats	Impoundments, lack of reproduction.
Range	Illinois, Iowa, Missouri, Arkansas, Kentucky, Louisiana, Mississippi, Tennessee, Kansas, Montana, Nebraska, North Dakota, South Dakota

Description

The pallid sturgeon is a large, slow-maturing, long-lived freshwater fish. It has a flattened, shovel-like head, five rows of bony plates, and an unequally lobed tail. There is a row of sensory barbels in front of its ventral, toothless mouth.

This sturgeon is distinguished from the more common shovelnose sturgeon *(Scaphirhynchus platorhynchus)* by a number of characteristics. The pallid is lighter in color and attains a larger size. It appears smoother overall and has a longer nose. The most notable difference is the length and placement of the barbels. The pallid sturgeon's barbels are situated about a third of the distance from the mouth to the nose; those of the shovelnose sturgeon are at the midpoint between the two. The inner barbels of the pallid sturgeon are about half the length of the outer barbels; all the shovelnose sturgeon's barbels are about the same length. The species has also been known as *Parascaphirhynchus albus,* and by the common name of white sturgeon.

Behavior

Like other sturgeon species, the pallid is an opportunistic bottom feeder, consuming mollusks, crustaceans, worms, aquatic insects, and other fish. The barbels are sensory organs, and are important in the fish's feeding process.

The reproductive cycle of this sturgeon is not well known, although it is probably similar to other North American sturgeon species. Fish reach sexual maturity at about five years of age and spawn every few years thereafter. When spawning, small batches of sticky eggs are periodically released over a period of about 12 hours.

Habitat

The pallid sturgeon is found in large, turbid, free-flowing rivers with rocky or sandy bottoms. It inhabits swifter flowing waters than the related shovelnose sturgeon.

Distribution

The pallid sturgeon has been reported from the mouth of the Mississippi River to the mouth of the Missouri River; from the Missouri River as far as Fort Benton, Montana; and from the lower reaches of the Yellowstone River. The total length of the species' historic range was over 3,500 mi (5,600 km) and involved river habitat in 13 states: Louisiana, Mississippi,

Pallid Sturgeon, photograph. U. S. Fish and Wildlife Service. Reproduced by permission.

Arkansas, Tennessee, Kentucky, Missouri, Illinois, Iowa, Kansas, Nebraska, South Dakota, North Dakota, and Montana. While it appears that the pallid sturgeon was never abundant, it was once considered fairly common. As late as 1967, researchers were able to capture several fish in a single net set, and fishermen reported taking hundreds of pallid sturgeon as the reservoirs on the Missouri River filled.

The species still occurs in dramatically reduced numbers throughout much of its historic range. This decline is graphically illustrated by the number of pallid sturgeon sightings over the last three decades. In the 1960s, about 500 observations were made; in the 1970s, there were 209 sightings. In the 1980s, the number of observations fell to 65. The decline has been especially notable from the impounded sections of the Missouri River above the Gavins Point Dam along the South Dakota/Nebraska border.

Remnant populations probably exist in the Missouri River near the mouth of the Yellowstone River below Fort Peck, Montana; in the upper end of Lake Sharpe near Pierre, South Dakota, and between the

mouth of the Platte River in Nebraska and Gavins Point Dam. Scattered sightings in the Mississippi River in the 1980s indicate that a small number of pallids may survive there.

Threats

The decline in pallid sturgeon populations has been caused by the alteration of virtually its entire river habitat by channelization and impoundment. About 51% has been channelized, 28% impounded, and the remaining 21% affected by the upstream impoundments.

The Mississippi and Missouri rivers have had an important role in the development of the nation's commerce, and since the early 1800s, they have been modified for commercial navigation. In the 1950s and 1960s, a series of dams were constructed on the Missouri River in North and South Dakota, in effect, turning the free-flowing river into a series of long narrow impoundments. This has led to a number of habitat changes which have apparently interfered with pallid sturgeon reproduction. Studies of the fish populations of the impoundments have consistently failed to document any young pallid sturgeon. There has been no documented reproduction in a decade, and the aging remnant population seems headed for extinction.

The dams block the normal movement of the sturgeon to historic spawning or feeding areas and have destroyed some spawning and nursery areas. They have produced changes to the water quality, temperature, and flow rates, which may affect reproduction and food sources.

Conservation and Recovery

Studies are underway, using the short-nose sturgeon as a surrogate species, to determine the feasibility of propagating the pallid sturgeon in captivity. During recent years, researchers have been developing new techniques to locate and caputure pallid sturgeon in preparation for a captive propagation program.

Since the federal government is heavily involved with the river habitats of the pallid sturgeon, agencies involved in dam operations and river channel maintenance will be consulting with the Fish and Wildlife Service on recovery of the species.

Natural reproduction has failed for at least one generation throughout the pallid sturgeon's range. Artificial propagation is being used to supplement wild populations until suitable spawning conditions in the wild can be restored. About 7,000 hatchery-reared pallids were released into the Mississippi River in 1994. To avoid potential hazards associated with inbreeding, domestication, and exposure to disease, extreme care is being taken in handling cultured stocks.

Attempts to spawn pallids taken from the Missouri and Yellowstone rivers in Montana have not been successful to date. When young are produced, the plan is to release them above Fort Peck Reservoir in a portion of the Missouri where 27 pallids have been recorded since 1990. The pallid sturgeon population in the Missouri River above Fort Peck is estimated at less than 100.

In the Missouri River, below Fort Peck Dam downstream to Lake Sakakawea (including the Yellowstone River below the mouth of the Powder River), 150 pallids have been handled since 1990 (this number includes 40 recaptures). The population estimate for these river stretches is 250 pallids.

Contacts

U.S. Fish and Wildlife Service
Division of Endangered Species
Denver Federal Center
P.O. Box 25486
Denver, Colorado 80225
http://www.r6.fws.gov/

U.S. Fish and Wildlife Service
Division of Endangered Species
Federal Building
Ft. Snelling
Twin Cities, Minnesota 55111
http://www.midwest.fws.gov/

U.S. Fish and Wildlife Service
Division of Endangered Species
1875 Century Blvd., Ste 200
Atlanta, Georgia 30345
http://www.southeast.fws.gov/

References

Carlson, D. M., et al. 1985. "Distribution, Biology, and Hybridization of *Scaphirhynchus albus* and *S. platorynchus* in the Missouri and Mississippi Rivers." *Environmental Biology of Fishes* 14:51-59.

Deacon, J. E., G. Kobetich, J. D. Williams, and S. Contreras. 1979. "Fishes of North America, Endangered, Threatened, or of Special Concern." *Fisheries* 4(2):29-44.

Gilbraith, D. M., M. J. Schwalbach, and C. R. Berry. 1988. "Preliminary Report on the Status of the Pallid Sturgeon, *Scaphirhynchus albus*, a Candidate Endangered Species." South Dakota State University, Brookings, South Dakota.

Hallemeyn, L. W. 1983. "Status of the Pallid Sturgeon (*Scaphirhynchus albus*)." Fisheries 8(1):3-9.

Hesse, L. W. 1987. "Taming the Wild Missouri River: What Has It Cost?" *Fisheries* 12(2):2-9.

Keenlyne, K. D. 1989. "A Report on the Pallid Sturgeon." U.S. Fish and Wildlife Service, Pierre, South Dakota.

Whitley, J. R., and R. S. Campbell. 1974. "Some Aspects of Water Quality and Biology of the Missouri River" *Transactions of the Missouri Academy of Science* 7-8:60-670.

Blue Shiner

Cyprinella caerulea

Status	Threatened
Listed	April 22, 1992
Family	Cyprinidae (Minnow)
Description	Medium-sized dusky blue minnow with pale yellow fins.
Habitat	Clear, cool water over sand and gravel substrate among cobble.
Food	Insects.
Reproduction	Spawns from early May to late August.
Threats	Degradation of water quality due to sewage pollution, strip-mining activity, urbanization.
Range	Alabama, Georgia, Tennessee

Description

The blue shiner, *Cyprinella (=Notropis) caerulea,* is a medium-sized minnow attaining a length of about 4 in (10 cm). Coloration is dusky blue with pale yellow fins. The species has a distinct lateral line and diamond-shaped scales outlined with melanophores.

Behavior

Isolation and fragmentation characterize present populations of the blue shiner. This species spawns from early May to late August.

Habitat

The blue shiner occurs in the east and central farming and forest region. The average annual precipitation is 40-50 in (101-127 cm) and the average annual temperature is 48.2-63°F (9-17°C). The topography of nearly one-half of this region consists of steeply sloping, mainly forest land, used for both recreation and timber production. Udults and Udalfs are the most extensive soils. Fluvents occur along streams and are cropped intensively throughout the region, but do not occur extensively.

Small farms are characteristic of this region and primarily grow corn, soybeans, small grains, and hay.

Specifically, the blue shiner occurs in clear, cool water over sand and gravel substrate among cobble.

Distribution

This species is historically known from the Cahaba and Coosa River systems. It is likely that the species once occupied most of the upper Coosa and Alabama Rivers. In 1971, the minnow was last collected from the Cahaba River system.

Currently, the species is found in Alabama in Weogufka and Choccolocco Creeks and the lower reaches of Little River. Also found in Tennessee, the species ranges in the Conasauga River and the tributary, Minnewauga Creek. In Georgia, the blue shiner is found in the Conasauga and Coosawattee Rivers, including various tributaries. The species no longer exists in Big Wills Creek, a tributary of the upper Coosa River.

Threats

The reason for the decline of the blue shiner is likely a result of water quality degradation due to urbanization, sewage pollution, and strip-mining activity in the upper Cahaba River basin.

Increases in blue-green algae and losses of vascular plants are indicators of the degradation of the water quality in the Cahaba River. Low oxygen lev-

Blue Shiner, photograph. U. S. Fish and Wildlife Service. Reproduced by permission.

els coupled with high levels of total inorganic nitrogen and total phosphorous have also been documented on the river. These modifications in habitat have had adverse effects on the species.

Other factors that have reduced the species' range are reservoirs for flood control, hydropower, and impoundment. Such human alterations of the environment have caused the isolation of the blue shiner populations. Fragmented populations may be more vulnerable to environmental changes, and genetic diversity might be lowered as fewer mating pairs form.

As a result of all of these factors, the species is not nearly as pervasive as it once was. Rather, the species occurs in the Coosawattee River, the Turniptown Creek, and at seven sites on the Conasauga River, including three of its tributaries. Several of these populations do not come in contact with other populations, and it is speculated that distance, topography, and sites with poor water quality acting as barriers may isolate one population from another.

Conservation and Recovery

The blue shiner survives in only six populations occurring in headwater streams of the Coosa River drainage, where it requires water of high quality and not subject to excessive siltation or other kinds of pollution. The U. S. Fish and Wildlife Service published a Recovery Plan for the blue shiner in 1995. Actions to be taken under the plan include monitoring of the existing populations of the blue shiner, research to determine its habitat needs, the development and implementation of a plan to conserve its critical habitat, and efforts to reintroduce the species into suitable habitats from which it has been extirpated.

Contact

U. S. Fish and Wildlife Service
Regional Office, Division of Endangered Species
1875 Century Blvd., Suite 200
Atlanta, Georgia 30345
http://southeast.fws.gov/

References

U. S. Fish and Wildlife Service. 1995. Blue Shiner Recovery Plan. Jackson, Mississippi. 20 pp.

U. S. Fish and Wildlife Service. 22 April 1992. "Endangered and Threatened Wildlife and Plants: Threatened Status for Two Fish, the Goldline Darter (*Percina aurolineata*) and the Blue Shiner (*Cyprinella (=Notropis) caerulea*)." *Federal Register* 57 (78): 14786-14789.

Beautiful Shiner

Cyprinella formosa

Status	Threatened
Listed	August 31, 1984
Family	Cyprinidae (Minnows)
Description	Small, silvery minnow with a metallic iridescence and red-orange hues.
Habitat	Riffles in small streams.
Food	Terrestrial and aquatic insects, algae.
Reproduction	Probably spawns in late spring through late summer.
Threats	Water diversion, groundwater depletion, hybridization.
Range	Arizona, New Mexico; Mexico (Sonora and Chihuahua)

Description

The beautiful shiner, *Cyprinella formosa*, is a small, silvery minnow with an elliptical, compressed, elongated body that has a metallic iridescence, large eyes, large scales, and a pointed snout. Its length is 3-6 in (7.5-15 cm) in length. The belly, fins, and tail are diffused with an attractive red-orange coloration. The caudal fin is deeply notched with pointed lobes. The shiner is tan dorsally and metallic or silver laterally with some orange on the body. Breeding males are brilliantly colored, with orange or yellow fins and a bright greenish-blue body. The dorsal and anterior surfaces have a wash of yellow or orange. Females remain a drab yellowish-brown with colorless, clear, or slightly yellowed fins throughout the year. This species has also been classified as *Notropis formosa*.

Behavior

The male scoops a nest out of gravel in shallow, fast-flowing water, where the female deposits her eggs, probably in late spring through late summer. Life span is up to three years. The beautiful shiner feeds mostly on terrestrial and aquatic insects, augmented with algae and other plant matter.

Habitat

The beautiful shiner occurs in a variety of stream habitats, but the largest concentrations are found in the riffles of smaller streams. Aquatic habitats in the region are subject to severe drying in summer and sudden flooding in the rainy season. Streams flow intermittently during the dry season, and the shiner seeks refuge in permanent, spring-fed pools.

Distribution

This species is endemic to the Rio Yaqui basin of southeastern Arizona, northwestern Sonora, Mexico, and portions of eastern Chihuahua, Mexico. It was also found in the various closed drainages of the Guzman basin, including Rio Mimbres in New Mexico and the Casa Grandes, Santa Maria, and Del Carment, just east of the Rio Yaqui. It was first collected from San Bernardino Creek in extreme southeastern Arizona. The beautiful shiner survived in San Bernardino Creek until spring flows diminished because of groundwater pumping, and the creek dried up. Remaining habitat there was severely trampled by drinking livestock, making it uninhabitable. The water flow of the Mimbres River has been depleted by diversion and groundwater pumping. This species is now considered extirpated

Beautiful Shiner, photograph by John Rinne, USFS. Reproduced by permission.

from the United States. Stock collected under permit from the Mexican government in 1989 from Rio Moctezuma was released in the San Bernardino National Wildlife Reserve in 1990 and survives as reproducing populations in three ponds. Contract biologists from the Arizona State University and the University of Michigan surveyed the Rio Yaqui basin in 1979 and found populations of the beautiful shiner seriously depleted in the Mexican portion of its historic range. It was found to be absent from Arizona and New Mexico.

Threats

The range and numbers of the beautiful shiner have decreased significantly because of habitat modifications, such as arroyo cutting, water diversion, dam construction, and excessive pumping of groundwater from the aquifers. Many rivers in the lowlands of Mexico, formerly inhabited by the beautiful shiner, have been modified into an artificially channeled canal system to support irrigation agri-

culture. This has destroyed many of the pools used by fishes to survive a drought. Water quality has declined due to chemical and sewage contamination. The beautiful shiner currently receives no legal protection from the Mexican government. Of particular danger to the beautiful shiner is the indiscriminate release into the watershed of the closely related red shiner (*Notropis lutrensis*), a fish used as bait for sport fishing. The expanding population of the red shiner appears to be reducing the beautiful shiner by competition and interbreeding.

Conservation and Recovery

If sufficient habitat can be secured and maintained in the San Bernardino National Wildlife Refuge (Cochise County, Arizona) or reclaimed in the Mimbres River (Luna County, New Mexico), the beautiful shiner could be reintroduced at either place, using Mexican stock. The aquatic habitats of the wildlife refuge are considered in jeopardy because of generally lowered water tables in the region. The U. S. Bureau of Land Management (BLM) has issued leases for geothermal resources on lands adjacent to the San Bernardino National Wildlife Refuge. Biologists fear that exploration and development of these leases could cause further depletion of the underground aquifers or create channels for pollution of groundwater. The BLM will examine these threats in consultation with the U. S. Fish and Wildlife Service.

Contact

U. S. Fish and Wildlife Service
Regional Office, Division of Endangered Species
P.O. Box 1306
Albuquerque, New Mexico 87103-1306
Telephone: (505) 248-6911
Fax: (505) 248-6915
http://southwest.fws.gov/

References

Hendrickson, D. S., et al. 1980. "Fishes of the Rio Yaqui Basin, Mexico and United States." *Journal of the Arizona-Nevada Academy of Science* 15 (3): 65-106.

Miller, R. R. 1977. "Composition of the Native Fish Fauna of the Chihuahuan Desert Region." In *Transactions of the Symposium on the Biological Resources of the Chihuahuan Desert Region*, edited by Wauer and Riskind. Transactions of Proceedings Series No. 3. U. S. Department of the Interior, Washington, D. C.

Spotfin Chub

Cyprinella monacha

Status	Threatened
Listed	September 9, 1977
Family	Cyprinidae (Minnow)
Description	Small, dusky green chub.
Habitat	Flowing water over clean substrate.
Food	Insects
Reproduction	Unknown.
Threats	Habitat degradation, pollution.
Range	Alabama, North Carolina, Tennessee, Virginia

Description

The spotfin chub, *Cyprinella (=Hybopsis) monacha*, is a small species growing to a maximum size of 3.6 in (9.2 cm) in length. The body is elongate; the mouth inferior; usually there is one pair of minute, terminal labial barbels; scales moderate to somewhat small in size; a distinctive large black spot is present in the caudal region. Juveniles and adult females are olive above with the sides largely silvery and the lower parts white. Large nuptial males have brilliant turquoise-royal blue coloring on the back, side of the head, and along the mid-lateral part of the body; lesser blue is found in at least some fins; all fins are tipped with satiny white during peak development of color. Based on observations and morphological comparisons, it appears that the spotfin chub is a sight feeder, selecting minute insect larvae from clean substrates. An examination of nine specimens revealed that diptera were the dominant food items, comprising 93.4% of the total, with the remaining food items consisting of immature mayflies, stoneflies, and caddisflies.

Behavior

This fish's age at sexual maturity and number of years sexually active are unclear. Its maximum life span is suspected to be less than four years. No observations of reproductive behavior are known. Capture dates of specimens in nuptial condition suggest that spawning occurs in June, possibly beginning in May and extending into July. It is highly unlikely that nests are constructed and eggs are guarded because none of the close relatives of the spotfin chub are known to do so.

Habitat

The spotfin chub inhabits moderate to large streams, 49-230 ft (15-70 m) average width, with a good current, clear water, and cool to warm temperatures. These streams have pools frequently alternating with riffles. The fish has been taken from a wide variety of substrates, although rarely, if ever, from significantly silted substrates.

Distribution

The spotfin chub is restricted to the Tennessee River drainage where it once occurred widely in 12 tributary systems distributed over five states. Presently, this species is known only from the lower North Fork of the Holston River, Virginia and Tennessee; the Emory River System in Cumberland, Fentress, and Morgan Counties, Tennessee; and the upper Little Tennessee River, North Carolina. Efforts are underway to transplant the species to Abrams Creek in Blount County, Tennessee. No quanitiative estimates of its current population density are available. Indices of relative abundance indicate that the spotfin chub was captured with

William Roston

greater frequency prior to about 1950, although it has been generally uncommon or rare since its discovery. This fish was reportedly abundant only in Chickamauga Creek, Georgia, when it was last taken there in 1877.

Threats

The reasons for the decline in some populations are uncertain. Other populations have been adversely affected by such factors as damming, runoff from coal mining operations, municipal and industrial wastes, and siltation.

Conservation and Recovery

Since the exact cause for the decline in some populations is unknown, it is impossible to make meaningful recommendations for these situations. Otherwise, it appears that the best strategy for the conservation of the spotfin chub would be maintain and possibly upgrade habitat in the three river systems containing extant populations.

Contacts

Regional Office of Endangered Species
U. S. Fish and Wildlife Service
1875 Century Blvd., Suite 200
Atlanta, Georgia 30345
http://southeast.fws.gov/

Regional Office of Endangered Species
U. S. Fish and Wildlife Service
Federal Building
Ft. Snelling
Twin Cities, Minnesota 55111
http://midwest.fws.gov/

Asheville Ecological Services Field Office
U.S. Fish and Wildlife Service
160 Zillicoa St.
Asheville, North Carolina 28801-1082
Telephone: (828) 258-3939
Fax: (828) 258-5330

References

Freeman, J. C. 1980. "A Quantitative Survey of Fish and Macroinvertebrates of the Holston River Basin: August-September 1973." Report WR (70)-40-80.1. Tennessee Valley Authority, Division of Water Resources.

Jenkins, R. E., and N. M. Burkhead. 1982. "Description, Biology and Distribution of the Spotfin Chub, a Threatened Cyprinid Fish of the Tennessee River Drainage." Report. U. S. Fish and Wildlife Service, Atlanta.

U. S. Fish and Wildlife Service. 1983. "Recovery Plan for the Spotfin Chub." U. S. Fish and Wildlife Service, Atlanta.

Devils River Minnow

Dionda diaboli

Status	Threatened
Listed	October 20, 1999
Family	Cyprinidae
Description	A small minnow.
Habitat	Spring-fed streams in semi-arid terrain.
Food	Algae.
Reproduction	Lays untended, externally fertilized eggs.
Threats	Habitat destruction and introduced predators.
Range	Texas, Mexico

Description

The Devils River minnow is a small fish, with adults reaching a body length of 1.0-2.1 in (25-53 mm). It has a wedge-shaped spot near the tail and a pronounced lateral stripe with double dashes extending through the eye to the snout but not reaching the lower lip. The species has a narrow head with prominent dark markings on scale pockets above the lateral line; this produces a cross-hatched appearance when viewed from the top.

Behavior

The Devils River minnow is thought to feed primarily on algae. It is probably a broadcast spawner, with externally fertilized eggs that sink to the bottom substrate for untended incubation.

Habitat

The Devils River minnow occurs in stream habitat characterized by channels of fast-flowing, spring-fed waters over gravel substrates. It occurs in junctions where spring flow enters a stream, rather than in the spring outflow itself. Its habitat is periodically subjected to extreme water-flow variations caused by extended drought and flash floods. The general landscape is semi-desert.

Distribution

The Devils River minnow is a local (or endemic) species that is only known from three locations in Val Verde and Kinney Counties, Texas, and one in Coahuila, Mexico. It is native to tributary streams of the Rio Grande in Val Verde and Kinney Counties, Texas, and Coahuila, Mexico.

Threats

The Devils River minnow is part of a unique fish community and ecosystem of the Chihuahuan Desert of Mexico and Texas that contains a large number of threatened species. About half of the native fishes of that ecosystem are considered threatened and at least four species are recently extinct, mostly because of habitat destruction and the effects of introduced species of fish. The specific range of the Devils River minnow has been reduced and fragmented through habitat destruction caused by the construction of dams, the dewatering of springs, and other causes of ecological degradation. The population size at known critical habitats has declined greatly. In 1989, only seven individuals were collected from five sites at 24 sampling locations within the historical range of the species. The Devils River minnow was once one of the most abundant fish in the Devils River, but is now one of the least abundant. The status of the Devils River minnow in Mexico is not known for certain, but it is thought to be greatly reduced there. The decline of the Devils River minnow in its surviving habitats is likely due to unsustainable predation by introduced smallmouth bass (*Micropterus dolomieu*), a game fish. Areas where the Devils River minnow occurs are mostly privately owned. Exceptions include the Devils River State Natural Area located north of Dolan Falls and managed by the state of Texas, and land adjoining portions of San Felipe Creek owned by the City of Del Rio. The Nature Conservancy, a private environmental organization, owns the Dolan Falls Preserve, in the middle portion of the Devils River. Primary land uses within the watersheds supporting the Devils River minnow are cattle, sheep, and goat ranching.

Conservation and Recovery

The Devils River minnow is listed as a threatened species by the U. S. Fish and Wildlife Service (FWS), by the State of Texas, and by the government of Mexico. A Conservation Agreement in support of protection and management for the Devils River minnow has been signed between the FWS, the Texas Parks and Wildlife Department, and the City of Del Rio. This action has resulted in the implementation of protection and habitat management for the rare fish. Actions to be implemented in support of this minnow include: surveys and monitoring of its populations; maintenance of a genetically representative captive population at two fish hatchery facilities, for use in captive propagation to provide stock for reintroduction efforts and as insurance against extinction; establishment of new populations through reintroduction; protection of the San Felipe Creek watershed by the City of Del Rio; provision of technical assistance to landowners on riparian protection and management; review of live-bait harvest and selling practices in the Devils River area to develop a strategy to prevent the take of threatened species and introduction of non-native ones; studies of the abundance and range of exotic fish in the Devils River, and in San Felipe, Las Moras, and Sycamore creeks; studies of hydrology in critical habitats; and studies of the biology and habitat needs of the Devils River minnow, including interactions with the smallmouth bass.

Contacts

U. S. Fish and Wildlife Service
Regional Office, Division of Endangered Species
P.O. Box 1306
Albuquerque, New Mexico 87103-1306
Telephone: (505) 248-6911
Fax: (505) 248-6915
http://southwest.fws.gov/

U. S. Fish and Wildlife Service
Austin Ecological Services Field Office
Harland Bank Building
10711 Burnet Road, Suite 200
Austin, Texas 78758-4460
Telephone: (512) 490-0057

Reference

U. S. Fish and Wildlife Service. 20 October 1999. "Endangered and Threatened Wildlife and Plants: Final Rule To List the Devils River Minnow as Threatened." *Federal Register* 64 (202):56596-56609.

Desert Dace

Eremichthys acros

Status	Threatened
Listed	March 11, 1967
Family	Cyprinidae (Minnows)
Description	Olive-green above and silvery below with a dull yellow reflection on the sides.
Habitat	Thermal springs and outflow streams.
Food	Algae, diatoms, snails, insects.
Reproduction	Spawns year round with peak fecundity in April and May.
Threats	Channelization of outflows, predation by other fish, geothermal exploration.
Range	Nevada

Gary Vinyard, Nevada Dept. of Wildlife

Description

The desert dace, *Eremichthys acros*, the only member of the genus *Eremichthys*, is about 2.5 in (7 cm) long. Under optimal conditions, individuals may occasionally reach a length of 10 in (25 cm). The desert dace is olive-green above and silvery below with dull yellow reflections along the sides. Some individuals, especially the young, have a pronounced dark streak along the middle of each side. The side scales reflect bluish and greenish iridescent in sunlight. An unusual aspect of this fish's anatomy is the presence of prominent horny sheaths on the jaws, which probably allow the fish to scrape algae from rocks. No other cyprinid possesses such a feeding adaptation.

Behavior

The desert dace feeds on algae, diatoms, and sometimes snails and insects. The horny sheaths on the jaws are probably used for grazing.

It is notable for its tolerance for high temperatures, often surviving in waters as hot as 100°F (38°C).

The desert dace probably breeds year-round and has been observed to spawn in November, March, and May. Some mature eggs are carried throughout the year but reach the highest fecundity in March and April. Captive-bred dace began producing young at an age of 13 months.

Habitat

The desert dace inhabits thermal springs and their outflows, including small irrigation ditches, where waters are warmer than 67°F (19°C). Water temperature appears to be a major factor controlling the distribution of desert dace within a spring system. In very hot springs, the dace finds its temperature range in the cooler outflow streams. Its preferred water temperature is 73.4-84.2°F (23-29°C), but it has been observed in water as hot as 105°F (40.5°C), the highest temperature ever recorded for a minnow habitat in North America.

Outflows from the numerous small springs terminate either in marshy areas or coalesce into Mud Meadow Wash. Pools that the desert dace occupy include spring pools up to 8 ft (2.4 m) in depth with little or no current and peripheral vegetation, and in small, flowing, natural channels and irrigation ditches with dense vegetation, including pondweed, saltgrass, spikerushes, and bulrush.

Distribution

The desert dace is endemic to a group of thermal springs in the Soldier Meadows area of Humboldt County, Nevada where it survives in eight of 20 or more springs.

Threats

Most of the desert dace's habitat is privately owned. At many of the Soldier Meadows springs, water has been diverted from natural channels into concrete-lined ditches, primarily to water livestock. Channelization changes the temperature gradient of the outflows and interferes with the dace's need to locate optimal water temperatures. Additionally, artificial channels do not readily support the abundance of tiny life forms, which supply the bulk of the desert dace's diet. Two reservoirs, located 3 mi (5 km) from the habitat springs, contain many non-native fishes, such as channel catfish and smallmouth bass. There is danger that these fishes will escape into the springs and prey upon the dace.

Because Soldier Meadows is recognized for having significant geothermal resources, there is some threat of regional exploration and development of this alternative energy source. Such activities would severely disturb the thermal aquifer that feeds the local springs. Tentative geothermal wells were drilled several years ago but were eventually abandoned.

Conservation and Recovery

Critical Habitat has been designated for the desert dace to include all thermal springs and outflows within Soldier Meadows, an area of about 8 sq mi (21 sq km). Current ongoing activities consist of a joint effort between Bureau of Land Management (BLM) and the Nevada Department of Wildlife to transplant desert dace into two springs on BLM-administered land. BLM maintains a water temperature and flow recorder on the two springs. More research needs to be conducted to determine habitat requirements of juveniles, foods and feeding habits, population dynamics, current distribution and abundance, and interaction with native and introduced species. Once these data are collected, they can be applied to the life history and ecological requirements of the species.

Contact

Regional Office of Endangered Species
U.S. Fish and Wildlife Service
Eastside Federal Complex
911 N. E. 11th Ave.
Portland, Oregon 97232
http://pacific.fws.gov/

References

Hubbs, C. L. and R. R. Miller. 1948. "Two New, Relict Genera of Cyprinid Fishes from Nevada." *Occasional Papers of the Museum of Zoology*, University of Michigan, Vol. 507.

Ono, R. D., J. D. Williams, and A. Wagner. 1983. *Vanishing Fishes of North America*. Stonewall Press, Washington, D.C.

U.S. Fish and Wildlife Services. 1985. "Determination of Threatened Status and Designation of Critical Habitat for the Desert Dace." *Federal Register* 50:50304-50309.

Slender Chub

Erimystax cahni

Status	Threatened
Listed	September 9, 1977
Family	Cyprinidae
Description	Small, elongated, olive to brown minnow.
Habitat	Warm springs with shoals.
Food	Insects, mollusks.
Reproduction	Spawns from mid-April to early June.
Threats	Dam construction, siltation, pollution.
Range	Tennessee, Virginia

Description

The slender chub, *Erimystax (=Hybopsis) cahni*, has a moderately elongated body and reaches a maximum length of about 3 in (7.7 cm). It has a long snout, large eyes, and a slightly underhanging mouth. Olive to brown above, it has silvery sides, a whitish underside, and a dark lateral stripe.

Behavior

Little is known of the slender chub's reproductive behavior. Spawning probably begins in mid to late April and extends into early June. Young mature in three to four years and die shortly after. It feeds primarily on insects and mollusks.

Habitat

From April to September the slender chub inhabits large warm streams, 100-413 ft (30-125 m) wide, which have wide shoals of clean gravel. The fish's winter habitat is unknown.

Distribution

The slender chub is endemic to the upper Tennessee River basin and has been recorded from the Clinch, Powell, and Holston rivers. It was collected from the Holston River only one time, in 1941, and has not been seen there since.

The slender chub has one of the smallest ranges of any eastern North American minnow. Today, it is found in nine population centers on the Powell and Clinch Rivers in Tennessee and Virginia. It occurs in sections of the main channel of the Powell River from Lee County, Virginia, downstream to Norris Lake, Tennessee. In the Clinch River it is found in localized populations from Scott County, Virginia, downstream to Norris Lake.

Threats

The Holston River population was lost when the Cherokee Reservoir was completed by the Tennessee Valley Authority (TVA) in the 1940s. The river above the reservoir is now silted and polluted by industrial discharges from Kingsport, Tennessee. The habitat below the reservoir is affected by cold water releases. Clinch River populations have also suffered from reservoir development and from chemical spills and discharges in the 1960s and 1970s.

The Powell River headwaters arise in the heart of coal mining country, and the affects of runoff from the mines are evident in the river and its tributaries. Coal silt has been measured as deep as 3.3 ft (1 m) in pools and backwaters at McDowell Ford. These conditions are only expected to worsen in the near future. Gravel shoals in the Clinch and Powell rivers have been dredged, further disturbing slender chub habitat.

Slender Chub, photograph. U. S. Fish and Wildlife Service. Reproduced by permission.

Conservation and Recovery

The recovery of the slender chub and other aquatic life in the Powell River hinges entirely on the cooperation of mining companies in decreasing coal silt runoff into the streams. Other impacts that should be monitored include toxic spills, pesticides, herbicides, siltation from road construction, and decreased water flow due to slurry pipelines. The TVA, the Tennessee Wildlife Resources Agency, the Tennessee Heritage Program, and the Virginia Commission of Game and Inland Fisheries have consulted to determine the adequacy of existing legislation for lessening contamination in the Upper Tennessee watershed.

It is possible that successful reintroduction of the fish back into its historic range can occur once the Holston River has been stabilized. Portions of the habitat may have to be rehabilitated before the expansion or reintroduction of populations can occur. Protecting existing populations is essential to any potential success of introduced fish.

Contacts

Regional Office for Endangered Species
U.S. Fish and Wildlife Service
1875 Century Blvd., Suite 200
Atlanta, Georgia 30345
http://southeast.fws.gov/

Regional Office for Endangered Species
U. S. Fish and Wildlife Service
300 Westgate Center Dr.
Hadley, Massachusetts 01035
http://northeast.fws.gov/

References

Burkhead, N. M., and R. E. Jenkins. 1982. "Five-year Status Review of the Slender Chub, *Hybopsis cahni*, a Threatened Cyprinid Fish of the Upper Tennessee Drainage." U.S. Fish and Wildlife Service Report. Newton Corner, Massachusetts.

U. S. Fish and Wildlife Service. 1983. "Slender Chub Recovery Plan." U.S. Fish and Wildlife Service, Atlanta.

Hutton Spring Tui Chub

Gila bicolor ssp.

Status	Threatened
Listed	March 28, 1985
Family	Cyprinidae (Minnow)
Description	Silvery sided chub with a dusky olive back.
Habitat	Springs and outflows.
Food	Snails, insects, and amphipods.
Reproduction	Spawns between April and June.
Threats	Limited numbers, groundwater pumping, contamination.
Range	Oregon

Description

The silvery sided Hutton tui chub ranges from 4.7-6 in (12-15 cm) in length. It has a dusky olive back and white belly. Its head is longer, the dorsal fin smaller, and the eyes larger than closely related chubs. Tui chubs in general have only one row of teeth on the pharyngeal bone, and the teeth of this tui chub are exceptionally robust. The Hutton Spring tui chub has been proposed for classification as *Gila bicolor oregonensis*.

Behavior

The omnivorous Hutton tui chub feeds on a wide range of snails, terrestrial and aquatic insects, amphipods, and perhaps algae. It prefers deeper pools and spawns in shallower water over beds of aquatic vegetation. Females deposit eggs between April and June, which hatch after about nine days.

Habitat

The Hutton tui chub is confined to two freshwater springs and associated outflow streams. It requires clean water of constant temperature. Hutton Spring was widened and diked in the 1970s to create a pool about 40 ft (12 m) wide and 15 ft (5 m) deep. Dredging removed most aquatic vegetation, except for a dense stand of rushes in the center of the pool. The Hutton Spring tui chub is currently the only fish inhabiting the spring.

Distribution

Populations of the Hutton Spring tui chub have been found in two spring pools and related outflow streams and marshes in Lake County, Oregon. The springs are situated at the northwestern edge of the dry Alkali Lake.

The Hutton Spring tui chub is known only from Hutton Spring and Three Eighths Spring—a smaller spring located slightly southeast of Hutton Spring. The chub population in Hutton Spring is thought to number about 300 individuals, and Three Eighths Spring supports an additional 150 chubs.

Threats

Surviving populations of the Hutton Spring tui chub are threatened by groundwater pumping for irrigation, which has caused spring discharges and water levels in the region to fall. The property owner has generally been protective of Hutton Spring and has fenced the area to exclude livestock. Three Eighths Spring remains unfenced and has been slightly disturbed by cattle. Both springs are vulnerable to habitat modification, either by dredging or diversion of water into artificial channels. Although it has not yet occurred, the introduction of non-native fishes into the springs would have a disastrous effect on the Hutton tui chub because of the narrow confines of the pools.

P. Harris

A nearby dump is a repository for an estimated 25,000 55-gal (208.2 l) drums of highly toxic chemicals. Residues from these improperly disposed wastes have leached into the surface and groundwater of the Alkali Lake area. It is possible that the springs inhabited by the Hutton Spring tui chub will become contaminated within the foreseeable future if the corroded storage drums continue to leak.

Conservation and Recovery

The Bureau of Land Management, the Environmental Protection Agency, and the Oregon Department of Environmental Quality are working with the property owner to further protect the habitat and spring area, and these agencies are examining ways to reclaim the toxic waste disposal site. One problem is to prevent siltation, erosion, water drawdown and vegetation destruction of the habitat caused by the property owner's spring back-hoe work for water control. And although the property

owner has fenced the immediate vicinity of the spring, vegetative damage caused by cattle trampling has generally caused erosion and sedimentation in the area.

Groundwater contamination, the greatest threat to the spring, was caused by toxic herbicide material that was improperly disposed of about 1.75 mi (2.8 km) from the spring, and state and federal agencies are using their authority to require cleanup of the dump site. The use of heavy equipment at the dump site also caused modification of the spring area.

Contact

Regional Office of Endangered Species
U.S. Fish and Wildlife Service
Eastside Federal Complex
911 N.E. 11th Ave.
Portland, Oregon 97232
http://pacific.fws.gov/

References

Bills, F. 1977. "Taxonomic Status of Isolated Populations of Tui Chub Referred to as *Gila bicolor oregonensis* [Snyder]." M.A. Thesis. Oregon State University, Corvallis, Oregon.

Bond. C. E. 1973. "Keys to Oregon Freshwater Fishes." *Technical Bulletin No. 58.* Agricultural Experiment Station, Oregon State University.

Bond, C. E. 1974. "Endangered Plants and Animals of Oregon; Fishes." *Special Report No. 205.* Agricultural Experiment Station, Oregon State University.

U.S. Fish and Wildlife Service. 1985. "Determination of Threatened Status for Hutton Tui Chub and Foskett Speckled Dace." *Federal Register* 50:12302-12306.

Mohave Tui Chub

Gila bicolor mohavensis

Status	Endangered
Listed	October 13, 1970
Family	Cyprinidae (Minnows)
Description	Olive to brown with a chunky body, large head, and short snout.
Habitat	Deep pools fed by alkaline mineral springs.
Food	Plankton, insect larvae, detritus.
Reproduction	Spawns in spring.
Threats	Hybridization, habitat degradation.
Range	California

Description

The Mohave tui chub, *Gila bicolor mohavensis*, is a moderate to large subspecies of the tui chub, 2-3.7 in (5-9.2 cm) long. It has a thick, chunky body with a large head and short snout, an oblique mouth, and short, rounded fins. In older fish, a distinct hump sometimes develops behind the head. This chub is bright brassy-brown to dusky-olive on the sides and bluish-white to silver on the belly. The fins are olive to rich brown.

The Mohave tui chub is similar in appearance to the Endangered Owens tui chub (*G. b. snyderi*) and the Lahontan tui chub (*G. b. obesa*).

Behavior

The Mohave tui chub is adapted for feeding on plankton and also consumes insect larvae and detritus. It spawns in March or April when water warms to 65°F (18°C) and may spawn again in the fall. Females affix fertilized eggs to aquatic plants, primarily the ditchgrass. Fry form schools in the shallows, but mature fish are solitary. The life span is probably no more than two years.

Habitat

The Mohave tui chub occurs in mineralized, alkaline waters in deep pools or more shallow outflow streams. It was once found in the mainstream of the Mohave River but prefers lakes and mineral spring pools. Dominant plants in the habitat include ditchgrass, bulrush, cattail, rush, saltgrass. Because it does not withstand flooding well, it is dependent on populations in lakes and pools to replenish fish that are washed downstream and out of the river.

Distribution

The Mohave tui chub is the only fish known to be endemic to the Mohave River basin in southwestern California. During the Pleistocene, the river was fed by three large lakes—Mohave, Little Mohave, and Manix—which supplied ideal habitat for this chub. When the climate grew more arid and the lakes dried, the Mohave tui chub became restricted to the Mohave River downstream from Victorville, and to a series of springs between Victorville and the river sources.

The Mohave tui chub is currently found in three extensively modified pools at Soda Springs, situated near the southeastern edge of the dry bed of Soda Lake in San Bernardino County. The springs were an important water stop for travelers on the Mohave Road, which was a supply road from Los Angeles to Ft. Mohave on the Colorado River. In 1940 Lake Tuendae, the largest pool, was excavated and channeled for a health spa which operated until 1974. Groundwater pumping has decreased the size of the other pools.

Mohave Tui Chub, photograph by Phil Pister. Reproduced by permission.

In the 1970s Mohave tui chubs were transplanted to Lark Seep Lagoon on the China Lake Naval Weapons Center. This is now the largest existing population, consisting of several thousand individuals. The Desert Research Station Pond near Hinkley, about 10 mi (16 km) northwest of Barstow, supports a transplanted population of 1,500-2,000.

Threats

When the Arroyo chub (*G. orcutti*) was introduced as a baitfish into the Mohave River during the 1930s, the Mohave tui chub entered a precipitous decline. The two fish interbred so extensively that the Mohave tui chub was almost eliminated as a unique subspecies by 1967. In addition, construction of dams and reservoirs at the headwaters altered water flow in the mainstream and provided better habitat for many non-native fishes, which compete more aggressively for food.

Conservation and Recovery

After a string of failures, the success of recent relocation efforts has generated cautious optimism for the recovery of the Mohave tui chub. The U. S. Fish and Wildlife Service plans to establish three more protected populations of at least 500 fish each. Likely transplant sites are along the Mohave River at Camp Cady Wildlife Area, Afton Canyon Campground, and Mohave Narrows Regional Park. Once these transplants are deemed successful, biologists will consider removing this chub from the federal list. Biologists are currently assessing the feasibility of removing the Arroyo chub from the Mohave River and restocking the river with the indigenous Mohave tui chub.

Contact

Regional Office of Endangered Species
U.S. Fish and Wildlife Service
Eastside Federal Complex
911 N. E. 11th Ave.
Portland, Oregon 97232
http://pacific.fws.gov/

References

Hoover, F., and J. A. St. Amant. 1983. "Results of Mohave Tui Chub, *Gila bicolor mohavensis*, Relocations in California and Nevada." *California Fish and Game* 69:54-56.

U.S. Fish and Wildlife Service. 1984. "Recovery Plan for the Mohave Tui Chub, *Gila bicolor mohavensis*." U.S. Fish and Wildlife Service, Portland.

Owens Tui Chub

Gila bicolor snyderi

Status	Endangered
Listed	August 5, 1985
Family	Cyprinidae (Minnows)
Description	Olive and white chub with lateral blue and gold reflections.
Habitat	Streams, rivers, irrigation ditches.
Food	Insects.
Reproduction	Spawns when water temperature reaches 64°F (17.8°C).
Threats	Water diversion, competition from non-native fishes, hybridization.
Range	California

Description

The Owens tui chub, *Gila bicolor snyderi*, is a moderate to large subspecies of *G. bicolor*, with males reaching 4 in (10 cm) and females slightly more than 5 in (13 cm) in length. It is olive above and whitish below, with lateral blue and gold reflections. The side of the head is noticeably gold. Its mouth lining and tongue are purplish. It has a large head and eyes, and the greatest body depth is just behind the head. It has the heaviest, strongest pharyngeal teeth of any known *G. bicolor* species.

The Owens tui chub has been known since the late 1800s, but was not described as a new subspecies until 1973.

Behavior

Little is known about this chub's reproductive characteristics, but it is thought that spawning occurs when water temperature reaches 64°F (17.8°C). Juveniles appear to use shallow margins as nursery areas.

Little is known about food requirements as well, but comparing the Owens tui chub with sympatric species, it is assumed that juveniles are insectivorous and adults are omnivorous.

Some periodicity has been recorded. It has been observed invading newly flooded shallows in the evening and returning to deeper water in the morning. It also appears that spawning fish migrate to more shallow areas in the spring and summer, and return to deeper water in the fall and winter.

Habitat

Based on past collections, the Owens tui chub occupied various habitats ranging from thermal spring pools, supporting only a few hundred individuals, to the mainstream of the Owens River, where the population numbered in the tens or hundreds of thousands. Primary habitat requirements appear to be clear, clean water, adequate cover in the form of rocks, undercut banks, or aquatic vegetation, and sufficient insect food. Preferred habitat conditions seem to include streams with a slow current, mud bottoms, clear water, and submerged vegetation.

Distribution

The Owens tui chub has been recorded in Owens Lake, Owens River, tributary streams, and irrigation ditches throughout the Owens River basin (Inyo and Mono Counties), California. Because of extensive hybridization throughout the basin, genetically pure populations of the Owens tui chub are now known from only two locations in Mono County—in the source springs of Hot Creek, and a

Owens Tui Chub, photograph by B. "Moose" Peterson/WRP. Reproduced by permission.

8-mi (13-km) stretch of the Owens River below Long Valley Dam. Both sites are within the Inyo National Forest but are owned by the city of Los Angeles. The present distribution represents less than 1% of its historic range.

Threats

Demand for water from the Owens River basin for irrigation and human consumption is high. The river has been dammed at several places and much of its water is diverted through aqueducts to Los Angeles, more than 260 mi (415 km) to the south. The resulting reduction of stream flow has degraded water quality and greatly restricted available habitat for this chub.

The surviving Owens tui chub populations are also threatened by predators, such as the introduced brown trout, and by interbreeding with the Lahontan tui chub (*G. b. obesa*). This non-native chub was introduced illegally into the Owens River as a baitfish.

Conservation and Recovery

The California Department of Fish and Game, Bureau of Land Management, and the U. S. Fish and Wildlife Service (FWS) have repeatedly tried to reintroduce the Owens tui chub to Fish Slough in Mono County. To date, however, transplanted chubs have not survived. Further reintroduction efforts will be based on the results of ongoing research into the chub's habitat preferences.

In 1986 the FWS and the state Department of Fish and Game reached an agreement to maintain the chub's habitat at Hot Creek Springs.

Contact

Regional Office of Endangered Species
U.S. Fish and Wildlife Service
Eastside Federal Complex
911 N.E. 11th Ave.
Portland, Oregon 97232
http://pacific.fws.gov

References

Miller, R. R. 1973. "Two New Fishes, *Gila bicolor sny-deri* and *Catostomus fumeiventris,* from the Owens River Basin, California." *Occasional Papers of the Museum of Zoology, University of Michigan* 667:1-19.

Pister, E. P. 1981. "The Conservation of Desert Fishes." In R. J. Naiman and D. L. Solts, eds., *Fishes in North American Deserts.* John Wiley and Sons, New York.

U.S. Fish and Wildlife Service. 1985. "Determination of Endangered Status and Critical Habitat Designation for Owens Tui Chub." *Federal Register* 50(150):31592-31587.

Borax Lake Chub

Gila boraxobius

Status	Endangered
Listed	October 5, 1982
Family	Cyprinidae (Minnows)
Description	Dwarf chub with an olive green back and silvery sides and black flecking.
Habitat	Mineralized lake fed by thermal springs.
Food	Diatoms, aquatic invertebrates, terrestrial insects.
Reproduction	Spawns year round.
Threats	Water diversion, geothermal exploration.
Range	Oregon

Description

The Borax Lake chub, *Gila boraxobius*, is a dwarf chub, ranging from 1.3-2.4 in (3.3-6 cm) in length. It has an olive green back with a dark mid-line, and silvery sides with black flecking, and a purplish iridescence. The eyes are large and protuberant. The jaw is elongated.

Behavior

This chub is an opportunistic omnivore, feeding on diatoms, tiny crustaceans, insects and larvae, and detritus. It spawns throughout the year with peaks in spring and fall. Young are prominent in the shallow coves around the lake margin in May and June. Individuals live from one to three years.

Habitat

Borax Lake is a 10.2-acre (4.1-hectare), highly mineralized natural lake, characterized by shallow waters (3.3 ft; 1 m), sparse aquatic vegetation, and a constant inflow from thermal springs. Outflow from the lake maintains a small pond and, in the past, extensive marshes between the lake and the pond. Over time, precipitation of salts from the spring water has raised the perimeter of the lake approximately 30 ft (9 m) above the valley floor, isolating the chub from the surrounding watershed.

From 1898 to 1907 the extensive salt deposits of the area were mined for borax. The lake is the site of the original Twenty Mule Team Borax Works, which shipped borax in wagons hauled by 20-mule teams to the railroad at Winnemucca, Nevada.

Distribution

It is thought that this species evolved within the last 10,000 years in Harney County, Oregon. Alford Lake, a large pluvial lake, once covered this area. About 10,000 years ago the lake began to dry, and native fishes were restricted to remaining springs, lakes, and creeks. An ancestral stock became isolated in the springs of Borax Lake and adapted to the extreme conditions of the habitat, evolving into the form now recognized as the Borax Lake chub.

The Borax Lake chub is found only in Borax Lake, its outflow, and Lower Borax Lake, situated in the Alvord Basin of south-central Oregon (Harney County). Population estimates for Borax Lake made in 1986 and 1987 ranged between 6,000 and 14,000. There are thought to be an additional 8,000-10,000 chubs in Lower Borax Lake. The Borax Lake chub apparently experiences large swings in population caused by hot weather die-offs. Renewed spawning activity in the fall signals a rebound to pre-summer levels.

Borax Lake Chub, photograph by Jack Williams. Reproduced by permission.

Threats

Borax Lake is a fragile aquatic ecosystem, which is particularly sensitive to alteration. In 1980 a modification of the lake perimeter to divert water lowered the water level by about 1 ft (0.3 m). This decreased the total area of chub habitat and increased the average water temperature of the lake. Much of the adjacent marsh dried up as a result of this diversion. Marshes around the lower lake retain water from permanent seepage.

The entire Alvord Basin is geothermally active, and the Bureau of Land Management (BLM) has leased geothermal exploration rights to private companies. Biologists fear that exploratory drilling in the area will disrupt interconnecting channels within the aquifer, lower water pressure, and cause the lake, which is above the valley floor, to go dry.

Conservation and Recovery

Within an area defined as habitat critical to the survival of the Borax Lake chub, the BLM owns 320

acres (130 hectares). Another 320 acres (130 hecatres) is privately owned, including the lake itself. In 1983 the Nature Conservancy secured a 10-year lease to the lake and—with the assistance of the Oregon Department of Fish and Wildlife and the BLM—has undertaken a program to rehabilitate the marshes by returning lake outflows to previous levels.

Contact

Regional Office of Endangered Species
U.S. Fish and Wildlife Service
Eastside Federal Complex
911 N.E. 11th Ave.
Portland, Oregon 97232
http://pacific.fws.gov/

References

Ono, R. D., J. Williams, and A. Wagner. 1983. *Vanishing Fishes of North America*. Stonewall Press, Washington, D.C.

Williams, J. E., and C. E. Bond. 1980. "*Gila boraxobius*, a New Species of Cyprinid Fish from Southeastern Oregon with a Comparison to *Gila alvordensis* Hubbs and Miller." *Proceedings of the Biological Society of Washington* 92(2):291-298.

U.S. Fish and Wildlife Service. 1987. "Recovery Plan for the Borax Lake Chub, *Gila boraxobius*." U.S. Fish and Wildlife Service, Portland.

Humpback Chub

Gila cypha

Status	Endangered
Listed	March 11, 1967
Family	Cyprinidae (Minnows)
Description	Large olive brown chub with a hump behind the head.
Habitat	Swift currents and deep channels.
Food	Bottom feeder.
Reproduction	Spawns May to July.
Threats	Dam construction, competition with non-native fish.
Range	Arizona, Colorado, Utah

Description

The humpback chub, *Gila cypha*, is a large chub, between 12 and 15 in (30-38 cm) in length, with a prominent dorsal hump behind the head. It has a flat, fleshy snout, and small eyes. It is olive or brown on the back and silvery on the sides and belly. So odd looking is this fish that it has been described as "remarkable" and "bizarre" even in official publications.

Behavior

Spawning in the Little Colorado River occurs in May to July when the water temperature is 60.8-66.2°F (16-19°C), and May through June in the Black Rocks area of the Colorado River when water temperatures reach 52.7-61.7°F (11.5-16.5°C). Spawning occurs over boulder, sand, and possibly gravel substrates.

The chub's underhanging mouth suggests bottom feeding; it is known to feed on Chironomids, Simuliids, plankton, crustaceans, diatoms, and other small invertebrates.

Habitat

The humpback is adapted to the Colorado River system, one of the most severe swift-water fish habitats in North America. Its specific habitat requirements are not known, but it has generally been associated with fast currents and deep channels. Juveniles prefer a slower current, a silt substrate, and a depth of less than 3.3 ft (1 m).

Distribution

The humpback chub was probably found throughout much of the Colorado River basin. It has been documented from the Colorado River from its headwaters in Colorado to its lower reaches along the Arizona-California border; the Green River from its Wyoming headwaters to confluence with the Colorado River in Utah; the lower Yampa River, a Colorado tributary of the Green River; and the White River in Utah.

When Flaming Gorge Dam was completed in Daggett County, Utah, in 1962, the humpback chub was eliminated from long stretches of the Green River above and below the dam. The cold tailwaters of Glen Canyon Dam (built in Coconino County, Arizona) have caused reductions in both the distribution and abundance of humpback chubs in Marble and Grand canyons. Populations are located in the Colorado, Little Colorado, Green, and Yampa rivers. The largest population is located in the Little Colorado River in the Grand Canyon.

Threats

The humpback chub has declined significantly since the Flaming Gorge and Glen Canyon dams

Humpback Chub, photograph. U. S. Fish and Wildlife Service. Reproduced by permission.

were completed, but populations were probably lost in the 1930s when the Hoover Dam was built. When the dam reservoirs were filled, cold tailwaters forced out the humpback chub, which prefers warmer waters. Below the dams, water flows were significantly decreased. The U. S. Fish and Wildlife Service (FWS) has determined that any additional diversion of water from the Colorado River would jeopardize the survival of the humpback chub, the bonytail chub (*G. elegans*), and the Colorado squawfish (*Ptychocheilus lucius*).

Conservation and Recovery

When these fishes were granted protection under the Endangered Species Act, the western states threatened a protracted confrontation with the federal government over water rights. In 1984 the FWS convened the Upper Colorado River Basin Coordinating Committee. Members included representatives of the FWS, the Bureau of Reclamation, the states of Colorado, Utah, and Wyoming, and private water development interests.

In 1988 all parties agreed on a recovery program for the Colorado River basin and established a committee to oversee implementation. The unprecedented agreement calls for maintaining an adequate stream flow throughout the system. On the Colorado and Green Rivers prescribed releases from federal reservoirs will provide the needed water. On the Yampa and White Rivers, the FWS will purchase water rights to assure an adequate flow. The agreement also contains provisions for habitat rehabilitation, restocking of native fishes, and continued monitoring of wildlife populations.

A captive propagation program has been established to stock reclaimed portions of the Colorado River with native fishes. Fish hatcheries in the region, such as Rifle Falls State Fish Hatchery and the Hotchkiss National Fish Hatchery, will probably be expanded to include facilities for the humpback chub. In 1989 in a multi-agency cooperative effort, 1,800 humpbacks were captured in the Little Colorado; 450 were tagged with radio transponders to enable biologists to track the fish's movements in the river.

The second revised Recovery Plan for the species, released in 1990, noted that the recovery goal is the protection or restoration of five viable, self-sustaining populations within the Colorado River basin and the protection of the habitat utilized by these populations.

Downlisting will occur when these five populations have been located or reestablished. To achieve this goal, the FWS recommended a number of actions, including the resolution of taxonomic problems in defining the populations of the Colorado Basin *gila*; the identification and definition of humpback chub populations; and research into the life history and ecological requirements of the fish. The plan also calls for the protection of humpback chub populations and their habitats, the assessment of potential reintroduction and augmentation sites, and the implementation of stocking. Promoting and encouraging improved communication and information dissemination was also advised.

On March 21, 1994, the FWS published the final rule designating Critical Habitat for the Humpback Chub in portions of the Upper Basin of the Colorado, Green, and Yampa rivers; and in the Colorado and Little Colorado rivers in the Lower Basin.

Contacts

Regional Office of Endangered Species
U.S. Fish and Wildlife Service
P.O. Box 1306
Albuquerque, New Mexico 87103
http://southwest.fws.gov/

Regional Office of Endangered Species
U.S. Fish and Wildlife Service
P. O. Box 25486
Denver Federal Center
Denver, Colorado 80225
http://www.r6.fws.gov/

References

U.S. Fish and Wildlife Service. 1979. "Humpback Chub Recovery Plan." U.S. Fish and Wildlife Service, Albuquerque.

Sonora Chub

Gila ditaenia

Status	Threatened
Listed	April 30, 1986
Family	Cyprinidae
Description	A small minnow.
Habitat	Streams and shallow rivers.
Food	Small invertebrates and algae.
Reproduction	Lays externally fertilized eggs.
Threats	Habitat destruction and degradation.
Range	Arizona; Mexico

Sonora Chub, photograph by C. Allan Morgan. Reproduced by permission.

Description

The Sonora chub is a fine-scaled, medium-sized minnow. Adults are less than 3.2 in (12.5 cm) in body length, and are generally stout in appearance. They are dark-colored, with two dark lateral bands and a caudal (or tail) spot. Their small body scales are oval to rectangular in shape, and have numerous radii. During the breeding season the fins of the male develop brilliant red coloration, with a milky border on the outer margins, and their underside turns orange. The female develops a less bright coloration.

Behavior

The Sonora chub feeds on small aquatic invertebrates, terrestrial insects, and algae grazed from rocks and other solid substrates. Not much is known about its breeding, but the Sonora chub probably spawns in September to October.

Habitat

The Sonora chub inhabits streams and shallow rivers in dry regions. Its habitat elements include clean permanent water, pools and riffle areas, and a riparian zone of shading vegetation. It is most abundant in deeper pools.

Distribution

The Sonora chub is a locally evolved (or endemic) fish that is only known from southern Arizona and nearby areas of northern Sonora state, Mexico.

Threats

Some of the original habitat of the Sonora chub was damaged by the construction of an impoundment and by the disturbance of riparian vegetation. The remaining habitat is potentially threatened by pollution by silt and nutrients, by the potential influences of recreation and mining, and by the introduction of predatory non-native fishes (such as the green sunfish, *Lepomis cyanellus*) and parasites. The surviving critical habitat of the Sonora chub in Arizona is in areas of Sycamore Creek, including Yank's Spring, Penasco Creek, and an unnamed tributary. This reach of only about 4.7 mi (7.5 km) of the Sycamore Creek drainage is located within the Coronado National Forest, in Santa Cruz County, Arizona. In Mexico, it occurs in the Rio Concepcion.

Conservation and Recovery

The Sonora chub is relatively secure in its critical habitat in Arizona, due to Federal ownership and the special-use designation provided its habitats in the Coronado National Forest. However, because of the very limited amount of suitable habitat in Arizona, it is likely that significant population enhancement of the rare chub can only be accomplished by protecting parts of its critical habitat in Sonora, Mexico. Studies are being undertaken of the biology and ecology of the Sonora chub, and of the factors limiting its abundance. Human activities near its Arizona habitats are generally restricted to bird-watching, hiking, and other forms of outdoor recreation, with access limited to hiking and horseback trails. However, the canyons containing the critical habitat receive heavy visitor use, and include a trailhead parking lot for visitors. Although the chub habitat occurs within an area zoned for livestock grazing, the steep and rocky topography generally precludes this use along stream banks within the riparian zone of the critical habitat. Moreover, the U.S. Forest Service restricts grazing by domestic animals in the vicinity. The remaining portion of the Sycamore Creek Critical Habitat flows through the Gooding Research Natural Area, which was established in 1970 to protect unique species, and precludes any grazing or mineral mining. Because of its small range and population size, the Sonora chub is threatened by catastrophic population loss due to extreme weather or another cause. Consideration is being made of establishing a refugium population in a nearby fish hatchery. Neither the habitat or the chub receive official protection in Mexico.

Contacts

U. S. Fish and Wildlife Service
Regional Office, Division of Endangered Species
P.O. Box 1306
Albuquerque, New Mexico 87103-1306
Telephone: (505) 248-6911
Fax: (505) 248-6915
http://southwest.fws.gov/

U. S. Fish and Wildlife Service
Arizona Ecological Services Field Office
2321 West Royal Palm Road, Suite 103
Phoenix, Arizona 85021-4915
(602) 640-2720

References

Conservation Management Institute. "Sonoma Chub 2000." Virginia Tech, Blacksburg, VA. http://fwie.fw.vt.edu/WWW/esis/lists/e252018.htm

U.S. Fish and Wildlife Service. 1986. "Endangered and Threatened Wildlife and Plants; Final Rule to Determine the Sonora Chub to be a Threatened Species and Determine its Critical Habitat." *Federal Register* 51: 16042-16047.

Bonytail Chub

Gila elegans

Status	Endangered
Listed	April 23, 1980
Family	Cyprinidae (Minnows)
Description	Large, silver chub with greenish back.
Habitat	Turbid, swift-flowing rivers.
Food	Insects and algae.
Reproduction	Spawns in the spring.
Threats	Dam construction, water diversion, competition with non-native fishes.
Range	Arizona, California, Colorado, Nevada, Utah

Description

The bonytail chub, *Gila elegans*, is a relatively large chub, averaging 12 in (30 cm) in length. Its chunky body is silver with a greenish tinge along the back. The head is flattened, the back slightly humped, the eyes very small and of little use. The narrow tail terminates in a V-shaped caudal fin. The breeding male's belly turns bright orange-red. The bonytail chub was once considered a subspecies of the roundtail chub (*G. robusta*) but has since been accorded full species status.

Behavior

The bonytail chub is omnivorous, feeding mainly on terrestrial insects, larvae, algae, and detritus. In spring it spawns in schools over rocky shoals of smaller tributaries.

Habitat

This species is found in larger rivers and displays a high tolerance for turbidity. It is most frequently associated with eddies just outside the main river current. The bonytail chub is susceptible to changes in water temperature and flow, and low levels of chemical pollution.

Distribution

The bonytail chub was once abundant throughout the Colorado River and its larger tributaries. It has been collected from the Green River in Wyoming and Utah, Yampa and Gunnison Rivers in Colorado, the Colorado River in Arizona, Nevada and California, and the Gila and Salt Rivers in Arizona.

In the 1960s a dramatic decline in bonytails was recorded in the Green River after the Flaming Gorge Dam was completed. The Bureau of Reclamation has since adjusted water flows from the dam to improve downstream habitat, but no corresponding recovery of the bonytail has been noted. Recent surveys indicate that the bonytail chub may survive only in Lake Mohave along the Arizona-Nevada border. The surviving wild population appears to consist of older fish that are not reproducing.

Threats

Massive reservoir impoundment and hydroelectric dams have changed the character of the Colorado River basin. Many stretches of river—for example, the Dolores River below the McPhee Dam—are dry through portions of the year. Massive amounts of water are diverted each year for irrigation and human consumption. The U. S. Fish and Wildlife Service (FWS) has determined that any additional diversion of water from the Colorado River would jeopardize the survival of the bonytail chub, humpback chub (*G. cypha*), and the Colorado squawfish (*Ptychocheilus lucius*).

Bonytail Chub, photograph by John Rinne, USFS. Reproduced by permission.

Introduction of exotic fishes into the river basin has also contributed to the bonytail chub's decline. Predation on larval chubs by red and redside shiners may account for the absence of bonytail fry. Non-native fishes now outnumber native fishes in the Colorado River basin.

In 1984 the FWS convened the Upper Colorado River Basin Coordinating Committee to defuse controversy over the federal listing of several Endangered fishes. The committee, a forum for discussion and negotiation, consisted of representatives of the FWS, the Bureau of Reclamation, the states of Colorado, Utah, and Wyoming, and private water development interests. In 1988 the committee forged an unprecedented regional agreement to improve water flow and quality in the Colorado River basin.

Conservation and Recovery

In 1986, the FWS and the Division of Refuge Management initiated a cooperative effort to hold Endangered Colorado River fish in refuges along the lower Colorado River. Use of these refuges—typically riverside ponds with controlled river access—permits fish fry to be reared to subadult size before being released into the river, improving survival chances. The bonytail chub was the first fish to be transplanted to a pond at Imperial National Wildlife Refuge in Arizona, using stock from the Dexter National Fish Hatchery.

Bonytail fry have also been stocked in ponds at the Havasu, Cibola, and Buenos Aires national wildlife refuges and subsequently returned to the river with promising results, but the bonytail chub is still a long way from recovery. The Colorado River Fishes Recovery Team recommended in 1987 that all bonytails netted in the wild be transported to the Dexter facility for use in the captive propagation effort.

The 1994 revised Recovery Plan for the species noted that the recovery goal, in the short-term, is to prevent extinction, and in the long-term, to address quantitative goals for downlisting and eventual delisting. Recovery criteria will be developed after the completion of various actions, including the prevention of extinction by establishing a genetically diverse captive population for reintroduction into the wild. The revised plan also calls for the gathering of essential information about the life history and habitat requirements of the fish; the resolution of taxonomic problems in Colorado River basin chubs (the bonytail as well as the humpback and roundtail); and the development of quantitative recovery goals and a long-term habitat protection strategy.

On March 21, 1994 the FWS published the final rule designating Critical Habitat for the bonytail chub in portions of the Upper Basin of the Colorado, Green, and Yampa Rivers; and in the Colorado River in the Lower Basin.

Contacts

Regional Office of Endangered Species
U.S. Fish and Wildlife Service
Eastside Federal Complex
911 N.E. 11th Ave.
Portland, Oregon 97232
http://pacific.fws.gov/

Regional Office of Endangered Species
U.S. Fish and Wildlife Service
P.O. Box 1306
Albuquerque, New Mexico 87103
http://southwest.fws.gov/

Regional Office of Endangered Species
U.S. Fish and Wildlife Service
P. O. Box 25486
Denver Federal Center
Denver, Colorado 80225
http://www.r6.fws.gov/

References

Ono, R. D., J. D. Williams, and A. Wagner. 1983. *Vanishing Fishes of North America.* Stonewall Press, Washington, D.C.

Sigler, W. F., and R. R. Miller. 1963. *Fishes of Utah.* Utah State Department of Fish and Game, Salt Lake City.

U.S. Fish and Wildlife Service. 1990. "Bonytail Chub Revised Recovery Plan." U.S. Fish and Wildlife Service, Denver.

Chihuahua Chub

Gila nigrescens

Status	Threatened
Listed	October 11, 1983
Family	Cyprinidae (Minnows)
Description	Medium-sized, dusky brown chub.
Habitat	Deep pools in small streams.
Food	Insects, aquatic invertebrates, plant matter.
Reproduction	Spawns in April or May.
Threats	Water diversion, dam construction, pollution.
Range	New Mexico; Chihuahua, Mexico

Description

The Chihuahua chub, *Gila nigrescens*, is a medium-sized minnow, ranging from 3-6 in (8-15 cm) long. It is a dusky brown above and whitish beneath. During the breeding season an orange-red color develops around the mouth and lower fins. In the past, this species has also been variously classified as *G. pulchella* and *Tigoma nigrescens*. To add to the confusion, the name *G. nigrescens* has been applied by some authors to a different chub found in the Rio Grande and Pecos rivers.

Behavior

The Chihuahua chub, like a trout, takes insects from the surface of the water. It feeds also on small, aquatic invertebrates, fish fry, and some plant matter. Chubs spawn in April and May over beds of aquatic vegetation in deeper, quiet pools. The habitat is subject to extreme drying in summer and violent flash floods in the rainy season. Seven centuries ago when the watershed was more stable, the Mimbres Indians took large numbers of these chubs for food and used the fish as a design element on their pottery.

Habitat

This species inhabits smaller streams in canyonlands. Average water depth is only about 3 ft (1 m), but the shallow stream beds are often interspersed with deeper pools. This chub prefers overhanging vegetation, undercut banks, or submerged trees for cover. Associated with the Chihuahua chub in some of the same streams is the Endangered beautiful shiner (*Notropis formosus*).

Distribution

The Chihuahua chub once ranged throughout the Guzman basin, which includes the Mimbres River of southwestern New Mexico and the Rio Casas Grandes, Rio Santa Maria, and Laguna Bustillos Rivers of Chihuahua, Mexico.

When surveys for the Chihuahua chub were conducted in 1979, one small, relict population of about 100 fish was found in the Mimbres River in Grant County, New Mexico. In 1981 and 1982 the New Mexico Department of Game and Fish discovered a second small population in the mainstream of the river. The presence of all age grades suggests that successful reproduction has continued despite severe flooding of previous years.

Threats

The Mimbres River of New Mexico has been significantly modified by agricultural and flood control developments. Chihuahua chub populations have declined because of the diversion of water for

James E. Johnson

irrigation, dam and levee construction, and artificial stream channelization. The excessive pumping of groundwater has caused many springs in the region to dry up. These conditions have restricted the Chihuahua chub to one small section of the river. Continuing flood reclamation work, irrigation diversions, and channelization will undoubtedly contribute to further decline.

Water pollution has been responsible for eliminating the chub from most of its range in Mexico. Development of hydroelectric facilities, diversion of surface waters for irrigation, and excessive pumping from the underground aquifers have completely dried up many streams and springs in the region.

Conservation and Recovery

The delisting of this fish could only be considered when conservation easements are in place along the springfed headwaters of the river and two additional populations have been reestablished within its former range. The Chihuahua chub is currently being propagated at the Dexter National Fish

Hatchery at Dexter, New Mexico, for use as reintroduction stock.

Contact

Regional Office of Endangered Species
U.S. Fish and Wildlife Service
P.O. Box 1306
Albuquerque, New Mexico 87103
http://southwest.fws.gov/

References

Hatch, M. D. 1980. "Management Plan for the Chihuahua Chub, *Gila nigrescens* (Girard, 1856), in New Mexico." New Mexico Department of Game and Fish, Santa Fe.

Hubbard, J. P., *et al.* 1978. *Handbook of Species Endangered in New Mexico.* New Mexico Department of Game and Fish, Santa Fe.

U.S. Fish and Wildlife Service. 1986. "Chihuahua Chub Recovery Plan." U.S. Fish and Wildlife Service, Albuquerque.

Yaqui Chub

Gila purpurea

Status	Endangered
Listed	August 31, 1984
Family	Cyprinidae (Minnows)
Description	Medium-sized silvery minnow with a dark side band and a dark spot at the base of the tail.
Habitat	Flowing streams and pools.
Food	Insects and plant matter.
Reproduction	Spawns in March.
Threats	Water diversion, groundwater depletion, predation and competition from other fishes.
Range	Arizona; Mexico (Chihuahua and Sonora)

Description

A medium-sized silvery minnow, the Yaqui chub, *Gila purpurea,* ranges in size from 5-6 in (12.5-15 cm). Its streamlined shape terminates in a narrow tail and V-shaped caudal (tail) fin. Dark-colored overall but lighter below, it displays a single dark band on its side, and a dark spot at the base of the tail. Fins are enlarged and nearly fan-shaped.

Behavior

This chub feeds on insects, arachnids, plant matter, detritus, and small fish. It uses backwaters of streams and springs beneath undercut and overgrown banks for feeding and shelter. Breeding behavior has not been described, but the fish probably spawns in deep pools, where there is aquatic vegetation. Spawning occurs in March. Males become steel-blue in coloration while females are straw-colored.

Habitat

The Yaqui chub requires clean, narrow, permanent streams and spring pools, free of introduced fishes. Streams typically consist of deep pools separated by riffles and flowing stretches of moderate current. The chub is associated with a variety of shrub and brush rangeland of the Rio Sonora Basin but prefers cut banks along pool margins, downed logs of mature trees, and rock overhangs in association with perennial flows. Larger individuals prefer deep pools and smaller individuals prefer intermediate riffles and smaller pools. The chub appears to inhabit deep pools and fast runs during floods and shallower isolated pools during dry seasons. Associated vegetation includes watercress, willow, seep-willow, cottonwood, velvet ash, and tobosa grass.

Distribution

This species is endemic to the Rio Yaqui basin of southeastern Arizona, northwestern Sonora, and portions of eastern Chihuahua, Mexico. This chub has also been recorded from the Rio Sonora and Rio Matape on the Pacific slope of Mexico. It was first collected from San Bernardino Creek, just south of the Arizona-Sonora border. The Yaqui chub survived in San Bernardino Creek in Arizona until spring flows diminished and the creek dried up. Remaining habitat was severely trampled by livestock seeking water, making it uninhabitable.

Surviving Arizona populations are known from a few springs on the San Bernardino National Wildlife Refuge and Leslie Creek in Cochise

James E. Johnson

County. Contract biologists from the Arizona State University and the University of Michigan surveyed the Rio Yaqui basin in 1979 and found only a single chub, signaling a serious decline in numbers. The status of the Mexican populations is largely unknown beyond the fact that a severe decline in numbers has occurred. A large percentage of existing populations resulted from reintroductions, which have created large and viable stocks in diverse habitats throughout its historical range.

Threats

The range of the Yaqui chub decreased significantly because of habitat modifications, such as arroyo cutting, water diversion, dam construction, and excessive pumping of groundwater from aquifers. The American Fisheries Society proposed protection for the Yaqui chub as early as 1979, and in 1983 the Desert Fishes Council petitioned the U. S. Fish and Wildlife Service (FWS) to list the chub on the basis of its disappearance from San Bernardino Creek.

The U. S. Bureau of Land Management (BLM) has issued leases for geothermal resources on lands adjacent to the San Bernardino National Wildlife Refuge. Biologists fear that exploration and development of these leases could cause further depletion of the underground aquifers or create channels for pollution of groundwater. The BLM will examine these threats in consultation with the FWS.

Introduced predatory fishes, such as largemouth bass, bluegill, black bullhead, channel catfish, and green sunfish are present in some portions of the Rio Yaqui basin and probably feed on the Yaqui chub. Other springs and outflow streams within the San Bernardino National Wildlife Refuge may provide suitable habitat for the Yaqui chub. The FWS surveyed sites there in preparation for a translocation effort.

Many rivers in Mexico, formerly inhabited by the Yaqui chub, have been highly modified into an artificially channeled canal system to support irrigation agriculture. Water quality has declined drastically because of chemical and sewage contamination. The Yaqui chub receives no legal protection from the Mexican government.

Conservation and Recovery

Yaqui chubs from the Dexter National Fish Hatchery in New Mexico were stocked on San Bernardino Ranch in 1980, immediately following the purchase of the ranch by the Nature Conservancy. Two of three stockings succeeded. The Dexter stock failed in 1984 for unknown reasons and was immediately reinstated with 100 fish from the North Pond stock established in 1980. House Pond was renovated in 1984-85 to remove mosquitofish, a species incompatible with topminnows. It was restocked with chubs and topminnows in 1986. Also in 1986, because secure populations were established within the San Bernardino National Wildlife Refuge, Yaqui chubs were removed from the Dexter National Fish Hatchery and stocked in West Turkey Creek, where they established.

Yaqui chub reappeared in Black Draw in 1987, either from the 1980 stocking or through upstream dispersal from Mexico. Considerable FWS effort had by then been expended in erosion control and revegetation, and the positive results of this—coupled with consecutive wet years and the appearance of Mexican stone rollers (a cyprinid fish)—helped reestablish the Yaqui chub to its historic habitat.

Contact

U. S. Fish and Wildlife Service
Regional Office, Division of Endangered Species
P. O. Box 1306
Albuquerque, New Mexico 87103-1306
Telephone: (505) 248-6911
Fax: (505) 248-6915
http://southwest.fws.gov/

References

Hendrickson, D. A., et al. 1980. "Fishes of the Rio Yaqui Basin, Mexico and United States." *Journal of the Arizona-Nevada Academy of Science* 15 (3): 65-106.

Silvey, W. 1975. "Statewide Fisheries Investigations: Fishes of Leslie Creek, Cochise County, Arizona." Statewide Survey of Aquatic Resources, Federal Aid Project F-7-R-17. Arizona Fish and Game Department, Phoenix.

U. S. Fish and Wildlife Service. 1979. "Environmental Assessment of the Proposed Land Acquisition of San Bernardino Ranch, Cochise County, Arizona." U. S. Fish and Wildlife Service, Albuquerque.

Pahranagat Roundtail Chub

Gila robusta jordani

Status	Endangered
Listed	October 13, 1970
Family	Cyprinidae (Minnow)
Description	Medium to large, greenish chub with black blotches.
Habitat	Thermal waters with mud or sand substrate.
Food	Mostly plant matter; some detritus and insects.
Reproduction	Spawns in the spring.
Threats	Habitat destruction, competition with exotic species.
Range	Nevada

Description

The Pahranagat roundtail chub, *Gila robusta jordani*, also known as the Pahranagat bonytail chub, is a medium-sized fish, growing to about 10 in (25 cm). It has an elongated body with a narrow tail and a deeply cleft caudal fin. Its coloring is greenish with black blotches.

The Pahranagat roundtail chub is most similar in appearance to the common roundtail chub (*G. r. robusta*), which is found in the Colorado River and its larger tributaries.

Behavior

The patchy distribution of Pahranagat roundtail chub in the Pahranagat Creek/Ditch suggests that this fish requires specific foraging habitat. Pahranagat roundtail chub typically congregate in pools below a portion of the river that is typically narrow and has increased water velocity. Fallen trees or branches are common to these areas, and increase water turbulence. The distinctive hydraulic conditions that Pahranagat roundtail chub occupy probably provide optimum opportunities for encountering food items with minimal energy expenditure. Pahranagat roundtail chub generally enter slightly faster water velocities when striking at a food item.

Pahranagat roundtail chub forage primarily on drifting invertebrates and secondarily, though infrequently, by pecking at substrate. The species rarely preys on other fish, although a Pahranagat roundtail chub was observed to successfully consume a mosquitofish. Rates of adult drift feeding vary, with more food consumed in the winter than in summer. The lower food consumption rate during the summer corresponds to a reduced availability of food items during the summer. The summer appears to be a period of austerity for adults, characterized by high metabolic demands due to warmer water temperatures and low food availability.

There is no relationship between feeding rate and relative food item abundance for two size classes of adult Pahranagat roundtail chub, although there is a relationship between feeding rate and water temperature for larger adults. Large Pahranagat roundtail chub may feed more selectively with increasing water temperatures, preferring bigger and energetically more efficient prey items. During winter, retrieval of smaller prey items in cooler water requires the expenditure of less metabolic energy.

Pahranagat Chub, photograph by John Rinne, USFS. Reproduced by permission.

Pahranagat roundtail chub have been observed spawning at three sites in the Pahranagat Creek, all approximately 2.0-2.2 mi (3.2-3.5 km) below Ash Springs. Adult Pahranagat roundtail chub begin to congregate in mid-January, although spawning generally does not start until late January. Peak daytime spawning activity generally occurs during early to mid-February, and although congregations persist through March, spawning usually does not occur after mid-February. In May 1988 spawning congregations appeared on two of the spawning sites, but no spawning activity was observed, and no larvae were produced.

Male and female Pahranagat roundtail chub are readily distinguishable by their reproductive behavior, which is similar to other cyprinids. The persistent and insistent behavior of a fish in the spawning congregation suggests that it is a male. Females are fewer in number and receive substantial attention in the form of male pursuit. When the female is ready to spawn, she swims down to the gravel bottom where she is attended by a group of two to 10 males. The spawning group vibrates violently for three to six seconds. The female generally swims away and is pursued by males until ready to spawn again. It is believed that females only appear on the spawning site when prepared to spawn, which occurs intermittently over several days.

Spawning occurs in relatively fast water in gravel-covered pool bottoms at water depths ranging from 1.9-3.4 ft (58-104 cm). Water temperatures during the spawning months range from 63-76°F (17-24.5°C).

Pahranagat roundtail chub eggs are broadcast over gravel substrates and apparently fall into the cracks. Convict cichlids and speckled dace have been observed picking at the spawning beds, presumably in search of eggs. Larvae reach "swim-up" stage approximately 28 days after eggs are deposited in the gravel bed. It takes 28-53 days for all larvae to leave the spawning beds, with peak emigration occurring on the 30th day. Larval emigration generally occurs between 6:00 p.m. and midnight, with the majority of emigration occurring between 7:00 and 8:00 p.m.

Habitat

This species lives in pools where water temperatures range from (81-86°F (27-30°C). Aquatic vegetation includes algae, *Chara zeylania, Compsopogon coeruleus, Najas marina,* and a variety of diatoms. It inhabits water with bottoms ranging from mud to firm sand.

During the winter of the study, Pahranagat roundtail chub congregate at the confluence of Crystal Springs and Pahranagat Creek to forage because ostracods (seed shrimps) and other invertebrates are abundant in the cooler water. During the summer, chub congregate in the occasional pockets of cool water created by irrigation runoff from adjacent pastures and forage on food items carded by the runoff. Because they reduce their active metabolism during the summer season, they may move into slower to reduce energy expenditures.

Distribution

The Pahranagat roundtail chub is endemic to the Pahranagat Valley in Lincoln County, Nevada. Precise limits of the historic range are not known because the valley waters were extensively altered before the fish was discovered. However, it is known to have occurred in Crystal, Hiko, and Ash Springs, and in the Pahranagat River. Two other Endangered fishes are found in the Pahranagat Valley-White River springfish (*Crenichthys baileyi baileyi*) and Hiko White River springfish (*C. b. grandis*). These fishes were historically the most abundant species found in Crystal, Hiko and Ash Springs.

The Pahranagat roundtail chub is considered one of the rarest fish in North America. Less than 75 adult chubs and, perhaps, 200 yearlings are thought to survive in approximately 7,590 ft (2,300 m) of an unmodified portion of the Pahranagat River downstream from Ash Springs on Burns Ranch. Fry and juveniles are sometimes found in irrigation ditches, where they usually do not survive.

Threats

When the Pahranagat roundtail chub was listed as Endangered in 1970, a published summary of the factors affecting the species and the reasons for its listing was not required. However, it is probable that the species was granted Endangered status because it had been extirpated from two of three historically occupied spring systems, and was considered to be extremely rare. Degradation of the riparian habitat due to grazing, crop production in adjacent habitat, and loss of riverine canopy was believed to be contributing to the declining Pahranagat roundtail chub population. Though these activities may have contributed to decline of the fishes in the past, recent field visits suggest that habitat conditions have improved. However, improvements in the current habitat conditions, while maintaining current land use practices, will be needed before the fish can be recovered.

The introduction of non-native fishes to the watershed are primarily responsible for the decline of the Pahranagat roundtail chub. Streams in the Pahranagat Valley have been extensively altered to accommodate irrigation. The present restricted habitat of the Pahranagat roundtail chub is one of the few stream reaches that has not been lined with concrete. Non-native fishes competing with the chub include the convict cichlid, carp, mosquitofish, and the shortfin molly.

In the Pahranagat Valley habitat overlap between Pahranagat roundtail chub and shortfin molly occurs primarily during the Pahranagat roundtail chub larval stage. Convict cichlids were believed to be the more formidable threat to larval Pahranagat roundtail chub based on gut analysis and observations of them picking at gravel spawning beds of adult Pahranagat roundtail chub. In laboratory experiments using a castostomid (sucker) larvae as a substitute for the Endangered Pahranagat roundtail chub, shortfin mollies were discovered to be extremely effective larval predators. Mollies are now considered a greater threat to larval Pahranagat roundtail chub than cichlids because of their tendency for greater spatial overlap. Fortunately, Pahranagat roundtail chub reproduction occurs in late winter when populations of non-natives are depressed and in reaches of river with the smallest non-native populations.

Conservation and Recovery

In the years immediately following publication of the 1985 Recovery Plan for the Pahranagat roundtail chub, much effort was directed toward establishing the captive population at Dexter National Fish Hatchery and identifying the ecology of the Pahranagat roundtail chub. The U. S. Fish and Wildlife Service's (FWS) National Fisheries Research Center-Reno completed many research tasks specified in the 1985 plan, including Pahranagat roundtail chub life history, abundance and distribution, food habits, habitat use, movement patterns, population dynamics, and inter- and intraspecific interactions. This research also provided information on White River and Hiko White River spring fishes.

Twenty chubs relocated to the Endangered Fish Facility at Shoshone Ponds in Nevada failed to reproduce, but in 1985 the FWS successfully established a captive population of the Pahranagat roundtail chub at the Dexter National Fish Hatchery. Alerted to severe drying of an inhabited irrigation ditch, personnel from the Nevada Department of Wildlife and the Great Basin Complex netted about 50 juveniles, held them overnight in a live trap in a stream, and transferred them the next day in plastic sacks filled with stream water to the airport at Las Vegas. From there the fish were flown to Roswell, New Mexico, and handed over to hatchery personnel. The facility is located south of Roswell near Dexter in Chaves County. Previous attempts to translocate the chub to the hatchery had failed.

It is hoped that this captive stock can be used as the basis for a reintroduction effort when suitable habitat can be located or significant stretches of the Pahranagat River rehabilitated.

The Pahranagat roundtail chub may be considered for reclassification from endangered to threatened when:

1) Pahranagat Creek/Ditch contains adequate cool water pools, for chub to persist through the summer months;

2) a self-sustaining Pahranagat roundtail chub population (comprising three or more age-classes, a stable or increasing population size, and documented reproduction and recruitment) is present in a combined total of approximately 75% of either 4.7 mi (6.8 km) of the Crystal Spring outflow stream through its confluence during the winter months with the Ash Springs outflow stream, or 6.2 (10 km) of Pahranagat Creek/Ditch below the confluence for three complete generations (or a minimum of 15 consecutive years); and

3) impacts to the species and its habitat have been reduced or modified to a point where they no longer represent a threat of extinction or irreversible population decline.

The Pahranagat roundtail chub may be considered for delisting provided that all reclassification criteria have been met and when:

1) a minimum year round in-stream flow of 1.75 cu ft (49.5 l) per second is present, at the point where Pahranagat Ditch starts, to sustain a Pahranagat roundtail chub population;

2) the riparian corridor along the outflow stream of Crystal Spring has been enhanced;

3) all impacts to its habitat have been neutralized or reduced sufficiently for both the species and land uses to coexist; and

4) a Pahranagat roundtail chub population as defined in the downlisting criteria inhabits both approximately 75% of both the Crystal Spring outflow stream through its confluence during the winter months with the Ash Springs outflow stream, and approximately 75% of Pahranagat Creek/Ditch from the beginning of Crystal and Ash Springs outflows to Upper Pahranagat Lake.

Contact

Regional Office of Endangered Species
U.S. Fish and Wildlife Service
Eastside Federal Complex
911 N. E. 11th Ave.
Portland, Oregon 97232
http://pacific.fws.gov/

References

Courtenay, W. R., Jr., *et al.* 1985. "Comparative Status of Fishes Along the Course of the Pluvial White River, Nevada." *Southwestern Naturalist* 30:503-524.

Deacon, J., C. Hubbs, and B. Zahuranec. 1964. "Some Effects of Introduced Fishes on the Native Fish Fauna of Southern Nevada." *Copeia* 2:384-388.

U.S. Fish and Wildlife Service. 1985. "Recovery Plan for the Pahranagat Roundtail Chub, *Gila robusta jordani.*" U.S. Fish and Wildlife Service. Portland.

U.S. Fish and Wildlife Service. 1998. "Recovery Plan for the Aquatic and Riparian Species of Pahranagat Valley." U.S. Fish and Wildlife Service, Portland. 92 pp.

Virgin River Chub

Gila robusta seminuda

Status	Endangered
Listed	August 24, 1989
Family	Cyprinidae (Minnow)
Description	Medium-sized, silvery minnow with a narrow tail and deeply cleft caudal fin.
Habitat	Deep, swift currents over sand or gravel bottoms.
Food	Algae, insects, crustaceans, organic detritus.
Reproduction	Little known.
Threats	Impoundments, water diversion, predation by introduced species.
Range	Arizona, Nevada, Utah

Description

The Virgin River chub (*Gila robusta seminuda*) is a silvery fish in the minnow family that usually grows to about 8 in (20 cm) but has been known to attain a length of 18 in (45 cm). It has an elongated body with a narrow tail and deeply cleft caudal fin. It is distinguished from other subspecies of *G. robusta* by the number of rays in the dorsal, anal, and pelvic fins (9-10) and the number of gill rakers (24-31). It has small, embedded scales on its back, breast, and belly that are difficult to see, which accounts for the subspecific name *seminuda.*

Behavior

The Virgin River chub is omnivorous, feeding on algae, aquatic and terrestrial insects, crustaceans, and organic detritus. Little is known about its spawning behavior.

Habitat

This chub prefers deep, swift-flowing water, where there are boulders or other cover. It is tolerant of high salinity and turbidity and occurs over sand and gravel bottoms in water less than 86°F (30°C).

Distribution

It is believed that the Virgin River chub once inhabited about 134 mi (215 km) of the Virgin River, from its confluence with the Colorado River upstream to La Verkin Creek, near Hurricane, Utah. In the late nineteenth century it was considered common. Today, this subspecies is restricted to a 50-mi (80-km) portion of the Virgin River, between Mesquite, Nevada, and La Verkin Creek, near Hurricane, Utah. The land bordering this stretch of the river is both public and privately owned. In Arizona, the federal Bureau of Land Management (BLM) administers about 80-90% of the river frontage; privately owned land is concentrated in the vicinity of Littlefield. In Utah, about 13 mi (21 km) are managed by BLM; the state owns four small parcels and the rest is privately owned. In Nevada, land north of the town of Mesquite is in private hands.

Threats

The original range of the Virgin River chub was reduced almost 60% by nineteenth-century water diversions and the construction of Hoover Dam and Lake Mead. The chub is currently threatened by further water removal and impoundments, reduced reproduction, and competition from introduced fish species.

Although the Virgin River chub has survived a major reduction of its habitat caused by dams and water diversions, additional impoundments or diversions may drive the subspecies toward extinction. Federal listing as an Endangered species will require the Washington County Conservancy District (which has identified four potential reservoir sites) and the federal Soil Conservation Service (an agency of the Department of Agriculture which is planning flood control and irrigation projects) to make provisions for the conservation of the chub and its habitat.

The population of many river species often fluctuates because of changing environmental conditions, many of which are poorly known. However, it is clear that the species' survival is heavily dependent on the frequency of successful reproductive years. Recent studies have indicated that between 1984 and 1988, the Virgin River chub had only one good reproductive year.

Several other recent events have affected Virgin River chub populations. In 1988, an attempt was made to eradicate the exotic red shiner *(Notropis lutrensis)* from the Virgin River from the Washington Fields diversion downstream to the Virgin River Gorge. This introduced species is a major threat to native species. In 1985, it became established in the St. George area and within a year became the dominant fish species. After first salvaging 1,200 Virgin River chub, all remaining fish in that 21-mi (33-km) stretch of the river were eradicated and a barrier dam was installed at the head of the Virgin River Gorge to prevent return of the shiner.

Another 1988 event had a major impact on Virgin River fish populations. A dike at the Quail Creek Reservoir failed, releasing 25,000 acre-feet (30 billion l) of water into the river. This scouring flood is believed to have had a devastating effect on the entire fish population of the Virgin River.

Conservation and Recovery

In 1995, a Recovery Plan was released for the Virgin River chub in the Virgin River. Necessary actions identified in the recovery plan include habitat acquisition and protection, regulation of flows from the Quail Creek Reservoir System, and monitoring and research studies of the rare fish. Critical habitat of the Virgin River chub in the Virgin River was designated in 2000, an action that will focus recovery efforts for the rare fish. The recently discovered population of the Virgin River chub in the Muddy River is covered within the context of all rare aquatic species in the Recovery Plan for the Muddy River ecosystem, released in 1996. As part of the recovery process, a captive population of Virgin River chub is held at the Dexter National Fish Hatchery as insurance against extinction and as a source of fish for restocking efforts.

Contacts

U. S. Fish and Wildlife Service
Regional Office, Division of Endangered Species
Eastside Federal Complex
911 N. E. 11th Ave.
Portland, Oregon 97232-4181
Telephone: (503) 231-6121
http://pacific.fws.gov/

U. S. Fish and Wildlife Service
Regional Office, Division of Endangered Species
P.O. Box 1306
Albuquerque, New Mexico 87103-1306
Telephone: (505) 248-6911
Fax: (505) 248-6915
http://southwest.fws.gov/

U. S. Fish and Wildlife Service
145 East 1300 South, Suite 404
Salt Lake City, Utah 84115-6110
Telephone: (801) 524-5009
Fax: (801) 524-5021

References

Cross, J. N. 1975. "Ecological Distribution of the Fishes of the Virgin River (Utah, Arizona, Nevada)." Master's thesis. University of Nevada, Las Vegas.

Heckman, R. A., J. E. Deacon, and P. D. Gregor. 1966. "Parasites of the Woundfin Minnow, *Plagopterus argentissimus,* and Other Endemic Fishes from the Virgin River, Utah." *Great Basin Naturalist* 46(4): 663-676.

Hickman, T. J. 1988. "Study of Fishes in the Virgin River (Utah)." Annual Report for 1987. Western Ecosystems, St. George, Utah.

Rinne, John N., and W. L. Minckley. 1991. *Native Fishes and Arid Lands: Dwindling Resource of the Desert Southwest.* USDA Forest Service, Fort Collins, Colorado.

U. S. Fish and Wildlife Service. 1995. "Virgin River Fishes Recovery Plan." U. S. Fish and Wildlife Service, Denver, Colorado.

U. S. Fish and Wildlife Service. 1996. "Recovery Plan for the Rare Aquatic Species of the Muddy River Ecosystem." U. S. Fish and Wildlife Service, Portland, Oregon.

Rio Grande Silvery Minnow

Hybognathus amarus

Status	Endangered
Listed	July 20, 1994
Family	Cyprinidae (Minnow)
Description	Stout silvery minnow with moderately small eyes and a small, slightly oblique mouth.
Habitat	Low velocity currents in slack backwater areas at least 18 in (45.7 cm) deep with shifting sandy substrates.
Food	Algae.
Reproduction	Spawns during high spring flow, normally in June.
Threats	Degradation of habitat due to river diversion; water degradation caused by municipal,industrial, and agricultural discharges; competition from exotic fish.
Range	New Mexico, Texas

Description

The Rio Grande silvery minnow is a stout fish with moderately small eyes and a small, slightly oblique mouth. Adults may reach 3.5 in (8.9 cm) in total length. The dorsal fin of the silvery minnow is distinctly pointed with the front located slightly closer to the tip of the snout than to the base of the tail. Life color is silver with emerald reflections. The belly is silver-white, fins are plain, and barbels absent.

Behavior

The silvery minnow spawns during the high spring flow, normally in June, as a result of snow runoff and reservoir release. The eggs are spawned in currents, then drift along the flow edge for about 24 hours before hatching. The drift time, however, is temperature dependent. After hatching, the fry seek slack water areas for safety; not being strong swimmers at birth, they attempt to find areas with no or low moving currents. Although there are no predators for the eggs, they are vulnerable to being sucked in by irrigation diversion.

The silvery minnow feeds on algae growing in shallow water in bright sunlight. Until recently, it was thought that the minnow did not reach sexual maturity until age two, but recent observations suggest that under ideal feeding conditions, the silvery minnow grows at a tremendous rate and can reach sexual maturity in one year.

Habitat

The silvery minnow prefers low velocity currents in slack backwater areas at least 18 in (45.7 cm) deep with shifting sandy substrates. However, construction of the Cochiti Dam altered the Rio Grande substrate to gravel, and water diversion sometimes leaves this reach of the river dry. The waters in the middle of the river are murky, partly as a result of natural siltation and partly from irrigation return flow.

In the past, during periods of extremely low flow, the species survived in areas where irrigation water returned to the river, in seepage and leakage pools located downstream of irrigation diversion dams, and, prior to the construction of Co-

Rio Grande Silvery Minnow, photograph by Gerald L. Burton. Reproduced by permission.

chiti Dam, in the canyon of the Rio Grande up-stream of Cochiti.

Distribution

This species was historically one of the most abundant and widespread fishes in the Rio Grande basin, occurring from Espanola, New Mexico, to the Gulf of Mexico. It was also found in the Pecos River, a major tributary of the Rio Grande, from Santa Rosa, New Mexico, downstream to its confluence with the Rio Grande in south Texas.

Collection data indicate that the species occupies about 5% of its historical range. It has been completely extirpated from the Pecos River and from the Rio Grande downstream of Elephant Butte Reservoir. Currently, it is found only in a 170-mi (274-km) reach of the middle Rio Grande, New Mexico, from Cochiti Dam, Sandoval County, to the headwaters of Elephant Butte Reservoir.

Thought to be extinct in 1969, the silvery minnow's population varies greatly from one year to the next, depending on food supply and water depths. In 50 fish collections made between Bernalillo and Elephant Butte Reservoir between 1987 and 1988, the silvery minnow was the second most abundant species, but by 1989-92 it had become the least abundant native fish species. If there is continual water flow year-round, the silvery minnow will become the dominant species within its reach, as was the case in 1994, but the U. S. Fish and Wildlife Service believes that without protection the species will likely become extinct.

Threats

Throughout much of its historic range, the decline of the silvery minnow may be attributed to modifications of stream desiccation by impoundments, water diversion for agriculture, stream channelization, and introduced exotic species. Its decline in the Pecos River, where it was replaced by a congener, the plains minnow (*H. placitus*), occurred in 1968 when the plains minnow was introduced as bait. In less than a decade the silvery minnow was extirpated.

Decline in the Rio Grande probably began in 1916 when the gates at the Elephant Butte Reservoir were closed. Elephant Butte was one of five major dams constructed in the silvery minnow's Rio Grande habitat; it and the other dams were used to divert the flow of water for agriculture, and often the diversion caused reaches to dry up and destroy all fish life. Concurrent with building the dams was stocking the reservoirs with non-native fish, some of which made their way into streams and outcompeted native species.

Conservation and Recovery

The success of the silvery minnow is entirely dependent on water flow, which in the middle Rio Grande is controlled by the Rio Grande Compact Commission, established in 1929 to ensure the equitable apportionment of flows. The commission meets annually to review compliance during the preceding year and to consider water control implications. Federal agencies involved in determining water flows are the International Boundary and Water Commission, the Bureau of Reclamation, and the Corps of Engineers. All federal agencies are responsible for complying with the Endangered Species Act and as such must consider the survival of vulnerable fish in the Rio Grande. However, because water diversion is such a controversial issue, there has been much opposition from the agricultural sector. Under a 1906 charter with Mexico, the United States is required to deliver 600,000 acre feet annually to Mexico from the Rio Grande, which dictates certain water diversion decisions.

The growth of agriculture and cities along the Rio Grande may have adversely affected the quality of the river's water. During low flow periods, a large percentage of the river's flow consists of municipal and agricultural discharge.

Although New Mexico state law lists the silvery minnow as an endangered species, state law does not include provisions for acquisition of instream water rights for protection of fish and wildlife and their habitats. This has been a major factor affecting the survival of species dependent upon the presence of instream flow. Under the existing water rights administration, two native Rio Grande fish have become extinct and two others have been extirpated.

Contact

U. S. Fish and Wildlife Service
Regional Office, Division of Endangered Species
P.O. Box 1306
Albuquerque, New Mexico 87103-1306
Telephone: (505) 248-6911
Fax: (505) 248-6915
http://southwest.fws.gov/

Reference

U. S. Fish and Wildlife Service. 20 July 1994. "Final Rule to List the Rio Grande Silvery Minnow as an Endangered Species." *Federal Register* 59 (138).

White River Spinedace

Lepidomeda albivallis

Status	Endangered
Listed	September 12, 1985
Family	Cyprinidae
Description	A colorful, medium-sized minnow.
Habitat	Cool, spring-fed creeks and streams.
Food	Small invertebrates and organic detritus.
Reproduction	Lays eggs in gravel.
Threats	Habitat loss and predation and competition with introduced fishes.
Range	Nevada

Description

The White River spinedace is a medium-sized minnow, which can attain a total length of 6 in (15 cm). The males are brightly colored, with bright brassy-green to olive above, silvery with sooty blotches on the sides, and silvery white below. The dorsal and caudal fins are pale olive-brown to pinkish-brown, with deep-olive rays and membranes flushed with rose. The pectorals are yellowish with orange-red axils. The anal and pelvic fins are bright orange-red. The lower edge of the caudal peduncle (or fin) is speckled with orange-red. There is some coppery red to red on the sides of the face, and the lateral line is strongly gilt-colored. The coloration of females is similar, but less intense.

Behavior

The breeding characteristics of the White River spinedace have not been studied, but it probably spawns over fine gravel, from early spring to summer. It probably becomes sexually mature at about one year of age. It is an omnivorous feeder, eating a variety of bottom-dwelling and drifting animals and plant matter.

Habitat

The White River spinedace occurs in cool freshwater springs and small outflows.

Distribution

The White River spinedace historically occurred in the White River Valley, in White Pine and Nye Counties, Nevada. It was also reported from the lower Colorado River, California, and from Railroad Valley, Nevada. However, these were non-indigenous occurences, resulting from the use of the rare fish as bait. These extralimital populations no longer exist.

Threats

The White River spinedace has been extirpated from most of its original natural range. Its only surviving population is at Flag Springs in Nye County, northeastern Nevada. A study in 1993 found only about 50 individuals in this critically endangered population. The White River spinedace is highly vulnerable to the effects of habitat alterations and the introduction of exotic, predatory and competing fishes. Prominent among the latter threats are brown trout (*Salmo trutta*), brook trout (*Salvelinus fontinalis*), rainbow trout (*Oncorhynchus mykiss*), cutthroat trout (*O. clarki*), largemouth bass (*Micropterus salmoides*), guppy (*Poecilia reticulata*), mosquitofish (*Gambusia affinis*), and goldfish (*Carassius auratus*).

Conservation and Recovery

The only surviving critical habitat of the White River spinedace is located in the Kirch Wildlife

White River Spinedance, photograph by John Rinne, USFS. Reproduced by permission.

Area, owned and controlled by the Nevada Department of Wildlife. It is crucial that this habitat be fully protected from any potentially damaging influences. Predatory largemouth bass have been released into downstream reservoirs and have spread upstream to threaten the endangered spinedace. Fish barriers have been erected and initial habitat improvements completed to improve survivorship of the rare fish. A captive-breeding program will be necessary to produce stock for release into other suitable habitats, once the non-native fishes have been eradicated from the critical habitat.

Contacts

U. S. Fish and Wildlife Service
Regional Office, Division of Endangered Species
Eastside Federal Complex
911 N. E. 11th Ave.
Portland, Oregon 97232-4181
(503) 231-6121
http://pacific.fws.gov/

U. S. Fish and Wildlife Service
Snake River Basin Office
1387 South Vinnell Way, Suite 368
Boise, Idaho 83709-1657
Telephone: (208) 378-5243
Fax: (208) 378-5262

References

Biological Resources Research Center. 1997. "*Lepidomeda albivallis:* White River spinedace." Biological Resources Research Center at University of Nevada, Reno. (http://www.brrc.unr.edu/data/fish/lepialbi.html).

Conservation Management Institute. 14 March 1996. White River Spinedace. *Virginia Tech, Endangered Species Information System.* (http://fwie.fw.vt.edu/WWW/esis/lists/e251019.htm). Date Accessed: July 6, 2000.

Big Spring Spinedace

Lepidomeda mollispinis pratensis

Status	Threatened
Listed	March 28, 1985
Family	Cyprinidae (Minnows)
Description	Small, silver minnow with two spiny rays in the dorsal fin.
Habitat	Clear, clean, shallow stream.
Food	Probably omnivorous.
Reproduction	Undescribed.
Threats	Limited distribution.
Range	Nevada

Spinedace, photograph. U.S. Fish and Wildlife Service. Reproduced by permission.

Description

The Big Spring spinedace, *Lepidomeda mollispinis pratensis*, is a small, minnow-like fish, characterized by two weak, spiny rays in the dorsal fin. Bright silver in color, it ranges from 2-3 in (5-7.6 cm) in total length. This subspecies is one of seven taxa belonging to the Plagopterini, a unique tribe of fishes that is restricted to the lower Colorado River system.

Behavior

This species has been little studied and its behavior and breeding biology are largely undescribed. It is probably omnivorous.

Habitat

The Big Spring spinedace inhabits a clear, clean, shallow stream fed by perennial springs. When first discovered, it appeared restricted to a spring-fed marsh that has since dried up.

Distribution

The ancestors of this species became isolated in remote, spring-fed meadows of southern Nevada at the end of pluvial times, when the climate became warmer and drier. The region where the spinedace is found—Meadow Valley Wash—once contained Lake Carpenter and Carpenter River, which flowed into the Colorado River more than 10,000 years ago. The Big Spring spinedace was first discovered in a large marsh adjacent to Big Spring near the town of Panaca (Lincoln County), Nevada. Subsequently, diversion of water from the spring for irrigation caused the marsh to dry up, and the Big Spring dace was thought to be extinct. In 1978 personnel from the Nevada Department of Wildlife discovered a small population of the Big Spring spinedace in Condor Canyon, just northeast of Panaca. Condor Canyon comprises about 4 mi (6.5 km) of Meadow Valley Wash with perennially flowing water. In 1980 state biologists transplanted spinedace above a barrier falls to establish the fish in all portions of the available habitat, although by the time the 1994 Recovery Plan for the species was published, distribution was described as being limited to a 5 mi (8 km) section of Meadow Valley Wash, which flows through public and private lands. The fish is fairly abundant within this limited habitat of Condor Canyon, but actual population size has not been determined. The fish has been extirpated from the Panaca (Big) Spring outflow stream, due to habitat modification and non- native species introduction.

Threats

The Big Spring spinedace is threatened by its very limited distribution, which prevents any expansion of the population, by the danger of catastrophic destruction of this limited habitat, and by the introduction of non-native species. In some places the stream in Condor Canyon is only a few feet wide and could be disrupted by water diversion, use by livestock, or prolonged drought.

Conservation and Recovery

The Bureau of Land Management administers about 75% of the canyon and includes most of the land in a grazing allotment. The allotment has been inactive for some time, however, and is not expected to be renewed. The Nature Conservancy owns about 40 acres (16 hectares) of land at the upper end of Condor Canyon and has agreed to cooperate with the U.S. Fish and Wildlife Service (FWS) to recover this species.

On the basis of ongoing research, state and federal biologists will determine a suitable transplant location within the fish's historic range and attempt to establish a new population. In the meantime, every effort will be made to prevent accidental or purposeful introduction of the mosquitofish—a non-native pest found in many regional waters—into Condor Canyon. Based on previous experience, the mosquitofish could eliminate the spinedace population in short order. The 1994 U.S. Fish and Wildlife Service Recovery Plan for the Big Spring spinedace has as its goal delisting of the species by 2006. The fish may be proposed for delisting when a self-sustaining population exists in Meadow Valley Wash in Condor Canyon for at least five consecutive years and its habitat is secured from all known threats. Recovery efforts should include restoration of habitat between Condor Canyon and Panaca Spring to allow the Big Spring spinedace population to expand into its historic habitat. Additionally, one or more self-sustaining refugia populations should be established to prevent the extinction of the species should unforseen catastrophic events severely impact or eliminate the Condor Canyon population. The Recovery Plan recommends that the Condor Canyon habitat be secured by obtaining conservation agreements with private landowners and instream water flow rights. Populations should also be monitored and the habitat enhanced; and the public should be educated through an outreach program.

Contact

U.S. Fish and Wildlife Service
Regional Office, Division of Endangered Species
Eastside Federal Complex
911 N.E. 11th Ave.
Portland, Oregon 97232-4181
(503) 231-6121
http://pacific.fws.gov/

References

Deacon, J. E., C. Hubbs, and B. Zahuranec. 1964. "Some Effects of Introduced Fishes on the Native Fish of Southern Nevada." *Copeia* 1964: 384-388.

Hardy, T. 1980. "Interbasin Report to the Desert Fishes Council." *Proceedings of the Desert Fishes Council* 10: 5-21; 11: 68-70.

Miller, R. R., and C. Hubbs. 1960. "The Spiny-Rayed Cyprinid Fishes of the Colorado River System." *Miscellaneous Publications of the Museum of Zoology, University of Michigan* 115: 1-39.

U.S. Fish and Wildlife Service. 1994. "Big Spring Spinedace Recovery Plan." U.S. Fish and Wildlife Service, Portland.

Little Colorado Spinedace

Lepidomeda vittata

Status	Threatened
Listed	March 11, 1967
Family	Cyprinidae (Minnows)
Description	Small, olive and silver minnow with a small head and large eyes.
Habitat	Streams with gravel or mudsilt bottoms.
Food	Insects, detritus.
Reproduction	Spawns in early summer.
Threats	Dams, groundwater pumping, competition with introduced fish.
Range	Arizona

Description

The Little Colorado spinedace, *Lepidomeda vittata*, is a small minnow, about 4 in (10 cm) long. It is olive above and silvery below, with a lateral band. The back is olive or bluish to lead gray. It has a small head and relatively large eyes.

Behavior

This spinedace spawns primarily in early summer, continuing at a reduced rate until early fall. In courtship behavior, males pursue females, nibbling them about the vent. Like other minnows, the Little Colorado spinedace feeds on small insects and detritus.

Habitat

This spinedace inhabits pools in narrow to moderately sized streams where the water flows over a fine gravel or silt-mud bottom. During droughts, it retreats to springs and intermittent stream bed pools. During flooding, it spreads throughout the stream once again.

Distribution

The Little Colorado spinedace occurred throughout the upper portions of the Little Colorado River drainage in Arizona. It was first described in 1874, from specimens taken from the river between the mouth of the Zuni River and Sierra Blanca in Arizona.

It is now found only in portions of the Little Colorado River and East Clear, Chevelon, Silver, and Nutrioso creeks in Coconino, Navajo, and Apache Counties, Arizona.

Threats

The decline of the Little Colorado spinedace is the result of habitat alteration associated with human settlement. Dam building, water pumping, stream channeling, and road building have radically altered the water system within the spinedace's habitat. Introduced fish species also prey upon and compete with the spinedace.

Proposed water projects would further reduce viable habitat for this fish. For example, Wilkin's Dam at the confluence of Clear and East Clear Creeks is proposed as part of the Bureau of Reclamation's larger Mogollon Mesa project. Wilkin's Dam would inundate about 8 mi (13 km) of stream, significantly decreasing downstream flows. The project is currently inactive and is not expected to be reactivated in the near future. The best protection for spinedace

James E. Johnson

at the moment is federal ownership of much of its habitat. The East Clear Creek population is located within the Coconino and Apache-Sitgreaves National Forests, as are portions of the Little Colorado River, Silver and Nutrioso creeks populations.

Conservation and Recovery

The Fish and Wildlife Service has declared portions of East Clear Creek, Chevelon Creek, and Nutrioso Creek as habitat critical to the continued existence of the Little Colorado spinedace.

Contact

U.S. Fish and Wildlife Service
Division of Endangered Species
P.O. Box 1306
Albuquerque, New Mexico 87103
http://southwest.fws.gov/

References

Miller, R. R. 1983. "Distribution, Variation and Ecology of *Lepidomeda vittata*, a Rare Cyprinid Fish Endemic to Eastern Arizona." *Copeia* 1963:1-5.

Minckley, W. L. 1973. *Fishes of Arizona*. Sims Printing, Phoenix.

Spikedace

Meda fulgida

Status	Endangered
Listed	July 1, 1986
Family	Cyprinidae (Minnows)
Description	Slender, silvery fish with sharp spines in dorsal and pelvic fins.
Habitat	Stream pools and riffles in flowing water.
Food	Insect larvae, plant matter.
Reproduction	Spawns in the spring.
Threats	Dam construction, channelization, water diversion, groundwater pumping.
Range	Arizona, New Mexico

Description

The only species in the genus *Meda*, the spikedace, *Meda fulgida*, is a small, slender fish, less than 3 in (7.5 cm) in length. It is characterized by silvery sides and sharp spines in the dorsal and pelvic fins. Breeding males develop a brassy golden color, especially around the head and ventral fins.

Behavior

The highly mobile spikedace has a high reproductive potential but periodically experiences large fluctuations in population size. It spawns in spring and feeds on a range of insects, larvae, and plant matter.

Habitat

The spikedace is found in stream pools and shallow riffles with gravel or rubble substrates and moderate to swift currents. It is tolerant of periodic flooding, which gives it a competitive edge over other native fishes in the watershed. An omnivorous fish, it feeds on tiny animal and plant organisms including detritus, bacteria, filamentous algae, crustaceans, worms, fish, zooplankton, and aquatic insects. Vegetative communities found adjacent to occupied streams include cottonwood dominated riparian communities, ponderosa pine forests, desert shrublands, desert grasslands, and pinyon/ juniper rangelands

Distribution

The spikedace is endemic to the Gila River basin upstream (east) of the city of Phoenix, Arizona. It was once common in the Verde, Aqua Fria, Salt, San Pedro, San Francisco, and Gila Rivers. The historic range may have included the upper San Pedro River in Sonora, Mexico, where habitat no longer exists. The spikedace has been extirpated from most of its historic range in the Gila River basin. It is presently found only in the upper Gila River in New Mexico, and in Aravaipa and Eagle Creeks and the upper Verde River in Arizona. All existing populations are under threat. Land ownership in the remaining sections of occupied river reaches is mixed and includes: private individuals; conservation organizations including The Nature Conservancy (TNC); Arizona and New Mexico State lands; National Park Service (Gila Cliff Dwellings National Monument); U.S. Forest Service (Gila National Forest, Prescott National Forest); and the Bureau of Land Management (BLM) (Aravaipa Canyon Wilderness).

Threats

The distribution and numbers of the spikedace have been greatly reduced by dam construction, ar-

Meda Spikedace, photograph by John Rinne, USFS. Reproduced by permission.

tificial channeling of stream beds, water diversion, and groundwater pumping. The San Pedro River in Mexico has been almost totally de-watered by diversion of water to support irrigation agriculture. The species is also threatened by the spread of non-native predators and competitors, such as rainbow trout, smallmouth bass, channel catfish, and red shiner. An additional possible threat to fish is the construction of a major new dam on the mainstream Gila River by the federal Bureau of Reclamation, to control flooding and supply water for irrigation and municipal development. Federal listing of the spikedace aroused opposition from the Southwest New Mexico Industrial Development Corporation, the Hooker Dam Association, the Arizona Cattle Growers Association, the Arizona Mining Association, the Town of Silver City, New Mexico, and the Soil Conservation Service of New Mexico, among others. Many opponents expressed the opinion that the listing of the spikedace was premature or was being used as a pretext to stop dam construction, flood control efforts, and municipal development.

The Fish and Wildlife Service (FWS), however, replied that the listing was based on sound biological evidence.

Conservation and Recovery

The BLM owns portions of spikedace habitat on Aravaipa Creek and the Gila River and will assess the effects of its land use strategies—in particular, livestock grazing—on the species. Most spikedace habitat on the Verde River falls within the Prescott National Forest, administered by the Forest Service. The spikedace is offered some protection in New Mexico by its occurrence within the Gila National Forest, Gila Wilderness, and Gila River Research Natural Area. Although the population status has been listed as stable, the FWS has given this species a recovery priority rating of "4C" which means the degree of threat to this species is high and the recovery potential is low. In 1990, a barrier to upstream movement of non-native fishes was announced for Aravaipa Creek in Graham and Pinal

Counties, Arizona. The barriers are a multi-agency effort with primary funding and expertise being furnished by the Bureau of Reclamation under their new Enhancement Initiative. The BLM in cooperation with the FWS and Arizona Game and Fish Department, initiated a program to remove exotic fish species (e.g., green sunfish—*Lepomis cyanellus*, bullheads—*Ictalurus* spp.) from stock tanks on BLM lands within the Aravaipa Creek watershed in Arizona. These species need to be removed to prevent their spread into Aravaipa Creek. The 1991 Spikedace Recovery Plan called for the protection of existing populations, the restoration of populations in portions of historic habitat, and the eventual delisting of the species, perhaps by 2011. The plan sets forth mechanisms to obtain information necessary to determine quantitative criteria for describing a spikedace population capable of sustaining itself in perpetuity. Delisting is dependent on the establishment of such populations. Undoubtedly, demise of spikedace has been a result of combined effects of habitat change and introduced fishes. Because relative importance of the two factors has yet to be established, both must be considered in management toward recovery of this threatened species.

Contact

U. S. Fish and Wildlife Service
Regional Office, Division of Endangered Species
P.O. Box 1306
Albuquerque, New Mexico 87103-1306
Telephone: (505) 248-6911
Fax: (505) 248-6915
http://southwest.fws.gov/

References

Barrett, P. J., *et al.* 1985. "Draft Upper Verde River Aquatic Study." U.S. Fish and Wildlife Service, Arizona Game and Fish Department, and U.S. Bureau of Reclamation.

LaBounty, J. F., and W. L. Minckley. 1972. "Native Fishes of the Upper Gila River System, Mew Mexico." In *Symposium on Rare and Endangered Wildlife of the Southwestern United States.* New Mexico Department of Game and Fish, Santa Fe.

Propst, D. 1986. "Distribution Status and Biology of the Spikedace in the Gila River Basin, New Mexico." New Mexico Department of Game and Fish, Santa Fe.

U.S. Fish and Wildlife Service. 1986. "Determination of Threatened Status for Spikedace." *Federal Register* 51(126): 23769-23780.

U.S. Fish and Wildlife Service. 1991. "Spikedace Recovery Plan." U.S. Fish and Wildlife Service, Albuquerque.

Moapa Dace

Moapa coriacea

Status	Endangered
Listed	March 11, 1967
Family	Cyprinidae (Minnows)
Description	Gold or bronze minnow with a dark mid-dorsal stripe.
Habitat	Thermal springs and pools.
Food	Insects and plants.
Reproduction	Spawns year-round.
Threats	Habitat reduction, introduced competitors.
Range	Nevada

Description

The Moapa dace, *Moapa coriacea*, measures 3 in (7.6 cm) in length. The back and sides are an iridescent gold or bronze, marked by a dark mid-dorsal stripe. There is a distinctive black spot at the base of the caudal fin. It is similar in profile to both the roundtail chub (*Gila robusta*) and the Moapa speckled dace (*Rhinichthys osculus moapae*) but can be easily distinguished by its markings. The specific name, *coriacea*, refers to its decidedly leathery appearance.

Behavior

The Moapa dace feeds primarily on insects but also eats plant matter. Stomach contents have included beetles, moths, butterflies, true flies, leaf hoppers, true bugs, mayflies, dragonflies, worms, crustaceans, snails, algae, vascular plants, and detritus. It seems to feed primarily on drift items, but adults forage from the substrate as well. Larval dace feed on plankton. Moapa dace actively feed 24 hours a day, but peak feeding is at dawn and dusk.

Like other desert fishes that inhabit thermal springs, it spawns year-round with a peak in late spring or early summer. Moapa dace successfully breed in water temperatures of 86-89.6°F (30-32°C), and it must migrate upstream from the Muddy River into thermal tributaries to spawn successfully.

Habitat

The Moapa dace inhabits clear, warm, slow-flowing waters, fed by thermal springs. Spring pools and outflow streams may have sand, gravel, pebble, or mud bottoms. Algae in these waters is abundant, and overhanging vegetation includes mesquite, tamarist, and the only palm tree native to Nevada (*Washingtonia filifera*).

Distribution

This species has probably always been restricted to the sources and headwaters of Nevada's Muddy (Moapa) River system. Before 1933, it was considered common in 25 springs and up to 10 mi (16 km) of outflow streams and river channel.

The Moapa dace occupies approximately 6 mi (9.5 km) of stream habitat in five thermal headwater spring systems and the main stem of the upper Muddy (Moapa) River in Clark County, Nevada. A range-wide survey documented 3,841 Moapa dace in August 1994.

Threats

During the 1950s and 1960s, most of the springs on the Desert Oasis Warm Springs Resort and the former 7-12 Resort were cemented, graveled, channeled, chlorinated, and otherwise cleared of vege-

Moapa Dace, photograph by John Rinne, USFS. Reproduced by permission.

tation, actions severely restricting Moapa dace habitat. In addition, studies indicate a strong correlation between the decline of the Moapa dace and the introduction of the predatory shortfin molly sometime around 1963.

Conservation and Recovery

In 1972, an unsuccessful attempt was made to transplant 20 Moapa dace to Shoshone Ponds near Ely, Nevada, a Bureau of Land Management facility for conserving endangered fishes. In 1979 the U. S. Fish and Wildlife Service (FWS) purchased the 7-12 Resort and established the Moapa National Wildlife Refuge to protect the dace. In 1988 the National Fisheries Research Center in Seattle completed a three-year study on the life history and habitat requirements for the Moapa dace so that suitable habitat can be provided at the refuge.

A serious fire (reportedly started by a cigarette or fireworks) in the Moapa Dace National Wildlife Refuge in late June 1994 may have wiped out a num-

ber of Moapa—prior to the fire, the refuge supported more than 500 Moapa dace. On July 5, 1994, however, only one could be found on the refuge. But the following month, a range-wide survey found nearly 3,850 adults. Intensive management will be needed to prevent the loss of this monotypic genus. Personnel from the Desert National Wildlife Refuge complex, the FWS Reno Office, and the Reno Field Office of the National Biological Survey (NBS) removed fire debris from the stream channels in an attempt to accelerate rehabilitation of Moapa dace habitat. NBS biologists will monitor habitat conditions and the populations of affected aquatic species.

In 1996, the FWS released the Recovery Plan for the Rare Aquatic Species of the Muddy River Ecosystem, which covers not only the Moapa dace but also seven aquatic species of concern (three fish, two snails and two insects.) The plan notes that the Moapa dace will be considered for downlisting (from Endangered to Threatened) when three major critieria are met. Existing stream flows and historical habitat in three of the five occupied spring systems and the upper Muddy River must be protected through conservation agreements, easements, or fee title acquisitions. In addition, 4,500 adult Moapa dace must be present among the five spring systems and upper Muddy River; and the Moapa dace population must be comprised of three or more age classes, with reproduction and recruitment documented from three spring systems.

After downlisting is achieved, the species will be considered for delisting (removal from the Endangered Species list altogether). For this to occur, 6,000 adult Moapa dace must be present among the spring systems and upper Muddy River for five consecutive years; 75% of the historical habitat of the five spring systems and upper Muddy River must provide Moapa dace spawning, nursery, cover and/or foraging habitat; and non-native fishes and parasites must no longer adversely affect the long-term survival of the Moapa dace. These recovery criteria are preliminary and may be revised on the basis of new information.

Reclassification of Moapa dace from Endangered to Threatened could be initiated in 2000, if recovery criteria for threatened status are met. Delisting could be initiated in 2009 if reclassification to Threatened status occurs as scheduled.

Contact

Regional Office of Endangered Species
U.S. Fish and Wildlife Service
Eastside Federal Complex
911 N.E. 11th Ave.
Portland, Oregon 97232
(503) 231-6118
http://pacific.fws.gov/

References

Cross, J. N. 1976. "Status of the Native Fish Fauna of the Moapa River, Clark County, Nevada." *Transactions of the American Fisheries Society* 105(4):503-508.

La Rivers, I. 1962. *Fishes and Fisheries of Nevada.* Nevada State Fish and Game Commission, Reno.

U.S. Fish and Wildlife Service. 1983. "The Moapa Dace Recovery Plan." U.S. Fish and Wildlife Service, Portland, Oregon.

U.S. Fish and Wildlife Service. 1996. "Recovery Plan for the Rare Aquatic Species of the Muddy River Ecosystem." U.S. Fish and Wildlife Service, Portland, Oregon.

Palezone Shiner

Notropis albizonatus

Status	Endangered
Listed	April 27, 1993
Family	Cyprinidae (Minnow)
Description	A small, slender, translucent, straw-colored minnow with a dark midlateral stripe.
Habitat	Large creeks and small rivers in the Tennessee and Cumberland River systems.
Food	Not known; probably feeds on small aquatic invertebrates.
Reproduction	Not known; probably lays eggs in a benthic nest.
Threats	Siltation and other pollution from poor land use practices, coal mining and waste discharge.
Range	Alabama, Kentucky

Description

The Palezone shiner, *Notropis albizonatus*, is a small slender minnow with a translucent and straw-colored with a dark midlateral stripe.

Behavior

The Palezone shiner probably feeds on small aquatic invertebrates. It matures at a body length of about 1.5 in (38 mm). Breeding males develop tubercles by mid-May, and peak spawning condition occurs in June and may last into early July. Females have an extended abdomen which contain large, cream to yellow-colored ova in mid-May through late June. These observations suggest a spawning period from late-May through June and perhaps early July. Other aspects of spawning behavior are unknown.

Habitat

This *Notropis* species inhabits large creeks and small rivers in the Tennessee and Cumberland River systems and inhabits flowing pools and runs with sand, gravel, and bedrock substrates. This Palezone shiner's distribution overlaps the Oak-Hickory Ecosystem and Nashville Basin. The elevation is about 660 ft (200 m) and most of the outer part of the Basin is deeply dissected and consists of steep slopes between narrow rolling ridgetops and narrow valleys. The inner part of the Basin is predominantly undulating and rolling. The average annual precipitation is about 35-45 in (89-114 cm). The soils of this ecosystem are varied, have a thermic temperature regime, an udic moisture regime and a clay subsoil.

Distribution

This *Notropis* species has only been collected from four rivers, despite extensive collection efforts in the Tennessee and Cumberland River Systems. These rivers are the Paint Rock River, Jackson County, Alabama; the Little South Fork Cumberland River, Wayne and McCreary Counties, Kentucky; Marrowbone Creek, Cumberland County, Kentucky; and Cove Creek, Clinch River drainage, Campbell County, Tennessee.

Palezone Shiner, photograph by Ronald R. Cicerello. Reproduced by permission.

Threats

Generally the Palezone shiner is threatened by water quality degradation as a result of siltation and other pollution from poor land use practices, coal mining and waste discharge. The Tennessee and Cumberland Rivers are renowned as two of the most severely altered riverine systems due to many anthropogenic activities. Most of the main stem of both rivers and many tributaries are impounded. In addition, there has been a loss of the riverine habitat and impoundments usually alter downstream aquatic habitats. Siltation and toxic runoff have been the result of coal mining activities which unavoidably have adversely affected many reaches. Runoff from urban areas has also degraded water and substrate quality. The aquatic faunal diversity has declined due to this habitat destruction. Due to the limited distribution of this species a stochastic event such as an accidental toxic chemical spill could cause extirpation. As the populations are separated by impoundments natural recolonization of an extirpated population would be virtually impossible. Future activities which could impact this species are the issuance of permits for hydroelectric facility construction and operation, coal mining, reservoir construction, stream alterations, wastewater facility development, pesticide registration and road and bridge construction. The Tennessee Valley Authority has indicated that the Point Rock River population is in the timber-sourcing area for three proposed wood-chip mills. Any large-scale timber harvesting could lead to population-level effects. Three wood-processing companies have applied to the Nashville District, U.S. Army Corps of Engineers for permits under section 10 of the Rivers and Harbors Act and section 404 of the Clean Water Act and to the Tennessee Valley Authority for shoreline leases and section 26-A permits to construct and operate wood-chip mills located between Bridgeport, Alabama and New Hope, Tennessee.

Conservation and Recovery

A Recovery Plan for the Palezone shiner has been outlined. In order to ensure the continued survival of this species existing State and Federal legislation and regulation must be enforced. It will also be necessary to research the life history of the Palezone shiner, including spawning season and behavior, habitat requirements, age and growth, and food habits. Research should also be done concerning propagation and reintroduction techniques and habitat improvement techniques. In addition, efforts need to be made to reestablish other spawning populations, promote the safe use of pesticides by local farmers, regulate water quality, and monitor spawning areas. The date for the downlisting of the Palezone shiner is 2007, if all the recovery criteria have been met.

Contacts

U. S. Fish and Wildlife Service
Asheville Ecological Services Field Office
160 Zillicoa Street
Asheville, North Carolina 28806-1082
Telephone: (828) 258-3939
Fax: (828) 258-5330

U. S. Fish and Wildlife Service
Regional Office, Division of Endangered Species
1875 Century Blvd., Suite 200
Atlanta, Georgia 30345
http://southeast.fws.gov/

References

U.S. Fish and Wildlife Service. 27 April 1993. "Endangered and Threatened Wildlife and Plants; Determination of Endangered Status for the Duskytail Darter, Palezone Shiner and Pygmy Madtom." *Federal Register*

U. S. Fish and Wildlife Service. 1996. "Palezone Shiner (*Notropis* sp.)." Endangered and Threatened Species of the Southeastern United States (The Red Book) FWS Region 4. http://endangered.fws.gov/i/e/sae33.html

U.S. Fish and Wildlife Service. 1997. "Recovery Plan for Palezone Shiner (*Notropis albizonatus*)." Atlanta, GA.

Cahaba Shiner

Notropis cahabae

Status	Endangered
Listed	October 25, 1990
Family	Cyprinidae
Description	Small, delicate-bodied, silvery-colored fish.
Habitat	Large shoal areas of the main channel of the Cahaba River.
Food	Small crustaceans, insect larvae, algae.
Reproduction	Spawn from late May through June.
Threats	Pollution, siltation.
Range	Alabama

Description

Notropis cahabae, Cahaba shiner, is a small, delicate-bodied, silvery-colored fish about 2.5 in (6 cm) long with a peach colored narrow stripe over the dark lateral stripe. This species differs from the minic shiner, a closely related species, by a lateral stripe that does not expand before the caudal spot and by the absence of a predorsal dark blotch. Also, the Cahaba shiner's dorsal, caudal peduncle scales are uniformly dark and pigmented and its peduncle scales are broadly outlined and diffuse.

Behavior

This shiner probably requires a river with sufficient small crustaceans, insect larvae, and algae for food, similar to its close relative, the mimic shiner. The Cahaba shiner seems consistent with other fish in the mimic shiner group, spawning much later than do other North American cyprinids. They appear to spawn from late May through June and seem to have a more limited spawning period than do many fish which reach a rather small adult size.

Habitat

This species' habitat appears to be large shoal areas of the main channel of the Cahaba River. The Cahaba shiner is found in the quieter waters less than 1.6 ft (0.5 m) deep, just below swift riffle areas. The Cahaba shiner seems to prefer patches of sandy substrate at the edge of or scattered throughout gravel beds or downstream of larger rocks and boulders. The Cahaba shiner does not occupy deep water habitats or any other sites other than that of large, shallow shoals.

Distribution

The Cahaba shiner is the only North American large stream fish that is endemic to one main stem of one river. Its entire current range encompasses 60 mi (100 km) of the Cahaba River in Alabama, from 3 mi (5 km) northeast of Heiberger to 3.75 mi (6 km) above Booth Ford. In the recent past, the Cahaba shiner has been collected in about 76 mi (122 km) of the Cahaba River from 3 mi (5 km) northeast of Heiberger in Perry County to Highway 52 bridge near Helena in Shelby County. This range reduction of over 20% occurred between 1969 and 1977. Further reductions in total populations are evident with the stronghold for the species now limited to about 15 river mi (24 river km) between the Fall Line and Piper Bridge or 20% of the historic range. The Cahaba shiner once had a wider historical distribution which may have included the Coosa River.

Robert A. Stiles

In 1989 and 1990, in an effort to document population levels, fish were collected at known population sites. Within the stronghold of the species, an average of 3.2 Cahaba shiners were captured, as compared with an average of 38.5 during the period of 1981 to 1986. The ratio of Cahaba shiners to the closely related and more widespread mimic shiner in the earlier sampling was about one to one. In the 1990 survey, the ratio was about 16 mimic shiners to each Cahaba shiner. In addition to the change in ratio, the abundance of both species has decreased, with the Cahaba shiner possibly the less adaptable of the two species.

Threats

Located within the Mobile Basin, the 212 mile Cahaba river supports 132 species and is one of the most diverse, free-flowing rivers of its size in the continent. Lately, however, the populations of several species have severely declined or have been eliminated largely because of pollution. One fish species, the blue shiner, has already been extirpated. Water quality has been degraded from sewage treatment plants, limestone quarries, and strip mining. The effect on the fauna of water rich in dissolved nutrients can be magnified in still pools during low flows and high temperatures when dissolved oxygen drops to low levels. Virtually all of the water flow in some stretches of the Cahaba River during low flows consists of treated sewage effluent. Siltation can have an adverse effect on water quality. Recent fish collections in the Cahaba River have shown a significant decrease in species diversity and numbers of specimens with an apparent increase in siltation. Chlorination from sewage could have an adverse impact on the Cahaba shiner. They are possibly more sensitive to chlorine than other *Notropis* species.

Methane gas extraction is of considerable interest in the Cahaba River Basin. While preliminary information indicates that the Cahaba shiner can tolerate permitted chloride levels, the potential for the discharge of wastewater from these wells in excess of permitted levels and the impact on the

Cahaba shiner is of concern. The impact of other pollutants that may be in wastewater from methane gas wells is unknown.

Conservation and Recovery

The Alabama Department of Conservation and Natural Resources recognizes the Cahaba shiner as an endangered species. In addition, the counties of Perry and Dallas, which border over a third of the Cahaba River's lower main channel, passed resolutions in 1981 establishing scenic corridors as buffer zones. Parties planning activities which might impact the environment in these corridors are required to obtain a permit from their County Commission. A Cahaba River Society, comprised of biologists, conservationists, land-owners and business leaders, has also been organized to protect the river. Since the Cahaba shiner is now a federally-listed, endangered species, Federal agencies are required to ensure that any activities they authorize, fund, or implement are not likely to jeopardize its continued existence. If a Federal action might affect this species, the responsible Federal agency must enter into formal consultation with the U.S. Fish and Wildlife Service.

Contacts

U. S. Fish and Wildlife Service
Jackson Ecological Services Field Office
6578 Dogwood View Parkway, Suite A
Jackson, Mississippi 39213-7856
Telephone: (601) 965-4900
Fax: (601) 965-4340

U. S. Fish and Wildlife Service
Regional Office, Division of Endangered Species
1875 Century Blvd., Suite 200
Atlanta, Georgia 30345
http://southeast.fws.gov/

References

Howell, W.M., R.A. Stiles, and J.S. Brown. 1982. "Status Survey of the Cahaba Shiner (*Notropis D.*) and Goldline Darter (*Percina aurolineata*) in the Cahaba River from Trussville to Booth Ford." Alabama

Mayden, R.L., and B.R. Kuhajda. 1989. "Systematics of *Notropis cahabae*, a New Cyprinid Fish Endemic to the Cahaba River of the Mobile Basin." *Bulletin of the Alabama Museum of Natural History* 9:16.

Pierson, J.M., W.M. Howell, R.A. Stiles, M.F. Mettee, P.E. O'Neal, R.D. Suttkus, and J.S. Ramsey. *Fishes of the Cahaba River System in Alabama.* Geological Survey of Alabama.

Stiles, R.A. 1990. "A Preliminary Report on the Current Status of the Goldline Darter, *Percina aurolineota*, and the Cahaba shiner, *Notropis cahabae*, in the Little Cahaba and Cahaba Rivers of Alabama." A Report to the U.S. Fish and Wildlife Service.

U.S. Fish and Wildlife Service. 25 October 1990. "Endangered Status Determined for the Fish Cahaba Shiner *Notropis cahabae*." *Federal Register* 55(207): 42961-42966.

Arkansas River Shiner

Notropis girardi

Status	Threatened
Listed	November 23, 1998
Family	Cyprinidae (Minnows)
Description	Small, light tan fish with a small, dorsally flattened head, round snout, and small subterminal mouth.
Habitat	Main channels of wide, shallow, sandy-bottomed rivers and larger streams of the Arkansas River basin.
Food	Detritus, aquatic invertebrates, sand and silt.
Reproduction	Spawns in July; usually lays 120-274 eggs.
Threats	Habitat destruction, modification, depletion; competition with the non-indigenous Red River shiner; drought.
Range	Arkansas, Kansas, New Mexico, Oklahoma, Texas

Description

The Arkansas River shiner, *Notropis girardi*, is a small, robust shiner with a small, dorsally flattened head, rounded snout, and small subterminal mouth. Adults attain a maximum length of 2 in (5 cm). Dorsal, anal, and pelvic fins all have eight rays, and there is usually a small, black chevron present at the base of the caudal fin. Dorsal coloration tends to be light tan, with silvery sides gradually grading to white on the belly.

Behavior

The Arkansas River shiner is a generalist feeder in which no particular invertebrate dominates the diet. Adults may prefer to wait on the lee sides of sand ridges and feed upon organisms washed downstream. In the Canadian River of Texas, the diet of Arkansas River shiner was dominated by detritus, aquatic invertebrates, and sand and silt. With the exception of the winter season when larval flies were consumed much more frequently than other aquatic invertebrates, no particular invertebrate taxa dominated the diet. The Arkansas

River shiner feeds on both items suspended in the water column and items lying on the substrate. In the Pecos River, fly larvae, copepods, immature mayflies, insect eggs, and seeds were the dominant items in the diet.

The Arkansas River shiner spawns in July, usually coinciding with flood flows following heavy rains. It appears that the Arkansas River shiner is in peak reproductive condition throughout the months of May, June, and July and may actually spawn several times during this period. Arkansas River shiner eggs are nonadhesive and drift with the swift current during high flows.

The number of mature eggs for Arkansas River shiners in Texas varied between 120 and 274, with some large females containing more than 400. Hatching occurs within 24-48 hours after spawning. The larvae are capable of swimming within three to four days; they then seek out backwater pools and quiet water at the mouth of tributaries where food is more abundant. This species will not spawn unless conditions are favorable to the survival of the larvae.

Life span is unknown, but is likely less than three years in the wild.

Habitat

The Arkansas River shiner historically inhabited the main channels of wide, shallow, sandy-bottomed rivers and larger streams of the Arkansas River basin. Adults are uncommon in quiet pools or backwaters, and almost never occur in tributaries having deep water and bottoms of mud or stone. Water depth, sand ridge and midchannel habitats, dissolved oxygen, and current are the environmental variables most strongly associated with the distribution of Arkansas River shiner within the channel. Juvenile Arkansas River shiners associate most strongly with current, conductivity (total dissolved solids), and backwater and island habitat types.

Distribution

Historically, the Arkansas River shiner was widespread and abundant throughout the western portion of the Arkansas River basin in Kansas, New Mexico, Oklahoma, and Texas. In New Mexico, surveys and collection records establish that the Arkansas River shiner historically inhabited the Canadian River from the Texas-New Mexico state line as far upstream as the Sabinoso area in central San Miguel County, New Mexico, a distance of more than 120 river-mi (193 river-km). The Arkansas River shiner also occurred in Ute and Revuelto Creeks and the Conchas River.

In Texas, the Arkansas River shiner occurred throughout the Canadian River from state line to state line, a distance of about 230 river-mi (370 river-km). The first reported captures of Arkansas River shiner from Texas were in 1954. The species was captured at several sites extending from near the Texas-New Mexico state line at the Matador Ranch in Oldham County downstream to the Texas-Oklahoma state line.

As of the late 1990s, the Arkansas River shiner was almost entirely restricted to about 500 mi (800 km) of the Canadian River in Oklahoma, Texas, and New Mexico. An extremely small population may still survive in the Cimarron River in Oklahoma and Kansas, based on the collection of only nine individuals since 1985. A non-native population of the Arkansas River shiner has become established in the Pecos River of New Mexico in the late twentieth century. The decline of this species throughout its historical range may primarily be attributed to inundation and modification of stream discharge by impoundments, channel desiccation (drying out) due to water diversion and excessive groundwater pumping, stream channelization, and introduction of non-native species.

Threats

The Arkansas River basin population is threatened by habitat destruction and modification from stream dewatering or depletion due to diversion of surface water and groundwater pumping, construction of impoundments, and water quality degradation. Competition with the nonindigenous Red River shiner (*N. bairdi*) contributed to diminished distribution and abundance in the Cimarron River. Incidental capture of the Arkansas River shiner during pursuit of commercial bait fish species may also contribute to reduced population sizes. Drought and other natural factors also threaten the existence of the species.

Conservation and Recovery

Kansas lists the Arkansas River shiner as a state endangered species and has designated portions of the main stem Cimarron, Arkansas, South Fork Ninnescah, and Ninnescah Rivers as critical habitat. A permit is also required for public actions that have the potential to destroy listed individuals or their critical habitat. Subject activities include any publicly funded or state or federally assisted action, or any action requiring a permit from any other state or federal agency. The penalty for violations is a maximum fine of US$2,500 and confinement for a period not to exceed one year. Kansas does not permit the commercial harvest of bait fish from rivers and streams.

New Mexico also lists the Arkansas River shiner as a state endangered species. This listing prohibits the taking of fish without a valid scientific collecting permit but does not provide habitat protection. Oklahoma lists the Arkansas River shiner as a state threatened species, but like New Mexico, this listing does not provide habitat protection. The states of Arkansas and Texas provide no special protection for the species or its habitat.

While Kansas, New Mexico, and Oklahoma protect the Arkansas River shiner from take and/or possession, only Kansas addresses the problem of habitat destruction or modification. Only New Mexico provides significant protection from the potential introduction of non-native, competitive species. Licensed commercial bait dealers in New Mexico may sell bait minnows only within the drainage where they have been collected and cannot sell any state-listed fish species.

The U. S. Geological Survey has initiated a water quality assessment of the High Plains aquifer under the National Water Quality Assessment program. Through this project the U. S. Geological Survey planned to evaluate existing water quality problems in the aquifer and provide information that will help protect water quality in the aquifer.

The Canadian River Municipal Water Authority, the nonfederal sponsor of the Lake Meredith Salinity Control Project, has agreed to implement certain conservation actions for the Arkansas River shiner. It has agreed to: (1) conduct routine evaluations of flow conditions within the immediate project area, (2) adjust operation of the salinity control project to minimize any potential effect upon the Arkansas River shiner, and (3) monitor water quality within the affected stream segment. It also has agreed to cooperate with the U. S. Fish and Wildlife Service and the State of New Mexico in scheduling releases from Ute Reservoir to benefit the Arkansas River shiner. The Canadian River Municipal Water Authority initiated releases in June 1997, and researchers at Texas Tech University are evaluating the effect of these releases on reproductive ecology of the Arkansas River shiner, and will provide recommendations for scheduling any future releases.

Contacts

U. S. Fish and Wildlife Service
Regional Office, Division of Endangered Species
P.O. Box 1306
Albuquerque, New Mexico 87103-1306
Telephone: (505) 248-6911
Fax: (505) 248-6915
http://southwest.fws.gov/

U. S. Fish and Wildlife Service
Regional Office, Division of Endangered Species
1875 Century Blvd., Suite 200
Atlanta, Georgia 30345
http://southeast.fws.gov/

U. S. Fish and Wildlife Service
Regional Office, Division of Endangered Species
P.O. Box 25486
Denver Federal Center
Denver, Colorado 80225
http://www.r6.fws.gov/

U. S. Fish and Wildlife Service
Oklahoma Ecological Services Field Office
222 South Houston, Suite A
Tulsa, Oklahoma 74127-8909
Telephone: (918) 581-7458
Fax: (918) 581-7467
http://ifs2es.fws.gov/Oklahoma/

Reference

U. S. Fish and Wildlife Service. 23 November 1998. "Final Rule to List the Arkansas River Basin Population of the Arkansas River Shiner (*Notropis girardi*) as Threatened." *Federal Register* 63 (225): 64771-64799.

Cape Fear Shiner

Notropis mekistocholas

Status	Endangered
Listed	September 25, 1987
Family	Cyprinidae (Minnow)
Description	Small, silvery-yellow minnow with a dark lateral stripe.
Habitat	Pools, slow riffles, and runs.
Food	Plant matter.
Reproduction	Undescribed.
Threats	Dam construction.
Range	North Carolina

Description

Cape Fear shiner (*Notropis mekistocholas*) is a pale metallic-yellow minnow that rarely exceeds 2 in (5.1 cm) in length. A black lateral stripe runs the length of the side. The fins are yellow and pointed, the upper lip is black, and the lower lip bears a thin black bar along its margin.

Behavior

This shiner, unlike most other members of the large genus *Notropis*, feeds extensively on plant matter, and its digestive tract has a long, convoluted intestine. Nothing is known of its breeding biology.

Habitat

Cape Fear shiner is usually found in pools, riffles, and runs over gravel, cobble, or boulder bottoms. It is frequently associated with schools of related species but is never the most numerous. Juveniles are often found in slack water, among midstream rock outcrops, and in side channels and pools.

Distribution

Cape Fear shiner has been documented from nine rivers and streams in central North Carolina: Bear and Robeson Creeks and Rocky River (Chatham County); Fork Creek (Randolph County); Deep River (Moore, Randolph, Chatham, and Lee Coun-

ties); and Cape Fear River and Kenneth, Neals, and Parkers Creeks (Hartnett County). This shiner is now restricted to only four North Carolina populations. The largest and most stable population is located near the confluence of the Rocky and Deep Rivers in Chatham and Lee Counties. A second population center is found in Chatham County above the Rocky River hydroelectric dam, and a third inhabits the Deep River system in Randolph and Moore Counties above the Highfalls hydroelectric reservoir. In 1987 a viable population was discovered in Neals Creek in Harnett County.

Threats

Cape Fear shiner may always have been rare, but there is no doubt that the population has suffered a sharp decline. Construction of dams along the Cape Fear River system has inundated portions of the shiner's riverine habitat and fragmented the population. Potential future threats could come from road construction, channel modification, additional damming, and waste water discharges, with proposed dam projects in the area posing further threats to the shiner's habitat.

Conservation and Recovery

Because "critical habitat status" has been designated for Cape Fear shiner, certain options are available for habitat management. The recovery plan recommends 1) searching for additional populations

Cape Fear Shiner, photograph. U. S. Fish and Wildlife Service. Reproduced by permission.

and habitat suitable for reintroducing species; 2) reintroducing captive bred individuals back into the original habitat; and 3) monitoring population and habitat conditions. The habitat is also somewhat protected by state and federal laws from disturbance by construction activities.

Contacts

U. S. Fish and Wildlife Service
Regional Office, Division of Endangered Species
1875 Century Blvd., Suite 200
Atlanta, Georgia 30345
(404) 679-4000
http://southeast.fws.gov/

U. S. Fish and Wildlife Service
Asheville Ecological Services Field Office
160 Zillicoa St.
Asheville, North Carolina 28801-1082
Telephone: (828) 258-3939
Fax: (828) 258-5330

References

Pottern, G. B., and M. T. Hulsh. 1985, 1986, 1987. "Status Surveys of the Cape Fear Shiner (*Notropis mekistocholas*)." U. S. Fish and Wildlife Service, Atlanta.

Snelson, F. F. 1971. "*Notropis mekistocholas*, a New Cyprinid Fish Endemic to the Cape Fear River Basin, North Carolina." *Copeia* 1971: 449-462.

U. S. Fish and Wildlife Service. 1987. "Determination of Endangered Status and Critical Habitat for the Cape Fear Shiner." *Federal Register* 52: 36034-36039.

U. S. Fish and Wildlife Service. 1988. "Cape Fear Shiner Recovery Plan." U. S. Fish and Wildlife Service, Atlanta.

Pecos Bluntnose Shiner

Notropis simus pecosensis

Status	Threatened
Listed	February 20, 1987
Family	Cyprinidae (Minnows)
Description	Small silvery minnow with a rounded blunt snout.
Habitat	Shallow flowing water over sandy bottom.
Food	Probably insects, algae, and other plant matter.
Reproduction	Thought to spawn spring to autumn.
Threats	Dam construction, water diversion.
Range	New Mexico

Description

Pecos bluntnose shiner (*Notropis simus pecosensis*) is a small minnow, reaching an adult length of up to 3.5 in (8.9 cm). It has a slender, silvery body and a large mouth overhung by a bluntly rounded snout. This shiner was first thought to be part of a single species (*Notropis simus*), whose range extended throughout the Rio Grande river basin. In 1982 biologists determined that the species was made up of two subspecies—Rio Grande (*N. s. simus*) and Pecos (*N. s. pecosensis*). The Rio Grande subspecies, once commonly used as a baitfish, has not been collected since 1964 and is believed extinct.

Behavior

Little information on the life history of this species is available. It is thought to feed mostly on terrestrial and aquatic insects, augmented with algae and plant matter. It probably spawns from spring to autumn.

Habitat

Pecos bluntnose shiner inhabits the main channel of the Pecos River, a slow-flowing, shallow (16 in [41 cm]) river with a sandy bottom. Younger fish have been found in backwaters, riffles, and pools. Natural springs such as those in the Santa Rosa and Lake McMillan areas also support small populations.

Distribution

This subspecies was first collected in 1874 from the Rio Grande near San Ildefonso, New Mexico. It was subsequently found in the Pecos River between Santa Rosa and Carlsbad.

Pecos bluntnose shiner occurs in the Pecos River (in New Mexico) in two river segments totaling some 100 mi (161 km). The first segment extends from approximately 10 mi (16 km) south of Fort Sumner downstream about 64 mi (103 km) into Chaves County; the second, shorter, segment of about 37 mi (60 km) stretches between Hagerman and Artesia in Chaves and Eddy counties.

Within these two stretches, abundance of the species is uneven. The largest populations occur in seepage areas of the river upstream from Highway 70 crossing to Fort Sumner, and, to a lesser extent, in the reach between Hagerman and Artesia.

The species is now far less common than it once was. A 1982 survey netted only 76 specimens, compared with 818 in 1941 and 1,482 in 1939. Collections made in 1986 at five historic sites contained a total of 131 Pecos bluntnose shiners. Additional collections have been made systematically since that

Pecos Bluntnose Shiner, photograph by Brooks M. Burr. Reproduced by permission.

time and have shown varying degrees of population decline and recovery.

The waters of the Pecos River are administered by the states of New Mexico and Texas through the Pecos River Compact. The Bureau of Reclamation and the Army Corps of Engineers operate dams on the river in accordance with the compact. Land along the Pecos River is mostly privately owned. Federal land includes a few small parcels between Fort Sumner and Roswell, administered by the Bureau of Land Management. A short section of the river flows through the Bitter Lakes National Wildlife Refuge.

Threats

Though very little is known about the reasons for the species' decline, it seems apparent that the cause is related to, if not exclusively the result of, habitat modifications. Changes to Pecos bluntnose shiner's environment since the mid-1980s include the habitat's physical alteration, its pollution, and the intro-

duction of non-native species. This is part of a general pattern of decline in small, short-lived fishes that are native to the large riverine waters of the Southwest.

The U. S. Fish and Wildlife Service (FWS) has expressed concern over the status of this shiner since 1978, when it was determined that the waterflows in the Rio Grande and Pecos rivers had been greatly reduced by dam construction and diversion of water for irrigation. The FWS believed for a time that Pecos bluntnose shiner was already extinct. Efforts to list the fish as endangered were stalled until specimens were rediscovered in New Mexico.

Conservation and Recovery

The FWS has designated two sections of the Pecos River in New Mexico as critical for the survival of the Pecos bluntnose shiner: 1) 64 mi (103 km) from Fort Sumner downstream into Chaves County and 2) 37 mi (59.5 km) between Hagerman and Artesia. Both areas support relatively abundant, reproducing populations of the shiner, but flow in the river below Fort Sumner could be radically reduced by further dam construction.

In the 1980s the New Mexico Parks and Recreation Commission was granted a permit to establish a permanent recreation pool in Santa Rosa Reservoir that would reduce flows below Alamogordo Reservoir. Construction on the Brantley Dam in that area commenced in 1983. The Pecos River is already highly managed, with dams and diversion structures along most of its course. Most structures on the river have been built by the Army Corps of Engineers, which has stated that future flood control measures can be managed to preserve Pecos bluntnose shiner.

The State of New Mexico has provided some legal protection for this species through the New Mexico Wildlife Conservation Act, which prohibits taking of any listed species without a scientific collecting permit. The state also has a limited ability to protect the habitat through the Habitat Protection Act, water pollution legislation, and tangentially through a legal provision that protects areas used by game fish.

The 1992 recovery plan for the species (from the FWS) considers species' stabilization to be the primary recovery goal. Recovery criteria involve maintaining viable populations throughout the 100 mi (160.9 km) of habitat where the species still occurs. To achieve this goal, the FWS recommended 1) monitoring, maintaining, and enhancing existing populations; 2) reintroducing the fish into historic habitats; 3) enforcing statutes that protect existing populations and their habitats; and 4) developing and implementing public information programs. If stabilization is achieved, delisting objectives will be determined by the FWS in 2002.

Contact

U. S. Fish and Wildlife Service
Regional Office, Division of Endangered Species
P. O. Box 1306
Albuquerque, New Mexico 87103-1306
Telephone: (505) 248-6911
Fax: (505) 248-6915
http://southwest.fws.gov/

References

Chernoff, B., R. R. Miller, and C. R. Gilbert. 1982. "*Notropis orca* and *Notropis simus*, Cyprinid Fishes from the American Southwest." *Occasional Papers of the Museum of Zoology, University of Michigan* 698: 1-49.

New Mexico Department of Game and Fish. 1982. "The Status of *Notropis simus pecosensis* in the Pecos River of New Mexico." Office of Endangered Species, Albuquerque.

U. S. Fish and Wildlife Service. 1987. "Determination of Threatened Status for Pecos Bluntnose Shiner." *Federal Register* 52: 5295-5303.

U. S. Fish and Wildlife Service. 1992. "Recovery Plan for Pecos Bluntnose Shiner." U. S. Fish and Wildlife Service, Albuquerque.

Topeka Shiner

Notropis topeka

Status	Endangered
Listed	December 15, 1998
Family	Cyprinidae
Description	Small, olive-green stout minnow with a distinct dark stripe preceding the dorsal fin.
Habitat	Small, headwater, prairie streams with good water quality and cool temperatures.
Food	Insects, zooplankton.
Reproduction	Spawns on silt-free substrates.
Threats	Habitat destruction, degradation, modification, and fragmentation resulting from siltation, reduced water quality, tributary impoundment, stream channelization, and stream dewatering; and introduced predatory fishes.
Range	Iowa, Kansas, Minnesota, Missouri, Nebraska, South Dakota

Description

The *Notropis topeka* (Topeka shiner) is a small, stout minnow, not exceeding 3 in (8 cm) in length. The head is short with a small, moderately oblique (slanted or sloping) mouth. The eye diameter is equal to or slightly longer than the snout. The dorsal (back) fin is large, with the height more than one half the predorsal length of the fish, originating over the leading edge of the pectoral (chest) fins. Dorsal and pelvic fins each contain eight rays (boney spines supporting the membrane of a fin). The anal and pectoral fins contain seven and 13 rays respectively, and there are 32-37 lateral line scales. Dorsally the body is olivaceous (olive-green), with a distinct dark stripe preceding the dorsal fin. A dusky stripe is exhibited along the entire longitudinal length of the lateral line. The scales above this line are darkly outlined with pigment, appearing cross-hatched. Below the lateral line the body lacks pigment, appearing silvery-white. A distinct chevron-like spot exists at the base of the caudal (tail) fin.

Behavior

The Topeka shiner swims independent of currents and is an insectivore (insect eater). It is primarily a diurnal (daytime) feeder on insects, with midges, true flies, and mayflies, making up the bulk of the diet. However, zooplanktons also contribute significantly to the species' diet. The Topeka shiner is reported to spawn in pool habitats, over green sunfish and orange spotted sunfish nests, from late May through July in Missouri and Kansas. Males are reported to establish small territories near these nests. The Topeka shiner is an obligate (essential) spawner on silt-free sunfish nests, but it is unlikely that the species is solely reproductively dependent on sunfish; the shiner also utilizes other silt-free substrates as spawning sites. Maximum lifespan for

Topeka Shiner, photograph. U. S. Fish and Wildlife Service. Reproduced by permission.

the Topeka shiner is three years; however, only a very small percentage lives to the third summer.

Habitat

The Topeka shiner occupies small, headwater, prairie streams with good water quality and cool temperatures. These streams generally exhibit year round flow, but some have periodic flow during summer. At times when surface flow ceases, pool levels and cool water temperatures are maintained by seepage through the streambed, spring flow and/or groundwater seepage. The predominant substrates within these streams are clean gravel, cobble and sand. However, bedrock and clay hard-pan (layer of hard soil) overlain by a thin layer of silt are not uncommon. Topeka shiners most often occur in pool and run areas of streams, seldom being found in choppy water. They are pelagic (living in open water) in nature, occurring in mid-water and surface areas, and are primarily considered a schooling fish. Occasionally, individuals of

this species have been found in larger streams, downstream of known populations, presumably as strays.

Distribution

The Topeka shiner is a small fish presently known from small tributary streams in the Kansas and Cottonwood River basins in Kansas; the Missouri, Grand, Lamine, Chariton, and Des Moines River basins in Missouri; the North Raccoon and Rock river basins in Iowa; the James, Big Sioux and Vermillion River watersheds in South Dakota; and, the Rock and Big Sioux River watersheds in Minnesota.

Historically, the Topeka shiner was widespread and abundant throughout low order tributary streams of the central prairie regions, including portions of Iowa, Kansas, Minnesota, Missouri, Nebraska, and South Dakota. The number of known occurrences of Topeka shiner populations has been reduced by approximately 80%, with approximately 50% of this decline occurring within the last 25 years. The species now primarily exists as isolated and fragmented populations.

In Missouri, 42 of the 72 sites historically supporting Topeka shiners were re-surveyed in 1992; shiners were collected at eight of the 42 surveyed locales. In 1995, the remaining 30 historical sites not surveyed in 1992 and an additional 64 locales, thought to have potential to support the species, were sampled. Topeka shiners were found at six of the 30 remaining historical locations and at six of the 64 additional sites sampled. In total, recent sampling in Missouri identified Topeka shiners at 14 of 72 historic localities, and at 20 of 136 total sites sampled. In Iowa, 24 locales within four drainages were sampled in 1994 at or near sites from which the species was reported extant between 1975 and 1985. The Topeka shiner was captured at three of 24 sites, with these three captures occurring in the North Raccoon River basin. There were six collections of the species in 1994 and 1995, also from the same drainage. In Kansas, extensive stream surveys completed from 1995 through 1997 identified 10 new localities for Topeka shiners and reconfirmed the species in a historic locale where it was previously believed extirpated.

In South Dakota in 1997, surveys identified several specimens from two streams in Brookings County, South Dakota. In the James River basin, three new localities for the species were identified, and the species was reconfirmed from a historic locality. Two of the new locations were in Beadle County, where 29 and 4 individual Topeka shiners were captured. The other new location was in Hutchinson County, where one Topeka shiner was captured. The reconfirmed historic locale was in Davison County, where one Topeka shiner was captured. In Minnesota, 14 streams in the range of the Topeka shiner were surveyed between 1985 and 1995. The species was collected from five of nine streams with historic occurrences, and was not found in the five streams with no historic occurrences. These locales were in the Rock River drainage. In 1997, additional surveys were completed with the species being captured at 15 sites in eight streams, including a stream in the Big Sioux River basin.

In Nebraska, in 1989, the shiner was discovered in the upper Loup River drainage, where two specimens were collected. In 1996, a single specimen was collected from a stream in the Elkhorn River basin. These were the first collections of Topeka shiners in Nebraska since 1940.

Threats

The Topeka shiner is threatened by habitat destruction, degradation, modification, and fragmentation resulting from siltation, reduced water quality, tributary impoundment, stream channelization, and stream dewatering. The species also is impacted by introduced predaceous fishes.

Intensive land-use practices, maintainence of altered waterways, dewatering of streams, and continuing tributary impoundment and channelization represent the greatest existing threats to the Topeka shiner. Over-grazing of riparian zones (banks of a natural course of water) and the removal of riparian vegetation to increase tillable acreage greatly diminish a watershed's ability to filter sediments, organic wastes and other impurities from the stream system. Irrigation draw-down of groundwater levels affects surface and subsurface flows which can impact the species. At present, both Federal and State planning for development of watershed impoundments and channelization and/or its maintenance continue in areas with populations of Topeka shiners. Several impoundments are planned for construction on streams with abundant numbers of the species. Portions of these stream reaches will be inundated by the permanent pools of the reservoirs, imperiling the species' future existence in these localities. Prior to the planning of the impoundments, these populations of Topeka shiners were considered to be the most stable range-wide, due to their occurrence in watersheds dominated by high quality prairie with generally very good grazing management and land stewardship.

Conservation and Recovery

A number of Federal agencies have jurisdiction and responsibilities potentially affecting the Topeka shiner. Federal involvement is expected to include the Corps of Engineers throughout the species' range with respect to its administration of the Clean Water Act. The U.S. Environmental Protection Agency will need to consider the Topeka shiner in the registration of pesticides, adoption of water quality criteria, and other pollution control programs. The U.S. Department of Transportation, Federal Highway Administration, will need to consider the effects of bridge and road construction at locations where known habitat may be impacted. The U.S. Department of Agriculture, Natural Resources Conservation Service and Farm Service Agency, will need to consider the effects of structures and channelization projects installed under the Watershed Protection and Flood Prevention Act, the Farm Bill programs, and other activities which may impact water quality, quantity, or timing of flows. The Federal Energy Regulatory Commission will need to consider potential impacts to the Topeka shiner and its habitat resulting from gas pipeline construction over streams and from hydroelectric development.

Contacts

U. S. Fish and Wildlife Service
Kansas Ecological Services Field Office
315 Houston Street, Suite E
Manhattan, Kansas 66502-6172
Telephone: (913) 539-3474
Fax: (913) 539-8567

U. S. Fish and Wildlife Service
Regional Office, Division of Endangered Species
1 Federal Drive
BHW Federal Building
Fort Snelling, Minnesota 55111
Telephone: (612) 713-5360
http://midwest.fws.gov/

U. S. Fish and Wildlife Service
Regional Office, Division of Endangered Species
P.O. Box 25486
Denver Federal Center
Denver, Colorado 80225
http://www.r6.fws.gov/

References

U. S. Fish and Wildlife Service. 15 December 1998. "Final Rule To List the Topeka Shiner as Endangered." *Federal Register* 63(240):69008-69021.

Oregon Chub

Oregonichthys crameri

Status	Endangered
Listed	October 18, 1993
Family	Cyprinidae (Minnow)
Description	Small brownish-yellow minnow.
Habitat	Low-velocity water flow with depositional substrates.
Food	Copepods, cladocerans, larvae.
Reproduction	Spawning occurs from April to August; females produce 147-671 eggs.
Threats	Elimination of its backwater habitats, creation of flood control structures, chemical spills, competition.
Range	Oregon

Description

The Oregon chub, *Oregonichthys crameri*, is a small minnow measuring up to 1.4 in (3.5 cm). The scales on the lower body are brownish-yellow, while the upper scales are brown to white. The fins are almost clear and almost transparent. This species has also been classified as *Hybopsis crameri*.

Behavior

Males, which measure more than 1.4 in (3.5 cm) in standard length, defend territories in or near aquatic vegetation. The number of eggs produced per female ranges from 147 to 671. Spawning occurs from the end of April through early August when water temperatures range from 60.8°F to 82.4°F (16°C to 28°C). Adults feed primarily on copepods, cladocerans, and chironomid larvae.

Habitat

The Oregon chub was once distributed through sloughs and overflow ponds. Population sites typically feature low- or zero-velocity water flow, depositional substrates, and abundant aquatic, or overhanging riparian, vegetation.

Distribution

The Oregon chub was formerly distributed throughout the lower elevation backwaters of the Willamette River drainage. Populations of the chub are now restricted to the Middle Fork of the Willamette River near Dexter and Lookout Point Reservoirs in Lone County, Oregon. Small numbers of the chub have also been observed on the lower North Santiam River, which forms the boundary between Linn and Marion Counties and in Gray Creek within the Finley National Wildlife Refuge in Benton County. In 1992 an additional population was discovered in a tributary to Lake Creek in Linn County.

Threats

It is believed the Oregon chub has been adversely affected by changes in and elimination of its backwater habitats. The main stem of the Willamette River was formerly a braided channel with numerous secondary channels, meanders, oxbows, and overflow ponds that may have provided habitat for the chub. The construction of flood control projects and revetments, however, have altered historical flooding patterns and eliminated much of the river's braided channel pattern. The period of construction

Dale Skeesick

of flood control structures directly coincides with the period of decline of this species. Habitat loss has also resulted from siltation of shallow habitats from logging and construction activities, unauthorized fill activities, and changes in water level or flow conditions from construction, diversions, or natural desiccation. This species is also threatened by chemical spills and competition. Direct mortality is a potential threat from chemical spills from overturned trucks or oil tankers, runoff or accidental spills of brush control and agricultural chemicals, and overflow from chemical toilets in campgrounds. Competition for resources and predation may be a result of intentional or accidental introductions of non-indigenous fish species.

Conservation and Recovery

Conservation measures provided to species listed as endangered or threatened pursuant to the Endangered Species Act include recognition, recovery actions, requirements for federal protection, and prohibitions against certain practices. Recognition through listing encourages conservation measures by federal, international, and private agencies, groups, and individuals.

Contact

U. S. Fish and Wildlife Service
Regional Office, Division of Endangered Species
Eastside Federal Complex
911 N. E. 11th Ave.
Portland, Oregon 97232-4181
Telephone: (503) 231-6121
http://pacific.fws.gov/

Reference

U. S. Fish and Wildlife Service. 18 October 1993. "Determination of Endangered Status for the Oregon Chub." *Federal Register* 58 (199): 53800-53804.

Blackside Dace

Phoxinus cumberlandensis

Status	Threatened
Listed	June 12, 1987
Family	Cyprinidae (Minnows)
Description	Small, green-gold minnow with a black lateral stripe and bright yellow fins.
Habitat	Well developed riparian areas with undercut stream banks, large rocks, and deep pools.
Food	Algae, detritus, insects.
Reproduction	Spawns in May to June.
Threats	Stream siltation, competition with the redbelly dace.
Range	Kentucky, Tennessee

Description

The blackside dace, *Phoxinus cumberlandensis*, is a small fish less than 3 in (8 cm) long with a single black lateral stripe, a green-gold back with black specks, and a pale or sometimes brilliant scarlet belly. The fins are often bright yellow with metallic silver surrounding the base of the pelvic and pectoral fins.

Behavior

The life history of this species has not been well-documented. It spawns in May and June in nests that have been constructed or adopted. One nest that was observed occurred in a shallow pit composed of gravel, with fine gravel for spawning. The blackside dace has been observed grazing on rocks, and it is thought that it feeds on algae, detritus, and sometimes insects.

Habitat

The blackside dace prefers well-developed riparian areas with undercut stream banks, large rocks, and deep pools. The largest populations occur in areas where the banks are lined with lush vegetation and the canopy cover exceeds 70%. The plant life helps to maintain cool water temperatures and remove silt from areas downstream of the riffles. The stream current must be swift enough to sweep away silt.

Distribution

Because this fish was only recently discovered, its historic range is not known. However, it may have been extirpated from as many as 52 streams within Kentucky and Tennessee before it was discovered and described.

The blackside dace is found in small streams in the upper Cumberland River basin, primarily above Cumberland Falls, in Pulaski, Laurel, McCreary, Whitley, Knox, Bell, Harlan, and Letcher Counties in Kentucky; and Scott, Campbell, and Claiborne Counties in Tennessee. In spite of its seeming widespread distribution, it now occupies little more than 14 mi (23 km) of about 30 streams.

Threats

Siltation caused by coal mining, timber harvesting, acid mine drainage, siltation from strip mining, agriculture, and road-construction runoff are responsible for the decline of this fish. Many of the streams, which continue to support blackside dace, remain threatened by these activities. The blackside

Blackside Dace, photograph. U. S. Fish and Wildlife Service. Reproduced by permission.

dace also faces competition from an introduced dace—the southern redbelly dace (*P. erythrogaster*)—which may have displaced it in warmer waters within its range.

Conservation and Recovery

The states of Kentucky and Tennessee prohibit taking this fish for any purpose. Some conservation measures include translocating wild individuals, restricting timber harvesting, herbicide and pesticide use, controlling pollution and road maintenance practices, reducing stream bank modification and channelization, and reintroducing captive bred fish to suitable habitat. The U. S. Fish and Wildlife Service hopes that each of the 24 streams providing habitat for the dace receives some kind of protection, either through public agencies or private conservation organization ownership. Noticeable improvements have been made in the coal-related problems, and the quality of the substrates has improved as well throughout the Cumberland River

Basin. The dace has successfully recolonized in some stream reaches within the Basin. Because of the number of populations that are present on public lands, the potential for recovering the species is good. State and federal regulations are in place for expanding the species into new habitats.

Contact

Regional Office of Endangered Species
U.S. Fish and Wildlife Service
1875 Century Blvd, Suite 200
Atlanta, Georgia 30345
http://southeast.fws.gov/

References

O'Bara, C. J. 1985. "Status Survey of the Blackside Dace (*Phoxinus cumberlandensis*)." U.S. Fish and Wildlife Service, Asheville, North Carolina.

Starnes, W. C., and D. A. Etnier. 1980. "Fishes." In Enger and Hatcher, eds., *Tennessee's Rare Wildlife*;

Vol. 1, *The Vertebrates*. Tennessee Wildlife Resources Agency and Tennessee Conservation Department, Knoxville.

Starnes, W. C., and L. B. Starnes. 1978. "A New Cyprinid of the Genus *Phoxinus* Endemic to the Upper Cumberland River Drainage." *Copeia* 1978:508-516.

U. S. Fish and Wildlife Service. 1988. "Recovery Plan for the Blackside Dace." U.S. Fish and Wildlife Service, Atlanta.

Woundfin

Plagopterus argentissimus

Status	Endangered
Listed	October 13, 1970
Family	Cyprinidae (Minnows)
Description	Silvery minnow with a flat head and sharp, dorsal spine.
Habitat	Shallow water near riffles.
Food	Omnivorous.
Reproduction	Spawns in May.
Threats	Dam construction, water diversion.
Range	Arizona, Nevada

Description

The silvery blue woundfin, *Plagopterus argentissimus*, which grows to a length of about 3 in (7.5 cm), has a flattened head, giving it a torpedo shape. Its sharp dorsal spine is responsible for its name. It is scaleless, except for small plates of bone in the leathery skin, and has barbels (sensors) on its lips like a catfish.

The woundfin is a member of the unique tribe, Plagopterini, which is endemic to the lower basin of the Colorado River and its ancestral tributary, the White River. This tribe has only three genera, two of which consist of a single species.

Behavior

The woundfin's reproductive cycle is probably triggered by increasing temperature, lengthening daylight, and declining spring runoff in late May. Spawning females leave pools to join groups of males in swifter flowing water over cobble or gravel beds. After spawning, the females return to pools.

Woundfins are omnivorous and eat algae, detritus, seeds, insects, and larvae.

Habitat

Adult and juvenile woundfin inhabit runs and quiet waters adjacent to riffles with sand and sand/gravel substrates. Adults are generally found in habitats with water depths between 6 in and 1.4 ft (15 and 43 cm) and with velocities between 0.8 and 1.6 ft/second (24 and 49 cm/second). Juveniles select areas with slower and deeper water, while fry are found in backwaters and stream margins which are often associated with growths of filamentous algae. Spawning areas have a swifter flow and sand or mud substrates.

Distribution

Based on early records, the original range of the woundfin extended from near the junction of the Salt and Verde Rivers at Tempe, Arizona, to the mouth of the Gila River at Yuma, Arizona. Woundfin were also found in the mainstem Colorado River from Yuma upstream to the Virgin River in Nevada, Arizona, and Utah and into La Verkin Creek, a tributary of the Virgin River in Utah. However, there is reason to believe that the woundfin occurred further upstream in the Verde, Salt, and Gila Rivers in Arizona.

Except for the mainstem of the Virgin River, woundfin were extirpated from most of their historical range. Woundfin presently range from Pah Tempe Springs (also called La Verkin Springs) on the mainstem of the Virgin River and the lower portion of La Verkin Creek in Utah, downstream to Lake Mead. A single specimen was taken from the middle Muddy (Moapa) River, Clark County,

Woundfin, photograph by John Rinne, USFS. Reproduced by permission.

Nevada, in the late 1960s and since that time no additional specimens have been collected. Population numbers remain unclear.

Threats

The woundfin declined when the flow of the Virgin River was altered by dams, reservoirs, canals, and other diversion structures. Many spawning streams have been depleted by the diversion of water for irrigation and municipal uses. Remaining populations are threatened by the introduction of non-native fish, notably the red shiner (*Notropis lutrensis*), which has completely replaced the woundfin in some areas. In 1988, Fish and Wildlife Service regional personnel, in cooperation with the Utah Division of Wildlife Resources and the Washington County Water Conservancy District, eliminated red shiners from a 21-mi (34-km) portion of the upper Virgin River.

Conservation and Recovery

During the 1970s the state of Arizona attempted to transplant the woundfin to a number of rivers and creeks. These initial transplants, however, appear to have been unsuccessful. The Endangered Species Act allows "experimental populations" to be established through transplantation, and plans for reintroducing the woundfin into its original range and other suitable habitat are now being developed.

In 1995, the FWS proposed the designation of 94.8 mi (151.7 km) of critical habitat for the woundfin (approximately 13.5% of its historical range); the same proposal also recommended the designation of critical habitat for two rare fishes that share its habitat, the endangered Virgin River chub *Gila seminuda* and the threatened Virgin spinedace (*Lepidomeda mollispinis mollispinis*). The majority of the land to be designated as critical habitat is under Federal or private ownership. The proposed critical habitat designation incorporates portions of the mainstem Virgin River and its tributaries, including the 100-year floodplain.

Contacts

U.S. Fish and Wildlife Service
Division of Endangered Species and Habitat Conservation
2105 Osuna Road N.E.
Albuquerque, New Mexico 87113-1001
Telephone: (505) 346-2525
E-mail: r2esweb@fws.gov
http://ifw2es.fws.gov/

U.S. Fish and Wildlife Service
Upper Colorado River Endangered Fish Recovery Program
Denver Federal Center
P.O Box 25486
Lake Plaza North
134 Union Boulevard
Denver, Colorado 80228-1807
Telephone: (303) 236-2985
Fax: (303) 236-5262

References

Deacon, J. E., and W. L. Minckley. 1973. "A Review of Information on the Woundfin, *Plagopterus argentissimus* Cope (Pisces: Cyprinidae): Progress Report on Population Dispersion and Community Structure of Fishes of the Virgin River System." U.S. Fish and Wildlife Service, Salt Lake City.

U.S. Fish and Wildlife Service. 1985. "Recovery Plan for Woundfin, *Plagopterus argentissimus* Cope." U.S. Fish and Wildlife Service, Albuquerque.

Sacramento Splittail

Pogonichthys macrolepidotus

Status	Threatened
Listed	February 8, 1999
Family	Cyprinidae
Description	A large minnow with barbels and a deeply forked tail.
Habitat	Rivers, sloughs, and fresh and brackish tidal waters.
Food	Feed on the bottom on invertebrates and detrital matter.
Reproduction	Spawn large numbers of eggs in aquatic vegetation.
Threats	Habitat destruction and degradation caused by hydrological changes associated with water diversions, as well as agricultural chemicals and other stressors.
Range	California

National Geographic Society

Description

The Sacramento splittail, *Pogonichthys macrolepidotus*, is a large cyprinid fish that can exceed 16 in (41 cm) in length. The name splittail refers to the distinctive tail of the fish. *Pogon-ichthys* means bearded fish, referring to the small barbels (whisker-like sensory organs) on the mouth of the fish, unusual in North American cyprinids. *Macro-lepidotus* means large-scaled. Adults are characterized by an elongated body, distinct nuchal hump (on the back of the neck), and small, blunt head, usually with barbels at the corners of the slightly subterminal mouth. The enlarged dorsal lobe of the caudal fin distinguishes the splittail from other minnows in the Central Valley of California. Sacramento splittails are dull, silvery-gold on the sides and olive-gray dorsally.

During spawning season, pectoral, pelvic, and caudal (tail) fins are tinged with an orange-red color. Males develop small white nuptial tubercles on the head. Breeding tubercles (nodules) also appear on the base of the fins.

Behavior

Splittails are relatively long-lived, frequently reaching five to seven years of age. An analysis of hard parts of the splittail indicate that larger fish may be eight to ten years old. Females are highly fecund, with the largest females producing over 250,000 eggs. Populations fluctuate annually depending on spawning success, which is highly correlated with freshwater outflow and the availability of shallow-water habitat with submerged vegetation. Fish usually reach sexual maturity by the end of their second year. The onset of spawning is associated with rising water levels, increasing water temperatures, and increasing day length. Peak spawning occurs from the months of March through May, although records of spawning exist for late January to early July. In some years, most spawning may take place within a limited period of time. For instance, in 1995, a year of extraordinarily successful spawning, most splittail spawned over a short period in April, even though larval splittail were captured from February through early July. Within each spawning season, older fish reproduce first, followed by younger individuals. Spawning occurs over flooded vegetation in tidal freshwater and euryhaline habitats of estuarine marshes and sloughs and slow-moving reaches of large rivers. Larvae remain in shallow, weedy areas close to spawning sites for 10 to 14 days and move into deeper water as they mature and swimming ability increases.

Splittails are benthic (bottom) foragers. In Suisun Marsh, they feed primarily on opossum shrimp, benthic amphipods, and harpactacoid copepods, although detrital material makes up a large percentage of their stomach contents. In the Delta, clams, crustaceans, insect larvae, and other invertebrates also are found in the diet. Predators include striped bass and other piscivores.

Habitat

In recent years, they have been found most often in slow-moving sections of rivers and sloughs and dead-end sloughs. Reports from the 1950s, however, mention Sacramento River spawning migrations and catches of splittail during fast tides in Suisun Bay. Because they require flooded vegetation for spawning and rearing, splittail are frequently found in areas subject to flooding. In 1995, after an unusually wet winter, over five million juvenile splittail were salvaged at the Central Valley Project and State Water Project indicating the magnitude of spawning success in favorable water years. They are year-round residents in Suisun Marsh, concentrat-

ing in the dead-end sloughs that typically have small streams feeding into them. They tend to be most abundant where other native fishes are abundant as well. In spring, both adult and young splittail are frequently found in shallow, flooded areas, such as the Yolo and Sutter bypasses, low riverine parts of delta islands, and river mouths. Historically, the major flood basins distributed throughout the Sacramento and San Joaquin valleys provided spawning and rearing habitat. These flood basins have all been reclaimed or modified for flood control purposes, including Yolo and Sutter bypasses. Although primarily a freshwater species, splittail can tolerate salinities as high as 10 to 18 parts per thousand. California Department of Fish and Game survey data from 1979 through 1994 indicate that the highest abundances occurred in shallow areas of Suisun and Grizzly bays.

Recent research indicates that splittail will use the Yolo and Sutter bypasses during the winter and spring months for foraging and spawning. However, the Yolo Bypass may only be used by splittail during wet winters, when water from the Sacramento River over-tops the Fremont Weir and spills over the Sacramento Weir into the Bypass. In 1998, the Yolo and Sutter bypasses provided good habitat for fish, particularly splittail, when they were flooded for several weeks in March and April. In order to provide spawning habitat for splittail, water must remain on the bypasses until fish have completed spawning, and larvae are able to swim out on their own, during the draining process.

Distribution

The Sacramento splittail is native to the Central Valley of California, where it was once widely distributed. Historically, it was found as far north as Redding on the Sacramento River, as far south as the present-day site of the Friant Dam on the San Joaquin River, and up tributaries of the Sacramento River as far as the current Oroville Dam on the Feather River and the Folsom Dam on the American River.

Threats

The Sacramento splittail was once part of the diet of Native Americans living in the Central Valley. Recreational anglers reported catches of 50 or more per day prior to the damming of its riverine habitats. They were captured in the past in southern San

Francisco Bay and at the mouth of Coyote Creek in Santa Clara County, but the species is no longer present there.

The splittail is primarily threatened by the altered hydraulics and reduced Delta outflow caused by the export of freshwater from the Sacramento and San Joaquin rivers through operation of the State and Federal water projects. These operations include not only the export of water from the Delta but also diversion of water to storage during periods of high run-off, which reduce instream flows and available submerged aquatic habitat for spawning and rearing. These hydrological effects, coupled with severe drought years, introduced aquatic species, the loss of shallow-water habitat to reclamation activities, and other human-caused actions, have reduced the species' capacity to recover from natural seasonal fluctuations in hydrology for which it was adapted. Additional threats to this species include

(1) direct and indirect mortality at power plants and in-Delta water diversion sites;

(2) reduced river flows and changes in the seasonal patterns of flows in the Sacramento and San Joaquin rivers and their tributaries;

(3) the loss of spawning and nursery habitat as a consequence of draining and diking for agriculture;

(4) the loss of shallow-water habitat due to levee slope protection, marina construction, and other bank-oriented construction activities;

(5) the reduction in the availability of highly productive brackish-water habitat;

(6) the presence of toxic substances, especially agricultural and industrial chemicals and heavy metals in their aquatic habitat;

(7) human and natural disturbance of the food web through altered hydrology and introduction of exotic species;

(8) flood control operations that strand eggs, larvae, juveniles, and adults;

(9) the increase in severity of these effects by several years of drought; and

(10) entrainment (pulling) of fish through unscreened or inadequately screened munici-

pal and agricultural diversions. The Sacramento splittail is now restricted to a small portion of its former range. However, during wet years, the species migrates up the Sacramento River as far as the Red Bluff diversion dam in Tehama County, and into the lowermost reaches of the Feather and American rivers. Overall, its abundance has declined by about 60% from 1984 through 1993. The greatest declines (over 80%) occurred in the shallow Suisun Bay area, the center of the range of the species. Splittail populations are now 35%-60% of what they were in the 1940s.

Conservation and Recovery

Protective measures currently being implemented to benefit the delta smelt may benefit the splittail, such as restrictions on pumping under certain conditions. However, the ecological requirements of these species differ, especially with respect to timing of important development stages and habitat uses. Unlike delta smelt, splittail require flooded lowland habitat for spawning and are particularly vulnerable to disturbance or destruction of marshy habitat.

Contacts

U. S. Fish and Wildlife Service
Regional Office, Division of Endangered Species
Eastside Federal Complex
911 N. E. 11th Ave.
Portland, Oregon 97232-4181
Telephone: (503) 231-6121
http://pacific.fws.gov/

U. S. Fish and Wildlife Service
Sacramento Fish and Wildlife Office
2800 Cottage Way, Room W-2605
Sacramento, California 95825-1846
Telephone: 916-414-6600
Fax: 916-460-4619

References

U. S. Fish and Wildlife Service. 8 February 1999. "Determination of Threatened Status for the Sacramento Splittail." *Federal Register* 64(25): 5963-5981.

Colorado Pikeminnow

Ptychocheilus lucius

Status	Endangered
Listed	March 11, 1967
Family	Cyprinidae (Minnows)
Description	Largest of the minnow family; dark olive above, whiter below, with a pointedsnout and large mouth.
Habitat	River eddies and pools.
Food	Aquatic invertebrates, insect larvae, fish.
Reproduction	Upstream or downstream migration to spawn in late spring.
Threats	River flow reduction, competition.
Range	Arizona, California, Colorado, Utah, Wyoming

Description

The Colorado pikeminnow, *Ptychocheilus lucius*, is the largest of the large Cyprinidae (minnow) family, sometimes attaining a length of 5 ft (1.5 m) and a weight of 80 lb (36 kg). It is long and slender, with a pointed snout and flattened head. Adults are dark olive above, whiter below. A voracious predator, it has a large mouth with long, fragile gill arch wells that are designed for grasping prey. This fish is also called the Colorado squawfish.

Behavior

Pikeminnows are predatory feeders. Newly hatched young feed on zooplankton and insect larvae. On reaching 4 in (10 cm), they begin to prey on other fish. A long-lived fish, spawning occurs in females at about 15 years of age during the months of July and August. The pikeminnow is migratory, undertaking long-distance spawning migrations of 250 mi (400 km), round trip; homing behavior has also been noted by researchers. Pikeminnows migrate either upstream or downstream for spawning in late spring, and eggs hatch in less than four days at water temperatures of about 70°F (21°C). Newly hatched larvae drift downstream immediately after hatching, and there is apparently a long-term upstream movement of juveniles that repopulates and maintains the upstream populations of adults.

Habitat

This species has adapted to a watershed known for its variable flow, high silt loads, and turbulence. Adults spend most of their time in eddies, pools, and protected pockets just outside of the main current. Young fish are found in quieter water, usually over silt or sand bottoms.

Distribution

The pikeminnow was once found in the Colorado River basin throughout the mainstream and major tributaries from Arizona to Wyoming. By states, its range included: the Gila River basin in Arizona; the Colorado River from the Mexican border to the Nevada state line in California; the Colorado River and lower reaches of the Gunnison, White, Yampa, Dolores, San Juan, Uncompahgre, and Animas Rivers in Colorado; the San Juan and Animas Rivers in New Mexico; the Colorado River mainstream in Nevada; the entire reach of the Colorado and Green Rivers, and the San Juan, White, and Dolores Rivers in Utah; and the Green River in Wyoming.

Pikeminnow, photograph. U. S. Fish and Wildlife Service. Reproduced by permission.

Remaining Colorado pikeminnow occur for the most part in the Green River in Utah, and in the Yampa and Colorado Rivers in Colorado and portions of Utah. The first Colorado pikeminnow reported from Wyoming in nearly 30 years was captured, identified, and released unharmed in August 1990 by a zoology professor from Arizona State University. The adult pikeminnow was found in the Little Snake River a few miles north of the Colorado-Wyoming border. Although this report was significant and prompted new sampling in the Wyoming section of the Upper Colorado River basin, biologists were only cautiously optimistic because adult pikeminnows have been known to migrate long distances during spawning periods; one theory was that the fish was a member of an unknown Wyoming population, but it also could have been far upstream from its normal range.

The fish is thought to be absent from the lower Colorado River and rare throughout the remainder of the range. It was probably extirpated from the Gila River basin in Arizona by 1990, but rein-

troduction of the species is ongoing. The U. S. Fish and Wildlife Service lists the species as endangered in Arizona, California, Colorado, Utah, and Wyoming.

Threats

The Colorado River was once one of the world's most turbulent rivers. Fish thriving in its turbid and highly mineralized waters were specially adapted to these extreme conditions, and the pikeminnow was plentiful. Many early settlers preferred the "white, flaky, and sweet" flesh of the pikeminnow over any of the native trout.

Since the construction of Hoover Dam in the 1930s and subsequent massive water control projects on the Colorado, water flow has been greatly reduced, radically altering the riverine environment. The decline in pikeminnows has been especially pronounced in areas below reservoirs, which are characterized by extreme water temperature fluctuations, altered flow patterns, lower turbidity, higher salinity, and the presence of introduced fishes, such as the red shiner, redside shiner, and green sunfish.

Conservation and Recovery

As a part of the effort to recover the Colorado pikeminnow, the U. S. Fish and Wildlife Service (FWS) and the Arizona Game and Fish Department began a collaborative project to establish experimental populations in Arizona's Salt and Verde Rivers. In 1985 over 175,000 fingerlings from the Dexter National Fish Hatchery in New Mexico were introduced into those rivers. In 1987, 100,000 more were released.

Also in 1987, the FWS proposed that a third experimental population be established in the main Colorado channel between Imperial Dam and Parker Dam. Under this plan, 100,000 fingerlings would be released the first year, followed by annual restockings over the next 10 years. The FWS hopes to establish a sport fishery for the pikeminnow in the lower Colorado River. A special FWS regulation will allow anglers to take pikeminnows in this stretch of the river, as long as they comply with all other state regulations.

In March 1994, the FWS published the final rule designating critical habitat for the Colorado pikeminnow in portions of the upper basin of the Colorado, Green, Yampa, White, and San Juan Rivers; there is no critical habitat designated in the lower basin. The critical habitat designation will help to focus conservation activities by identifying areas that contain primary constituent elements. In determining which areas to designate as critical habitat for a species, the FWS considers physical and biological attributes that are essential to the Colorado pikeminnow.

Contacts

U. S. Fish and Wildlife Service
Regional Office, Division of Endangered Species
Eastside Federal Complex
911 N. E. 11th Ave.
Portland, Oregon 97232-4181
Telephone: (503) 231-6121
http://pacific.fws.gov/

U. S. Fish and Wildlife Service
Regional Office, Division of Endangered Species
P.O. Box 1306
Albuquerque, New Mexico 87103-1306
Telephone: (505) 248-6911
Fax: (505) 248-6915
http://southwest.fws.gov/

U. S. Fish and Wildlife Service
Regional Office, Division of Endangered Species
P.O. Box 25486
Denver Federal Center
Denver, Colorado 80225
http://www.r6.fws.gov/

References

Stalnaker, C. B., and P. B. Holden. 1973. "Changes in Native Fish Distribution in the Green River System, Utah-Colorado." *Utah Academy Proceedings* 50 (1): 25-32.

U. S. Fish and Wildlife Service. 1978. "Colorado Squawfish Recovery Plan." U. S. Fish and Wildlife Service, Denver.

Vanicek, C. D., and R. H. Kramer. 1969. "Life History of the Colorado Squawfish and the Colorado Chub in the Green River in Dinosaur National Monument." *Transactions of the American Fisheries Society* 98 (2): 193-208.

Loach Minnow

Rhinichthys cobitis

Status	Threatened
Listed	October 28, 1986
Family	Cyprinidae (Minnows)
Description	Slender, olive-colored minnow with an oblique mouth and upturned eyes.
Habitat	Swift-flowing, perennial streams and rivers.
Reproduction	Unknown.
Food	Insects and plant matter.
Threats	Habitat destruction, degradation of water quality, competition with introduced fishes.
Range	Arizona, New Mexico

Description

The slender, olive-colored loach minnow, *Rhinichthys (=Tiaroga) cobitis,* is the only species in its genus. It is typically less than 3.1 in (7.9 cm) in length. It is characterized by a highly oblique terminal mouth, eyes that point markedly upward, and a group of dirty white spots at the base of the dorsal and tail fins. Breeding males develop vivid red-orange markings, particularly on the belly.

Behavior

The loach minnow has not been studied thoroughly. It is omnivorous, feeding on the stream bottom on filamentous algae, zooplankton, crustaceans, and aquatic insects.

Habitat

The loach minnow inhabits streams with perennial flow and is concentrated in shallow, turbulent riffles over a cobble substrate. Recurrent flooding keeps the substrate free of silt and sediments and, because it is better adapted to strong currents, allows the loach minnow to maintain its population against encroaching non-native fishes. The semi-desert to desert region the fish inhabits is composed of plateaus, plains, basins, and many isolated mountain ranges.

Distribution

This species was once common locally throughout much of the Verde, Salt, San Pedro, San Francisco, and Gila River systems. It inhabited mainstreams and tributaries up to about 7,200 ft (2,195 m) in elevation. It is thought that the fish once inhabited about 1,750 mi (2,816 km) of stream habitat.

The loach minnow now inhabits a greatly reduced range. In Arizona it is found in Aravaipa Creek (Graham and Pinal counties), the Blue River (Greenlee County), and the White River near the confluence of the mainstem and the East Fork (Navajo County). In New Mexico it survives in the headwaters of the Gila River (Gila, Grant, and Catron Counties) and in portions of the San Francisco and Tularosa rivers and Whitewater Creek (Catron County).

The loach minnow population in the East Fork and mainstem White River on the White Mountain Apache Indian Reservation in Arizona was sampled during the summer and fall of 1989. Not much was known about this population, which was rediscovered in 1985. Researchers concluded that the loach minnow was much more abundant and widespread in the East Fork than previously thought. Still, the current range totals only about 15% of the historic

Loach Minnow, photograph by John Rinne, USFS. Reproduced by permission.

range for this fish. This species occurred historically in the San Pedro River in Sonora, Mexico, but habitat there has been largely destroyed by diversion of water for irrigation.

Threats

This species' range and population size have been reduced by habitat destruction and the introduction of exotic fish species that prey upon it or compete for food and space resources.

Habitat loss has occurred as a result of river and stream alterations (dams, diversions, channelization, groundwater pumping, mining, timber production, grazing) that 1) reduce or alter stream flows (including changing flooding patterns), 2) increase and decrease water temperatures, 3) increase erosion and siltation, and 4) result in the destruction of marshes and backwaters and the removal of riparian vegetation.

The loach minnow is especially sensitive to sedimentation, reductions in stream flow, and im-

poundments that flood required flowing water habitats.

Other fishes in the habitat are also threatened by these changing conditions. By the late 1980s more than a third of the basin's endemic fishes were classified as endangered or threatened under federal law, and an additional 35% were considered in jeopardy by state wildlife offices.

Conservation and Recovery

In March 1994 the U. S. Fish and Wildlife Service (FWS) designated critical habitat for the loach minnow in approximately 159 miles (257 km) of portions of the Gila River in Grant and Catron Counties, New Mexico; the San Francisco and Tularosa Rivers and Dry Blue Creek, Catron County, New Mexico; the San Francisco and Blue Rivers and Campbell Blue Creek, Greenlee County, Arizona; and Aravaipa Creek in Graham and Pinal Counties, Arizona.

Large sections of the remaining inhabited streams occur on public lands. Seventy-five percent of Aravaipa Creek is protected by its designation as the Aravaipa Canyon Wilderness. Defenders of Wildlife administers portions of the headwaters as the George Whittell Wildlife Preserve. The Blue River is contained within the Apache-Sitgreaves National Forest. The Gila River flows through the Gila National Forest, which includes the Gila Wilderness, the Lower Gila River Bird Habitat Management Area, and the Gila River Research Natural Area—all managed by the Forest Service. The Forest Service also administers major portions of the San Francisco and Tularosa Rivers and Whitewater Creek. The White River population occurs on the Fort Apache Indian Reservation and has been the focus of recovery efforts conducted by the tribal council and with the Bureau of Indian Affairs.

The Middle Box Canyon on the Gila River (Grant County, New Mexico) was proposed as the site for construction of the Conner Dam and Reservoir. The Southwest New Mexico Industrial Development Corporation, the Hooker Dam Association, the Arizona Cattle Growers Association, the Arizona Mining Association, the Town of Silver City, New Mexico, and the Soil Conservation Service of New Mexico, among others, opposed federal listing of the loach minnow because it might stop or slow construction of the dam. Central Arizona Project Upper Gila Water Supply damming/impoundment plans also threatened the species. The continued conflict over water rights in the region propelled the loach minnow and other Gila River fishes into the limelight of controversy at the beginning of the twenty-first century.

Studies to determine the feasibility of reintroduction of the fish to the San Pedro River continued as funding allowed. In addition, a cooperative project (Bureau of Land Management, FWS, and Arizona Game and Fish Department) was initiated to remove exotic fishes from and prevent their movement back into Aravaipa Creek.

Contact

U. S. Fish and Wildlife Service
Regional Office, Division of Endangered Species
P.O. Box 1306
Albuquerque, New Mexico 87103-1306
Telephone: (505) 248-6911
Fax: (505) 248-6915
http://southwest.fws.gov/

References

Propst, D. L. 1986. "Distribution, Status, and Biology of the Loach Minnow in the Gila River Basin." New Mexico Department of Game and Fish, Santa Fe.

U. S. Fish and Wildlife Service. 1986. "Determination of Threatened Status for the Loach Minnow." *Federal Register* 51 (208): 39468-39478.

U. S. Fish and Wildlife Service. 1991. "Loach Minnow Recovery Plan." U. S. Fish and Wildlife Service, Albuquerque.

U. S. Forest Service. 1985. "Proposed Gila National Forest Plan." USFS Southwestern Region, Albuquerque.

Foskett Speckled Dace

Rhinichthys osculus ssp.

Status	Threatened
Listed	March 28, 1985
Family	Cyprinidae (Minnows)
Description	Silvery dace with dark blotches.
Habitat	Freshwater springs and outflows.
Food	Detritus, fish eggs.
Reproduction	Spawns in June and July.
Threats	Limited distribution, habitat destruction, pollution.
Range	Oregon

Description

The silvery Foskett speckled dace ranges from 1.8-3.1 in (4.5-8 cm) in length. It has large eyes and is often marked with dark blotches on its rear half. The belly may turn orange or red during breeding season. Breeding behavior has not been observed but it is thought that the species spawns on hard substrates between late May and early June.

Behavior

This dace, which lives to 3 years, appears to be non-territorial but collects in small schools and is rarely found singly. It is a bottom browser, feeding on insects, detritus, and other fishes' eggs. It spawns in June and July.

It is not know if this species is migratory but larvae and juvenile dace have been observed in the marsh 6-10 ft (1.8-3.1 m) away from the adult population, and so either the adults migrated to spawn or the larvae or juveniles migrated.

Habitat

This species is restricted to a single spring system, comprised on Foskett Spring and Dace Spring, and the overflow rivulets with mud substrates. Most of the population occurs in the springhole, which is about 6 ft (1.8 m) in diameter and 6-12 in (15.2-30.5 cm) deep. The outflow rivulets are only a few inches (or centimeters) wide and deep. A few individuals have been observed in the cattle tracks where water seeps continuously. The spring brook eventually turns into a marsh and finally dries up before reaching the bed of Coleman Lake.

The area around the spring supports grasses and other aquatic vegetation, including cattails. Cover that the fishes utilize include overhanging grasses, grass roots, and algae. The water is clear, of fairly constant temperature, and with slow but significant currents.

Distribution

The Foskett speckled dace is endemic to a small spring system in the Coleman Basin on the west side of Warner Valley (Lake County) in arid south-central Oregon.

Foskett speckled dace still occurs in portions of the Foskett Spring system. In 1982, an attempt was made to transplant the fish to other ponds in the region with indifferent success. When this species was federally listed in 1985, less than 1,500 individuals survived, and the number has not appreciably increased. In 1998, the population was estimated at 200 individuals in the source pool, 700 in the spring brook, and 27,000 in the shallow pool marsh.

Threats

This species is threatened by actual or potential modification of its springs habitat. Ground water

Foskett Speckled Dace, photograph. U. S. Fish and Wildlife Service. Reproduced by permission.

levels in the area have been lowered by pumping to support irrigation agriculture and may eventually decrease the flow of the Foskett Spring, which is already considered minimal. Ditching or otherwise tampering with the pools and outflows would probably destroy the entire spring system. Trampling by livestock that come to drink at the spring is a particular problem.

The spring hole was excavated and damned at some point to form a small reservoir, and the dace population may have reached its peak when the reservoir was functional. The population seems to be restricted by the size of the habitat, and Foskett Spring itself will probably never support more than 2,000 individuals. The wetland on the edge of normally dry Coleman Lake may have formerly provided some habitat, but it is now either occupied by cattails or trampled by cattle.

Other threats include encroachment of vegetation (cattails and rushes), decreases in the level of dissolved oxygen, pumping of groundwater, chan-

nelization, decreased water levels and flow, and erosion and siltation.

Conservation and Recovery

The Foskett speckled dace has been transplanted to an excavated area at the spring source, Dace Spring, located just south of Foskett Spring. This artificial habitat is in a muddy, well-vegetated situation. Attempts to transplant the fish into other nearby protected springs will continue. Both springs that contain the dace are in a geothermal area, so it is probable that other suitable habitat is available.

The Bureau of Land Management owns Dace Spring and expects to acquire Foskett Spring through a land exchange with the private owner. This will permit fencing of the habitat, removal of cattle that trample the area, monitoring spring water, and modifying the habitat to create deeper water with moderate vegetative cover.

Contact

Regional Office of Endangered Species
U.S. Fish and Wildlife Service
Eastside Federal Complex
911 N. E. 11th Ave.
Portland, Oregon 97232-4181
Telephone: (503) 231-6121
http://pacific.fws.gov/

References

Bond. C. E. 1973. "Keys to Oregon Freshwater Fishes." Technical Bulletin 58. Oregon State University, Agricultural Experiment Station.

Bond, C. E. 1974. "Endangered Plants and Animals of Oregon; Fishes." Special Report 205. Oregon State University, Agricultural Experiment Station.

U.S. Fish and Wildlife Service. 1985. "Determination of Threatened Status for Hutton Tui Chub and Foskett Speckled Dace." *Federal Register* 50: 12302-12306.

Independence Valley Speckled Dace

Rhinichthys osculus lethoporus

Status	Endangered
Listed	October 10, 1989
Family	Cyprinidae (Minnow)
Description	Small minnow with olive green back, silvery belly, and black spots.
Habitat	Spring and outflow.
Food	Insects.
Reproduction	Presumably spawns in mid-summer.
Threats	Limited distribution, low numbers, water diversion, introduced fish species.
Range	Nevada

Description

The Independence Valley speckled dace, *Rhinichthys osculus lethoporus*, is distinguished from other speckled dace by a more laterally compressed body. It differs from the Clover Valley speckled dace, found in nearby springs, by a less developed lateral line, fewer number of pectoral fin rays, and a straighter, more oblique mouth.

Behavior

The speckled dace is an adaptable species, able to occupy a variety of habitats, from cold streams and rivers with rocky bottoms to thermal springs with silt bottoms. This adaptability has enabled it to survive in environments too harsh for other species. The isolation of populations has led to a large number of forms that are recognized as subspecies. They feed primarily on insects, and are presumed to spawn in mid-summer.

Habitat

Independence Valley speckled dace are found in a temperate, permanent desert stream/marsh fed by numerous springs. Although known as Independence Valley Warm Springs, these springs are not cited as thermal waters. The speckled dace are found primarily in the shallow water of the marsh of this spring system among the sedges and grasses. It is believed that they also occupied the stream, but were forced out due to predation by non-native fish species such as rainbow trout, largemouth bass, and bluegill. No data exist on the flow velocities or temperatures of habitat currently occupied by Independence Valley speckled dace, but preliminary data show the speckled dace inhabit a large portion of the marsh as well as two seep areas northeast of the marsh.

The flows from Independence Valley Warm Springs are impounded into two reservoirs. The upper, and shallower of the two, is roughly 5 ft (1.5 m) deep and 98 ft (30 m) wide. The lower reservoir is approximately 10 ft (3 m) deep with a diameter of approximately 148 ft (45 m). A dense mat of vegetation consisting mostly of stonewort with some water milfoil and hornwort covered the bottom of the large reservoir. The edges of the pond are lined with pondweed. When flows are high, all flows from the upper reservoir enter the lower one. Water flows from the lower impoundment through a looping channel for 200 ft (70 m) before entering a marsh. Once entering the marsh, the channel disappears, becoming eroded and shallow. Water depth in the channel ranges from 4 to 18 in (10 to 46 cm), with a shallower water depth in the marsh. Several small ponds occurred in the marsh area, one approximately 500 ft (152 m) northeast of the lower reservoir and one approximately 1,000 ft (305 m) to the southeast. Approximately 25 speckled dace were observed in October 1994. Several springheads located further south of this system have not been extensively mapped.

Distribution

Independence Valley warm springs was surveyed in 1983, and only 33 Independence Valley speckled dace were minnow trapped from the lower marsh. The Nevada Division of Wildlife surveyed the area in 1992 and captured only one speckled dace in the shallowest area of the marsh. In October 1994, Nevada Division of Wildlife and U. S. Fish and Wildlife Service personnel collected and released five individuals and observed approximately 20 more in the extensive marsh area.

Based on general habitat characteristics of other closely related dace species, the Independence Valley speckled dace should have been found throughout the Independence Valley Warm Springs system, not just the marshy area below the springs. It is believed that the historical range of the Independence Valley speckled dace was throughout the spring system and its associated marsh. The vast marsh area has not been intensively surveyed in the past 11 years so the current distribution is unknown. It is unclear whether the distribution of the Independence Valley speckled dace has expanded or diminished since the subspecies was listed.

Threats

The building and manipulation of reservoirs for irrigation was thought to be a serious threat to both speckled dace due to the reduction of available stream/outflow habitat and pond/reservoir habitat when water levels were regulated. At the turn of the twenty-first century, in Independence Valley no lands were being irrigated for crop production and no land had been used for crop production for over 10 years. The reservoirs and stream outflows had not been used for irrigation for approximately the same amount of time. The landowner stated that no plans exist for irrigation to occur on the property the fish presently occupy.

Conservation and Recovery

The reservoirs at Independence Valley Warm Springs continue to be a popular fishing area. Bluegill were established years ago and are still found in the reservoir. Despite the largemouth bass and bluegill in the reservoir and outflow, speckled dace persist in the marsh, but determining how the population is affected remains to be resolved. Removal of the normative fish and establishment of an alternative fishery at another location remains the most viable option for both speckled dace recovery and meeting anglers needs. Essential to the recovery of the Independence Valley speckled dace is the removal and relocation of the largemouth bass and bluegill that inhabit the stream, segments of the marsh, and the reservoir at Independence Valley Warm Springs. Since the ranch is a fairly popular fishing area, the bass could be relocated nearby to protect the Independence Valley speckled dace and still provide a sport fishery.

Contacts

U. S. Fish and Wildlife Service
Regional Office, Division of Endangered Species
Eastside Federal Complex
911 N. E. 11th Ave.
Portland, Oregon 97232-4181
http://pacific.fws.gov/

U. S. Fish and Wildlife Service
4600 Kietzke Lane, Building C
Reno, Nevada 89502

References

Hubbs, C. L., R. R. Miller, and L. C. Hubbs. 1974. *Hydrographic History and Relict Fishes of the North Central Great Basin.* Memoirs of the California Academy of Sciences. Volume 7.

McNatt, R. M. 1988. "Field Trip Report on Investigation of Three Speckled Dace Sites in Clover Valley, Nevada." U. S. Fish and Wildlife Service, Great Basin Complex, Reno, Nevada.

Vinyard, G. L. 1984. "A Status Report about the Independence Valley Speckled Dace (*Rhinichthys osculus lethoporus*), Independence Valley Tui Chub (*Gila bicolor isolata*), and Clover Valley Speckled Dace (*Rhinichthys osculus oligoporus*); Three Fishes Restricted to the Northeastern Portion of Nevada." U. S. Fish and Wildlife Service, Reno, Nevada.

Ash Meadows Speckled Dace

Rhinichthys osculus nevadensis

Status	Endangered
Listed	September 2, 1983
Family	Cyprinidae (Minnows)
Description	Small, plain fish with blotches on the sides.
Habitat	Warm springs and outflows.
Food	Aquatic fauna.
Reproduction	Spawns in early spring and late summer.
Threats	Groundwater pumping, predation by introduced fish species.
Range	Nevada

Peter Sanchez

Description

The *Rhinichthys osculus nevadensis* (Ash Meadows speckled dace) is a small silvery slender minnow about 3 in (7 cm) long. It is plain except for its poorly defined blotches and speckles on the sides. It has small eyes, small, irregularly place scales, and a small subterminal mouth with a barbel at each corner. All fish in the genus have a double row of teeth in the pharynx. Body coloration varies widely within a population. Generally, the dorsum is olive-gray blending ventrally to golden. Black spots frequently cover the body and there may be one or two distinct, black lateral strips. It reaches a maximum length of approximately 3.9 in (10 cm) and may live as long as four years.

This fish was first described in 1893 as a full species, *Rhinichthys nevadensis.* However, in 1948, it was determined to be a subspecies of *Rhinichthys osculus.*

Behavior

The Ash Meadows speckled dace reaches maturity in the second summer. It spawns once in early spring and again in late summer. It feeds on a variety of small aquatic animals that inhabit the thermal springs.

Speckled dace generally prefer flowing streams where they feed on drifting insects. Spawning occurs primarily during the spring and summer over stream riffles where eggs are broadcast by females and fertilized as they drift to the substrate.

Habitat

The Ash Meadows speckled dace occurs in spring systems and aquatic habitats formed by the spring waters. It is known to occur in headwater spring pools, spring outflow creeks, and marshes formed by the spring flows. It also occurs in irrigation ditches and canals that utilize the spring flows for irrigation. The seeps and springs comprising Ash Meadows formerly flowed into an extensive marsh that was drained in the mid-1960s. Thunderstorms occasionally cause flood waters to discharge from Ash Meadows into the Amargosa River.

Distribution

The Ash Meadows speckled dace has not been found outside of Ash Meadows. It formerly inhabited much of the interconnected surface warm springs and outflows.

Dace populations and suitable habitat have been severely reduced by agricultural and residential development and groundwater pumping. Manipulation of springs and their outflows reduced the number of populations so that speckled dace are presently found only in the Bradford Springs, Big Spring, Tubbs Springs, and Jackrabbit Spring. The population in Jackrabbit Spring was estimated at zero and 11 in 1982 and 1983, respectively, and the population in Big Spring was estimated at 15 and 13 in these same two respective years. Speckled dace populations continued downstream some distance from both of these springs when these estimates were made, however, no estimate of population size in these streams was attempted. Tubbs Spring spring pool population was estimated at 35. No population estimates have been made in Bradford Springs. The total population size of Ash Meadows speckled dace is estimated at 500. The habitats occupied by dace, and 164 ft (50 m) on both sides of the aquatic environment, are designated critical habitat for the speckled dace. Much of this area is also critical habitat for the Ash Meadows Amargosa pupfish and spring-loving centaury. Critical habitat for the speckled dace includes approximately 36 acres (14 hectares).

Threats

A number of exotic fish species, such as the mosquitofish and black molly have been introduced to Ash Meadows where they compete with and prey on native fishes. The Ash Meadows killifish (*Empetrichthys merriami*), now extinct, was eliminated by predation from introduced species.

Conservation and Recovery

The critical habitat of the Ash Meadows speckled dace is now owned by the Fish and Wildlife Service and is protected against development. However, non-native fish should be eliminated from its habitat. The populations of the Ash Meadows speckled dace should be monitored, and research undertaken into its biology and habitat needs. A captive-breeding population should be establishes, and consideration given to reestablishing extirpated populations where the habitat is suitable.

Contact

U. S. Fish and Wildlife Service Regional Office
Division of Endangered Species
Eastside Federal Building
911 N. E. 11th Ave.
Portland, Oregon 97232-4181
Telephone: (503) 231-6121
http://pacific.fws.gov/

U.S. Fish and Wildlife Service
Nevada Fish and Wildlife Office
1340 Financial Boulevard, Suite 234
Reno, Nevada, 89502-7147
Telephone: (775) 861-6300

References

Gilbert, C. H. 1983. "Report on the Fishes of the Death Valley Expedition Collected in Southern California and Nevada in 1891 with Descriptions of New Species." *North American Fauna* 7:220-234.

Soltz, D. L., and R. J. Naiman, eds. 1978. "The Natural History of Native Fishes in the Death Valley System" *Natural History Museum of Los Angeles County, Science Series* 30:17.

U.S. Fish and Wildlife Service. 1983. "Determination of Endangered Status and Critical Habitat for Two Fish Species in Ash Meadows, Nevada," *Federal Register* 48(172): 40178-40186.

Williams, J. E. and D. W. Sada. 1985. "Status of Two Endangered Fishes from Two Springs in Ash Meadows, Nevada." *Southwestern Naturalist* 30(4): 475-484.

Clover Valley Speckled Dace

Rhinichthys osculus oligoporus

Status	Endangered
Listed	October 10, 1989
Family	Cyprinidae (Minnow)
Description	Small minnow with olive-green back, silvery belly, and black spots.
Habitat	Springs and outflows.
Food	Insects.
Reproduction	Presumably spawns in mid-summer.
Threats	Limited distribution, water diversion, introduced fish species.
Range	Nevada

Description

Clover Valley speckled dace, *Rhinichthys osculus oligoporus*, is a small minnow that grows to 4 in (10.2 cm). It has an olive-green back, silver or gold abdomen, and a random pattern of black spots. It is distinguished from other speckled dace by its less developed lateral stripe, the location of its pectoral fins, and the number of pectoral fin rays.

Behavior

The speckled dace is an adaptable species, able to occupy a variety of habitats, from cold streams and rivers with rocky bottoms to thermal springs with silt bottoms. This adaptability has enabled it to survive in environments too harsh for other species. The isolation of populations has led to a large number of forms that are recognized as subspecies. They feed primarily on insects and are presumed to spawn in mid-summer.

Habitat

Clover Valley speckled dace are found primarily in reservoirs and outflows of the three spring systems: Clover Valley Warm Springs, Wright Ranch Spring, and Bradish Spring. There do not appear to be any associated marshes with these springs, only the outflows that have been heavily modified. The introduction of rainbow trout appears to have affected the speckled dace in the past. Because access to the properties for conducting studies has not been permitted, details of Clover Valley speckled dace seasonal habitat requirements, population size, distribution over time, reproductive potential, and available habitat are unknown.

Ground water in Clover Valley is derived principally from precipitation on the east slope of the East Humboldt Range and to a lesser extent from the north side of Spruce Mountain and the west slope of the Chase Spring Mountains. Gravity-fed springs and seeps issue from the lower alluvial slopes along the west side of the valley and are used primarily for supplemental irrigation of meadows. The three spring systems in the valley currently inhabited by the Clover Valley speckled dace are Clover Valley Warm Springs, Wright Ranch Spring, and Bradish Spring. All of these springs are privately owned and have been modified to provide water for agricultural purposes.

Clover Valley Warm Spring is impounded immediately downstream of the springhead into a small reservoir approximately 10 ft (3 m) wide and 2 ft (0.6 m) deep. Temperatures recorded in the spring system have ranged from 65 to 67°F (18.3 and 19.4°C) to and seem to change accordingly with ambient air temperature further downstream.

There are two outflows from the reservoir. The riparian areas in the first are composed primarily of sedges and grasses, while rush and hard-stem bulrush are common. Several types of mesic forbs were

Gary Vinyard

found only occasionally in the riparian zone. Aquatic vegetation was mostly watercress and algae. Surveys found this section to be relatively rich in aquatic insects. Leeches, scuds (amphipod crustaceans, such as beach fleas), caddis flies, and native snails were all abundant in the channel. While dragon fly larvae were common, non-native snails were found occasionally, and giant water bugs were rarely encountered.

The second section of the original channel has been divided with irrigation ditches. The irrigated section shows signs of heavy livestock use, resulting in compaction. The aquatic plants and insects are in lower abundance than in the first section. In the past, irrigation practices completely dewatered the natural stream channel.

Distribution

In October 1995, the Nevada Division of Wildlife surveyed the Clover Valley Warm Springs area and the two outflows for distribution and population

numbers of Clover Valley speckled dace. There are two outflows for this spring: presumably the original channel and an irrigation ditch. The resulting population estimates were 13,500 for the first section and 10,440 for the second. The Wright Spring population was estimated at 1,500 individuals occupying the pond and 12,500 inhabiting the outflows. The Brandish Spring population could not be surveyed because permission to access the property could not be obtained.

Threats

Initial surveys for Clover Valley speckled dace in 1934 indicated that springs occupied by the speckled dace had been altered at a much earlier date. Outflows from the springs had been impounded into reservoirs before being distributed to various irrigation ditches. The habitat below the reservoirs was periodically dewatered on the irrigation schedule. At the time of listing, the irrigation usage continued, and speckled dace populations were restricted to habitats within the reservoirs and seasonally in the outflows. In the most recent survey of 1995, populations of speckled dace were present at both the Clover Valley Warm Springs and Wright Ranch Spring areas. The outflows that were the most stable or had the greatest flow of water also had the largest number of speckled dace.

Conservation and Recovery

This dace is threatened by its limited distribution, diversion of the spring water, and predation by introduced fish species. These springs have long been impounded for irrigation purposes, limiting the dace to the outflow and certain sections of the reservoir. Often the reservoirs are stocked with sport fish, such as rainbow trout (*Salmo gairdneri*), largemouth bass (*Micropterus salmoides*), and bluegill (*Lepomis machrochirus*), which feed on the dace, forcing it to retreat to areas safe from the predatory species.

So far the owners of the springs have not been willing to sign agreements to conserve the species. One has indicated an intention to increase the use of a spring for irrigation, while another plans to introduce game fish into a reservoir, despite the danger to the Clover Valley speckled dace. The U. S. Fish and Wildlife Service hopes that it will be able to obtain conservation easements and manage the springs to protect the dace.

Contacts

U. S. Fish and Wildlife Service
Regional Office, Division of Endangered Species
Eastside Federal Complex
911 N. E. 11th Ave.
Portland, Oregon 97232-4181
(503) 231-6121
http://pacific.fws.gov/

U. S. Fish and Wildlife Service
4600 Kietzke Lane, Building C
Reno, Nevada 89502

References

Hubbs, C. L., R. R. Miller, and L. C. Hubbs. 1974. *Hydrographic History and Relict Fishes of the North Central Great Basin.* Memoirs of the California Academy of Sciences. Volume 7.

McNatt, R. M. 1988. "Field Trip Report on Investigation of Three Speckled Dace Sites in Clover Valley, Nevada." U. S. Fish and Wildlife Service, Great Basin Complex, Reno, Nevada.

Minckley, W. L., and J. E. Deacon. 1968. "Southwestern Fishes and the Enigma of Endangered Species.'" *Science* 159: 1424-1432.

Vinyard, G. L. 1984. "A Status Report about the independence Valley Speckled Dace (*Rhinichthys osculus lethoporus*), Independence Valley Tui Chub (*Gila bicolor isolata*), and Clover Valley Speckled Dace (*Rhinichthys osculus oligoporus*); Three Fishes Restricted to the Northeastern Portion of Nevada." U. S. Fish and Wildlife Service, Reno, Nevada.

Kendall Warm Springs Dace

Rhinichthys osculus thermalis

Status	Endangered
Listed	October 13, 1970
Family	Cyprinidae (Minnows)
Description	Small fish; males are bright purple, females are olive green.
Habitat	Warm springs and seeps.
Food	Aquatic insects.
Reproduction	Spawns several times a year.
Threats	Water pollution, habitat destruction.
Range	Wyoming

Description

The Kendall Warm Springs dace, *Rhinichthys osculus thermalis*, is a small minnow about 2 in (5.4 cm) long. Breeding males are often a bright purple color; females are typically dull olive green.

This dace was first given the name *Apocope osculus thermalis.* The 1970 revision of Wyoming Fishes considered the Kendall Warm Springs dace and the Green River dace (*R. o. yarrowi*) to make up a single species. However, further comparison showed that the Kendall dace differed by having fewer scales and fin rays, a larger head and fins, and a smaller body. Its taxonomic status remains unclear.

Behavior

Although the Kendall Warm Springs dace has not been closely studied, spawning probably occurs several times a year, if not year round. It is thought that females lay several hundred eggs. Dace usually gather in small schools, due either to space limitations or to an inborn behavioral preference. A skittering flight to the nearest clump of plants is a typical reaction to danger, although some flee to the deeper, turbulent areas in the main current of its spring habitat.

Although the diet of the Kendall Warm Springs dace has not been confirmed, other *R. osculus* species are omnivorous with insects comprising an important food source.

Habitat

Kendall Warm Springs in Wyoming consists of numerous seeps and springs scattered along the north face of a limestone ridge at an elevation of 7,840 ft (2,390 m) in the Bridger-Teton National Forest. The spring outflow flows southwest for 984 ft (300 m) before cascading into the Green River over an embankment formed by the water's mineral deposits. Water from the springs has a constant temperature of 85°F (29°C). It is slightly alkaline, mineralized, and high in dissolved solids.

Vegetation near the spring complex is limited to various grasses, forbs, and low-growing shrubs and trees, such as willow and sagebrush. Monkeyflower and moss are the dominant aquatic plants in the upper pool; below that area, sage pondweed, moss, and stonewart predominate. Overhanging vegetation is essential for the dace's cover.

Distribution

The Kendall Warm Springs dace has probably always been restricted to the Kendall Warm Springs near the Green River drainage in Sublette County, Wyoming.

Kendall Warm Springs Dace, photograph by William R. Gould. Reproduced by permission.

Because of the fish's small size and the inefficiency of survey techniques, population figures are uncertain. In 1934, biologists estimated the total population as between 200,000 and 500,000 individuals. Recent observations suggest that even the lower figure may have been exaggerated. It is thought that the current maximum population is only a few thousand individuals.

Threats

Over the course of many years, human activities have altered the Kendall Warm Springs dace's habitat. A road built across the creek built before 1934 is still the main access route to the upper Green River and the northern Bridger Wilderness. A culvert divides the upper half of the dace population from the lower. Several rock dams have been built over the years to provide small bathing and soaking pools, and people have used the pools to wash clothes. The presence of detergents in the water has probably had a detrimental effect on the fish populations.

Conservation and Recovery

To preserve water quality, the Forest Service closed the springs to bathing and prohibited the use of soaps, detergents, and bleaches. For many years, fishermen used Kendall dace as fish bait until prohibited by the Wyoming Game and Fish Department in the early 1960s. One hundred sixty acres (64 hectares) have been designated by the Forest Service as the Kendall Warm Springs Biological Management Unit. The boundaries include most of the small watershed and surrounding land. Because of this designation, mineral exploration, seining, and trapping are prohibited. The immediate area around the springs has been fenced and interpretive signs posted. To control traffic along the creek, vehicle access has been blocked.

The thermal spring and surrounding land may qualify as a research natural area. If so, a formal designation could provide more complete habitat protection.

Contact

Regional Office of Endangered Species
U.S. Fish and Wildlife Service
P.O. Box 25486
Denver Federal Center
Denver, Colorado 80225
http://www.r6.fws.gov/

References

Baxter, G. T., and J. R. Simon. 1970. "Wyoming Fishes." Bulletin 4. Game and Fish Department, Cheyenne.

Binns, N. A. 1978. "Habitat Structure of Kendall Warm Springs, with Reference to the Endangered Kendall Warm Springs Dace." Fisheries Technical Bulletin No. 3, Wyoming Game and Fish Department, Cheyenne.

U.S. Fish and Wildlife Service. 1982. "Kendall Warm Springs Dace Recovery Plan." U.S. Fish and Wildlife Service, Denver.

Modoc Sucker

Catostomus microps

Status	Endangered
Listed	June 11, 1985
Family	Catostomidae (Sucker)
Description	Dwarf, olive-gray or olive-green with a white to yellow belly.
Habitat	Small streams with shallow pools and good cover.
Food	Aquatic invertebrates, algae, detritus.
Reproduction	Spawns May and June.
Threats	Siltation, hybridization, habitat alteration.
Range	California

Description

The Modoc sucker, *Catostomus microps*, is a dwarf species of the family Catostomidae. Individuals begin to mature at 2.75-3.3 in (7-8.5 cm) with few adults exceeding 4.2 in (18 cm) in length. The Modoc sucker is deep gray to bluish or green-brown to deep gray-olive above. The sides lighten to yellow or white on the belly. It is cream-colored to white ventrally, with caudal, pelvic and pectoral fins that are a light yellowish orange. A bright orange band appears on the sides of the males during spawning season.

Behavior

The Modoc sucker feeds on bottom-dwelling invertebrates, algae, and detritus. Stomach contents have revealed that half the diet may be detritus supplemented with diatoms, filamentous algae, chironomid larvae, crustaceans, and aquatic insects.

Adult suckers usually remain close to the bottom. Large numbers of papillae and taste buds on the downward turned mouth, limited eyesight, and the position of the eyes in the middle of the head equip the sucker for bottom feeding.

During the spring, spawning runs from mid-April to the end of May, it ascends creeks or tributaries that may be dry during summer months. Depending on temperature and water quality, the spawning fish travel up to a mile upstream. When spawning, which may occur from mid-morning to late afternoon, two or three males surround a single female who releases eggs, which probably adhere to the gravel substrate. Males may or may not stimulate females with breeding tubercles.

Sexual maturity usually occurs at age three although males may mature sooner. Life expectancy is four and the oldest known specimen was five years old.

Habitat

The Modoc sucker prefers small streams with low or intermittent flow having soft sediments, clear water, and large shallow pools with overhanging trees or cliffs and undercut banks. The vegetation in the valley and meadowland habitat includes sagebrush and western juniper. Forested habitat areas contain ponderosa pine, Jeffrey pine, California black oak, California incense cedar, and white fir. The riparian areas contain cottonwood trees, aspen, willows, and tall grasses, which provide cover for the streams. Portions of Rush Creek run through a residential subdivision, farmland and pastures.

Distribution

The Modoc sucker has been found in small tributary streams of the Pit River in Modoc and Lassen counties, California. A 1978 California Department of Fish and Game survey reported the species from eight creeks: Washington, Hulbert, Turner, Willow, Ash, Dutch Flat, Johnson, and Rush. At one time, the species inhabited additional streams, but because it is restricted to small, often intermittent streams it was probably never common.

Presently, the species is restricted to portions of Turner and Rush Creeks, two small drainage systems in Modoc County. The federal government manages about half of the land and the rest is privately owned. Recent information indicates that genetically pure Modoc suckers are restricted to Turner Creek and its tributaries, Washington, Hulbert, and Johnson creeks, and to smaller unnamed feeder streams. About 1,300 individuals are estimated to inhabit this creek system.

Threats

The recent decline of the Modoc sucker can largely be attributed to habitat degradation and to hybridization with the more common Sacramento sucker (*Catostomus occidentalis*).

Severe erosion, caused by overgrazing by livestock, has increased the amount of silt carried by streams, dramatically degrading water quality. Grazing sheep and cattle trampled streambanks causing increased erosion. The flooding of pastures and channelization resulted in non-native fish hybridizing with *C. microps* reducing the purity of the populations, and diversion of water used in irrigation reduced the number and size of pools available to the sucker. Introductions of *Salmo trutta* and brown trout added competitive pressure to the Modoc sucker. Even before the federal listing of this species, the Bureau of Lands Management voluntarily removed many riparian areas from grazing, which has improved water quality in the watershed to some degree.

Waterfalls, steep gradients, and rocky rapids always separated the Modoc sucker from the Sacramento sucker, which ranges downstream in the larger creeks and reservoirs of the Pit River system. When the Sacramento sucker moved upstream to spawn, these natural barriers prevented its encroachment into Modoc sucker habitat. Artificial channeling of these streams removed many natural barriers, and now the two species are interbreeding. Ongoing hybridization could eliminate the Modoc sucker as a separate and distinct species from many streams. Redirection of stream flow has also allowed predator fish access to the Modoc sucker's habitat.

Conservation and Recovery

Critical Habitat was designated in Modoc County to include 26 mi (42 km) of stream bed and a buffer zone along the banks of Turner, Washington, Hulbert, and Johnson creeks. Through cooperation of Fish and Wildlife Service, the Forest Service, and the California Department of Fish and Game, the Modoc sucker has been reintroduced into Turner Creek, and plans have been developed to rehabilitate Rush Creek and reintroduce the Modoc sucker there.

The Recovery Plan calls for the protection of existing populations and the establishment of at least two additional populations. To achieve these goals, FWS recommends reducing timber rights near the habitat; revegetate and rehabilitate habitat; restrict agricultural practices that cause siltation; restrict road maintenance activities; maintain the water table and flow; remove exotic brown trout from the habitat and prevent its return; restrict cattle that damages vegetation; and prevent stream bank and channel modification. FWS also hopes that new populations can be established by acquiring private land along Johnson and Dutch Flat Creeks; fencing and stabilizing Dutch Flat Creek; and translocating wild individuals to both locations.

Contact

U.S. Fish and Wildlife Service
Division of Endangered Species
Eastside Federal Complex
911 N.E. 11th Ave
Portland, Oregon 97232
http://pacific.fws.gov/

References

California Department of Fish and Game. 1980. *At the Crossroads: A Report on the Status of California's Endangered and Rare Fish and Wildlife*. State of California Resources Agency, Sacramento.

Martin, M. 1972. "Morphology and Variation of the Modoc Sucker, *Catostomus microps* Rutter, with Notes on Feeding Adaptations." *California Fish and Game* 58:277-284.

Mills, T. J. 1980. "Life History, Status, and Management of the Modoc Sucker, *Catostomus microps* (Rutter) in California, with a Recommendation for Endangered Classification." Endangered Species Program Special Publication 80-6. California Department of Fish and Game, Inland Fish.

Moyle, P. B. and A. Marciochi. 1975. "Biology of the Modoc Sucker, *Catostomus microps*, in Northern California." *Copeia* 1975:556-560.

U.S. Fish and Wildlife Service. 1983. "Action Plan for the Recovery of the Modoc Sucker." U.S. Fish and Wildlife Service, Sacramento. 14 pp.

Warner Sucker

Catostomus warnerensis

Status	Threatened
Listed	September 27, 1985
Family	Catostomidae (Sucker)
Description	Small eyes, large scales, and a conical snout with heavy, almost blotchy mottling color; breeding males display a bright orange or reddish lateral stripe.
Habitat	Lakes, streams, and associated wetlands.
Food	Bottom feeder on algae, larvae, insects, and crustaceans.
Reproduction	Spawns upstream in the spring.
Threats	Introduced predators, dams and obstacles in spawning streams.
Range	Oregon

Description

The Warner sucker is a moderate-sized sucker, reaching a maximum length of about 20 in (51 cm). It matures at three to four years of age at a length of 5.1-6.3 in (13-16 cm). A bright orange lateral stripe is present on adults during spawning runs. The Warner Sucker is a species that was isolated in the remaining waters of a Pleistocene lake that previously covered much of the Warner Basin floor. When glaciers retreated and the climate became drier, the lake gradually disappeared.

Behavior

Although primarily lacustrine (lake-dwelling), in spring this species spawns in the headwaters of streams that feed the lakes. It requires a silt-free, gravel stream bed for spawning. Breeding probably begins when the fish reaches sexual maturity at three years of age and continues until death, possibly to nine years of age. Typical spawning usually involves one female attended by two or more males. Larvae is deposited upstream and juveniles merge in about four weeks, and the young remain in creeks near the spawning areas for several months to two years before descending to larger bodies of water. Because of dams that obstruct passage and because some populations occur in pools close to suitable spawning areas, the know migrations are short, although some individuals are known to have migrated several miles.

The diet of the Warner sucker probably consists of algae, midge larvae and other small insects, zooplankton and other small crustaceans, and organic debris. This species is primarily a nocturnal feeder and is not active during the day.

Habitat

The habitat of the Warner sucker encompasses large natural lakes and associated marshes. Early residents in the area recalled when suckers were very abundant and ascended the creeks in masses to spawn. Specimen have been collected from lakes, reservoirs, irrigation and diversion canals, streams with various substrate types, and springs. The preferred non-breeding habitat seems to be slow or still water with a high concentration of organic material. Preferred breeding habitat is gravel substrates in streams or springs. Larvae find refuge in still water at the edge of streams of ditches, sometimes in very shallow water only 1-2 in (2-5 cm) deep.

Distribution

The Warner sucker is endemic to the streams and lakes of the Warner Basin in south-central Oregon.

Warner Sucker, photograph provided by Bureau of Land Management, Alan Munhall, photographer. Reproduced by permission.

It now inhabits portions of Crump and Hart Lakes, the spillway canal north of Hart Lake, and portions of Snyder, Honey, Twentymile, and Twelvemile Creeks—all in Lake County, Oregon. Portions of Crump and Hart Lakes are included within the Hart Mountain National Wildlife Refuge. Much of the stream habitat is held by the Bureau of Land Management. Land on the valley floor is for the most part privately owned.

Between 1977 and 1991, eight surveys were conducted to locate Warner sucker populations. These surveys have shown that when adequate water is present, Warner suckers inhabit all the lakes, sloughs, and potholes in the Warner Valley. In 1992, a population estimate was conducted for the Honey Creek and Twentymile Creek drainages, resulting in estimates of 2,500 adults, 2,800 individuals, and 4,400 fry.

In 1992, drought conditions caused Hart Lake to dry up, and as many Warner suckers as could be salvaged were transported to other habitats. In 1996, the Hart Lake population had become reestablished with an estimated 500 individuals.

Threats

Dams and diversion structures, some in place since before the turn of the twentieth century, have prevented this sucker from reaching its spawning and rearing grounds in the stream headwaters. Water pollution and siltation at the few remaining spawning sites also threaten the survival of eggs and hatchlings.

Hart Lake and a portion of Crump Lake dried up in the early 1930s and again in the early 1960s, but periodic fluctuations in lake levels seem to be a natural feature of the Warner Valley. The Warner sucker survives these droughts by seeking refuge in streams that feed the lakes, but at a high cost in population mortality. Increased irrigation demands during such periods aggravate and prolong natural drought conditions, keeping both the water table and sucker population levels low.

Conservation and Recovery

In early 1991, the threat of a fifth consecutive drought year prompted the agencies responsible for managing the Warner sucker to plan a salvage operation to establish a refuge population of suckers at the Dexter National Fish Hatchery and Technology Center in New Mexico. Salvage operations consisted primarily of intensive trap netting in Hart Lake to collect suckers, then transportation of the captured fish to a temporary holding facility (a series of five small earth ponds linked by a 600-ft (183-m) ditch at Oregon Department of Fish and Wildlife's Summer Lake Wildlife Management Area. The suckers were held at Summer Lake Wildlife Management Area for five months until September 1991, when 75 adults were recaptured and transported to Dexter.

While being held at Summer Lake Wildlife Management Area, the suckers from Hart Lake spawned successfully, leaving an estimated 250+ young in the Summer Lake Wildlife Management Area holding ponds after the adults were taken to Dexter. The young suckers did well in the ponds, growing approximately 3.3 in (8.4 cm) during their first summer and reaching sexual maturity at the age of only two years. Sucker larvae were observed in the ponds during the summer of 1993, just over two years after the original wild suckers from Hart Lake were held there. Approximately 30 of the two-year-old suckers were captured and released in Hart Lake in September 1993. In June 1994, more than one hundred 4-7 in (10.2-17.8 cm) Warner suckers were observed in the Summer Lake Wildlife Management Area ponds. In 1996, nine adult fish were observed in these ponds along with about 20 larvae.

The suckers taken to Dexter were reduced from 75 to 46 individuals between September 1991 and March 1993, largely due to anchor worm infestation. In March 1993, the 46 survivors (12 males and 34 females) appeared ready to spawn, but the females did not produce any eggs. In May 1994, five males and seven females spawned, producing a total of approximately 175,000 eggs. However, for reasons that are not clear, none of the eggs were successfully fertilized. The remaining 20 fish at Dexter died in 1995. In November of 1995, approximately 65 more suckers from Summer Lake Wildlife Management Area were transferred to Dexter for spawning purposes but as yet no attempts to spawn these fish have occurred.

In 1991, the Bureau of Land Management installed a modified steep-pass Denil fish passage facility on the Dyke diversion on lower Twenty-

mile Creek. The Dyke diversion. structure is a 4 ft (1.2 m) high irrigation diversion that was impassable to suckers and trout before the fishway was installed. It blocked all migration of fishes from the lower Twentymile Creek, Twentymile Slough and Greaser Reservoir populations from moving upstream to spawning or other habitats above the structure.

An evaluation of fish passage alternatives has been done for diversions on Honey Creek which identifies the eight dams and diversions on the lower part of the creek that are barriers to fish migration. In May 1994, a fish passage structure was tested on Honey Creek. It consisted of a removable fishway and screen. The ladder immediately provided passage for a small redband trout. These structures were removed by Oregon Department of Fish and Wildlife shortly after their installation due to design flaws that did not pass allocated water.

Critical habitat was designated for the Warner sucker at the time of listing in 1985.

Contact

U.S. Fish and Wildlife Service
Regional Office, Division of Endangered Species
Eastside Federal Complex
911 N.E. 11th Ave.
Portland, Oregon 97232-4181
(503) 231-6121
http://pacific.fws.gov/

References

Bond. C. E. 1973. "Keys to Oregon Freshwater Fishes." Technical Bulletin 58. Oregon State University, Agricultural Experiment Station.

Bond, C. E. 1974. "Endangered Plants and Animals of Oregon, I. Fishes." Special Report 205. Oregon State University, Agricultural Experiment Station.

Coombs, C. I., C. E. Bond, and S. F. Drohan. 1979. "Spawning and Early Life History of the Warner Sucker (*Catostomus warnerensis*)." Report to U.S. Fish and Wildlife Service, Sacramento. 52 pp.

U.S. Fish and Wildlife Service. 27 September 1985. "Determination That the Warner Sucker is a Threatened Species and Designation of Critical Habitat." *Federal Register* 50 (188): 39117-39123.

Shortnose Sucker

Chasmistes brevirostris

Status	Endangered
Listed	July 18, 1988
Family	Catostomidae (Sucker)
Description	Sucker with a terminal oblique mouth and vestigial papillae on the lips.
Habitat	Lakes; streams for spawning.
Food	Bottom feeder on plants and detritus.
Reproduction	Spawns in the spring.
Threats	Dam construction; hybridization.
Range	California, Oregon

Description

The shortnose sucker, *Chasmistes brevirostris*, can grow as long as 25 in (64 cm) at maturity. It is distinguished from other members of the genus *Chasmistes* by its terminal, oblique mouth, which has no (or only vestigal) papillae on the lips.

Behavior

In the spring, the shortnose sucker moves from its lake habitat to stream headwaters to spawn. Suckers are adapted to feed by suction, siphoning and filtering food from lake bottoms. The species is long-lived; several fish have been netted that were over 40 years old. Most shortnose suckers reach sexual maturity at age six or seven. The shortnose sucker was a food fish for the Klamath Indians for thousands of years.

Habitat

The shortnose sucker is lake-dwelling and prefers the freshwater reservoirs of mountainous, southeastern Oregon. It requires free-flowing streams for spawning. Shoreline river and lake habitats with vegetative structure are known to be important during larval and juvenile rearing.

Distribution

The shortnose sucker was once found throughout the Klamath Basin of south-central Oregon and north-central California. A shortnose sucker population in Lake of the Woods, Oregon, was lost during a program to eradicate carp and perch in 1952. A population in the Clear Lake Reservoir shows distinct evidence of interbreeding with the Klamath largescale sucker, creating a genetically impure hybrid. Specimens collected from Copco Reservoir in 1962, 1978, and 1979 were found to have hybridized with the Klamath smallscale sucker.

The current distribution of the shortnose sucker includes Upper Klamath Lake and its tributaries, Klamath River downstream to Iron Gate Reservoir, Clear Lake Reservoir and its tributaries, Gerber Reservoir and its tributaries, the Lost River, and Tule Lake. Gerber Reservoir represents the only habitat with a shortnose sucker population that does not also host the equally endangered Lost River sucker. In the Upper Klamath Lake watershed, shortnose sucker spawning runs are primarily limited to the Sprague and Williamson Rivers, although spawning runs may also occur in the Wood River and in Crooked Creek. Shortnose sucker spawning has been documented in the Clear Lake watershed.

Drastic population declines in the 1980s caused the species to be placed on the state's protected species list and to be listed as Endangered by the FWS, along with the Lost River sucker (*Deltistes luxatus*), another rare Klamath Basin fish. Populations for both sucker species have declined by some 95% due to sport-fishing, water quality degradation, al-

Joseph Tomelleri.

gae-induced fish-kills, and the combined effects of river damming, instream flow diversions, draining of marshes, dredging of Upper Klamath lake, and other water manipulations.

The dramatic decline of the mid-1980s was documented beginning in 1984, when a survey estimated the number of spawning shortnose suckers swimming out of Upper Klamath Lake at 2,650 individuals. Surveys in 1985 and 1986 found significantly fewer fish. The catch of shortnose suckers declined 34% between the 1984 and 1985 spawning runs. In 1986, the spawning run declined 74% compared to 1985. No significant recruitment of young into the population has been documented in the last two decades.

Threats

Through the 1970s, runs of suckers moving from Upper Klamath Lake to spawning areas in the Williamson and Sprague Rivers were great enough to support a popular sport fishery. Sharp declines

were noted in 1984-1986 and the sport fishery was closed in 1987.

The primary cause of this decline was the overall reshaping of the Klamath Basin through dams, water diversion, dredging, and the elimination of marshes. Once, the Upper Klamath Basin had over 350,000 acres (141,641 hectares) of wetlands, with extensive riparian corridors, and functional floodplains that handled storm runoff, dampened sharp peaks in the hydrograph, reduced erosion forces, removed organic and inorganic nutrients, and improved water quality. Currently, less than 75,000 acres (30,352 hectares) of wetlands remain in the Basin, and the loss of these wetlands has had large scale detrimental effects to the quality and quantity of suitable sucker habitat.

Although reservoirs provide suitable habitat for the shortnose sucker, the dams block the fish's spawning runs. Surviving suckers are almost all older fish. There has been no significant addition of

Shortnose Sucker, photograph. U. S. Fish and Wildlife Service. Reproduced by permission.

young to the population since the Sprague River Dam was constructed at Chiloquin, Oregon, in 1970, cutting off 85% of the spawning range.

Fish ladders, installed at the Sprague River Dam, have been little or no help. Although the shortnose sucker is a strong swimmer, it cannot leap the rungs of the ladders. Damming has also facilitated hybridization with other sucker species in the dam's tailwaters. Non-native fishes have also contributed to shortnose sucker decline through hybridization and competition.

Conservation and Recovery

The Klamath Indian Tribe and local biologists alerted the Oregon Fish and Wildlife Commission to the critical situation of both the shortnose sucker and the Lost River sucker. If these species are to be recovered, these groups and the Fish and Wild-life Service must continue to cooperate in efforts to restore a breeding range for these endangered fish. The National Wildlife Refuge System (FWS) re-

leased the Sucker Critical Habitat Proposal in 1996 to preserve and restore the Klamath Basin habitat critical to both shortnose and Lost River suckers.

Contact

U.S. Fish and Wildlife Service
Division of Endangered Species
911 N.E. 11th Ave.
Portland, Oregon 97232
http://pacific.fws.gov/

References

Coots, M. 1965. "Occurrences of the Lost River Sucker, *Deltistes luxatus* (Cope), and Shortnose Sucker, *Chasmistes brevirostris* (Cope) in Northern California." *California Fish and Game* 51:68-73.

Miller, R. R., and G. R. Smith. 1981. "Distribution and Evolution of *Chasmistes* (Pisces: Catostomidae) in Western North America." *Occasional Papers of the Museum of Zoology*, University of Michigan 696:1-46.

Moyle, P. B. 1978. *Inland Fishes of California.* University of California Press, Berkeley.

U.S. Fish and Wildlife Service. 1988. "Determination of Endangered Status for the Lost River Sucker and Shortnose Sucker." Federal Register 53(137): 27130-27133.

U. S. Fish and Wildlife Service. 1993. "Recovery Plan for the Lost River Sucker and Shortnose Sucker." U.S. Fish and Wildlife Service, Portland.

White, R. and K. Stubbs, 1996. "The Sucker Critical Habitat Proposal." U.S. Fish and Wildlife Service, Portland.

Cui-ui

Chasmistes cujus

Status	Endangered
Listed	March 11, 1967
Family	Catostomidae (Sucker)
Description	Olive to blackish-brown sucker.
Habitat	Lakes; headwaters for spawning.
Food	Bottom feeder.
Reproduction	Spawns in the spring.
Threats	Dam construction, degraded water quality.
Range	Nevada

Cui-ui, photograph. U. S. Fish and Wildlife Service. Reproduced by permission.

Description

The cui-ui, *Chasmistes cujus*, is a is a plump, robust sucker, which attains a maximum length of about 25 in (64 cm) and a maximum weight of about 7 lbs (3.2 kg). It has a plump, robust body, and coarse scales. The head is large and blunt with small eyes. The mouth, atypical for a sucker, is oblique, rather than rounded, with thin lips and weak or nearly absent papillae. The cui-ui is pale olive to blackish-brown above, and white below. Breeding males have reddish sides. Females have a more bluish cast than males, attain greater length and weight than males, are more stocky in appearance, and have proportionally shorter fins. The female's vent becomes swollen and extended during spawning.

Behavior

Spawning occurs once a year, primarily between April and late June, peaking in May. Temperature and flow characteristics of the Truckee River seem to determine timing of spawning, which occurs primarily at night in clusters of two to seven fish, most frequently with a female flanked on either side by a male. The demersal, adhesive eggs and sperm are broadcast over a large area. Males and females spawn repeatedly, often more than 100 times, each spawning act lasting three to six seconds. Males spawn actively over four to five days and females two and one-half to four days. There is no aggression among spawners and females spawn with different combinations of males.

Spawning has also been reported in Pyramid Lake at the entrance of freshwater streams on fine to coarse gravel and in the Marble Bluff fishway where the substrate is predominately compacted soil. Upstream migrating pre-spawning adults require pool environments, typically log jam pools, as refuge during the day.

The only migratory behavior reported for cui-ui involves adults ascending the Truckee River from Pyramid Lake to spawn, and their return to the lake and downstream migration of hatched larvae. Adults migrate to the south end of Pyramid Lake from late winter to early spring (February to May) where pre-spawning adults congregate off the mouth of the river. Young fish migrate downstream shortly after hatching, primarily from mid-May through mid-July, usually within about one month of peak adult migration.

Habitat

The cui-ui spends its adult life in lakes and rivers and swims upstream in the spring to spawn.

Distribution

The cui-ui was once plentiful throughout Truckee River and Pyramid Lake (Nevada); Klamath Lake and its tributaries (Oregon and California); and Utah Lake (Utah).

This species is now extremely rare or absent throughout its historic range. Although no population figures are available, the most viable remaining population of cui-ui appears to occur only in Pyramid Lake, Nevada. Adults migrate from Pyramid Lake up the lower Truckee River in spring to reproduce, and return to Pyramid Lake immediately following spawning. Larvae emigrate to Pyramid Lake shortly after hatching.

Threats

The natural habitat of the cui-ui has been drastically altered since the turn of the century by the construction of dams and water diversion channels. Water quality has steadily declined as flows decreased and the influx of silt and pollutants increased. Non-native fish species have preyed on cui-ui young, significantly reducing the population.

The Cui-ui Recovery Plan, completed by the U. S. Fish and Wildlife Service (FWS) in 1992, has the stated objective of improving the status of cui-ui so that the species has at least a 0.95 probability of persisting for 200 years. This objective necessitates securing spawning habitat in the lower Truckee River and rearing habitat in Pyramid Lake as well as an avenue of passage for spawners and larvae.

The plan calls for restoring a portion of the Truckee River and Pyramid Lake to a natural and balanced condition. If a significant portion of this essential habitat can be reclaimed, the cui-ui stands a good chance of surviving. A captive breeding pro-

gram is underway with the goal of restocking cui-ui in Pyramid Lake.

Until April 1987, Nevada's Truckee River population was cut off from its spawning grounds at the river's headwaters. Then the Marble Bluff Fish Facility, designed to pass spawning fish of all types upstream past the Truckee River Dam, was opened. Almost immediately biologists observed a run of the endangered Lahontan cutthroat trout (*Salmo clarki henshawi*) through the facility, soon followed by more than 4,000 cui-ui.

Continuing and future threats to the cui-ui include egg-hungry Lahontan redsides and alterations in the habitat, including channelization projects of the lower Truckee River by the Army Corps of Engineers, which have in the past resulted in the loss of protective cover, leaving many areas exposed to direct sunlight and solar heating.

Conservation and Recovery

In October 1996, the United States signed the Truckee River Water Quality Settlement Agreement with the cities of Reno and Sparks, Washoe County, the state of Nevada, and the Pyramid Lake Paiute Tribe. The agreement resolves litigation over approval and operation of the Reno-Sparks water treatment facility brought by the Pyramid Lake Paiute Tribe against Reno, Sparks, the state of Nevada, and the U.S. Environmental Protection Agency.

The FWS is preparing a wetlands management plan detailing actions necessary to best manage water being acquired to sustain 25,000 acres (10,117 hectares) of wetland habitat, including the timing of water applications to wetlands, and the volumes of acquired water to be applied.

In virtually the closing moments of the 101st legislative session in November 1990, Congress enacted a new law intended to help recover the cui-ui and Lahontan cutthroat trout and restore National Wildlife Refuge wetlands in Nevada vital to migratory waterfowl and shorebirds using the Pacific Flyway.

In addition to its progressive strategies for fish and wildlife, Public Law 101-618 confronts many long-standing water problems in the Truckee and Carson River basins of western Nevada: allocation of water between California and Nevada, coordination of water storage in Federal and private reservoirs, water management at one of the first Bureau of Reclamation irrigation projects, and resolution of certain Native American water rights disputes. Most significant for the conservation of endangered species and wetlands is a directive to acquire water rights expressly for fish and wildlife. The purchase of water at market rates should encourage the voluntary reallocation of water resources to benefit fish and wildlife in a manner that is equitable and most likely to enjoy local support.

Just as it addresses wetland restoration, Public Law 101-618 pursues the recovery of listed fishes in Pyramid Lake. In perhaps the most significant provision for these species, the Secretary of the Interior is directed to negotiate a formal Operating Agreement with the states of California and Nevada to govern management of the Truckee River reservoirs. Among other purposes, such an agreement may improve spawning conditions in the lower river through coordinated reservoir operations.

Contact

Regional Office of Endangered Species
U.S. Fish and Wildlife Service
Eastside Federal Complex
911 N. E. 11th Ave.
Portland, Oregon 97232
http://pacific.fws.gov/

Reference

U.S. Fish and Wildlife Service. 1992. "Cui-ui Recovery Plan: Revision." U.S. Fish and Wildlife Service, Portland.

June Sucker

Chasmistes liorus

Status	Endangered
Listed	March 31, 1986
Family	Catostomidae (Sucker)
Description	Small sucker with an under-hanging mouth.
Habitat	Shallow, saline waters.
Food	Bottom feeder.
Reproduction	Spawns in June.
Threats	Predation, water diversion.
Range	Utah

Description

Named for its peak spawning time, the June sucker is a small fish, attaining a mature length of only about 1.25 in (3 cm). It has often been confused with the Utah sucker but can be readily distinguished by its underhanging mouth, relatively smooth, divided lips, a broad skull, and greater numbers of gill rakers.

The species as it exists today, differs slightly from specimens collected in the 1800s. It is hypothesized that the June and Utah suckers interbred during a prolonged drought in the 1930s when their populations were seriously stressed. The name *Chasmistes liorus liorus* was assigned to specimens collected in the 1800s, and *C. l. mictus* to those collected after 1939. To avoid confusion, the June sucker is now being classified as a full species—*C. liorus*. It has retained its distinct characteristics and is not actively interbreeding with any other species today.

Behavior

In spite of its former abundance, biological data for this bottom-feeding species is mostly wanting. The adult June sucker ascends the Provo River during the second or third week of June and completes spawning within five to eight days.

Habitat

The June sucker thrives in the shallow, saline waters of Utah Lake, Utah, a 94,000-acre (38,000-hectare) remnant of ancient Lake Bonneville. The lake's average depth is 10 ft (3 m) and maximum depth only about 14 ft (4 m). Its turbid waters are slightly saline. The June sucker spawns in the Provo River, the largest tributary of the lake, with limited activity in the Spanish Fork River.

Distribution

The species historically occupied the Spanish Fork River and possibly other tributaries of Utah Lake. Millions of June suckers were reported in Utah Lake in the late 1800s and composed an important part of the commercial fish harvest. During the early 1930s, hundreds of tons of suckers were lost when the lake was nearly drained because the water was needed for irrigation. In 1951, the June sucker was considered the second most abundant species in Utah Lake; by 1959 it was considered fourth in abundance; by 1970 it ranked seventh.

The June sucker is restricted to Utah Lake and the lower portion of the Provo River (Utah County). Spawning is restricted because the fish can travel only about 5 mi (8 km) upstream to where a diversion barrier blocks further movement.

Though less than a decade ago, fewer than 1,000 adult June suckers were known to survive (and of those, none were younger than 15 years of age), recent recovery efforts have dramatically increased the population numbers. A cooperative propagation effort by the Bureau of Reclamation, Central Utah Wa-

June Sucker, photograph. Utah Department of Natural Resources. Reproduced by permission.

ter Conservancy District, Provo water users, Utah Division of Wildlife Resources and the U.S. Fish and Wildlife Service, has resulted in the production of 6,000 fry. The Utah Correction Institute has been converted to a June sucker rearing facility and more than 400 fish are being raised there with excellent results.

Threats

The species decline is believed to result from several events, including significant alterations in the species' lake and river habitat. Dams and water diversions constructed on the rivers flowing into Utah Lake have reduced water flows, altered flow regimes within the river, and dramatically increased fluctuations in the level of the lake. Increased pollution and nutrient inflow, caused by urban development surrounding Utah Lake, have degraded water quality within the lake and destroyed shoreline vegetation. In addition, over 20 non-native fishes have been introduced into Utah Lake, including white bass, largemouth bass, walleye, black bullhead, channel catfish, and carp that compete with the June sucker

for food and prey upon juvenile June suckers. The combination of these factors has apparently reduced the survival of young fish to the point that most fish found today, other than the newly introduced fry, are between 20 and 43 years old.

The Central Utah Water Conservancy District, the Provo River Water Users Association, and several other groups questioned the efficacy of listing the June sucker as Endangered. These groups feared that listing would interfere with the Central Utah Project, an ongoing, federally funded, construction project designed to supply more water for irrigation and human use. The Governor of Utah supported the listing. Subsequently, the Fish and Wildlife Service (FWS) determined that existing plans to dike Goshen and Provo bays and to create further upstream reservoirs would result in habitat losses.

Conservation and Recovery

The state of Utah is currently implementing sections of a June Sucker Management Plan to ensure the survival of the species and attempt to overcome the impacts of predation. The Bonneville Chapter of the American Fisheries Society has been involved in the recovery effort, and the Utah Correction Institute has been converted to a June sucker rearing facility, where more than 400 fish are being raised.

In 1995, a draft Recovery Plan was announced by the FWS, with the goal of increasing reproduction and survival of young June suckers to increase population numbers and ensure the species' survival. Recovery actions recommended to facilitate recovery of the species include identification of habitat requirements, coordination of efforts to restore required water flows and other appropriate habitat conditions, and identification and amelioration of the effects of predation by non-native fish species.

Contact

U.S. Fish and Wildlife Service
Division of Endangered Species
Denver Federal Center
P.O. Box 25486
Denver, Colorado 80225
http://www.r6.fws.gov/

References

Bureau of Reclamation. 1979. "Central Utah Project, Bonneville Unit, Municipal and Industrial System, Final Environmental Statement, Volume I." Bureau of Reclamation, Salt Lake City.

Radant, R. D. 1983. "Fisheries Impact Analysis of Utah Lake Diking Plan, Irrigation and Drainage System, Bonneville Unit, Central Utah Project." Utah Division of Wildlife Resources with the Bureau of Reclamation, Salt Lake City.

Radant, R. D., and T. J. Hickman. 1984. "Status of the June Sucker." In *Proceedings of the Desert Fishes Council 15th Annual Symposium*. Bishop, California.

Lost River Sucker

Deltistes luxatus

Status	Endangered
Listed	July 16, 1988
Family	Catostomidae (Sucker)
Description	Large sucker growing to 10 lbs (4.5 kg).
Habitat	Lakes; flowing streams for spawning.
Food	Bottom feeder on plant matter and detritus.
Reproduction	Spawns in the spring.
Threats	Dam construction.
Range	California, Oregon

Description

The Lost River sucker, known locally as mullet, is one of the larger members of the sucker family, growing to 25 in (60 cm) in length and weighing as much as 10 lbs (4.5 kg). It has a short, terminal mouth, a hump on its snout, and triangular gill rakers (bony appendages that direct food into the gullet). Once classified in the genus *Chasmistes*, the species was moved into a separate genus, *Deltistes*, in 1896 based on the shape of its gill rakers.

Behavior

The Lost River sucker leaves its lake habitat in the spring and swims into smaller mountain streams to spawn. Sexual maturity for Lost River suckers sampled in Upper Klamath Lake occurs between the ages of 6-14 years with most maturing at age 9. Maximum life span is about 45 years. It is a bottom feeding species, adapted to siphoning sediments for plant matter and detritus.

Habitat

This lake-dwelling species spawns in the headwaters of small, flowing streams in spring.

Distribution

The Lost River sucker ranged in the lakes that fed the Lost and Klamath Rivers in the Klamath Basin of south-central Oregon and north-central California. Before the region was heavily farmed, beginning in the late 19th century, large numbers of spawning suckers were taken from Sheepy Creek, a tributary of Sheepy Lake. The Sheepy, Lower Klamath, and Tule Lakes were drained temporarily in 1924, eliminating Lost River suckers from these waters.

Once very plentiful in Klamath and Tule Lakes, the species' population has been reduced by as much as 95%. The present distribution of the Lost River sucker includes Upper Klamath Lake and its tributaries, Clear Lake Reservoir and its tributaries, Tule Lake and the Lost River up to Anderson-Rose Dam, the Klamath River downstream to Copco Reservoir and probably to Iron Gate Reservoir. In the Upper Klamath Lake watershed, Lost River sucker spawning runs are primarily limited to Sucker Springs in Upper Klamath Lake, and the Sprague and Williamson Rivers. Spawning runs also occur in the Wood River and in the Crooked Creek watershed. An additional run may occur in Sheepy Lake in the Lower Klamath Lake watershed, and spawning has been documented in the Clear Lake watershed.

In the 1980s, the numbers showed a decline severe enough to spark the Endangered listing in 1988. A 1984 survey estimated the number of spawning suckers moving out of Upper Klamath Lake to be 23,120. By 1985, the number had declined to 11,860.

Lost River Sucker, photograph. U. S. Fish and Wildlife Service. Reproduced by permission.

The species had been almost eliminated from the river's Copco Reservoir in Siskiyou County, California. Despite an intensive search, only one specimen was collected there in 1987.

Threats

Early surveys of the Klamath Basin found Lost River suckers in sufficient abundance to constitute a major food source for the Klamath Indians and early settlers. In the late 1890s a cannery was operated near Olene, Oregon, to commercially harvest the fish.

The Upper Klamath Basin once had over 350,000 acres (141,641 hectares) of wetlands, extensive riparian corridors, and functional floodplains that could intercept storm runoff, dampen sharp peaks in the hydrograph, reduce erosion forces, remove organic and inorganic nutrients, and improve water quality. The loss of these wetlands has had large scale detrimental effects to the quality and quantity of suitable sucker habitat. Currently, less than 75,000 acres (30,352 hectares) of wetlands remain in the Basin.

The entire Klamath River basin has been transformed by dam construction, water diversion, and dredging. Although the large artificial reservoirs technically provide new habitat for lake-dwelling fish, the dams block the fishes' spawning runs. The most significant event in the decline of the Lost River sucker was construction of the Sprague River Dam at Chiloquin, Oregon, in 1970, which cut off the species from more than 95% of its historical spawning habitat. Since this dam was built, significant numbers of young have not been added to the population. Most living fish are at least 19 years old.

In 1988, thousands of Lost River suckers in Upper Klamath Lake were killed because of blue-green algal blooms. These toxic algal blooms occur in particularly hot, dry years. Pollution of the lake and decreased summer inflows aggravate this problem. Such large-scale die-offs are clearly a contributor to this species' current status, though they don't occur every year.

Fish ladders, constructed to assist fish over the dams, have not aided the Lost River sucker, a fish that does not leap. Unless some way is found to lift this fish over the dams and into spawning waters, the species is doomed. The Oregon Fish and Wildlife Commission placed the Lost River sucker on the state's list of protected species in 1987, and California law recognizes it as Endangered.

Conservation and Recovery

In 1996, the FWS (National Wildlife Refuge System) released the *Sucker Critical Habitat Proposal*, with the goal of defining, preserving and restoring the habitat of the Klamath Basin, critical to both the Lost River and shortnose sucker—the latter of which shares the habitat and is also listed as Endangered.

Contact

U.S. Fish and Wildlife Service
Division of Endangered Species
911 N.E. 11th Ave
Portland, Oregon 97232
http://pacific.fws.gov/

References

Coots, M. 1965. "Occurrences of the Lost River Sucker, *Deltistes luxatus* (Cope), and Shortnose Sucker, *Chasmistes brevirostris* (Cope) in Northern California." *California Fish and Game* 51:68- 73.

Moyle, P. B. 1978. *Inland Fishes of California*. University of California Press, Berkeley.

U.S. Fish and Wildlife Service. 1988. "Determination of Endangered Status for the Lost River Sucker and Shortnose Sucker." Federal Register 53(137): 27130-27133.

U. S. Fish and Wildlife Service. 1993. "Recovery Plan for the Lost River Sucker and Shortnose Sucker." U.S. Fish and Wildlife Service, Portland.

Razorback Sucker

Xyrauchen texanus

Status	Endangered
Listed	October 23, 1991
Family	Catostomidae (Sucker)
Description	Robust fish with a sharp, dorsal ridge behind the head.
Habitat	River channels, gravel bars.
Food	Algae, plankton, insects.
Reproduction	Spawns in the spring.
Threats	Lack of recruitment of young, loss of habitat.
Range	Arizona, California, Colorado, Nevada, Utah

Description

The razorback sucker is a large freshwater fish, often exceeding 6 lbs (2.7 kg) in weight and 24 in (61 cm) in length. Adults have an abrupt, sharp-edged dorsal ridge behind the head and a fleshy mouth situated on the underside the head. Younger fish, less than 6 in (15 cm) long, lack the distinctive keel. This species was originally placed in the genus *Catostomus*. It has also been known by the common name, humpback sucker.

Behavior

In the lower Colorado River basin, razorback suckers spawn from late January through April; in the upper basin spawning takes place mostly in May and June.

After migrating considerable distances to spawning areas, females are accompanied by several males over clean gravel bars. The collection of fertilized eggs and young larvae indicates that the species is reproducing successfully. However, almost no larvae over about 0.5 in (1.3 cm) in length have been found, indicating that the species is not successfully recruiting young to the population. Adult razorback suckers feed primarily on algae, but also eat plankton, insects, and decaying organic matter

Habitat

The razorback sucker shows different habitat preferences depending on the season. During the spring spawning season it is found mostly over sand, gravel, and cobble runs; flooded bottomlands; and the eddies formed at the flooded mouths of tributary streams.

In winter, the fish take up a relatively sedentary position in deeper water or the main stream channel. Studies with radio-tagged fish indicate that during the winter fish travel only about 3 mi (0.8 km) over the course of several months. Because they have not been seen by researchers, the habitat requirements of larvae and young fish are largely unknown.

Distribution

First described in 1861, the razorback sucker was once an abundant species throughout the 3,500 mi (5,600 km) Colorado River basin. It is believed to have occurred in Arizona, California, Colorado, Nevada, New Mexico, Utah, Wyoming, and in the Mexican states of Baja California, Norte, and Sonoma. A significant commercial fishery for the species existed in southern Arizona during the early 1900s, and in Colorado thousands were observed during spring runoffs during the 1930s and early 1940s.

Razorback Sucker, photograph. U. S. Fish and Wildlife Service. Reproduced by permission.

In recent decades the razorback sucker has undergone a steady decline in both range and numbers. It now occurs in about 750 mi (1,200 km) of the upper Colorado River basin and in about 200 mi (320 km) of the lower basin. The largest population of adult fish—an estimated 60,000—survives in Lake Mohave, on the Arizona-Nevada border. Small numbers of the species are also found in Lake Mead and Senator Wash Reservoir. In the upper Colorado basin an estimated 750-1,200 individuals inhabit the upper Green River and some of its tributaries in Utah and Colorado. Razorbacks are also found in the upper Green River, Utah; lower Yampa River, Colorado; and the Colorado River, near Grand Junction, Colorado. The species is present but very rare in the San Juan, Dirty Devil, and Colorado arms of Lake Powell.

Threats

Since the early 1900s, construction of dams on the Colorado River and its major tributaries have radically altered the river system, impounding nearly the entire lower basin and greatly decreasing water flows. The once abundant razorback sucker has progressively declined as the natural flow of the river has been disrupted. The changes in flow caused by dams has reduced available spawning areas and rendered other parts of the river too cold to support the species. However, of most concern to researchers is the fact that despite successful reproduction, the young are not surviving. It is believed that the present population consists almost entirely of adults. If this situation continues, the extinction of the species in the near future is a certainty.

It appears that the main causes of the death of razorback sucker larvae are predation by nonnative fish species and a lack of food availability. A number of predatory species, including carp, channel catfish, flathead catfish, largemouth bass, smallmouth bass, and bluegill, feed on razorback sucker eggs and larvae. In addition, recent studies in Lake Mohave have suggested that there is not sufficient zooplankton in the lake to support the growing larvae.

Conservation and Recovery

The conservation and recovery of federally listed fish species in the Colorado River basin—the Colorado squawfish *(Ptychocheilus lucius)*, humpback chub *(Gila cypha)*, bonytail chub *(Gila elegans)*, and razorback sucker—has been coordinated by the Colorado River Endangered Fishes Recovery Implementation Committee, which consists of representatives from a number of federal agencies. Protective measures for the razorback sucker will now be included in the committee's work. As part of the recovery process, a captive population of razorback suckers is held at the Dexter National Fish Hatchery as insurance against extinction and a population source for an ongoing restocking effort. Unfortunately, this effort does not appear to be succeeding. Over the last ten years, over 13 million razorback sucker fry have been stocked in over 50 sites in Arizona. It is believed that these juveniles were heavily preyed upon by introduced non-native fishes.

Alteration of the Colorado River system is continuing and the Fish and Wildlife Service has been in consultation with over 100 federally funded or regulated projects in the upper Colorado basin over the last decade. Among the more prominent projects are the Central Utah Project, which will divert water from the Green River, and the Two Forks Project, which will divert water from the Colorado River. These will affect listed fish species by decreasing the flow in most of the remaining riverine habitat.

Contacts

U.S. Fish and Wildlife Service
Regional Office, Division of Endangered Species
Denver Federal Center
P.O. Box 25486
Denver, Colorado 80225
http://www.r6.fws.gov/

U.S. Fish and Wildlife Service
Regional Office, Division of Endangered Species
Eastside Federal Complex
911 N.E. 11th Ave.
Portland, Oregon 97232
http://pacific.fws.gov/

References

Bozek, M. A., L. J. Paulson, and J. E. Deacon. 1984. "Factors Affecting Reproductive Success of Bonytail Chubs and Razorback Suckers in Lake Mohave.~ Final Report," 1416-0002-81-251. Bureau of Reclamation, Boulder City, Nevada.

Loudermilk, W. E. 1985. "Aspects of Razorback Sucker *(Xyrauchen texanus,* Abbott) Life History which Help Explain Their Decline." *Proceedings of the Desert Fishes Council* 13(1981):67-72.

Marsh, P. C., and W. L. Minckley. 1989. "Observations on Recruitment and Ecology of Razorback Sucker: Lower Colorado River, Arizona-California." *Great Basin Naturalist* 49(1):71-78.

Minckley, W. L., et al. 1991. "Management Toward Recovery of Razorback Sucker *(Xyrauchen texanus)*." In *Battle Against Extinction*, edited by W. L. Minckley and J. E. Deacon. University of Arizona Press, Tucson.

Papoulis, D. 1986. "The Effect of Food Availability on Growth and Mortality of Larval Razorback Sucker, *Xyrauchen texanus*." U.S. Fish and Wildlife Service, Albuquerque, New Mexico.

Rinne, John N., and W. L. Minckley. 1991. *Native Fishes and Arid Lands: Dwindling Resource of the Desert Southwest.* USDA Forest Service, Fort Collins, Colorado.

Tyus, H. M. 1987. "Distribution, Reproduction, and Habitat Use of the Razorback Sucker in the Green River, Utah, 1979-986." *Transactions of the American Fisheries Society* 116:111-116.

Tyus, H. M., and C. A. Karp. 1989. "Habitat Use and Stream-flow Needs of Rare and Endangered Fishes, Yampa River, Colorado." U.S. Fish and Wildlife Service, *Biological Report* 89(14).

Yaqui Catfish

Ictalurus pricei

Status	Threatened
Listed	August 31, 1984
Family	Ictaluridae (Catfish)
Description	Mottled brown back, silvery sides, and reddish coloration on the head, fins, and tail.
Habitat	Large streams in slow to moderate current.
Food	Bottom feeder.
Reproduction	Spawns in late spring.
Threats	Water diversion, groundwater depletion, hybridization.
Range	Arizona, Mexico (Chihuahua and Sonora)

Description

The Yaqui catfish, *Ictalurus pricei,* is a medium-sized catfish, with a length of 6-8 in (15-20 cm). The back is a lightly mottled brown. Sides are silvery. A reddish coloration is prominent beneath the head, and on the fins and tail. The body is profusely speckled in the young, becoming a more unicolored, dark gray to black dorsally, and white to grayish beneath. The barbels are jet black except on the immediate chin, where they are gray to whitish.

Behavior

Similar to the channel catfish, the Yaqui catfish spawns in late spring. Eggs are laid in a nest, which is constructed on the bottom and guarded by the male. He incubates the eggs by fanning away silt. Hatchlings collect in small schools that are protected by the male. This catfish feeds opportunistically on insects and larvae, crustaceans, plant matter, and detritus—almost anything that is found on the bottom of the stream.

Habitat

The Yaqui catfish inhabits large streams in areas of slow to moderate current. It feeds over mud or sandy gravel bottoms in pools and backwaters. Aquatic habitats in the region are subject to severe drying in summer and sudden flooding in the rainy season. Streams flow intermittently during the dry season, and the catfish seeks refuge in permanent, often spring-fed, pools.

Distribution

This species is endemic to the Rio Yaqui basin of southeastern Arizona, northwestern Sonora, and portions of eastern Chihuahua, Mexico. It was first collected from San Bernardino Creek in extreme southeastern Arizona. The Yaqui catfish survived in San Bernardino Creek until spring flows diminished because of groundwater pumping, and the creek dried up. Remaining habitat there was severely trampled by livestock seeking water, making it uninhabitable. This species is considered by some to be extirpated in the United States. The U. S. Fish and Wildlife Service (FWS) has assigned the Threatened status to the species.

Contract biologists from the Arizona State University and the University of Michigan surveyed the Rio Yaqui basin in 1979 and found populations of the Yaqui catfish seriously depleted in the Mexican portion of its historic range and absent from Arizona. In 1991, it was considered imperiled in the Rio Yaqui basin due to habitat modifi-

Yaqui Catfish, photograph by John Rinne, USFS. Reproduced by permission.

cation and hybridization with channel and blue catfish.

Yaqui catfish were captured under permit from the Mexican government in 1987 and 1990, and are being cultivated at the Dexter National Fish Hatchery in New Mexico in anticipation of reintroductions.

Threats

The range and numbers of the Yaqui catfish have decreased significantly because of habitat modifications, such as arroyo cutting, water diversion, dam construction, and excessive pumping of groundwater from aquifers. Many rivers in Mexico, formerly inhabited by the Yaqui catfish, have been modified into an artificially channeled canal system to support irrigation agriculture. Water quality has declined due to chemical and sewage contamination. The Yaqui catfish receives no legal protection from the Mexican government.

The Yaqui catfish appears to be interbreeding with two non-native catfish, the channel catfish (*I. punctatus*) and the blue catfish (*I. furcatus*), which have become established in the Rio Yaqui system. If hybridization continues, the distinctive characteristics of this species could be lost.

Conservation and Recovery

If sufficient habitat can be secured and maintained in the San Bernardino National Wildlife Refuge (Cochise County, Arizona), the catfish could be reintroduced there, using Mexican stock. Habitat at the wildlife refuge, however, is considered in jeopardy because of generally lowered water tables in the region. The U. S. Bureau of Land Management (BLM) has issued leases for geothermal resources on lands adjacent to the refuge. Biologists fear that exploration and development of these leases could cause further depletion of the underground aquifers or create channels for pollution of groundwater. The BLM will examine these threats in consultation with the FWS.

Contact

U. S. Fish and Wildlife Service
Regional Office, Division of Endangered Species
P.O. Box 1306
Albuquerque, New Mexico 87103-1306
Telephone: (505) 248-6911
Fax: (505) 248-6915
http://southwest.fws.gov/

References

Hendrickson, D. A., et al. 1980. "Fishes of the Rio Yaqui Basin, Mexico and United States." *Journal of the Arizona-Nevada Academy of Science* 15 (3): 65-106.

Miller, R. R. 1977. "Composition of the Native Fish Fauna of the Chihuahuan Desert Region." In *Transactions of the Symposium on the Biological Resources of the Chihuahuan Desert Region*, edited by Wauer and Riskind. Transactions of Proceedings Series, no. 3. U. S. Department of the Interior, Washington, D.C.

Smoky Madtom

Noturus baileyi

Status	Endangered
Listed	October 26, 1984
Family	Ictaluridae (Catfish)
Description	Small, light brown catfish.
Habitat	Mountain streams in riffles and pools.
Food	Aquatic insects.
Reproduction	Spawns during the spring and summer.
Threats	Limited distribution, mineral exploration.
Range	Tennessee

Description

The Smoky madtom, *Noturus baileyi*, is a small, light brown catfish with a somewhat elongated, bow-shaped body, small eyes and a rounded caudal fin. The largest known specimen was 2.9 in (7 cm) long.

Behavior

The Smoky madtom has been found in various stages of breeding condition during the spring and summer. Nests containing an average of 35 eggs have been located during July under large slab rocks in pool areas. This fish is probably nocturnal and is thought to feed on aquatic insects.

Habitat

From May to November this small catfish is generally found beneath slab rocks at either the crest or base of riffles. It utilizes silt-free riffles during other times of the year.

Distribution

The Smoky madtom was both discovered and nearly extirpated at the same time. In 1957 a U. S. Fish and Wildlife Service crew was treating Abrams Creek in the Great Smoky Mountains National Park (Blount County, Tennessee) with a fish toxicant. The purpose of the operation was to remove non-native fish from the watershed before closure of the Chilhowee Dam. Five dead Smoky madtom specimens were taken from the creek and provided the basis for its scientific description. The species was thought to be extinct until it was rediscovered in Citico Creek in the Cherokee National Forest in 1980.

The only known population of the Smoky madtom is the rediscovered population inhabiting a 6.5-mi (10.4-km) stretch of Citico Creek in Monroe County, Tennessee. The habitat is administered by the Forest Service.

Since the Smoky madtom population trend from 1990 through 1994 appeared stable to upward, co-operating conservation organizations decided to continue with attempts to restore the species to Abrams Creek in the Great Smoky Mountains National Park. Aquarium-reared fry were released each year from 1990 to 1992. Night snorkeling surveys in Abrams Creek located a few surviving Smoky madtoms in 1990 and 1991, but none were observed in 1992. No evidence of natural reproduction had been documented by 1994, but once successful spawning occurs, the likelihood of finding individual Smoky madtoms will increase greatly.

Smoky Madtom, photograph. U. S. Fish and Wildlife Service. Reproduced by permission.

Threats

Because Citico Creek holds the only known Smoky madtom population, it is imperative to reestablish this species in another stream within its historic range.

The Smoky madtom's limited range is threatened by logging activities, road and bridge construction, and mineral exploration within the Citico Creek watershed, where formations of anakeesta shale have been found. On contact with water, this type of shale forms poisonous sulfuric acid. The acidic water also leaches metals-particularly aluminum-from the soil, which are extremely toxic to aquatic species. Any activities that expose the shale may result in acid contamination of Citico Creek.

When shale was exposed during construction of the Tellico-Robbinsville highway in the 1970s, acidic runoff increased the concentration of sulfates, heavy metals, and acidity in Grassy Branch, a tributary of the South Fork Citico Creek. Later surveys of Grassy Branch revealed no fish life.

Several species of madtoms have been eliminated from portions of their range for unknown reasons. Biologists think that, in addition to more obvious habitat degradation, they are unable to cope with even trace amounts of complex organic chemicals that may have been added to their habitat. Organic pollution is minimal in the Citico Creek system, but any increase could jeopardize this small, isolated population.

Conservation and Recovery

Since the early 1980s, biologists with the Cherokee National Forest have studied and monitored the populations of the fish in cooperation with the University of Tennessee, Tennessee Wildlife Resources Agency, U.S. Fish and Wildlife Service, Great Smoky Mountains National Park, and a private organization, Conservation Fisheries, Inc. Research on the life histories of the species was funded by these cooperators. Annual population monitoring began in 1986. Collection of nests with eggs, followed by captive propagation in aquariums, came next.

Although successful spawning in aquariums had not been achieved as of 1994, wild-collected eggs have hatched in captivity, and fry have been reared to a size large enough for release. The fry are being stocked into Abrams Creek in the Great Smoky Mountains, another stream in which both species are believed to have occurred. If populations can be established in Abrams Creek, the species will be brought a step back from the brink of extinction.

Contacts

Regional Office of Endangered Species
U.S. Fish and Wildlife Service
1875 Century Blvd., Suite 200
Atlanta, Georgia 30345
http://southeast.fws.gov/

References

Bauer, B. H., G. R. Dinkins, and C. A. Etnier. 1983. "Discovery of *Noturus baileyi* and *N. flavipinnis* in Citico Creek, Little Tennessee River System." *Copeia* 1983:558-560.

Dinkins, G. R. 1982. "Status Survey of the Smoky Madtom (*Noturus baileyi*)." U.S. Fish and Wildlife Service, Asheville, North Carolina.

U.S. Fish and Wildlife Service. 1985. "Smoky Madtom Recovery Plan." U.S. Fish and Wildlife Service, Atlanta.

Yellowfin Madtom

Noturus flavipinnis

Status	Threatened
Listed	September 9, 1977
Family	Ictaluridae (Catfish)
Description	Small catfish tinged with yellow.
Habitat	Moderately flowing, warm streams.
Food	Aquatic insects.
Reproduction	Spawns in the spring.
Threats	Water diversion, pollution, siltation.
Range	Georgia, Tennessee, Virginia

Description

The yellowfin madtom, *Noturus flavipinnis*, is a small, elongated catfish that grows to a maximum length of about 3.6 in (9 cm). It has large eyes, a rounded caudal fin, and a dark spot on the upper sides just in front of the tail fin. The body, especially the fins, are tinged with yellow.

Behavior

Very little is known of the yellowfin madtom's reproductive behavior since few specimens have been collected during spawning. However, it is thought they spawn in the late spring, and like other madtoms, deposit their eggs on the underside of stones upstream from the usual habitat. The yellowfin madtom feeds on a variety of aquatic insects, and is most active at night.

Habitat

This small catfish inhabits moderately flowing streams with clean, warm water, adequate plant cover, and little siltation. At night, the nocturnal yellowfin madtom is likely to be found on the streambed away from the banks and riffle areas.

Distribution

The yellowfin madtom was probably widely distributed throughout many of the lower streams of the Tennessee River basin above Chattanooga, Tennessee at one time. It has been collected from six streams—Chickamauga Creek, Hines Creek, the North Fork of the Holston River, Cooper Creek, Powell River, and Citico Creek.

Only three known populations remain in Citico Creek (Monroe County) and Powell River (Hancock County) in Tennessee, and Copper Creek (Scott and Russell counties) in Virginia. An experimental population has been established on the Holston River in Tennessee and Virginia.

In 1990, the population trend for the yellowfin madtom appeared to be a steep downward slope. Cooperating conservation groups therefore decided to take only one yellowfin nest from Citico Creek in 1991; to stock all of the juveniles that were reared back into Citico Creek (68 total); and not take any nests from Citico Creek in 1992. In 1993, the yellowfin madtom population index suggested a strong upward trend. Two nests were collected, and all 113 of the juveniles produced were released back into Citico Creek. At the time of the 1994 survey, the number of yellowfins looked promising, indicating a continuing trend toward successful recovery.

Threats

Three of the six historical populations have been lost because of water impoundment and pollution. At present, the Powell River site is threatened by coal siltation. Even if all coal mining stopped now,

Yellowfin Madtom, photograph. U. S. Fish and Wildlife Service. Reproduced by permission.

previously deposited siltation would continue to threaten yellowfin madtom habitat. The Citico Creek locality in the Cherokee National Forest is probably the most secure, but faces some danger of acid contamination because of the nature of shale strata in the region.

Conservation and Recovery

The U. S. Fish and Wildlife Service (FWS) has finalized plans to establish a "non- essential experimental" population on the North Fork of the Holston River in Washington County, Tennessee. A non-essential experimental population is one whose survival is not considered essential to the survival of the species. This designation allows scientists more management flexibility. Authority over the experiment is assigned to the state of Virginia.

Since the early 1980s, biologists with the Cherokee National Forest have studied and monitored the populations of the fish in cooperation with the University of Tennessee, Tennessee Wildlife Resources

Agency, U.S. Fish and Wildlife Service, Great Smoky Mountains National Park, and a private organization, Conservation Fisheries, Inc. Research on the life histories of the species was funded by these cooperators. Annual population monitoring began in 1986. Collection of nests with eggs, followed by captive propagation in aquariums, came next.

Although successful spawning in aquariums had not been achieved as of 1994, wild-collected eggs have hatched in captivity, and fry have been reared to a size large enough for release. The fry are being stocked into Abrams Creek in the Great Smoky Mountains, another stream in which both species are believed to have occurred. If populations can be established in Abrams Creek, these species will be brought a step back from the brink of extinction.

Since the late 1980s, the FWS has been working with the National Park Service to reintroduce the yellowfin madtom in Abrams Creek within the Great Smoky Mountains National Park (Blount County, Tennessee). When this population is established, FWS will turn its efforts to the Holston River reintroduction.

During 1989-1991, when the yellowfin madtom population index was so low, it was comforting to know that some individuals were being held in an experimental captive breeding program. Full recovery of this species and several others in the southern Appalachian Mountains will be assured only by habitat restoration, successful captive breeding programs, and the establishment of reintroduced populations.

Contact

U.S. Fish and Wildlife Service
Regional Office, Division of Endangered Species
1875 Century Blvd., Suite 200
Atlanta, Georgia 30345
http://southeast.fws.gov/

References

Bauer, B. H., G. L. Denkins, and D. A. Etnier. 1983. "Discovery of *Noturus baileyi* and *N. flavipinnis* in Citico Creek, Little Tennessee River System." *Copeia* 1983:558-560.

Taylor, W. R., R. E. Jenkins, and E. A. Lachner. 1971. "Rediscovery and Description of the Ictalurid Catfish, *Noturus flavipinnis*." *Proceedings of the Biological Society of Washington* 83:469-476.

U.S. Fish and Wildlife Service. 1983. "Yellowfin Madtom Recovery Plan." U.S. Fish and Wildlife Service, Atlanta.

Neosho Madtom

Noturus placidus

Status	Threatened
Listed	May 22, 1990
Family	Ictaluridae
Description	A small catfish.
Habitat	Streams and small rivers with a gravel bottom.
Food	Aquatic invertebrates.
Reproduction	Lays externally fertilized eggs.
Threats	Habitat destruction and water pollution.
Range	Kansas, Missouri, Oklahoma

Description

The Neosho madtom is a small, flat-headed catfish with a body length less than about 3.2 in (8.7 cm). Its body color is yellowish, with four brownish saddles on the back and scattered mottling on the sides.

Behavior

The Neosho madtom feeds on aquatic insects such as mayfly larvae (Ephemeroptera), usually during the several hours before sunset. Little is known of its reproductive habits, although it is thought to spawn in June and July.

Habitat

The Neosho madtom is found in stream riffles over a loosely-packed gravel bottom. Adults prefer swift, shallow currents while young fish inhabit deeper water with slower currents.

Distribution

The Neosho madtom occurs in reaches of the Neosho, Cottonwood, and Spring Rivers, in the Arkansas River drainage in Kansas, Missouri, and Oklahoma.

Threats

Much of the original habitat of the Neosho madtom has been destroyed by the construction of dams and reservoirs, which inundate habitat and destroy the gravel riffles and the swift currents the fish needs to live. Cold water released from the Tenkiller Dam killed off all Neosho madtoms on the Illinois River in Oklahoma. New impoundments are a potential threat to the Neosho madtom, by altering flow and other habitat characteristics and isolating populations. Commercial dredging for gravel removes riffle habitat and may also destroy madtoms. Organic and nutrient pollution from feedlots, runoff from agricultural fields, municipal and industrial sewage effluent, accidental spills from roads, the Wolf Creek Nuclear Generating Station, and the Cherokee County Superfund Site cleanup operations are also a threat.

Conservation and Recovery

Various actions have been undertaken on behalf of the Neosho madtom. Studies have been made of its habitat use and distribution in four selected river reaches. Oklahoma State University conducted a survey of the Neosho River, resulting in two additional site records within the known range of the rare fish. Consultations with the Federal Highway Administration resulted in a highway bridge being constructed over the Neosho River in a way that avoided impacts to the madtom. The U. S. Fish and Wildlife Service also consulted with the Soil Conservation Service on the construction of a dam on a tributary watershed within the Cottonwood River Basin, re-

Neosho Madtom, photograph by Suzanne L. Collins and Joseph T.Collins, VTC Enterprises, Inc. Reproduced by permission.

sulting in design changes and a monitoring program to try to avoid damages, and to determine what residual effects may have occurred. Continuing needs include studies of population size and mobility, and assessment of the degree of competition with other species, especially the slender madtom (*Noturus exilis*). Protecting critical habitat in the Neosho, Cottonwood, and Spring Rivers is also crucial.

Contacts

U. S. Fish and Wildlife Service
Regional Office, Division of Endangered Species
P.O. Box 1306
Albuquerque, New Mexico 87103-1306
Telephone: (505) 248-6911
Fax: (505) 248-6915
http://southwest.fws.gov/

U. S. Fish and Wildlife Service
Regional Office, Division of Endangered Species
1 Federal Drive
BHW Federal Building
Fort Snelling, Minnesota 55111

Telephone: (612) 713-5360
http://midwest.fws.gov/

U. S. Fish and Wildlife Service
Regional Office, Division of Endangered Species
P. O. Box 25486
Denver Federal Center
Denver, Colorado 80225
http://www.r6.fws.gov/

U. S. Fish and Wildlife Service, Northern Prairie
Wildlife Research Center
8711 37th Street Southeast
Jamestown, North Dakota 58401

Reference

Northern Prairie Wildlife Research Center. 2000. "Status of Listed Species and Recovery Plan Development: Neosho Madtom." *Northern Prairie Wildlife Research Center.* (http://www.npwrc. usgs.gov/resource/distr/others/recoprog/states/ species/notuplac.htm). Date Accessed: July 6, 2000.

Pygmy Madtom

Noturus stanauli

Status	Endangered
Listed	April 25, 1993
Family	Ictaluridae (Catfish)
Description	Smallest member of the catfish family; an unusually long adipose fin.
Habitat	Moderate to large rivers on shallow pea-size gravel shoals with moderate to strong current.
Threats	Siltation and other pollution from poor land use practices, coal mining and waste discharge.
Range	Tennessee

Description

The madtoms are the smallest members of the catfish family. Madtoms can be distinguished by their small size and an unusually long adipose fin and round tail fin.

The *Noturus stanauli* (pygmy madtom) is the smallest of the known madtoms, growing to a maximum length of 1.5 in (3.8 cm). Its head is flat and is a dark brownish gray, except for the unpigmented areas around the tip of the snout and nares. It has a very distinctive pigmentation pattern, dark brown or black above the midline of the body and pale yellow or white below. Also, most or all of its fins are unpigmented, It has eight soft pectoral fin rays and 14-16 anal rays. The pectoral spines have strong recurred posterior serrae and well-developed anterior serrae.

Behavior

Much of the species' life history is unknown However, much can be inferred from comparisons with closely related species, According to most recent phylogenies, the pygmy madtom's closest relatives are members of a group including the least madtom (*Noturus hildebrandi*) and the smoky madtom (*Noturus baileyi).*

The average life span of most madtoms is two or three years. However, members of the subgenus Rabida, of which the pygmy madtom is a member, are the shortest-lived madtoms, living only one to two years.

Pygmy madtom reproductive behavior is probably similar to that of closely related madtom species. Related madtoms nest in cavities beneath slabrocks and at times use other cover objects, such as cans and bottles. As native mussels are abundant in pygmy madtom habitat, it is possible that this species might use empty mussel shells for nesting cover. Reproduction likely occurs from spring to early summer; smoky madtom and least madtom reproduction occurs between late May and mid-July. Males guard eggs and young within their territories for several weeks, until the young are actively feeding. Other riffle-dwelling madtom species have been observed nesting in shallow heads or foots of pools, including the closely related smoky madtom and least madtom.

Madtoms almost exclusively prey on aquatic insect larvae. Most authors have suggested that they are primarily opportunistic feeders and take prey items in proportion to their abundance.

These fish possess a dangerous venomous pectoral spine with which they will not hesitate to inflict a wound in self-defense.

Habitat

This species is found in moderate to large rivers on shallow pea-size gravel shoals with moderate to

J. R. Shute

strong current. Although there are no observations of seasonal habitat shifts, the closely related smoky madtom is known to switch from riffles in summer and fall to overwinter in shallow pools. Many individuals are also found in the flowing portions of pools during the reproductive season.

This species' distribution overlaps the Oak-Hickory Ecosystem and Nashville Basin. The elevation is about 660 ft (200 m). Most of the outer part of the Basin is deeply dissected and consists of steep slopes between narrow rolling ridgetops and narrow valleys. The inner part of the Basin is predominantly undulating and rolling. The average annual precipitation is about 35-45 in (89-114 cm). The soils of this ecosystem are varied, have a thermic temperature regime, an udic moisture regime and a clay subsoil.

Distribution

The fish fauna of the Tennessee River valley has been extensively surveyed; however, the pygmy madtom, which was likely once more widespread in the Tennessee River system, has been collected from only two short river reaches separated by about 600 river miles (965 river km). It has been taken from the Duck River, Humphreys and Hickman Counties, Tennessee, and from the Clinch River, Hancock County.

Threats

Generally this species of the pygmy madtom is threatened by water quality degradation as a result of siltation and other pollution from poor land use practices, coal mining and waste discharge.

The Tennessee and Cumberland Rivers are renowned as two of the most severely altered riverine systems due to many anthropogenic activities. Most of the main stem of both rivers and many tributaries are impounded. In addition, there has been a loss of the riverine habitat and impoundments usually alter downstream aquatic habitats.

Siltation and toxic runoff have been the result of coal mining activities which unavoidably have adversely affected many reaches. Runoff from urban areas has also degraded water and substrate quality. The aquatic faunal diversity has declined due to this habitat destruction.

Because the two known populations are isolated from each other by impoundments, recolonization of any extirpated population is not be possible without human intervention. The absence of natural gene flow among populations of these fishes leaves the long-term genetic viability of these isolated populations in question. Additionally, several madtom species have, for unexplained reasons, been extirpated from portions of their range. In addition to visible habitat degradation, a variety of complex organic chemicals that may occur only in trace amounts have been added to the waters. Many madtoms are apparently restricted to only the best remaining riverine systems, suggesting that their specialized reproductive habits are impaired by contaminated water.

Due to the limited distribution of this species, a stochastic event such as an accidental toxic chemical spill could cause extirpation. As the populations are separated by impoundments natural recolonization of an extirpated population would be virtually impossible.

The pygmy madtom is not generally protected from threats other than take without a State permit.

Future activities which could impact this species are the issuance of permits for hydroelectric facility construction and operation, coal mining, reservoir construction, stream alterations, wastewater facility development, pesticide registration and road and bridge construction.

Conservation and Recovery

The U.S. Fish and Wildlife Service published a Recover Plan for the pygmy madtom in 1994. This endangered fish only survives in one short reach of a stream in the Tennessee River drainage: the Clinch River (it is probably recently extirpated from the Duck River). The objective of the recovery plan is to search for additional surviving populations, and to ensure the protection of the habitat of the known one. The plan also has criteria for enhancing the known habitat, monitoring the populations of the pygmy madtom, and conducting research into its biology and habitat needs, including methods of beneficial management. Crucial to the survival of the pygmy madtom is the improvement of its habitat, especially through better land-use practices that would reduce erosion and stabilize streambanks. It is also essential to take actions to prevent any potential spills of toxic chemicals into the Clinch River, as such an occurrence could cause the extinction of the pygmy madtom. The rare fish should be bred in captivity, to provide stock for the establishment of one or more additional wild populations in suitable habitat.

Contacts

U. S. Fish and Wildlife Service
Asheville Ecological Services Field Office
160 Zillicoa Street
Asheville, North Carolina 28801-1082
Telephone: (828) 258-3939

U. S. Fish and Wildlife Service
Regional Office, Division of Endangered Species
1875 Century Blvd., Suite 200
Atlanta, Georgia 30345
http://southeast.fws.gov/

References

U.S. Fish and Wildlife Service. 27 April 1993. "Endangered and Threatened Wildlife and Plants; Determination of Endangered Status for the Duskytail Darter, Palezone Shiner and Pygmy Madtom." *Federal Register* http://endangered.fws.gov/r/fr93502.html

U.S. Fish and Wildlife Service. 1994. "Pygmy Madtom Recovery Plan." Atlanta, GA.

Scioto Madtom

Noturus trautmani

Status	Endangered
Listed	September 25, 1975
Family	Ictaluridae (Catfish)
Description	Small dusky olive or dark brown catfish with a milky white belly and four dark-saddle markings across its back.
Habitat	Stream riffles or moderate flow over gravel substrate.
Food	Bottom browsing on plant matter and detritus.
Reproduction	Probably spawns in summer, depositing eggs in nests.
Threats	Critically low numbers.
Range	Ohio

Description

The Scioto madtom, *Noturus trautmani*, is a small catfish ranging from 1.4 to 2.3 in (3.6 to 6 cm) in length. Its coloration is a dusky olive or dark brown, mottled with gray. There are four distinct, dark saddle markings across the back. The belly is unspotted and milky white. The caudal (tail) fin is marked by a dark bar or crescent while the adipose fin is yellowish. It has a slender, scaleless body, broad flat head, long barbels around the mouth, and sharp, heavy pectoral and dorsal spines. Pricks from these spines are strongly irritating to humans.

Behavior

It is assumed that the Scioto madtom is a bottom browser and, like most of its relatives, feeds on plant and animal detritus. Feeding occurs primarily at night and food items are identified by the barbels. The madtom becomes inactive during the day and remains hidden in the substrate.

Although breeding sites have not been located, this species is thought to spawn in summer and migrate downstream in the fall. Madtoms deposit eggs in nests located in depressions or cavities. The male guards both the nest and the young for up to several weeks following hatching.

Habitat

Based on habitat conditions in its former range, it would appear that the Scioto madtom prefers stream riffles of moderate flow over a substrate of gravel. Water is of generally high quality with little suspended sediment.

Distribution

This species was first collected in 1943 from Big Darby Creek (Pickaway County), a tributary of the Scioto River basin. It is thought to be endemic to this central Ohio watershed. Only 18 specimens have ever been netted, most in a single stretch of creek near the village of Fox.

Few rare fish have been sought as avidly as the Scioto madtom, but it has not been collected since 1957, and many biologists have declared it extinct. If this madtom still exists, it survives in very low numbers. Intensive surveys in suitable habitats in adjacent drainages between 1981 and 1985 failed to located any specimens of the Scioto madtom. Only 18 specimens are known to have been collected at all, and most of these were from a fairly small area of Big Darby Creek.

Threats

Because no population centers have ever been located, it is difficult to determine what, if any, environmental factors have contributed to the Scioto madtom's decline. However, the construction of impoundments on Big Darby Creek and the Scioto River increased siltation, and the pollution level has generally increased, both of which could have contributed to the madtom's decline.

Conservation and Recovery

Although this fish may be extinct, the Fish and Wildlife Service has deemed it prudent to maintain its Endangered status. If a population is rediscovered, it will be afforded immediate protection under the provisions of the Endangered Species Act. If the species is removed from the list and then rediscovered, the entire listing process would have to be reinitiated.

Contact

Regional Office of Endangered Species
U.S. Fish and Wildlife Service
Federal Building, Fort Snelling
Twin Cities, Minnesota 55111
http://midwest.fws.gov/

Reference

Trautman, M. B. 1981. *The Fishes of Ohio.* The Ohio State University Press, Columbus.

Mexican Blindcat

Prietella phreatophila

Status	Endangered
Listed	June 2, 1970
Family	Ictaluridae
Description	Small, blind catfish.
Habitat	Freshwater pools in caves.
Food	Organic detritus and small inverte-brates.
Reproduction	Externally fertilized eggs.
Threats	Habitat damage caused by pollution.
Range	Mexico

Description

The Mexican blindcat is a small catfish, achieving a length of up to 0.5 in (1.2 cm). Its eyes are greatly reduced and non-functional, and its skin lacks pigmentation.

Behavior

The Mexican blindcat does not have functional eyes, and perceives its environment through its tactile barbels and probably also by sensing electrical fields. The male digs a shallow nest, where the female lays eggs, which are fertilized externally by milt (sperm) excreted by the male. The developing eggs in the nest are guarded until they hatch. The Mexican blindcat has been maintained in captivity, but it has not been induced to breed.

Habitat

The Mexican blindcat occurs in dark, underground, freshwater pools and wells in tropical areas. This unusual aquatic habitat is known as "hypogeous," or underground habitat. The underground habitat is periodically subject to rapid changes in water volume, due to flows associated with surface rains and underground streams passing through bedrock fractures.

Distribution

The Mexican blindcat was first discovered in underground cave-pools and wells in central Coahuila State, Mexico. Recent discoveries of populations of congeneric (same genus) blindcats in northern and eastern Mexico have expanded the range of this fish. Initial taxonomic research considers that these populations represent at least two different species.

Threats

Some populations of the Mexican blindcat have been severely affected by habitat damage caused by pollution by nutrients and pesticides, and perhaps by excessive collecting.

Conservation and Recovery

Recent fieldwork in northern Mexico has found additional populations of the Mexican blindcat, so the species may not be as endangered as once thought. However, all of its known habitats are vulnerable to pollution and disturbance. The habitats of the Mexican blindcat are not protected.

Contact

Instituto Nacional de Ecología
Av. Revolución, 1425
Col. Campestre, C.P. 01040, Mexico, D.F.
http://www.ine.gob.mx/

References

Borowsky, R. 1996. "The sierra de El Abra of north-eastern Mexico: blind fish in the world's largest cave system." *Tropical Fish Hobbyist* 44(7): 178-188

Parzefall, J. 1993. "Behavioural ecology of cave-dwelling fishes." In *Behaviour of Teleost Fishes*, edited by T. J. Pitcher. Chapman & Hall, London. pp. 573-606.

Delta Smelt

Hypomesus transpacificus

Status	Endangered
Listed	March 5, 1993
Family	Osmeridae (Smelt)
Description	Slender-bodied translucent fish with steely-blue sheen.
Habitat	Fresh and brackish shallow water with low salinity.
Food	Copepods, amphipods and opossum shrimp.
Reproduction	1,200-2,600 eggs between February and June.
Threats	Drought, chemicals.
Range	California

Description

The delta smelt is a slender-bodied fish typically 2.4-2.8 in (6.1-7.1 cm) long. Some individuals may reach a standard length of 4.7 in (11.9 cm). Live specimens are nearly translucent and have a steely-blue sheen to their sides. Occasionally there may be one chromatophore between the mandibles, but usually none are present. Its mouth is small, with a maxilla that does not extend past the mid-point of the eye. The eyes are relatively large; the orbit width is contained about 3.5-4 times in the head length. Small, pointed teeth are present in the upper and lower jaws. The first gill arch has 27-33 gill rakers and there are seven branchiostegal rays. There are nine to ten dorsal fin rays, eight pelvic fin rays, ten to 12 pectoral fin rays, and 15-17 anal fin rays. The lateral line is incomplete and has 53-60 scales along it. There are four to five pyloric caeca.

Behavior

Delta smelt inhabit open, surface waters of the Delta and Suisun Bay, where they presumably school. Spawning takes place between January and July, as inferred from larvae collected during this period. Timing and length of the spawning season may vary. Spawning usually takes place from late March through mid-May in tow outflow years. Spawning pulses have not been detected. Spawning occurs in sloughs and shallow edge-waters of channels in the upper Delta.

Laboratory observations have indicated that delta smelt are broadcast spawners and that the eggs sink to the bottom and stick to hard substrates such as: rock, gravel, tree roots or submerged branches, and submerged vegetation. At 57-61°F (14-16°C), embryonic development to hatching takes nine to 14 days and feeding begins four to five days later.

Newly hatched delta smelt have a large oil globule that makes them semi-buoyant, allowing them to maintain themselves just off the bottom, where they feed on microscopic crustaceans and other microscopic prey. Once the swimbladder (a gas-filled organ that allows fish to maintain neutral buoyancy) develops, larvae become more buoyant and rise up higher into the water column. At this stage, most are presumably washed downstream until they reach the mixing zone or the area immediately upstream of it.

Growth is rapid and juvenile fish are 1.6-2 in (4-5 cm) long by early August. By this time, young-of-year fish dominate trawl catches of delta smelt, and adults become rare. Delta smelt reach 2.2-2.8 in (5.6-7.1 cm) standard length in seven to nine

Delta Smelt, photograph by B. "Moose" Peterson/WRP. Reproduced by permission.

months. Growth during the next three months slows down considerably, presumably because most of the energy ingested is being directed towards gonadal development. There is no correlation between size and fecundity, and females between 2.3-2.8 in (5.8-7.1 cm) standard length lay 1,200-2,600 eggs, which is low when compared to two other species of Osmeridae occurring in California that exhibit fecundities from 5,000 to 25,000 eggs per female. The abrupt change from a single-age, adult cohort during spawning in spring to a population dominated by juveniles in summer suggests strongly that most adults die after they spawn.

The primary foods for all life stages of the delta smelt are nauplius, copepodite, copepodid, and adult stages of the euryhaline copepod *Eurytemora affinis*. Pelagic larvae are zooplanktivores and feed on copepods, cladocerans, and amphipods. Adults consume *E. affinis* during all times of the year. The opossum shrimp (*Mysis relicta*) is secondarily important as food for adults, and cladocerans are consumed seasonally.

Habitat

H. transpacificus is the only smelt endemic to California and the only true native estuarine species found in the Sacramento-San Joaquin estuary, known as the Delta. It is a euryhaline species, a species adapted to living in fresh and brackish water, that occupies estuarine areas with salinities below 2 grams per liter. It rarely occurs in estuarine waters with more than 10-12 ppt salinity, about one-third sea water.

Delta smelt is adapted for life in the mixing zone of the Sacramento-San Joaquin estuary. The estuary is an ecosystem where the mixing zone and salinity levels are determined by the interaction of river outflow and tidal action. Individuals appear to be most abundant in shallow, low salinity water associated with the mixing zone, except when they spawn.

The larvae require the high microzooplankton densities produced by the mixing zone environment. The best survival and growth of larvae occurs when the mixing zone occupies a large geographic area, including extensive shoal regions that provide suitable spawning substrates within the euphotic zone (depths less than 13 ft, or 4 m).

During periods of drought and increased water diversions, the mixing zone and associated delta smelt populations are shifted farther upstream in the Delta. The mixing zone is now primarily located in river channels during the entire year because of increased water exports and diversions. When located upstream, the mixing zone becomes confined to the deep river channels, becomes smaller in total surface area, contains very few shoal areas of suitable spawning substrates, may have swifter, more turbulent water currents, and lacks high zooplankton productivity. Reproduction of the species is very likely adversely affected now that the mixing zone is located in the main channels of the Delta.

Distribution

The delta smelt is endemic to California and the only true native estuarine species found in the Delta. Historically, the fish occurred from Suisun Bay upstream into the Sacramento and San Joaquin Rivers. The species historically congregated in upper Suisun Bay and Montezuma Slough when the Sacramento and San Joaquin river flows were high. During very high river outflows, some individuals would be washed into San Pablo Bay.

The species is now rare in Suisun Bay, and virtually absent from Suisun Marsh where it was once seasonally common. The center of the species abundance has shifted to the Sacramento River channel in the Delta. They occur in the Delta primarily below Isleton on the Sacramento River, below Mossdale on the San Joaquin River, and in Suisun Bay. They move into freshwater when spawning (ranging from January to July) and can occur in: (1) the Sacramento River as high as Sacramento, (2) the Mokelumne River system, (3) the Cache Slough region, (4) the Delta, and, (5) the Montezuma Slough area of the estuary. During high outflow periods, they may be washed into San Pablo Bay, but they do not establish permanent populations there. Since 1982, the center of delta smelt abundance has been the northwestern Delta in the channel of the Sacramento River. However, high outflows in the winter of 1992-93 allowed delta smelt to recolonize Suisun Bay in 1993. Delta smelt are captured seasonally in Suisun Marsh.

Delta smelt were once one of the most common pelagic (living in open water away from the bottom) fish in the upper Sacramento-San Joaquin estuary. Delta smelt abundance from year to year has fluctuated greatly in the past, but between 1982 and 1992 their population was consistently low. The decline became precipitous in 1982 and 1983 due to extremely high outflows and continued through the drought years 1987-92. In 1993, numbers increased considerably, apparently in response to a wet winter and spring. During the period 1982-92, most of the population was confined to the Sacramento River channel between Collinsville and Rio Vista. This was still an area of high abundance in 1993, but delta smelt were also abundant in Suisun Bay. The actual size of the delta smelt population is not known. In 1990, the estimated population was 280,000. The pelagic life style of delta smelt, short life span, spawning habits, and relatively low fecundity indicate that a fairly substantial population probably is necessary to keep the species from becoming extinct.

Threats

The delta smelt occurs only in Suisun Bay and the Sacramento-San Joaquin estuary near San Francisco Bay in California. The species has declined nearly 90% over the last 20 years, and is primarily threatened by large freshwater exports from the Sacramento River and San Joaquin River diversions for agriculture and urban use. Prolonged drought, introduced nonindigenous aquatic species, reduction in abundance of key food organisms, and agricultural and industrial chemicals also threaten this species.

The decline in the species' population was concurrent with increased human changes to seasonal Delta hydrology, freshwater exports, and the accompanying changes in the temporal, spatial, and relative ratios of water diversions. Delta water diversions and exports presently total up to about nine million acre-feet per year. State and Federal projects presently export about six million acre-feet per year when there is sufficient water available, and in-Delta agricultural uses result in diversion of about three million additional acre-feet per year. The U. S. Fish & Wildlife Service is currently aware of another 21 major Central Valley Project, State Water Project, or private organizations' proposals that will result in increased water exports from the Delta. This will reduce water inflow to the Delta, changing the timing and volume of Delta inflow, or increasing heavy metal contamination into the Delta.

Since 1983, the proportion of water exported from the Delta during October through March has been higher than in earlier years. The timing of these proportionally higher exports have coincided with the species' spawning season. During periods of high export pumping and low to moderate river outflows, reaches of the San Joaquin River reverse direction and flow to the pumping plants located in the southern Delta. During this reversal flow, out-migrating larval and juvenile fish of many species become disoriented. Large mortalities occur as a result of entrainment and predation by striped bass at the various pumping plants and other water diversion sites. Net positive riverine flows and estuarine outflows of sufficient magnitude are required for *H. transpacificus* larvae to be carried downstream into the upper end of the mixing zone of the estuary rather than upstream to the pumping plants.

During periods of drought and increased water diversions, the mixing zone and associated delta smelt populations are shifted farther upstream in the Delta. When located upstream, the mixing zone becomes confined to the deep river channels, becomes smaller in total surface area, contains very few shoal areas of suitable spawning substrates, may have swifter, more turbulent water currents, and lacks high zooplankton productivity.

Harvesting of the species is not known to be a major limiting factor, though some individuals are harvested as a non-target by-catch in commercial bait fisheries for other baitfish species. Predation by striped bass, as mentioned above, has become a limiting factor coupled with the reversal of flow in riverine habitats.

Poor water quality may also be limiting factor. All major rivers in the species' range are exposed to large volumes of agricultural and industrial chemicals that are applied in the California Central Valley watersheds. Agricultural chemicals and their residues, and chemicals originating in urban runoff, find their way into the rivers and estuaries. In the Colusa Basin Drainage Canal, significant toxicity has been documented in striped bass embryos and larvae, medaka larvae, the major food organism of the striped bass larvae and juveniles, and the opossum shrimp. Some heavy metal contaminants have been released into the Delta from industrial and mining enterprises. These compounds could adversely affect the species' survival.

Nonindigenous aquatic species have been introduced into the Delta by untreated discharges of ship ballast water. Several introduced species adversely affect the delta smelt. An Asian clam, introduced as larvae at the beginning of the present drought, was first discovered in the Suisun Bay in October of 1986. By June of 1987, the Asian clam was nearly everywhere in Suisun, San Pablo, and San Francisco Bays irrespective of salinity, water depth, and sediment type at densities greater than 10,000 individuals per square meter. This clam could potentially play an important role in affecting the phytoplankton dynamics in the estuary. It may have an affect on the fish by decreasing phytoplankton and by directly consuming the smelt's primary food. Weakened larvae due to reduced food availability or feeding efficiency causing decreased food ingestion rates makes the species more vulnerable to starvation or predation.

Water diversions throughout the species' range has been the major cause of the species decline. Future diversions must be carefully considered so as not to further jeopardize the species. Stricter regulation on chemical runoff into the Delta region needs to be established. Discharges of ship ballast water must be properly treated to inhibit further introduction of nonindigenous species into the habitat. Stocking of the area with striped bass should be discontinued due to the increased predation threat caused by this species. Reintroduction of *E. affinis*, the species' main food source, should be instigated to lessen the chance of the smelt's starvation. Captive breeding programs for the species should be implemented to increase the genetic variance and increase the species' chance for survival.

The waters of the estuary receive a variety of toxic substances, including agricultural pesticides, heavy metals, and other products of urbanized society. The effects of these toxic compounds on larval fishes and their food supply are poorly known, but there is growing evidence that larval striped bass are suffering direct mortality or additional stress from low concentrations of toxic substances. There is also evidence that planktonic organisms upon which delta smelt feed may be depleted on occasion by brief aperiodic flushing of high concentrations of pesticides through the system. It is not known if these substances also are affecting delta smelt.

Although delta smelt has managed to coexist with introduced bass and other competitors in the past, it is quite possible that at low population levels interactions with them could prevent recovery.

In particular, inland silversides are usually collected in areas where delta smelt may spawn and they could be major predators on eggs and larvae. Since 1988, chameleon gobies have increased dramatically in the Delta, and adults of this species and yellowfin goby may prey on delta smelt eggs and larvae.

In past years, efforts to enhance striped bass populations by planting large numbers of juveniles from hatcheries could have had a negative effect on other pelagic fishes in the estuary once bass have reached a size where predation begins on these fish. The enhanced predator populations, without a concomitant enhancement of prey populations such as delta smelt, may have resulted in excessive predation pressure on prey species. In 1992, planting of juvenile striped bass was halted indefinitely because of potential effects of predation on juvenile winter-run chinook salmon.

Conservation and Recovery

Delta smelt adults seek shallow, fresh or slightly brackish backwater sloughs and edgewaters for spawning. To ensure egg hatching and larval viability, spawning areas also must provide water with low concentrations of pollutants, and adequate substrates for egg attachment comprised of submerged tree roots and branches and submersed vegetation.

To ensure that delta smelt larvae are transported from the area where they are hatched to shallow, productive rearing or nursery habitat, the Sacramento and San Joaquin Rivers and their tributary channels must be protected from physical disturbance, such as sand and gravel mining, diking, dredging, and levee or bank protection and maintenance, and flow disruption. Adequate river flow is necessary to transport larvae from upstream spawning areas to rearing habitat in Suisun Bay.

Delta smelt larvae and juveniles must be provided a shallow, protective, food-rich environment in which to protect larval, juvenile, and adult delta smelt from entrainment in the water projects. Protection of rearing habitat conditions may be required from the beginning of February through the summer.

Adult delta smelt must be provided unrestricted access to suitable spawning habitat in a period that may extend from December to July. Adequate flow and suitable water quality may need to be maintained to attract migrating adults in the Sacramento and San Joaquin River channels and their associated tributaries. These areas should be protected from physical disturbance and flow disruption during migratory periods.

Delta smelt culture techniques and facilities are being developed. Initial efforts to breed delta smelt in captivity have been successful, although rearing beyond the larval stage so far has not been possible. However, if hatchery propagation is to be successful, fish must be released into an environment that provides ample food, low levels of toxic compounds, and low entrainment losses.

Contact

U.S. Fish and Wildlife Service
Regional Office, Division of Endangered Species
Eastside Federal Complex
911 N. E. 11th Ave.
Portland, Oregon 97232-4181
Telephone: (503) 231-6121
http://pacific.fws.gov/

Reference

U.S. Fish and Wildlife Service. 5 March 1993. "Endangered and Threatened Wildlife and Plants; Determination of Threatened Status for the Delta Smelt." *Federal Register* 58 (42): 12854-12863.

Little Kern Golden Trout

Oncorhynchus aguabonita whitei

Status	Threatened
Listed	April 13, 1978
Family	Salmonidae (Trout)
Description	Olive-backed trout with red cheeks and belly, and a golden underside.
Habitat	Clear, cool flowing water.
Food	Insects.
Reproduction	Spawns in late June.
Threats	Competition and hybridization with rainbow trout, pollution.
Range	California

Description

The Little Kern golden trout, *Oncorhynchus aguabonita whitei*, a subspecies of the golden trout, reaches an adult size of 8-12 in (20-31 cm) and weighs up to 1 lb (0.45 kg). It is olive above a broad reddish lateral line, golden yellow below, and has red cheeks and belly.

Behavior

The golden trout usually spawns in late June in gravel riffle areas. Males reach sexual maturity in about two years, females in three. The trout's diet consists primarily of aquatic insects.

Habitat

This trout inhabits clear, cool, swift-flowing streams.

Distribution

The Little Kern golden trout has been found only in the Little Kern River (Tulare County), California. Genetically pure populations of Little Kern golden trout now survive only in headwater streams that were not stocked with rainbow trout or that have falls preventing upstream migration

of rainbow trout. There are no current population figures.

Threats

In the 1930s rainbow trout were introduced into the Little Kern River system and hybridization with the golden trout resulted. Additional threats to the Little Kern golden trout are the possibility of water quality degradation from off-road vehicle use in the area, improper road construction, careless logging, pollution from mining operations, and overgrazing in the drainage basin.

Conservation and Recovery

The staff of the Sequoia National Forest has consulted informally with the Fish and Wildlife Service (FWS) to determine the best way to harvest timber in the forest without disturbing the golden trout's habitat.

The main channel and tributary streams of the Little Kern river above the barrier falls have been designated by the FWS as habitat critical for the survival of the Little Kern golden trout. The state Department of Fish and Game has established the Golden Trout Wilderness Area, encompassing the FWS-designated area in the Sequoia National For-

Little Kern Golden Trout, photograph by B. "Moose" Peterson/WRP. Reproduced by permission.

est, and has developed a management plan for the species.

Contact

U.S. Fish and Wildlife Service
Division of Endangered Species
Eastside Federal Complex
911 N.E. 11th Ave
Portland, Oregon 97232
http://pacific.fws.gov/

References

Behnke, R. J. 1980. *Monograph of the Native Trouts of the Genus* Oncorhynchus *of Western North America.* U.S. Fish and Wildlife Service, Denver.

Moyle, Peter. 1976. *Inland Fishes of California.* University of California Press, Berkeley.

U.S. Fish and Wildlife Service. 1989. *Endangered Species Technical Bulletin.* Vol XIV, No. 5: 2-9.

Apache Trout

Oncorhynchus apache

Status	Threatened
Listed	March 11, 1967
Family	Salmonidae (Trout)
Description	Medium-sized yellowish trout with dark brown spots.
Habitat	Headwaters of high, cold mountain streams.
Food	Insects.
Reproduction	Spawns from March to mid-June.
Threats	Competition from other trout species; hybridization.
Range	Arizona

Description

Also known as the Arizona trout, the Apache trout, *Oncorhynchus apache*, has a deep, compressed body with a large dorsal fin. It grows to a mature length of between 7-9 in (18-23 cm). The yellowish or yellow-olive back and sides are covered with uniformly spaced dark brown spots.

Behavior

The Apache trout feeds principally during the day on terrestrial and aquatic insects, taking them from the surface. Alternative food sources may include other fish, crustaceans, mollusks, and snails. After reaching three years of age, females spawn from March through mid-June, depositing eggs in several reeds. In Big Bonita Creek, fry did not emerge for 60 days, which limited growth before the severe winter set in and contributed to mortality of the young. Newly emerged fry migrate at night to reduce the risk of predation.

Habitat

The Apache trout inhabits small, cold, high gradient, fast-flowing mountain streams with boulders, rocks, and gravel substrates. The streams flow through mixed coniferous forest at altitudes above 8,250 ft (2,500 m). Water temperature ranges from 32-72°F (0-22 °C). The upper lethal temperature for the Apache trout is 73°F (23 °C), and most fish refuse to eat at temperatures above 68°F (20 °C). The severe winters typically deplete trout populations, which must recover sufficiently the following summer.

Distribution

This species was known historically from the headwaters of the Little Colorado, Salt, San Francisco, White and Black River systems in the White Mountains of eastern Arizona (Greenlee County) and western New Mexico (Catron County).

Currently, the headwaters of the White and Black river systems on the Fort Apache Indian Reservation support the greatest concentrations of the Apache trout. Streams in the Gila and Apache-Sitgreaves national forests have been rehabilitated to support reintroduced populations. Several thousand of the fish have been counted in Bonita Creek on the East Fork White River. Before reintroductions began, the range of the Apache trout was reduced to about 30 mi (48 km) of stream, less than five percent of the historic range.

Threats

Competition with introduced, non-native fishes has been the major factor in the decline of the Apache trout. Brook, rainbow, and brown trouts were introduced into many streams in the region as game

Apache Trout, photograph. U. S. Fish and Wildlife Service. Reproduced by permission.

fishes and expanded their populations to the detriment of the Apache trout. The Apache trout also has the ability to interbreed with the brown trout, and hybrids were spreading into many streams. Continuing hybridization would have meant the extinction of the Apache trout as an identifiable species. In the late 1970s the Fish and Wildlife Service (FWS) began a project to rehabilitate streams on the Fort Apache Indian Reservation. Ord Creek was treated repeatedly to remove introduced trout, and Apache trout from Bonita Creek were relocated there. But in spite of precautions, the brook trout reappeared in the stream the following year.

Conservation and Recovery

Biologists have erected artificial barriers in several streams to separate the species and reduce hybridization, and the Bureau of Indian Affairs and the White Mountain Apache Tribe have cooperated extensively in reintroduction efforts. In 1984, Dry Creek in the Gila National Forest was rehabilitated

to accept a transplanted population of Apache trout. The stream was sampled and found to still contain trout hybrids that would dilute the genetic purity of transplanted Apaches. The project was delayed until hybrids could be removed. In 1986-87, five streams were scheduled for restoration, and in 1988 and 1990, barriers were constructed on Little Bonita Bay and three streams were restocked with pure species.

In 1986 the Williams Creek National Fish Hatchery succeeded for the first time in raising the Apache trout in captivity. Personnel at the facility designed an innovative feeding system that simulates natural stream conditions and automatically dispenses brine shrimp for the fry. The Hatchery hopes to raise 50,000 Apache trout fingerlings each year for restocking streams on the Fort Apache Reservation and Apache-Sitgreaves National Forest Service. The success of this hatchery program and continuing reintroduction efforts virtually ensure the long-term survival of the Apache trout.

Contact

U.S. Fish and Wildlife Service
Division of Endangered Species
P.O. Box 1306
Albuquerque, New Mexico 87103
http://southwest.fws.gov/

References

Alcorn, S. R. 1976. "Temperature Tolerances and Upper Lethal Limits of *Salmo apache*." *Transaction of the American Fishery Society* 105(2): 294-295.

Apache Trout Recovery Team. 1983. "Apache Trout Recovery Efforts." U.S. Fish and Wildlife Service, Albuquerque.

U.S. Fish and Wildlife Service. 1979. "Recovery Plan for the Arizona Trout, *Salmo apache*." U.S. Fish and Wildlife Service, Albuquerque.

Umpqua River Cutthroat Trout

Oncorhynchus clarki clarki

Status	Delisted
Listed	August 9, 1996, Endangered
Delisted	April 26, 2000
Family	Salmonidae
Description	Profusion of small to medium-sized spots of irregular shape; not brilliantly colored.
Habitat	Two to five months in saltwater.
Food	Invertebrates.
Reproduction	Ideal spawning in cool streams with moderate flows and little change in water temperature.
Threats	Degradation of habitat due to logging, recreational fishing, drought.
Range	Oregon

Description

The Umpqua River cutthroat trout, *Oncorhynchus clarki clarki,* is a distinct population segment of the coastal cutthroat trout. Coastal cutthroat trout differ from all other trout by their profusion of small to medium-sized spots of irregular shape. In addition, they do not develop the brilliant colors associated with inland cutthroat trout, which are a separate species. In the sea-run populations, spots and colors are further obscured by the silvery skin deposit common to sea-run trout. Non-anadromous (resident) fish tend to be darker, with a copper or brass sheen.

Behavior

Coastal cutthroat trout have the most complex and flexible life history of the Pacific salmonids, one characterized by three patterns of migratory behavior. These behaviors are termed anadromy, potamodromy, and residency, and examples of each are presently found in the Umpqua River. Anadromy is a common life-history trait of Pacific salmonids, and is exemplified by a species that migrates from freshwater to the ocean and then returns to freshwater as an adult to spawn. Potamodromy, a relatively uncommon life-history trait, is exemplified by a species that undertakes freshwater migrations of varying length without entering the ocean. Residency, a relatively common life-history trait, is exemplified by a species that remains within a relatively small freshwater range throughout its entire life cycle.

Coastal cutthroat trout that sea-run, unlike other anadromous salmonids, do not overwinter in the ocean, and they only rarely make extended migrations across large bodies of water. They migrate in the near-shore marine habitat, rarely going farther than 6 mi (9 km) from land. Most anadromous cutthroat trout enter seawater as two- or three-year olds, although some may remain in freshwater up to five years before entering the sea. Other cutthroat trout may never out-migrate at all, remaining residents of small headwater tributaries. Still other cutthroat trout may migrate only into rivers and lakes, even when they have access to the ocean.

Habitat

The Umpqua River cutthroat trout spends two to five months in salt water, usually close to shore near estuaries and beaches. Because they spend less time in a marine environment, ocean conditions have a

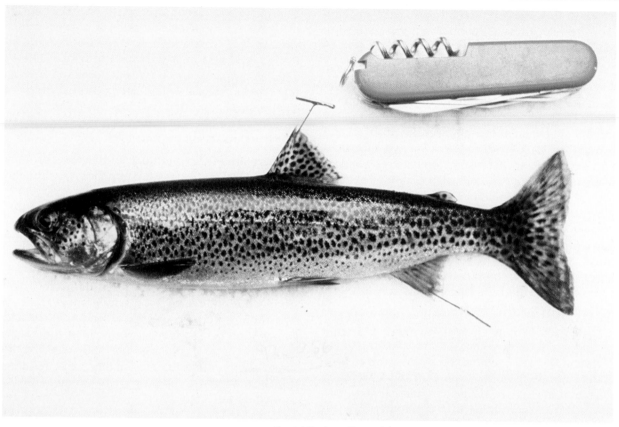

Coastal Cutthroat Trout, photograph by T. H. Williams. Reproduced by permission.

lesser impact on the cutthroat than on other salmon species, and during periods of poor ocean conditions, such as rises in water temperature as a result of El Nino, the cutthroat will return to a freshwater habitat.

For adequate spawning conditions to occur, streams must be cool with moderate flows and little change in water temperature. The lowest cutthroat populations occur in streams whose forest canopy has been removed by silviculture (clearing of forest), which caused fluctuation of water temperatures leading to outbreaks of disease, altered timing of migration, and accelerated maturation. The removal of streamside vegetation decreases woody debris that provides cover for the cutthroat and interrupts the food chain for other species that comprise the cutthroat's diet. Cutthroats require a fairly clean gravel substrate, and siltation will hinder the emergence of fry, as well as limit the production of invertebrates that are a part of the cut-

throat's diet. Logging also alters the oxygen content of the water, and changes the velocity and depth.

Distribution

Each salmonid species has had a unique evolutionary history and utilizes ecological niches different from all other species. The coastal cutthroat trout subspecies, native to western North America, is found in the coastal temperate rainforests from southeast Alaska to northern California.

The Umpqua River cutthroat trout, a distinct population segment of the coastal cutthroat trout, inhabits a large coastal basin draining in the southwestern Oregon coast. The Umpqua River cutthroat trout lives and spawns in the main-stem Umpqua River, the North Umpqua River, the South Umpqua River, and their respective tributaries—the chief of which are the Smith River and Calapooya, Elk, and Scholfield Creeks. The estuary of the Umpqua River is one of the largest on the Oregon coast, and any factors that degrade its productivity and quality are likely to decrease the Umpqua River cutthroat trout population.

The historical range of anadromous cutthroat trout may have extended up to Toketee Falls on the North Umpqua River, with populations most likely inhabiting areas above both Soda Springs and Galesville Dams. Natural barriers form gene flow barriers, resulting in a distinction between resident cutthroat trout populations above natural barriers and migrating populations below such barriers. However, the isolated cutthroat trout populations created several decades ago by these impassable barriers are believed to be still genetically similar to those cutthroat trout residing below the artificial barriers, so the populations residing above Galesville and Soda Springs Dams are listed as Umpqua River cutthroat trout.

The North Umpqua River has larger and healthier populations of cutthroat trout than the South Umpqua River, as determined by Winchester Dam counts, although ladder counts at the Winchester Dam indicate that the sea-run population of the cutthroat trout has declined to precipitously low levels. Although no long-term surveys of cutthroat trout were conducted in the South Umpqua River before 1993, a very small, wild cutthroat trout population probably exists in the South Umpqua River system. The South Umpqua River appears to have always been less conducive to cold-water dependent species like the cutthroat trout than the North Umpqua River. The North Umpqua River begins farther inland and flows for a substantial distance at a higher elevation than most other Oregon coastal rivers; as a result, the North Umpqua River has historically had cooler water temperatures and larger summer water flows than other local rivers. The South Umpqua River also begins at a relatively high altitude but stays there only for a short time. Its rapid drop in elevation leads to higher water temperatures and lower summer flows than the North Umpqua River. Present conditions in the North Umpqua River continue to be more favorable for cutthroat trout production than those found in the South Umpqua River.

Threats

The extremely low numbers of adult cutthroat trout counted at Winchester Dam on the North

Umpqua River signal a high risk of extinction for the species. The primary threats to the survival of the Umpqua River cutthroat trout are recreational fishing, and loss or degradation of habitat due to logging. Drought, which leads to decreased streamflows and increased water temperatures, is the principal natural condition that may have contributed to reduced numbers of cutthroat trout, especially in the seven dry years prior to 1996.

There are other conditions and factors that may have affected cutthroat trout populations, although they are less well-established as active agents than the ones cited above. These include the following: predation by marine competitors and birds; adverse environmental conditions resulting from natural factors such as floods and poor ocean conditions; pollution caused by agriculture and urban development; disease outbreaks caused by hatchery introductions and warm water temperatures; mortality resulting from unscreened irrigation inlets; and competition in estuaries between native and hatchery cutthroat trout; and loss of habitat caused by the construction of dams. Non-native fish and pinnipeds are known to prey on or compete with salmonids but there is no specific information regarding the impact of predation on Umpqua River cutthroat trout. Disease is not believed to be a critical factor in the decline of cutthroat trout.

The documentary evidence available suggests that land-use practices in Oregon have generally contributed to the curtailment, modification, and destruction of habitat diversity and complexity there. This habitat attrition has reduced salmonid production and accelerated the frequency and magnitude of both flooding and drought. Estuarine habitats, highly productive environments vital to the life cycle of the Umpqua River cutthroat trout, have been especially affected. There, degradation and loss through dredging, filling, and diking for agricultural, commercial, and municipal uses have substantially contributed to the decline in cutthroat trout.

At least 60% of the Oregon streams used by anadromous salmonids are rated as having low or very low habitat quality. These poorly rated streams are all found in watersheds that have been moderately to heavily harvested for lumber, while those streams rated good are found almost exclusively in drainages that have had little or no history of timber harvest and road construction. This strongly suggests that silviculture has degraded water quality and contributed heavily to the decline of the Umpqua River cutthroat trout. Silviculture is practiced on approximately 70% of the federal, state, and private timberland within the Umpqua River basin area, and more than 80 of the basin's river reaches are designated as being of limited water quality.

Commercial logging and other forest and rangeland management practices often have multiple adverse effects on the habitats that support the cutthroat trout. The removal of forest canopy can cause an increase in both the maximum and the diurnal fluctuation of water temperatures, leading to disease outbreaks, altered timing of migration, and accelerated maturation. The removal of streamside vegetation can deplete the bank area of potential new woody debris that provides cover for cutthroat trout. Loss of riparian areas can also result in decreased invertebrate production and detritus sources, both of which are key components of the species' food chain. Siltation, another result of some logging practices, is known to hinder fry emergence from the gravel, and may limit production of benthic invertebrates. Logging can also decrease the dissolved oxygen content of both surface and intragravel water while changing stream flow regimes, adversely affecting water velocity and depth characteristics.

The riparian habitat loss attributed to logging can also affect river temperature and acidity in ways that are harmful for cutthroat trout. Summer water temperatures and the frequency of winter flooding have increased in the Umpqua River watershed since the mid-1950s, presumably as a result of poor logging practices. Summer water temperatures are often above the preferred range for cutthroat trout and other salmonid populations (about 44-61°F [6-16°C]) in portions of the river. The riparian forest canopy has begun to recover recently in the North Umpqua River watershed, but maximum water temperatures are still higher than those preferred by cutthroat trout. This recovery has been slower in the South Umpqua River watershed and conditions for cutthroat trout have remained poorer than in the North Umpqua River. Data indicates that pH levels in various tributaries of the Umpqua River basin exceed the state of Oregon's water quality standards, and these pH levels can be attributed to the effects of logging.

Recent increased timber harvest on federal land could increase the chance of further damage to aquatic resources in the Umpqua River basin. The emergency salvage timber sale provisions of a 1995 appropriations act have resulted in harvest of at least seven timber sales in the Umpqua River basin. The impacts of such sales are especially great in the South Umpqua River basin since existing habitat and water quality conditions are recognized as poor in this area.

Cutthroat trout are not harvested commercially—though they are believed to be the victims of undocumented illegal harvest—but they are a popular gamefish throughout the Pacific Northwest. Recreational fishing has likely contributed to the general decline in Umpqua River cutthroat trout populations. Current fish hatchery practices may also play a role in the decline of native cutthroat trout. A long-standing fishery in the lower main-stem Umpqua River aimed at hatchery-reared cutthroat trout probably promoted an incidental harvest of native Umpqua River cutthroat trout. Extensive releases of Alsea River hatchery-reared cutthroat trout have occurred near the Umpqua River estuary in the Smith River from 1975 to 1994 and in Scholfield Creek from 1983 to the present time. Until recently, approximately 12,000 hatchery-reared cutthroat trout per year have been released into the Smith River. Releases of approximately 4,000 hatchery-reared cutthroat trout per year continue to occur into Scholfield Creek. Given the life history of cutthroat trout, their extensive use of estuaries, their susceptibility to angling, and the potential impact of recreational fishing to native fish stocks, it is likely that these releases have had a substantial impact on native populations.

Cutthroat trout upstream migrations historically extended from June through January. It has been observed that currently migration may only be possible during late July and August, the period of highest water temperatures in the Umpqua River. This may be detrimental to the cutthroat trout because the adults experience delays during the spawning migration from the lower Umpqua River estuary to the North and South Umpqua Rivers. The high water temperatures on the main-stem Umpqua River in late July and August may have had a significant impact on the survival and time of arrival of cutthroat trout at Winchester Dam. Ongoing Oregon Department of Fish and Wildlife radio-tagging studies are expected to provide more insight into this issue.

Conservation and Recovery

Several recovery efforts are underway that may slow or reverse the decline of Umpqua River cutthroat trout. These include the Northwest Forest Plan, Coastal Salmon Restoration Initiative, and Umpqua River Basin Fisheries Restoration Initiative. There are several current trapping efforts underway in the Umpqua River basin to trap juvenile cutthroat trout for population inventory. There may be other ongoing research to determine population presence and abundance.

In August 1996, the U. S. Fish and Wildlife Service (FWS) added the species to the List of Endangered and Threatened Wildlife. The National Marine Fisheries Service, which has jurisdiction for this population, has determined that the Umpqua River cutthroat trout, which was identified as an ESU (Evolutionarily Significant Unit) of the species, is part of a larger population segment that is not endangered or threatened. The Umpqua River cutthroat trout was removed from the list effective April 26, 2000, and the FWS has removed the protections given to this species by the Endangered Species Act.

Contacts

Regional Office of Endangered Species
U. S. Fish and Wildlife Service
Eastside Federal Center
911 N. E. 11th Ave.
Portland, Oregon 97232-4181
Telephone: (503) 231-6121
http://pacific.fws.gov/

National Marine Fisheries Service
Environmental and Technical Services Division
525 NE Oregon St.—Suite 500
Portland, Oregon 97232-2737
Telephone: (503) 231-2005

Office of Protected Resources
1315 East-West Highway
Silver Spring, Maryland 20910
Telephone: (301) 713-1401

Reference

National Marine Fisheries Service. 9 August 1996. "Endangered Status for Umpqua River Cutthroat Trout in Oregon." *Federal Register* 61 (155):41514-41522.

Lahontan Cutthroat Trout

Oncorhynchus clarki henshawi

Status	Threatened
Listed	Endangered: October 13, 1970
Reclassified	Threatened: July 16, 1975
Family	Salmonidae (Trout)
Description	Green to greenish blue with a bright red cutthroat mark.
Habitat	Cool, well-oxygenated water.
Food	Aquatic insects.
Reproduction	Spawns in April and May.
Threats	Dam construction, degradation of water quality, competition with other trout.
Range	California, Nevada

Description

The Lahontan cutthroat trout, *Oncorhynchus clarki henshawi*, a subspecies of the cutthroat trout, can be distinguished by its relatively larger size. This trout ranges from 10-15 in (25-38 cm) in length and usually has a bright red stripe, or "cutthroat" mark, under each side of the lower jaw. The body is elongated and compressed with a relatively long head. The back is green to greenish blue. The head, fins, and sides may be yellowy, and the belly is silvery. Some biologists consider the Lahontan a separate subspecies only because of its geographic isolation from other cutthroat trout.

The species was originally listed as Endangered in 1970, and reclassified as Threatened in 1975 to facilitate management and allow regulated angling. There is no designated critical habitat for the species.

Behavior

The life history of the Lahontan cutthroat is similar to that of other cutthroat trout, which feed on aquatic insects and spawn from the middle of April to late May. The eggs hatch in six to eight weeks.

Habitat

This species inhabits lakes and streams and requires cool, well-oxygenated water during all its life stages. Flowing water with clean gravel substrates is necessary for spawning. The Lahontan subspecies is adapted to the highly mineralized waters found in many of the region's lakes.

Distribution

The Lahontan cutthroat trout is endemic to the enclosed Lahontan basin of west-central Nevada and adjacent portions of California. It once inhabited Winnemucca Lake, which is now dry, and was eliminated from Lake Tahoe by competing species.

In Nevada, the Lahontan cutthroat trout exists in about 155 streams and six lakes and reservoirs in Nevada, California, Oregon, and Utah. The species has been introduced outside its native range, primarily for sport fishing purposes. As of 1995, the fish occupied approximately 0.4 % of its former lake habitat and 10.7% of its former stream habitat within native range. Independence and Summit Lakes support the only remaining reproducing lacustrine form of Lahontan cutthroat trout within native range. Many of the fluvial populations occupy iso-

Lahontan Cutthroat Trout, photograph by B. "Moose" Peterson/WRP. Reproduced by permission.

lated stream segments of larger river systems with no opportunity for natural recolonization. No current population estimates have been made.

A captive population of the Lahontan trout, used to replenish stocks in Pyramid Lake, is maintained at the Verdi Hatchery, Nevada. The California Department of Fish and Game has established a captive population at its Kernville Hatchery.

Threats

The Lahontan cutthroat trout declined throughout its range because of damage to its spawning beds caused by timber harvesting, forest fires, and grazing livestock. Streams have been dammed and water diverted for irrigation or municipal uses. Construction of the Marble Bluff Dam closed off spawning grounds in the headwaters of the Truckee River until recent construction of a fish ladder there. Water pollution, particularly downstream from Reno and Carson City, has also been a limiting factor.

Conservation and Recovery

In 1986 U.S. Fish and Wildlife Service (FWS) personnel assisted more than 1,400 Lahontan cutthroat trout over the Marble Bluff Dam, the largest trout run in the fish facility's history. These spawning trout were expected to contribute to the recovering natural population in the Truckee River.

In 1987 FWS personnel conducted an emergency operation to salvage some 200 Lahontan cutthroats from drought-depleted sections of By-Day Creek in Mono County, California. These fish were transferred to a headwater stream in the East Walker River basin, then used to restock Slinkard Creek the following year.

With planned recovery activities nearly 50 percent complete, the FWS accelerated its stream rehabilitation efforts in 1989, spurred by successes in artificial propagation at the Kernville Hatchery. According to the 1995 Recovery Plan, the species will be considered for delisting when management has been instituted to enhance and protect habitat required to sustain appropriate numbers of viable, self-sustaining populations. Recovery objectives protect all existing populations until research and analysis can validate population requirements by basin.

Because fluvial and lacustrine adapted forms of the Lahontan cutthroat have different behavior, ecology, and habitat use, recovery criteria necessary to delist the species may be modified after population viability anaysis has been conducted. The ecological and genetic importance of Pyramid and Walker Lakes in recovery of the lacustrine form will be determined after research has been conducted.

Actions needed to recover the species include the identification and coordination of interagency activities to secure, manage and improve habitat for all existing populations; the revision of the Recovery Plan based on genetic, population viability and other research; and the development and imple-

mentation of reintroduction plans. Lahontan cutthroat trout harvests should also be regulated to maintain viable populations. Self-sustaining populations existing outside of native range should be managed until their need is completed.

Contact

U.S. Fish and Wildlife Service
Division of Endangered Species
Eastside Federal Complex
911 N.E. 11th Ave.
Portland, Oregon 97232
http://pacific.fws.gov/

References

Behnke, R. J. 1980. *Monograph of the Native Trouts of the Genus* Oncorhynchus *of Western North America.* U.S. Fish and Wildlife Service, Denver.

Moyle, P. B. 1976. *Inland Fishes of California.* University of California Press, Berkeley.

Paiute Cutthroat Trout

Oncorhynchus clarki seleniris

Status	Threatened
Listed	March 11, 1967
Family	Salmonidae (Trout)
Description	Purplish pink trout with few or no body spots and a cutthroat mark under the jaw.
Habitat	Cool, well-oxygenated streams.
Food	Insects.
Reproduction	Spawns in early summer.
Threats	Limited distribution, hybridization.
Range	California

Description

The Paiute cutthroat trout, *Oncorhynchus clarki seleniris*, is a subspecies of the cutthroat trout, growing 10-12 in (25-30 cm). Its body is elongated and compressed, its head is relatively long, and it has a bright red stripe, or "cutthroat" mark, under each side of the lower jaw. Distinguishing characteristics of the Paiute cutthroat are its purplish pink color and the absence (or near absence) of body spots. Before being reduced to subspecies status in 1947, it was classified as a full species (*Oncorhynchus seleniris*).

Behavior

The Paiute cutthroat trout matures sexually at two years and spawns during the early summer in flowing waters above a clean gravel stream bed. The female excavates a nest and spawns with the dominant male. Eggs hatch in six to eight weeks when the water temperature is 42-52°F (6-11°C). The number of eggs produced is proportional to the female's length. An 8 in (20 cm) female will spawn 250-400 eggs. Fingerlings often move into tributary streams until large enough to survive in the main streams. The largest fish vigorously defend stream pools, driving smaller ones into runs and riffles in available unoccupied habitat.

The Paiute, like other trout, are opportunistic feeders of aquatic insects throughout the year and terrestrial insects during the summer. Although the Paiute cutthroat cannot successfully compete with other trout species for food, food is not a limiting factor for establishing a new environment as long as no other trout species are present.

Habitat

The Paiute cutthroat trout requires cool, well-oxygenated water during all its life stages and prefers streams with moderate current in meadow areas. It can survive in lakes, but must have access to flowing water for spawning. There are no unique cover or shelter requirements.

The Silver Creek habitat above Llewellyn Falls is a large mountain meadow at 8,000 ft (2,500 m) elevation. At the highest elevation of Silver Creek the dominant vegetation is pine and red fir. Stands of aspen trees occur throughout the watershed. The stream is mainly riffles with few large pools; the temperature ranges from 32°F (0°C) in winter to 65°F (18°C) in summer. North Fork Cottonwood Creek is smaller than Silver Creek and receives less precipitation but the habitat conditions are similar.

Distribution

This subspecies was first collected above Llewellyn Falls in Alpine County, California, and

Paiute Cutthroat Trout, photograph by B. "Moose" Peterson. Reproduced by permission.

has an extremely limited range. Historically, it was found only in Silver King Creek in the East Fort Carson River watershed in the Toiyabe National Forest. Silver King Creek is a headwater tributary of the enclosed Lahontan basin of Nevada.

The Paiute cutthroat trout was eliminated from much of its range in the early twentieth century because of interbreeding with the introduced rainbow trout. Several small populations had previously been transplanted into the upper reaches of Silver King Creek above Llewellyn Falls, an impassable barrier for other trout. Some of these fish were transplanted into other California lakes and streams, and at least two populations survive outside the native drainage—Cottonwood Creek (Mono County), and Stairway Creek (Modero County). Recent estimates placed the number of Paiute cutthroat trout at about 2,550. Except for one small inholding in the Silver King basin, the major habitat streams are within the Toiyabe National Forest.

Threats

Probably the greatest threat to this subspecies, besides its limited distribution, is competition and interbreeding with other non-native trout. Where other trout have invaded its habitat, the Paiute cutthroat trout has been displaced or hybridized out of existence. Waters managed for the Paiute cutthroat trout must be protected from the natural or accidental introduction of other trout.

Conservation and Recovery

The extremely limited native range—approximately 9 mi (15 km) in three streams—has complicated recovery efforts. Recovery activities have focused on protecting existing habitat, rehabilitating new sections of streams by removing non-native fishes, and reintroducing the Paiute. State and federal personnel have cooperated to reduce sedimentation and promote the regrowth of native streambank vegetation in the watershed.

In 1988, the U.S. Fish and Wildlife Service (FWS), in cooperation with the Forest Service, completed the first phase of planned recovery activities for Paiute cutthroat trout populations in the Toiyabe National Forest. Several low, instream dams were constructed to improve spawning habitat; a barrier was built to prevent competing trout from intermingling with the Paiute on Fourmile Creek; sections of river bank were recontoured to decrease erosion and promote regrowth of natural vegetation; work was completed on the banks of a tributary to reduce sedimentation in Silver King Creek; and solar-powered electric fences were installed to exclude cattle and protect the growth of willow trees along streams. Volunteers donated more than 1,100 hours of labor to these projects.

Contact

U.S. Fish and Wildlife Service
Division of Endangered Species
Eastside Federal Complex
911 N.E. 11th Ave.
Portland, Oregon 97232
http://pacific.fws.gov/

References

Behnke, R. J. 1980. *Monograph of the Native Trouts of the Genus* Oncorhynchus *of Western North America.* U.S. Fish and Wildlife Service, Denver.

Diana, J. S., and E. D. Lane. 1978. "The Movement and Distribution of Paiute Cutthroat Trout in Cottonwood Creek, California." *Transactions of the American Fisheries Society* 107:444-448.

U. S. Fish and Wildlife Service. 1985. "Paiute Cutthroat Trout Recovery Plan." U. S. Fish and Wildlife Service, Portland.

Greenback Cutthroat Trout

Oncorhynchus clarki stomias

Status	Threatened
Listed	March 11, 1967 Endangered
Reclassified	April 18, 1978 Threatened
Family	Salmonidae (Trout)
Description	Heavily spotted trout; males often have a blood-red belly
Habitat	Flowing mountain streams.
Food	Aquatic insects.
Reproduction	Spawns in the spring.
Threats	Competition with non-native trout, habitat degradation from mining and logging, water diversion.
Range	Colorado

Description

The greenback cutthroat trout, *Oncorhynchus clarki stomias*, typically ranges from 10-15 in (25-38 cm) in length. The largest individuals may weigh up to 4 lbs (1.5 kg). The body and head are elongated. Of all cutthroat trout subspecies, the greenback generally has the largest spots and the most numerous scales. It displays a dark "cutthroat" mark under each side of the jaw. The belly of the mature male is often a vivid, blood-red color.

Behavior

The greenback cutthroat trout feeds on aquatic insects in streams and zooplankton, benthic crustaceans, and insects in lakes. Larger individuals may feed on larval tiger salamanders and darters. If food supplies are adequate and suitable spawning gravel is available near the female's home range, there is no migration. Because trout are an opportunistic feeder, the quantity and quality of food are not a serious limiting factor to the species' survival.

The greenback cutthroat trout reaches sexual maturity at 2-3 years of age. Spawning occurs annually in the spring and early summer until death, at 4-5 years in streams and 8-10 years in lakes. Females construct nests in gravel substrates while the males observe her progress. The dominant male constantly drives away subordinate males, and he fertilizes the eggs during spawning. Other males may fertilize the eggs as well. Females construct nests in suitable gravel and spawn several times over a 2-3 day period. After the eggs are spawned and fertilized, the female covers the eggs with gravel and abandons the nest. Spawning peaks when daily water temperature exceeds 45°F (7°C). The average fecundity of females is 700-1,000 eggs per pound of body weight. The incubating eggs require adequate water flow to maintain sufficient oxygen levels.

In head-to-head competition with the brook trout, the greenback cutthroat is invariably the loser. Although adults rarely interact, brook trout juveniles are more aggressive and drive greenback juveniles out of shallow, protective streams into larger creeks and rivers, where they are devoured by predators.

Habitat

This trout inhabits undisturbed headwaters at elevations of 7,000-11,000 ft (2,100-3,200 m) in the Rocky Mountain National Park and in one spring-fed pond at Fort Carson. It prefers clear, swift-

Greenback Cutthroat Trout, photograph. U. S. Fish and Wildlife Service. Reproduced by permission.

flowing mountain streams but the greenback cutthroat can survive in any habitat and tolerate any water conditions that support other species of trout. Young and juvenile fish occupy shallow, more open habitat, while older fish prefer deeper water with more cover, particularly overhanging banks and vegetation. Riffle areas are used for spawning. Juveniles tend to shelter in shallow backwaters until large enough to fend for themselves in the mainstream.

Distribution

The greenback cutthroat trout is the only trout endemic to the Rocky Mountain sources of the South Platte and Arkansas River systems of north-central and central Colorado. Its range extended from the headwaters of both rivers to the foothills along the Front Range.

The greenback cutthroat trout is found in the headwater streams above barriers that prevent non-native trout from invading the habitat. The species

occurs in the South Platte River, including the east slope drainage of the Rocky Mountain National Park (Cow, Hidden Valley, Pear Reservoir, West and Fern Creeks, Fern, Bear, Caddis and Odessa Lakes, and the Big Thompson River). It is known from Como Creek in the North Boulder Creek watershed (Boulder County), South Boxelder Creek (Douglas County), and the South Fork of Cache la Poudre River in Roosevelt National Forest and Black Hollow Creek (Larimer County). The headwaters of the Arkansas River, including South Huerfano and Cascade Creeks in San Isabel National Forest, and Hourglass Creek, also support populations of the greenback cutthroat trout.

There are no recent estimates, but the greenback population has increased because of successful reintroduction efforts.

Threats

In the late nineteenth century, the greenback cutthroat's numbers were dramatically reduced by toxic mine pollution and water diversion for agricultural irrigation, so that by 1937 the species was thought to be extinct. The agricultural practices resulted in water diversion, reduced water levels, altered water temperature, siltation, and erosion. Logging activities altered the vegetation and hydroelectric power diverted stream flows. Physical damage was inflicted on the watershed by highway construction, ski resort development, and housing projects. Most threatening to the greenback cutthroat was the widespread introduction of nonnative trout—brook, rainbow, brown, and other subspecies of cutthroat—throughout the range of the greenback cutthroat. Brook trout quickly replaced the greenback in small tributary streams and brown trout replaced it in rivers. Rainbow trout hybridized with the greenback and the purity of the species was lost in many populations.

Conservation and Recovery

Efforts to conserve the greenback began as early as 1959, when fingerlings from the Forest Canyon headwaters of the Big Thompson River were stocked in Fay Lake after non-native trout were removed. Unable to survive in Fay Lake, the trout managed to establish a self-sustaining population in Caddis Lake, immediately downstream. In 1967, a brook trout population was eliminated from Black Hollow Creek, and the greenback cutthroat was reintroduced, using stock from Como Creek. A barrier was constructed to prevent the return of brook trout, and the stream was designated a sanctuary for greenback cutthroat trout.

After brook trout were eliminated from Hidden Valley Creek in 1973 and barriers were constructed to prevent the return of competitive species, the greenback population in the stream recovered. In 1975, state and federal biologists successfully transplanted greenbacks to Bear Lake after removing brook trout. Because of these successes, the greenback cutthroat trout was "downlisted" from Endangered to Threatened in 1978. Recovery efforts continue under the direction of the U.S. Fish and Wildlife Service and the Park Service with cooperation of researchers at Colorado State University.

Contact

U.S. Fish and Wildlife Service
Division of Endangered Species
Denver Federal Center
P.O. Box 25486
Denver, Colorado 80225
http://www.r6.fws.gov/

References

Gagnon, J. G. 1973. "The Greenback." *Trout: Quarterly Publication of Trout Unlimited* 144:12, 13-28, 30.

U.S. Fish and Wildlife Service. 1977, 1983 Revision. "Greenback Cutthroat Trout Recovery Plan." U.S. Fish and Wildlife Service, Denver.

Gila Trout

Oncorhnynchus gilae

Status	Endangered
Listed	March 11, 1967
Family	Salmonidae (Trout)
Description	Iridescent, golden trout with prominent, irregular spotting.
Habitat	Headwater streams with cover and riffle areas.
Food	Aquatic invertebrates.
Reproduction	Spawns in the spring.
Threats	Restricted range, hybridization.
Range	Arizona, New Mexico

Description

The Gila trout, *Oncorhnychus gilae,* grows 10-14 in (25-34 cm) in length and is readily identified by its iridescent golden sides, which grade to a dark copper on the gill covers. Irregular spotting is prominent on the back and sides. Dorsal, pelvic, and anal fins have white to yellowish tips. During spawning season, the normally white belly may be streaked with yellow or orange.

Behavior

Spawning occurs in April and May when midday water temperatures reach 46-54°F (8-12°C). Gila trout are opportunistic predators, feeding on insects and aquatic invertebrates.

Habitat

The Gila trout inhabits clear, cool headwater streams with moderate current and sufficient depth and cover to provide refuge during severe droughts. Gila trout usually congregate in deeper pools and in shallow water only where there is protective debris or plant beds.

Distribution

The Gila trout is native to the Mogollon Plateau of New Mexico and Arizona. It was once common in the Gila and San Francisco Rivers and tributary streams, in southwestern New Mexico, and in the Verde and Agua Fria drainages in Arizona. By the 1960s, it was eliminated from the Verde and Agua Fria drainages.

When the Recovery Plan was completed in 1978, native populations of the Gila trout were confined to five streams in New Mexico—Diamond, South Diamond, McKenna, Spruce, and Upper Iron Creeks. In addition, two other streams in Mexico and Arizona harbored introduced populations— McKnight and Sheep Corral Creeks. The 1992 population numbers were for fewer than 10,000 individuals; many were stunted because of crowding or insufficient food sources. Fortunately, healthy breeding populations survived on protected land in the Gila Wilderness Area, providing a strong base for reintroduction efforts.

Threats

The Gila trout declined in its native waters because of degraded water quality, heavy fishing, and hybridization with non-native trout, which were introduced as game fish into the watersheds. Dam building, water pumping, stream channeling, road building, and logging have radically altered the water system within the Gila trout's range.

Gila Trout, photograph by John Rinne, USFS. Reproduced by permission.

Conservation and Recovery

Recovery efforts have focused on removing non-native trouts from selected sections of higher quality streams, erecting barriers to prevent their return, and then restocking the waters with populations of the Gila trout. This strategy essentially creates refuges within the streams, where the Gila trout is the preferred and dominant trout species. The U.S. Fish and Wildlife Service (FWS), the Forest Service, New Mexico Department of Game and Fish, and New Mexico State University have collaborated on recovery.

By the end of 1987, biologists had restored seven populations in designated wilderness areas—six within the Gila National Forest in New Mexico, and one in Prescott National Forest in Arizona. Restoration has been so successful that the FWS has proposed to "downlist" the Gila trout from Endangered to Threatened, although by the time the 1993 Recovery Plan revision was released, that action had not yet taken place. The revision estimated that

downlisting could be possible by 2000 if continuous progress was made.

The recovery team has attracted the support of local residents and sport fishermen by emphasizing the Gila trout's potential as a game fish. Because many of the habitat streams are at or near their carrying capacity, sport fishing is not expected to interfere with the recovery of the Gila trout. If unforeseen problems developed, the sport season could be terminated.

Recovery efforts have had varying levels of success. In the late 1980s, for instance, FWS biologists implemented a captive propagation program by transferring 36 adult fish and 1,800 eggs to Mescalero National Fish Hatchery in New Mexico. Captive-raised fingerlings will be used to build a brood stock and restock new streams. Future efforts will concentrate on rehabilitating and restocking larger streams to expand the Gila trout's range.

Other recovery efforts have included replication of the five relictual populations, completion of several biological and ecological studies, initiation of development of hatchery techniques, and the development of a population monitoring protocol. Survey efforts are continuing in an attempt to locate new populations, and studies are being conducted to establish the degree of genetic divergence among the five indigenous populations and related fish. Public information efforts about the plight of the Gila trout and the need for its recovery have included brochures, a slide series and videotape, and publication of public education articles.

The goal of the Gila Trout Recovery Plan is to improve the status of the fish to the point where survival of all indigenous lineages is secured and maintained. To accomplish this goal, a large array of factors was considered, including the species' historical distribution, its habitat requirements and preferences, and available management alternatives.

The 1993 revised plan outlined two possible strategies for recovery; the first involves the preservation of the Gila trout as a relictual species in a few small, isolated headwater streams without expanding distribution within the historic range to any appreciable degree. The second, preferred strategy, is to accelerate expansion of current distribution of Gila trout within its historic range into larger, more stable, resilient habitats. Adoption of this strategy would greatly reduce the likelihood of local extinction caused by natural, stochastic events and human-induced disturbances.

Contact

U.S. Fish and Wildlife Service
Division of Endangered Species
P.O. Box 1306
Albuquerque, New Mexico 87103
http://southwest.fws.gov/

References

Behnke, R. J., and M. Zarn. 1976. *Biology and Management of Threatened and Endangered Western Trouts.* U.S.D.A. Forest Service General Technical Report RM-23 Rocky Mountain Forest and Range Experiment Station, Fort Collins.

Minckley, W. L. 1973. *Fishes of Arizona.* Arizona Game and Fish Department, Phoenix.

U.S. Fish and Wildlife Service. 1979. "Gila Trout Recovery Plan." U.S. Fish and Wildlife Service, Albuquerque.

Chum Salmon

Oncorhynchus keta

Status	Threatened
Listed	August 2, 1999
Family	Salmonidae
Description	An anadromous salmonid fish.
Habitat	Breeds in cool, clean streams; grows to maturity in the ocean.
Food	Aquatic invertebrates and smaller fish.
Reproduction	Lays eggs in freshwater; young fish migrate to the ocean; adults return to the natal stream to spawn.
Threats	Destruction and degradation of breeding streams by forestry, road building, and other developments; overfishing at sea and during the landward migration.
Range	Oregon, Washington

Description

Chum salmon belong to the family Salmonidae and are one of eight species of Pacific salmonids in the genus *Oncorhynchus*. Chum salmon grow to be among the largest of Pacific salmon, second only to chinook salmon in adult size, with individuals reported up to 42 lbs (19 kg) in weight. Average size for the species is around 8-15 lbs (3.6-6.8 kg). Chum salmon are semelparous (they spawn only once and then die). They spawn in freshwater, and exhibit obligatory anadromy (adults migrate from the ocean to freshwater streams to spawn and die), as there are no recorded landlocked or naturalized freshwater populations. The chum salmon is best known for the canine-like fangs and striking body color of spawning males: a calico pattern, with the anterior two-thirds of the flank marked by a bold, jagged, reddish line and the posterior third by a jagged black line. Females are less flamboyantly colored and lack the extreme dentition of the males.

Behavior

Chum salmon usually spawn in coastal streams. Juveniles out-migrate to seawater almost immediately after emerging from the gravel that covers their redd (spawning bed). This ocean-type migratory behavior contrasts with the stream-type behavior of coastal cutthroat trout, steelhead, coho salmon, and most types of chinook and sockeye salmon, which usually migrate to sea at a larger size, after months or years of freshwater rearing. This means that survival and growth in juvenile chum salmon depend less on freshwater conditions than on favorable estuarine and marine conditions.

Another behavioral difference between chum other salmon that rear extensively in freshwater is that chum salmon form schools, presumably to reduce predation, especially if their movements are synchronized to swamp predators. Age at maturity appears to follow a latitudinal trend, in which a greater number of older fish occur in the northern portion of the range.

Age at maturity has been investigated in many studies, and in both Asia and North America it appears that most chum salmon mature between three and five years of age, with 60-90% of the fish maturing at four years of age. However, a higher proportion of five-year-old fish occurs in the north, and a higher proportion of three-year-old fish occurs in the south: British Columbia, Washington, Oregon.

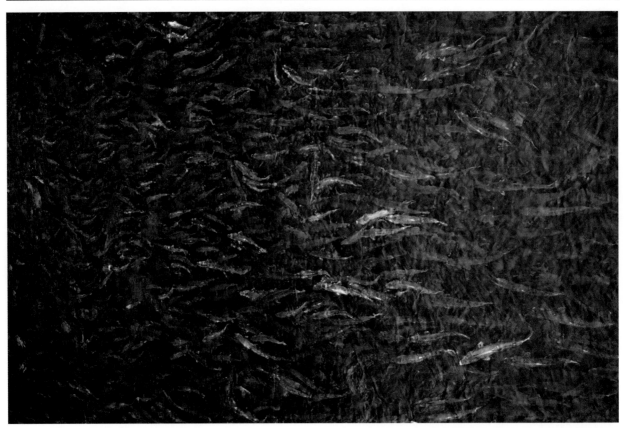

George Cassidy

Habitat

Chum salmon usually spawn in the lower reaches of rivers typically within 60 mi (96 km) of the ocean. Redds are usually dug in the mainstream or in side channels of rivers. In some areas, particularly in Alaska and northern Asia, they typically spawn where upwelling groundwater percolates through the redds.

Chum salmon are believed to spawn primarily in the lower reaches of rivers because they usually show little persistence in surmounting river blockages and low falls. However, in some systems, such as the Skagit River in Washington, chum salmon routinely migrate over long distances upstream, as far as 100 mi (160 km). In two other rivers, the species swims a much greater distance. In the Yukon River, Alaska, and the Amur River, between China and Russia, chum salmon migrate more than 1,500 mi (2,400 km) inland. Although these distances are impressive, both of these rivers have low gradients and are without extensive falls or other blockages to

migration. In the Columbia River basin, there are reports that chum salmon may historically have spawned in the Umatilla and Walla Walla Rivers, more than 180 mi (288 km) from the sea. However, these fish would have had to pass Celilo Falls, a web of rapids and cascades, which presumably were passable by chum salmon only at high water flows.

During the spawning migration, adult chum salmon enter natal river systems from June to March, depending on characteristics of the population or geographic location. Groups of fish entering a river system at particular times or seasons are often identified by the season in which they "run," and run timing has long been used by the fishing community to distinguish sea-run populations of salmon, steelhead, and sea-run cutthroat trout. In Washington, a variety of seasonal runs of chum salmon are recognized, including summer, fall, and winter-run populations. Fall-run chum predominate, but summer runs are found in Hood Canal, the Strait of Juan de Fuca, and in southern Puget Sound. Only two rivers have chum returning so late in the sason that they are designated as winter-run, and both of these are in southern Puget Sound. Adult chum salmon spend their time feeding at sea. However, not much is known about this pelagic stage of their life history.

Distribution

Chum salmon have the widest natural geographic and spawning distribution of any Pacific salmonid. This is primarily because its range extends farther along the shores of the Arctic Ocean than that of the other salmonids. Chum salmon have been documented to spawn from Korea and the Japanese island of Honshu, east around the rim of the North Pacific Ocean, to Monterey Bay in southern California. The range in the Arctic Ocean extends from the Laptev Sea in Russia to the Mackenzie River in Canada. Historically, chum salmon were distributed throughout the coastal regions of western Canada and the United States as far south as Monterey, California. Presently, major spawning populations are found only as far south as Tillamook Bay on the northern Oregon coast.

Chum salmon may historically have been the most abundant of all salmonids. Prior to the 1940s, chum salmon comprised almost 50% of all salmonids in the Pacific Ocean.

The National Marine Fisheries Service has identified four genetically distinct populations of chum salmon (or Evolutionarily Significant Units; ESU). Two of the four are listed as threatened: Hood Canal summer-run chum and Columbia River chum. The other two populations (Puget Sound/Strait of Georgia and Pacific Coast) are distinct populations but are not considered in danger of extinction.

Puget Sound/Strait of Georgia ESU: Not threatened: The Puget Sound/Strait of Georgia ESU includes most U.S. populations of chum salmon outside Alaska. It includes all chum salmon populations from Puget Sound and the Strait of Juan de Fuca. This region also includes Canadian populations from streams draining into the Strait of Georgia. Chum salmon from the west coast of Vancouver Island are not considered part of this ESU, in part because available genetic information suggests these fish are distinct from Puget Sound/Strait of Georgia fish. Chum salmon populations in the Puget Sound/Strait of Georgia ESU have four recognized summer-run populations and two recognized winter-run populations.

Pacific Coast ESU: Not threatened: This region includes all natural chum salmon populations from the Pacific coasts of Washington and Oregon, as well as populations in the Strait of Juan de Fuca west of the Elwha River. This ESU is defined primarily on the basis of life-history and genetic information. Coastal populations form a coherent group that show consistent differences between other fall-run populations in Washington and British Columbia.

The spawning escapements for this population appear to be increasing, to about 35,000 spawners on the Washington coast. The harvest of chum salmon from coastal fisheries combined had averaged 96,000 fish per year from 1988-1992. This suggests a total abundance level on the order of 150,000 adults.

Hood Canal Summer-Run ESU: Threatened: This ESU includes summer-run chum salmon populations in Hood Canal in Puget Sound and in Discovery and Sequim Bays on the Strait of Juan de Fuca. It may also include summer-run fish in the Dungeness River, but the existence of that run is uncertain. Distinctive life-history and genetic traits are the most important factors in identifying this ESU.

Hood Canal summer-run chum salmon spawn from mid-September to mid-October. Fall-run chum salmon spawn from November through December or January. Run timing data from as early as 1913 indicated temporal separation between summer and fall chum salmon in Hood Canal, and recent spawning surveys show that this temporal separation still exists. Genetic data indicate strong and long-standing reproductive isolation between chum salmon in this population and other chum salmon populations in the United States and British Columbia. Hood Canal is also geographically separated from other areas of Puget Sound, the Strait of Georgia, and the Pacific Coast.

In general, summer-run chum salmon are most abundant in the northern part of the range, where they spawn in the mainstreams of rivers. Farther south, water temperatures and stream flows during late summer and early fall become unfavorable for salmonids. These conditions do not improve until the arrival of fall rains in late October/November. Presumably for these reasons, few summer chum populations are recognized south of northern British Columbia. Summer-run chum salmon populations from Washington must return to fresh water and spawn during periods of peak high water temperature, suggesting an adaptation to specialized environmental conditions that allow this life-history strategy to persist in an otherwise inhospitable environment. Therefore, these populations contribute substantially to the ecological/genetic diversity of the species as a whole.

Genetic data indicate that summer-run populations from Hood Canal and the Strait of Juan de Fuca are part of a much more ancient lineage than summer-run chum salmon in southern Puget Sound.

Although summer-run chum salmon in this region have experienced a steady decline since the late-1960s, escapement in 1995-96 increased dramatically in some streams. Spawning escapement of summer-run chum salmon in Hood Canal numbered over 40,000 fish in 1968, but was reduced to only 173 fish in 1989. In 1991, only seven of 12 streams that historically contained spawning runs of summer-run chum salmon still had escapements. Then in 1995-96, escapement increased to more than 21,000 fish in northern Hood Canal, the largest run since the late 1960s.

Summer runs of chum salmon in the Strait of Juan de Fuca did not demonstrate the marked declining trend that has characterized the summer-run populations in Hood Canal in recent years, although they are at very low population levels. Further, though escapement of summer-run chum salmon to Salmon Creek increased in 1996, the other two populations in the Strait of Juan de Fuca did not show similar increases, and the overall trend in the strait populations was one of continued decline.

Of the 12 streams in Hood Canal that had supported spawning populations of summer chum salmon in recent times, five may have become extinct by 1994, and six of the remaining seven showed strong downward trends in abundance. However, in 1995 and 1996, new information demonstrated substantial increases of returning summer chum to some streams. Several factors may have contributed to the dramatic increase in abundance, including hatchery supplementation, reduction in harvest rate, increase in marine survival, and improvements in freshwater habitat.

Columbia River ESU: Threatened Historically, chum salmon were abundant in the lower reaches of the Columbia River and may have spawned as far upstream as the Walla Walla River, over 300 mi (480 km) inland. Only remnant chum salmon populations still exist in the lower Columbia River. They are few in number, low in abundance, and of uncertain stocking history. Genetic data are available for only two small Columbia River populations, which differ substantially from each other as well as from all other chum populations.

During the first half of the twentieth century, commercial fishers harvested as many as 500,000 chum salmon a year. Today, there may be a few thousand, perhaps up to 10,000, chum spawning annually in the Columbia River basin. The chum salmon run size in the Columbia River has been relatively stable since the run collapsed in the mid-1950s. The minimal run size in 1995 was 1,500 adult fish.

Threats

The present depressed condition of many populations of naturally reproducing chum salmon throughout its range is the result of habitat degradation, water diversions, excessive harvesting, and artificial propagation. These factors exacerbate the adverse affects of competition, predation, drought and poor ocean conditions. Habitat modification is a large factor that affects the chum salmon.

Chum salmon depend less on freshwater habitats than some other Pacific salmonids. However, their spawning areas still extend up to 50 miles (80 km) upstream in many rivers, and their requirements for successful spawning and rearing, such as cold, clean water and relatively sediment-free spawning gravel, are similar to those of other Pacific salmon.

Alterations and loss of freshwater habitat for salmonids have been extensively documented in many regions, especially in urban areas or habitat associated with construction of large dams. Since about 1975, a major issue in stream restoration has been the role that large woody debris plays in creating and maintaining Pacific salmon spawning and rearing habitat. Descriptions of pre-development conditions of rivers in Washington and Oregon that had abundant salmonid populations suggest that even big rivers had large amounts of instream woody debris. This debris not only blocked most rivers to navigation, but also contributed to trapping sediments and nutrients, impounding water, and creating many side channels and sloughs. Many streams consisted of a network of sloughs, islands, and beaver ponds with no main channel. For example, portions of the Willamette River reportedly flowed in five separate channels, and many coastal Oregon rivers were so filled with logjams and snags they could not be ascended by early explorers.

Besides clearing rivers for navigation, extensive stream improvements were accomplished to facilitate log drives. Historically, some of the more adverse impacts on the estuarine and freshwater habitats used by chum salmon resulted from stream improvements in the 1800s and early 1900s, when logs were transported down streams and stored in main stems of rivers, lakes, and estuaries. These activities included blocking off sloughs and swamps to keep logs in the mainstream and clearing boulders, trees, logs, and snags from the main channel. Smaller streams required the building of splash dams to provide sufficient water to carry logs. Scouring, widening, and unloading of main-channel gravel during the log drive may have caused as much damage as the initial stream cleaning. Stream cleaning continued through the mid-1970s in many areas not only for flood control and navigation, but also as a fisheries enhancement tool. Debris in streams was viewed as something that would either impede or block fish passage and as a source of channel destruction by scour during storm-induced log-jam failures.

Stream modification with the most impacts on chum salmon are: (1) Water withdrawal, conveyance, storage, and flood control, resulting in insufficient flows, stranding, juvenile entrainment, and instream temperature increases; (2) logging and agriculture leading to the loss of woody debris, sedimentation, loss of riparian vegetation, habitat simplification; (3) mining, especially gravel removal, dredging, pollution; and (4) urbanization leading to stream channelization, increased runoff, pollution, habitat simplification.

Chum salmon generally spend only a short time relative to other salmonids in streams and rivers before migrating downstream to estuarine and nearshore marine habitats. Because of this, the survival of early life history stages depends more on the health and ecological integrity of estuaries and nearshore environments than it does for most other Pacific salmon. Another facotor that effects the survival of the chum salmon is harvest.

Incidental harvest in salmon fisheries in the Strait of Juan de Fuca and coho salmon fisheries in Hood Canal pose a significant threat for the Hood Canal summer-run ESU. Historically, summer chum salmon have not been a primary fishery target in Hood Canal, as harvests have focused on chinook, coho, and fall chum salmon. However, summer chum salmon have a run timing that overlaps with those of chinook and coho salmon, and they have been incidentally harvested in fisheries directed at those species. Prior to 1974, Hood Canal was designated a commercial salmon fishing preserve, with the only net fisheries in Hood Canal occurring on the aboriginal Skokomish Reservation. In 1974, commercial fisheries were opened in Hood Canal, and incidental harvest rates on summer chum salmon began to increase rapidly. By the late 1970s, incidental harvest rates had increased to 50-80% in most of Hood Canal.

Exploitation rates on summer-run chum salmon in Hood Canal have been greatly reduced since 1991 as a result of closures of the coho salmon fishery and of efforts to reduce the harvest of summer chum salmon. Between 1991 and 1996, harvests removed an average of 2.5% of the summer-run chum salmon returning to Hood Canal, compared with an average of 71% in the period from 1980-1989.

The Columbia River historically contained large runs of chum salmon that supported a substantial commercial fishery in the first half of this century. These landings represented a harvest of more than 500,000 chum salmon in some years. There are presently neither recreational nor directed commercial fisheries for chum salmon in the Columbia River, although some chum salmon are taken incidentally in the gill-net fisheries for coho and chinook salmon and there has been minor recreational harvest in some tributaries.

Predation by juvenile coho salmon is a primary another cause of mortality to chum salmon. Artificial propagation is another threat to the chum salmon.

For almost 100 years, hatcheries in the U.S. Pacific Northwest have produced chum salmon for the purpose of increasing the harvest and rebuilding depleted runs. Potential problems associated with hatchery programs include genetic alteration of indigenous, naturally reproducing populations, disease transmission, predation of wild fish, difficulty in determining wild stock status due to incomplete marking of hatchery fish, depletion of wild stock to increase brood stock, and replacement rather than supplementation of wild stocks through competition and continued annual introduction of hatchery fish. All things being equal, the more hatchery fish that are released, the more likely natural populations are to be impacted by hatchery fish. Similarly, the more genetically similar hatchery fish are to natural populations they spawn with, the less change there will be in the genetic makeup of future generations in the natural population.

Conservation and Recovery

The Northwest Forest Plan is a federal interagency cooperative program to coordinate ecosystem management strategy for federal lands administered by the U. S. Forest Service and Bureau of Land Management within the range of the Northern spotted owl, which overlaps considerably with the range of chum salmon.

The most significant element of the Northwest Forest Plan for ocean-run fish is an aquatic ecosystem conservation strategy that includes special land allocations, such as key watersheds and riparian reserves, to provide aquatic habitat refuge; and new watershed analysis, watershed restoration, and monitoring processes.

Several state conservation plans will also benefit the chum salmon: the Washington Wild Stock Restoration Initiative, which implements plans to monitor and evaluate critical populations of salmon and steelheads; Washington Wild Salmonid Policy, which provides habitat protection principles, escapement objectives, harvest management, and genetic conservation for all state agencies; and the Hood Canal/Strait of Juan de Fuca Chum Salmon Conservation Plan.

Exploitation rates on summer-run chum salmon in Hood Canal have been greatly reduced since 1991 as a result of closures of the coho salmon fishery and of efforts to reduce the harvest of summer chum salmon. Between 1991-1996, harvests removed an average of 2.5% of the summer-run chum salmon returning to Hood Canal, compared with an average of 71% in the period from 1980-1989. The harvest restrictions have included an array of specific measures endorsed by both state and tribal fisheries managers, including area closures, restrictions in the duration and timing of chinook and coho salmon fisheries, mesh size restrictions and live-release requirements in net fisheries, catch-and-release requirements for recreational fisheries, and selective gear fisheries that should minimize impacts to summer chum salmon.

Contact

U. S. Fish and Wildlife Service
Regional Office, Division of Endangered Species
Eastside Federal Building
911 N. E. 11th Ave.
Portland, Oregon 97232-4181
Telephone: (503) 231-6121
http://pacific.fws.gov/

References

National Marine Fisheries Service. March 10, 1998. "Proposed Threatened Status and Designated Critical Habitat for Hood Canal Summer-Run Chum Salmon and Columbia River Chum Salmon." *Federal Register* 63(46): 11774.

National Marine Fisheries Service. March 25, 1999. "Threatened Status for Two ESUs of Chum Salmon in Washington and Oregon." *Federal Register* 64(57): 14508.

U. S. Fish and Wildlife Service. 2 August 1999. "Endangered and Threatened Wildlife and Plants; Listing of Nine Evolutionarily Significant Units of Chinook Salmon, Chum Salmon, Sockeye Salmon, and Steelhead." *Federal Register* 64(147): 41835-41839.

Coho Salmon

Oncorhynchus kisutch

Status	Threatened
Listed	November 20, 1996 (Central California); June 18, 1997 (Southern Oregon/Northern California Coasts)
Family	Salmonidae
Description	A salmonid (trout-like) fish.
Habitat	Freshwater streams, northeastern Pacific Ocean.
Food	Invertebrates, smaller fish.
Reproduction	Lays eggs in freshwater.
Threats	Habitat destruction and degradation, and overfishing of adults.
Range	California, Oregon

Description

The coho salmon, also known as the silver salmon, has a trout-like, elongated, moderately compressed body. The mouth is terminal and large. The upper jaw extends beyond the back of the eye, and the snout is narrowly rounded. The upper jaw becomes strongly hooked in spawning males. Coho have well-developed teeth in both jaws, and also on the palate and tongue. Pre-spawning adult coho are colored metallic blue on the back, and silvery on the sides and belly. They have irregular black spots on the back and upper lobe of the caudal fin. The flesh along the base of the teeth on the lower jaw is pale, and the body flesh is colored pink to red. The sexually mature males in freshwater have a brilliant red stripe on their sides, bright green on the back and head, and are often dark on the belly. The females are less strongly colored, and are usually bronze to pinkish-red on the sides.

Behavior

Coho salmon are born in the headwaters of rivers, and spend the first 18 months of their life there. They then migrate to the ocean, where they feed and grow for several years. When they reach sexual maturity, they return to the headwaters of their natal stream, where they breed, and die. Coho feed on aquatic invertebrates when small, graduating to smaller fish, and then to bigger fish as the salmon become larger predators.

Habitat

The freshwater habitat of coho in headwater streams is characterized by cool, clean water. They breed in beds of clean gravel, and this is also where the larvae live. Fingerling-sized and larger life stages in freshwater live in deeper water, such as pools. During the marine phase of their life history, coho live in open-water (or pelagic), cool-temperate regions of the northeastern Pacific Ocean.

Distribution

The historic range of the coho in the lower 48 states included coastal streams of California, Oregon and Washington, plus the much larger Sacramento and Columbia river systems, reaching as far inland as Idaho. It also occurs in rivers throughout coastal British Columbia and western Alaska.

Threats

During the twentieth century, the coho has decreased to as little as 1% of its former abundance in its southern range (in California and Oregon). It is

Ann and Rob Simpson

extirpated in more than half of its native rivers in that region. The decline of the coho stocks of California and Oregon has been caused by several, interacting factors. Much of their freshwater habitat has been degraded by siltation and temperature increases caused by logging and other disturbances in the watersheds of their breeding and rearing habitats in headwater streams. Clear-cut logging in the riparian (or stream-side) zone results in large increases in the summertime water temperature, which can be lethal for these cool-water fish. In addition, the erosion of soil from destabilized streambanks and at road crossings results in the deposition of silt into the gravel spawning and larval-rearing habitat of salmon, which smothers the eggs and larvae. Moreover, many rivers have had hydroelectric dams constructed on them, and this prevents or impedes the migration of coho to and from the sea. Other threats to coho include erosion associated with overgrazing of livestock, in-river mining of gravel or gold, urban and industrial pollution, agricultural diversions, and urbanization. In addition, stocks of coho salmon are heavily fished at sea and when they

are migrating to their breeding habitat. In many cases, the fishing pressure is excessive (this is known as overfishing), and is a further reason why stocks are declining. These factors have affected coho salmon throughout their range on the Pacific coast, but the damages have been most intense for stocks breeding on coastal rivers in California and Oregon. Overall, the coho has become extirpated over about 56% percent of its historic range in the lower 48 states, endangered in about 13%, threatened in about 20%, and of special concern in 5%. In California, for example, about one-half million coho inhabited rivers in the state in the 1940s, but only a few thousand survived in the 1990s. The coastal rivers of Oregon produced about 1.4-million coho in 1900, but fewer than 20,000 in the 1990s. In Washington, the 1.2 million coho that once lived in the Columbia basin are virtually extinct.

Conservation and Recovery

Listing of the threatened stocks of coho in California and Oregon has been a highly contentious and politicized process. The environmental and fishing communities have exerted pressure to list these stocks under the Endangered Species Act. However, this action been resisted by interests in the timber industry, agribusiness, and state governments, who fear restrictions on their activities in order to conserve coho habitat. Finally, in 1999, the National Oceanic and Atmospheric Administration (NOAA) listed the status of coho as "threatened" in the following regions: Central California; Southern Oregon/Northern California Coasts; and Oregon Coast. In addition, coho were judged as "Candidate for Listing" in the following regions: Puget Sound/Strait of Georgia; and Lower Columbia River/Southwest Washington. The key to saving the threatened and depleted stocks of coho in coastal California, Oregon, and Washington is to preserve their small remaining areas of high-quality freshwater habitat in headwater streams. In large part, this requires close restrictions on logging and road building in the watersheds. Moreover, many degraded habitats will have to be managed to improve conditions, particularly in terms of mitigating heavily silted gravel beds. It will also be necessary to restock some populations that have been extirpated, and to strictly prohibit continued fishing of adult coho until the stocks have been rebuilt.

Contacts

U. S. Fish and Wildlife Service
Regional Office, Division of Endangered Species
Eastside Federal Complex
911 N. E. 11th Ave.
Portland, Oregon 97232-4181
Telephone: (503) 231-6121
http://pacific.fws.gov/

National Marine Fisheries Service, Protected Resources Division
525 N. E. Oregon Street, Suite 500
Portland, Oregon 97232
Telephone: (503) 230-5400

References

National Oceanic and Atmospheric Administration. April 18, 2000. "West Coast Salmon and the Endangered Species Act. Listing Status: Coho." *Protected Resources NOAA Fisheries and National Marine Fisheries Service: The Endangered Species Act.* (http://www.nwr.noaa.gov/1salmon/salmesa/cohoswit.htm). Date Accessed: July 6, 2000.

Sierra Club. 1999. "Spotlight on Species, Coho Salmon: *Oncorhynchus kisutch.*" *Sierra Club.* (http://www.sierraclub.org/habitat/coho.asp). Date Accessed: July 6, 2000.

Steelhead Trout

Oncorhynchus mykiss

Status	Endangered (Selected rivers in California and Washington); Threatened (Selected rivers in California, Idaho, Oregon, and Washington)
Listed	June 17, 1998 (Parts of California, Idaho, Oregon, and Washington); August 2, 1999 (Parts of Oregon and Washington)
Family	Salmonidae
Description	A trout that is steel blue above and silvery on the sides and belly in salt water and olive green on the back and less silver on the sides and belly in freshwater.
Habitat	May migrate as juveniles to the ocean and return to freshwater to spawn or may spend entire life in freshwater.
Food	Trout feed on aquatic and terrestrial insects, small fish insects and their eggs, and crustaceans.
Reproduction	Spawns between December and June in freshwater.
Threats	Habitat loss and degradation, disease, and dams making spawning sites inaccessible.
Range	California, Idaho, Oregon, Washington

Description

At sea, *Oncorhynchus mykiss* (steelhead) are steel blue above with bright silvery sides and belly. Sharply defined black spots mark back, head, sides, dorsal, and caudal fins. The spots are small, rarely over 0.125 in (0.32 cm) in diameter, and highly variable in number. After entering freshwater, steelhead develop a broad pink or red stripe on each side of the body. This stripe fades away at the edges rather than being sharply outlined. In freshwater, steelhead gradually take on more of an appearance of a stream rainbow trout; the back gradually becomes olive green and the sides and belly become less silvery. Steelhead lack the red streaks beneath the jaw that characterize the cutthroat trout. The mouth lining is white. Juveniles are covered with small, oval to round parr marks. Steelhead typically do not have the pair of red or orange streaks on the underside of the jaw that are characteristic of cutthroat trout.

Most steelhead usually weigh less than 10 lbs (4.5 kg), but an individual weighing 42 lbs (19 kg) was caught in Alaska, and a 23 lb (10 kg) individual was caught in California. Immature sea-run individuals returning after less than a year in the ocean are called "half-pounders" and weigh from 0.5-1.5 lbs (230-680 g). The life span from this species is about seven years, but older individuals have been recorded.

Behavior

The steelhead exhibit one of the most complex suites of life history traits of any salmonid species. Steelhead may exhibit anadromy (migration as juveniles from freshwater to the ocean, and then re-

Innerspace Visions

turning to spawn in freshwater) or freshwater residency (residing their entire lives in freshwater). Freshwater forms are usually referred to as rainbow or redband trout, while anadromous life forms are termed steelhead. Few detailed studies have been conducted regarding the relationship between resident and anadromous steelhead and, as a result, the relationship between these two life forms is poorly understood. Recently the scientific name for the biological species that includes both steelhead and rainbow trout was changed from *Salmo gairdneri* to *O. mykiss*. This change reflects the premise that all trout from western North America share a common lineage with Pacific salmon.

Steelhead typically migrate to marine waters after spending two years in freshwater. They then reside in marine waters for typically two or three years prior to returning to their natal stream to spawn as four- or five-year olds. Unlike other Pacific salmon, steelhead are iteroparous, meaning they are capable of spawning more than once before they die. However, it is rare for steelhead to

spawn more than twice before dying; most that do so are females. Steelhead adults typically spawn between December and June. Depending on water temperature, steelhead eggs may incubate in redds (nesting gravels) for 45 days to four months before hatching as alevins (a larval life stage dependent on food stored in a yolk sac). Following yolk-sac absorption, young juveniles or fry emerge from the gravel and begin actively feeding. Juveniles rear in freshwater from one to four years, then migrate to the ocean as smolts.

Biologically, steelhead can be divided into two reproductive ecotypes, based on their state of sexual maturity at the time of river entry and the duration of their spawning migration. These two ecotypes are termed "stream maturing" and "ocean maturing." Stream maturing steelhead enter freshwater in a sexually immature condition and require several months to mature and spawn. Ocean maturing steelhead enter freshwater with well-developed gonads and spawn shortly after river entry. These two reproductive ecotypes are more commonly referred to by their season of freshwater entry.

Two major genetic groups or subspecies of steelhead occur on the West Coast of the United States: a coastal group and an inland group, separated in the Fraser and Columbia River basins approximately by the Cascade crest. These genetic groupings apply to both anadromous and non-anadromous forms of steelhead. Both coastal and inland steelhead occur in Washington and Oregon. California is thought to have only coastal steelhead while Idaho has only inland steelhead.

Under certain conditions, anadromous and resident steelhead are capable not only of interbreeding, but also of having offspring that express the alternate life history form; that is, anadromous fish can produce non-anadromous offspring, and vice versa. There is evidence that in very cold streams juvenile steelhead have difficulty attaining mean threshold size for smoltification and therefore do not emigrate downstream early in life. They are thermally-fated to a resident life history regardless of whether they were the offspring of anadromous or resident parents.

Freshwater populations can help buffer extinction risks to sea-faring steelhead populations by providing offspring that migrate to the ocean and enter the breeding population of steelhead, and by providing a reserve gene pool in freshwater that may persist through times of unfavorable conditions for anadromous fish. In spite of these potential benefits, presence of resident populations is not a substitute for conservation of anadromous populations. A particular concern is isolation of resident populations by human-caused barriers to migration.

Habitat and Distribution

Historically, steelhead were distributed throughout the North Pacific Ocean from the Kamchatka Peninsula in Asia to the northern Baja Peninsula. Presently, the species distribution extends from the Kamchatka Peninsula, east and south along the Pacific coast of North America, to approximately Malibu Creek in southern California. There are infrequent anecdotal reports of steelhead occurring as far south as the Santa Margarita River in San Diego County. Historically, steelhead likely inhabited most coastal streams in Washington, Oregon, and California as well as many inland streams in these States and Idaho. However, during the twentieth

century, over 23 indigenous, naturally reproducing stocks of steelhead are believed to have been extirpated, and many more are thought to be in decline in numerous coastal and inland streams in Washington, Oregon, Idaho, and California. Forty-three stocks have been identified as being at moderate or high risk of extinction.

Of the 15 Evolutionary Significant Units (ESUs) the National Marine Fisheries Service has identified, two have been listed as endangered, seven as threatened, three as candidates for listing, and three as viable and not in danger of extinction.

One is the Lower Columbia River ESU listed as Threatened on June 17, 1998. This coastal steelhead ESU occupies tributaries to the Columbia River between the Cowlitz and Wind Rivers in Washington, inclusive, and the Willamette and Hood Rivers in Oregon, inclusive. Excluded are steelhead in the upper Willamette River basin above Willamette Falls, and steelhead from the Little and Big White Salmon Rivers in Washington. Rivers draining into the Columbia River have their headwaters in increasingly drier areas, moving from west to east. Columbia River tributaries that drain the Cascade Mountains have proportionally higher flows in late summer and early fall than rivers on the Oregon coast.

Steelhead populations in this ESU are of the coastal genetic group, and a number of genetic studies have shown that they are part of a different ancestral lineage than inland steelhead from the Columbia River Basin. Genetic data also show steelhead from this ESU to be distinct from steelhead from the upper Willamette River and coastal streams in Oregon and Washington.

There have been almost universal, and in many cases dramatic, declines in steelhead abundance since the mid-1980s in both winter-run and summer-run steelhead runs in the Lower Columbia River. Of 21 wild winter-run and summer-run steelhead stocks on the northern side of this region, only two are healthy and the remaining 19 are depressed. The primary exception to the declines is the Toutle River winter-run steelhead stock, which has increased following decimation by the eruption of Mount St. Helens in 1980. In some cases, chinook salmon populations in the same streams have not shown such dramatic declines. No clear explanation presently exists for these declines in steelhead, but not chinook salmon. The National Marine Fisheries Service (NMFS) is unable to identify any natural populations of steelhead in this ESU that could be considered healthy.

Summer-run steelhead are native to the Hood, Lewis, Washougal and Kalama Rivers in this ESU. However, summer-run fish have also been introduced into the Sandy and Clackamas Rivers. Furthermore, naturally spawning winter-run steelhead populations have been negatively impacted by introductions of non-native summer-run steelhead due to interbreeding and/or competition.

Another ESU is the Central Valley, California, ESU which was listed as Threatened on June 17, 1998. This coastal steelhead ESU occupies the Sacramento and San Joaquin Rivers and their tributaries. Excluded are steelhead from San Francisco and San Pablo Bays which are part of the Central California Coast ESU. In the San Joaquin basin, the best available information suggests that the current range of steelhead has been limited to the Stanislaus, Tuolumne, and Merced Rivers tributaries and the mainstream San Joaquin River to its confluence with the Merced River by human alteration of formerly available habitat. The Sacramento and San Joaquin Rivers offer the only migration route to the drainages of the Sierra Nevada and southern Cascade mountain ranges for anadromous fish. The distance from the Pacific Ocean to spawning streams can exceed 180 mi (290 km), providing unique potential for reproductive isolation among steelhead. The Central Valley is much drier than the coastal regions to the west, receiving on average only 4-20 in (10-50 cm) of rainfall annually. The valley is characterized by erosive soils, and native vegetation was dominated by oak forests and prairie grasses prior to agricultural development. The coastal vegetation is redwood forests. Steelhead within this ESU have the longest freshwater migration of any population of winter-run steelhead. There is essentially one continuous run of steelhead in the upper Sacramento River. River entry ranges from July through May, with peaks in September and February. Spawning begins in late December and can extend into April.

Ecological information provides additional insight into species diversity within this region. First, the Central Valley as a whole can be divided into three ecoregions based largely on elevation and associated changes in climate and rainfall: (1) A mountainous region, averaging about 3,280 ft (1,000 m) in elevation, that includes the headwaters of the Sacramento and tributaries to the San Joaquin

Rivers; (2) a region of tablelands and hills at intermediate elevation, through which the tributary rivers flow; and (3) the valley itself, which includes broad, flat lands that border the Sacramento and San Joaquin Rivers. Geologically, the upper Sacramento River basin, which arises from the volcanic Cascade Range, differs from the lower Sacramento and San Joaquin River basins, which flow out of the northern and southern Sierra Nevada. The upper Sacramento River basin is also hydrologically distinct, and it supports native subspecies of resident steelhead. The southern part of the San Joaquin River basin is also very distinct ecologically, and genetic data indicate that, as a group, Central Valley steelhead are quite distinct from all coastal populations.

Various reports indicate that naturally spawning steelhead are distributed throughout a number of streams in the Central Valley region, but that they occur in small numbers. Furthermore, many populations are of non-native, mixed, or uncertain origin. In 1994, the recent total run size to the upper Sacramento River basin is probably less than 10,000 steelhead per year, and it is believed that less than 2,000 of those fish were the result of natural production from native populations.

Long-term declines in abundance, small population sizes in the Sacramento River, and the high risk of interbreeding between hatchery and naturally spawned steelhead as major concerns for steelhead in this region. Additionally, the significant loss of historic habitat, degradation of remaining habitat from water diversions, reduction in water quality and other factors, and the lack of monitoring data on abundance are other important risk factors.

A third ESU is the South-Central California Coast ESU, listed as Threatened on June 17, 1998. This coastal steelhead ESU occupies rivers from the Pajaro River, located in Santa Cruz County. Most rivers in this ESU drain the Santa Lucia Mountain Range, the southernmost unit of the California Coast Ranges. The climate is drier and warmer than in the north, which is reflected in the vegetation change from coniferous forest to chaparral and coastal scrub. Another biological transition at the north of this area is the southern limit of the distribution of coho salmon. The mouths of many of the rivers and streams in this area are seasonally closed by sand berms that form during periods of low flow in the summer. The southern boundary of this ESU is near Point Conception, a well-known transition area for the distribution and abundance of marine flora and fauna.

A fourth ESU is the Southern California ESU, which was listed as Endangered on June 17, 1998. This coastal steelhead ESU occupies rivers from the Santa Maria River, San Luis Obispo County to the southern extent of the species' range. Available data indicate that Malibu Creek, Los Angeles County is the southernmost stream generally recognized as supporting a persistent, naturally spawning population of anadromous steelhead.

Migration and life history patterns of southern California steelhead depend more strongly on rainfall and stream flow than is the case for steelhead populations farther north. River entry ranges from early November through June, with peaks in January and February. Spawning primarily begins in January and continues through early June, with peak spawning in February and March. Average rainfall is substantially lower and more variable in this ESU than regions to the north, resulting in increased duration of sand berms across the mouths of streams and rivers and, in some cases, complete dewatering of the marginal habitats. Environmental conditions in marginal habitats may be extreme, including elevated water temperatures, droughts, floods, and fires, and presumably impose selective pressures on steelhead populations. Steelhead use of southern California streams and rivers with elevated temperatures suggests that populations within this ESU are able to withstand higher temperatures than those to the north. The relatively warm and productive waters of the Ventura River resulted in more rapid growth of juvenile steelhead than occurred in northerly populations. However, relatively little life history information exists for steelhead from this ESU.

There are less than 200 adults comprising total run size for each of the six streams in this ESU. Populations have been extirpated from all streams south of Ventura County, with the exception of Malibu Creek in Los Angeles County.

The fifth steelhead ESU is the Upper Columbia River Basin ESU which is Endangered and was listed on June 17, 1998. This inland steelhead region comprises the Columbia River basin upstream from the Yakima River, Washington, to the U.S.-Canada border. The geology of these provinces is somewhat similar and very complex, developed from marine invasions, volcanic deposits, and glaciation. The

river valleys in this region are deeply dissected and maintain low gradients except in extreme headwaters. The climate in this area includes extremes in temperatures and precipitation, with most precipitation falling in the mountains as snow. Stream flow in this area is provided by melting snowpack, groundwater, and runoff from alpine glaciers. It is a harsh environment for fish, much different from the benign, coastal streams of the Pacific Northwest. Life history characteristics for Upper Columbia River basin steelhead are similar to those of other inland steelhead ESUs; however, some of the oldest smolt ages for steelhead, up to seven years, are reported from this region. This may be associated with the cold stream temperatures. Based on limited data available from adult fish, smolt age is dominated by two-year olds. Steelhead from the Wenatchee and Entiat Rivers return to freshwater after one year in salt water, whereas Methow River steelhead are primarily two-ocean residents.

In 1939, the construction of Grand Coulee Dam on the Columbia River blocked over 1,120 mi (1,800 km) of river from access by anadromous fish. In an effort to preserve fish runs affected by Grand Coulee Dam, all anadromous fish migrating upstream were trapped at Rock Island Dam from 1939-1943 and either released to spawn in tributaries between Rock Island and Grand Coulee Dams or spawned in hatcheries and the offspring released in that area. Through this process, smolts of all anadromous salmonids, including steelhead, which were historically native to several separate subbasins above Rock Island Dam, were redistributed among tributaries in the Rock Island-Grand Coulee reach without regard to their origin.

Estimates of historical (pre-1960s) abundance are available from fish counts at dams. Counts at Rock Island Dam from 1933-1959 averaged 2,600-3,700, suggesting a pre-fishery run size in excess of 5,000 adults for tributaries above Rock Island Dam. Runs may already have been depressed by lower Columbia River fisheries at this time. The 1989-1993 average natural escapements numbered 800 for the Wenatchee River, and 450 for the Methow and Okanogan Rivers. Recent average total escapements for these stocks were 2,500 and 2,400, respectively. Average total run size at Priest Rapids Dam for the same period was approximately 9,600 adult steelhead.

Habitat degradation, juvenile and adult mortality in the hydrosystem, and unfavorable environmental conditions in both marine and freshwater habitats have contributed to the declines and represent risk factors for the future. Harvest in lower river fisheries and genetic homogenization from composite broodstock collections are other factors that may contribute significantly to risk to the Upper Columbia region.

Hatchery populations, considered part of this ESU, include the Wells Hatchery stock of summer-run steelhead. Although this stock represents a mixture of native populations, it probably retains the genetic resources of steelhead populations above Grand Coulee Dam that are now extinct from those native habitats. Operations at the Wells Hatchery have utilized large numbers of spawning adults and have incorporated about 10% of naturally spawning adults into the broodstock each year, procedures that should help minimize the negative genetic effects of artificial propagation. Because of the incorporation of naturally spawning adults into the hatchery broodstock and the large number of hatchery propagated fish that spawn naturally, there is a close genetic resemblance between naturally spawning populations and the Wells Hatchery stock that could be used for recovery purposes.

Another ESU is the Snake River Basin ESU, listed as Threatened on June 17, 1998. This inland steelhead region includes the Snake River basin of southeast Washington, northeast Oregon, and Idaho. The Snake River flows through terrain that is warmer and drier on an annual basis than the upper Columbia basin or other drainages to the north. Geologically, the land forms are older and much more eroded than most other steelhead habitat. The eastern portion of the basin flows out of the granitic geological unit known as the Idaho Batholith. The western Snake River basin drains sedimentary and volcanic soils of the Blue Mountains complex. Collectively, the environmental factors of the Snake River basin result in a river that is warmer and more turbid, with higher pH and alkalinity, than is found elsewhere in the range of inland steelhead. Snake River basin steelhead are summer steelhead, as are most inland steelhead, and have been classified into two groups, A-run and B-run, based on migration timing, ocean age, and adult size. Snake River basin steelhead enter freshwater from June to October and spawn in the following spring from March to May. Snake River basin steelhead usually smolt at an age of 2-3 years. Each has several life history differences, including spawning size, run time, and habitat type.

The Imnaha River Hatchery stock was recently founded from an undiluted stock with no previous history of non-native hatchery releases for the purpose of preserving the native genetic resources of this area. Therefore, this stock represents an important component of the evolutionary legacy of this ESU. Although the Oxbow Hatchery stock has been under artificial propagation for several generations and has been propagated almost entirely from hatchery-derived adults, this stock represents the only source of a unique genetic resource.

Prior to Ice Harbor Dam completion in 1962, there were no counts of Snake River basin naturally spawned steelhead. However, Lewiston Dam counts during the period from 1949-1971 averaged about 40,000 steelhead per year in the Clearwater River, while the Ice Harbor Dam count in 1962 was 108,000, and averaged about 70,000 until 1970. Although there is little information for most stocks within this ESU, there are recent run size or escapement estimates for several stocks. The 1990-1994 average escapement above Lower Granite Dam was approximately 71,000.

The Central California Coast ESU was listed as Threatened on June 17, 1998. Only two estimates of historical (pre-1960s) abundance are available: an average of about 500 adults in Waddell Creek in the 1930s and early 1940s, and an estimate of 20,000 steelhead in the San Lorenzo River before 1965. In the mid-1960s, 94,000 steelhead were estimated to be spawning in many rivers of this ESU, including 50,000 and 19,000 fish in the Russian and San Lorenzo Rivers, respectively. More recent estimates for the Russian River is 7,000 fish and 500 fish in the San Lorenzo River. These estimates indicate that recent total abundance of steelhead in these two rivers is less than 15% of their abundance 30 years ago. Additional recent estimates for several other streams indicate individual run sizes are 500 fish or less. Steelhead in most tributary streams in San Francisco and San Pablo Bays have been extirpated. Steelhead in this ESU may be exhibiting slight increases in abundance in recent years. Updated abundance data for the Russian and San Lorenzo Rivers indicate increasing run sizes over the past two to three years, but it is not possible to distinguish the relative proportions of hatchery and natural steelhead in those estimates. Additional data from a few smaller streams in the region also show general increases in juvenile abundance in the 1964-1975 period. Data from the Carmel River show increases in adult and juvenile steelhead abundance over the past two to five years.

The Middle Columbia River ESU listed as Threatened since August 2, 1999 occupies the Columbia River basin and tributaries from above the Wind River in Washington and the Hood River in Oregon upstream to, and including, the Yakima River, in Washington. Geology within this province is dominated by the Columbia River Basalt formation, stemming from lava deposition. This intermontane region includes some of the driest areas of the Pacific Northwest, generally receiving less than 16 in (40 cm) of rainfall annually.

Current population sizes are substantially lower than historic levels, especially in the rivers with the largest steelhead runs: the John Day, Deschutes, and Yakima Rivers. At least two extinctions of native steelhead runs have occurred in the Deschutes River basin. Trends in natural escapement in the Yakima and Umatilla Rivers have been highly variable since the mid to late 1970s, ranging from abundances of 2,000-3,000 steelhead during peaks that indicate relatively healthy runs to those that are cause for concern, approximately 500 fish during the low points.

The serious declines in abundance in the John Day River basin are especially troublesome because the John Day River has supported the largest populations of naturally spawning summer steelhead in the ESU. Populations in the Yakima River basin are at a small fraction of historical levels, with the majority of production coming from a single stream. The number of naturally spawning fish in the Umatilla River has been relatively stable in recent years, but this has been accomplished with substantial supplementation of natural spawning by hatchery-reared fish. Naturally produced steelhead have declined precipitously in the Deschutes River over the past decade. The most optimistic observation that can be made for steelhead in this area is that some populations have shown resiliency to bounce back from even more depressed levels in the past.

The Upper Willamette River ESU listed as Threatened on August 2, 1999 comprises the Willamette River and its tributaries, upstream from Willamette Falls to the Calapooia River. The Willamette River basin is geographically complex. In addition to its connection to the Columbia River, the Willamette River historically has had connections with coastal basins through stream capture and headwater transfer events.

Steelhead from the upper Willamette River are genetically distinct from those in the lower river. Reproductive isolation from lower river populations may have been facilitated by Willamette Falls, which is known to be a migration barrier to some anadromous salmonids. For example, winter steelhead and spring chinook salmon occurred historically above the falls, but summer steelhead, fall chinook salmon, and coho salmon did not.

The native steelhead of this basin are late-migrating winter-run, entering freshwater primarily in March and April, whereas most other populations of West Coast winter steelhead enter freshwater beginning in November or December.

As early as 1885, fish ladders were constructed at Willamette Falls to aid the passage of anadromous fish. The ladders have been modified and rebuilt, most recently in 1971, as technology has improved. These fishways facilitated successful introduction of Skamania stock summer steelhead and early-migrating Big Creek stock winter steelhead to the upper basin. Another effort to expand the steelhead production in the upper Willamette River was the stocking of native steelhead in tributaries not historically used by that species. Native steelhead primarily used tributaries on the east side of the basin, with cutthroat trout predominating in streams draining the west side of the basin.

Steelhead in the Upper Willamette River ESU are distributed in a few, relatively small, natural populations. Over the past several decades, total abundance of natural late-migrating winter steelhead ascending the Willamette Fails fish ladder has fluctuated several times over a range of approximately 5,000-20,000 spawners. However, the last peak occurred in 1988, and this peak has been followed by a steep and continuing decline. Abundance in each of the last five years has been below 4,300 fish, and the run in 1995 was the lowest in 30 years. Declines also have been observed in almost all natural populations, including those with and without a substantial component of naturally spawning hatchery fish.

The Oregon Coast ESU is a candidate for listing. This coastal steelhead occupies river basins on the Oregon coast north of Cape Blanco, excluding rivers and streams that are tributaries of the Columbia River. Most rivers in this area drain the Coast Range Mountains, have a single peak in flow in December or January, and have relatively low flow during summer and early fall. The coastal region receives fairly high precipitation levels, and the vegetation is dominated by Sitka spruce and western hemlock. Upwelling off the Oregon coast is much more variable and generally weaker than in areas south of Cape Blanco. While marine conditions off the Oregon and Washington coasts are similar, the Columbia River has greater influence north of its mouth, and the continental shelf becomes broader off the Washington coast.

The Oregon Coast ESU primarily contains winter-run steelhead; there are only two native stocks of summer-run steelhead. Summer-run steelhead occur only in the Siletz River, above a waterfall, and in the North Umpqua River, where migration distance may prevent full utilization of available habitat by winter-run steelhead. Alsea River winter-run steelhead have been widely used for steelhead broodstock in coastal rivers. Populations of non-anadromous steelhead are relatively uncommon on the Oregon coast, as compared with other areas, occurring primarily above migration barriers and in the Umpqua River basin. Age structure appears to be similar to other West Coast steelhead, dominated by four-year-old spawners. Iteroparity is more common among Oregon coast steelhead than in populations to the north.

Another candidate for listing is the Klamath Mountains Province (KMP) ESU. This coastal steelhead ESU occupies river basins from the Elk River in Oregon to the Klamath and Trinity Rivers in California, inclusive. Geologically, this region includes the KMP, which is not as erosive as the Franciscan formation terrains south of the Klamath River basin. Dominant vegetation along the coast is redwood forest, while some interior basins are much drier than surrounding areas and are characterized by many endemic species. Elevated stream temperatures are a factor affecting steelhead and other species in some of the larger river basins. With the exception of major river basins, such as the Rogue and Klamath, most rivers in this region have a short duration of peak flows. Strong and consistent coastal upwelling begins at about Cape Blanco and continues south into central California, resulting in a relatively productive nearshore marine environment.

Steelhead within this ESU include both winter-run and summer-run steelhead as well as the unusual half-pounder life history, characterized by immature steelhead that return to freshwater after only two to four months in saltwater, overwinter-run in rivers without spawning, then return to saltwater the following spring.

The Northern California ESU is also a candidate for listing which occupies river basins from Redwood Creek in Humboldt County to the Gualala River. Dominant vegetation along the coast is redwood forest, while some interior basins are much drier than surrounding areas and are characterized by many endemic species. This area includes the extreme southern end of the contiguous portion of the Coast Range Ecoregion. Elevated stream temperatures are a factor in some of the larger river basins (greater than 68°F [20°C]) but not to the extent that they are in river basins farther south. Precipitation is generally higher in this geographic area than in regions to the south, averaging 40-80 in (100-200 cm) of rainfall annually. With the exception of major river basins, such as the Eel, most rivers in this region have peak flows of short duration. Strong and consistent coastal upwelling begins at approximately Cape Blanco and continues south into central California, resulting in a relatively productive near-shore marine environment.

This region includes both winter- and summer-run steelhead, including what is presently considered to be the southernmost population of summer-run steelhead, in the Middle Fork Eel River. Half-pounder juveniles also occur in this geographic area, specifically in the Mad and Eel Rivers; however, adults with the half-pounder juvenile life history may not spawn south of the Klamath River basin. As with the Rogue and Klamath Rivers, some of the larger rivers in this area have migrating steelhead year round, and seasonal runs have been named. River entry ranges from August through June, and spawning from December through April, with peak spawning in January in the larger basins and late February and March in the smaller coastal basins.

Threats

Steelhead on the West Coast of the United States have experienced declines in abundance in the past several decades as a result of natural and human factors. Forestry, agriculture, mining, and urbanization have degraded, simplified, and fragmented habitat. Water diversions for agriculture, flood control, domestic, and hydropower purposes have greatly reduced or eliminated historically accessible habitat. Studies estimate that during the last 200 years, the lower 48 states have lost approximately 53% of all wetlands and the majority of the rest are severely degraded. Washington's and Oregon's wetlands are estimated to have diminished by one-third, while California has experienced a 91% loss of its wetland habitat. Loss of habitat complexity has also contributed to the decline of steelhead. For example, in national forests in Washington, there has been a 58% reduction in large, deep pools due to sedimentation and loss of pool-forming structures, such as boulders and large wood. Similarly, in Oregon, the abundance of large, deep pools on private coastal lands has decreased by as much as 80%. Sedimentation from land-use activities is recognized as a primary cause of habitat degradation in the range of West Coast steelhead.

Steelhead support an important recreational fishery throughout their range. During periods of drought conditions or summer low flow, the impacts of recreational fishing on trout stocks may be heightened. Although steelhead are not generally targeted in commercial fisheries, high seas drift-net fisheries in the past may have contributed slightly to a decline of this species in local areas, but could not be solely responsible for the large declines in abundance observed along most of the Pacific coast over the past several decades. A particular problem occurs in the main stem of the Columbia River where naturally spawned steelhead from the Upper Columbia and Snake River basin ESUs migrate at the same time and are subject to the same fisheries as hatchery-produced steelhead, chinook, and coho salmon. Incidental harvest mortality in mixed-stock sport and commercial fisheries may exceed 30% of naturally spawned populations.

Infectious diseases constitute one of many factors that can influence adult and juvenile steelhead survival. Steelhead are exposed to numerous bacterial, protozoan, viral, and parasitic organisms in spawning and rearing areas, hatcheries, migratory routes, and the marine environments. Specific diseases, such as bacterial kidney disease, ceratomyxosis, columnaris, furunculosis, infectious hematopoietic necrosis virus, redmouth and black spot disease, erythrocytic inclusion body syndrome, and whirling disease, among others, are present and are known to affect steelhead and salmon. Studies have shown that naturally spawned fish tend to be less susceptible to pathogens than hatchery-reared fish.

Introductions of non-native species and habitat modifications have resulted in increased predator populations in numerous river systems, thereby increasing the level of predation experienced by salmonids. Predation by marine mammals is also of concern in some areas experiencing dwindling steelhead run sizes.

Hatchery programs and harvest management have strongly influenced steelhead populations. Established hatchery programs that were designed to replenish stocks that had declined because of habitat losses have complicated the conservation efforts in recent times. Some of the hatcheries have maintained relatively pure stocks that are very similar to wild-run populations, while other hatcheries have re-stocked streams with hybrids that may or may not be genetically pure. Loss of genetic purity causes some populations to become less viable, more susceptible to disease, and less valuable for scientific research.

The departments of fish and game in Washington, Oregon, and California have adopted and are implementing natural salmonid policies designed to limit hatchery influences on natural, indigenous steelhead. Sport fisheries now focus on harvest of marked, hatchery-produced steelhead, and sport fishing regulations are designed to protect wild fish. While some limits have been placed on hatchery production of anadromous salmonids, more careful management of current programs and scrutiny of proposed programs are necessary in order to minimize impacts on listed species.

Natural climatic conditions have exacerbated the problems associated with degraded and altered riverine and estuarine habitats. Persistent drought conditions have reduced already limited spawning, rearing, and migration habitat. Climatic conditions appear to have resulted in decreased ocean productivity which, during more productive periods, may help offset degraded freshwater habitat conditions.

Conservation and Recovery

The state of Washington is currently in the process of developing a statewide strategy to protect and restore wild steelhead and other salmon and trout species. In 1997, the Joint Natural Resources Cabinet was created to restore healthy salmon, steelhead, and trout populations by improving those habitats on which the fish rely. The cabinet's current activities include development of the Lower Columbia Steelhead Conservation Initiative, which is intended to comprehensively address protection and recovery of steelhead in the lower Columbia River area.

The Oregon Plan for Salmon and Watersheds, established in 1996, calls for research to determine the decline of coastal coho and steelhead, most notably, those factors relating to harvest, habitat, and hatchery activities; a comprehensive monitoring plan; and tap local efforts to improve understanding of freshwater and marine conditions, determine populations trends, and evaluate the effects of artificial propagation in restoring the salmon.

In 1998, the state of Oregon implemented changes to its fishing regulations that will help conserve steelhead. These regulation include: (1) Elimination of steelhead retention fisheries; (2) creation of sanctuary areas for rearing steelhead where no angling is permitted; (3) elimination of the use of bait in trout fisheries that could negatively impact juvenile steelhead; (4) implementation of season closures for trout species during juvenile steelhead outmigration; and (5) modification of gear requirements to protect juvenile steelhead in trout fisheries. Current harvest regulations and hatchery programs will be modified in the future if monitoring results indicate that changes are needed.

The state of California's program for steelhead conservation consists of several major programs: (1) The CALFED Bay-Delta program; (2) the Governor's Watershed Restoration and Protection Council to implement the watershed planning and habitat; and (3) CDFG strategic management plans for steelhead in the and Northern California ESUs.

The plans for Klamath Mountain and Northern California steelhead identify a wide range of existing and new hatchery management measures that are intended to reduce the impacts of hatchery steelhead programs on wild steelhead populations in these ESUs. These measures include: requiring a minimum 6 in (15 cm) size before releasing hatchery fish; marking all hatchery fish and conducting spawning surveys to assess the extent hatchery fish stray into natural spawning areas; reducing hatchery releases if they are found to stray; placing a cap on hatchery production; and conducting regular health checks during each rearing cycle to detect and destroy diseased fish that cannot be effectively treated.

Significant steps have been taken over the past two years in the Central California Valley towards the largest ecological restoration project yet undertaken in the United States. The CALFED program in coordination with other Central Valley efforts have implemented numerous habitat restoration actions that benefit Central Valley steelhead. Emphasis has been placed on addressing tributary drainages with high potential for steelhead production.

Contacts

Protected Resources Division
National Marine Fisheries Service, Northwest Region
525 N.E. Oregon Street, Suite 500
Portland, Oregon 97232-2737
Telephone: (503) 230-5400

U. S. Fish and Wildlife Service
Regional Office, Division of Endangered Species
Eastside Federal Building
911 N. E. 11th Ave.
Portland, Oregon 97232-4181
Telephone: (503) 231-6121
http://pacific.fws.gov/

References

National Marine Fisheries Service. August 18, 1997. "Listing of Several ESUs of West Coast Steelhead." *Federal Register* 62(159): 43937

National Marine Fisheries Service. March 19, 1998. "Threatened Status for Two ESUs of Steelhead in Washington, Oregon, and California." *Federal Register* 63(53): 13347-13371.

National Marine Fisheries Service. March 25, 1999. "Threatened Status for Two ESUs of Steelhead in Oregon and Washington." *Federal Register* 64(57): 14521.

Sockeye Salmon

Oncorhynchus nerka

Status	Endangered, Snake River ESU
Listed	January 3, 1992
Status	Threatened, Ozette Lake ESU
Listed	March 25, 1999
Family	Salmonidae
Description	An anadromous salmonid fish.
Habitat	Breeds in cool, clean streams; grows to maturity in the ocean.
Food	Aquatic invertebrates and smaller fish.
Reproduction	Lays eggs in freshwater; young fish migrate to the ocean; adults return to the natal stream to spawn.
Threats	Destruction and degradation of breeding streams by forestry, road building, and other developments; overfishing at sea and during the landward migration.
Range	Idaho, Washington

Description

Adult *Oncorhynchus nerka* (sockeye salmon) are typically bright red, with a green head. During the ocean and adult migratory phase they often have bluish backs and silver sides, giving rise to another common name, "bluebacks." The name "sockeye" is thought to have been a corruption of the Indian word "sukkai."

Behavior

Sockeye salmon exhibit a wide variety of life-history patterns that reflect varying dependency on the freshwater environment. With the exception of certain river-type and sea-type populations, the vast majority of sockeye salmon spawn in or near lakes, where the juveniles rear for one to three years prior to migrating to the ocean. For this reason, the major distribution and abundance of large sockeye salmon stocks are closely related to the location of rivers that have accessible lakes in their watersheds for juvenile rearing.

Growth influences the duration of stay in the nursery lake and is influenced by intra- and inter-specific competition, food supply, water temperature, thermal stratification, migratory movements to avoid predation, lake turbidity, and length of the growing season. Lake residence time usually increases the farther north a nursery lake is located. In Washington and British Columbia, lake residence is normally one or two years, whereas in Alaska some fish may remain three or four years in the nursery lake, prior to smoltification. Adaptation to a greater degree of utilization of lake environments for both adult spawning and juvenile rearing has resulted in the evolution of complex timing for incubation, fry emergence, spawning, and adult take entry that often involves intricate patterns of adult and juvenile migration and orientation not seen in other salmon species.

Upon emergence from the substrate, sockeye salmon alevins exhibit a varied behavior that appears to reflect local adaptations to spawning and rearing habitat. For example, lake-type sockeye salmon juveniles move either downstream or upstream to rearing lakes. Periods of streambank holding are limited for most juvenile sockeye salmon, as emergents in streams above or between connecting

Sockeye Salmon, photograph by Diane Ronayne/Idaho Department of Fish & Game. Reproduced by permission.

lakes use the current to travel to the nursery lake. Predation on migrating sockeye salmon fry varies considerably with spawning location. Sockeye salmon fry mortality due to predation by other fish species and birds can be extensive during downstream and upstream migration to nursery lake habitat, and is only partially reduced by the nocturnal migratory movement of some fry populations. Juveniles emerging in streams downstream from a nursery lake can experience periods of particularly high predation compared with other juvenile sockeye. Juvenile sockeye salmon in lakes are visual predators, feeding on zooplankton and insect larvae. Smolt migration typically occurs between sunset and sunrise, beginning in late April and extending through early July, with southern stocks migrating the earliest. Once in the ocean, sockeye salmon feed on copepods, euphausiids, and amphipod crustaceans, fish larvae, squid, and pteropods. The greatest increase in length is typically in the first year of ocean life, whereas the greatest increase in weight is during the second year.

Northward migration of juveniles to the Gulf of Alaska occurs in a band relatively close to shore, and offshore movement of juveniles occurs in late autumn or winter.

Among other Pacific salmon, sockeye salmon prefer cooler ocean conditions. Lake- or river-type will spend from one to four years in the ocean before returning to freshwater to spawn. Adult sockeye salmon home precisely to their natal stream or lake habitat. Stream fidelity in sockeye salmon ensures that juveniles will encounter a suitable nursery lake.

Habitat

On the Pacific coast, sockeye salmon inhabit riverine, marine, and lake environments from the Columbia River and its tributaries north and west to the Kuskokwim River in western Alaska. There are also sockeye salmon life forms that are non-anadromous, meaning that members of the form spend their entire lives in freshwater. Non-anadromous sockeye salmon in the Pacific Northwest are known as kokanee. Occasionally, a proportion of the juveniles in an anadromous sockeye salmon population will remain in their rearing lake environment throughout life and will be observed in the spawning grounds together with their anadromous siblings. "Residual sockeye" refers to these resident, non-migratory progeny of anadromous sockeye salmon parents.

Among the Pacific salmon, sockeye salmon exhibit the greatest diversity in selection of spawning habitat and great variation in river entry timing and the duration of holding in lakes prior to spawning. The vast majority of sockeye salmon typically spawn in inlet or outlet tributaries of lakes or along the shoreline of lakes where upwelling of oxygenated water through gravel or sand occurs. However, they may also spawn in suitable stream habitat between lakes; along the nursery lakeshore on outwash fans of tributaries or where upwelling occurs along submerged beaches; and along beaches where the gravel or rocky substrate is free of fine sediment and the eggs can be oxygenated by wind-driven water circulation. All of these spawning habitats may be used by the lake-type sockeye salmon.

Sockeye salmon also spawn in main-stem rivers without juvenile lake-rearing habitat. These are referred to as "river-type" and "sea-type" sockeye salmon. In areas where lake-rearing habitat is unavailable or inaccessible, sockeye salmon may utilize river and estuarine habitat for rearing or may forgo an extended freshwater rearing period and migrate to sea as underyearlings. Riverine spawners that rear in rivers for one or two years are termed "river-type" sockeye salmon. Riverine spawners that migrate as fry to sea or to lower river estuaries in the same year, following a brief freshwater rearing period of only a few months, are referred to as "sea-type" sockeye salmon. River-type and sea-type sockeye salmon are common in northern areas and may predominate over lake-type sockeye salmon in some river systems.

Within the range of West Coast sockeye, there often exist populations of resident lake-type non-anadromous sockeye salmon. Non-anadromous sockeye salmon are commonly referred to as "kokanee," whose parents, for several generations back, have spent their whole lives in freshwater. Several native and introduced populations of kokanee within the geographic range of West Coast sockeye salmon may be genetically distinct and reproductively isolated from one another and from other salmon populations. It has long been known that kokanee can produce sea-type young. However, the number of sea-type out-migrants that successfully return as adults is typically quite low.

A portion of the juvenile anadromous sockeye salmon will occasionally remain in their lake rearing environment throughout life and will be observed on the spawning grounds together with their anadromous cohorts. These fish are defined as resident sockeye salmon to indicate that they are the progeny of anadromous sockeye salmon parents, spend their adult life in freshwater, but spawn together with their anadromous siblings.

Distribution and Threats

In considering the ESU (Evolutionarily Significant Units) status of resident forms of sockeye salmon, the key issue is the evaluation of the strength and duration of reproductive isolation between resident and sea-type forms. Many kokanee populations appear to have been strongly isolated from sympatric sockeye salmon populations for long periods of time.

The National Marine Fisheries Service has identified seven evolutionary significant units for the sockeye salmon, and has listed the Ozette Lake ESU as threatened and the Snake River ESU as endangered.

(1) Okanogan River: This ESU consists of sockeye salmon that return to Lake Osoyoos through the Okanogan River via the Columbia River and spawn primarily in the Canadian section of the Okanogan River above Lake Osoyoos. The Okanogan River sockeye is distinguished by a) the very different rearing conditions encountered by juvenile sockeye salmon in Lake Osoyoos, b) the tendency for a large percentage of 3-year-old returns to the Okanogan population, c) the apparent one-month separation in juvenile run-timing between Okanogan and Wenatchee-origin fish, and d) the adaption of Okanogan River sockeye salmon to much higher temperatures during adult migration in the Okanogan River.

(2) Lake Wenatchee: This ESU consists of sockeye salmon that return to Lake Wenatchee through the Wenatchee River via the Columbia River and spawn primarily in tributaries above Lake Wenatchee. The Lake Wenatchee sockeye salmon pop-

ulation is distinguished by: a) Very different environmental conditions encountered by sockeye salmon in Lake Wenatchee compared with those in Lake Osoyoos, b) the near absence of 3-year-old sockeye returns to Lake Wenatchee, and c) the apparent one-month separation in juvenile run-timing between Okanogan and Wenatchee-origin fish.

(3) Quinault Lake: This ESU consists of sockeye salmon that return to Quinault Lake and spawn in the main-stem of the upper Quinault River, in tributaries of the upper Quinault River, and in a few small tributaries of Quinault Lake itself. The Quinault Lake sockeye salmon is considered a separate ESU based on its unique life history. Historical estimates ranged between 20,000-250,000 in the 1920s; the five year average 1991 to 1995 is estimated at 32,000 adults.

(4) Baker River: This ESU consists of sockeye salmon that return to the barrier dam and fish trap on the lower Baker River after migrating through the Skagit River. They are trucked to one of three artificial spawning beaches above either one or two dams on the Baker River and are held in these enclosures until spawning. Sockeye salmon in this population enter the Quillayute River in May through September and hold in the Sol Duc River before entering Lake Pleasant, usually in early November, when sufficient water depth is available in Lake Creek. Historical estimates in 1900 were 20,000; the five year average 1991 to 1995 is estimated at 2,700 adults.

(5) Lake Pleasant: Sockeye salmon in this region enter the Quillayute River in May through September and hold in the Sol Duc River before entering Lake Pleasant, usually in early November, when sufficient water depth is available in Lake Creek. Spawning occurs on beaches from late November to early January. Sockeye salmon in Lake Pleasant are smaller than other salmon populations, weighing no more than 3 lbs (1.4 kg). In some brood years, a majority of Lake Pleasant sockeye spend two years in freshwater prior to migrating to sea. In the 1930s, more than 500,000 sockeye fry were released into Lake Pleasant, but these hatchery fish do not seem to have altered the genetic integrity of the wild population. Sockeye escapement to Lake Pleasant was 760-1,500 fish during the early 1960s.

(6) Ozette Lake: Threatened. This ESU consists of sockeye salmon that return to Ozette Lake through the Ozette River and currently spawn primarily in lakeshore upwelling areas in Ozette Lake. Minor spawning may occur below Ozette Lake in the Ozette River or in Coal Creek, a tributary of the Ozette River. Sockeye salmon do not presently spawn in tributary streams to Ozette Lake, although they may have spawned there historically. Genetics, environment, and life history are the primary factors in distinguishing this ESU. Ozette Lake sockeye salmon are genetically distinct from all other sockeye salmon stocks in the Northwest, and Ozette Lake kokanee are the most genetically distinct salmon stock in the contiguous United States. However, Ozette Lake kokanee are closely allied to several sockeye salmon stocks on Vancouver Island.

Kokanee are very numerous in Ozette Lake and spawn in inlet tributaries, characteristics and the degree of genetic differentiation from other sockeye salmon populations. The distinctive early river-entry timing, protracted adult-run timing, long three- to 10-month lake-residence period prior to spawning, unusually long spawn timing, and genetic differences from other coastal Washington sockeye salmon are important factors in identifying this ESU. In addition, the relative absence of red skin pigmentation and the presence of an olive-green spawning coloration by the majority of the Quinault stock appear to be unique among major sockeye salmon stocks in Washington. Historical records estimate a few thousand sockeye in 1926, and a few hundred in the mid-1960s. The 1992-1996 average escapement was about 700.

Threats to the Ozette Lake ESU: The declines in sockeye salmon are likely the result of a combination of factors, including introduced species, predation, loss of tributary populations, decline in quality of beach-spawning habitat, temporarily unfavorable oceanic conditions, excessive historical harvests, and introduced diseases.

Recent hatchery production in Ozette Lake has been primarily from local stock, with the exception of 120,000 Quinault Lake sockeye salmon juveniles released in 1983. The release of 14,398 kokanee/sockeye salmon hybrids in 1991-1992 may have had deleterious effects on genetic integrity of the ESU because Ozette Lake kokanee are genetically dissimilar to Ozette Lake sockeye salmon. Sockeye salmon on the West Coast of the United States have experienced declines in abundance in the past several decades as a result of natural and human factors. Forestry, agriculture, mining, and urbanization have degraded, simplified, and fragmented habitat. Water diversions for agriculture, flood control, domestic, and hydropower have greatly reduced or eliminated historically accessible habitat. Studies indicate that in most western states, about 80-90% of the historical riparian habitat has been eliminated. Further, it has been estimated that, during the last 200 years, the lower 48 states have lost approximately 53% of all wetlands and the majority of the rest are severely degraded. Washington's and Oregon's wetlands are estimated to have diminished by one-third. Sedimentation from land use activities is recognized as a primary cause of habitat degradation in the range of West Coast sockeye salmon.

Sockeye salmon have supported important commercial fisheries through much of their range. Harvest restrictions to protect sockeye in the Columbia River basin have reduced harvest rates for these sockeye. Sockeye salmon from the Washington coast and Puget Sound are harvested in Puget Sound and near-shore fisheries targeting larger sockeye populations originating in British Columbia.

Introductions of non-native species and habitat modifications have resulted in increased predator populations in numerous river and lake systems, thereby increasing the level of predation experienced by salmonids. Predation by marine mammals is also of concern in areas experiencing dwindling sockeye run sizes.

Natural climatic conditions have served to exacerbate the problems associated with degraded and altered riverine and estuarine habitats. Persistent drought conditions have reduced the already limited spawning, rearing, and migration habitat. Further, climatic conditions appear to have resulted in decreased ocean productivity which, during more productive periods, may help offset degraded freshwater habitat conditions.

In an attempt to mitigate the loss of habitat, extensive hatchery programs have been implemented throughout the range of sockeye on the West Coast. While some of these programs have been successful in providing fishing opportunities, the impacts of these programs on native, naturally reproducing stocks are not well understood. Competition, genetic introgression, and disease transmission resulting from hatchery introductions may significantly reduce the production and survival of naturally spawned sockeye. Furthermore, collection of native sockeye for hatchery broodstock purposes

may result in additional negative impacts to small or dwindling natural populations.

Harbor seals migrate up the Ozette River into Ozette Lake and have been seen feeding on adult sockeye salmon off the spawning beaches in Ozette Lake. The numbers of seals and of salmon taken by each seal is unknown. Seal predation on sockeye salmon at the river mouth and during the salmon's migration up the Ozette River may also be occurring. The upriver migration of harbor seals to feed on adult sockeye occurs commonly in British Columbia, occurring 100 mi (160 km) upriver on the Fraser River at Harrison Lake and up to 200 mi (320 km) inland on the Skeena River. Sockeye migrate up to Ozette Lake in less than 48 hours, and the majority of the adults travel at night. Given the precarious state of West Coast sockeye salmon stocks, including Ozette Lake, any marine mammal predation may have a significant effect on particular stocks, and these effects need to be more fully understood.

Outside the Olympic National Park, virtually the entire watershed of Ozette Lake has been logged. A combination of past overfishing and spawning habitat degradation associated with timber harvest and road building, have been major causes of this stock's decline.

The exotic plant, reed canary grass, has been encroaching on sockeye spawning beaches in Ozette Lake, particularly on the shoreline north of Umbrella Creek, where sockeye spawning has not occurred for several years. This plant survives overwinter submergence in up to 3 ft (1 m) of water and may possibly provide cover for predators of sockeye salmon fry. Suitable lakeshore spawning habitat for sockeye salmon is reported to be extremely limited in Ozette Lake. High water temperatures in Ozette Lake and River and low water flows in the summer may create a thermal block to migration and influence timing of sockeye migration. Water temperatures in late-July and August in the Ozette River near the lake outlet have exceeded the temperature range over which sockeye are known to migrate.

(7) Snake River: Endangered. The Snake River sockeye salmon shares its spawning habitat, Redfish Lake, Idaho, with kokanee, which are non-migrating sockeye salmon that spend their entire lifespan in the lake. Studies have indicated that kokanee and the sockeye do not interbreed. Adult Snake

River sockeye salmon enter the Columbia River in June and July and ascend the river system at the rate of about 13 mi (21 km) per day. Fish do not feed once they enter freshwater, but live off their accumulated body flesh. Those fish that complete their spawning journey usually arrive at Redfish Lake, Idaho, in August, and take four to eight weeks preparing to spawn. During this period the fish develop a reddish orange body color, the females swell with maturing eggs, and the males develop hooked jaws. In October, females construct nests, known as redds, in gravel areas of the eastern shoreline of the lake. Using her tail, the female digs a depression in the gravel and deposits between 50-100 eggs, which are then fertilized by sperm released by the male. The process continues until the female has deposited about 2,000 eggs. The adults die within a few weeks of spawning. The eggs incubate in the redds until April or May, when the young sockeye emerge. They remain in the gravel and feed from attached yolk sacs. After exhausting this food source the young fry swim up from the gravel and begin to feed on plankton.

In late April or early May, after spending one or two years in Redfish Lake, the juvenile sockeye, now known as smolt, begin their migration to the Pacific. While migrating, fish undergo chemical changes that will allow them to survive in a saltwater environment. Those that successfully reach the Pacific disperse widely for one to three years before attempting the return journey to spawn. Snake River sockeye salmon inhabit both salt- and freshwater at different stages of their life histories. Successful reproduction requires loose gravel that can serve for the construction of redds. Juvenile sockeye require unobstructed passage to the ocean and a water flow strong enough to bring them to saltwater in time to coincide with their physiological changes.

Historically, Idaho's sockeye salmon are known from lakes in the Stanley basin of the Salmon River and the Snake River basin. In the Stanley basin they were produced in at least five lakes: Redfish, Alturas, Stanley, Yellow Belly, and Petit. They also spawned in Big Payette Lake on the North Fork Payette River and in Wallowa Lake on the Wallowa River. For centuries sockeye salmon were a staple food resource of the Shoshone and Bannock Indian tribes. In the late 1800s miners and other settlers arrived in the area and began taking sockeye for food. Between 1870 and 1880 several commercial sockeye fisheries operated at Payette Lake, and plans were

made to establish a cannery at Redfish Lake. In the early twentieth century construction of dams on the Salmon and Payette Rivers sharply reduced sockeye salmon in the Snake River basin.

Today the Snake River sockeye salmon is almost extinct in the wild. Only Redfish Lake has supported a spawning sockeye population and the number of fish returning in recent years has steadily approached zero. Access to other lakes in the Stanley basin which have supported the sockeye in the past have been blocked by irrigation diversions and fish barriers. The Sunbeam Dam, which initially blocked access to the Stanley basin lakes in 1913, was partially removed in 1934 and sockeye populations began to recover. By 1942, 200 sockeye spawned in Redfish Lake. The population increased yearly and reached a peak of almost 4,500 in 1955.

However, the construction of a series of hydropower dams on the lower Snake River in the 1960s created additional obstacles to migration and the population began a steady decline. By 1989 only two fish returned to Redfish Lake. None were seen the following year and in 1991 only four fish returned.

Threats to the Snake River ESU: While many factors have contributed to the decline in the Snake River sockeye salmon, including predation, drought, and overharvesting, the overwhelming threat to this race of salmon, as for all Pacific Northwest salmon, is the network of hydroelectric dams and irrigation projects that has obstructed the fishes' passage and disrupted the historic pattern of spring water flows. Out-migrating juveniles must deal with eight hydropower dams along the lower Snake and Columbia Rivers. Studies have found that 77-96% of migrating juveniles die on their voyage to the ocean. Upstream-migrating adults also face high mortality because of the dams; between 34-57% percent of adults never reach their spawning ground.

Conservation and Recovery

Although there have been a number of attempts to institute a program to conserve Pacific coast salmon and steelhead, the most comprehensive was mandated by the Pacific Northwest Electric Power Planning and Conservation Act of 1980. This federal law established the Northwest Power Planning Council, which in turn developed a Fish and Wildlife Program with provisions to conserve the Snake River sockeye and other salmon runs. Conservation methods, which involved increased spring water releases from the dams, have met with only limited success, mainly because the timing and amount of releases are not mandated and have been resisted by hydropower producers, who would have to forgo some electrical generation. Attempts to capture juvenile sockeye and transport them around the dams have failed because most have died from the stresses of handling, transport, and overcrowding.

Most experts believe that the only way to promote the recovery of the Snake River sockeye and other threatened salmon runs is to greatly speed up water flow during the spring migration. This would require the drawing down of reservoirs behind the four lower Snake River dams: Lower Granite, Little Goose, Lower Monumental, and Ice Harbor. Water dedicated to salmon conservation would then be used to replenish the reservoirs. This long-term solution would involve the modification of existing fish passage facilities and, since it would also require changes in irrigation practices, river transportation, and patterns of recreational use such as boating and fishing, would encounter significant political opposition and require a lengthy phase-in period. And perhaps more importantly, any change in operation of the hydroelectric dams could affect the production and pricing of electricity in the region.

In the short term, while these issues are being debated, efforts to conserve the Snake River salmon will involve the production of hatchery-spawned fish and strategies to increase the spring flow from available sources. The Idaho Department of Fish and Game and the Shoshone-Bannock Indian tribes, with funding from the Bonneville Power Administration, has begun a hatchery program to increase sockeye production. Young sockeye from Redfish Lake have been trapped and placed in a hatchery. The only female in the group of four fish that returned to the lake in 1991 was captured to conserve the genetic traits of the wild sockeye in hatchery-raised fish.

While the extremely low number of Snake River sockeye have led many researchers to conclude that the run is functionally extinct already, they hope that conservation policies and methods developed for this species will help preserve other imperiled Pacific salmon runs in the future. Researchers have recently identified 101 Pacific salmon runs that they

regard as at "high risk of extinction" and another 58 runs that are at "moderate risk."

Contact

U. S. Fish and Wildlife Service
Regional Office, Division of Endangered Species
Eastside Federal Building
911 N. E. 11th Ave.
Portland, Oregon 97232-4181
Telephone: (503) 231-6121
http://pacific.fws.gov/

References

Bjornn, T. C., D. R. Craddock, and D. R. Corley. 1968. "Migration and Survival of Redfish Lake, Idaho, Sockeye Salmon, *Oncorhynchus nerka*." *Transactions of the American Fisheries Society* 37: 360-373.

Chapman, D. W., et al. 1990. "Status of Snake River Sockeye Salmon." Final Report for Pacific Northwest Utilities Conference Committee. 101 SW Main Street, Suite 810, Portland, Oregon 97204.

National Marine Fisheries Service. 20 November 1991. "Endangered Status for Snake River Sockeye Salmon." *Federal Register* 56(224): 58619.

National Marine Fisheries Service. 28 December 1993. "Designated Critical Habitat: Snake River Sockeye Salmon, Snake River Spring/Summer Run Chinook Salmon, and Snake River Fall Chinook Salmon." *Federal Register* 58(247): 68543.

National Marine Fisheries Service. 10 March 1998. "Proposed Threatened Status for Ozette Lake and Designated Critical Habitat for Ozette Lake, Washington Sockeye Salmon." *Federal Register* 63(46): 11750.

National Marine Fisheries Service. 25 March 1999. "Threatened Status for Ozette Lake Sockeye Salmon in Washington." *Federal Register* 64(57): 14528.

Nehlson, W., J. E. Williams, and J. A. Lichatowich. 1991. "Pacific Salmon at the Crossroads: Stocks at Risk from California, Oregon, Idaho, and Washington." *Fisheries* 16 (2):4-21.

Chinook Salmon

Oncorhynchus tshawytscha

Status

The following nine "evolutionarily significant populations," or distinctive stocks, have been designated as at risk in the United States:

1. Sacramento River, CA; winter-run population; Endangered; Listed: April 6, 1990

2. Snake River, ID, OR, WA; mainstem and subbasins in the Tucannon River, Grande Ronde River, Imnaha River, Salmon River, and Clearwater River; fall-run natural populations; Threatened; Listed: April 22, 1992

3. Snake River, ID, OR, WA; mainstem and subbasins in the Tucannon River, Grande Ronde River, Imnaha River, and Salmon River; spring/summer-run natural populations; Threatened; Listed: April 22, 1992

4. All naturally spawned populations from rivers and streams flowing into Puget Sound, WA, including the Straits of Juan de Fuca from the Elwha River eastward, and Hood Canal, South Sound, North Sound and the Strait of Georgia; Threatened; Listed: August 2, 1999

5. All naturally spawned populations in OR and WA from the Columbia River and its tributaries upstream from its mouth to a point east of the Hood River, and White Salmon River to Willamette Falls in Oregon, excluding the spring run in the Clackamas River; Threatened; Listed: August 2, 1999

6. All naturally spawned populations in OR in the Clackamas River and the Willamette River and its tributaries above Willamette Falls; Threatened; Listed: August 2, 1999

7. All naturally spawned populations in WA in the Columbia River tributaries upstream of Rock Island Dam and downstream of Chief Joseph Dam, excluding the Okanogan River, and the Columbia River from a line between the west end of Clatsop Jetty, OR, and the west end of Peacock Jetty, WA, upstream to Chief Joseph Dam, including spring-run hatchery stocks (and their progeny) in Chiwawa River, Methow River, Twisp River, Chewuch River, White River, and Nason Creek; Threatened; Listed: August 2, 1999

8. All naturally spawned spring-run populations in CA from the Sacramento-San Joaquin Rver mainstem and its tributaries; Threatened; Listed: December 29, 1999

9. All naturally spawned populations in CA from Redwood Creek south to Russian River, inclusive of all populations in main-stems and tributaries; Threatened; Listed: December 29, 1999

Family

Salmonidae (Salmon)

Description

A large, silvery fish with black spots on the body.

Habitat

Adults live in the ocean, but ascend rivers to spawn on gravel bottom. Juveniles live in freshwater habitat, then descend to the ocean where the adults live in pelagic habitats.

Food

Juveniles feed on aquatic invertebrates and small fish. Adults feed on large invertebrates and smaller fish.

Reproduction

Spawns in freshwater at various times of year, depending on the stock.

Threats

Loss or degradation of spawning habitat, excessive fishing at sea and during the spawning migration.

Range

California, Idaho, Oregon, Washington

Chinook Salmon, photograph. U. S. Fish and Wildlife Service. Reproduced by permission.

Description

The chinook salmon, also known as the king salmon, is the largest species of salmon in the world. Large individuals can reach a weight exceeding 50 lbs (23 kg) and a body length of more than 58 in (147 cm). One individual caught in Alaska weighed an enormous 126 lbs (57 kg). Adults have a silvery body marked with irregular black spots on the back, on both lobes of the caudal (or tail) fin, and on the dorsal (top) and adipose (top back) fins. Chinook salmon have 10 to 14 major dorsal fin rays, 14-19 anal fin rays, 14-19 pectoral fin rays, and 10 to 11 pelvic fin rays. The gill rakers are rough and widely spaced, with six to 10 rakers on the lower half of the first gill arch. Reproductive adults are uniformly olive brown to dark maroon in color, but males are darker than females and have a hooked upper jaw and an arched back.

Behavior

The chinook salmon is an anadromous species of fish, meaning it spends most of its adult life at sea,

but migrates to breed in freshwater rivers and streams. The eggs are laid in clean, well-aerated gravel beds, where they hatch and the fry (or alevins) live for about one month. Juveniles then emerge and feed on aquatic invertebrates for an additional eight to 12 weeks until reaching 3-4 in (7-10 cm) fork length. The juveniles then undergo a metamorphic change known as smolting, which is necessary for undertaking the transition from freshwater to saltwater habitats. The transformed stage, known as smolts, then migrate down tributaries and to the river estuary, where they enter the marine environment. Adult chinook salmon live at sea for two to four years before returning to their birth river to spawn. The adults are exhausted by the breeding effort and die soon afterward. However, the particulars of behavior and life history vary significantly in different parts of the range of the chinook salmon. Some species run up-river in the autumn, and others in the winter or springtime. For example, winter-run chinook salmon that spawn on the Sacramento River ascend the river between December and May. The run consists of mostly three-year-old fish along with smaller numbers of two- and four-year-old individuals. In the late spring and summer each female excavates a gravel nest, known as a redd, in water 9-42 in (23-107 cm) deep. The redd is an approximately 1 ft-deep (30 cm) depression dug by the female turning on its side and rapidly flexing its tail to dislodge gravel, which settles slightly downstream. The female then extrudes eggs into the depression; these are fertilized by one or more attending males. The female then moves slightly upstream and excavates another redd, with the dislodged gravel covering the eggs in the first depression. This process continues until all of the eggs of the female, usually numbering 4,000-5,000, have been deposited and fertilized. Both males and females die after spawning; the females usually remain on the redd, while the males move downstream. Newly hatched alevins emerge from the eggs after about four months. They remain buried in the gravel for another one to four months, nourished by their yolk sac. The salmon fry spend only a short time in their rearing areas before beginning their out-migration to the ocean, passing through the river's estuary between December and April.

Habitat

Chinook salmon need streams or rivers with a clean gravel bottom and an adequate flow of well-oxygenated water to aerate their eggs and alevins. The water temperature must be cooler than about 56°F (13°C) for eggs to hatch. Adults live in the open ocean, in cool temperate and boreal habitats.

Distribution

The general distribution of the chinook salmon is western North America and northeastern Asia. In western North America it occurs from the Ventura River in California, and north to Point Hope, Alaska, and the Mackenzie River area in Canada. In northeastern Asia it occurs from Hokkaido, Japan, to the Anadyr River, Russia. Adults occur in waters of the northern Pacific Ocean. Within this broad range, the chinook salmon can be divided into numerous distinct breeding stocks, or evolutionarily significant units, including the ones considered in this entry on endangered and threatened populations of the United States.

Threats

The chinook salmon has suffered large population declines throughout most of its range. Much of its breeding habitat has been degraded or destroyed by siltation and warm-water conditions associated with forestry practices in the watershed of the river or stream. In other cases habitat damage has been caused by nearby urbanization, industrialization, mining activities, road building, or agricultural practices (including pesticide use). Many historical breeding habitats are now inaccessible to migratory fish because of the construction of impassable hydroelectric dams or other kinds of impoundments. In addition, most stocks of pelagic and migrating fish are being harvested excessively, resulting in decreasing populations of breeding adults. Juvenile salmon are threatened by various factors, including predatory fish species (especially in estuarine habitats), diversion into irrigation projects that draw water from rearing rivers or streams, and mortality caused by water-intake pipes and turbines of hydroelectric facilities.

Conservation and Recovery

The U. S. Fish and Wildlife Service, National Marine Fisheries Service, state agencies, and other organizations are undertaking various actions on behalf of populations of chinook salmon. Similar actions are being undertaken to enhance breeding populations in other countries, including Canada, Japan, and Russia. Management practices include actions undertaken to improve spawning habitat (for example, by providing clean gravel), mitigation of obstructions associated with dams and impoundments (for example, by constructing fish ladders; in some cases, dams are being removed to restore migratory runs), or by relaxing the fishing pressure. In addition, many agencies are attempting to enhance the reproductive efforts of wild fish by rearing eggs and alevins in hatcheries, later releasing the fingerlings in suitable habitat to fend for themselves. In some areas, these actions are helping to maintain or increase the numbers of wild chinook salmon. In many other areas, however, overfishing and habitat damage (the latter often associated with forestry operations) are continuing to have severe effects on the species and its populations continue to decline.

Contacts

U. S. Fish and Wildlife Service
Boise Ecological Services Field Office
4696 Overland Road, Room 576
Boise, Idaho 83705
Telephone: (208) 334-1931
Fax: (208) 334-9493

U. S. Fish and Wildlife Service
Division of Endangered Species
4401 North Fairfax Drive
Arlington, Virginia 22203
Telephone: (703) 358-2171

National Marine Fisheries Service
Protected Resources Division
525 N.E. Oregon Street, Suite 500
Portland, Oregon 97232
Telephone: (503) 231-2005

National Marine Fisheries Service
Office of Protected Resources
1315 East West Highway
Silver Spring, Maryland 20910
Telephone: (301) 713-1401

References

National Marine Fisheries Service. 1992. "Endangered and Threatened Species; Threatened Status for Snake River Spring/Summer Chinook Salmon, Threatened Status for Snake River Fall Chinook Salmon." *Federal Register* 57 (78):14653-14663.

National Oceanic and Atmospheric Administration. 1999. "Designated Critical Habitat: Revision of Critical Habitat for Snake River Spring/Summer Chinook Salmon." *Federal Register* 64 (55):57339-57403.

National Oceanic and Atmospheric Administration. 1999. "Endangered and Threatened Species: Regulations Consolidation; Final Rule." *Federal Register* 64 (55):14051-14077.

National Oceanic and Atmospheric Administration. 2000. "Designated Critical Habitat: Critical Habitat for 19 Evolutionarily Significant Units of Salmon and Steelhead in Washington, Oregon, Idaho, and California." *Federal Register* 65:7764-7787.

U. S. Fish and Wildlife Service. 1999. "Endangered and Threatened Wildlife and Plants; Determination of Threatened Status for Two Chinook Salmon Evolutionarily Significant Units (ESUs) in California." *Federal Register* 64 (249):72960-72961.

U. S. Fish and Wildlife Service. 1999. "Endangered and Threatened Wildlife and Plants: Listing of Nine Evolutionarily Significant Units of Chinook Salmon, Chum Salmon, Sockeye Salmon, and Steelhead." *Federal Register* 64 (147):41835-41839.

Waples, R., R. P. Jone, Jr., B. R. Beckman, and G. A. Swan. 1991. *NOAA Technical Memorandum NMFS F/NWC-201. Status Review for Snake River Fall Chinook Salmon.* National Marine Fisheries Service, 73 pp.

Bull Trout

Salvelinus confluentus

Bull Trout, photograph by Hollingsworth. U.S. Fish and Wildlife Service. Reproduced by permission.

Status	Threatened (Klamath River and Columbia River Distinct Population Segments)
Listed	June 10, 1998
Status	Threatened (Jarbidge River, Coastal-Puget Sound, and St. Mary-Belly River Distinct Population Segments)
Listed	November 1, 1999
Family	Salmonidae
Description	A salmonid fish with small, pale-yellow to crimson spots on a darker background, which ranges from olive green to brown above, fading to white on the belly.
Habitat	Rivers and streams; some populations migrate to the ocean.
Food	Invertebrates and smaller fish.
Reproduction	Lays eggs in gravel; some populations are anadromous.
Threats	Habitat destruction by impoundment and dams, and degradation by siltation and other kinds of pollution.
Range	Idaho, Montana, Nevada, Oregon, Washington

Description

The *Salvelinus confluentus* (bull trout), a member of the family Salmonidae, is native to the Pacific northwest of the United States and western Canada. It was first described as *Salmo spectabilis* in 1856 from a specimen collected on the lower Columbia River, then subsequently described under names like *Salmo confluentus* and *Salvelinus malma*. Until 1980, bull trout and Dolly Varden (*Salvelinus malma*) were considered a single species, but various kinds of evidence have been presented to demonstrate important differences between these species. Although bull trout and Dolly Varden co-occur in several northwestern Washington river drainages, there is little evidence of introgression, and the two species appear to be maintaining distinct genomes.

Bull trout and Dolly Varden look very similar. Both have small, pale-yellow to crimson spots on a darker background, which ranges from olive green to brown above, fading to white on the belly. Spawning adults develop varying amounts of red on the belly. Both species exhibit differences in size, body characteristics, coloration, and life-history behavior across their range. The elongated body is somewhat rounded with the greatest body depth below the dorsal fin. The head is long, the eyes large, the snout blunt and pointed, and the mouth terminal. Freshwater forms grow 12-18 in (30-46 cm), and the anadromous forms grow 18-24 in (46-60 cm). The color varies with size, locality, and habitat. In sea-run adults the back and upper sides are dark blue and the lower sides are silvery to white. In freshwater populations the back and upper sides are olive green to brown; the sides are a paler color. The dorsal surface and sides are marked with yellow, orange, or red spots a little smaller than the size of the eye. The paired fins and anal fin are white or creamy without spots. Spawning males, espe-

Bull Trout, photograph by Wade Fredenberg, U. S. Fish and Wildlife Service. Reproduced by permission.

cially in anadromous populations, turn red on the ventral surface and tip of the snout. The lower jaw and parts of the head are black, and the back turns olive-brown. The spots become a more vivid orange-red, and the pectoral, pelvic, and anal fins are red-black with a white leading edge. The snout thickens and the lower jaw turns up. Females change less.

Behavior

The bull trout feeds on aquatic invertebrates, terrestrial insects that fall into its streams, and small fish. It breeds in beds of clean gravel, which are known as redds. The eggs incubate in the gravel and the larvae also live there initially. The small fish and adults live elsewhere in their stream and riverine habitat, often in pools. Some populations run to the sea, but most are landlocked and cannot do this.

Habitat

The bull trout occurs in clean, cool, freshwater rivers and streams in forested terrain. It spawns in gravel beds.

Distribution

The bull trout occurs in several geographically distinct populations, or "distinct population segments," which are isolated and do not interbreed.

The Klamath River distinct population segment (or DPS) occurs in the Klamath River. This river originates in south-central Oregon near Crater Lake National Park, flows southwest into northern California where it meets the Trinity River, and then empties into the Pacific Ocean. Bull trout in this drainage are reproductively isolated and genetically and evolutionarily distinct from those in other large rivers in the region. Bull trout were once widely distributed in the Klamath River basin, but are now limited to only seven isolated stream areas.

The Columbia River DPS occurs throughout the Columbia River basin within the United States and its tributaries (but excluding bull trout found in the Jarbidge River, Nevada; see below). Although bull trout in the upper and lower Columbia River have different lineages, no discrete geographical boundary has been established between the two groups. The Columbia River DPS is significant because the overall range of the species would be substantially reduced if this discrete population were lost. The Columbia River DPS includes bull trout residing in portions of Oregon, Washington, Idaho, and Montana. Bull trout are estimated to have once occupied about 60% of the Columbia River basin, and they presently occur in only 45% of the historical range. The Columbia River DPS is composed of 141 subpopulations. The U.S. Fish and Wildlife Service has divided the Columbia River basin area into the lower Columbia River, the mid-Columbia River, upper Columbia River, and the Snake River and its tributaries. Each division has its own set of subpopulations.

The Jarbidge River, a tributary of the Snake River located in southwest Idaho and northern Nevada, currently contains the southernmost habitat occupied by bull trout. Bull trout range in Nevada covers the East Fork Jarbidge and West Fork Jarbidge Rivers, along with Slide, Dave, Pine, and Jack Creeks. This DPS is discrete because it is segregated from other bull trout in the Snake River basin by a gap in suitable habitat of greater than 150 mi (240 km) and by several impassable dams on the main-stem Snake River.

The Coastal-Puget Sound bull trout DPS encompasses all Pacific Coast drainages within the coterminous United States north of the Columbia River in Washington, including those flowing into Puget Sound. This DPS is discrete because it is geographically segregated from other subpopulations by the Pacific Ocean and the crest of the Cascade Mountain Range. This DPS is significant to the species as a whole because it is thought to contain the only anadromous forms of bull trout in the coterminous United States, thus, occurring in a unique ecological setting.

The St. Mary-Belly River DPS is located in northwest Montana east of the Continental Divide. Both the St. Mary and Belly Rivers are tributaries of the Saskatchewan River basin in Alberta, Canada. This DPS is discrete because it is segregated from other bull trout by the Continental Divide and is the only population found east of the Continental Divide in the coterminous United States. This DPS is significant because its loss would result in a significant reduction in the range of the taxon within the coterminous United States. Bull trout in this population segment migrate across the international border with Canada.

Threats

Bull trout have been extensively displaced by introduced brook trout (*Salvelinus fontinalis*), and hybrids of the two species have been verified in several streams. The brown trout (*Salmo trutta*) is another introduced salmonid that is affecting some populations of bull trout. Where brook trout or brown trout co-occur with bull trout, its distribution has contracted and that of the introduced salmonids expanded. Negative effects of introduced salmonids is the most pervasive threat to bull trout subpopulations in the Columbia River basin, 62% of which are threatened by competition, predation, or displacement by non-native species. The harm caused by non-native species to the bull trout is often exacerbated by habitat conditions, water temperature, and isolation.

Many bull trout habitats have been degraded by intensive livestock grazing, mostly in lowland meadows and to a lesser extent in forested areas. Livestock grazing in the vicinity of streams and rivers promotes bank instability and erosion, and diminishes the availability of undercut banks used a trout for resting habitat. For example, of the 141 subpopulations of bull trout identified in the Columbia River DPS, about 50% are threatened by ongoing livestock grazing.

Extensive timber harvesting is another important factor degrading aquatic habitats. Activities such as clear-cutting, partial cutting with overstory removal, and selective logging for old-growth timber result in temporarily reduced riparian cover and increased water temperature. Roads built for access to timber cause increased erosion, sedimentation, and siltation of breeding habitat. For example, about 74% of the habitat in the Columbia River basin has been affected by forestry and associated roads. Latent threats of forestry are thought responsible for

Photo Researchers Inc., William H. Mullins

many of the 2,300 landslides that took place in the Clearwater and Spokane river basins during high runoff events in 1995 and 1996, which correlated closely with high logging-road density on national forest lands. These same runoff events also triggered an estimated 2,000 land slides on adjacent non-federal timber-lands in the Clearwater River basin. The effects of timber harvesting and roads on streams are long lasting, and recovery is slow. The legacy left by past forestry practices limits bull trout populations and restoration in all major watersheds. In the Wenatchee National Forest, Washington, bull trout spawning and rearing are correlated with streams not subject to past timber harvest, while in the Tucannon River Drainage timber harvesting has been responsible for the decline and isolation of bull trout in Pataha Creek.

Dams and impoundments are another important threat to bull trout, particularly on the Columbia River distinct population segment. Bull trout passage is prevented or inhibited at hydroelectric, flood-control, and irrigation dams on almost every major river in the Columbia River basin except the Salmon River in Idaho.

The direct harvesting (by fishing) of bull trout has also been an important factor in its demise, although the directed harvest has been stopped where the species is threatened. However, there is still by-catch mortality associated with recreational fishing for other trout species and salmon.

Other factors affecting bull trout in some areas include the construction and maintenance of county and state roads, the past and ongoing effects of agricultural activities, residential developments, hydrological diversions for irrigation, channelization, mining activities in the watershed, and pollution by sewage, nutrients, and toxic chemicals.

Conservation and Recovery

Federal, state, and local conservation and recovery actions have been undertaken to reverse the long-term declining trend for the threatened population segments of the bull trout. The actions include restrictive angling regulations, the adoption of various land-management rules, and interagency conservation programs. Federal programs that include land management plans, timber sales, and livestock grazing allotments are assessed to determine if they jeopardize the continued existence of bull trout. These actions have already begun to improve habitat conditions and reduce threats for the bull trout in some regions. Overall, however, the implementation and enforcement of existing federal and state laws designed to conserve fishery resources, maintain water quality, and protect aquatic habitat have not been sufficient to prevent the past and continuing habitat degradation that is primarily responsible for bull trout declines.

Examples of positive actions are the efforts of the Klamath Basin Working Group to: eradicate brook trout in Long, Sun and Three-Mile Creeks; reduce livestock grazing along bull trout streams; assess watershed conditions; and monitor bull trout status. Bull trout conservation in the Klamath basin has also benefited from habitat restoration activities initiated by the Upper Klamath Basin Working Group, which began in 1994. Weyerhauser Timber Company began a program of improved road maintenance in 1994 to reduce sediment inputs from roads on its lands adjacent to occupied bull trout stream reaches in the Klamath River basin, and U. S. Timberlands is continuing the practice. Timber harvests on U.S. Timberlands property occurred along Boulder Creek in 1994 and Long Creek in 1995. A review of the activities concluded that leaving buffer strips and restoring disused roads left the riparian habitat in better condition than before the timber harvest. No timber harvests are currently planned for areas adjacent to streams occupied by bull trout in the Klamath River basin. However, six of the seven bull trout subpopulations in the Klamath River basin have been affected by past forest management practices.

The bull trout in the Columbia River basin is the focus of protection efforts that will be important to its long term conservation and recovery there. However, threats continue and subpopulation improvements throughout the Columbia River have yet to be demonstrated. Chemical eradication programs were initiated in 1992 for brook trout in Sun Creek, but this also killed a number of bull trout. Ongoing

management actions in Three-Mile and Long Creeks focus on brook trout eradication via selective electrofishing, snorkel-spearing, trapping, and chemical treatments with the objective of expanding bull trout range. Brook trout have declined in Three-Mile Creek, but there has been no measurable change in numbers in Long Creek.

A local Bull Trout Task Force was formed in 1994 to gather and share information on bull trout in the Jarbidge River. The task force was successful in 1997 in replacing the Jack Creek culvert with a concrete bridge to facilitate bull trout passage into Jack Creek. However, the task force has not yet developed a comprehensive conservation plan addressing all threats to bull trout in the Jarbidge River basin. The Humboldt National Forest plan was amended in 1995 to include the Inland Native Fish Strategy. This fish and wildlife habitat policy sets a no net loss objective and is currently guiding Forest Service planning of possible reconstruction of a portion of the Jarbidge Canyon Road. In June 1998, Humboldt National Forest issued the Jarbidge River Environmental Assessment for Access and Restoration between Pine Creek Campground and the Jarbidge Wilderness. Conservation actions have also been taken in support of the St. Mary-Belly River Coastal-Puget Sound bull trout DPSs.

Contacts

U.S. Fish and Wildlife Service
Snake River Basin Office
1387 S. Vinnell Way, Room 368
Boise, Idaho 83709-1657
Telephone: (208) 378-5243
Fax: (208) 378-5262

U. S. Fish and Wildlife Service
Regional Office, Division of Endangered Species
Eastside Federal Building
911 N. E. 11th Ave.
Portland, Oregon 97232-4181
Telephone: (503) 231-6121
http://pacific.fws.gov/

U. S. Fish and Wildlife Service
Regional Office, Division of Endangered Species
P. O. Box 25486
Denver Federal Center
Denver, Colorado 80225
http://www.r6.fws.gov/

Reference

U.S. Fish and Wildlife Service. 1 Nov. 1999. "Endangered and Threatened Wildlife and Plants; Determination of Threatened Status for Bull Trout in the Coterminous United States; Final Rule." *Federal Register* 64(210):58909-58933.

Ozark Cavefish

Amblyopsis rosae

Status	Threatened
Listed	November 1, 1984
Family	Amblyopsidae (Cavefish)
Description	White, blind cavefish about 2 in (5.1 cm) long.
Habitat	Cave streams.
Food	Bat guano, plankton, small invertebrates.
Reproduction	Fertilization occurs February to April producing 20-25 eggs.
Threats	Groundwater pollution; disturbance of caves.
Range	Arkansas, Missouri, Oklahoma

Description

The Ozark cavefish, *Amblyopsis rosae*, is a true troglobitic (cave-dwelling) fish. It is a small (2 in, or 5.1 cm), pinkish-white fish with a broad flattened head, small scales, and a projecting lower jaw. The dorsal and anal fins are located far back on the body, the caudal fin is rounded, and the pelvic fins are absent. The Ozark cavefish has only vestigal eyes. It uses sensory papillae, which occur in two or three rows on its tail fin, to "feel" its way through its environment.

The only other species in the genus *Amblyopsis* is the Northern cavefish (*A. spelea*), found in southern Indiana and west central Kentucky. The northern and southern species are not readily distinguishable, and they differ mainly in the arrangement of their sensory organs. How they differ greatly is their degree of cave adaptation, with the Ozark cavefish being much more selective and less adaptable.

Behavior

This species is rarely seen and little is known of its life history. Free swimming fry have been observed at five to six months of age, and first reproduction begins at three to four years. Fertilization probably occurs from February to April, although only one-fifth of the females breed in a season. Females produce 20-25 eggs. The young are carried in the gill cavity until they lose their yolk sac at age four to five months.

The most available food source is bat guano, but the cavefish also feeds on copepods, cladocerans, isopods, amphipods, crayfish, crickets, larval salamanders, and young cavefish.

Habitat

The Ozark cavefish inhabits the caves that honeycomb the highly soluble Boone and Burlington limestone formations of the Ozark Mountains. Food supply in these stable, yet fragile, cave habitats is limited in diversity and quantity because of the lack of light. Larger populations of the Ozark cavefish occur in caves used by the endangered gray bat (*Myotis grisescens*), where bat guano is the primary energy source. The caves occasionally flood, and the introduced waters also carry some food resources. Organic matter enters the cave entrances via wind and some food may enter through sinkholes.

Distribution

The Ozark cavefish is the only cavefish within the Springfield Plateau of southwest Missouri, northwest Arkansas, and northeast Oklahoma. Early studies of the southern cavefish (*Typhlichthys*

Ozark Cavefish, photograph by Russell Norton. Reproduced by permission.

subterraneus) often confused it with the Ozark cavefish, and it is difficult to sort out actual sightings. Historic records place the Ozark cavefish in at least nine counties and possibly in an additional five. There are reports of the cavefish occurring in 52 caves; only 24 historic localities are confirmed, however.

As of 1990, there were 9 known populations of the Ozark cavefish in Missouri and 21 populations range-wide, including populations in at least 14 caves in six counties in Arkansas, Missouri, and Oklahoma. Discoveries of new populations in Missouri in 1989 and 1990 delighted researchers. In 1989, the presence of cavefish in Jackson Cave (Greene County) was confirmed by Dr. Steven Jones of Drury College. Another population was found in Hayes Spring Cave (Stone County). Although this population is located within the historic range of the cavefish, upon its discovery it was the only known population in Stone County. It was believed that the cavefish had been extirpated from Fantastic Caverns (Greene County), but a single cavefish was ob-

served there in 1989, marking the first time the species had been observed in the caverns since 1981. Finally, in January 1990, cavefish were observed in a spring at the Neosho National Fish Hatchery at Neosho, Missouri.

Threats

The decline of the Ozark cavefish may be due to degradation of subsurface or groundwater. Northwest Arkansas is an area of heavy agricultural use where animal waste from poultry and swine seep into the groundwater. Sinkholes in the soluble limestone bedrock increase the possibility of direct contamination of the groundwater. Researchers from the Arkansas Department of Pollution Control and Ecology have detected nitrate and ammonia levels in regional wells that are probably toxic to the cavefish. Industrial and residential development of Greene County, Missouri, have also caused water contamination. Toxic levels of nickel from urban wastes have been found in at least one cave system.

A low reproduction rate and a confined habitat make the Ozark cavefish vulnerable to even casual collecting. There are several documented instances of scientific collectors taking large numbers of Ozark cavefish. A scientific collection in the 1930s from one Arkansas cave may be responsible for reducing that population to a very low level. Pet stores often display blind cavefish (possibly Ozarks) for sale to aquarists. Another threat to the cavefish is disturbance caused by groups of amateur spelunkers. Protection of cavefish requires that human disturbance be kept to a minimum. The populations in caves where cavefish were once known to occur disappeared when the caves were opened to spelunkers.

Conservation and Recovery

Cave Springs Cave in Arkansas is now owned by the state, providing some protection for the largest known cavefish population. Missouri purchased Turnback Creek Cave which, although it contains only a small Ozark cavefish population, has considerable cavefish habitat and may support a reintroduction effort. The Nature Conservancy and Arkansas Natural Heritage Commission have also purchased caves with small populations of cavefish.

Maintaining the openings into the caves so that bats can freely come and go is crucial for the continuing supply of food resources. Cave water supplies, which include drainage basins and aquifers, must be protected from surface runoff. The Recovery Plan recommends monitoring regional hydraulic patterns so that water quality can be controlled and the water table and flow can be maintained; installing gates to cave entrances to de-

crease disturbance by spelunkers; introduce bat populations into uncolonized recovery caves; and educate spelunkers to the harm they can inflict upon cavefish.

Contacts

Regional Office of Endangered Species
U.S. Fish and Wildlife Service
P. O. Box 1306
Albuquerque, New Mexico 87103
http://southwest.fws.gov/

Regional Office of Endangered Species
U.S. Fish and Wildlife Service
Federal Building
Fort Snelling, Minnesota 55111
http://midwest.fws.gov/

Regional Office of Endangered Species
U.S. Fish and Wildlife Service
1875 Century Blvd, Suite 200
Atlanta, Georgia 30345
http://southeast.fws.gov/

References

Poulson, T. L. 1963. "Cave Adaptation in Amblyopsid Fishes." *American Midland Naturalist* 70(2):257-290.

U.S. Fish and Wildlife Service. 1986. *Recovery Plan for the Ozark Cavefish,* Amblyopsis rosae. U.S. Fish and Wildlife Service. Atlanta, 52 pp.

Willis, L. D., and A. V. Brown. 1985. "Distribution and Habitat Requirements of the Ozark Cavefish, *Amblyopsis rosae.*" *American Midland Naturalist* 114(2):311-317.

Alabama Cavefish

Speoplatyrhinus poulsoni

Status	Endangered
Listed	September 9, 1977: Threatened
Reclassified	September 28, 1988: Endangered
Family	Amblyopsidae (Cavefish)
Description	Small, eyeless, albino cavefish.
Habitat	Underground pools and streams in caves.
Food	Aquatic invertebrates and cavefish.
Reproduction	Probably incubates eggs under the gills.
Threats	Low numbers; degradation of groundwater quality.
Range	Alabama

Description

The Alabama cavefish, *Speoplatyrhinus poulsoni*, is about 3 in (8 cm) long and has no discernible pigmentation, appearing pinkish-white. It is eyeless and has transparent fins and skin. It has a large head, which makes up more than one-third of its length.

The Alabama cavefish is the rarest American cavefish and one of the rarest freshwater fishes in North America.

Behavior

Although little is known about the Alabama cavefish, it probably incubates eggs within a chamber underneath the gills. There's some evidence to suggest that it matures late and reproduces until the end of its life. It feeds on small aquatic invertebrates and smaller cavefish and has a life span of five to 10 years.

Habitat

The cavefish's only known habitat is Key Cave in Alabama. The cave has cool, year-round temperatures and receives no direct light. It is located within the Warsaw limestone formation, which is a large, stable aquifer and an excellent conveyer of groundwater. The Warsaw limestone rests on underlying rock strata that are honeycombed with channels to allow passage of groundwater.

Flooding is generally responsible for washing organic matter into the pools and streams within the caves, providing food for cave fauna, which in turn provides food for higher lifeforms. In Key Cave, the guano of the gray bat is probably the major source of the organic matter at the bottom of the food chain.

The aquatic community in this cave includes fairly large populations of two cave-adapted crayfish, as well as numerous isopods and amphipods.

Distribution

The Alabama cavefish has been found only in Key Cave in Lauderdale County, Alabama. Only nine specimens have ever been collected. Because the underground water system in the area is so widespread, it was hoped that the cavefish had been dispersed to other sites. However, studies of 120 other caves in the area, conducted since 1977, have failed to locate any other cavefish populations. The number of individuals in the Key Cave population is estimated to be less than 100. In 1988 the Alabama cavefish was reclassified from Threatened to Endangered.

Threats

The quality of the groundwater directly affects the fragile ecology of the cave. When water is degraded by fertilizers, pesticides, or sewage run-off, the food supply for the cavefish diminishes, which

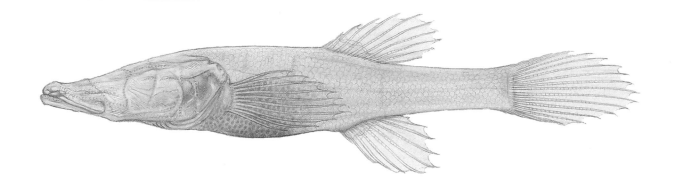

Cimmaron Trading Co.

in turn reduces its longevity and reproductive capabilities. The U. S. Fish and Wildlife Service (FWS) is working with the Environmental Protection Agency to control sources of groundwater pollution in the area and to advise about the impact of any construction on the runoff patterns. The population level of the gray bat within the cave also affects the Alabama cavefish. In recent years, bat numbers have declined, reducing guano, and lessening habitat viability. Food availability is the primary limiting factor on population, which is directly related to the viability of the bat inhabitants of the cave. In Key Cave the bat population diminished by half over a 10-year period.

Conservation and Recovery

FWS personnel are currently exploring management techniques for stabilizing the population of the Endangered gray bat (_Myotis grisescens_; see separate entry). As the Gray Bat Recovery Plan is implemented, it will also benefit the cavefish. Further re-

search is needed to plan the recovery of the Alabama cavefish. The little that is currently known, however, is not encouraging. Captive breeding of cave-dwelling species has invariably failed in the past, and it is not considered a viable recovery strategy for the Alabama cavefish. Transplanting the fish to other sites is not considered feasible, and biologists' options are limited.

The Recovery Plan calls for determining the recharge requirements of Key Cave; monitoring the Key Cave aquifer and water quality; determining the impact of the loss of bats in Shelta Cave; prohibiting human disturbance of the caves; and controling agricultural practices in the recharge area.

Contact

Regional Office of Endangered Species
U.S. Fish and Wildlife Service
1875 Century Blvd, Suite 200
Atlanta, Georgia 30345
http://southeast.fws.gov/

References

Cooper, J. E., and R. A. Kuehne. 1974. *"Speoplatyrhinus poulsoni,* a New Genus and Species of Subterranean Fish from Alabama." *Copeia* 2:486-493.

Poulson, T. L. 1963. "Cave Adaptation in Amblyopsid Fishes." *American Midland Naturalist* 70(2):257-290.

U.S. Fish and Wildlife Service. 1985. "Revised Alabama Cavefish Recovery Plan." U.S. Fish and Wildlife Service, Atlanta.

Waccamaw Silverside

Menidia extensa

Status	Threatened
Listed	April 8, 1987
Family	Atherinidae (Silverside)
Description	Small, slender, almost transparent fish.
Habitat	Shallow, open water over dark bottoms.
Food	Plankton.
Reproduction	Spawns April to July.
Threats	Water pollution.
Range	North Carolina

Description

Waccamaw silverside (*Menidia extensa*), also known as the skipjack or glass minnow, is a small, slender, almost transparent fish with a silvery stripe along each side. It has large eyes, and its jaw is angled sharply upward. Adults reach about 2.5 in (6.4 cm) in length.

Behavior

Waccamaw silverside is a lake dweller. It forms schools near the lake surface over shallow, dark-bottomed shoals. The species reaches sexual maturity at one year of age and spawns from April through July; the spawning peak is reached when water temperature is 68-72°F (20-22.2°C). Neither sex exhibits any physical characteristics of spawning conditions; most silversides die shortly after spawning, but a few may survive a second winter. Females may develop eggs as early as November and will ultimately produce about 150 eggs.

The adults feed on plankton, primarily crustaceans, at the surface in open water. Feeding occurs day and night, and no seasonal behavior has been noted. If waters are rough, the silverside remains close to shore. Silversides are an important food source for larger fishes in Lake Waccamaw.

Habitat

This silverside's habitat, Lake Waccamaw, is rich in its diversity of aquatic fauna and flora. The Waccamaw basin supports more unique nonmarine mollusks than any other locale in North Carolina. About 50 fish species, including many popular game fish, are found in the lake and its drainages. Many endemic species are of special interest to biologists.

The lake has a surface area of 9,000 acres (3,642 hectares) and an average depth of only 7.5 ft (2.3 m). Although fed by acidic swamp streams, it has a virtually neutral pH. This neutral condition of the water, unusual among North Carolina's coastal plain lakes, is believed to be caused by the buffering effect of the calcareous Waccamaw Limestone formation, which underlies the lake and is exposed on the north shore. Lake Waccamaw is a registered North Carolina Natural Heritage Area and has been proposed as a National Natural Landmark.

Distribution

Waccamaw silverside is endemic to North Carolina's Waccamaw basin. Lake Waccamaw's 85-sq mi (220-sq km) watershed is predominantly rural, dominated by small farms and forested tracts owned by large timber companies.

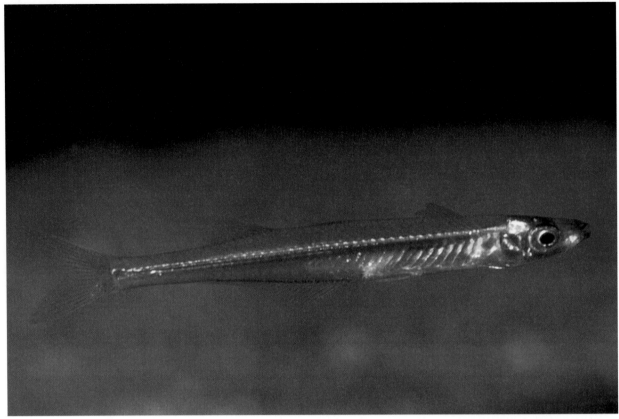

Waccamaw Silverside, photograph by James F. Parnell. Reproduced by permission.

This species inhabits Lake Waccamaw (Columbus County) and its feeder stream, Big Creek, upstream to the County Road 1947 crossing. It is found downstream only during periods of high water, when individuals are washed over Lake Waccamaw Dam into the river (where they do not appear to survive). The state of North Carolina administers the lake and Lake Waccamaw State Park, a relatively undeveloped 273-acre (110.5-hectare) tract. With the exception of the state park, the remainder of the lake shoreline is privately owned.

Threats

Studies of Lake Waccamaw and its fish and mussel fauna, conducted between 1979 and 1981 and funded through the North Carolina Wildlife Resources Commission, indicated that increasing amounts of organic matter and agricultural chemicals are being washed into the lake. Silt from upstream logging activities has also increased. This slow but steady deterioration in water quality could threaten much of Lake Waccamaw's fauna and, particularly, the silverside, which uses the clean, sandy bottom of the lake for spawning.

Because the lake is so shallow, changes in the level of the water table would change the chemical balance and cause the fish's extinction. Non-native aquatic weeds are a potential threat to the stability of the water, as is pesticide use anywhere within the watershed.

Because the population virtually turns over each year, the silverside is vulnerable to catastrophic events that could prevent it from reproducing in a season and thereby wipe out the species. Although the silverside is a major food source for the larger fish in the lake, it has adapted to heavy predation, and this does not seem to be a major threat.

Conservation and Recovery

In 1987 the U. S. Fish and Wildlife Service (FWS) initiated a program of water-quality monitoring to compile baseline data for the lake so that serious problems could be discovered at an early stage. All federally funded activities that might affect the fish's habitat currently require a consultation with the FWS to limit harm to the silverside.

Contact

U. S. Fish and Wildlife Service
Regional Office, Division of Endangered Species
1875 Century Blvd., Suite 200
Atlanta, Georgia 30345
Telephone: (404) 679-4000
http://southeast.fws.gov/

References

Cooper, J. E., ed. 1977. *Endangered and Threatened Plants and Animals of North Carolina.* North Carolina Museum of Natural History, Raleigh.

Davis, J. R., and D. E. Louder. 1969. "Life History of *Menidia extensa." Transactions of the American Fisheries Society* 98 (3):466-472.

Lindquist, D. G. 1981. "Endemic Fishes of Lake Waccamaw." *Kin'Lin* 2 (5):38-41.

U.S. Fish and Wildlife Service. 1987. "Endangered and Threatened Wildlife and Plants; Determination of Threatened Status and Critical Habitat for the Waccamaw Silverside." *Federal Register* 52 (67):11277-11286.

White River Springfish;
Hiko White River Springfish

Crenichthys baileyi baileyi
Crenichthys baileyi grandis

Status	Endangered
Listed	September 27, 1985
Family	Cyprinodontidae (Killifish)
Description	Greenish above and silvery below with a dark lateral stripe.
Habitat	Hot desert springs.
Food	Plant material, especially algae, detritus, animal matter.
Reproduction	10-17 eggs produced with each spawning.
Threats	Low numbers, restricted range, predation by other fish.
Range	Nevada

Description

The White River springfish reaches a maximum length of about 2.5 in (6.3 cm). It has a large, steeply sloping head, which is very broad in older individuals. Its mouth is small and straight with bicuspid teeth. Dorsal and anal fins are set far back from the caudal base, and no pelvic fins are present. The caudal fins are straight in terminal outline. Coloring ranges from olivaceous above to silvery on lower sides and bottom. These fish usually have two lengthwise series of coarse black spots, one along the middle line of the body, the other on a level with the caudal peduncle. The White River springfish is a thermal endemic fish, i.e., it originates in warm, isolated water and is adapted to the living conditions there. Cold water acts as a barrier that prevents these fish from moving away from the warm water springs where they originated.

Crenichthys baileyi is one of two species within the genus *Crenichthys*. Distinctive characteristics of the genus include a lack of pelvic fins and bicuspid teeth, a long, coiled intestine, and restricted range. Fishes in this genus have been of particular scientific interest because of their adaptation to extremely high temperatures and low dissolved oxygen. White River springfish and Hiko White River springfish are uniquely adapted for surviving in environments of extreme temperatures and low dissolved oxygen content.

The White River springfish and Hiko White River springfish were described in 1981 as two of five subspecies of *C. baileyi*. These two subspecies are visually similar. Greenish above and silvery below, both have a dark lateral stripe, comprised of double rows of spots on the sides that may be connected, that runs from behind the gills to the tail fin. Breeding males exhibit more intense coloration than females, with mid-dorsal markings becoming very dark (almost black) in contrast to the light, sometimes yellow, sides above the fused spots.

Behavior

Individual female springfish will spawn at different times of the year. Most females average two spawning periods a year, while the spawning season of the entire population extends over a long pe-

White River Springfish, photograph by John Rinne, USFS. Reproduced by permission.

riod of time each year. Moapa White River spring-fish spawn year-round with peak spawning activity from April through August. The period of spawning activity may be regulated by the production of food in the spring system. During the spawning season the males are more brightly colored than the females; courting behavior and breeding occur in and around dense vegetation, which provides cover for the attached eggs; copulation occurs in an S-shaped clasp and the male's anal fin is folded under the female's ovipositor to enhance sperm transfer; one egg at a time is laid and fertilized; 10-17 eggs are produced by each spawning; and the incubation period is five to seven days. Males aggressively defend territories in order to monopolize reproductive females. Springfish forage along the substrate and in plants, as evidenced by the ingestion of bottom-dwelling invertebrates, plant fragments, and detritus.

Because simple, short food chains in the desert springs do not permit diet specialization, *C. baileyi* is probably an opportunistic feeder whose diet consists of half plant matter, primarily filamentous algae, supplemented by detritus, midges, caddisfly larvae, and animal matter, including gastropoda, amphipoda, trichoptera, and lepidoptera. During the winter when invertebrates are not available, the diet becomes herbivores. Smaller fish need to consume a large percentage of their body weight in food every day to meet their metabolic demands, which vary directly with water temperature. White River springfish inhabiting warm water have respiratory rates four times greater than springfish in cool waters.

The White River springfish appears to exhibit a pronounced daily activity cycle with a peak in activity occurring in mid-afternoon and reduced activity levels at night. It is possible that stress caused by interaction with exotic fish may be responsible for the observed reduction in activity levels in *C. b. baileyi* compared to other *C. baileyi* subspecies. *C. baileyi grandis* is most active at sunrise and sunset.

Habitat

Both subspecies are known from single populations in springs in the Pahranagat Valley in Lincoln County, Nevada. The White River spinefish occurs in the headwater pool of Ash Spring whose predominant substrate is sand and silt with some areas of gravel. Pastureland adjacent to the outflow stream has been planted with saltgrass for cattle grazing; the upper end of the outflow stream consist of ash trees, cottonwoods, willows, and wild grape. Mats of filamentous algae become abundant in the spring pool during spring and summer, which provides an important source of cover.

Hiko and Crystal Springs, habitat for the Hiko White River spinefish, have relatively deep source pools and associated effluent streams. Aquatic vegetation, especially filamentous algae, is abundant during spring and summer. Shoreline vegetation includes spikerush and cattails, ash trees, cottonwoods, and willows.

Distribution

The species is endemic to the remnant waters of the White River system in eastern Nevada; these two subspecies are restricted to the Pahranagat Valley. During pluvial times, 10,000-40,000 years ago, a far larger White River flowed into the Colorado River by way of the Virgin River. When the White River dried up, the springfishes were restricted to the remaining permanent springs and outflows.

The White River springfish is presently found only in Ash Springs, which is used for public swimming and is principally inhabited by non-native fishes. Recent surveys indicate a severe reduction in numbers. The Hiko White River springfish was extirpated from Hiko Spring when game fishes were introduced in 1967, and it now survives as a single population of less than 100 individuals in Crystal Springs. The springs and most of the surrounding lands are privately owned, but a small portion is managed by the Bureau of Land Management. The Hiko White River springfish occurs in Hiko and Crystal Springs located in the Pahranagat Valley in the northern Mohave Desert.

At the time of its listing, this subspecies existed only as a single, small population restricted to Crystal Springs. Predation by largemouth bass had caused its extirpation from Hiko Spring in the 1960s. In 1985 *C. b. grandis* was re-introduced into Hiko Spring and is apparently now well established while the population in Crystal Springs is quite small.

A program sponsored by the University of Nevada introduced *Crenichthys baileyi baileyi* into Blue Link Spring in Mineral County to establish a refuge population, which is now well established. When last surveyed in 1995 less than 125 individuals were observed in Crystal Spring but the population in Hiko Spring was approximately 5,500 and in Blue Link Springs 12,000.

Threats

White River springfish and Hiko White River springfish were listed as endangered species with critical habitat in 1985. At that time, the one known population of the White River springfish and the single remaining population of the Hiko White River springfish were threatened by habitat alteration and the presence of non-native species, which compete and prey upon the springfishes. Populations of both subspecies of springfish continue to face threats to their existence from continued presence of non-native species, diseases not previously found in native fish populations, habitat manipulation, and loss of genetic material exchange between populations.

The greatest spatial overlap between native and introduced fishes is between springfish (both subspecies) and shortfin molly, followed by springfish and convict cichlids. Both springfish species larvae overlapped most with adult mollies. Mollies and cichlids are thermophilic (warm temperature loving), like the springfish, and are abundant in the areas occupied by springfish. In laboratory experiments, both the convict cichlid and shortfin molly were found to be extremely adept at larval predation. Competition for food between springfish and shortfin molly is minimal, although both forage at or near the bottom, because of the molly's tendency towards herbivory. The greatest competition for food resources occurs between cichlids and springfish as they are both omnivorous and thermophilic.

Recent experiments, using the Moapa White River springfish as a substitute for the two listed species, clarified behavioral relationships between the springfish, the shortfin molly, and the convict cichlid. Springfish are more aggressive amongst themselves in the presence of shortfin molly, which increased mortality among springfish. Mollies were also observed preying upon newly laid springfish eggs. Springfish were most often the target of aggressive cichlid attacks, resulting in significant springfish mortality. When springfish were confined with both non-native species, the aforementioned practices became more intense. Experimental reproductive data confirmed severely reduced larval production and recruitment for springfish cohabiting with convict cichlids and shortfin mollies.

The desert springs inhabited by these springfishes are extremely localized and vulnerable to alteration by diversion of water or introduction of non-native fishes. Efforts to restock the Hiko White River springfish in Hiko Spring have been made in recent years but the long-term viability of this restocking effort is questionable. Most of the restocked springfish have fallen prey to the numerous exotic fishes that inhabit the spring, such as the convict cichlid and mosquitofish. The introduced fish also carry parasites, most notably the copepod *Lernea*, which infects the springfish.

Conservation and Recovery

Critical Habitat was designated for both subspecies to include Ash Springs for the White River springfish, and Crystal and Hiko Springs for the Hiko White River springfish. The Desert Fishes Council opposed designation of Critical Habitat because it feared that the action would attract undue animosity from local landowners.

Specific conservation measures should include removing feral and exotic animals from the lands around the springs, controlling and restricting agricultural practices, restricting construction and development in areas near the habitat that could affect water quality, prohibiting stream bank and stream channel modification, and limiting human access to the area.

The White River springfish may be considered for delisting when: a self-sustaining White River springfish population (comprising three or more age-classes, a stable or increasing population size, and documented reproduction and recruitment) is

present in the spring pools of Ash Spring for three complete generations (or a minimum of six consecutive years); and impacts to the species and its habitat have been reduced or modifed to a point where they no longer represent a threat of extinction or irreversible population decline.

The Hiko White River springfish may be considered for delisting when: a self-sustaining Hiko White River springfish population (comprising three or more age-classes, a stable or increasing population size, and documented reproduction and recruitment) is present in the spring pools of Hiko and Crystal Springs for three complete generations (six consecutive years).

Contact

U. S. Fish and Wildlife Service
Regional Office, Division of Endangered Species
Eastside Federal Building
911 N. E. 11th Ave.
Portland, Oregon 97232-4181
Telephone: (503) 231-6121
http://pacific.fws.gov/

References

Constantz, G. D. 1981. "Life History and Patterns of Desert Fishes." In: *Fishes of the American Desert.* New York: John Wiley: 137-290.

Deacon, J. E., C. Hubbs, and B. J. Zahuranec. 1964. "Some Effects of Introduced Fishes on the Native Fish Fauna of Southern Nevada." *Southwestern Naturalist* 12:31-44.

La Rivers, I. 1994. *Fishes and Fisheries of Nevada.* University of Nevada Press, Reno, Nevada.

U.S. Fish and Wildlife Service. 1985. "Determination of Endangered Status for Two White River Springfish." *Federal Register* 50:37194-37197.

U. S. Fish and Wildlife Service. 1998. "Recovery Plan for the Aquatic and Riparian Species of Pahranagat Valley." U.S. Fish and Wildlife Service, Portland.

Williams, J. E., and G. R. Wilde. 1981. "Taxonomic Status and Morphology of Isolated Populations of the White River Springfish, *Crenichthys baileyi*

(Cyprinodontidae)." *Southwestern Naturalist* 25: 485-503.

Williams, J. E., and G. R. Wilde. 1985. "Endangered Aquatic Ecosystems in North American Deserts with a List of Vanishing Species in the Region." *Journal of the Arizona-Nevada Academy of Sciences* 20(1): 1-61.

Railroad Valley Springfish

Crenichthys nevadae

Status	Threatened
Listed	March 31, 1986
Family	Cyprinodontidae (Killifish)
Description	Robust killifish, greenish above and silvery beneath.
Habitat	Thermal springs.
Food	Insects and plant matter.
Reproduction	Spawns year round but highest during summer.
Threats	Predation, water diversion.
Range	Nevada

Description

The robust-bodied Railroad Valley springfish, *Crenichthys nevadae*, is about 3 in (7 cm) long. It has a large, heavy head that is flattened above the eye; both the dorsal and anal fins are located far back, almost to the tail. Its color is greenish above and silvery beneath. Like other members of the order Cyprinodontiformes, the Railroad Valley springfish lacks spines in the fins; unlike other members of the order, its color is much less mottled and the lateral blotches are much bolder.

Behavior

Springfish live out their short lives within a narrowly defined, geographic area, feeding on insects and plant matter. From March through May, it is primarily herbivorous, then switches to a carnivorous diet of primarily ostracods. Breeding occurs year-round but ovary production documented from Big Warm Spring was greatest during the summer, declined in spring and fall, and was poorly developed in winter. When water temperatures were especially high, no larval fish were produced in any season. Reproduction seems to be severely restricted in water temperatures above 95°F (35°C). The ratio of males to females is even in the spring but the number of females almost doubles in the summer and fall.

Habitat

The Railroad Valley springfish is found in warm spring pools, outflow streams, and adjacent marshes. Outflows tend to be shallow and less than 3 ft (1 m) wide except for Big Warm Spring, which is several yards wide. The substrate of the head pools is typically sand, gravel or pebble with some decaying organic matter. Portions of some outflows contain dense mats of a nitrogen-fixing blue-green algae. Dense vegetation lines the pools and outflows; salt grass is common in marshy areas. The springs and outflows at Lockes Ranch contain duckweed and pondweed. Water temperatures in the headsprings range from 64-100°F (18.3-38.3°C). The critical maximum temperature of the Railroad Valley springfish has been recorded at 100°F (38.2°C).

Distribution

The Railroad Valley springfish is native to four thermal springs—Big, North, Hay Corral, and Reynolds—near Locke's Ranch and two thermal springs on the Duckwater Shoshone Indian Reservation—Big Warm and Little Warm. Additionally, the species has been introduced into Chimney

Springs, about 6 mi (10 km) south of Locke's Ranch. This is a seepage area which forms small thermal ponds at Sodaville in Mineral County, Nevada. The springfish has also been introduced into springs at the source of Hot Creek, 40 mi (64 km) west of Locke's Ranch. The Big Warm Springs population no longer occurs in the headspring pool or in much of the outflow where it was once observed.

Threats

All of the springs inhabited by the Railroad Valley springfish have been physically altered, primarily to serve as watering holes for grazing livestock, and the species has declined in numbers as a result. Spring pools have been diked, waters diverted, and outflows channeled, reducing the amount of suitable habitat. Vegetation around some of the springs (particularly, North Spring) have also been trampled by the cattle. Habitats are further threatened by groundwater pumping, which causes a decrease in spring discharges. In 1981, the introduced springfish population at Chimney Springs was lost after spring discharge ceased altogether. Springfish were reintroduced into Chimney Springs when flows resumed. Several other springs in the region have also failed.

Non-native fishes, which have been introduced into the limited habitat, also threaten this springfish. Guppies have become established in Big Warm Spring and have nearly eliminated springfish from the main pool. Development of one outflow channel of Big Warm Spring as a fish farm resulted in escape of catfish into the spring system.

Conservation and Recovery

Critical Habitat has been designated for the springfish in Nye County to include six springs and associated streams and marshes within the historic range of the springfish. The designated area does not include habitat in the outflow creek of Big Warm Spring. Unauthorized introduced populations near Sodaville, in Chimney Springs, and Hot Creek are not included in the designation.

Conservation measures should include federal management of habitat at Locke's Ranch and the Duckwater Indian Reservation to control agricul-

tural wastes that might affect groundwater quality and cattle grazing that degrades the habitat; modify the operation of the commercial catfish facility at Big Warm Springs to prohibit the escape of catfish into spring outflows; protection of the aquifer feeding the springs; and establishing new populations within the historical range of the species.

Federal listing of the Railroad Valley springfish has had some impact on the leasing of Bureau of Land Management lands for livestock grazing and mineral exploration.

Contact

U.S. Fish and Wildlife Service
Division of Endangered Species
911 N.E. 11th Ave.
Portland, Oregon 97232-4181
http://pacific.fws.gov/

References

Deacon, J. E., C. Hubbs, and B. J. Zahuranec. 1964. "Some Effects of Introduced Fishes on the Native Fish Fauna of Southern Nevada." *Southwestern Naturalist* 12:31-44.

Deacon, J. E., and J. E. Williams. 1982. "Summer Food Habits of Fishes from Two Springs in East-Central Nevada." *Southwestern Naturalist* 27(4): 437-445.

Deacon, J. E., and J. E. Williams. 1984. "Annotated List of the Fishes of Nevada." *Proceedings of the Biological Society of Washington* 97(1):103-118.

Hubbs, C., and J. E. Deacon. 1964. "Additional Introduction of Tropical Fishes into Southern Nevada." *Southwestern Naturalist* 9:249-251.

U.S. Fish and Wildlife Service. 1986. "Determination of Threatened Status and Designation of Critical Habitat for the Railroad Valley Springfish." *Federal Register* 51: 10857-10865.

Williams, C. D. 1986. "Life History of the Railroad Valley Springfish, *Crenichthys nevadae* Hubbs, of East-Central Nevada." M.S. Thesis, California State University, Sacramento. 124 pp.

Leon Springs Pupfish

Cyprinodon bovinus

Status	Endangered
Listed	August 15, 1980
Family	Cyprinodontidae (Killifish)
Description	Small, robust, dusky gray to iridescent blue fish.
Habitat	Shallow, open streams.
Food	Invertebrates, detritus, diatoms, and vascular plants.
Reproduction	Spawning may occur twice a day during summer and less actively as water temperature cools.
Threats	Oil pollution, groundwater pumping, hybridization.
Range	Texas

Description

Leon Springs pupfish, *Cyprinodon bovinus*, is a small, robust-bodied fish, about 1.5 in (4 cm) long at maturity. Its color varies from dusky gray to iridescent blue. It has a wider head and body than other *Cyprinodon* species and is further distinguished in the following characteristics. *C. variegatus,* the sheepshead minnow, has pronounced vertical bars on its sides and trunk which are absent in *C. bovinus*; *C. elegans* (the Commanche Springs pupfish [see separate entry]) has a speckled color pattern uniques among *Cyprinodon*; *C. pecosensis* (the Pecos pupfish) does not have the fully scaled abdomen and the bright yellow pigment on the dorsal and caudal fins in breeding males that occur in *C. bovinus*.

Behavior

Pupfish do much of their feeding from the muddy bottom. Their diet consists of tiny invertebrates, detritus, diatoms, and vascular plants, especially algae.

Although breeding occurs throughout the year, spawning is most active during the summer. When water temperature is warm enough, spawning may occur twice a day. The male pupfish dig pits in the feeding areas and aggressively defend the territory from other males. They guard small spawning areas in shallow water, where the females deposit eggs. Development of the eggs is dependent upon water temperature; hatching occurs in two to three weeks, or longer. Newly hatched fry move near the creek edge or into the outskirts of a marsh margin.

C. bovinus mates readily with other *Cyprinodon* species, and hybridization has severely reduced the number of pure individuals. There is some evidence that female *C. bovinus* prefer males of other *Cyprinodon* species.

Habitat

The Leon Springs pupfish inhabits quiet shallow saline springs, pools, and outflow streams. The pupfish has an extended breeding season, wide salinity and temperature tolerances, and broad food habits, and appears to thrive in a simple community with few competing species. Where there is high salinity, few trees grow along the banks but filamentous algae is abundant during parts of the year. Substrates are primarily hard clay or soft mud, which is washed away during heavy rains. During extended cold periods the pupfish may either migrate upstream to thermal spring seeps or bury into the warmer mud substrate.

Leon Springs Pupfish, photograph. U. S. Fish and Wildlife Service. Reproduced by permission.

Distribution

This pupfish was discovered in 1851 at Leon Springs, 8 mi (13 km) west of Fort Stockton in southwestern Texas. Sometime before 1938, the pupfish disappeared from the spring and was thought to be extinct. In 1958, Leon Springs dried up because of excessive groundwater pumping. In 1965 the species was rediscovered at Diamond Y Spring in Pecos County, 9 mi (14.5 km) north of Fort Stockton.

The Leon Springs pupfish probably survives only in Diamond Y Spring and Leon Creek, its outflow stream. Recently, this small population has been stable with summer densities reaching three or more fish per square meter.

Threats

Much of the original habitat of this pupfish was destroyed by diversion of water for irrigation and excessive groundwater pumping. In recent years,

the Diamond Y Spring has experienced diminishing flow and will probably dry up if pumping continues at the present rate. In addition, the springs area is in the midst of an active oil and gas field. A refinery is located upstream from the main spring head for the pupfish's habitat. The oil companies have acted to minimize leakage into Diamond Y Spring and Leon Creek, but past oil spills have caused considerable fish mortality, and the potential for further accidents still exists. In 1974 the common sheepshead minnow was released into Leon Creek. Interbreeding between it and the Leon Springs pupfish resulted in extensive hybridization, threatening the genetic purity of the species. The pupfish competes for territorial sites with the plains killifish and with all other fish in the spring flows for food. Because most *Cyprinodon* species historically occurred in isolation from other members of its genus, they have not adapted well to the presence of other fish. The Pecos pupfish, *C. pecosensis*, is a particular threat because its salinity tolerance is similar to *C. bovinus*.

Conservation and Recovery

Springs and seeps feeding the pupfish's habitat have some salinity that makes the water less suitable for human needs and these springs have not gone dry as have other springs tapped for irrigation purposes. The survival of the species depends upon the continued water depth of these springs. These springs also provide a safe haven against competitive fish species unless non-native fish are introduced by humans.

A carefully supervised fish poisoning program and intensive selective seining efforts successfully removed all sheepshead minnows and hybrids by August 1978. Although the present Leon Springs pupfish population seems to be genetically pure, the habitat remains accessible and still vulnerable to the release of harmful exotic fishes.

The entire known range of this species from the head of Diamond Y Spring downstream to above the State Highway 18 crossing has been designated as Critical Habitat. In cooperation with the Soil Conservation Service, the Trans-Pecos Soil and Water Conservation District constructed a protective dike around one of the springs to ensure that an oil spill would not reach the habitat.

The Recovery Plan calls for a number of proactive conservation measures. They include: 1) continued cooperation with private landowners, the Texas Parks and Wildlife Service, and oil and gas companies drilling in the habitat areas in order to protect the springs and the aquifer from contaminants or from reduction in water levels; 2) construction of dikes to prevent groundwater flow into the springs; 3) with signs around the habitat, warn visitors of the extreme danger of introducing exotic fish; 4) establish emergency actions in case of spring failure; 5) maintain the captive population at Dexter National Fish Hatchery and conduct research as to the *C. bovinus*'s reproductive requirements, disease and parasites, and the effect of changes in stream flow. Wild populations should be studied for the effects of competition and predation by other fish, survivorship, and the effect of the physical characteristics of the habitat on the species.

Contact

U. S. Fish and Wildlife Service
Regional Office, Division of Endangered Species
P. O. Box 1306
Albuquerque, New Mexico 87103-1306
Telephone: (505) 248-6911
Fax: (505) 248-6915
http://southwest.fws.gov/

References

Echelle, A. A., and C. Hubbs. 1978. "Haven for Endangered Pupfish." *Texas Parks and Wildlife Magazine* 36: 9-12.

Kennedy, S. E. 1978. "Life History of the Leon Springs Pupfish, *Cyprinodon bovinus*." *Copeia* 1977: 93-103.

U. S. Fish and Wildlife Service. 1985. "Leon Springs Pupfish Recovery Plan." U. S. Fish and Wildlife Service, Albuquerque.

Devil's Hole Pupfish

Cyprinodon diabolis

Status	Endangered
Listed	March 11, 1967
Family	Cyprinodontidae (Killifish)
Description	Tiny pupfish with long tail, and a large head and eyes.
Habitat	Limestone cavern.
Food	Algae.
Reproduction	Breeds year round.
Threats	Groundwater depletion, siltation.
Range	Nevada

Description

The Devil's Hole pupfish, *Cyprinodon diabolis*, is the most distinctive member of its genus, characterized by its extremely small size, which rarely exceeds 0.8 in (2 cm) in length, its absence of pelvic fins, and the lack of vertical crossbars in mature males. It has a long tail, and a large head and eyes. It is distinguished from other members of the genus *Cyprinodon* by its lack of pelvic fins and scales in the preorbital region, and vertical crossbars in males, as well as by its posterior dorsal fin, long anal fin, and large head and eye.

Behavior

Little is known of Devil's Hole pupfish behavior. Its food supply is thought to consist entirely of algae. Algae growth, in turn, depends on the amount of sunlight that strikes the surface of the shelf pool within Devil's Hole. During the summer, the shelf receives about four hours of sunlight a day; no direct sunlight reaches the water surface during winter. Any decline in water level directly affects the amount of sunlight reaching the water, and thus food availability for the pupfish.

The Devil's Hole pupfish is primarily an annual species, living about one year, whose population fluctuates during the course of each year. Natural population fluctuations have been recorded from a maximum of 553 fish in the summer to a minimum of 127 fish in the winter.

Spawning occurs throughout the year, but reaches a peak in the spring. Fertilization occurs when eggs are singly deposited onto the substrate where they incubate. Growth during the spring varies between 0 and 0.025 in (0.06 cm)/wk, and little or no growth occurs during the winter.

Stomach analyses show they are opportunistic feeders whose diet includes *Spirogyra* or diatoms, depending on the season. Stomachs also contained invertebrates such as amphipods, ostracods, and protozoans.

Habitat

The spring pool of Devil's Hole (Nevada) is located some 60 ft (18 m) below the land surface, where there is a shallow rock shelf approximately 8 ft (2.4 m) by 16 ft (5 m). Just beyond the shelf, the spring descends to an unknown depth into a myriad of chasms, mostly unexplored. Most of the pupfish's reproductive and feeding activity takes place on the shallow shelf.

Distribution

This pupfish has probably been isolated within its current habitat, a limestone cave situated on the east central border of Ash Meadows, for many thousands of years. Small refugium populations have been established in the Amargosa Pupfish Station in Ash Meadows and in facilities constructed by the Bureau of Reclamation located near the base of

Devil's Hole Pupfish, photograph. Photo Researchers, Inc. Reproduced by permission.

Hoover Dam along the Colorado River. Devil's Hole is a deep, water-filled limestone cavern. Probable population is from 300-900 individuals.

Threats

Throughout the 1960s, pumping groundwater for irrigation lowered the water level within Devil's Hole. The reduction was so serious that in 1972, 27 Devil's Hole pupfish were moved to the Hoover Dam Refugium (Clark County), Nevada, to establish a captive breeding population. This captive population is reproducing, and numbers have fluctuated from 48-69 pupfish in recent years.

The primary threat to the pupfish's survival in the wild continues to be reduction of water levels needed to maintain the habitat. Other potential threats include surface runoff, which carries sand and silt into the underground caverns. Devil's Hole is part of the Ash Meadows National Wildlife Refuge, which has acquired water rights in the region.

Conservation and Recovery

The first goal of recovery is to stabilize the Devil's Hole habitat, but the species will probably remain threatened, even if pristine conditions are reestablished. For this reason, it is important to maintain the captive population. Scientists are concerned that the Hoover Dam population is not genetically pure, since these pupfish are larger in body size than the Devil's Hole population.

The status of the species has improved considerably in the past 10 years, but its populations are persistently small and localized. Prior to this, the removal of groundwater from wells pumping to support a cattle and alfalfa ranch reduced the water level within Devil's Hole. This decline was immediately evidenced in a decrease in the fish population attributed to the drying of areas utilized by the fish for feeding and reproduction. Litigation initiated by the U. S. Department of the Interior to protect Devil's Hole ended with a ruling by the U. S. Supreme Court which upheld a lower court decision mandating the maintenance of a minimum water level. The level being enforced today measures 2.7 ft (0.8 m) below a benchmark on the wall within Devil's Hole.

Recovery criteria include the requirement that all listed and candidate species be present in all locales they historically occupied within Ash Meadows; that listed species have reached self-sustaining populations; that the essential habitat be free of threats from all non-native animals, exotic plants and detrimental human disturbances; and that the springs have returned to historic discharge rates and water flow is reestablished into historic channels. In addition, the Devil's Hole minimum water level must be 1.4 ft (0.4 m) below the copper washer with a minimum pupfish population of 300 individuals during winter and 700 during late fall; two refugia populations must be established for the Devil's Hole pupfish; and native plant and aquatic communities and have been reestablished to historic structure and composition within all essential habitat.

To achieve these goals, the 1990 Recovery Plan recommends a variety of needed actions, including the securing of habitat and water resources for the Ash Meadows ecosystem; research on the biology of the species; management activities within the essential habitat; the reestablishment of populations and/or monitoring of new and existing populations; and the determination and/or verification of recovery objectives.

Contact

U. S. Fish and Wildlife Service
Regional Office, Division of Endangered Species
Eastside Federal Complex
911 N. E. 11th Ave.
Portland, Oregon 97232-4181
Telephone: (503) 231-6121
http://pacific.fws.gov/

References

Miller, R. R. 1961. "Man and the Changing Fish Fauna of the American Southwest." *Papers of the Michigan Academy of Science, Arts and Letters* 46: 365-404.

Minckley, C. O., and J. E. Deacon. 1975. "Foods of the Devil's Hole Pupfish." *Southwestern Naturalist* 20(1): 105-111.

U. S. Fish and Wildlife Service. 1980. "Devil's Hole Pupfish Recovery Plan." U. S. Fish and Wildlife Service, Albuquerque.

U. S. Fish and Wildlife Service. 1990. "Recovery Plan for the Endangered and Threatened Species of Ash Meadows, Nevada." U. S. Fish and Wildlife Service, Portland.

Williams, J. E. 1977. "Observations on the Status of the Devil's Hole Pupfish in the Hoover Dam Refugium." Report REC-ERC- 77-11. U. S. Fish and Wildlife Service, Albuquerque.

Comanche Springs Pupfish

Cyprinodon elegans

Status	Endangered
Listed	March 11, 1967
Family	Cyprinodontidae (Killifish)
Description	Silvery brown pupfish with two lateral stripes and bluish-turquoise fins.
Habitat	Springs and outflows.
Food	Plant matter and insects.
Reproduction	Spawns in pools.
Threats	Water diversion, competition with other pupfish.
Range	Arizona, California, Mexico

Description

Fish in the genus *Cyprinodon* average about 2.8 in (7 cm) in length. The Comanche Springs pupfish, *C. elegans*, is one of the most distinctive species of pupfish. Both sexes are silvery brown and lack vertical bars; males exhibit a "speckled" color pattern. Two rows of lateral stripes, comprised of squarish black blotches that are tangent to but not touching each other, run from behind the head to the tail. The top edge of the upper stripe runs along the spine while the lower edge of the bottom stripe is about two-thirds down the side. The top fanlike fin and the tail fin are bluish-turquoise.

Behavior

This pupfish has not been extensively studied and little is known of its behavior. It spawns in spring outflows and in small pools of standing water. It feeds on insects and plant material in all areas of its habitat.

Habitat

The Comanche Springs pupfish prefers freshwater shallow runs with slow current. Since most other pupfishes occupy more saline waters, long isolation from other species of the genus is probable.

Distribution

The Comanche Springs pupfish was known to inhabit two isolated spring systems, 114 mi (190 km) apart, in the Pecos River drainage of southwestern Texas. The first included Comanche Springs and the headwaters (now dry) of a group of streams that presently fall within the city limits of Fort Stockton (Pecos County). Comanche Springs dried up during the 1950s, completely destroying that pupfish population. The second spring system was found near Balmorhea in Reeves County, Texas. These springs and associated marshes have been extensively modified to support an irrigation network.

The species is known to occur only in Reeves County in Giffin and San Solomon Springs, an irrigation network fed by Phantom Lake, and Toyah Creek. The water from Phantom Lake Spring is diverted by a system of earthen dams into concrete irrigation ditches. Water is directed down a canal to merge with flows from San Solomon Spring and then enters two major channels for diversion into agricultural fields. The pupfish population is locally numerous but generally sparse throughout most of the network. Fish are seen sporadically near the mouth of a concrete irrigation canal entering Lake Balmorhea. No current population estimates have been made.

James E. Johnson

Threats

Other pupfish have been introduced into the same water system and threaten the Comanche Springs pupfish in two ways: by direct competition for limited food supplies; and by possible inter-breeding and hybridization. The main threat to the Comanche Springs pupfish, however, remains the artificial conditions of water flow within its habitat. Seasonal drying can strand and kill large numbers of fish, and recovery efforts have focused on methods to moderate the extreme pattern of drying and flooding of the stream and irrigation network.

Conservation and Recovery

To support the long-term survival of the species, some means must be found to stabilize the water table in the area. Increased pumping of groundwater for agriculture and human use has lowered water levels and reduced spring flows. Large artesian springs near Balmorhea are dimin-

ishing in flow, and Phantom Lake Spring is expected to dry up within 50 years. In fact, most large springs of West Texas have measurably diminished.

The Texas Parks and Wildlife Department has constructed a refuge at Balmorhea State Recreation area to provide stable flowing water for several thousand Comanche Springs pupfish. The Dexter National Fish Hatchery in New Mexico maintains a genetic stock of the pupfish, which will be used for reintroduction if the wild population is eliminated by drought or other cause.

Contact

U. S. Fish and Wildlife Service
Regional Office, Division of Endangered Species
P. O. Box 1306
Albuquerque, New Mexico 87103-1306
Telephone: (505) 248-6911
Fax: (505) 248-6915
http://southwest.fws.gov/

References

Davis, J. R. 1979. "Die-Offs of an Endangered Pupfish, *Cyprinodon elegans* (Cyprinodontidae)." *Southwestern Naturalist* 24: 534-536.

Hubbs, C. 1957. "Distributional Patterns of Texas Fresh-Water Fishes." *Southwestern Naturalist* 2: 89-104.

U. S. Fish and Wildlife Service. 1980. "Comanche Springs Pupfish (*Cyprinodon elegans*) Recovery Plan." U.S. Fish and Wildlife Service, Albuquerque.

Desert Pupfish

Cyprinodon macularius

Status	Endangered
Listed	March 31, 1986
Family	Cyprinodontidae (Killifish)
Description	Small, laterally compressed pupfish; males are blue and yellow when mating.
Habitat	Desert streams and rivers.
Food	Plant matter and insects.
Reproduction	Spawns in spring and summer.
Threats	Dam construction, predation.
Range	Arizona, California, Mexico

Description

The desert pupfish, *Cyprinodon macularius*, is a small, laterally compressed fish with a smoothly rounded body. The larger male rarely grows longer than 3 in (7.5 cm). During the reproductive season males turn bright blue on the head and sides and yellow on the caudal fin and tail. Females and juveniles usually have tan to olive backs and silvery sides. Adults have narrow, vertical, dark bars on the side, which are often interrupted to give the impression of a disjunct, lateral band.

Behavior

The desert pupfish matures rapidly and may produce up to three generations per year. Spawning occurs throughout the spring and summer months. Females lay eggs on submerged plants in shallow water. Males defend the eggs, which hatch within about three days. After a few hours, the young begin to feed on small plants and insects. Individuals survive for about a year.

Habitat

This species is adapted to a harsh desert environment and is capable of surviving extreme conditions, sometimes living in water with temperatures in excess of 110°F (43.3°C). It is capable of withstanding oxygen levels as low as 0.1 parts per million, and salinities nearly twice that of seawater.

Distribution

The desert pupfish was described in 1853 from specimens collected in the San Pedro River of Arizona. It was once common in the desert springs, marshes, and tributary streams of the lower Gila and Colorado River drainages in Arizona, California, and Mexico. It was also found in the slow-moving reaches of some large rivers, including the Colorado, Gila, San Pedro, and Santa Cruz.

The desert pupfish is composed of two subspecies in the United States: a Colorado River form and a Quitobaquito form. Natural populations of the Colorado River form have been extirpated from Arizona, and are restricted to three natural locations in California and the non-natural irrigation drains around the Salton Sea in California—San Felipe Creek and San Sebastian Marsh (Imperial County), and Salt Creek (Riverside County). It is also found in shoreline pools and irrigation drains in the region. Surveys of Salt Creek and related irrigation ditches indicate that the populations there may no longer be viable.

In Arizona, the Quitobaquito form persists in a single, modified spring at the Organ Pipe Cactus National Monument (in Pima County). The pupfish is also thought to survive in low numbers in the Rio Sonoyta of Sonora, Mexico, but little is known of this Mexican population.

Desert Pupfish, photograph by B. "Moose" Peterson/WRP. Reproduced by permission.

Threats

The construction of dams on the Gila, Colorado, and Salt Rivers for irrigation and flood control dewatered the lower Gila and Salt Rivers and eliminated many of the marshy pools in which the Colorado River desert pupfish bred. The desert pupfish was then forced into mainstream channels where it was preyed upon by larger fishes. Although it is extremely hardy in many respects, the desert pupfish cannot tolerate competition and is readily displaced by introduced fishes, such as tilapia, shortfin mollies, mosquitofish, and largemouth bass.

Many historic pupfish localities have been dried by groundwater pumping (affecting both spring and stream discharges), channel erosion, and arroyo formation (resulting in marshland drainage, the creation of sheer banks and lateral habitat loss). An additional threat comes from poor grazing practices by domesticated livestock, which may reduce terrestrial vegetative cover, enhancing watershed erosion, exacerbating problems of arroyo cutting, and

increasing sediment loads and turbidity in receiving waters. Habitats may be further impacted by trampling where cattle feed or drink, in or adjacent to water.

Conservation and Recovery

Breeding populations of desert pupfish have been established in Arizona at Bog Hole and Research Ranch, Arizona-Sonora Desert Museum, Boyce Thompson Arboretum, and Arizona State University. In California, captive populations were established at Salton Sea State Park, the Living Desert Reserve, and Anza-Borrego State Park. Most of these small populations are maintained in artificial refugia.

Desert pupfish are also held at Dexter National Fish Hatchery in Dexter, New Mexico. These fish, obtained from Santa Clara Slough, were used to stock reintroduction efforts in Arizona. Populations were also introduced into three springs on Bureau of Land Management land in Arizona at Peoples

Canyon in the Bill Williams River (Yavapai County), Howard Well in the Gila River (Graham County), and Mesquite Spring (Pinal County).

The 1993 U. S. Fish and Wildlife Service (FWS) recovery plan for the desert pupfish calls for the eventual downlisting of the Colorado River form (its delisting, however, is not considered feasible in the foreseeable future), and the protection of the two other subspecies (downlisting of the Quitobaquito form appears to be unattainable). To achieve the goals of downlisting and protection by 2009, the plan calls for a variety of actions, including the protection of natural populations and their habitats, the re-establishment of populations, and the establishment of a refugium population of the Quitobaquito form. The plan also calls for the development of a protocol for exchange of genetic material, the monitoring of natural and replicated populations, and the determination of factors affecting population persistence. As with all recovery efforts, the FWS also calls for a public information and education program to spread the word about the importance of protecting the species.

Contacts

U. S. Fish and Wildlife Service
Regional Office, Division of Endangered Species
Eastside Federal Complex
911 N. E. 11th Ave.
Portland, Oregon 97232-4181
Telephone: (503) 231-6121
http://pacific.fws.gov/

Regional Office of Endangered Species
U. S. Fish and Wildlife Service
P. O. Box 1306
Albuquerque, New Mexico 87103
http://southwest.fws.gov/

References

Black, G. F. 1980. "Status of the Desert Pupfish, *Cyprinodon macularius*, in California." Special Publication 80-1. State of California, Department of Fish and Game, Sacramento.

Kynard, B. E. 1981. "Study of Quitobaquito Pupfish: Systematics and Preservation." Final Report. National Park Service.

McMahon, T. E., and R. R. Miller. 1985. "Status of the Fishes of the Rio Sonoyta Basin, Arizona and Sonora, Mexico." *Proceedings of the Desert Fishes Council*, Vol. 14. Bishop, California.

U. S. Fish and Wildlife Service. 1993. "Desert Pupfish Recovery Plan." U. S. Fish and Wildlife Service, Albuquerque.

Ash Meadows Amargosa Pupfish

Cyprinodon nevadensis mionectes

Status	Endangered
Listed	May 10, 1982 (Emergency listing)
Reclassified	September 2, 1983
Family	Cyprinodontidae (Killifish)
Description	Small, iridescent silver-blue minnow.
Habitat	Thermal springs.
Food	Insects, aquatic invertebrates.
Reproduction	Spawns year round.
Threats	Water diversion, competition with introduced fishes.
Range	Nevada

Description

The Ash Meadows Amargosa pupfish, *Cyprinodon nevadensis mionectes*, is a small minnow, rarely exceeding 2.75 in (6.9 cm) in length. Normally silver gray and darker across the back, breeding males turn an iridescent silver-blue.

Behavior

This pupfish breeds throughout the year with peak periods in spring and early summer. Like other pupfish, it feeds on insects and small, aquatic invertebrates.

Habitat

The Ash Meadows Amargosa pupfish occupies 10 spring areas within Ash Meadows, all of which are designated as critical habitat. It is established outside of its native range in clay ponds located approximately 3.75 mi (2.25 km) west of the Area of Management Concern boundary. Most of these habitats lie on public land within the boundaries of Ash Meadows Refuge and include spring sources and outflow channels occupied by the species. The size of its habitats range from Crystal Pool, with a spring pool measuring 49 ft (15 m) in diameter and 20 ft (6 m) deep and discharging 62.9 gal (238.2 l)/

sec, to small springs in the Five Springs complex that have no spring pool and discharge less than 0.02 gal (0.09 l)/sec. The outflows from many springs occupied by this pupfish combine with one another. These confluences, however, are restricted to springs lying relatively close together and do not occur between springs separated by great distances.

Distribution

The Amargosa pupfish is endemic to the Ash Meadows region, an unusual desert wetland east of the Amargosa River in western California and eastern Nevada. These wetlands are maintained by springs and seeps fed by an extensive groundwater system.

The pupfish is restricted to the 10 spring areas within Ash Meadows, all of which are designated as critical habitat (Big Spring, Bradford Spring #2, Jack Rabbit Spring, Point of Rocks Spring, Tubbs Spring, Crystal Pool, Crystal Reservoir, Lower Crystal Marsh, Longstreet Spring, Five Springs, Rogers Spring, Fairbanks Spring, Peterson Reservoir, Clay Pits Spring, and Forest Spring).

The Amargosa pupfish occurs in a wide variety of habitats, including shallow and deep streams from springs. It lives in large springs and outflows

John and Karen Hollingsworth

at Ash Meadow, including Fairbanks, Rogers, Longstreet, Jack Rabbit, Big, and Point of Rocks Springs, Crystal Pool, and two springs of the Bradford Springs group. Most of these habitats lie on public land within the boundaries of Ash Meadows Refuge.

Population estimates made during June 1982 and July 1982 recorded 568 and 1,189 pupfish, respectively, in Jack Rabbit Spring and 1,189 and 1,822 pupfish, respectively, in Big Spring. Quantitative estimates have not been made for other populations nor have these old estimates been updated.

Threats

Since habitats of this pupfish provide most of the surface water in the area, they were the most altered during agricultural development. All have been altered by diversion into earthen or concrete channels, impoundment, drying due to pumping of local groundwaters, and/or elimination of riparian veg-

etation during ground leveling. They also support the widest variety of introduced organisms. These alterations eliminated fish populations from Soda Spring and Point of Rock Pool #1, and depressed the size of remaining populations by decreasing the amount of available habitat.

Conservation and Recovery

Critical Habitat for the Ash Meadows Amargosa pupfish has been designated in the following springs and their outflows in Nye County, Nevada: Fairbanks, Rogers, Longstreet, Crystal Pool, Bradford, Jack Rabbit, Big, Point of Rocks, and three unnamed springs. The Critical Habitat designation also includes a buffer zone immediately surrounding these springs. The buffer zone is essential to the conservation of the fish because it provides vegetative cover that contributes to providing the uniform water and feeding conditions preferred by the pupfish.

Contact

U. S. Fish and Wildlife Service
Regional Office, Division of Endangered Species
Eastside Federal Complex
911 N. E. 11th Ave.
Portland, Oregon 97232-4181
Telephone: (503) 231-6121
http://pacific.fws.gov/

References

Miller, R. R. 1948. "The Cyprinodont Fishes of the Death Valley System of Eastern California and Southwestern Nevada." *Miscellaneous Publications of the Museum of Zoology, University of Michigan* 68:1-155.

Soltz, D. L., and R. J. Naiman, eds. 1978. "The Natural History of Native Fishes in the Death Valley System." *Natural History Museum of Los Angeles County, Science Series* 30:17.

U.S. Fish and Wildlife Service. 2 September 1983. "Determination of Endangered Status and Critical Habitat for Two Fish Species, Ash Meadows, Nevada." *Federal Register* 48(172):40178-40186.

Warm Springs Pupfish

Cyprinodon nevadensis pectoralis

Status	Endangered
Listed	October 13, 1970
Family	Cyprinodontidae (Killifish)
Description	Silvery sided pupfish; males are bright blue.
Habitat	Thermal springs.
Food	Omnivorous.
Reproduction	Spawns year round.
Threats	Groundwater pumping.
Range	Nevada

Description

The warm springs pupfish, *Cyprinodon nevadensis pectoralis*, the smallest of the four extant subspecies of the Nevada pupfish, ranges from 1.5-2.5 in (3.7-6.2 cm) long. Females and juveniles are silvery; males are bright blue.

Behavior

Because of its rarity, little is known of the life history of this pupfish. The spawning season runs for most of the year, with a peak from April through June. Like other pupfish, the warm springs subspecies is probably omnivorous, feeding on insects and plant matter.

Habitat

Although these pupfish reside in the outlet streams of all of their habitat springs, they do not reproduce there. Essential habitat for the warm spring pupfish is the springs' physically stable source pools or headwaters.

Distribution

The warm springs pupfish has only been found in the Ash Meadows region of Nevada. The species was never very widespread. Today, it is found in Lovell's Spring, sometimes referred to as School's Spring, 0.6 mi (1 km) northwest of Devil's Hole at Ash Meadows (Nye County), Nevada. It is also found in five additional spring flows, all within 0.6 mi (1 km) of Lovell's Spring. The U. S. Fish and Wildlife Service (FWS) estimates that the total warm springs pupfish population is less than 500 fish, with almost half living in School Spring. With the establishment of the Ash Meadows Refuge, four of the six habitats lie on public land withdrawn for wildlife management. Essential habitat for this species includes 2,240 acres (896 hectares) surrounding all of its habitat.

Threats

The warm springs pupfish is especially threatened by groundwater pumping that is lowering the water table throughout the region. Because the springs are quite small, they dry quickly when the water level falls. Competition with the introduced mosquitofish could become a problem if they penetrate any further into spring pools. Some predation on the warm springs pupfish is occurring, especially by birds such as the belted kingfisher.

Essential for the continued existence of the warm springs pupfish is protection of its very limited habitat, especially spring water levels. This will involve procuring and enforcing water rights so that spring water levels can be maintained, the control of emergent vegetation around the springs, and the addition of supplemental water whenever necessary.

In 1977 agricultural interests sold about 23 sq mi (60 sq km) of land at Ash meadow to a real estate developer. Attempts by the developer to construct a residential community at Ash Meadow for 55,000 people resulted in widespread land disturbance and water diversions. In May 1982, the FWS used emergency provisions of the Endangered Species Act to invoke protection of several fishes at Ash Meadows. In 1984, after attempts by the FWS to negotiate adequate conservation agreements failed, the developer sold about 11,000 acres (4,450 hectares) to the Nature Conservancy. The property was later purchased by the federal government to establish the Ash Meadows National Wildlife Refuge.

Conservation and Recovery

The FWS published a revised Recovery Plan for the warm springs pupfish in 1990. Much of its remaining critical habitat is protected in the Ash Meadows National Wildlife Refuge. Two additional habitats are privately owned and are potentially threatened by development and other activities. These habitats should be acquired and designated as ecological reserves, or conservation easements negotiated with the private owners. The habitats will also have to be managed to eradicate or reduce the abundance of non-native fish and crayfish. Other necessary actions include monitoring of the abundance of the warm springs pupfish and research into its biology and habitat needs. There should also be a public education campaign to develop a broad base of support for the protection of its rare warm-spring habitats.

Contacts

U.S. Fish and Wildlife Service
Office of the Regional Director
911 N.E. 11th Ave.
Portland, Oregon 97232-4181
Telephone: (503) 321-6118
Fax: (503) 231-2122

Regional Office of Endangered Species
U.S. Fish and Wildlife Service
Lloyd 500 Building, Suite 1692
500 N.E. Multnomah Street
Portland, Oregon 97232
http://pacific.fws.gov/

References

Miller, R. R., and J. E. Deacon. 1973. "New Localities of the Rare Warm Springs Pupfish, *Cyprinodon nevadensis pectoralis*, from Ash Meadows, Nevada." *Copeia* (1973):137-140.

Soitz, D. L. 1974. "Variation in Life History and Social Organization of Some Populations of Nevada Pupfish, *Cyprinodon nevadensis*." Ph.D. Dissertation. University of California, Los Angeles.

U.S. Fish and Wildlife Service. 1976. "Warm Springs Pupfish Recovery Plan." U.S. Fish and Wildlife Service, Albuquerque.

U.S. Fish and Wildlife Service. 1990. "Recovery Plan for the Endangered and Threatened Species of Ash Meadows, Nevada." U.S. Fish and Wildlife Service, Portland, Oregon.

Owens Pupfish

Cyprinodon radiosus

Status	Endangered
Listed	March 11, 1967
Family	Cyprinodontidae (Killifish)
Description	Short, thick body; females are silvery with dark vertical bars; males are olive above and slate gray beneath.
Habitat	Springs and small streams with silt or sand bottoms and heavily vegetation.
Food	Algae, aquatic insects, crustaceans, plankton.
Reproduction	50-200 eggs deposited in spring.
Threats	Water diversion, groundwater pumping, introduced predators.
Range	California

Description

The Owens pupfish, *Cyprinodon radiosus*, is a small (2.5 in; 6.4 cm) deep-bodied fish with a laterally compressed shape. The sexes display differing size and color patterns. The larger males are olive above and slate gray beneath, with an overall bluish cast. Their lateral bars are deep purplish with posterior bars having some gold. The lower head is silver and blue, and the dorsal and anal fins are blue with an orange-amber border. The smaller females are deep olive with brown lateral blotches and purplish vertical bars.

Behavior

Pupfish are omnivorous and feed on algae, aquatic insects, crustaceans, and plankton. The spawning season begins in April when water temperatures reach 68°F (20°C). When spawning, males turn bright blue and become territorial, defending their spawning area from other male pupfish and from other fish species. Females can deposit 50-200 eggs during the season but rarely lay more than one or two eggs at a time. Eggs hatch in seven to 10 days, depending on water temperature. Newly hatched pupfish larvae begin feeding the day they hatch. Pupfish fry, which live along the shoreline where warmer water supports abundant food, mature in three to four months.

Habitat

Basic habitat requirements for the Owens pupfish consists of good quality water, aquatic vegetation, and a silt- or sand-covered bottom. It is normally found near the margins of bulrush marshes, in wide, well-vegetated shallow sloughs, or in spring pools.

Distribution

The Owens pupfish has been found in east-central California in the Owens River and adjacent springs as far south as the springs around Owens Lake in Inyo County. In 1915 the species was plentiful along the Big Bend areas of the Owens River northeast of Bishop, but had mostly disappeared by 1934. During the 1940s the Owens pupfish was considered extinct. In 1956, however, a small population was discovered in Fish Slough. This population has been the source for all Owens pupfish populations that have been reestablished and exist today.

The Owens pupfish is now confined to four springs in the Fish Slough area north of Bishop

Owens Pupfish, photograph by B. "Moose" Peterson/WRP. Reproduced by permission.

(Mono County), California. The protected area includes the Owens Valley Native Fish Sanctuary and a Bureau of Land Management spring refuge. There are no current population estimates.

Threats

Most Owens pupfish habitat was destroyed when dams and upstream diversions on the Owens River prevented seasonal flooding of shallow marshy areas. Groundwater pumping for irrigation continues to threaten aquifers supplying water to the remaining spring habitats, and vandals have destroyed structures built to help maintain the habitats.

Conservation and Recovery

The sanctuary at Fish Slough was created in the late 1960s to provide protected habitat for the speck-

led dace, the Owens sucker, and the federally listed Owens tui chub (*Gila bicolor snyderi*) as well as the pupfish. Fish Slough, a unique wetland in an arid environment, contains a number of rare species besides the Owens pupfish, including the Fish Slough milkvetch and an undescribed species of mollusk. Recently, recovery efforts at the sanctuary received a setback, when it was discovered that the predatory largemouth bass had penetrated the Owens pupfish refuge at Fish Slough. In a single year, the bass managed to invade all four habitat springs. California Fish and Game personnel suspect that the bass were purposely introduced above fish barriers to threaten the survival of the pupfish. Repeated efforts to eradicate the bass have been only partially successful. Because much of the habitat within the historic range can never be restored, U. S. Fish and Wildlife Service personnel hope to transplant the fish to the adjacent Adobe Valley, where good habitat still exists.

Contact

U. S. Fish and Wildlife Service
Regional Office, Division of Endangered Species
Eastside Federal Complex
911 N. E. 11th Ave.
Portland, Oregon 97232-4181
Telephone: (503) 231-6121
http://pacific.fws.gov/

References

Brown, J. H. 1971. "The Desert Pupfish." *Scientific American* 225: 104-110.

Soltz, D. L., and R. J. Naiman. 1978. "The Natural History of Native Fishes in the Death Valley System." *Natural History Museum of Los Angeles County Science Series* 30:1-76.

U. S. Fish and Wildlife Service. 1984. "Recovery Plan for the Owens Pupfish, *Cyprinodon radiosus*." U. S. Fish and Wildlife Service, Portland.

Pahrump Poolfish

Empetrichthys latos latos

Status	Endangered
Listed	March 11, 1967
Family	Cyprinodontidae (Killifish)
Description	Slender fish, greenish above and silvery green below, with a broad mouth and ashort slender head.
Habitat	Alkaline mineral springs.
Food	Insects and plant matter.
Reproduction	Peak spawning in the spring.
Threats	Decreased spring discharge.
Range	Nevada

Description

The Pahrump poolfish, *Empetrichthys latos latos,* is a slender fish, reaching a length of 3 in (8 cm). It has a broad mouth, a short and slender head, and no pelvic fins. Both sexes are greenish above and silvery green below. During spawning season males appear lightly washed with blue. The Pahrump poolfish is the only surviving species in the genus *Empetrichthys,* following the extinction in the late 1940s of the Ash Meadows killifish (*E. merriami*). The Pahrump poolfish is also called the Pahrump killifish.

Behavior

Young Pahrump poolfish are more active during daylight while adults are more active at night. Peak spawning occurs in the spring, although different groups will spawn throughout the year. During her breeding cycle, the female seeks seclusion for egg-laying in remote corners of the springs. The fry remain near the bottom or in areas that offer protection from predation. This fish is omnivorous and eats a wide variety of insects, plant matter, and detritus.

Habitat

The Pahrump poolfish is adapted to alkaline mineral springs and outflow streams. Adults prefer deeper pools; juveniles are found near the surface in shallower areas of the springs, where there is aquatic vegetation. The ancestral spring of this species maintained a constant, year-round temperature of 76°F (24.4°C).

Distribution

The Pahrump poolfish and two subspecies inhabited separate springs in the Pahrump Valley in Nevada. Both of the other subspecies (*E. l. concavus* and *E. l. pahrump*) are now extinct. Originally, this fish was known only from Manse Spring on the Manse Ranch in Nye County. It was eliminated from this spring in 1975 when the water dried up. An early transplant site at Latos Pools near Boulder City was lost to a flood in 1975. Two transplanted populations of the Pahrump poolfish survive—in Corn-Creek Springs Pond on the Desert National Wildlife Range northwest of Las Vegas in Clark County, and in the Shoshone Pond southeast of Ely in White Pine County. No more than several hundred of these fish are thought to survive.

Threats

The Manse Spring dried up because of excessive groundwater pumping for irrigation. The drying of the spring had been predicted by biologists, who

Poolfish, photograph. Photo Researchers, Inc. Reproduced by permission.

moved the fish to other localities. The Corn-Creek Springs population may eventually be threatened by increased groundwater pumping related to the growth of the Las Vegas metropolitan area. Because habitat in Shoshone Pond is considered less than optimal, U. S. Fish and Wildlife Service (FWS) biologists consider the site a temporary holding pool.

Conservation and Recovery

Low numbers and restricted distribution make the Pahrump poolfish greatly vulnerable to extinction. The major recovery strategy will be to protect the two existing populations until further transplant sites can be located. The FWS hopes to establish at least three protected populations, each of 500 or more adults. Success in this effort would warrant delisting the species. An attempt is currently being made to rehabilitate Manse Spring, the Pahrump poolfish's ancestral pool.

Contact

U. S. Fish and Wildlife Service
Regional Office, Division of Endangered Species
Eastside Federal Complex
911 N. E. 11th Ave.
Portland, Oregon 97232-4181
Telephone: (503) 231-6121
http://pacific.fws.gov/

References

La Rivers, Ira. 1962. *Fishes and Fisheries of Nevada.* Nevada State Fish and Game Commission, Reno.

U. S. Fish and Wildlife Service. 1980. "Pahrump Killifish Recovery Plan." U. S. Fish and Wildlife Service, Portland.

Big Bend Gambusia

Gambusia gaigei

Status	Endangered
Listed	March 11, 1967
Family	Poeciliidae (Livebearer)
Description	Small, yellowish gambusia with dark bars under its eyes and chin, and a faint lateral stripe.
Habitat	Clear, shallow spring-fed water.
Food	Insect larvae and small invertebrates.
Reproduction	Bears live young.
Threats	Limited habitat, introduced competitors.
Range	Texas

Description

The Big Bend gambusia, *Gambusia gaigei*, grows to a length of about 1.2 in (3 cm). It is yellowish overall, with dark bars beneath the eye and chin and a faint lateral stripe. The male's anal fin is adapted as a sex organ for transferring sperm to the female.

Behavior

The gambusia is a livebearer. Eggs hatch inside the mother's body and are born alive. It is thought that females store sperm for several months after being impregnated. Big Bend gambusia's feeding habits are unknown but it is assumed that it feeds on insect larvae and small invertebrates such as zooplankton and worms.

Habitat

The Big Bend gambusia's natural habitat is clear, shallow streams and marshes fed by warm springs. This fish is most abundant amid shoreline vegetation, where there are overhanging trees.

Distribution

The Big Bend gambusia is known only from springs in Big Bend National Park in Texas. Biologists surmise that at least two separate populations originally existed—at Boquillas Spring, and at Spring 4, east of the present Rio Grande Village campground. It probably existed in other springs in the vicinity of Rio Grande Village. The Boquillas Spring population and the original Spring 4 population have been extirpated.

Currently, the Big Bend gambusia is restricted to the outflow stream of a single spring near Rio Grande Village in the Big Bend National Park (Brewster County), Texas. Descendants of the original Spring 4 population are being maintained in a natural holding pool nearby.

As of 1994, the gambusia population was stable in the refugium and in two other warm water spring ponds in the area.

Threats

Surface runoff and flooding of the Rio Grande River continually threaten the Big Bend gambusia's survival. Periods of high rainfall increase the amount of silt carried by surface runoff, increasing stream turbidity and bottom deposition. Floods provide an avenue for mosquitofish (*G. affinis*) and other competitors to invade the Big Bend gambusia's pools. Over the years, federally sponsored projects, designed to enhance the "oasis image" of the Rio Grande Village area, have diverted spring outflows into artificial ditches and ponds. Groundwa-

Big Bend Gambusia, photograph. U. S. Fish and Wildlife Service. Reproduced by permission.

ter levels have been lowered, decreasing the flow from the gambusia's springs.

Conservation and Recovery

At one time, the gambusia population was reduced to one female and two males held in captivity. To ensure the species' future, the artificial refugium was modified to receive piped-in warm water on a day-to-day, year-round basis. Population stabilization has been achieved at the refugium and in two other warm water spring ponds. Park personnel regularly monitor the habitats. Continued threats to the species include proposed campground expansion, floods on the Rio Grande (which could allow invasion of the pond by competing or predatory fish species), and anglers transferring fish to the gambusia habitats. Captive populations of the Big Bend gambusia are maintained at the U. S. Fish and Wildlife Service's Dexter National Fish Hatch-

ery in New Mexico and the University of Texas at Austin as a precaution against extinction of the wild population.

The Park Service's current management goals for recovery of the species include supplementing spring flows from wells in the dry season, and rehabilitating sections of two spring outflows to approximate pre-development conditions. Plans also call for eradication of mosquitofish from springs and streams in the campground area and the eventual establishment of this gambusia in other suitable locations.

Contact

Regional Office of Endangered Species
U.S. Fish and Wildlife Service
P.O. Box 1306
Albuquerque, New Mexico 87103
http://southwest.fws.gov/

References

Brune, G. 1981. *Springs of Texas.* Branch-Smith, Fort Worth.

Hubbs, C., and J. G. Williams. 1979. "A Review of Circumstances Affecting the Abundance of *Gambusia gaigei,* an Endangered Fish Endemic to Big Bend National Park." In R. Linn, ed., *Proceedings of the First Conference on Scientific Research in the National Parks.*

Minckley, W. L. 1962. "Two New Species of Fishes of the Genus *Gambusia* (Poeciliidae) from Northeastern Mexico." *Copeia* 1962:391-396.

U. S. Fish and Wildlife Service. 1984. "Big Bend Gambusia Recovery Plan." U.S. Fish and Wildlife Service, Albuquerque.

San Marcos Gambusia

Gambusia georgei

Status	Endangered
Listed	July 14, 1980
Family	Poeciliidae (Livebearer)
Description	Small, faintly striped gambusia with lemon-yellow fins.
Habitat	Quiet, shallow waters of constant temperatures.
Food	Invertebrates.
Reproduction	Bears live young.
Threats	Aquifer depletion, degradation of water quality.
Range	Texas

Description

Gambusia is well-defined and mature males may be distinguished from related genera by their thickened upper pectoral fin rays. Only a limited number of *Gambusia* are native to the United States and of this subset, San Marcos gambusia, *G. georgei*, has one of the most restricted ranges.

The San Marcos gambusia ranges in length from 1-1.6 in (2.5-4 cm). It is subtly different from the western mosquitofish, *G. affinis*. Scales tend to be strongly crosshatched in contrast to the less-distinct markings on the scales of *G. affinis*. In addition, San Marcos gambusia tend to have a prominent dark pigment stripe across the distal edges of their dorsal fins. A diffuse mid-lateral stripe extending posteriorly from the base of the pectoral fin to the caudal peduncle is also often present, especially in dominant individuals. As in *G. affinis*, a dark subocular bar is visible and is elicited easily from frightened fish. Compared to *G. affinis*, *G. georgei* has fewer spots and dusky pigmented regions on the caudal fin. The median fins (i.e., unpaired fins: dorsal, caudal, and anal fins) of wild-caught specimens of San Marcos gambusia tend to be lemon yellow under certain behavioral patterns (when they are not under stress). In a dominant or high male, this color can approach a bright yellowish-orange, especially around the gonopodium. A bluish sheen is evident in more darkly pigmented individuals, especially near the anterior dorsolateral surfaces of adult females.

Behavior

The San Marcos gambusia is a livebearer, which means eggs hatch inside the female's body and emerge alive. The female is capable of bearing up to 60 young in a single brood. This gambusia feeds on insect larvae and other invertebrates in slow-moving waters that are shaded by overhanging trees or bridges.

Hybridization between *G. georgei* and *G. affinis* was first noted in 1969 and the production of hybrid individuals between them has continued for many years without obvious introgression of genetic material into either of the parental species. Given the history of hybridization between these two species, this factor was not thought to be of primary importance in considerations of the status of *G. georgei*. It was thought that so long as the proportion of hybrids remained relatively low compared to the abundance of pure *G. georgei*, few problems associated with genetic swamping or introgression would occur. However, the series of collections taken during 1981-1983 indicate that hybrid individuals may have become many times more abundant than the pure *G. georgei*. It is possible that hybrid individuals may now be competing

San Marcos Gambusia, photograph. U. S. Fish and Wildlife Service. Reproduced by permission.

with *G. georgei,* placing an additional stress on the small native population.

Habitat

The San Marcos gambusia apparently prefers quiet waters adjacent to sections of moving water, but seemingly of greatest importance, thermally constant waters. *G. georgei* is found mostly over muddy substrates but generally not silted habitats, and shade from over-hanging vegetation or bridge structures is a factor common to all sites along the upper San Marcos River where apparently suitable habitats for this species occur. Introduced elephant ears have been noted in previously recorded localities for the species. Although the exact nature of the relationship between the occurrence and abundance of elephant ears and the disappearance of *G. georgei* is unknown, some investigators believe these non-native plants may have modified essential aspects of the gambusia's habitat.

Compared to *G. georgei, G. affinis* tends to show similar preferences for shallow, still waters, but dif-

fers strikingly from *G. georgei* in ability to colonize environments with greater temperature fluctuation. These environments include the partially isolated sloughs, intermittent creeks, and drainage ditches found in the upper San Marcos River, and in the nearby Blanco River and lower San Marcos River, as well.

The San Marcos gambusia apparently requires: 1) thermally constant water; 2) quiet, shallow, open water adjacent to sections of moving water; 3) muddy substrates without appreciable quantities of silt; 4) partial shading; 5) clean and clear water; and 6) food supply of living organisms.

Distribution

The gambusia's entire known range is restricted to the San Marcos River near the city of San Marcos (Hays County) in south-central Texas. Historically, the San Marcos gambusia populations have been extremely sparse.

The San Marcos gambusia is currently restricted to a 0.6-mi (1-km) section of the San Marcos River. Most specimens have been found between the Interstate Highway 35 crossing and Thompson's Island. This gambusia is extremely rare as determined by surveys conducted in 1978 and 1979 in the San Marcos River. Biologists netted more than 20,000 *Gambusia* specimens but counted only 18 San Marcos gambusia among them.

Intensive searches conducted in May, July, and September 1990 were unsuccessful in locating any pure San Marcos gambusia. More than 15,450 *Gambusia* were identified during the searches. One individual collected during the search—an immature fish with plain coloration—was visually identified as a possible backcross (hybrid) of the San Marcos gambusia *G. affinis.* According to the 1996 Recovery Plan for the species in the Comal Springs and San Marcos habitat, the decrease in San Marcos abundance along with their hybrids suggests the extinction of the species.

Threats

The San Marcos gambusia's very restricted distribution in the river and its absence from the headwaters at Spring Lake indicate very specific habitat requirements. It is extremely sensitive to any alteration of its habitat. Changes in water turbidity caused by runoff from land clearing and construction, an increase in water temperatures caused by lowered water flows, and excessive pumping of groundwater from the Edwards Aquifer, which supplies water to the city of San Antonio, could easily eliminate the species. The entire known range has been designated as habitat critical to the survival of the San Marcos gambusia.

The Texas Department of Water Resources forecast that groundwater pumping for human uses in the region will continue to increase well into the twenty-first century. At the current rate of increase, scientists predict that the Edwards Aquifer will be so depleted that flow from the San Marcos Springs will cease around 2000. Without the cooperation of all state and local agencies that manage use of the aquifer, recovery of the San Marcos gambusia and other endemic wildlife is considered a remote possibility.

Conservation and Recovery

The 1996 San Marcos/Comal (Revised) Recovery Plan, which covers the San Marcos gambusia and four other listed species, notes that recovery goals for the habitat's species include the survival of these species in their native ecosystems; the development of an ecosystem approach using strategies to address both local, site-specific and broad regional issues related to recovery; and the conservation of the integrity and function of the aquifer and spring-fed ecosystems that these species inhabit.

Delisting is considered unattainable for all five species (including the San Marcos gambusia) due to the potential for extinction from catastrophic events. Consequently, the revised Recovery Plan calls for the establishment and continued maintenance of refugia capability for all five species in case of a catastrophic event. Though downlisting is considered a possibility for several of the species, the plan notes that, because the San Marcos gambusia is teetering on the brink of extinction (indeed, it may have gone over the edge), it is unlikely the species could be reclassified from Endangered to Threatened in the foreseeable future. Interim conservation measures are recommended to measure progress toward preventing its extinction. Academic researchers, Texas Parks and Wildlife Department scientists and the U. S. Fish and Wildlife Service continue to search for the gambusia during all collection and research with fishes that is done on the San Marcos River.

Contact

U.S. Fish and Wildlife Service
Regional Office, Division of Endangered Species
P.O. Box 1306
Albuquerque, New Mexico 87103
http://southwest.fws.gov/

References

Brune, G. 1981. *Springs of Texas.* Branch-Smith, Fort Worth.

Hubbs, C., and A. E. Peden. 1969. "*Gambusia georgei* from San Marcos, Texas." *Copeia* 1969 (2):357-364.

U.S. Fish and Wildlife Service. 1984. "San Marcos River Recovery Plan." U.S. Fish and Wildlife Service, Albuquerque.

U.S . Fish and Wildlife Service. 1996. "San Marcos and Comal Springs and Associated Aquatic Ecosystems (Revised) Recovery Plan." U.S. Fish and Wildlife Service, Albuquerque.

Clear Creek Gambusia

Gambusia heterochir

Status	Endangered
Listed	March 11, 1967
Family	Poeciliidae (Livebearer)
Description	Small, stocky fish with a metallic sheen.
Habitat	Limestone springs.
Food	Aquatic invertebrates.
Reproduction	Bears up to six broods a year.
Threats	Limited distribution, hybridization.
Range	Texas

Description

The Clear Creek gambusia, *Gambusia heterochir*, is a stocky gambusia with a pronounced metallic sheen and distinctive, dark concentric markings on the back and sides. Females have a pronounced anal spot. Males are distinguished from other livebearers by a deep notch in the dorsal margin of the pectoral fin (behind the gills).

Behavior

The female Clear Creek gambusia may store sperm for several months after being inseminated by multiple males and is fertile for seven months of the year, from March through September. Males are semi-territorial during the breeding season, with the dominant males occupying territories with the lowest predation potential. Females abound in the preferred habitat, while less dominant males attract fewer receptive females. During the seven months in which the female is fertile, she is capable of producing about 50 young every 42 days, or six broods per year. After gestation of 40 days, eggs hatch inside the mother's body, and young emerge alive. Clutch size depends upon the size of the female, and up to 100 young may be produced per brood.

The primary food source, about 80%, for the Clear Creek gambusia is the amphipod, *Hyalella texana*, but it is an opportunistic feeder and will consume a wide variety of foods in the absence of am-phipods. This gambusia is active during the day in all seasons.

Habitat

This gambusia is restricted to shallow springs and outflow streams at the base of a limestone cliff with clear, clean water, low pH (acid), and nearly constant, year-round temperatures. It prefers areas of profuse aquatic vegetation. Upper Clear Creek rises from the Wilkinson Springs, a group of limestone springs that discharges water from the Edwards Aquifer.

Clear Creek has an elevational difference of about 48 ft (15 m) from headwaters to confluence, and the four dams that have been constructed have caused pools to form. The Clear Creek gambusia occurs in these isolated spring-fed pools that maintain a fairly constant temperature of around 68°F (20°C). The surrounding shrub/brush rangeland is classified as Texas savannah and is used primarily for ranching.

Distribution

The Clear Creek gambusia is endemic to the source pools and headwaters of Clear Creek, a small tributary of the San Saba River in Menard County, central Texas. Its existence was first documented in 1953, and it has been known only from this location.

Glen Mills, Texas Parks & Wildlife

The population is restricted to the main pools of the Wilkinson Springs at the headwaters of Upper Clear Creek on the Clear Creek Ranch, situated 10 mi (16 km) west of Menard near Ft. McKavett. The headspring pool covers an area of about 2.2 acres (1 hectare). The natural course of Upper Clear Creek has been modified extensively to provide water for livestock, irrigation, and humans. About 250 ft (75 m) downstream from the headsprings, a series of four dams impounds the creek into pools.

Threats

The main threat to this species is simply its extremely limited distribution and dependence on a single group of springs. Should the water table fall because of groundwater pumping or water flows become diverted to support more intensive human uses, the population would be eliminated. The Clear Creek gambusia is also threatened by its ready ability to interbreed with other more common gambu-

sia species, which are found in Clear Creek below the dams.

Conservation and Recovery

Of particular concern was the predatory mosquitofish (*G. affinis*), which in the 1970s found its way into some of the dam pools through a deteriorated section of an aging, earthen-concrete dam. This dam was extensively repaired in 1979 by U. S. Fish and Wildlife Service (FWS) personnel, and mosquitofish were removed. Although the site is privately owned, the FWS has reached a conservation agreement with the landowner to manage the habitat pools. Since the repairs to the dam were completed, the primary goal of recovery has been to maintain the status quo. Should the habitat be further jeopardized, for example, by sale of the ranch to resort developers, the FWS anticipates a more aggressive intervention.

Contact

Regional Office of Endangered Species
U.S. Fish and Wildlife Service
P.O. Box 1306
Albuquerque, New Mexico 87103
http://southwest.fws.gov/

References

Hubbs, Clark. 1957. "*G. heterochir*, a New Poeciliid Fish from Texas with an Account of Its Hybridization with *G. affinis.*" *Tulane Studies in Zoology* 5:1-16.

Minckley, W. L. 1962. "Two New Species of Fishes of the Genus *Gambusia* (Poeciliidae) from Northeastern Mexico." *Copeia* 1962:391-396.

Rosen, D. E., and R. M. Bailey. 1963. "The Poeciliid Fishes (Cyprinodontiformes): Their Structure, Zoogeography, and Systematics." *Bulletin of the American Museum of Natural History* 126:1-176.

U.S. Fish and Wildlife Service. 1980. "Recovery Plan for Clear Creek Gambusia *Gambusia heterochir.*" U.S. Fish and Wildlife Service, Albuquerque.

Pecos Gambusia

Gambusia nobilis

James E. Johnson

Status	Endangered
Listed	October 13, 1970
Family	Poeciliidae (Livebearer)
Description	Robust, silvery yellow fish with an arched back.
Habitat	Springs and outflow streams.
Food	Insects and other invertebrates.
Reproduction	Bears live young.
Threats	Fragmentation of habitat, dying springs.
Range	New Mexico, Texas

Description

The Pecos gambusia, *Gambusia nobilis*, also known as the Texas gambusia, is closely related to the common mosquitofish (*G. affinis*). It is a small, robust silvery yellow fish, and in profile, shows an arched back. Females have a black area on the abdomen that surrounds the anal fin. The anal fin of the male is modified as an organ to transfer milt during copulation.

Behavior

The Pecos gambusia gives birth to live young. It feeds on the surface, taking a wide variety of insects and small invertebrates. It shelters from predators in beds of aquatic vegetation.

Habitat

The Pecos gambusia is found in springs and outflow streams over a large geographic range in the Pecos River basin—from an elevation of 3,870 ft

(1,180 m) in the uplands of New Mexico to about 2,690 ft (820 m) in Texas. It is found in springheads, limestone sinks, spring-fed creeks, and sedge-covered marshes. Common factors among these habitats are: clear, clean water, stable flows, and fairly constant temperatures. The Pecos gambusia is intolerant of water temperatures above about 100°F (38°C).

Distribution

The Pecos gambusia is endemic to the Pecos River basin in southeastern New Mexico and western Texas, occurring from Fort Sumner in De Baca County, New Mexico, as far south as Fort Stockton in Pecos County, Texas. New Mexican populations, known from the Pecos River south of Fort Sumner and the North Spring River near Roswell, have been extirpated. Texas populations in Leon and Comanche Springs were eliminated when the springs dried up.

In New Mexico, populations occur in Ink Pot within the Salt Creek Wilderness Area, in a group of springs, sinkholes, and outflows at Bitter Lake National Wildlife Refuge (Chaves County), at Living Desert State Park, and in Blue Spring and its outflows (Eddy County). In Texas, populations are found near Balmorhea in East Sandia, Phantom Lake, and Giffin springs (Reeves County), and near Fort Stockton in Leon Creek and Diamond-Y Spring outflows (Pecos County).

In 1980, the total population of the Pecos gambusia was estimated at about two million fish, divided fairly equally among sites in New Mexico and Texas. The largest concentrations occurred in Pecos County, Texas. In spite of the seemingly large numbers, all populations are considered vulnerable because of alterations to the Pecos River.

Threats

Water diversion from the Pecos River for irrigation intensified after five major and three lesser dams were constructed along the main river channel. A new dam (Brantley Dam) to replace the existing McMillan Dam was recently proposed for construction.

Although the mainstream never provided preferred habitat for the Pecos gambusia, it enabled fish to migrate from dry springs to habitable ones during drought years. Dam construction and water diversion have reduced natural stream flows, increased salinity and turbidity, and altered water temperatures, prohibiting migration. The isolated gambusia populations now depend on uninterrupted spring discharges for survival. Introduction of non-native gambusia into the river system has been an additional factor in limiting the Pecos gambusia's range. Although it is better adapted to springs and outflows, its competitors are better suited to existing downstream conditions.

Conservation and Recovery

During the 1970s, U. S. Fish and Wildlife Service personnel attempted to transplant the Pecos gambusia to more than 20 springs and sinkholes within the Bitter Lake National Wildlife Refuge in an effort to expand its range and improve its chances of survival. Most of these attempts were unsuccessful, but small populations were established at Bitter Creek, Sago, and two smaller springs. In 1987 Bitter Creek and Sago Spring supported a population of about 500 gambusia.

In the past, the Dexter National Fish Hatchery in New Mexico successfully raised a captive population of the Pecos gambusia. Although this population was eventually released, the hatchery's success demonstrates that a captive stock could be used to replenish drought-depleted populations.

Contact

U.S. Fish and Wildlife Service
Regional Office, Division of Endangered Species
P.O. Box 1306
Albuquerque, New Mexico 87103
http://southwest.fws.gov/

References

Bednarz, J. C. 1979. "Ecology and Status of the Pecos Gambusia, *Gambusia nobilis* (Poeciliidae), in New Mexico." *Southwest Naturalist* 24:311-322.

U.S. Fish and Wildlife Service. 1983. "Pecos Gambusia Recovery Plan." U.S. Fish and Wildlife Service, Albuquerque.

Gila Topminnow
Yaqui Topminnow

Poeciliopsis occidentalis occidentalis
Poeciliopsis occidentalis sonoriensis

Status	Endangered
Listed	March 11, 1967
Family	Poeciliidae (Livebearer)
Description	Small guppy-like tan to olive fishes.
Habitat	Usually shallow, quiet waters.
Food	Plant and animal material; detritus.
Reproduction	Bears live young.
Threats	Water projects, competition.
Range	Arizona

Yaqui Topminnow, photograph. U. S. Fish and Wildlife Service. Reproduced by permission.

Description

The Gila topminnow, *Poeciliopsis occidentalis occidentalis*, is a guppy-like livebearer that averages 1.2-1.6 in (3-4 cm) in length; it is tan to olive above and white below. Breeding males darken to jet black and develop bright yellow fins and golden tints along the midline. The Gila topminnow species consists of two subspecies—the Gila topminnow (*P. o. occidentalis*) and the Yaqui topminnow (*P. o. sonoriensis*). Although the two subspecies are visually very similar, the Yaqui topminnow has a longer snout and its mouth is positioned higher on its head. Both subspecies are federally listed as endangered. The Yaqui topminnow has a slightly curved, elongated body with a rounded to almost square caudal fin. The males are small, rarely exceeding 1 in (2.5 cm) but the females may be twice as large. The anal fin of the male is elongated into a copulatory organ (gonopodium), extending forward past the tip of the snout when in copulatory position. The eggs are fertilized internally and the young develop within the female's body and are born alive. Gravid females show distended abdomens and darkened urogenital areas. The body color is tan to olivaceous, darker above, often white on belly. The scales on the dorsum are darkly outlined by melanophores, extending as specks to upper belly and pre-pectoral area. The dark lateral is continuous along the sides posterior, and the fin-rays are outlined with melanophores. Breeding males are black, with some gold on the predorsal midline and orange at base of the gonopodium and sometimes on the bases of dorsal and pelvic fins.

Behavior

Topminnow lifespan appears to be about one year. Onset of breeding is affected by water temperature, daylight, and food availability. Gestation

Gila Topminnow, photograph by John Rinne, USFS. Reproduced by permission.

varies from 24 to 28 days for the Gila topminnow and 12-14 days for the Yaqui subspecies. Young are born alive from the mother. Topminnows feed on a wide variety of plant and animal material and bottom detritus.

Habitat

Topminnows can live in a broad range of habitats. They prefer shallow, warm, fairly quiet waters, but can also be found in moderate currents and depths up to 3.3 ft (1 m). They inhabit permanent and intermittent streams, marshes, and may be found close to the banks of larger rivers. Preferred habitat contains dense mats of algae and debris, usually along stream margins or below riffles, with sandy substrates sometimes covered with mud and debris. They become most abundant in marshes, especially those fed by thermal springs or artesian outflows.

Distribution

The Gila topminnow was historically abundant throughout the Gila River system in Arizona, New Mexico, and northern Mexico. The species was first described in 1853 from a specimen collected from the Santa Cruz River near Tucson. The Yaqui subspecies was formerly abundant throughout the Rio Yaqui drainage in southeastern Arizona and in Sonora and Chihuahua, Mexico. Each subspecies

now occupies only a remnant of its historic U.S. range. Populations of this once abundant species are so small and suitable habitat so fragmented that there is a definite concern for the survival of the species in the United States.

Surveys conducted in 1989 showed the status of the Gila topminnow to be declining. In Arizona, the fish apparently is extirpated from two of the 11 sites where it once naturally occurred. One disappearance was due to an invasion of competing mosquitofish (*Gambusia affinis*) and the other was the result of unknown factors. Mosquitofish also reinvaded a third site from which they had been removed several years before, and their return threatened the native topminnow population there as well. The 1989 surveys also found that 14 reintroduced Gila topminnow populations had failed since the last survey in 1987. There remained approximately 50 topminnow populations, many of which were located in aquaria and other captive facilities. Several of the wild populations were introduced in 1989, including the first in the topminnow's historic range in New Mexico. The status of the topminnow in the Mexican portion of its range is believed to be stable, but information is sketchy.

Threats

Water projects have transformed all free-flowing southwestern rivers into intermittent, deeply cut streams or broad, sandy washes subject to flooding. As a result the Gila and Yaqui topminnows have been reduced to a fraction of their pre-1860s range. Beginning in the late 1800s, exotic fish species were introduced into the habitat. The aggressive and predatory mosquitofish (*Gambusia affinis*), introduced in 1926, has been the cause of much of the topminnow decline. The mosquitofish harasses adult topminnows and eats juveniles. Only when the habitat is sufficiently large and complex, can the two species coexist.

Conservation and Recovery

The Cottonwood Springs Partners for Wildlife project, located in southern Arizona on Sonoita Creek (a major tributary of the Santa Cruz River), continues to serve as an excellent opportunity for biodiversity restoration. This effort has improved habitat for the Gila topminnow, and the Huachuca water umbel (*Lilaeopsis schaffneriana* var. *recirva*), a plant proposed in 1995 for listing as endangered.

The U.S. Fish and Wildlife Service's (FWS) Arizona Ecological Services State Office hopes to use this Partners for Wildlife partnership and others nearby as examples to promote similar restoration efforts along the Santa Cruz River in Mexico.

Topminnow populations on the San Bernardino National Wildlife Refuge are well protected. The land for the refuge was purchased by the Nature Conservancy and donated to the FWS. The topminnow has been successfully reared at the Dexter National Fish Hatchery in New Mexico, and this stock will be used for reintroduction into the wild.

Contact

U.S. Fish and Wildlife Service
Regional Office, Division of Endangered Species
P.O. Box 1306
Albuquerque, New Mexico 87103-1306
Telephone: (505) 248-6911
Fax: (505) 248-6915
http://southwest.fws.gov/

References

Minckley, W. L. 1969. "Native Arizona Fishes: Live-bearers." *Wildlife Views* 16:6-8.

U.S. Fish and Wildlife Service. 1984. "Sonoran Topminnow (Gila and Yaqui) Recovery Plan." U.S. Fish and Wildlife Service, Albuquerque.

Unarmored Threespine Stickleback

Gasterosteus aculeatus williamsoni

Status	Endangered
Listed	October 13, 1970
Family	Gasterosteidae (Stickleback)
Description	Small, olive-brown fish with prominent dorsal spines.
Habitat	Vegetated, slow-flowing, shallow streams.
Food	Insects, larvae, and snails.
Reproduction	Spawns for three months.
Threats	Urbanization, hybridization, predation.
Range	California

Description

One of three subspecies of threespine stickleback in North America, the unarmored threespine stickleback, *Gasterosteus aculeatus williamsoni*, grows to a length of about 2.4 in (6 cm). Its streamlined body is olive-brown to dark green above and light yellow, white, or silvery below. The head, and sometimes the back, of breeding males turns bright red and they may exhibit some blue coloration. Most sticklebacks are heavily plated on the sides, but this subspecies is "zero plated" or unarmored. It is called "threespine" because two spiny projections replace the first dorsal fin, and a third spine protrudes in front of the rear back fin.

Behavior

The unarmored threespine stickleback is an opportunistic feeder, subsisting mostly on insects, insect larvae, snails, and some organic matter. It is more active during the day and probably completes most of its feeding cycle during daylight hours. Nesting males do not feed as often.

It reproduces throughout the year with a peak of activity corresponding to warm water temperature and minimal flood conditions. The male establishes a territory and constructs a nest from aquatic vegetation on the river bottom. Once the nest has been completed, the male attempts to attract females with a zig-zag "dance." A receptive female follows the male to the entrance of the nest and enters. He vibrates his snout against her exposed tail to stimulate her to release eggs. Then he drives her from the nest and fertilizes the eggs. This courtship ritual may take up to an hour to complete. He may then attempt to attract other females to the same nest for up to 24 hours, when he begins his parental duties. After the female lays eggs in the nest, the male fans the eggs for 24 hours to aerate them and aggressively drives away predators through combat. Under normal conditions eggs take about five days to hatch and males guard the fry for another six days. If the fry stray too far from the nest, the father captures them in his mouth and returns them to safety. After hatching, fry remain in the nest until large enough to fend for themselves. They will feed from the yolk of the large eggs for a couple of days and then begin foraging for food. Individuals live for one year.

Females may remain sexually active for up to three months and may be able to spawn every fifth day during this period, producing as many as 1,000 eggs per season. The length of her sexual activity depends upon favorable water conditions and availability of food. The male reproductive cycle requires two days for building the nest and attracting females, five days for the eggs to brood, and six days to guard the fry. In cooler waters this cycle takes up to 18 days. The availability of suitable nesting sites, rather than a paucity of males, seems to be the limiting factor for reproduction.

Unarmored Threespine Stickleback, photograph by B. "Moose" Peterson/WRP. Reproduced by permission.

Habitat

Optimum stickleback habitat consists of clean, clear-flowing streams in deeper pools where there is a slow, steady current. They do not occur in pools with no flow or in swifter flows. In stronger currents, adults shelter behind obstructions, particularly vegetation. They are most abundant in small impoundments, behind obstacles, and in riffles with vascular plants and filamentous algae. Breeding has been documented only in still waters and impoundments. Fry aggregate in the shallow margins of impoundments where vegetation provides protection from predators. Juveniles congregate in backwaters, hidden among aquatic plants. This fish is not found in waters that are even slightly turbid.

Distribution

Threespine sticklebacks are common throughout much of North America. The unarmored threespine stickleback, however, was found only in southern California. At one time, its range included the por-

tions of the Los Angeles, San Gabriel, and Santa Ana Rivers, which now pass directly through metropolitan Los Angeles (Los Angeles County). It also occurred in the headwaters of the Santa Clara River (northern Los Angeles County), and the Santa Maria River and San Antonio Creek (Santa Barbara County).

At present, the unarmored threespine stickleback survives in the headwaters of the Santa Clara River near the towns of Acton and Saugus, and in San Antonio Creek near Lompoc. A transplanted population is thought to survive in Honda Creek on the Vandenburg Air Force Base Reservation. A remnant population of the fish may have been located in Shay Creek (San Bernardino County).

Threats

This stickleback has been extirpated from the Los Angeles basin by urbanization. Groundwater pumping, water diversion, stream channelization, and degraded water quality have combined to permanently eliminate most of its historic habitat. Where it survives in San Antonio Creek, the unarmored threespine stickleback has interbred with another subspecies (*G. a. microcephalus*), which was accidentally introduced into the river system. If interbreeding continues, the unarmored threespine stickleback will lose its unique characteristics. Populations in the upper Santa Clara River have survived because the mountainous region is largely undeveloped, and natural barriers have prevented hybridization. In these headwaters, however, sticklebacks have been forced to compete for food and breeding sites with the introduced mosquitofish. Sometime in the 1970s, the African clawed frog (*Xenopus laevis*), which was a popular pet until prohibited, became established in a Santa Clara River tributary. This carnivorous frog is regarded as a threat to all native fishes. The U.S. Fish and Wildlife Service (FWS) has undertaken a project to eliminate the frog from streams in the region. In Southern California habitats, the stickleback young and some adults are preyed upon by aquatic insects, garter snakes, herons, and belted kingfishers. Some birds that prey on the stickleback carry tapeworms that destroy the fish's reproductive potential and copepods that cause fatal infections.

Conservation and Recovery

The FWS continues its research into the biology and ecology of the unarmored threespine stickleback and will attempt to reestablish additional populations within the historic range. Because several habitat streams are in danger of being dried up by groundwater pumping, the FWS has implemented a strategy to supply emergency water to these streams or to salvage fish populations if necessary. A major goal of the FWS Recovery Plan is to control the many non-native fishes and pests that abound in the watershed. Without some effort to remove these exotics, the native unarmored threespine stickleback will be unable to return to formerly inhabited streams.

Contact

U.S. Fish and Wildlife Service
Regional Office, Division of Endangered Species
Eastside Federal Complex
911 N.E. 11th Ave.
Portland, Oregon 97232-4181
Telephone: (503) 231-6121
http://pacific.fws.gov/

References

Irwin, J. F., and D. L. Soltz. 1982. "The Distribution and Natural History of the Unarmored Threespine Stickleback in San Antonio Creek, California". Report. U.S. Fish and Wildlife Service, Sacramento.

U.S. Fish and Wildlife Service. 1985. "Revised Unarmored Threespine Stickleback Recovery Plan." U.S. Fish and Wildlife Service, Portland.

Pygmy Sculpin

Cottus pygmaeus

Status	Threatened
Listed	September 28, 1989
Family	Cottidae (Sculpin)
Description	Small fish, grayish black to black, with 2 to 3 saddle markings.
Habitat	A single spring and spring run.
Food	Insects.
Reproduction	Spawns year-round.
Threats	Groundwater contamination, highway construction, limited range.
Range	Alabama

Description

The pygmy sculpin is a small freshwater fish about 1.8 in (4.6 cm) in length. Its coloration varies by maturity, sex, and breeding condition. Patterning consists of up to three dorsal saddles and spotted fins. Juveniles have a black head and a grayish black body with three light saddles. Mature fish have white heads and lighter bodies, with the grayish black color remaining in the form of two saddles. Breeding males become almost entirely black; spots in the dorsal fin enlarge and the margin becomes reddish orange. Breeding females are slightly darker than nonbreeding females.

Behavior

The pygmy sculpin feeds on a variety of insects and small aquatic crustaceans, with isopods being the most important food. The species spawns throughout the year, with a peak occurring in spring and summer. Usually more than one female deposits eggs in batches on the underside of rocks. These nests are probably guarded by the male.

Habitat

This species inhabits a single spring and spring run in Alabama. The spring flow averages 32 million gal (121 million l) per day, with a water temperature between 61 and 64°F (16 and 17.7°C). The

bottom of the spring pool and run is gravel and sand; large mats of vegetation occur in both the pool and the run.

Distribution

The pygmy sculpin was discovered in 1968 at Coldwater Spring and the spring run near Anniston, Alabama. The spring has been impounded and forms a one-acre pool, 2-4 ft (0.6-1.2 m) deep. The run is up to 60 ft (18 m) wide and flows for about 500 ft (152 m) where it is joined by Dry Creek. Below this point it is known as Coldwater Creek which flows into Choccolocco Creek. The pygmy sculpin is restricted to the spring and the spring run; it has not been found elsewhere. Coldwater Spring, which is owned by the City of Anniston, is the city's primary water supply, drawing about 16 million gal (60.5 million l) a day.

Threats

The main threats to the pygmy sculpin are groundwater contamination, the adverse impacts of highway construction on the source aquifer, and the species' restricted range.

Both the surface water and the underground aquifer have shown some degree of toxic contamination. The Anniston Army Depot is nearby and studies have indicated that toxic chemicals, includ-

Pygmy Sculpin, photograph by Richard Wallace and Noel Burkhead. Reproduced by permission.

ing chlorinated hydrocarbons, phenols, and hexa-valent chromium, have been found in groundwater at the depot. Although migration of these compounds is not an immediate threat, they may sink into the aquifer and have a future impact on the water quality of Coldwater Spring. The spring water itself contains high levels of trichloro-ethylene.

The Alabama Highway Department plans to construct a highway bypass from Interstate 20 to Anniston. Three alternative routes for the bypass have been proposed. The preferred route would run along the side of Coldwater Mountain, just above and to the east of Coldwater Spring. The use of explosives in cutting a mountain road might change the system of cracks and fissures that route water to and from the underground aquifer, thus affecting Coldwater Spring. The two other proposed routes present less risk to the spring.

Since only a single population of the pygmy sculpin is known to exist, the species is vulnerable to an unpredictable human or natural event. A toxic spill that would contaminate the spring's source aquifer is perhaps the most dangerous potential threat of this type.

Conservation and Recovery

The U. S. Fish and Wildlife Service published a Recovery Plan for the pygmy sculpin in 1991. The critical habitat of the threatened fish in Coldwater Spring and its run is owned and protected by the Anniston Water and Sewer Department. The key to the survival of the pygmy sculpin is the protection of the quantity and quality of groundwater in the recharge aquifer of its critical habitat. This means that threatening activities that could degrade hydrology or water chemistry must not be permitted. This protection is undertaken normally, since Coldwater Spring is the principal water supply of the town of Anniston. In addition, the populations of the pygmy sculpin should be monitored, and research undertaken into its biology, habitat needs, and beneficial management practices.

Contacts

Regional Office of Endangered Species
U. S. Fish and Wildlife Service
1875 Century Blvd., Suite 200
Atlanta, Georgia 30345
http://southeast.fws.gov/

Jackson Field Office
U. S. Fish and Wildlife Service
6578 Dogwood View Parkway, Suite A
Jackson, Mississippi 39213-7856
Telephone: (601) 965-4900
Fax: (601) 965-4340

References

Mount, R. H. 1986. "Vertebrate Animals of Alabama in Need of Special Attention." Alabama Agricultural Experiment Station.

U. S. Fish and Wildlife Service. 1991. "Pygmy sculpin (*Cottus pygmaeus*) Recovery Plan." Jackson, Mississippi.

Williams, J. D. 1968. "A New Species of Sculpin, *Cottus pygmaeus*, from a Spring in the Alabama River Basin" *Copeia* 1968:334-342.

Bluemask Darter

Etheostoma sp.

Status	Endangered
Listed	December 27, 1993
Family	Percidae (Perch)
Description	Small bright to dullish blue darter.
Habitat	Slow to moderate waters flowing over sand and fine gravel substrates.
Food	Unknown.
Reproduction	Unknown.
Threats	Siltation and pollutants from coal mining, gravel mining, poor land use practices, and waste discharges.
Range	Tennessee

Description

The bluemask darter is a small, slender fish that reaches a maximum size of 1.9 in (4.8 cm). Females and nonbreeding males are straw-yellow to tan. Along the sides there are seven to nine quadrate blotches formed by dark X-markings and faint blue pigment. Between the blotches and extending dorsally there are many small orange X-markings and spots. Dorsolaterally there are also many small brown markings. On the dorsum there are six dark brown saddles. The face and underside of the head are white to dusky, and there is blue pigment on the suborbital bar and operculum. The cheeks are fully scaled, and the lateral line is usually complete. The first dorsal fin contains a narrow dusky marginal band, a red-orange medial band, a dusky submedial band (males only), and a clear basal band. The second dorsal and caudal fins are mostly clear.

Breeding males are generally dusky with seven to nine bright cobalt blue bars on the side of the body. Between the bars, orange spots coalesce to form conspicuous splotches. Bright cobalt blue continuously covers the face, underside of the head, and branchiostegal membranes. The first dorsal fin contains a narrow gray to black marginal band, a bright red-orange medial band, a wide black submedial band, and a mostly clear basal band with black pigment in the posterior portions of the membranes. The second dorsal, caudal, anal, and pelvic fins are dusky gray to black.

The bluemask darter can be distinguished from *Etheostoma stigmaeum* and the blueside darter (*E. jessiae*) by: fully scaled cheeks; lateral line usually complete; premaxillary frenum absent; breeding males with bright cobalt blue pigment continuously covering the lower face and underside of the head; breeding males with soft dorsal and anal fins with no orange spots on rays or blue pigment in membranes; and palatine teeth absent.

Behavior

The bluemask darter occupies areas with slow to moderate flow over sand and fine gravel substrates. This type of habitat is seemingly limited within the Caney Fork River system of central Tennessee.

Habitat

Bluemask darters have been collected in slow to moderate current over clean sand and fine gravel at depths of 4-20 in (10.2-50.8 cm), typically just downstream of riffles or along the margins of pools and runs. They inhabit the lower free-flowing reaches of streams on the Highland Rim with substrates of limestone or chert bedrock, coarse chert gravel, and sand. Spawning males were collected from the

Bluemask Darter, photograph. U. S. Fish and Wildlife Service. Reproduced by permission.

Collins River in April 1991 over sand and gravel in moderately flowing runs. The closely related *E. stigmaeum*, which shares an affinity for sand and gravel substrates, spawns in early spring by burying eggs in gravel. The upper reaches of all four streams that support the bluemask darter flow underground during summer, with little to no surface flow. This limits perennial habitat for the species to the lower stream reaches.

Distribution

Historically this species was known from five rivers in the Caney Fork River system. Presently this darter is known from only four rivers in Van Buren, Warren, Grundy, and White Counties. The bluemask darter is thought to inhabit about 700 ft (213.4 m) of Cane Creek; 23 mi (37 km) of the Collins River; 2.7 mi (4.3 km) of the Rocky River; and 1.1 mi (1.8 km) of the upper Caney Fork River. The species may also seasonally occur in the 1.9-mi (301-km) reservoir fluctuation zone in the upper Caney Fork River and the 0.8-mi (1.3-km) fluctuation zone in Cane

Creek. Eight specimens were collected there on two occasions in the spring of 1990. Eight individuals were collected from the free-flowing portion of Cane Creek, just upstream of the Great Falls Reservoir in 1991.

The bluemask darter was collected at two localities in the Caney Fork River in the lower 1.1 river mi (1.8 km) above the Great Falls Reservoir. Twelve specimens were collected in relatively high flow along the margin of the stream over cobble and sparse gravel at a site 1.6 mi (2.6 km) east-southeast of Dodson, White County, during April 1991. On a return trip to the site in August 1991, the channel was completely dry, with the exception of widely scattered pools with substrates of large round boulders.

In the Caney Fork River, 14 bluemask darters were observed in a large pool over silty sand, detritus, and occasional small cobble in a large spring-fed isolated pool a short distance upstream of the site in waters temperature of 75-78°F (23.9-25.6°C). Large pools like this one, which are widely scattered, may be critical in sustaining populations through low flow periods. Because the perennial flow appears to be limited to the lower river, and because summer hold-over pools are widely scattered, this bluemask darter population must be extremely small and thus vulnerable to disturbance or habitat alteration.

Threats

The bluemask darter's distribution has been reduced by such factors as impoundments, water withdrawal, and the general deterioration of water quality resulting from siltation and pollutants contributed by coal mining, gravel mining, poor land use practices and waste discharges.

Because the existing bluemask darter populations inhabit only short stream reaches, they are vulnerable to extirpation from stochastic events, such as accidental toxic chemical spills. The valley along the Collins River is used extensively for commercial plant nurseries; this increases the chances of a toxic agricultural chemical spill and the buildup of contaminants in the stream sediment that could impact this population. Additionally, all existing bluemask darter populations are now isolated by the Great Falls Reservoir. Because the Cane Creek and upper Caney Fork River populations are extremely small and the Great Falls Reservoir presumably restricts gene flow among populations, the long-term genetic viability of all the populations is questionable.

Conservation and Recovery

U. S. Fish and Wildlife Service (FWS), in cooperation with willing landowners, has begun to implement programs to restore riparian habitat, fence cattle from stream reaches, develop alternative water supplies for cattle, and control agricultural run-off in other streams in the southeastern United States. These programs, which are designed to benefit both the landowner and the resource, help minimize soil erosion and enhance bluemask darter habitat.

Although the bluemask darter has been able to withstand some degree of habitat degradation, some of its habitat has been so severely altered that the species was extirpated from one stream, and other population segments have been reduced in size and vigor. The FWS is conducting research to determine the species' specific microhabitat requirements and ecological associations. Specific components of the species' habitat may be un-

known, and certain activities in the watershed may be adversely impacting the species. Habitat improvement programs may be needed to increase spawning success. Structures may be needed to provide cover and summer pool habitat and to stabilize the stream bank and streambed. Cooperative projects with landowners to provide alternative water sources may be needed to help minimize the impacts of water withdrawal projects.

The exact historic range of the bluemask darter is unknown. However, based on historic collection records, the species has been taken from only five rivers and creeks. The species is extirpated from the Calfkiller River, and because of significant habitat deterioration, including impoundments, siltation, and water quality degradation, it may not be possible to reintroduce the fish into this system. However, further study is needed to determine when water quality and physical habitat is suitable for reintroductions. Other streams may exist within the species' probable historic range that may be suitable for reintroduction, including the Barrens Fork River or lower reaches of Charles Creek or Mountain Creek in the Collins River system. If such streams exist, they might have potential for reintroduction success.

Contacts

U. S. Fish and Wildlife Service
Regional Office, Division of Endangered Species
1875 Century Blvd., Suite 200
Atlanta, Georgia 30345
http://southeast.fws.gov/

Cookeville Ecological Services Field Office
U. S. Fish and Wildlife Service
446 Neal St.
Cookeville, Tennessee 38501-4027
Telephone: (931) 528-6481
Fax: (931) 528-7075

References

U. S. Fish and Wildlife Service. 27 December 1993. "Endangered and Threatened Wildlife and Plants; Determination of Endangered Status for the Relict Darter and Bluemask (=Jewel) Darter." *Federal Register* 58 (246):68480-68486.

U. S. Fish and Wildlife Service. 25 July 1997. "Recovery Plan for Bluemask (=Jewel) Darter," U. S. Fish and Wildlife Service, Atlanta. 20 pp.

Slackwater Darter

Etheostoma boschungi

Status	Threatened
Listed	September 9, 1977
Family	Percidae (Perch)
Description	Darter with a blue-black bar under the eyes and prominent dorsal saddles.
Habitat	Streams with adjacent seepage areas.
Food	Insects, small crustaceans.
Reproduction	Spawns in March.
Threats	Loss of breeding habitat, degraded water quality.
Range	Alabama, Tennessee

Description

The slackwater darter, *Etheostoma boschungi*, was recently placed in a new subgenus, *Ozarka*. This group of medium-sized darters range from 1.6-3 in (4-7 cm) in length. The slackwater darter is distinguished from members of its group by a bold blue-black bar under the eyes and three prominent dark dorsal saddles.

Behavior

The slackwater darter feeds on insects and small crustaceans. Its life span is probably no more than three years.

Spawning usually begins in early March but may vary from year to year depending on temperature and rainfall. Water temperature must be warmer than 57°F (14°C), and rainfall must be heavy enough to lift adults into their spawning grounds. Each female attaches 100-300 eggs to Juncus and Eleocharis plants. Males aggressively defend egg-laden clumps of plants. Fry develop in late March and April and return to streams in late April or early May. Depending on rainfall and temperature conditions, the spawning activities progress as follows: November to January: adults aggregate for spawning migration; nuptial colors and gametes begin developing; there is strong evidence that individuals assemble in particular places downstream of the breeding site so that they can make their surge to the spawning

area in unison; January to the end of February: the spawning migration occurs and nuptial colors and gametes are fully developed; late February to the end of March: males establish territories, court females, and completes spawning; April: larvae develop in the breeding habitat; May: larvae leave the breeding habitat.

Habitat

The slackwater darter has distinct breeding and non-breeding habitats. It normally inhabits small to moderate, slow-flowing, upland streams, no more than 40 ft (12 m) in width and shallower than 6.6 ft (2 m). In wider streams, darters tend to gather in sluggish water beneath overhanging banks. It avoids riffles and rapids, and prefers substrates of gravel combined with silt or mud. It has not been observed over clean gravel substrates or in swift currents. It shows some preference for accumulated detritus, such as twigs and well-decayed leaves, but not large concentrations of newly fallen or compact leaves. Migration is not impeded by moderate riffles or shallow water, and the species is adaptable to changes in the oxygen level of the water as it changes during the summer.

Ready-to-spawn darters are lifted by heavy spring rains into seepage areas in open fields, pastures, and woods, where they spawn. Water in these seepages is typically no more than 3 in (8 cm) deep.

Slackwater Darter, photograph. U. S. Fish and Wildlife Service. Reproduced by permission.

The stream level must rise sufficiently to give spawning individuals access to the breeding grounds, whose elevations are between 620-840 ft (189-256 m).

Distribution

The remaining populations of the slackwater darter are probably remnants of a more widespread and continuous distribution throughout the smaller streams of the Tennessee River basin. Populations are currently found in five tributaries of the south bend of the Tennessee River: Buffalo River and Shoal Creek in Lawrence County, Tennessee; and Flint River (Madison County), Swan Creek (Limestone County), and Cypress Creek (Lauderdale County), Alabama. In 1984 the population was estimated at 3,600 in Cypress Creek, where the heaviest concentration of slackwater darters is found. Other streams may support only a few hundred of the fish. Biologists consider the population dangerously low.

Threats

The slackwater darter's breeding habitats have been in slow but steady decline for the past 200 years. Heavy use of groundwater for agriculture and human consumption has caused water tables to fall throughout the region, drying up many seepage areas that were historically used for spawning. Numerous spawning seepages have been diked to form agricultural ponds, and increased agricultural clearing has significantly increased siltation in the habitat.

Spreading urbanization is a potential threat to the habitat because of alteration in drainage that affects groundwater levels. The quality of groundwater is being degraded by pollutants, including insecticides, herbicides, fertilizers, industrial and chemical wastes from sewage lines and septic tanks seepage, and stockyard runoff. Because the breeding grounds are so limited, even a small spill could exterminate a breeding population. Much of the year the breeding grounds are too wet for crops, and so these areas are being turned into farm fish ponds. Probably many breeding sites have been eliminated by these farm fish ponds. Beavers have also dammed spawning streams and eliminated breeding areas.

Conservation and Recovery

The slackwater darter's specialized breeding habitats for the Buffalo and Flint Rivers, and Shoal and Swan Creeks, have not been fully mapped. This was the first task established by the U. S. Fish and Wildlife Service (FWS) Recovery Plan. The FWS hopes to purchase breeding sites or obtain management easements from private owners to protect breeding areas on at least three of currently inhabited streams. Without protection, it is feared that most seepage areas will disappear completely in the next 20 years.

Contact

U.S. Fish and Wildlife Service
Regional Office, Division of Endangered Species
1875 Century Blvd., Suite 200
Atlanta, Georgia 30345
http://southeast.fws.gov/

References

Page, Lawrence M. 1983. *Handbook of Darters.* T.H.F. Publishers, Neptune City, New Jersey.

U.S. Fish and Wildlife Service. 1984. "Slackwater Darter Recovery Plan." U.S. Fish and Wildlife Service, Atlanta.

Wall, B. R., and J. D. Williams. 1974. "*Etheostoma boschungi,* a New Percid Fish from the Tennessee River Drainage in Northern Alabama and Western Tennessee." *Tulane Studies in Zoology and Botany* 18(4):172-182.

Williams, J. D., and H. W. Robison. 1980. "*Ozarka*: A New Subgenus of *Etheostoma.*" *Brimleyiana* 4:149-156.

Relict Darter

Etheostoma chienense

Status	Endangered
Listed	December 27, 1993
Family	Percidae (Perch)
Description	Small darter with light colored backs and sides, with brown mottling and six to eight dark brown saddles.
Habitat	Headwater areas in slow-flowing pools, usually associated with gravel sand and leaf litter substrates.
Food	Unknown.
Reproduction	Spawning from late March to early June.
Threats	Channelization and deterioration of water quality.
Range	Kentucky

Description

The relict darter is one of the 10 recognized species in the *Etheostoma squamiceps* complex. It is a small (2.5 in; 6.4 cm) fish. The general body coloration of females and nonbreeding males consists of brown mottling on a light tan background. The dorsum coloration is variable, usually similar to the sides, but sometimes paler and crossed by six to eight small dark brown saddles. The venter is white and unmarked. The head has dark pre- and postorbital bars.

The most distinctive aspects of the relict darter are features of pigmentation and morphology of the dorsal fins of breeding males. The species can be distinguished with certainty only by examination of breeding males. Bright breeding colors do not develop. Breeding males are gray or dark brown on the dorsum and sides with light tan on the venter. The head and nape are greatly swollen and black, and the dark coloration obscures the nonbreeding pattern. Territorial and spawning males have alternating white and black bars on the side of the body. The first dorsal fin is black, except for a clear basal band, and has a small white knob on the tip of each spine; a small, clear triangle behind each knob that narrows into a thin, clear margin; and a small, clear

teardrop posterior to each spine located two-thirds the distance from the base of the fin to its margin. The caudal fin has a thin, clear margin and five to nine dark bands alternating with an equal number of clear to yellow bands that become increasingly wider and darker distally. The middle spot on the caudal fin base is darker than the other two fins. The anal and pelvic fins are dusky to black with narrow, clear margins.

Behavior

There is no published information on the reproduction of the relict darter, but it is assumed to be the same as other members of the genus. Males and females mature at one year of age at about 1.6 and 1.4 in (4.1 and 3.6 cm) standard length, respectively, but most males apparently do not spawn until their second year. Spawning occurs from late March to early June. Eggs averaging about 0.7 in (1.8 cm) are deposited on the undersides of submerged objects, usually flat stones. In the case of the relict darter, eggs are attached frequently to the undersides of sticks or logs; other related species spawn on the undersides of slab rocks. The female and male invert briefly during egg-laying and then both return to an upright position. Several females may spawn

Etheostoma sp., photograph. U. S. Fish and Wildlife Service. Reproduced by permission.

with a single male, and nests may contain as many as 1,500 eggs. The eggs are guarded by the male. Incubation periods range from about 125 hours at 71.6-78.8°F (22-26°C) to 270 hours at 64.4-71.6°F (18-22°C).

Habitat

Adults are concentrated in headwaters and creeks in quiet to gently flowing pools, usually over gravel mixed with sand and under or near cover such as fallen tree branches, undercut banks, or overhanging riparian vegetation.

Distribution

The relict darter is endemic to the Bayou du Chien system, a Mississippi River tributary, in extreme western Kentucky. This darter was "fairly common" in the high gradient reaches of Bayou du Chien in the early 1970s. In 1991 individuals were collected at five sites, but abundant at only two sites (18 individuals were collected at one site and 46 at

another). The other three sites yielded a total of only eight relict darters. Only one spawning area has been located—in a small tributary stream located in Graves County.

Threats

The most signicant factors in the relict darter's decline have likely been the poor land use practices in the area, which foster damaged silt to the creek, and canalization of the Bayou du Chien, which has significantly altered the darter's habitat. Improper pesticide use might also be a factor in the species' decline.

The Bayou du Chien system has been extensively channelized. Much of the streams' sinuosity was eliminated, undercut banks were lost, stream bank vegetation and in-stream cover were removed, and some smaller streams now flow only intermittently. This massive alteration of the relict darter's habitat reduced both relict darter numbers and the amount of suitable habitat. Aside from past channelization impacts, the area is extensively farmed and much of the watershed has been deforested. These alterations result in a fairly high silt load within the Bayou du Chien system that continues to degrade the habitat and further impacts the species. Because the relict darter inhabits only short stream reaches, it is vulnerable to extirpation from accidental, toxic chemical spills. This is especially true of the only known relict darter spawning site. Additionally, because the relict darter population has been drastically reduced in size, the species long-term genetic viability is questionable.

Conservation and Recovery

To save the relict darter, all existing state and federal legislation and regulations must be enforced. Relict darter research needs include: life history information (spawning season and behavior, habitat requirements, age and growth, and food habits); propagation and reintroduction techniques; and habitat improvement techniques. Management needs include: reestablishing spawning subpopulations in other tributaries; promoting the safe use of pesticides by local farmers; enforcing existing federal and state laws relating to water quality, and monitoring the species especially at spawning areas. Because suitable habitat has been reduced, especially spawning habitat, a program to improve habitat is one of the most important management needs. Additionally, management is needed to restore some of the species' habitat through repair of riparian habitat and control of nonpoint source pollution.

Contacts

U. S. Fish and Wildlife Service
Regional Office, Division of Endangered Species
1875 Century Blvd., Suite 200
Atlanta, Georgia 30345
http://southeast.fws.gov/

U. S. Fish and Wildlife Service
330 Ridgefield Court
Asheville, North Carolina 28806
Telephone: (704) 665-1195

References

Page, L. M., P. A. Ceas, D. L. Swofford, and D. G. Buth. 1992. "Evolutionary Relationships with the *Etheostoma squamiceps* Complex (Percidae: Subgenus *Catonotus*) with Descriptions of Five New Species." *Copeia* 1992 (3):615-646.

U. S. Fish and Wildlife Service. 1993. "Determination of Endangered Species Status for the Relict Darter." *Federal Register* 58 (246):68480-68486.

Warren, M. L. 1991. "Survey of the Relict Darter (*Etheostoma (Catonotus*) sp. cf *E. neopterum*)." Final Report Submitted to the U. S. Fish and Wildlife Service, Asheville, NC. 33 pp.

Webb, D. H., and M. E. Sisk. 1975. "The Fishes of West Kentucky. III. The Fishes of Bayou de Chien." *Transactions of the Kentucky Academy of Science.* 36:63-67.

Etowah Darter

Etheostoma etowahae

Status	Endangered
Listed	December 20, 1994
Family	Percidae
Description	A small brown or grayish-olive percid fish.
Habitat	Creeks or small rivers with moderate to high gradient and rocky bottoms.
Food	Small aquatic invertebrates.
Reproduction	Lays eggs.
Threats	Habitat loss by impoundments, and degradation by siltation and chemical pollution.
Range	Georgia

Description

The *Etheostoma etowahae* (Etowah darter) is a small-sized percid fish that is moderately compressed laterally, and has a moderately pointed snout with a terminal, obliquely angled mouth. The body ground shade is brown or grayish-olive. The side is usually pigmented with 13-14 small dark blotches just below the lateral line. The breast in nuptial males is dark greenish-blue. The Etowah darter has proven distinct from the greenbreast darter, *E. jordani*, a species with which it has previously been confused, by the absence of red marks on the sides and anal fins of male specimens.

Behavior

The Etowah darter feeds on or near the stream bottom on small aquatic invertebrates. It feeds in flowing water, and is intolerant of non-flowing conditions.

Habitat

The Etowah darter inhabits warm and cool, medium and large creeks or small rivers that are moderate or high gradient with rocky bottoms. It is found in relatively shallow riffles, with large gravel, cobble, and small boulder substrates. The Etowah darter is typically associated with the swiftest por-

tions of shallow riffles, but occasionally adults are taken at the tails of riffles. The sites having the greatest abundance of Etowah darters had clear water and relatively little silt in the riffles. The Etowah darter, like other members of the subgenus *Nothonotus*, shuns pool habitats and is intolerant of impoundment. The Etowah River system alone harbors at least 11 species of darters. Each species inhabits discrete portions of the drainage and specific habitats within its streams. The habitat requirements of the Cherokee darter differ significantly from those of the amber darter. However, the habitat requirements of the amber darter are similar, but not identical, to that of the Etowah darter.

Distribution

The Etowah darter is endemic to the upper Etowah River system in north Georgia, where it is restricted to the upper Etowah River main stem and two tributaries, Long Swamp and Amicalola Creeks. These streams drain both the Blue Ridge and Piedmont physiographic provinces. This distribution suggests habitat specialization; all streams inhabited by this species are geographically adjacent in the most upland portion of the river system. For a fish of moderate to large creeks or small rivers, the Etowah darter has one of the most restricted distributions in the southeast.

Etowah Darter, photograph by Noel M. Burkhead. Reproduced by permission.

Threats

The Etowah darter is only known from the upper Etowah River and two tributary systems. This rare fish has suffered habitat destruction caused by the construction of impoundments and ponds, and degradation by siltation caused by soil erosion in the watershed, agricultural runoff, discharges of sewage and other wastes, other pollutants, and increased urbanization. These factors continue to affect the Etowah darter and its habitat.

Conservation and Recovery

The critical habitat supporting the surviving populations of the Etowah darter must be protected against the construction of impoundments and other degrading influences. The privately owned land in watersheds of streams supporting the largest populations should be acquired and designated as ecological reserves, or conservation easements negotiated with the landowners. Threatening activities in the watersheds, such as road construction, timber harvesting, residential development, and the dumping of chemicals, sewage, or other pollutants must be strictly managed to prevent risks to the rare darter. Its populations should be monitored, and research undertaken into its biology and habitat needs.

Contacts

U.S. Fish and Wildlife Service Jacksonville Ecological Services Office
6620 Southpoint Drive South, Suite 310
Jacksonville, Florida, 32216
Telephone: (904) 232-2580
Fax: (904) 232-2404

U. S. Fish and Wildlife Service Regional Office
Division of Endangered Species
1875 Century Blvd., Suite 200
Atlanta, Georgia 30345
http://southeast.fws.gov/

Reference

U.S. Fish and Wildlife Service. 20 December 1994. "Endangered and Threatened Wildlife and Plants; Determination of Threatened Status for the Cherokee Darter and Endangered Status for the Etowah Darter." *Federal Register* (59).

Fountain Darter

Etheostoma fonticola

Status	Endangered
Listed	October 13, 1970
Family	Percidae (Perch)
Description	Tiny, reddish brown darter with dark horizontal lines on the side.
Habitat	Clear, quiet waters.
Food	Insect larvae, small crustaceans.
Reproduction	Spawns year-round.
Threats	Aquifer depletion, dam construction, recreational use of habitat.
Range	Texas

Description

The fountain darter, *Etheostoma fonticola*, is the smallest species of darter, usually less than 1 in (2.5 cm) in length, and is mostly reddish brown in life. The scales on the sides are broadly margined behind with dusky pigment. The dorsal region is dusted with fine specks and has about eight indistinct dusky cross-blotches. A series of horizontal stitch-like dark lines occur along the middle of the sides, forming an interrupted lateral streak. Three small dark spots are present on the base of the tail and there is a dark spot on the gill cover. Dark bars appear in front of, below, and behind the eye. The lower half of the spinous dorsal fin is jet-black; above this appears a broad red band, and above this band the fin is narrowly edged with black. Male fountain darters differ from females in four morphological characters: banding pattern, spinous dorsal fin coloration, genital papillae, and pelvic and anal fin nuptial tubercles.

Although the fountain darter has been characterized as the most advanced darter, the basis for this was an analysis of a very limited subset of traits, which appear to be highly influenced by environmental factors, such as temperature. The subgenus *Microperca*, to which *E. fonticola* belongs, is still thought to be the most derived (specialized) subgenus of *Etheostoma*. The evolutionary history of this group is presumed to involve an early separation of the presently recognized *E. proeliare* and *E. microperca* groups followed by a later isolation of a subset of an *E. proeliare*-like ancestor. This *E. proeliare*-like ancestor survived and became the presently recognized *E. fonticola* in only the San Marcos and Comal Rivers.

Behavior

Based on percent frequency of occurrence of food items in fountain darter stomachs sampled from the San Marcos River, juveniles and small fountain darters feed primarily on copepods; medium-sized feed mainly on dipteran and ephemeropteran larvae, and fully mature darters prefer ephemeropteran larvae. Food habit studies are currently underway for fountain darters in the Comal ecosystem.

Food habits of fountain darters in Spring Lake differ from the food habits of darters in the San Marcos River. Casual observations indicate that the overall invertebrate community in Spring Lake is different from the community in the river, which could explain the observed differences in food habits of darters in these two areas on the basis of availability of food items.

Fountain darters feed primarily during daylight and demonstrate selective feeding behavior. Those held in an aquarium feed on moving aquatic inver-

Fountain Darter, photograph by Roger W. Barbour. Reproduced by permission.

tebrates while disregarding immobile ones, suggesting that these darters respond to visual cues.

E. fonticola are headwater darters that breed in the relatively constant temperature of the San Marcos River. It has been recorded that fountain darters appear to spawn year-round and that the parents, after depositing eggs in vegetation, provided no further care to the young. After hatching, the fry were never free-swimming, due in part to the reduced size of their swim bladders. As in other darters, fountain darter eggs attach to moss and to algae and these eggs hatch in aerated aquaria. Breeding males display nuptial coloration and develop nuptial tubercles on their pelvic and anal fins. Tubercles on darters are thought to stimulate gravid females or to assist in maintaining the spawning position within the vegetation.

Natural populations of fountain darters have two temporal peaks of ova development, one in August and the other in late winter to early spring. There-

fore, fountain darters apparently have two major spawning periods annually. The monthly percentages of females with ovaries containing at least one mature ovum also demonstrate the two annual spawning peaks. However, females containing at least one mature ovum have been collected throughout the year, further suggesting year-round spawning. The ovary weight/body weight relationship and the testis width/square root of total length relationship also indicate the two peak spawning periods.

Most darters spawn in the spring or early summer. However, populations of *E. lepidum* and *E. spectabile*, which live in areas with slight annual water temperature variation, extend their breeding periods considerably (up to 10-12 months). The extension of the breeding season of *E. spectabile* throughout the summer is also known for a population inhabiting the Guadalupe River below Canyon Reservoir where releases from the bottom of the reservoir moderate water temperatures, especially during summer months. Since *E. fonticola* also lives in a relatively constant temperature environment, it is not especially surprising to find that this species spawns throughout the year.

Habitat

The fountain darter requires: 1) undisturbed stream floor habitats (including runs, riffles, and pools), 2) a mix of submergent vegetation (algae, mosses, and vascular plants) in part for cover, 3) clear and clean water, 4) a food supply of living organisms, 4) constant water temperatures within the natural and normal river gradients, and 5) most importantly, adequate springflows.

In general, *E. fonticola* prefers vegetated streamfloor habitats with a constant water temperature. Higher densities of the fish are found in mats of the filamentous green algae (*Rhizoclonium* sp.) and the moss *Riccia*. It is occasionally found in areas lacking vegetation. Fountain darters have also been observed among leaf litter in the Comal River

Critical habitat has been designated for the fountain darter as "Texas, Hays County; Spring Lake and its outflow, the San Marcos River, downstream approximately 0.5 mi (0.8 km) below Interstate Highway 35 bridge." A field identified of the downstream boundary is the defunct U.S. Geological Survey stream gauge.

Distribution

The historic range of the fountain darter included the sources, headwaters, and sections of the San Marcos and Comal Rivers in south-central Texas. Today, the fountain darter is found in the San Marcos River from Spring Lake (Hays County) to an area between the San Marcos wastewater treatment plant outfall and the confluence of the Blanco River. The fountain darter is also found virtually throughout the Comal River to its confluence with the Guadalupe River; the species had been previously eliminated from the Comal River when its habitat was reduced to isolated pools by excessive water removal, but reintroduction efforts were successful, and an established reproducing population now occupies the entire Comal aquatic ecosystem from Landa Lake to the vicinity of the Comal/Guadalupe River.

From 1974 until 1981 a stock of fountain darters taken from the San Marcos River near the Interstate Highway 35 crossing was cultured at the federal fa-

cility at Dexter, New Mexico, to ensure against a catastrophic loss of the species. This stock has since been discontinued; however, a new culture was established at the San Marcos National Fish Hatchery and Technology Center, now part of the National Biological Service, in 1988.

A 1993 study estimated the San Marcos River fountain darter population (excluding Spring Lake) to be 45,900. Over the past two decades, there has been a real decrease in fountain darter numbers in the San Marcos. 1976 estimates for the same area estimated a population of about 103,000 fish. A 1991 scuba-aided underwater survey of Spring Lake estimated at least 16,000 fountain darters at the springs openings and another 15,000 in the green algae habitat. A 1990 sampling of seven transects in Landa Lake and the Comal River reported a population estimate of about 168,078 darters above Torrey Mill Dam.

Threats

Actions that threaten the fountain darter include the destruction of aquatic vegetation in Spring Lake and the San Marcos River, recreational use of the San Marcos River, and long-term water depletion from the Edwards Aquifer. Swimmers and divers disturb the algae mats used by the darter for spawning, and the aquifer, which is part of a vast underground water system, supplies the water needs of more than one million people throughout the region, including the city of San Antonio. A dam on the lower portion of the San Marcos River apparently eliminated fountain darter habitat in that section of the river.

The Texas Department of Water Resources forecasts that groundwater pumping for human uses will continue to increase well into the twenty-first century. At the current rate of increase, scientists predict that the Edwards Aquifer will be so depleted that flow from the San Marcos Springs will cease around 2000 and flow from the Comal Springs will be severely reduced. Without the cooperation of state and local agencies to reduce the amount of groundwater extracted from the aquifer, recovery of the fountain darter is considered unlikely.

Conservation and Recovery

In 1993, the U.S. Fish and Wildlife Service (FWS) and several cooperators began studies in the Comal Springs ecosystem designed to study habitat use and to model instream flow requirements for the fountain darter and another potentially threatened species, the Comal Springs riffle beetle (*Heterelmis comalensis*). Results of the studies were not yet available when the revised Recovery Plan was published in 1996, but were expected to provide additional population and density estimates for the two species. In 1994, the FWS and cooperators initiated a similar study in the San Marcos system.

The 1996 San Marcos/Comal (Revised) Recovery Plan, which covers the fountain darter and four other listed species of the Upper San Marcos, notes that recovery goals for the habitats' species include the survival of these species in their native ecosystems; the development of an ecosystem approach using strategies to address both local, site-specific, and broad regional issues related to recovery; and the conservation of the integrity and function of the aquifer and spring-fed ecosystems that these species inhabit.

Delisting is considered unattainable for all five species (including the fountain darter) due to the potential for extinction from catastrophic events, especially from reduced water flows as a result of drought. Consequently, the revised Recovery Plan calls for the establishment and continued maintenance of refugia capability for all five species in case of a catastrophic event. Though delisting is considered unlikely, downlisting is considered a possibility for the fountain darter, possibly as early as 2025 if continuous progress is made.

Contact

U.S. Fish and Wildlife Service
P.O. Box 1306
Albuquerque, New Mexico 87103
http://southwest.fws.gov/

References

Schenck, J.R., and B.G. Whiteside. 1976. "Distribution, Habitat Preference and Population Size Estimate of *Etheostoma fonticola*." *Copeia* 1976:697-703.

U.S. Fish and Wildlife Service. 1980. "Determination of the Fountain Darter (*Etheostoma fonticola*) as Endangered." *Federal Register* 45:47355-47364.

U.S. Fish and Wildlife Service. 1984. "San Marcos River Recovery Plan." U.S. Fish and Wildlife Service, Albuquerque.

U.S. Fish and Wildlife Service. 1996. "San Marcos and Comal Springs and Associated Aquatic Ecosystems (Revised) Recovery Plan." U.S. Fish and Wildlife Service, Albuquerque.

Niangua Darter

Etheostoma nianguae

Status	Threatened
Listed	June 12, 1985
Family	Percidae (Perch)
Description	Slender fish with a long head that tapers into a slender, pointed snout; its basic color is yellowish-olive with seven or eight dark saddle bars on its back, and orange spots scattered on the upper sides.
Habitat	Shallow pools with silt-free bottoms.
Food	Aquatic insects.
Reproduction	Spawns in the spring.
Threats	Reservoir construction; stream channelization.
Range	Missouri

Description

The slender Niangua darter, *Etheostoma nianguae*, is a large, long (3-4 in, 7.5-10 cm) slender fish with a long head that tapers into a slender, pointed snout. Its basic color is yellowish-olive with seven or eight dark saddle bars on its back, and orange spots scattered on the upper sides. A series of U-shaped greenish blotches alternate with orange bars along the mid-side, and two small jet black spots at the base of the caudal fin. Breeding males exhibit an orange-red belly and a series of iridescent blue-green bars along the sides.

Behavior

The Niangua darter spawns in spring in swift currents over gravel bottoms. Breeding males (both males and females are sexually mature at one year of age) precede females to the spawning riffles to await their arrival. Encounters between the mating fish begin with head-bobbing by the female, followed by threat displays that include erection of the dorsal fin; encounters between males include a change in color patterns that heightens the contrast between the light background and darker markings, especially the saddle bar behind the pectoral fin.

Spawning occurs as the female lies buried in the gravel where she deposits eggs, with the male above. Most Niangua darters live to two years of age, although some survive to four.

The Niangua darter feeds almost exclusively on aquatic insects. Altough nine species of darters occur in association with the Niangua darter, competition for food is probably minimized because of different feeding strategies. The Niangua darter obtains its food by probing crevices with its slender snout.

Habitat

The species inhabits clear, medium-sized streams that run off hilly areas underlain by chert and dolomite. It is usually found in the margins of shallow pools with silt-free, gravel, or rocky bottoms, and occasionally boulders or bedrock. The greatest concentration of fish occurred in stream areas that had thick growths of water willow although it does not seem to have any dependence upon this vegetation.

Distribution

The Niangua darter is part of a diverse fish fauna, encompassing 107 species in the Osage basin. It is

William Roston

known only from a few tributaries of the Osage River in Missouri, where eight populations along 128 mi (205 km) of the river basin were reported in the early 1970s. These populations were in the Maries River and Lower Maries Creek (Osage County); Big Tavern Creek and upper Little Tavern Creek, Barren Fork, and Brushy Fork (Miller County); Niangua River and Greasy Creek (Dallas County); Little Niangua River, Starks Creek, Thomas Creek, and Cahoochie Creek (Camden, Hickory, and Dallas counties); Little Pomme de Terre River (Benton County); Pomme de Terre River (Green and Webster counties); Brush Creek (Cedar and St. Clair counties); and the North Dry Sac River (Polk County).

The Niangua darter population is believed to have declined at most Missouri sites in recent years. An intensive on-site habitat analysis concluded that the species is rare, localized in occurrence, and vulnerable to extinction.

Threats

Construction of the Truman Reservoir formed a barrier to the Niangua darter's movement between tributary streams, fragmenting its range. Migration between these tributary streams is considered important to the long-term survival of the species.

Highway and bridge construction projects frequently straighten and widen stream channels, and landowners channel streams to control local flooding. These practices have led to pervasive sedimentation and silt pollution throughout this darter's range. In addition to stream channelization, the practice of removing woody vegetation from stream banks causes increased erosion, changes in the character of the stream substrate, elimination of pools, and the alteration of stream flow, all of which seriously disrupt the stream ecosystem.

Spotted bass and rock bass were introduced into the Osage basin before 1940 and are now widely distributed. Diffusion of seven species of predatory fishes from reservoirs into tributary streams inhabited by the Niangua darter could further reduce the population.

Conservation and Recovery

Habitat considered critical for the darter's survival has been designated for portions of Camden, Cedar, Dallas, Greene, Hickory, Miller, and St. Clair Counties, Missouri. It encompasses some 90 mi (145 km) of inhabited stream and a 50-ft (15-m) streambank buffer zone.

The Recovery Plan calls for the long-term protection of riparian habitat, including land protection and aquisition; reducing adversely agricultural practices and stream bank modification; controlling the use of pesticides and herbicides; preventing channelization; eliminating passage barriers or providing fish passage devices; controlling the infiltration of predator fish; and reintroducing wild and captive fish to the habitat.

Contact

Regional Office of Endangered Species
U.S. Fish and Wildlife Service
Federal Building
Fort Snelling, Minnesota 55111
http://midwest.fws.gov/

References

Missouri Department of Conservation. 1974. "Rare and Endangered Species of Missouri." Pamphlet. Missouri Department of Conservation, Jefferson City.

Pflieger, W. L. 1971. "A Distributional Study of Missouri Fishes." *Museum of Natural History, University of Kansas Publications* 20(3):229-570.

Pflieger, W. L. 1975. "The Fishes of Missouri." Missouri Department of Conservation, Jefferson City.

Pflieger, W. L. 1978. "Distribution, Status, and Life History of the Niangua Darter, *Etheostoma nianguae.*" Aquatic Series No. 16. Missouri Department of Conservation, Jefferson City.

U.S. Fish and Wildlife Service. 1989. "Recovery Plan for the Niangua Darter." U.S. Fish and Wildlife Service, Twin Cities.

Watercress Darter

Etheostoma nuchale

Status	Endangered
Listed	October 13, 1970
Family	Percidae (Perch)
Description	Small darter; breeding males are blue with a red-orange belly.
Habitat	Deep, slow moving backwaters of springs.
Food	Insects, crustaceans, and snails.
Reproduction	Eggs are deposited in submerged vegetation.
Threats	Limited distribution, urbanization, water pollution.
Range	Alabama

Description

The watercress darter, *Etheostoma nuchale*, is a small, robust fish growing to a maximum length of 2 in (5 cm). Breeding males are blue above, red-orange below, and have blue and red-orange fins.

The spiny dorsal fin has an outer margin of blue followed by bands of red, blue, and red. This pattern is well-developed in breeding males, faint in females. The soft dorsal fin of males displays the same pattern, while the anal, basal portion of the caudal, and the paired fins are blue. In females, the soft dorsal, anal, caudal, and paired fins are speckled with small brown spots.

Behavior

This darter feeds on aquatic insects, crustaceans, and snails. Little is known about its behavior.

Males exhibit courtship behavior to all females encountered, and non-receptive females leave the area when approached by males. The courting male stays close to the receptive female and may rest his head on her back or neck, touch sides, or display his fins. Other males in the area try to displace the courting male. Larger males are generally successful. Eggs are deposited in submerged vegetation.

Habitat

The watercress darter inhabits deep, slow-moving backwaters of spring outflows. These areas support dense aquatic vegetation and particularly watercress (*Nasturtium officinale*), which attracts a large community of aquatic insects, the darter's principal food.

Distribution

The species was discovered in 1964 at Glenn Springs near Bessemer, Alabama. Because of its recent discovery, the historic range of the watercress darter is unknown.

The watercress darter has been found in three springs in Jefferson County, Alabama: Glenn Springs and Thomas' Spring in Bessemer, and Roebuck Springs in Birmingham. The species also occurs in Tapawingo Springs in Jefferson County, where it was successfully transplanted in 1988. Reproduction has since taken place, indicating that this new population introduction was a success. A similar transplantation was undertaken at Avondale Springs, also in Jefferson County, although no evidence of reproduction had been found by 1993. While not conclusive, limited population survey results indicate an apparent downward trend for all

Watercress Darter, photograph by Roger W. Barbour. Reproduced by permission.

of the naturally occurring populations, though the transplanted population seems to be doing well.

Threats

The greatest threats to this species appear to be habitat alteration and pollution. The growth of the Birmingham-Bessemer metropolitan area has resulted in extensive residential construction (notably apartment complexes and shopping malls) and the paving of large areas for streets and parking lots. The springs supporting the watercress darter depend on rainfall for recharging, much of which has now been diverted into drains and gutters. As a result, water levels in the springs tend to fluctuate widely.

Roebuck Spring, which had been a source for local drinking water, was condemned in the 1970s because of a level of bacteria too numerous to count. This contamination was possibly caused by seepage from nearby residential septic tanks. Darters in the spring suffer from gas bubble disease, which is caused by high levels of sewage-derived nitrogen in the water. Nitrogen gas builds up in the body of the fish, eventually killing it. This contamination of the Roebuck Springs habitat basin and its run has been identified along with an alarming decline in the watercress darter at the site. Concerned by the decline, in 1991 the U. S. Fish and Wildlife Service (FWS) conducted a contaminant investigation, and analysis of sediment and snail samples reported high levels of polycyclic aromatic hydrocarbons, a highly toxic substance to the fish.

The introduction of alien fish to the habitat has also affected the watercress darter populations. Grass carp were introduced into Thomas' Spring and by 1977 had removed all vegetation up to the shoreline and eliminated the natural darter population.

Conservation and Recovery

In 1980 the FWS purchased Thomas' Spring and 7 acres (2.8 hectares) of surrounding land for the

Watercress Darter National Wildlife Refuge, which is administered as part of the Wheeler National Wildlife Refuge. The grass carp were removed, the spring revegetated, and the watercress darter reintroduced from the Glenn Springs population. An additional pond has been built at the refuge and three small dams at Glenn Springs should restore the darter's habitat there. The owner of Glenn Springs signed an agreement allowing habitat management and conservation, and in 1988, 100 watercress darters were transplanted from Thomas' Spring into the newly constructed pond.

Successful recovery efforts include the January 1988 transplantation of 200 fish to Tapawingo Springs and Avondale Springs, both in Jefferson County. Reproduction has since occurred repeatedly in Tapawingo Springs, although by 1993, no watercress darters had been collected at Avondale Springs (collecting conditions are difficult at that site, however).

The 1993 recovery plan revision for the species notes that recovery goals are first reclassification (from Endangered to Threatened) and then delisting altogether. The species would be considered for reclassification when long-term protection has been achieved for the three known naturally occurring populations and one of the additional populations within the historic range, and when there are five years of data indicating that a minimum of four populations are viable. To delist the species, the FWS requires five years of data documenting the existence of six viable populations (each in separate discrete recharge areas) and the proven long-term protection of the discrete recharge area for each viable population.

To achieve these goals, the 1993 plan calls for a number of activities, including the implementation of actions to determine the genetic structure of the various populations; the correction of water quality and quantity problems; the transplantation of watercress darters to additional sites, augmenting the naturally occurring populations and protecting genetic diversity; and determination of the discrete recharge area for each viable population. The plan also calls for the achievement of long-term protection of the recharge area and the immediate habitat from threats to six viable populations.

Contact

Regional Office of Endangered Species
U.S. Fish and Wildlife Service
1875 Century Blvd., Suite 200
Atlanta, Georgia 30345
http://southeast.fws.gov/

References

Howell, W. M., and R. D. Caldwell. 1965. "*Etheostoma (Oligocephalus) nuchale*, a New Darter from a Limestone Spring in Alabama." *Tulane Studies in Zoology* 12 (4):101-108.

U.S. Fish and Wildlife Service. 1984. "Recovery Plan for the Watercress Darter (*Etheostoma nuchale*)." U.S. Fish and Wildlife Service, Atlanta.

U.S. Fish and Wildlife Service. 1993. "Revised Recovery Plan for the Watercress Darter (*Etheostoma nuchale*)." U.S. Fish and Wildlife Service, Atlanta.

Okaloosa Darter

Etheostoma okaloosae

Status	Endangered
Listed	June 4, 1973
Family	Percidae (Perch)
Description	Light-brown darter with dark olive stripes.
Habitat	Shallow streams of swift current.
Food	Insects and plant matter.
Reproduction	Spawning in April and May.
Threats	Road and dam construction, siltation, competition with other darters.
Range	Florida

Description

The Okaloosa darter, *Etheostoma okaloosae*, is a small fish with a divided dorsal fin, a rounded tail, and a slightly arched lateral line. This perch-like species' scales have darkly pigmented centers, giving an impression of long rows of spots. The cheek, throat, and chin are brown to yellowish brown with an olive-green cast ventrally and posteriorly. Along both sides there are usually a row of dark blotches. The first dorsal fin has an orange-red stripe near the outer margin and the tail itself usually has vertical bands of alternating light and reddish brown. The fish ranges from 3-4 in (7.5-10 cm) long. Fins are large and transparent.

Behavior

The Okaloosa darter feeds on aquatic insects and plant matter. Its primary spawning period is generally in late April or early May. The eggs are large in comparison to other Percidae. Males first establish territories, and females that enter the territories are mated. There does not seem to be a specified number of females for which males will spawn.

Habitat

The Okaloosa darter is an opportunistic species, in that it inhabits a variety of habitats within streams from sluggish, heavily vegetated areas to swift-flowing stretches over a sandy bottom. It seems to be most numerous in portions of the streams where currents are moderately swift and the depth of water is no more than 5 ft (1.5 m). Water temperatures range between 45 and 75°F (7 and 24°C). Much of the watershed drains pine and scrub oak, sand-hill habitat.

Distribution

The Okaloosa darter was first described in the 1940s from specimens taken from Little Rocky Creek in Okaloosa County. It is considered endemic to six Choctawhatchee Bay tributaries in Okaloosa and Walton counties in the Florida Panhandle. This watershed comprises nearly 113,000 acres (43,730 hectares), most of which falls within Eglin Air Force Base. Only about 12,000 acres (4,860 hectares) are privately owned.

This darter is found along about 190 mi (305 kilometers) of six stream systems flowing from Eglin Air Force Base through or near the cities of Niceville and Valparaiso into Boggy and Rocky Bayous on Choctawhatchee Bay, in Okaloosa and Walton counties, Florida. The habitat involves the main stems and tributaries of Tom's, East Turkey, Mill, Swift, and Rocky Creeks.

The U. S. Fish and Wildlife Service (FWS) has determined that the population has stabilized and is no longer in serious decline, according to a 1997 Re-

Okaloosa Darter, photograph by Roger W. Barbour. Reproduced by permission.

vised Draft Recovery Plan. The major responsibility for recovery of this species is with Eglin Air Force Base, which manages most of its known habitat.

Threats

The Okaloosa darter population has declined because of deterioration and loss of habitat, caused by road and dam construction, and siltation from land clearing. In addition, this species has suffered in competition with the more common brown darter, which has moved into headwaters formerly occupied exclusively by the Okaloosa darter.

Conservation and Recovery

Personnel from Eglin Air Force Base, the Florida Game and Freshwater Fish Commission, the Alabama Biological Survey, Florida State University, and the FWS collaborated on production of the 1981 Recovery Plan for the Okaloosa darter, which identified four primary recovery goals: to determine bi-

ological characteristics; protect extant populations and habitats; increase population sizes; and reestablish the species throughout its former range. In 1997, that plan was revised to reflect the success of the original plan: Studies recommended in the 1981 Recovery Plan have been completed, and Eglin Air Force Base is implementing habitat conservation measures, and plans to implement others.

Okaloosa darter populations have apparently stabilized. Downlisting this species from endangered to threatened could be considered in 2001 if Okaloosa darter populations in all six inhabited stream systems remain stable or increase, and if effective interagency agreements are established to protect the quality and quantity of water in these streams. Complete delisting may be considered when populations in all stream systems remain stable or increase for 20 years, and when effective and apparently permanent cooperative agreements to protect stream water quantity and quality have functioned for several years.

Contact

Regional Office of Endangered Species
U.S. Fish and Wildlife Service
1875 Century Blvd., Suite 200
Atlanta, Georgia 30345
http://southeast.fws.gov/

Reference

Crews, R. C. 1976. "Aquatic Baseline Survey on Selected Test Areas on Eglin Air Force Base Reservation, Florida." Report No. AFATL-TR-76-4. Eglin Air Force Base.

Duskytail Darter

Etheostoma percnurum

Status	Endangered
Listed	April 27, 1993
Family	Percidae (Perch)
Description	Darter 2.5 in (6.35 cm) in length and straw to olive colored.
Habitat	Gently flowing shallow pools and eddy areas of large creeks and moderately large rivers.
Food	Insects and vegetation.
Reproduction	Clutch of 23-150 eggs.
Threats	Siltation and other pollution from poor land use practices and coal mining.
Range	Tennessee, Virginia

Description

This slender bodied, 2.5-in (6.35-cm) fish has a straw to olivaceous colored body, the top of the head is medium to dark gray, and the belly is dingy white to pale gray. It has 10-15 long dark vertical bars on the sides of its body, 38-48 (usually 40-45) lateral scales, and 17-20 (usually 18-19) dorsal spines and rays. It is difficult to determine the sex of non-breeding individuals in the field. However, during the breeding season, the males become very distinctive. The head becomes dark and swollen, and the humeral spot and lateral vertical bars intensify. The first dorsal saddle and vertical bar form a particularly intense dark yoke. A dark border of melanophore develops along the pectoral and anal fin margins, and the anal fin whitens proximally. Brilliant gold, fleshy knobs develop on the tips of the dorsal fin spines and are conspicuous in contrast to the clear medial and dark basal portions of the fin membrane.

Behavior

The duskytail is primarily an insectivore. The youngest individuals consume microcrustaceans, chironomid larvae, and sometimes large quantities of heptageniid nymphs. Larger individuals are also mainly benthic insectivores, but they generally feed on larger prey items, such chironomid larvae,

ephemeropteran nymphs, microcrustaceans, and trichopteran larvae. Heptageniids were the dominant food item in the three largest duskytail size classes examined, and large duskytails sometimes feed on fish eggs. Because heptageniids occupy the interstices between rocks, duskytails may feed on the undersides of rocks. In the Little River, the spawning season occurs from late April or early May through June. In Copper Creek, the earliest spawning was observed as early as April 6 but most spawning occurs in May. Water temperatures were between 63.5 and 75°F (17.5 and 23.9°C). In the Little River, spawning occurs within the same habitat that the species occupies during the rest of the year. Many apparently breeding adults have been observed in a gravel/rubble run with moderate current in Copper Creek. In Citico Creek, nests and nest-guarding males have been found beneath slab rocks in the margins of pool areas, and in relatively swift shallow water in run areas, as long as appropriately sized slab rocks were available for nest cover.

Prior to the spawning act, the male chooses and cleans a spawning site under a rock. The male chases the female into the nest cavity, both fish invert their bodies, and the eggs are deposited individually into an egg cluster on the underside of the nest rock. Males stay at the nest site, guard the eggs, and may spawn with multiple females. The result

Duskytail Darter, photograph. U. S. Fish and Wildlife Service. Reproduced by permission.

is a clutch of 23-150 eggs. After several days, to allow for more ova to mature, the female can spawn with other males. Duskytail darters can spawn as one-year olds. About half of the individuals spawn at one year of age and do not survive to spawn again. The individuals that survive to spawn as two-year olds die shortly after spawning, and a very small percentage of the Little River population survived to age three.

Habitat

The duskytail darter inhabits gently flowing shallow pools and eddy areas of large creeks and moderately large rivers in the Tennessee and Cumberland River systems.

This species' distribution overlaps the Oak-Hickory ecosystem and Nashville basin. The elevation is about 6,400 ft (1,950 m). Most of the outer part of the basin is deeply dissected and consists of steep slopes between narrow rolling ridgetops and narrow valleys. The inner part of the basin is pre-

dominantly undulating and rolling. The average annual precipitation is about 35-45 in (89-114 cm). The soils of this ecosystem are varied, have a thermic temperature regime, an udic moisture regime, and a clay subsoil.

The duskytail inhabits the edges of gently flowing shallow pools, eddy areas, and slow runs in usually clear water of large creeks and moderately large rivers. Snorkel observations in Citico Creek and in the Little River, Copper Creek, and the Big South Fork of the Cumberland River indicate that they are apparently very discriminatory about preferred microhabitat type, being found over heterogeneous mixtures of rock sizes from pea gravel, rubble/cobble, slab-rock, and boulder substrates. The water is shallow, 4-30 in (10-76 cm) deep, with slow runs around edges of pools. Substrates are heterogeneous, with a wide range of rock sizes from pea gravel to cobble, slabrock, and boulders.

This apparent preference for a mixture of various substrate sizes often results in patchy distributions.

There may be locally dense clumps of individuals within a relatively short distance, and then long stretches can be surveyed without observing a single specimen. Adult duskytail darters have been observed only beneath the cover of rocks, except when moving between rocks. Young duskytails are highly territorial when cover rocks are scarce, but this behavior is greatly reduced when enough rocks of various sizes are available to provide cover for all individuals.

Duskytails are often found associated with detritus and are sometimes found on slightly silted substrates, but are rarely found in heavily silted areas, or in areas where silt does not fill or obscure the spaces between the cover rocks.

Distribution

Historically, this species has been collected from seven stream reaches; the duskytail darter is believed extirpated from Abrams Creek, Blount County, Tennessee, and South Fork Holston River, Sullivan County, Tennessee.

The duskytail darter is known from five reaches of the Tennessee and Cumberland River systems. The Little River population inhabits about 9 river mi (14.5 km). This population is potentially threatened by water withdrawal and increasing residential and commercial development in the watershed. In Citico Creek this species is affected by streamside habitat destruction.

This darter inhabits about 17 river mi (27.4 km) of Copper Creek and may comprise the largest population. This population is currently threatened by siltation, riparian erosion, and agricultural pollution.

The duskytail darter has been taken from one site on the Big South Fork of the Cumberland River. This particular population is faced with the threat of runoff as a result of coal mine activities in the upper watershed above Big South Fork National Recreational Area.

In the Little River, the duskytail darter population has been documented from two localities that are about 9 river mi (14.5 km) apart. Despite yearly intensive sampling, there have been very few collections of the species from the upstream Little River localities since their discovery there in the 1970s. The relative abundance in the upper reaches is much less than at the lower site in the Little River. In the Little River, the stronghold for the species may be limited to a short river reach just upstream

from the backwaters of the Fort Loudon Reservoir. Estimates were that this area was inhabited by more than 1,000 adult duskytail darters in the fall of 1993, but in other formerly occupied habitat, an extensive snorkel survey found no duskytails. The area was heavily silted, and extensive algal growth was noted in the rocky area normally inhabited by these darters. This degradation apparently resulted when flow was restricted by a logjam at a bridge: this allowed silt to settle in the slower current sections of the duskytail darter's preferred habitat.

Threats

Generally this species of *Etheostoma* is threatened by water quality degradation as a result of siltation and other pollution from poor land use practices, coal mining, and waste discharge.

The Tennessee and Cumberland Rivers are renowned as two of the most severely altered riverine systems due to many anthropogenic activities. Most of the main stems of both rivers and many tributaries are impounded; impoundments usually alter downstream aquatic habitats. In addition, there has been a loss of the riverine habitat.

Siltation and toxic runoff have been the result of coal mining activities which unavoidably have adversely affected many reaches. Runoff from urban areas has also degraded water and substrate quality. The aquatic faunal diversity has declined due to this habitat destruction.

Due to the limited distribution of this species, a stochastic event such as an accidental toxic chemical spill could cause extirpation. As the populations are separated by impoundments, natural recolonization of an extirpated population would be virtually impossible.

Conservation and Recovery

The duskytail population in the Big South Fork of the Cumberland River is within the National Park Service's jurisdiction, and the populations in the Little River and Citico Creek occur within, but mostly below, lands controlled by the National Park Service and U.S. Forest Service, respectively. These federal agencies are aware of these populations and have taken proactive measures to protect them. Populations with a federal connection have greater opportunities for protection under existing laws than the population in Copper Creek, which is totally on private lands.

Apparently, the duskytail darter has been able to withstand some degree of habitat degradation. However, some habitat has been so severely altered that the species is extirpated or the population is reduced in size and vigor. Knowledge of the species' specific microhabitat requirements and the ecological associations for each population is needed in order to focus management and recovery efforts on the specific problems within the species' habitat.

Contacts

Regional Office of Endangered Species
U. S. Fish and Wildlife Service
1875 Century Blvd., Suite 200
Atlanta, Georgia 30345
http://southeast.fws.gov/

Regional Office of Endangered Species
U. S. Fish and Wildlife Service
300 Westgate Center Dr.
Hadley, Massachusetts 01035
http://northeast.fws.gov/

References

U.S. Fish and Wildlife Service. April 27, 1993. "Determination of Endangered Status for the Duskytail Darter, Palezone Shiner and Pygmy Madtom." *Federal Register* 58(79):25758-25763.

U. S. Fish and Wildlife Service. March 30, 1994. "Recovery Plan for the Duskytail Darter." U.S. Fish and Wildlife Service, Atlanta, 25 pp.

Bayou Darter

Etheostoma rubrum

Status	Threatened
Listed	September 25, 1975
Family	Percidae (Perch)
Description	Brownish yellow darter with russet markings.
Habitat	Gravel bottoms in shallow flowing waters.
Food	Insects (mayfly larvae) and plant matter.
Reproduction	Spawns in the spring.
Threats	Limited range and habitat.
Range	Mississippi

Description

Only about 1.9 in (5 cm) long at maturity, the bayou darter, *Etheostoma rubrum*, displays russet markings on a field of dusky yellow. The back is a darker brownish yellow. Both males and females have a prominent double spot on the tail fin and a dark bar under the eyes. Males are decidedly larger than females.

The bayou darter is the second-smallest species in the subgenus *Nothonotus*, the smallest being the Tippecanoe darter (*E. tippecanoe*) found in the Ohio River system. The bayou darter is closely related to the yellow cheek darter (*E. moorei*) found in the Devil's Fork and Little Red River of Arkansas' White River system.

Behavior

The bayou darter spawns in mid-summer when it is about two years old, and probably lives three years. Darter fry hatch at the same time that mayfly larvae emerge in the same riffle habitat, and darter minnows are thought to feed almost exclusively on mayfly larvae. Adults feed on insects, small crustaceans, and plant matter.

Habitat

The watershed, where this darter is found, arises in coastal hills with elevations around 450 ft (137

m). From their sources, the creeks fall in steps to the coastal plain, where water flow has eroded through deposits of gravel, interspersed with sand. This has resulted in numerous gravel or sandstone riffles of moderate to swift current, which seem to be preferred by the bayou darter. The water in these riffles is typically only about 6 in (15 cm) deep.

Distribution

The bayou darter was first described in 1966 from specimens collected at Mississippi Highway 18 Bayou Pierre crossing. This species is probably endemic to the Bayou Pierre and its five major tributaries, a watershed that drains about 965 sq mi (2,500 sq km) of western Mississippi. The source of Bayou Pierre is a small seep near Brookhaven in Lincoln County.

The bayou darter has been found in Bayou Pierre and three of its tributaries (White Oak Creek, Foster Creek, and Turkey Creek). Range of the bayou darter seems to be limited upstream by waterfalls and downstream by the gradual loss of suitable riffle habitat. The largest concentration of bayou darters is in sections of Bayou Pierre and Foster Creek north of state highway 548 in Copiah County. Researchers consider the population to be limited but also report that they have not observed any significant decline in numbers in recent years. As of 1990, the U. S. Fish and Wildlife Service (FWS) con-

sidered the population stabilized, and the potential for recovery is good.

Threats

The major limitation on bayou darter numbers is its dependence on its specialized habitat—sand and gravel riffles. Some sand and gravel mining already occurs in the area, directly threatening the bayou darter's habitat. Agriculture is widespread in the region, particularly along portions of Turkey Creek and lower Bayou Pierre. In some places, streambank vegetation has been cleared, causing severe erosion and siltation. Nearby petroleum exploration may also pose some threat to water quality.

Conservation and Recovery

In the 1970s the Soil Conservation Service conceived the Bayou Pierre Watershed Project to dredge and straighten stream beds, build flood walls and dikes, and construct 24 dams to provide recreational pools. The project would have eliminated most of the bayou's habitat from the affected streams. After consultation with the FWS, the project's sponsors eliminated the dredging, channel work, and dams, and agreed to evaluate the effects of flood wall construction on downstream water quality. An agreement between the FWS and the Soil Conservation Service allowed construction of one dam on Turkey Creek above the Turkey Creek Falls.

The state of Mississippi has listed the darter as Endangered, providing it some protection from collection. It has been noted that clear-cutting along the stream banks could contribute to erosion and alter the water temperature. Timber companies operating in the area have been careful to provide buffer zones along streams, such as Bayou Pierre, as part of their stated policy of conserving riparian habitat.

In the 1990 revised Recovery Plan, the FWS included plans to implement a study on the fluvial geomorphic processes operating in Bayou Pierre. The species will be considered for delisting if recovery efforts are deemed successful, based on criteria that include a stable or increasing population (and habitat) over at least a 10-year period in Bayou Pierre and Foster Creek; evidence of the continued existence of the species in White Oak and Turkey Creeks; data on fluvial geomorphic processes operating in the Bayou Pierre system which supports the delisting of the species; an established continuing plan of periodic monitoring of population trends and habitat suitability; and continued protection of the darter's habitat. The 1990 revision listed the darter's population status as stable, and the FWS has given the species a recovery priority rating of 8C, which means the degree of threat to this species is moderate and the recovery potential is high.

Contact

Regional Office of Endangered Species
U.S. Fish and Wildlife Service
1875 Century Blvd., Suite 200
Atlanta, Georgia 30345
http://southeast.fws.gov/

References

Deacon, J. E., et al. 1979. "Fishes of North America: Endangered, Threatened, or of Special Concern." *Fisheries* 42:29-44.

U.S. Fish and Wildlife Service. 1983. "Bayou Darter Recovery Plan." U.S. Fish and Wildlife Service, Atlanta.

U.S. Fish and Wildlife Service. 1990. "Endangered and Threatened Species Recovery Program Report to Congress." U.S. Fish Wildlife Service, Washington, DC.

Cherokee Darter

Etheostoma scotti

Status	Threatened
Listed	December 20, 1994
Family	Percidae
Description	A small, white to pale yellow percid fish.
Habitat	Small to medium-sized, warm-water creeks with rocky bottoms.
Food	Aquatic invertebrates.
Reproduction	Lays eggs.
Threats	Habitat loss by impoundments, and degradation by siltation and chemical pollution.
Range	Georgia

Description

A small percid fish, the *Etheostoma (Ulocentra) scotti* (Cherokee darter), is subcylindrical in shape, and has a relatively blunt snout with a subterminal mouth. The body shade is white to pale yellow. The side of adults is pigmented with usually eight small dark olive-black blotches that develop into vertically elongate, slightly oblique bars in breeding adults, especially in males. The back usually has eight small dark saddles and intervening pale areas. The Cherokee darter has proven to be distinct from the Coosa darter, *E. coosae*, a species with which it was previously confused, by peak nuptial males never having five discrete color bands in the spinous dorsal fin.

Behavior

The Cherokee darter feeds on or near the stream bottom on small aquatic invertebrates. It feeds in flowing water, and is intolerant of non-flowing conditions.

Habitat

Cherokee darters inhabit small to medium-size warm-water creeks of moderate gradient, with predominately rocky bottoms. It is usually found in shallow water in sections of reduced current, typically in runs above and below riffles and at the ecotones of riffles and backwaters. The Cherokee darter is associated with large gravel, cobble, and small boulder substrates, and is uncommonly or rarely found over bedrock, fine gravel, or sand. It is most abundant in stream sections with relatively clear water and clean substrates (little silt deposition). The Cherokee darter is intolerant of heavy to moderate silt deposition. The Cherokee darter, like other members of the subgenus *Ulocentra*, is intolerant of impoundment.

Distribution

The Cherokee darter is endemic to the Etowah River system in north Georgia, where it is primarily restricted to streams draining the Piedmont physiographic province, and to a lesser extent, the Blue Ridge physiographic province. The Cherokee darter occurs in about 20 small to moderately large tributary systems of the middle and upper Etowah River system. However, only a few sites contain healthy populations of this species. The largest populations occur in northern tributaries upstream of Allatoona Reservoir. Populations are smaller in tributaries draining the southern portion of the system. The southern tributary systems tend to drain areas exhibiting less relief and are on the average much more degraded. Cherokee darter populations are

Cherokee Darter, photograph by Noel M. Burkhead. Reproduced by permission.

found primarily above Allatoona Reservoir. Downstream of Allatoona Dam, populations are restricted to two tributary systems. The Cherokee darter exhibits a disjunct and discontinuous distribution pattern indicating fragmentation and isolation of populations. The placement of Allatoona Reservoir in the middle Etowah River system has caused much of the fragmentation of this species' populations. One major tributary system in the upper Etowah system, Amicalola Creek, apparently naturally lacks populations of Cherokee darters, but contains a relatively close relative and also a narrow endemic, the holiday darter, *E. brevirostrum*. The Cherokee darter is allopatric (i.e., the ranges of the species do not overlap) with the other two *Ulocentra* species in the watershed, the holiday darter and Coosa darter.

Threats

The Cherokee darter is known from about 20 tributary systems of the Etowah River, but only a few sites have healthy populations. This rare fish

has suffered habitat destruction caused by the construction of impoundments, and degradation by siltation caused by soil erosion in the watershed, agricultural runoff, discharges of sewage and other wastes, other pollutants, and increased urbanization. These factors continue to affect the Cherokee darter and its habitat. It now occurs in relatively small, fragmented populations.

Conservation and Recovery

The critical habitat supporting the surviving populations of the Cherokee darter must be protected against the construction of impoundments and other degrading influences. The privately owned land in watersheds of streams supporting the largest populations should be acquired and designated as ecological reserves, or conservation easements negotiated with the landowners. Threatening activities in the watersheds, such as road construction, timber harvesting, and the dumping of chemicals, sewage, or other pollutants must be strictly managed to prevent risks to the rare Cherokee darter. Its populations should be monitored, and research undertaken into its biology and habitat needs.

Contacts

U.S. Fish and Wildlife Service
Jacksonville Ecological Services Office
6620 Southpoint Drive South, Suite 310
Jacksonville, Florida, 32216
Telephone: (904) 232-2580
Fax: (904) 232-2404

U. S. Fish and Wildlife Service
Regional Office, Division of Endangered Species
1875 Century Blvd., Suite 200
Atlanta, Georgia 30345
http://southeast.fws.gov/

Reference

U.S. Fish and Wildlife Service. 20 Dec 1994. "Endangered and Threatened Wildlife and Plants; Determination of Threatened Status for the Cherokee Darter and Endangered Status for the Etowah Darter." *Federal Register* (59).

Maryland Darter

Etheostoma sellare

Status	Endangered
Listed	March 11, 1967
Family	Percidae (Perch)
Description	Silvery darter with dark saddles across the back.
Habitat	Riffle areas in slow-moving streams.
Food	Insects, snails, some plant matter.
Reproduction	Spawns in April or May.
Threats	Dam construction, degradation of water quality.
Range	Maryland

Description

The silvery Maryland darter, *Etheostoma sellare*, reaches a maximum length of about 2.8 in (7 cm). It can be distinguished from closely related darters by four dark saddles across its back and a small dark spot behind the lower rear margin of its eye. The saddles may be poorly developed in juveniles and appear as a series of X-shaped blotches on the sides. The largest captured specimen may have been four years old.

Behavior

The Maryland darter is believed to spawn in late April or early May. Reproduction is probably similar to other members of its genus, which prefer riffle areas over a gravel substrate for spawning. The darter feeds on snails, insect larvae, aquatic insects, and some plant matter.

Habitat

Most specimens have been found in shallow riffle areas over a gravel or silt bottom in a single drainage system in Maryland. Normal flow velocities for streams in this basin are slight, scarcely maintaining a flow under drought conditions. Rooted aquatic plants are riverweed and water moss.

Distribution

The Maryland darter was originally described in 1913 from specimens collected in Swan Creek adjacent to Gasheys Run near Aberdeen, Maryland. It is believed to have once been more abundant in the lower Susquehanna River drainage.

The Maryland darter has been found only in the lower Susquehanna River basin near Aberdeen and Havre de Grace, Maryland, in Deer Creek, Swan Creek, and Gasheys Run. Biologists believe that the Deer Creek population may currently be the only viable population. Very few recent sightings of this species have been made. Field surveys at various locations in the early 1980s found only from one to 10 individuals at any location and no individuals have been observed since 1988.

Threats

The Maryland darter's range was reduced when the Susquehanna River was dammed in the twentieth century, causing extensive siltation, pollution, and water withdrawals of darter habitat. Associated threats are oxygen reduction and alteration of water temperature. It is probable that the lack of suitable habitat prevents the darter from breeding in Gasheys Run and that darters found there are stragglers from the Deer Creek population. Populations

Maryland Darter, photograph by Roger W. Barbour. Reproduced by permission.

in Deer Creek are potentially threatened by high turbidity caused by erosion and siltation; impoundments; insecticide, herbicide, and fertilizer runoff; and sewage plant malfunction resulting in flooding or untreated sewage being introduced into the stream.

Conservation and Recovery

The U. S. Fish and Wildlife Service has designated Critical Habitat for the Maryland darter to include: the Deer Creek main channel from Elbow Branch to the Susquehanna River; and Gasheys Run main channel from the Penn Central Railroad crossing south to Swan Creek. The most immediate threats to the Maryland darter are runoff into Deer Creek containing excessive nutrients or wastes and the possible construction of other dams and impoundments that would increase water turbidity. The Recovery Plan calls for monitoring water samples of the Susquehanna River drainage and upper Chesapeake Bay tributaries; restricting collection permits; establishing a state-owned refuge at the Deer Creek rifle; controlling water flows and water quality; and reducing sedimentation from road maintenance, construction, and agricultural pollution.

Contact

U.S. Fish and Wildlife Service
Regional Office, Division of Endangered Species
300 Westgate Center Dr.
Hadley, Massachusetts 01035
http://northeast.fws.gov/

References

Collette, B. B., and L. W. Knapp. 1966. "Catalog of Type Specimens of the Darters (Pisces, Percidae, Etheostomatini)." *Proceedings of the U.S. Natural History Museum* 119(3550):1-88.

Knapp, L. 1976. "Redescription, Relationships and Status of the Endangered Maryland Darter, *Etheostoma sellare* (Radcliffe and Welsh)." *Proceedings of the Biological Society of Washington* 89(6):99-117.

U. S. Fish and Wildlife Service. 1985. "Revised Maryland Darter Recovery Plan." U.S. Fish and Wildlife Service, Newton Corner, Massachusetts.

Boulder Darter

Etheostoma wapiti

Status	Endangered
Listed	September 1, 1988
Family	Percidae (Perch)
Description	Olive to gray darter with dark patches below and behind the eye.
Habitat	Deep, fast-moving water over boulder substrate.
Food	Probably immature aquatic insects.
Reproduction	Undescribed.
Threats	Dam construction.
Range	Alabama, Tennessee

Description

The boulder darter, *Etheostoma wapiti*, also known as the Elk River darter, is an olive to gray fish, reaching a maximum length of 3 in (7.6 cm). Females are generally lighter, but both sexes have dark patches below and behind the eye. The boulder darter lacks the red spots characteristic of closely related species. The species has also been classified in the genus *Nothonotus*.

Behavior

Less than 50 specimens of the boulder darter have ever been collected. Because of this rarity, nothing is known of its life history or breeding biology. It is probably a sight feeder of immature aquatic insects.

Habitat

The preferred habitat of the boulder darter is deep, fast-moving water over boulder and slab rock bottoms.

Distribution

This darter has been found in the Elk River from Fayetteville (Lincoln County, Tennessee) downstream through Giles County into Limestone County, Alabama. Specimens have also been col-lected from three Elk River tributaries: Indian and Richland creeks (Giles County, Tennessee) and Shoal Creek (Lauderdale County, Alabama). Biologists believe that the species once inhabited the southern bend of the Tennessee River, near its confluence with the Elk River.

The boulder darter is now restricted to about 23 mi (43 km) of the Elk River (Giles County, Tennessee, and Limestone County, Alabama) and 2 mi (3 km) of Indian and Richland creeks (Giles County, Tennessee). Within this restricted range, the darter is further limited by its specific habitat requirements.

Threats

The spotty occurrence of the boulder darter in the Elk River results in part from the rarity of its preferred habitat. As its common name suggests, the boulder darter lives among boulders. However, it is not found among boulders anywhere in the river bed; the location of the boulders is important. The boulders must occur in water 2-4 ft (0.6-1.2 m) in depth. Also, the boulders must occur in flowing water that is not too swift, such as in riffles or rapids, and not too slow, as in slightly flowing pools.

Most of the Elk River between the reaches affected by impoundment consists of long, heavily silted pools that have little or no boulder substrate. The relatively few riffles and runs are predominately floored with gravel and rubble substrates. At

Etheostoma sp., photograph. U. S. Fish and Wildlife Service. Reproduced by permission.

two of the six sites that harbor boulder darters, the boulders are in fact parts from old collapsed structures, a stone bridge and a spillway dam. The survival of the bolder darter is amazing considering the rarity of its preferred habitat and the severe and chronic degradation of the Elk River.

Extirpation of the boulder darter from the upper Elk River in Tennessee was likely due to cold water releases from Tims Ford Reservoir. The loss of the Shoal Creek population and any Tennessee River populations resulted from water impoundments behind Wheeler and Wilson Dams.

Although no new dams are currently planned for the watershed, other factors, such as increased siltation, improper pesticide use, toxic chemical spills, and phosphate mining could further threaten the species in the limited habitat it now occupies.

Conservation and Recovery

Biologists have long recognized the critical importance of knowing the reproductive biology of

any imperiled species, especially for developing conservation measures to protect and recover the species. Until recently, however, virtually nothing was known about the life history of the boulder darter. The first goal in researching the species was to observe its spawning behavior and to identify the area(s) of the river that served as spawning habitat. Unfortunately, observing boulder darter spawning behavior was not possible in the Elk River because of the water's consistent turbidity. Further, the river below Tims Ford Dam is subject to significant water level fluctuations resulting from power generation at the dam. In order to overcome the obstacles to studying the darter in its natural environment, ten darters were captured, transported to Gainesville, Florida, and placed in an artificial stream.

The artificial stream is a 4 by 8 ft (1.2 by 2.4 m) plexiglass aquarium generated by an electric trolling motor. Researchers mimicked important aspects of the boulder darter's habitat in the artificial stream, notably flow, temperature, photoperiod, and substrate composition. The boulder darters spawned in May and June 1991, yielding the first observations of reproduction for this endangered species. What was learned in this short period provided important insight into the inherent frailties of this darter at the critical point of creating the next generation.

Contact

Regional Office of Endangered Species
U.S. Fish and Wildlife Service
1875 Century Blvd., Ste. 200
Atlanta, Georgia 30345
http://southeast.fws.gov/

References

O'Bara, C. J., and D. A. Etnier. 1987. "Status Survey of the Boulder Darter." U.S. Fish and Wildlife Service, Asheville.

U. S. Fish and Wildlife Service. 1988. "Determination of Endangered Status for the Boulder Darter." *Federal Register* 53(170): 33996-33998.

U. S. Fish and Wildlife Service. 1989. "Boulder Darter Recovery Plan." U.S. Fish and Wildlife Service, Atlanta.

Amber Darter

Percina antesella

Status	Endangered
Listed	August 5, 1985
Family	Percidae (Perch)
Description	Small, golden brown darter with dark saddle-markings and a yellow belly.
Habitat	Riffle areas over sand and gravel bottoms.
Food	Aquatic insects.
Reproduction	Spawns in winter or early spring.
Threats	Dam construction, stream channelization.
Range	Georgia, Tennessee

Description

The amber darter, *Percina antesella*, is a short, slender-bodied fish generally less than 2.5 in (6 cm) long. The upper body is golden brown with dark saddle-markings; its belly is yellow-to-cream in color, and the throat of a breeding male is blue.

Behavior

In late winter or early spring, the amber darter swims up small streams to spawn in shallow marshy areas. It feeds primarily on gastropods (snails and limpets) and aquatic insects and larvae of caddisflies, mayflies, midges, beetles, and stoneflies. They also feed on fish eggs.

Habitat

The amber darter only inhabits areas of gentle riffles over sand and gravel bottoms. The species has not been observed in slack current in areas with debris or a mud bottom. As summer progresses, the amber darter uses the profuse vegetation that grows in the riffles for feeding and cover.

Distribution

A study completed in October 1983 concluded that the amber darter was restricted to the upper Conasauga River basin (a tributary of the Coosa River) in Georgia and Tennessee, with the exception of a small population in the Etowah River in Cherokee County, Georgia. The amber darter's preference for gentle riffles may explain why the species has not been found above the U.S. Highway 411 crossing in Polk County, Tennessee, where the Conasauga River's gradient steepens. Downstream, the amber darter's range is probably limited by heavy siltation.

As recently as 1982 and 1983, biologists could not find the amber darter in the Etowah River. If there is still a population in this river, it is very small. The only other collection record for the amber darter was from Shoal Creek, a tributary to the Etowah River (Cherokee County), Georgia, where the fish is no longer found. The Shoal Creek amber darter population was probably destroyed in the 1950s when Allatoona Reservoir inundated the lower portion of Shoal Creek.

The amber darter is now found along 33 mi (53 km) of the Conasauga River from the U.S. Highway 411 bridge near the town of Conasauga, Tennessee, downstream to the Tibbs Bridge in Murray County, Georgia. This stretch of the Conasauga River passes along the southern edge of Polk and Bradley counties, Tennessee, and curves south through Murray and Whitfield counties, Georgia. There is no current population estimate.

Amber Darter, photograph. U. S. Fish and Wildlife Service. Reproduced by permission.

Threats

The amber darter is threatened by runoff from agricultural and urban development in portions of the watershed. Because of its limited distribution, the amber darter could be jeopardized by a single catastrophic event. Heavy truck traffic across river bridges poses the threat of a toxic chemical spill that could eliminate a large percentage of the population. Increased tree farming activities, road and bridge construction, stream channel modifications, impoundments, changes in land use, and other projects in the watershed could have adverse impacts.

The impoundment of the Etowah River at Alatoona Reservoir has caused a great reduction of the population size in the Etowah River. Stream flow, water temperature, and siltation were all modified, especially during construction. And because of its limited distribution, the amber darter's ability to move to other suitable habitat was restricted by the impoundment's turbulent water.

The Etowah River system is subject to disturbance from potential changes in land use and activity, including silverculture, road and transmission lines maintenance, and pollution by herbicide and pesticide use.

Conservation and Recovery

The upper Conasauga River flows through the Chattahoochee and Cherokee national forests, and this undisturbed flow provides partial protection for the amber darter's downstream habitat. Further water control projects in the drainage require consultation with the U. S. Fish and Wildlife Service under provisions of the Endangered Species Act.

Contact

Regional Office of Endangered Species
U.S. Fish and Wildlife Service
1875 Century Blvd., Suite 200
Atlanta, Georgia 30345
http://southeast.fws.gov/

References

Etnier, D. A., B. H. Bauer, and A. G. Haines. 1981. "Fishes of the Gulf Coastal Drainage of North Georgia." Unpublished Report. U.S. Fish and Wildlife Service, Atlanta.

Freeman, B. J. 1983. "Final Report on the Status of the Trispot Darter and the Amber Darter in the Upper Coosa River System in Alabama, Georgia, and Tennessee." Report, Contract No. 14-16-0004-48. U.S. Fish and Wildlife Service, Atlanta.

Starnes, W. C., and D. A. Etnier. 1980. "Fishes." In D. C. Eagar and R. M. Hatcher, eds., *Tennessee's Rare Wildlife;* Vol. 1, *The Vertebrates.* Tennessee Heritage Program, Knoxville.

Goldline Darter

Percina aurolineata

Status	Threatened
Listed	April 22, 1992
Family	Percidae (Perch)
Description	Brownish-red darter with amber stripes and white belly.
Habitat	Gravel or sand substrate interspersed among cobble and small boulders.
Food	Unknown.
Reproduction	Unknown.
Threats	Reservoir construction, water pollution.
Range	Alabama, Georgia

Description

The *Percina aurolineata* (goldline darter) is a slender fish that reaches about 3 in (7 cm) in length. It is brownish-red with amber stripes along its pale to dusky upper back. It has a white belly with a series of square lateral and dorsal blotches that are separated by a pale or gold-colored longitudinal stripe.

Behavior

The fragmented populations the goldline darter in the upper Coosa and Cahaba Rivers appear to be reproducing. Any population that is stressed by a factor such as eutrophication, is more likely to succumb to disease and predation even if they are natural occurrences.

Habitat

The goldline darter can be found over a gravel or sand substrate that is interspersed among cobble and small boulders. It prefers a moderate to swift current, and water depths more than 2 ft (0.6 m).

Distribution

Historically, the goldline darter occurred in 49 mi (79 km) of the Cahaba River, and 7 mi (11 km) of the Little Cahaba River in Alabama. It has also been collected from the upper Coosa River drainage in the Coosawattee, Ellijay and Cartecay Rivers and tributaries, and in the Alabama River.

Presently, the goldline darter survives on fragmented populations in the upper Coosa River system in the Coosawattee River, Georgia, in 7 mi (11 km) of the Little Cahaba River, and in 27 mi (43 km) of the Cahaba River system in Alabama.

Threats

The range of this fish has declined due to water pollution and the construction of reservoirs. Water pollution is responsible for the decline of the goldline darter in the Cahaba River system. There are 10 municipal wastewater treatment plants in this basin, 35 mining areas, one coal bed methane and 67 other permitted discharges. During low flows, almost all of the water in some stretches of this river are treated sewage effluent. Nutrients in the sewage are contributing to eutrophication of the river, which removes oxygen from the water, and adversely affects the fish. Eutrophication is also responsible for the decline of vascular plants in the river, which also adversely affects this species. Increased siltation resulting from surface mining, the operation of limestone quarries and cement plants,

Goldline Darter, photograph by J. Malcolm Pierson. Reproduced by permission.

road construction, and site preparation for gas drilling operations all contribute to the degradation of water quality in this river. In the future, methane gas extraction in the basin could also affect the water quality.

In the Alabama and upper Coosa River, impoundments for hydropower, navigation, and flood control have probably wiped out all goldline darter populations in this area. These reservoirs have also fragmented and isolated the populations of this species in the Cahaba River system from those in the upper Coosa River tributary. Isolated populations are susceptible to environmental changes. This isolation threatens genetic variability as well as inhibits reproductive success.

Although some of the wastewater treatment facilities along the Cahaba river have recently been upgraded, this has not completely stopped the problem of enrichment.

Conservation and Recovery

Conservation of the goldline darter requires the protection of its remaining critical habitat, and improvement of the quality of the habitat. This will require the prevention of pollution associated with sewage, mining, and other sources. In addition, the surviving populations of the goldline darter must be monitored, and research undertaken into the biology of the species, its habitat needs, and necessary management practices.

Contacts

Ecological Services Field Office
Suite 310, 6620 Southpoint Drive, South
Jacksonville, Florida 32216-0958
Telephone: (904) 232-2580
Fax: (904) 232-2404

U. S. Fish and Wildlife Service
Regional Office, Division of Endangered Species
1875 Century Blvd., Suite 200
Atlanta, Georgia 30345
http://southeast.fws.gov/

Reference

U.S. Fish and Wildlife Service. 22 April 1992. "Endangered and Threatened Wildlife and Plants; Threatened Status for Two Fish, the Goldline Darter (*Percina aurolineata*) and Blue Shiner (*Cyprinella caerulea*)." *Federal Register* 57: 14786-14790.

Conasauga Logperch

Percina jenkinsi

Status	Endangered
Listed	August 5, 1985
Family	Percidae (Perch)
Description	Large darter with dark tiger stripes over a yellow body.
Habitat	Swift-flowing streams.
Food	Aquatic invertebrates.
Reproduction	Probably spawns in the spring.
Threats	Limited range, siltation, water pollution.
Range	Georgia, Tennessee

Description

The Conasauga logperch, *Percina jenkinsi*, also known as the reticulate logperch, is a large, slender darter, sometimes exceeding 6 in (15 cm) in length. It is characterized by tiger-like vertical dark stripes over a yellow upper body, small scales, narrow, dark bars with blotches between them, and a piglike snout. *P. jenkinsi* lacks the red, orange, or yellow colors found in the first dorsal fin of other logperch.

Behavior

Little is known of the behavior of this logperch. Collected specimens suggest that it spawns in the spring, most likely in fast-flowing riffles over gravel bottoms. It is non-migratory but changes its habitat from deep runs or flowing pools to deeper, slower pools in the fall. During the reproductive season it moves to shallow shoal areas with swift currents. The reproductive characteristics of *P. jenkinsi* are not known but the closely related *P. caprodes* has been well-studied. The non-territorial males gather in groups. When a receptive female swims through the school she is pursued by several males, one of which mates with her by burying in the sand, during which time 10-20 eggs are released, fertilized, and buried. The adults abandon the eggs and may spawn with several other mates. During a spring/summer reproductive season, *P. caprodes* females may lay as many as 3,000 eggs. Eggs hatch in five to nine days and the young fish may reach full maturity within a year.

It has been observed to forage for aquatic invertebrates by flipping over stones with its pig-like snout.

Habitat

The Conasauga logperch requires clean, unpolluted deep water or flowing pools with moderate to swift currents and substrates of clean rubble, sand, or gravel bottoms. Siltation, which often results when lands are cleared for agriculture or other uses, is a major threat to the quality of these stream habitats. Reproduction may occur in flowing pools with clean gravel substrates or in the swift currents of rivers. In lakes it spawns in more shallow sandy shoreline areas.

Distribution

This logperch has only been known from a single stretch of the Conasauga River in extreme southeastern Tennessee and north Georgia. Part of its range overlaps with that of the Endangered amber darter (*P. antesella*).

The Conasauga logperch is restricted to about 11 mi (18 km) of the upper Conasauga River. It has been found from just above the junction of Minnewauga Creek (Polk County), Tennessee, down-

Conasauga Logperch, photograph. U. S. Fish and Wildlife Service. Reproduced by permission.

stream through Bradley County, Tennessee, to the State Highway 2 bridge (Murray County), Georgia. The species has never been found outside this short stretch of river.

Threats

The upper Conasauga River flows through the Chattahoochee and Cherokee national forests, providing some protection for the downstream habitat where the logperch is found. However, agricultural and urban runoff from developed areas continue to jeopardize the habitat. Because of its limited range and clean water requirements, the Conasauga logperch could be jeopardized by a single catastrophic event, such as a toxic chemical spill.

A proposed reservoir project on the lower Conasauga River could also affect the fishes upstream. Fishes common to reservoirs, such as carp (*Cyprinus carpio*), dramatically increase in number after dam construction and could migrate upstream into the logperch's range. In 1982 an island

in the Conasauga River in Murray County, Georgia, was removed for flood control purposes. Before this channel work was done, Conasauga logperch were present but now cannot be located at the site.

Conservation and Recovery

Many organizations are now involved in helping to preserve the Conasauga River's ecosystem, which supports a number of rare fish and other species. The U.S. Fish and Wildlife Service's (FWS) field offices in Jacksonville, Florida, and Asheville, North Carolina, have provided funds to The Nature Conservancy to begin restoration work along the upper river corridor. Conservancy field offices in Tennessee and Georgia are working to identify areas with high biological diversity, map land-use patterns within those areas, and pinpoint threats to habitat quality. The U.S. Forest Service, which manages two national forests in the Conasauga headwaters (the Chattahoochee National Forest in Georgia and Cherokee National Forest in Tennessee), is monitoring rare fishes and has an interest in the well-being of other species at risk. Researchers at the University of Georgia's Institute of Ecology are mapping quality habitats and conducting studies on the status and life history of federally listed species.

The FWS has designated habitat critical to the survival of the Conasauga logperch to encompass its entire current range in Polk and Bradley Counties, Tennessee, and Murray County, Georgia. The water quality of this river section remains high; siltation and runoff are slight. FWS and state personnel are periodically monitoring the logperch population and are tracking developments that may potentially degrade the river. The FWS may attempt to introduce the logperch into another stream in the region to reduce the chances of accidental or catastrophic loss.

Contact

Regional Office of Endangered Species
U.S. Fish and Wildlife Service
1875 Century Blvd., Suite 200
Atlanta, Georgia 30345
http://southeast.fws.gov/

References

Ramsey, J. S. 1976. "Freshwater Fishes," In H. Boschung, ed., *Endangered and Threatened Plants and Animals of Alabama.* Bulletin of the Alabama Museum of Natural History. No. 2.

Thompson, B. A. 1985. *"Percina jenkinsi,* a New Species of Logperch (Pisces: Percidae) from the Conasauga River, Tennessee and Georgia." *Occasional Papers of the Museum Zoology Louisiana State University,* No. 62.

Leopard Darter

Percina pantherina

Status	Threatened
Listed	January 27, 1978
Family	Percidae (Perch)
Description	Small, olive green darter with dark eyes marked with gold, and a distinctive lateral band comprised of 10 or 11 black circles.
Habitat	Streams with rubble, boulder, or bedrock bottoms.
Food	Algae, invertebrates.
Reproduction	Spawns in the spring.
Threats	Low numbers, habitat alteration by impoundments, pollution.
Range	Arkansas, Oklahoma

Description

The leopard darter, *Percina pantherina*, is a small fish (3 in, 8 cm), light olive above and white below. It has dark eyes marked with gold flecks. The distinctive lateral band consists of 10 or 11 circular black spots connected by a fairly faint black band overlaid by an olive-yellow hue. Thirteen squarish blotches form saddles over the sides. The age of individuals can be determined by the prominence and color of the spots and blotches. The sexes are determined by enlarged midventral scales on the breast, which occur only in the males. Jet-black bands extend from the eyes through the nostrils, then begin to diminish. Closely related to the blackside darter (*P. maculata*), the leopard darter can be distinguished by its smaller scales.

Behavior

Early literature described the leopard darter as a riffle-dwelling species; more recent studies, however, found that moderately shallow pools are the preferred habitat of adult leopard darters, who may return to the riffles for spawning. Although little is known, biologists believe that the fish feeds on algae and small invertebrates.

Habitat

Adult leopard darters typically are found in pools in streams with relatively steep gradients that drain mountainous or hilly terrain and have rubble, boulder, and bedrock bottoms. They do not appear to inhabit the smaller headwater tributaries, and there is evidence that the species is most successful in intermediate-size streams rather than larger rivers.

Conditions surrounding occupied habitats include forests and farmland. The forests are generally oak-hickory, mixed pine-oak, and longleaf/slash and loblolly/shortleaf pine. The agricultural areas are chiefly hay fields, cattle pasture, and chicken houses. Any major impact on the Little River system, including the surrounding land, threatens the leopard darter.

Distribution

The leopard darter has been collected only from the Little River basin in southeastern Oklahoma and southwestern Arkansas.

Before 1977, 64 separate collecting efforts from 30 different locations resulted in a count of only 165 leopard darters. The largest population center was

Leopard Darter, photograph by Roger W. Barbour. Reproduced by permission.

in Glover Creek in Oklahoma. Since 1977, the leopard darter has been studied extensively in the Glover Creek drainage, and it appears to be the second most abundant darter species there. There are no current estimates for the size of this apparently stable population, but some observers believe the total population could be as low as 500 individuals.

Threats

A number of dams and reservoirs have been constructed on the Little River system: Pine Creek Reservoir, Broken Bow Lake, DeQueen Reservoir, Gillham Reservoir, and Dierks Reservoir. Only three leopard darters have ever been collected below these reservoirs. Further damming might well be fatal to the species because of its low numbers and restricted distribution. Spring flooding may also affect reproductive success by interrupting spawning and decreasing larval survival.

Impoundments pose the greatest threat to the leopard darter because of dissolved oxygen content,

reduced water flow, altered temperature, and the excessive discharge when water is released from the dams. Since only three leopard darters have been collected below reservoirs, and since they do not survive in lakes, the damming of streams has greatly reduced, and continues to extirpate the species from wide ranges of its historical habitat.

Silviculture, a major economic activity in the Little River basin, and the associated road construction, have caused many alterations in the watershed, including increased turbidity, erosion, and sedimentation in streams. As a result of industrial activity, the incidence of fish kills in the Little River is increasing. In one incident, creosote, flushed from a lumber treatment waste pond into the Cossatot River, poisoned 10 mi (16 km) of stream. Pollution from the use of herbicides, pesticides, and fertilizers on the agricultural lands surrounding some of the habitat threaten the water quality. Several gravel removal operations in the Little River system destroyed habitat and degraded water quality.

Conservation and Recovery

Very little can be done about the impoundments that have resulted from dam construction, and the increased demands for water by agricultural and municipal users, and flood control management may force further reservoir construction, several of which have been proposed. The strategy proposed in the Recovery Plan is to identify the most important populations and work to secure the stability of those habitats. Providing fish passages as part of the construction of new dams will help prevent populations from becoming isolated from each other and confined to waters below the reservoir where they seldom survive. Controlling water flow to provide sufficient depth for reproduction and growth during certain seasons would certainly increase populations.

The U. S. Fish and Wildlife Service has designated habitat critical to the survival of this species to include the main channel of the Little River in both Oklahoma and Arkansas, reaches of Black Fork Creek, the main channel of Glover Creek, including portions of the east and west forks, and the main channel of the Mountain Fork Creek. However, most of the land surrounding the Little River is privately owned, and the cooperation of the land owners is essential for conserving the habitats.

Research into the biology and population dynamics of this species is ongoing.

Contacts

Regional Office of Endangered Species
U.S. Fish and Wildlife Service
Box 1306
Albuquerque, New Mexico 87103
http://southwest.fws.gov/

Regional Office of Endangered Species
U.S. Fish and Wildlife Service
1875 Century Blvd., Suite 200
Atlanta, Georgia 30345
http://southeast.fws.gov/

References

Bailey, R. M., H. E. Winn, and C. L. Smith. 1954. "Fishes from the Escambia River, Alabama and Florida, with Ecologic and Taxonomic Notes." *Proceedings of the Academy of Natural Science, Philadelphia* 106:109-164.

Eleyy, R. L., J. C. Randolph, and R. J. Miller. 1975. "Current Status of the Leopard Darter, *Percina pantherina.*" *Southwest Naturalist* 20(3):343-354.

Miller, R. J., and H. W. Robison. 1973. *The Fishes of Oklahoma.* The Oklahoma State University Press, Stillwater.

Roanoke Logperch

Percina rex

Status	Endangered
Listed	August 18, 1989
Family	Percidae (Perch)
Description	Large darter, green above, yellowish white below; marked with dark patches, small saddles, and oval side markings.
Habitat	Pools and riffles with clear bottoms.
Food	Aquatic insect larvae.
Reproduction	Spawns in April and May.
Threats	Water pollution, low stream flow.
Range	Virginia

Description

The Roanoke logperch is a large darter that reaches a length of about 5.5 in (14 cm). It has an elongated cylindrical or slab-sided body with a complete lateral line. It has a dark green back, greenish yellow sides, and a white to yellowish belly. The sides and back are marked with numerous dark patches and distinct small saddles. It has oval markings on its side that are usually separated from the upper markings.

Behavior

The usual food of the Roanoke logperch is aquatic insect larvae. Individuals live for five to six years and become sexually mature at age four. Spawning occurs in April or May in deep runs over gravel.

Habitat

During the winter the Roanoke logperch inhabits deep pools where it usually finds shelter under boulders. In spring and summer, adults occupy gravel runs and riffles while juveniles gather in slower runs and shallow pools with clean sand bottoms.

Distribution

The Roanoke logperch was discovered in 1888 in the Roanoke River, near Roanoke, Virginia. It has been found only in the Roanoke River drainage (including tributaries) in south central Virginia and the Notoway River drainage in southeast Virginia.

Today, small populations of the Roanoke logperch inhabit rivers and streams in the two drainages of its historic range. In the Roanoke drainage, the largest and healthiest population occurs in the upper Roanoke River (Roanoke and Montgomery Counties) from within the City of Roanoke upstream into the North and South Forks and Tinker Creek. A scattered population occurs in the Pigg River in Pittsylvania and Franklin Counties and in Big Chestnut Creek, a tributary of the Pigg, in Franklin County. An extremely small population inhabits a 2.5-mi (4-km) section of the Smith River in Patrick County, upstream of Philpott Reservoir, and Town Creek, a tributary of the Smith River in Henry County.

In the Notoway River drainage, the Roanoke logperch is found in a 32-mi (51.5-km) reach of the river in Sussex County and in Stony Creek, a tributary in Dinwiddie and Sussex Counties. The population in this drainage is believed to be less than that in the Pigg River.

Threats

The main threat to the Roanoke logperch is degradation of the water quality. Expanding urban

Roanoke Logperch, photograph. U. S. Fish and Wildlife Service. Reproduced by permission.

and industrial development around Roanoke has a growing impact on the largest remaining population. Urban runoff and a variety of nonpoint-source pollutants—such as silt, oil, fertilizer, and toxic chemicals—are a growing threat to the species.

In addition, several proposed projects could have an adverse effect on this fish. The West Roanoke County Water Supply Project is intended to provide for the future needs of the county by taking water from the river. This could result in a low water flow for a 7-mi (11.3-km) section of the river, which is excellent logperch habitat. Low flow periods could possibly expose riffles, increase the water temperature during the summer and fall, and increase the concentration of pollutants while decreasing the amount of dissolved oxygen. Modifications to the original proposal may lessen some of the impacts to logperch habitat.

Conservation and Recovery

The U. S. Army Corps of Engineers has proposed the Upper Roanoke Flood Control Project,

which would modify the river's channel within the city limits. Even if efforts are made to avoid damage to logperch habitat, some adverse effects are expected.

The National Park Service has proposed construction of a Roanoke River Parkway. While this project is still in an early planning stage and its impact on the logperch cannot yet be evaluated, any road construction adjacent to the river is a cause for concern. The U. S. Fish and Wildlife Service will monitor all three of these projects to ensure that conservation of the Roanoke logperch is considered.

Contacts

U.S. Fish and Wildlife Service
Regional Office, Division of Endangered Species
300 Westgate Center Dr.
Hadley, Massachusetts 01035-9589
Telephone: (413) 253-8200
Fax: (413) 253-8300
http://www.northeast.fws.gov/

Chesapeake Bay Ecological Services Field Office
177 Admiral Cochrane Dr.
Annapolis, Maryland 21401-7307
Telephone: (410) 573-4500
Fax: (410) 263-2608

References

Burkhead, N. M. 1983. "Ecological Studies of Two Potentially Threatened Fishes (the Orangefin Madtom, *Noturus gilberti* and the Roanoke Logperch, *Percina rex)* Endemic to the Roanoke River Drainage." Report to Wilmington District Corps of Engineers, Wilmington.

Burkhead, N. M. 1986. "Potential Impact of the West County Reservoir Project on Two Endemic Rare Fish and the Aquatic Biota of the Upper Roanoke River, Roanoke County, Virginia." Report to Roanoke County Public Facilities Department, Roanoke.

Jenkins, R. E. 1979. "Freshwater and Marine Fishes." In *Endangered and Threatened Plants and Animals of Virginia.* Polytechnic Institute and State University, Blacksburg, Virginia.

Simonson, T. D., and R. J. Neves. 1986. "A Status Survey of the Orangefin Madtom *(Noturus gilberti)* and Roanoke Logperch *(Percina rex)."* Virginia Commission of Game and Inland Fisheries, Richmond, Virginia.

Snail Darter

Percina tanasi

Status	Threatened
Listed	October 9, 1975, Endangered
Reclassified	July 5, 1984, Threatened
Family	Percidae (Perch)
Description	Small brown darter with dark brown saddle marks.
Habitat	Vegetated streams with sandy bottoms.
Food	Invertebrates.
Reproduction	Spawns January to mid-March.
Threats	Dam construction, water pollution.
Range	Alabama, Georgia, Tennessee

Description

The snail darter, *Percina tanasi*, is a small, robust fish, rarely exceeding 3.4 in (9 cm) in length. Brown, with a faint trace of green above and white below, it has four dark brown, saddle-like patches across the back. The upper portion of its head is dark brown, the cheeks are mottled brown and yellow. A black bar extends vertically beneath the eyes, which have an orange-yellow iris. The median fins are mostly clear with black patterning tinged with yellow; the paired fins widely vary between individuals, from mostly clear to bright yellow-orange.

Behavior

Snail darters are relatively short-lived, reaching a maximum age of five or six years. The mortality rate between the first and second year is 75% to 80%. Snail darters spawn in the shallowest areas of river shoals between January and mid-March every year that they survive. Spawning is non-territorial with multiple, promiscuous mating after a courtship ritual in which the female visually solicits a single male, followed by touching and finally copulation. Spawning usually occurs on swift shallow shoals. About 600 eggs deposited in gravel or on rocks drift freely for 15-20 days before hatching. The larvae probably feed on tiny crustaceans and invertebrates. During this period the larvae are extremely vulnerable to predation by many species, including adult snail darters. Newly hatched darters drift downstream. The benthic juveniles are transformed into adults 15-30 days after hatching. As they grow, they move upstream to the shoal areas where they were spawned.

The snail dater feeds exclusively on gastropods, especially aquatic snails, during the fall and winter, and overall gastropods make up about 60% of the darter's food, although its diet tends to vary seasonally. Insects provide the other major food source during the spring and summer, and caddisfly may be the primary food source, supplemented by other insects and fish eggs. The diet of juveniles is the same as adults.

Habitat

Most snail darters prefer moderately flowing, vegetated streams with sandy bottoms and wide shoals for spawning, but because of the expansive range of the darter in three states, the habitats are associated with a wide variety of vegetation. Originally, oak-pine and oak-hickory forests surrounded the large streams and rivers, but these have largely been replaced by farm land.

The snail darter requires clean gravel-sand shoals for feeding and shallow, slow moving water for spawning. Spawning is delayed during times of flooding, suggesting that both water depth and water clarity are necessary for the mating ritual and

Snail Darter, photograph. U. S. Fish and Wildlife Service. Reproduced by permission.

egg deposit. Survival of eggs and larvae require slackwater areas, such as deep pools, downstream from the spawning site. Large, low-gradient, undisturbed rivers and streams with alternating pools and riffles provide the best spawning conditions.

Distribution

The snail darter was first collected in 1973 in the lower reaches of the Little Tennessee River in Loudon County, Tennessee, an area that was eventually inundated by completion of the Tellico Dam, a project of the Tennessee Valley Authority (TVA). According to the U. S. Fish and Wildlife Service (FWS), it is difficult to determine the range of the snail darter before construction of the dam. Snail darters were probably confined to the upper portions of the Tennessee River upstream from north-central Alabama, and the lower portions of the Hiwassee, Clinch, Little Tennessee, French Broad, and Holston Rivers.

The snail darter is now found in the main channel of the Tennessee River and in six of its tributaries. Darters have been found in small numbers in three Tennessee reservoirs—Watts Bar (Loudon County), Nickajack (Hamilton County), and Guntersville (Marion County). Only adult darters have been found and researchers think these fish migrated from tributary spawning grounds. No reproduction has been documented in these reservoirs.

In 1975 and 1976, snail darters were successfully transplanted to the Hiwassee River (Polk County). Surveys have indicated the population is thriving.

Additional snail darter populations have been located since the fish was initially described. In 1980 the first new naturally occurring population of snail darters was discovered in South Chickamauga Creek, which straddles the Tennessee-Georgia border (Hamilton County, Tennessee, and Catoosa County, Georgia). In 1981 small snail darter populations were discovered in the Sequatchee River

(Marion County) and Sewee Creek (Meigs County) in Tennessee. An additional population was found in September 1981 in the Paint Rock River (Jackson and Madison counties) in Alabama.

Threats

The snail darter declined because of habitat destruction resulting from impoundments throughout the Tennessee River drainage system. Siltation, channelization, and dredging, along with pollution from industrial and urban waste, and pesticides from agricultural practices, further compounded the adverse conditions of the river. Logging and mining activities, along with the conversion of forests to farm land, increased turbulence in the river system, and flood control and navigation management finally destroyed most of the darter's habitat.

Unknown to anyone before 1973, the snail darter became the focus of a major political controversy during the late 1970s when its existence halted the completion of the TVA's Tellico Dam on the Little Tennessee River. It was listed as an Endangered Species in 1975 with the Little Tennessee River designated as habitat critical to its survival. At the time of listing the only known population was threatened by the flooding of its habitat by the Tellico Dam.

In 1977 a federal appeals court ruled that the dam could not be completed since it would likely eliminate the snail darter. The following year, the U. S. Supreme Court upheld that decision, maintaining that the Endangered Species Act of 1973 was clear on the matter and that exceptions to the law must be made by the U. S. Congress, not the court.

In response to the Supreme Court's decision, Congress amended the Endangered Species Act in 1978, creating an Endangered Species Committee. The committee was given the responsibility for considering exemptions to the Act for resource development projects which had an unresolvable conflict with the Act. Since the committee was given the power to approve projects that would likely cause the extinction of a species, it soon became known as the God Committee.

In 1979, however, contrary to many expectations, the committee voted unanimously not to exempt the Tellico Dam from compliance with the Endangered Species Act. Congress responded by passing legislation, which was signed into law, exempting Tel-

lico Dam from the Act and mandating its completion. This act went on record as the first official U. S. government decision to extirpate a species.

Conservation and Recovery

Prior to the climax of the political controversy in 1979, the FWS attempted a number of transplants of the snail darter into other Tennessee waters. Only one transplant has proven successful. In 1975 and 1976, 710 snail darters were introduced into the Hiwassee River in Polk County. Regular surveys have confirmed reproduction, and the darter appears to be thriving there.

In 1980, following the exemption awarded the Tellico Dam by Congress, a new snail darter population was discovered in South Chickamauga Creek, in Tennessee and Georgia. Other small populations were subsequently discovered in Tennessee and Alabama.

In light of the discovery of additional snail darter populations, the FWS downlisted the snail darter from Endangered to Threatened in 1984. If substantial new snail darter populations are discovered or if current populations remain stable or increase over a 10-year monitoring period, the FWS Recovery Plan states the agency will consider removing the snail darter from the federal Endangered Species list.

Contact

Regional Office of Endangered Species
U.S. Fish and Wildlife Service
1875 Century Blvd., Suite 200
Atlanta, Georgia 30345
http://southeast.fws.gov/

References

Biggins, R. G. 1984. "Proposal to Reclassify the Snail Darter from an Endangered Species to a Threatened Species and Rescind Critical Habitat Designation." *Federal Register* 49 (35):6388-6389.

Etnier, D.A. 1976. "*Percina tanasi,* a New Percid Fish from the Little Tennessee River, Tennessee." *Proceeds of the Biological Society* 88 (44):469-645.

Hickman, G. D. and R. B. Fitz. 1978. "A Report on the Ecology and Conservation of the Snail Darter from 1875-1977." Tennessee Valley Authority Technical Note B28. 129 pp.

Starnes, W. C. 1977. "The Ecology and Life History of the Endangered Snail Darter." Ph.D. Dissertation, University of Tennessee, Knoxville. 143 pp.

U.S. Fish and Wildlife Service. 1983. "Snail Darter Recovery Plan." U.S. Fish and Wildlife Service, Atlanta.

Tidewater Goby

Eucyclogobius newberryi berryi

Status	Endangered
Listed	February 4, 1994
Family	Gobiidae (Goby)
Description	Small fish with large pectoral fins and a ventral suckerlike disk formed by the complete fusion of the pelvic fins.
Habitat	California lagoons with low salinity.
Food	Carnivorous small aquatic invertebrates.
Reproduction	Nesting activities commence in late April through early May.
Threats	Habitat alteration.
Range	California

Description

The tidewater goby is a small fish, rarely exceeding 2 in (5.1 cm) in length. It has large pectoral fins and a ventral suckerlike disk formed by the complete fusion of the pelvic fins.

Behavior

Peak nesting activities commence in late April through early May, when male gobies dig a vertical nesting burrow 4-8 in (10.2-20.4 cm) deep in clean, coarse sand. Suitable water temperatures for nesting are 75.6-79.6°F. (24.2-26.4°C) with salinity of five to 10 parts per thousand. Male gobies remain in the burrows to guard the eggs, which are hung from the ceiling and walls of the burrow until hatching. Larval gobies are found midwater around vegetation until they become benthic.

Habitat

The tidewater goby is almost unique among fishes along the Pacific coast of the United States in its restriction to waters with low salinity. All populations are generally found at the upper end of lagoons in salinity less than 10 parts per thousand, although gobies have been collected and reared in slightly higher salinity.

The tidewater goby occurs in loose aggregations of a few to several hundred individuals on the substrate in shallow water less than 3 ft (91 cm) deep, although they have been observed in depths up to 7.6 ft (2.3 m).

Distribution

Historically, the tidewater goby occurred in at least 87 of California's coastal lagoons. Since 1900 it has disappeared from approximately 50% of formerly occupied lagoons. The tidewater goby is discontinuously distributed throughout California, ranging from Tillas Slough (mouth of the Smith River) in Del Norte County south to Agua Hedionda Lagoon in San Diego County. Areas of precipitous coastlines that preclude the formation of lagoons at stream mouths have created three gaps in the distribution of the goby. Gobies are apparently absent from the Humboldt Bay and Ten Mile River; Point Arena and Salmon Creek; and Monterey Bay and Arroyo del Oso.

Threats

The major factor adversely affecting the tidewater goby is coastal development projects that have caused a loss of coastal saltmarsh habitat. Coastal marsh habitats have been drained and reclaimed for

Tidewater Goby, photograph by B. "Moose" Peterson/WRP. Reproduced by permission.

residential and industrial developments. Waterways have been dredged for navigation and harbors, resulting in permanent and direct loss of wetland habitats, as well as indirect losses due to changes in salinity. Coastal road construction projects have severed the connection between marshes and the ocean, resulting in unnatural temperature and salinity profiles that the tidewater goby cannot tolerate.

Furthermore, upstream water diversions adversely affect the tidewater goby by altering downstream flows, thereby diminishing the extent of marsh habitats that occurred historically at the mouths of most rivers and creeks in California. Alterations of flows upstream of coastal lagoons have already changed the distribution of downstream salinity regimes. Since the tidewater goby has relatively narrow salinity tolerances, changes in salinity distribution due to upstream water diversions may adversely affect both the size and distribution of goby populations.

Conservation and Recovery

No critical habitat or recovery plan has been designated. The Santa Ynez estuary, which is owned by the U.S. Air Force, is subject to the conservation mandate and prohibitions against jeopardy.

Roughly 10% of the coastal lagoons presently containing tidewater goby are under Federal ownership. Over 40% are entirely or partly owned and managed by the state of California. The remainder is privately owned.

Contacts

U. S. Fish and Wildlife Service
Regional Office, Division of Endangered Species
Eastside Federal Complex
911 N. E. 11th Ave.
Portland, Oregon 97232-4181
Telephone: (503) 231-6121
http://pacific.fws.gov/

U.S. Fish and Wildlife Service
Ventura Field Office
2493 Portola Road, Suite B
Ventura, California 93003-7726
Telephone: 805-644-1766

Reference

U.S. Fish and Wildlife Service. 4 February 1994. "Endangered and Threatened Wildlife and Plants; Determination of Endangered Status for the Tidewater Goby." *Federal Register* 59 (24): 5494-5498.

Snails

Slender Campeloma

Campeloma decampi

Status	Endangered
Listed	February 25, 2000
Family	Viviparidae
Description	Snail with prominently raised spiral lines on the shell.
Habitat	Soft sediment, detritus, or stream impoundments.
Food	Detritus.
Reproduction	Bears live young.
Threats	Siltation and pollution from waste discharges.
Range	Alabama

Description

The shell of the slender campeloma is medium to large, usually less than 1.4 in (35 mm) in length, narrow, relatively thin, and generally with prominently raised spiral lines. Lateral and marginal teeth of the shell are simple with very fine, difficult to distinguish points. The shell has no spiral nodules, spiral color bands or exaggerated angle of the opening to the outer margin of the shell.

The plate that closes the shell when the campeloma retracts is entirely concentric and does not reflect inward at the center.

Sexes are separate in this family, and males are distinguished by their modified right tentacle that serves as a copulatory organ. This tentacle is shorter and thicker than the left tentacle and the bilaterally symmetrical female tentacles.

The slender campeloma is distinquished from the closely related *Campeloma decisum* by the presence of faint striations and a relatively higher spire on the shell. The shell of the slender campeloma also tends to have strongly developed ridges, and ridges in the juveniles and early whorls of adults tend to be carinate (keel-shaped).

Behavior

The life history of the slender campeloma has not been studied by biologists, but many conclusions to their behaviors can be drawn by comparing this species to others in the genus and family.

All members of this family give birth to live young, rather than laying eggs like many other snails. Studies of the *Campeloma* genus show that May is the peak season for births, although the birthing season reaches into the beginning of September. They also carry young in the uterus over winter.

Habitat

The slender campeloma is often found burrowing in soft sediments or detritus, which is its main source of food. Detritus is made up of organic matter and rock fragments.

Historically, specimens have been found on stream impoundments.

Distribution

The historic range of the slender campeloma has been reduced by at least three-quarters. Habitat was once found along the north side of the Tennessee River in Jackson, Limestone, Madison, and Morgan Counties in Alabama.

Of the past populations, one was inundated by Wheeler Reservoir, and others cannot be found or reached.

Current population distribution is spotty. Existing populations are now isolated by Wheeler Reservoir, restricted to a few isolated sites along Round Island, Piney, and Limestone Creeks, three short stream reaches in Limestone County. Limestone Creek contains many listed species, indicating that this system has been severely impacted and undergone significant degradation.

Threats

Due to small population sizes and limited occupied habitat, the slender campeloma is extremely vulnerable. Threats include direct loss of habitat, siltation, altered water chemistry and chemical pollution.

The placement of Wheeler Reservoir has greatly impacted habitat for the slender campeloma. Dams and their impounded water can form barriers to snail movement, promote siltation and encourage changes in the flow of water and water chemistry. This reduces food and oxygen availability, affecting reproductive success and altering habitat.

In addition, when local water and habitat quality change, many isolated snail populations become more vulnerable to run-off and discharges into the watershed.

Additional sources of siltation include channel modification, agriculture, cattle grazing, logging, chip mills, unpaved road drainage, rock quarries, bridges and road expansion projects and industrial and residential development.

Discharges from polluting sources increase eutrophication, decrease dissolved oxygen concentration, increase acidity and conductivity, and create other changes in water chemistry. Some sources include leach from agricultural fields (especially cotton), residential lawns, livestock operations and leaking septic tanks which also contribute to changes in water quality.

Conservation and Recovery

Current conservation measures include the certain designation of critical habitat and a review of all projects affecting habitat. The Federal government is not requesting information about projects specifically affecting the habitat of the slender campeloma due to the listing of the armored snail which has a very similar range. After projects are reviewed appropriate conservation measures will be taken.

The U. S. Fish and Wildlife Service has determined that dams and their impoundments prevent the natural recolonization of surviving snail populations. Even if watershed impacts improve or even disappear, the damage will continue as long as the dams are present.

Contacts

U. S. Fish and Wildlife Service
Regional Office, Division of Endangered Species
1875 Century Blvd., Suite 200
Atlanta, Georgia 30345
http://southeast.fws.gov/

Asheville Field Office
U. S. Fish and Wildlife Service
160 Zillicoa Street
Asheville, North Carolina 28801-1082
Telephone: (828) 258-3939
Fax: (828) 258-5330

Reference

United States Department of the Interior. 25 February 2000. "Endangered and Threatened Wildlife and Plants: Endangered Status for the Armored Snail and Slender Campeloma." *Federal Register* 65 (38):10033-10039.

Cylindrical Lioplax

Lioplax cyclostomaformis

Status	Endangered
Listed	October 28, 1998
Family	Viviparidae
Description	A gill-breathing, freshwater snail.
Habitat	Lives in mud among rocks in fast-flowing streams and rivers.
Food	Filter-feeds on organic detritus.
Reproduction	Thought to brood its young in its gills.
Threats	Habitat destruction and degradation.
Range	Alabama

Description

The *Lioplax cyclostomaformis* (cylindrical lioplax), is a gill-breathing snail in the family Viviparidae. The shell is elongate, reaching about 1.1 in (2.8 cm) in length. Shell color is light to dark olivaceous-green externally, and bluish inside of the aperture (shell opening). The cylindrical lioplax is distinguished from other viviparid (eggs hatch internally and the young are born as juveniles) snails in the Mobil River Basin by the number of whorls, and differences in size, sculpture, microsculpture, and spire angle.

Behavior

The cylindrical lioplax is thought to brood its young and to filter-feed on organic detritus, as do better-known members of the Viviparidae. Life spans have been reported to be 3-11 years in other species of Viviparidae.

Habitat

Habitat for the cylindrical lioplax is unusual for the genus, as well as for other genera of viviparid snails. It lives in mud under large rocks in rapid currents over stream and river shoals. Other lioplax species are usually found in exposed situations or in mud or muddy sand along the margins of rivers.

Distribution

The cylindrical lioplax is currently known only from approximately 15 mi (24 km) of the Cahaba River above the Fall Line in Shelby and Bibb counties, Alabama. Survey efforts in 1974 failed to locate this snail in the Coosa or Alabama Rivers, and more recent survey efforts have also failed to relocate the species at historic localities in the Alabama, Black Warrior, Little Cahaba, and Coosa Rivers and their tributaries.

Threats

More than 90% of the historical habitat of the cylindrical lioplax has been destroyed by the extensive construction of numerous dams and inundation by impounded waters. Habitat downstream of impoundments has also been degraded by changes in hydrology, water quality, and eutrophication. Discharges associated with agriculture and municipal sources are also important in some areas. These are ongoing threats to the rare snail.

Conservation and Recovery

The cylindrical lioplax is currently known only from about 15 mi (24 km) of the Cahaba River. Its habitat is all on privately owned land. The remaining critical habitat of the cylindrical lioplax should

Lioplax (Snail), photograph by Art Bogan. Reproduced by permission.

be protected. This could be done by acquiring the private land and establishing ecological reserves, or by negotiating conservation easements with the landowners. The populations of the cylindrical lioplax should be monitored, and research undertaken into its biology and habitat needs, including methods of beneficial management. Additional populations of the rare snail should be established in areas with suitable habitat.

Contacts

U. S. Fish and Wildlife Service
Wildlife and Habitat Management Office
6578 Dogwood View Parkway
Jackson, Mississippi 39213
Telephone: (601) 965-4903

U. S. Fish and Wildlife Service
Regional Office, Division of Endangered Species
1875 Century Blvd., Suite 200
Atlanta, Georgia 30345
http://southeast.fws.gov/

Reference

U.S. Fish and Wildlife Service. 28 October 1998. "Endangered and Threatened Wildlife and Plants; Endangered Status for Three Aquatic Snails, and Threatened Status for Three Aquatic Snails in the Mobile River Basin of Alabama." *Federal Register* 63 (208): 57610-57620

Tulotoma Snail

Tulotoma magnifica

Status	Endangered
Listed	January 9, 1991
Family	Viviparidae (Live-bearing Snails)
Description	Aquatic snail with a globular shell, with spiral lines of knobs.
Habitat	Moderately flowing rivers with rocky bottoms.
Food	Filter-feeder.
Reproduction	Bears live young.
Threats	Alteration of habitat, water pollution, siltation.
Range	Alabama

Tulotoma Snail, photograph by J. Malcolm Pierson. Reproduced by permission.

Description

Tulotoma is a gill-breathing, operculate snail. Its shell is globular, reaching a size somewhat larger than a golf ball, and typically ornamented with spiral lines of knob-like structures. Its adult size and ornamentation distinguish it from all other freshwater snails in the Coosa-Alabama River system. Tulotoma is also distinguished by its oblique aperture with a concave margin.

Behavior

The tulotoma snail broods young and filter-feeds, as do other members of the Viviparidae.

Habitat

The tulotoma snail occurs in cool, well-oxygenated, clean, free-flowing waters, with the habitat including both the mainstem river and the lower portions of large tributaries. This species is found in riffles and shoals and has been collected by U.S. Fish and Wildlife Service (FWS) divers at depths of more than 15 ft (4.5 m) with strong currents. The species is strongly associated with boulder/cobble substrates and is generally found during daylight hours clinging tightly to the underside of large rocks. Other aspects of its biology are virtually unknown.

Distribution

The historic range of the tulotoma snail was from the Coosa River in St. Clair County, Alabama, to the Alabama River in Clarke and Monroe Counties, Alabama. Historic collecting localities in the Coosa River System included numerous sites on the river as well as the lower reaches of several large tributaries. This snail has only been recorded from two localities in the Alabama River System: the type locality near Claiborne, Monroe County, Alabama, and Chilachee Creek southwest of Selma, Dallas County, Alabama. Other than isolated archaeological relics, the species has never been recorded from the

Tombigbee, Black Warrior, Cahaba, or the Tallapoosa Drainages. Archaeological records from these drainages are doubtful since tulotoma snails were Indian food items with shells of ornamental value and were likely to be transported outside of their natural range. Collections from these drain-ages since the mid-nineteenth century have not verified the presence of this species.

The snail's current known range includes four localized populations in the lower, unimpounded portions of Coosa River tributaries: Kelly Creek, St. Clair and Shelby Counties; Weogufka and Hatchet Creeks, Coosa County; and Ohatchee Creek, Calhoun County. A single population continues to survive in the Coosa River between Jordan Dam and Wetumpka, Elmore County. All of these locations, with the exception of Ohatchee Creek where only a few snails have been observed, appear to have self-sustaining populations. The tulotoma snail has apparently been extirpated in the Alabama River.

Threats

The range reduction of tulotoma can be attributed to extensive channel modifications in the Coosa-Alabama River System for navigation and hydropower. Dredging of the Alabama River channel began in 1878 and continues to the present day. Locks and dams on that river were completed in the 1960s impounding tulotoma habitat from the lowermost known site near Claiborne, Alabama, to the confluence of the Coosa and Tallapoosa Rivers. The Coosa River has been impounded for hydropower from just above its confluence with the Tallapoosa for approximately 230 river mi (370 river km) by a series of six large dams constructed between 1914 and 1966. Most Alabama and Coosa River tributaries within the historic tulotoma range have been affected in their lower reaches by backwater from the impoundments.

Additional impacts on the species include pollution, siltation, and hydropower discharge. Industrial and municipal waste problems were found in the Coosa Drainage as well as the effects of excessive siltation. In a 1989 survey, Service biologists noted that tulotoma habitat in the river channel and tributaries affected by reservoir backwater may be limited by siltation.

Conservation and Recovery

The Alabama Power Company is conducting a multi-year life history and population study on the tulotoma snail in the Coosa River below Jordan Dam, Elmore County, Alabama. Information from this study should be used to access historic sites where the species no longer occurs. The suitability of the habitat would be evaluated for reintroduction of the snail. Known populations will be monitored and protected through existing legislation and regulations.

Contacts

U.S. Fish and Wildlife Service
Regional Office, Division of Endangered Species
1875 Century Blvd., Suite 200
Atlanta, Georgia 30334
http://southeast.fws.gov/

U.S. Fish and Wildlife Service
6578 Dogwood View Parkway
Jackson, Mississippi 39213
Telephone: (601) 965-4900

References

Hershler, R., J.M. Pierson, and R.S. Krotzer. 1990. "Rediscovery of *Tulotoma magnifica* (Conrad) (Gastropoda: Viviparidae)." *Proceedings of the Biological Society of Washington.* 103 (4): 815-824.

U.S. Fish and Wildlife Service. 9 January 1991. "Determination of Endangered Status for the Tulotoma Snail." *Federal Register* 56 (6): 797-800.

Utah Valvata Snail

Valvata utahensis

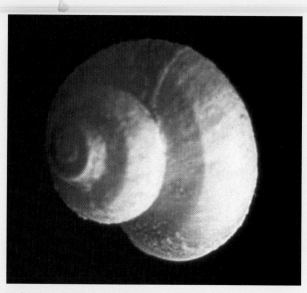

Status	Endangered
Listed	December 14, 1992
Family	Valvatidae
Description	A small freshwater snail.
Habitat	Cool, clean, flowing streams and rivers.
Food	Organic detritus and algae.
Reproduction	Lays eggs.
Threats	Habitat destruction and degradation by impoundments and water-flow control structures, dewatering for irrigation, and deterioration of water quality.
Range	Idaho, Utah

Utah Valvata Snail, photograph by Stephen D. Duke and William H. Mullins. Reproduced by permission.

Description

The Utah valvata snail has a turbinate shell (i.e., it is about equally high as wide), with up to four whorls, and as high as 0.2 in (4.5 mm).

Behavior

The Utah valvata snail feeds on dead plant biomass and on algae such as diatoms.

Habitat

The Utah valvata snail lives in deep pools near rapids or in perennial waters associated with large spring complexes. It occurs in areas with swift current, and prefers well-oxygenated water and a bottom substrate of mud or mud-sand among beds of submerged aquatic plants. A common associate is the macrophytic alga, *Chara*.

Distribution

The Utah valvata snail once occurred rather widely in prehistoric lakes and rivers in parts of Cal-

ifornia, Idaho, Nevada, Utah, and Wyoming. In the mid-1990s, it only occurred in a few spring and riverine sites in the Snake River, in the Hagerman Valley and below the American Falls dam to Burley, and near Minidoka Dam.

Threats

The Utah valvata snail has suffered habitat destruction and degradation through impoundment and flow-control activities on its streams and rivers. These have resulted in physical modification of its habitat and deteriorated water quality in terms of temperature, oxygen concentration, and nutrients.

Conservation and Recovery

One of the sites of the Utah valvata snail is in the Thousand Springs Preserve, a private protected area owned and managed by the Nature Conservancy. A recovery plan has been prepared for the rare snail, within the larger recovery plan for the Snake River. Its recovery depends upon achieving improvements in habitat and water quality in the Snake River. This would allow viable, naturally reproducing colonies of the snail to persist, and new ones to establish. Specific conservation measures include protection of the remaining free-flowing habitats from hydro-development, prevention of further diversions of water from the Snake River, achieving natural flow conditions, improving water quality, and enhancing watershed conditions.

Contacts

U. S. Fish and Wildlife Service
Regional Office, Division of Endangered Species
Eastside Federal Complex
911 N. E. 11th Ave.
Portland, Oregon 97232-4181
(503) 231-6121
http://pacific.fws.gov/

U. S. Fish and Wildlife Service
Regional Office, Division of Endangered Species
P. O. Box 25486
Denver Federal Center
Denver, Colorado 80225
http://www.r6.fws.gov/

U. S. Fish and Wildlife Service, Snake River Basin Office
1387 South Vinnell Way, Room 368
Boise, Idaho 83709-1657
Telephone: (208) 378-5243
Fax: (208) 378-5262

References

U. S. Fish and Wildlife Service. 1996. "Utah Valvata Snail (*Valvata utahensis*)." *U. S. Fish and Wildlife Service, Snake River Basin Sub-Ecoregion.* (http://www.fws.gov/r1srbo/Outreach/utahvsnl.htm). Date Accessed: July 7, 2000.

U. S. Fish and Wildlife Service. 1995. "Snake River Aquatic Species Recovery Plan." Boise, Idaho.

Idaho Springsnail

Fontelicella idahoensis

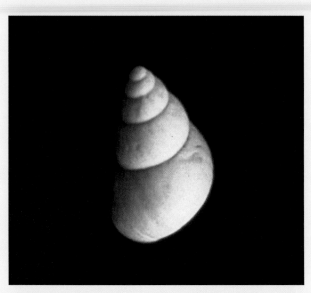

Status	Endangered
Listed	December 14, 1992
Family	Hydrobiidae
Description	A living fossil with a narrowly elongate shell with 5.5 to 6 whorls.
Habitat	Free-flowing cool spring alcoves.
Food	Plant debris or diatoms.
Reproduction	Lays eggs on the bottom of large rivers, probably early in the growing season.
Threats	Water quality degradation; New Zealand mudsnail.
Range	Idaho

Idaho Springsnail, photograph by William H. Mullins. Reproduced by permission.

Description

The Idaho springsnail is a relict of the Pleistocene Lake Idaho and is considered a "living fossil." It has a narrowly elongate shell reaching a length of 0.1-0.2 in (5-7 mm). This species is observed to have 5.5 to six whorls. The calcareous portion of the shell lacks a color pattern while the periostracus may or may not have a pattern. The aperture is holostomatous, without notches, canals, siphonal grooves, or denticulations. The foot is strong, mobile, truncate anteriorly and retractile. It bares lateral auriculate lobes and a mucous groove across the anterior edge; it is rounded and has a posterior pedal gland. The snail moves generally by gliding. The head bears filiform tentacles; the eyes are usually lateral at the outer bases of the tentacles. Body coloration is usually grayish-black. The species has also been classified as *Pyrgulopsis idahoensis*.

Behavior

This species is restricted to a diet of diatoms and plant debris which grazes along mud surfaces, rocky surfaces and macrophytes.

Habitat

The Idaho springsnail is found only in permanent, flowing waters of the mainstem Snake River. This snail is not found in any of the Snake River tributaries or marginal springs. It occurs on mud or sand associated with gravel to boulder-size substratum. This species often attaches itself to vegetation such as common associate *Potamogeton*, in riffles.

In addition to the Idaho springsnail, the Snake River and its tributaries provide essential habitat to sensitive native species such as the Shortface lanx or giant Columbia River limpet, the Shoshone sculpin, the Bliss Rapids snail, the Snake River physa snail, the Banbury Spring lanx, and the Utah Valvata snail. These areas contain some of the last mainstem Snake River habitats with the full range of native molluscan species present, and represent a unique aquatic community.

Distribution

Fossil records of the Idaho springsnail indicate this species to have been distributed throughout much of southern Idaho. This species is currently distributed discontinuously in the mainstem Snake River from sites from C. J. Strike Reservoir and upstream to Bancroft Springs in Owyhee and Elmore Counties, Idaho.

Threats

The free-flowing, cool water environments required by this species have been impacted by and are vulnerable to continued adverse habitat modification and deteriorating water quality from hydroelectric development, peak-loading effects from existing hydroelectric project operations, water withdrawal and diversions, water pollution, and inadequate regulatory mechanisms.

Water quality degradation continues from increased water use and withdrawal, aggravated by recent drought-induced low flows. The 121-mi (195-km) stretch of the Snake River is impacted by agricultural return flows; runoff from between 500 and 600 dairies and feed lots; effluent from over 140 private, state, and Federal fish culture facilities; and point source (e.g. municipal sewage) discharge. The ultimate impact of these factors are increased nutrient loads and concentrations which adversely affect the lotic fauna. Nutrient loading contributes to dense blooms of free-living and attached filamentous algae, which the species cannot utilize. This algae will often cover rock surfaces, effectively displacing suitable snail habitats and food resources.

A more recent threat is the discovery of the New Zealand mudsnail in the middle Snake River. The eurytopic mudsnail is experiencing explosive growth in the river and shows a wide range of tolerance for water fluctuations, velocity, temperature and turbidity. The mudsnail species seems to prefer warmer, polluted waters over pristine cold spring environments.

Conservation and Recovery

The U. S. Fish and Wildlife Service published a Recovery Plan for the Idaho springsnail and other endangered mollusks in the Snake River Basin in 1992. The conservation of this endangered snail requires the protection of its surviving critical habitat in the mainstem Snake River from impoundment, diversion, pollution, and other threatening activities. Moreover, where possible, habitat quality must be improved if the Idaho springsnail and other endangered species are to recover. Its populations should be monitored, and research undertaken into its biology and habitat needs.

Contacts

U. S. Fish and Wildlife Service
Regional Office, Division of Endangered Species
Eastside Federal Complex
911 N. E. 11th Ave.
Portland, Oregon 97232-4181
Telephone: (503) 231-6121
http://pacific.fws.gov/

Snake River Basin Fish and Wildlife Office
1387 South Vinnell Way, Suite 368
Boise, Idaho 83709-1657
Telephone: (208) 378-5243
Fax: (208) 378-5262

References

U. S. Fish and Wildlife Service. 14 December 1992. "Endangered and Threatened Wildlife and Plants: Determination of Endangered or Threatened Status for Five Aquatic Snails in South Central Idaho." *Federal Register* 57 (240): 59244-59257.

U. S. Fish and Wildlife Service. 1995. "Snake River Aquatic Species Recovery Plan." Snake River Basin Office, Ecological Services, Boise, Idaho.

Flat Pebblesnail

Lepyrium showalteri

Status	Endangered
Listed	October 28, 1998
Family	Hydrobiidae
Description	A small freshwater snail.
Habitat	Occurs in rapid currents of rocky river shoals.
Food	Probably feeds on algae growing on rocks.
Reproduction	Lays capsule of eggs on rocks.
Threats	Habitat destruction and degradation.
Range	Alabama

Description

The flat pebblesnail, *Lepyrium showalteri*, is a small snail in the family Hydrobiidae; however, the species has a large and distinct shell, relative to other hydrobiid species. This snail's shell is also distinguished by its depressed spire and expanded, flattened body whorl. The shells are ovate in outline, flattened, and grow to 0.1-0.2 in (2.5-5 mm) high and 0.2 in (5 mm) wide. The umbilical area is imperforate (no opening), and there are tow to three whorls which rapidly expand.

Behavior

Eggs are laid singly in capsules on hard surfaces. Little else is known of the natural history of this species. It probably feeds on algae growing on rocks.

Habitat

The flat pebblesnail is found attached to clean, smooth stones in rapid currents of river shoals.

Distribution

The flat pebblesnail was historically known from the mainstem Coosa River in Shelby and Talladega Counties, the Cahaba River in Bibb and Dallas Counties, and Little Cahaba River in Bibb County, Alabama.

Threats

The flat pebblesnail has suffered the loss of more than 90% of its original habitat through the construction of dams and impoundments, and to a lesser degree the degradation of water quality by sedimentation and pollution by nutrients. It not been found in the Coosa River portion of its range since the construction of Lay and Logan Martin Dams, and recent survey efforts have failed to locate any surviving populations outside of the Cahaba River drainage. The flat pebblesnail is currently known from one site on the Little Cahaba River, Bibb County, and from a single shoal series on the Cahaba River above the Fall Line, Shelby County, Alabama.

Conservation and Recovery

The only surviving critical habitats of the flat pebblesnail are on privately owned land. It is crucial that these habitats are protected from destruction by the construction of new dams or impoundments. Land-use in the watersheds of the habitats must be modified to reduce erosion and sedimentation, nutrient inputs, and other potentially degrading influences. This can be done by instituting best-management practices in local forestry, agriculture, and construction activities. The populations of the flat pebblesnail should be monitored, and research undertaken into its biology and habitat needs.

Contact

U.S. Fish and Wildlife Service
Jackson Ecological Services Field Office
6578 Dogwood View Parkway, Suite A
Jackson, Mississippi 39213
Telephone: (601) 965-4900
Fax: (601) 965-4340

Reference

U.S. Fish and Wildlife Service. 28 October 1998. "Endangered and Threatened Wildlife and Plants; Endangered Status for Three Aquatic Snails, and Threatened Status for Three Aquatic Snails in the Mobile River Basin of Alabama." *Federal Register* 63 (208): 57610-57620.

Bruneau Hot Springsnail

Pyrgulopsis bruneauensis

Status	Endangered
Listed	January 25, 1993
Family	Hydrobiidae
Description	Thin, transparent, white-clear shell with a black appearance.
Habitat	Plains and plateaus of the Snake River.
Food	Aquatic insects, diatoms.
Reproduction	Lays single round to oval eggs on hard surfaces throughout the year.
Threats	Drought, mining of aquifer system, cattle grazing.
Range	Idaho

Springsnail, photograph. U. S. Fish and Wildlife Service. Reproduced by permission.

Description

The Bruneau hot springsnail, *Pyrgulopsis bruneauensis*, have a small, globose to low-conic shell reaching a length of 0.22 in (0.5 cm) with 3.75 to 4.25 whorls. Fresh shells are thin, transparent, and white-clear, although appearing black due to pigmentation. In addition to its small size, less than 0.11 in (0.3 cm) shell height, distinguishing features include a verge (penis) with a small lobe bearing a single distal glandular ridge and elongate, muscular filament.

Behavior

The Bruneau hot springsnail appears to be an opportunistic grazer that feeds upon algae and other periphyton in proportions similar to those found in its habitat. However, snail densities are lowest in areas of bright green algal mats and highest where periphyton communities are dominated by diatoms, which may provide a more nutritious food source than other food types, thus contributing to this greater density. It logically follows from this that Bruneau hot springsnail may make food selections based on nutritional richness rather than just choosing "preferred" individual food items. Fluctuations in Bruneau hot springsnail abundance correspond with changes in food quality based on chlorophyll content.

Sexual maturity can occur within two months, with a sex ratio approximating 1:1. Reproduction occurs at temperatures between 75.2 and 95°F (24 and 35°C); this occurs throughout the year except when inhibited by high or low temperatures. At sites affected by high ambient temperatures during summer and early fall months, recruitment corresponds with cooler periods. Sites with cooler ambient temperatures also exhibit recruitment during the summer months. Springs with cooler minimum temperatures most likely get warmer than 68°F (20°C) in the summer, providing the species opportunities for increased growth and reproduction.

The Bruneau hot springsnail, whose individuals are dioecious, deposit its single round to oval eggs on hard surfaces such as rock substrates or other snail shells when suitable substrates are unavailable.

Biologists believe that some natural transfer of the Bruneau hot springsnail may occur among sites. The mechanisms for dispersal possibly include waterfowl passively carrying the Bruneau hot springsnail up or down the river corridor and spates, sudden overflows of water resulting from a downpour of rain or melting of snow, in the Bruneau River that would carry this taxon into other warm spring areas downstream. These mechanisms of dispersal would favor upstream to downstream genetic exchange.

Habitat

The hot spring and seep habitats of this snail are hydraulic outflows from the confined, regional geothermal aquifer that underlies Bruneau, Little, and Sugar valleys in north-central Owyhee County, an area of approximately 600 sq mi (155,400 hectares). This water flows through natural faults and fractures in the deep-lying volcanic and subsurface sedimentary rocks until it discharges at the surface through artesian vents, where the ground-level elevation is lower than the potentiometric or hydraulic head of the geothermal aquifer. The vast majority of the groundwater in this aquifer originates as natural recharge from precipitation in and around the Jarbidge and Owyhee mountains south of the Bruneau area. Ground water flows northward from volcanic rocks to sedimentary rocks where it is discharged as either natural springflow, well withdrawals, or leaves the area as underflow.

There also exists a shallow, unconfined coldwater aquifer within the upper layer of sedimentary rock. This second aquifer system is recharged from the infiltration of precipitation, streamflow, and applied irrigation water. Some scientists also believe that there may be recharge from upwardmoving geothermal water into the cold-water aquifer. There also may be additional shallow-water aquifer recharge occurring through leaks in irrigation wells.

The Bruneau hot springsnail occurs in flowing thermal springs and seeps along an 5-mi (8-km)

reach of the Bruneau River in water temperatures ranging from 60.3 to 98.4°F (15.7 to 36.9°C) This species has not been located outside the thermal plumes of hot springs entering the Bruneau River. The Indian Bathtub spring, the type locality, occurs at an elevation of 2,672 ft (814.4 m); the other thermal springs where this snail is found are at comparable elevations. The highest snail densities occur at temperatures ranging from 73 to 98°F (22.7 to 36.7°C). Some of the Bruneau hot springsnail colonies are separated by distances of less than 3.3 ft (1 m).

The Bruneau hot springsnail occurs in these habitats on the exposed surfaces of rocks, gravel, sand, mud, algal film and the underside of the water surface; however, during the winter period of cold ambient temperatures and icing, snails are most often located on the undersides of outflow substrates that are least exposed to cold temperatures. In madicolous habitats, those with thin sheets of water flowing over rock faces, the species has been found in water less than 0.39 in (1 cm) deep. Current velocity is not considered a significant factor limiting the distribution of this snail, since they have been observed to inhabit nearly 100% of the available current regimes. In a September 1989 survey of 10 thermal springs in the vicinity of the Hot Creek-Bruneau River confluence, the total number of Bruneau hot springsnails per spring ranged from one to 17,319. The species abundance fluctuates seasonally but is generally stable under persistent springflow conditions. Although on-site conditions are important, snail abundance is influenced primarily by temperature, spring discharge, and chlorophyll ratios.

Common aquatic community associates of the Bruneau hot springsnail include the molluscs *Physella gyrina*, *Fossaria exigua*, and *Gyraulus vermicularis*; the creeping water bug (*Ambrysus mormon minor*); and the skiff beetle (*Hydroscapha natans*). In addition, Hot Creek and several of the thermal springs along the Bruneau River support populations of *Poecilia reticulata* and *Tilapia* sp. These are exotic guppies that were apparently released into upper Hot Creek at the Indian Bathtub, from which they spread downstream and into nearby thermal springs and seeps along the Bruneau River.

Distribution

The most recent habitat survey in 1996 found Bruneau Hot Springsnails in 116 of 204 flowing thermal springs and seeps in their 5-mi (8-km) historical range along the Bruneau River. Eighty-six of these occupied springs are located upstream of the confluence of Hot Creek with the Bruneau River, 10 are at the confluence of Hot Creek, and 20 are downstream of the confluence of Hot Creek with the Bruneau River. Surveys conducted since 1991 indicate a moderate but significant decrease in suitable habitat and occupied pools. Since 1991, the total number of thermal springs in the Bruneau River has declined from 214 to 204, the number of springs occupied by Bruneau hot springsnails has declined from 130 to 116, and the population densities of occupied areas have declined from about 55 to 47 individuals per square foot (1 sq ft=0.09 sq m). Total site area, including all thermal springs and seeps whether occupied or unoccupied by Bruneau hot springsnails, increased by 4.3% from 1991 to 1996. Most of this increase was due to lower flows at one unoccupied spring site, resulting in more exposure of thermal outflow area below Buckaroo Dam, downstream of the majority of the occupied springs.

The Indian Bathtub area and most of the thermal springs along the Bruneau River upstream of Hot Creek are on lands administered by the Bureau of Land Management, while most Bruneau Hot Springsnail habitats downstream of the Indian Bathtub and Hot Creek confluence are on private land.

Threats

The primary threat to the Bruneau hot springsnail is a major reduction in its free-flowing thermal spring and seep habitats caused by agricultural-related ground water withdrawal and pumping. This activity has depleted and contiues to deplete the regional geothermal aquifer upon which snail habitat depends. Some scientist are convinced that leaks from uncased or poorly cased wells are also reducing water levels in the geothermal aquifer. The species and its habitat are also vulnerable to habitat modification from the sediments deposited by flash floods. In summary, the cumulative effects of water withdrawal continue to threaten the increasingly fragmented populations

of the Bruneau hot springsnail and their thermal habitats.

Ground water withdrawals from wells for domestic and agricultural purposes began in the area of the geothermal aquifer in the late 1890s. By the mid-1960s the decline in discharge from the Indian Bathtub spring became very noticeable, coinciding with the accelerated increase in ground water withdrawal to provide irrigation for croplands newly put into production.

The two most apparent effects of pumping stress are declines in hydraulic head and declines in spring discharge. Changes in discharge from thermal springs correlate with changes in hydraulic head, which fluctuate seasonally and are substantially less during late summer than in the spring.

Discharge fluctuations, which occur at most occupied springs, very frequently correspond with ground-water withdrawal rates; there are lower flows in the late spring to early fall when the need for pumping is greatest, and higher flows during late fall to spring when the need for pumping is lowest. Discharge from many of the thermal springs along Hot Creek and the Bruneau River has decreased or has been lost in the last 25 years, thus further restricting habitat for this taxon. The Hot Creek/Indian Bathtub spring site lost more than 90% of both its habitat and snail population during the period from 1954 to 1981. Rapidly dwindling spring flows were instrumental in this precipitous decline.

Spring discharge at the Indian Bathtub in 1964 was approximately 2,400 gal (9,085 l) per minute; by 1978, it had dropped to between 130-162 gal (492-613 l) per minute; and by the summer of 1990, discharge fell to zero through the early fall water withdrawal season. Visible spring discharge at the Indian Bathtub continues to be seasonal, intermittent most years, and quite low.

Snail population at the Indian Bathtub spring occur on vertical rockfaces protected from flash floods. In 1991, a flash flood sent huge amounts of sediment into the Hot Creek drainage, resulting in a 50% reduction in the size of the Indian Bathtub, a portion of which is now covered by approximately 10 ft (3 m) of sediment. Rockface habitat in the immediate vicinity of Indian Bathtub was also severely reduced and covered with sediment during this and other recent flash floods.

Ongoing population monitoring studies indicate a lack of movement or recruitment of Bruneau hot springsnails back to the Hot Creek/Indian Bathtub sites. Several factors have been cited as contributing to this situation, including silty substrate that lacks available rockface surfaces for reproduction, weak migration abilities, fish predation, and a lack of an upstream colonization that may have prevented the Bruneau hot springsnail from returning to the upper Hot Creek and Indian Bathtub sites.

Ground water withdrawals have generally declined over the past 15-20 years, primarily due to cropland retired from production through a cropland reclamation program. However, the volume of water pumped may increase significantly in the next few years as croplands will again be put into production. If present water management practices continue, if a substantial proportion of the croplands are returned to production, and if drier spring and summer climatic conditions return—all of which affect pumping rates and duration—water levels in the aquifer will either continue to decline or will eventually stabilize at a lower level, resulting in the further loss of Bruneau hot springsnail habitat.

While huge springflow declines have been documented at Indian Bathtub spring and several other springs, springflow data has not been collected in all the remaining 116 springs containing Bruneau hot springsnails. Some scientists believe that prior to the recent decline in water levels in the aquifer and the consequent fragmentation of remaining populations all of the springs and seeps supporting snails were connected, which allowed the natural dispersal and transfer of individuals. Studies done in the early 1990s indicate a general decline in the total number of thermal springs along the Bruneau River, the number of springs occupied by Bruneau hot springsnails, and the densities per unit area of Bruneau hot springsnails in occcupied pools. In 1993, dead Bruneau hot springsnails were found at one previously occupied spring site where flows had recently diminished and nine spring sites showed noticeable reductions in discharge. At this time there is no information available indicating how much lower water levels can continue to decline before all thermal springs along the Bruneau

River are lost. As potentiometric surfaces in the geothermal aquifer continue to decline, additional spring discharges will be reduced or lost, resulting in the continued loss of Bruneau hot springsnail habitat.

Cattle grazing has damaged Bruneau hot springsnail habitats and directly eliminated snails, especially along Hot Creek. Cattle have destroyed and displaced snails through trampling instream substrates, and their browsing removes heat-moderating riparian vegetation, allowing water temperatures to climb to levels that first damage reproduction and then can kill Bruneau hot springsnails. Livestock grazing in the watershed adjacent to Hot Creek, combined with ongoing drought conditions, contributed to an increase in sedimentation of that creek which eliminated Bruneau hot springsnail seep and spring habitats for almost 500 ft (152 m) in the Indian Bathtub/Hot Creek drainage. The Bureau of Land Management is going to control livestock grazing by installing fencing on the north end of Hot Creek drainage and the west side of the Bruneau River. The Bureau of Land Management also plans to install additional fencing along the east side of the Bruneau River. Both fencing projects, if properly maintained, will protect remaining snail habitat from the effects of livestock.

There are no current commercial uses for this species, although certain mollusc species have subsequently become vulnerable to illegal collection for scientific purposes after their rarity was widely publicized. Collection could now become a threat to this taxon because the distribution of the Bruneau hot springsnail is restricted and generally well-known.

There are no known diseases that affect Bruneau hot springsnails, but juvenile snails smaller are vulnerable to a variety of predators. Damselflies and dragonflies have been observed feeding upon Bruneau hot springsnails in the wild. The presence of wild guppie populations in Hot Creek and several of the other small thermal springs downstream along the west bank of the Bruneau River are a potential threat to this species, as they have been observed feeding upon these snails in the laboratory. In addition to guppies, a species of *Tilapia* has ascended into and reproduced in Hot Creek. The presence of this new potential exotic predator may constitute a threat to the Bruneau hot springsnail by restricting repopulation of the snail into Hot Creek and at other thermal spring sites that may be available to both species. The guppy and *Tilapia* are each capable of summer migration, when water temperatures are suitable, into the Bruneau River corridor, both upstream and downstream of Hot Creek. Movement of these exotic fish species into other thermal springs occupied by the Bruneau hot springsnail might affect their continued survival within individual spring sites. It should be noted that madicolous habitats support neither of these two exotic fishes or dragonflies, but do harbor numerous damselflies.

Sedimentation of Bruneau hot springsnail habitats is a significant threat to this species. Substantial sediments deposited by periodic flash floods cannot be flushed away by the remaining weak and declining springflows. Measures which could protect Bruneau hot springsnail habitats in the Indian Bathtub and Hot Creek areas from the effects of flash flooding have not been implemented. These measures include the construction of small retention dams in the Hot Creek watershed to trap runoff sediment while maintaining thermal seep habitats. Flooding and sedimentation therefore continue to threaten Bruneau hot springsnail habitat.

Conservation and Recovery

The Bureau of Land Management manages the public lands containing Bruneau hot springsnails and their habitats along Hot Creek and the Bruneau River. The Bureau of Land Management issues permits for livestock grazing on these lands and grants authorizations that could lead to the drilling of new wells and increased ground water use on Bureau of Land Management lands. In the past, the Bureau of Land Management has shown an interest in conserving this snail species by soliciting input from the U.S. Fish and Wildlife Service (FWS) regarding impacts that may result from any proposed activities. As discussed earlier, the Bureau of Land Management has implemented fencing to protect Bruneau hot springsnail habitats from grazing impacts.

The FWS entered into a short-term conservation agreement with Owen Ranches, Inc., the landowners of the Bruneau hot springsnail's habitat in Indian Bathtub spring. This conservation agreement included fencing, through funds provided by the FWS, to regulate livestock use and improve stream conditions. Although the agreement expired in October 1992, the current landowner has honored the terms of the agreement and voluntarily excludes livestock grazing from the Indian Bathtub spring.

The cropland reclamation program is a voluntary program that offers annual rental payments, incentive payments for certain activities, and cost-share assistance to establish approved cover on eligible cropland. This program encourages farmers to plant long-term resource-conserving covers to improve soil, water, and wildlife resources. The duration of the contracts are between 10 and 15 years; all of the current lands in the program have expired. It is unlikely that all those eligible for the new agreements will participate due to a dramatic drop in the rental rates currently offered through the program, declining from about US$50 per acre to about US$20 per acre (1 acre=0.4 hectare). Area landowners have indicated that this drop in rental fees will not provide the necessary incentive to continue participation.

After the Bruneau hot springsnail was list as endangered in January 1993, a joint lawsuit was filed by various Idaho plaintiffs to challenge that listing. In December 1993, the district court issued a ruling in favor of the Plaintiffs and set aside the final listing rule for the Bruneau hot springsnail. The district court decision was appealed by two intervening Idaho conservation groups and in 1995, the appellate court overturned the district court decision and reinstated the Bruneau hot springsnail to the endangered species list.

Contacts

U.S. Fish and Wildlife Service
Regional Office, Division of Endangered Species
Eastside Federal Complex
911 N.E. 11th Ave.
Portland, Oregon 97232-4181
(503) 231-6121
http://pacific.fws.gov/

Snake River Basin Office
U.S. Fish and Wildlife Service
1387 S. Vinnell Way, Room 386
Boise, Idaho 83709
(208) 378-5243

Reference

U.S. Fish and Wildlife Service. 17 June 1998. "Notice of Determination To Retain Endangered Status for the Bruneau Hot Springsnail in Southwestern Idaho Under the Endangered Species Act." *Federal Register* 63 (116): 32981-32996.

Socorro Springsnail

Pyrgulopsis neomexicana

Status	Endangered
Listed	September 30, 1991
Family	Hydrobiidae (Aquatic Snail)
Description	Minute aquatic snail with an elongated, tan spiral shell.
Habitat	Thermal spring.
Food	Algae and other organic detritus.
Reproduction	Eggs laid in spring and summer.
Threats	Limited range, destruction of habitat.
Range	New Mexico

Description

The Socorro springsnail is a minute aquatic snail with an elongated, light tan, spiral shell that measures only 0.1 in (0.25 cm) in length. Females are larger than males. The body and head are dark gray to black; the tentacles are dark at the base, lightening to pale gray at the tips. Snails of this family breathe through gills rather than lungs and have a lidlike structure on the foot called the operculum. *Pyrgulopsis* species are distinguished by characteristics of the structure of the male sexual organ. This snail has also been known as *Amnicola neomexicana* and *Fontelicella neomexicana*.

Behavior

The Socorro springsnail feeds on algae and elements of the organic film on the water. It lays eggs during the spring and summer.

Habitat

This snail species inhabits slowly flowing water near a thermal spring source. It is found on stones, among aquatic vegetation, and in the upper layer of organic muck on the bottom.

Distribution

The species was first described in 1916 from specimens taken from thermal springs west of Socorro (Socorro County), New Mexico. It no longer occurs in these springs.

The Socorro springsnail survives in a single spring in Socorro County. The main spring source has been impounded and only a single, small free-flowing source remains. The source pool measures less than a square meter in area; an outflow stream flows about 8 ft (2.5 m) to an irrigation ditch. The species inhabits the source pool and the outflow stream. The total population has been estimated at 5,000 individuals.

Threats

The greatest threat to the Socorro springsnail is its extremely limited distribution. Inhabiting a single small spring, the species is in danger of extinction through any change in its habitat. Pumping of the source pool, pollution, the introduction of predatory species, or vandalism, are threats to the species.

Conservation and Recovery

The spring is on private land and the owners did not object to the listing of the Socorro springsnail as Endangered.

Contact

U.S. Fish and Wildlife Service
Division of Endangered Species
P.O. Box 1306
Albuquerque, New Mexico 87103
http://southwest.fws.gov/

References

Hershler, R. and F. G. Thompson. 1987. "North American Hydrobiidae (Gastropoda: Rissoacea): Redescription and Systematic Relationships of *Tryonia* Stimpson, 1865 and *Pyrgulopsis* Call and Pilsbry. 1886." *Nautilus* 101(1):25-32.

New Mexico Department of Game and Fish. 1985. *Handbook of Species Endangered in New Mexico.* Santa Fe, New Mexico.

Taylor, D. W. 1987. *Fresh Water Mollusks from New Mexico and Vicinity.* Bulletin 116. New Mexico Bureau of Mines and Mineral Resources. Socorro, New Mexico.

Taylor, D. W. 1983. "Report to the State of New Mexico on a Status Investigation of Mollusca in New Mexico." New Mexico Department of Game and Fish, Santa Fe, New Mexico.

Royal Marstonia Snail

Pyrgulopsis ogmorhaphe

Royal Marstonia, photograph. U. S. Fish and Wildlife Service. Reproduced by permission.

Status	Endangered
Listed	April 15, 1994
Family	Hydrobiidae (Aquatic Snail)
Description	Small annual snail with a thin, conical-shaped shell.
Habitat	Leaves and twigs in the quieter pools downstream from the spring source.
Food	Diatoms and plant debris.
Reproduction	Annual life cycle.
Threats	Siltation contributed by coal mining, poor land use practices, and waste discharges.
Range	Tennessee

Description

The royal marstonia snail, *Pyrgulopsis (=Marstonia) ogmorhaphe,* is a small annual species, usually less than 0.25 in (6.4 mm) in length. It is distinguished from other closely related species by: 1) its relatively large size; 2) its large number of whorls (5.2 to 5.8); 3) its deeply incised, suture-producing, strongly shouldered whorls, which are almost flat above; 4) its complete aperture, which is broadly ovate in shape with a rounded posterior corner; 5) its outer lip, which is slightly arched forward in lateral profile; 6) its thin shell; 7) its conical terete shape; and 8) its enlarged bursa copulatrix with a completely exposed duct.

Behavior

This species eats diatoms and plant debris and has an annual life cycle.

Habitat

Royal marstonia snails are generally found in the diatomaceous "ooze" and on leaves and twigs in the quieter pools downstream from the spring source.

Distribution

The royal marstonia snail is known only from two spring runs in the Sequatchie River system in Marion County, Tennessee.

Because this species has an annual life cycle, the number of individuals varies from year to year, and the precise number of individuals is unknown. The royal snail has an extremely limited distribution and low numbers.

Threats

While no populations are known to have been lost, the general deterioration of the water quality that has resulted from siltation and other pollutants contributed by coal mining, poor land use practices, and waste discharges likely are impacting the species. This could result in serious, irreversible decline of the species. Additionally, both existing populations inhabit extremely limited areas, and they are very vulnerable to extirpation from accidental toxic chemical spills or vandalism. Other threats include road construction; agricultural, municipal, industrial, and mining runoff, both direct and from subsurface flows; cattle grazing; vandalism; and pollution from trash thrown into the spring. Also, timber harvesting for wood chip mills proposed for southeastern Tennessee and northeastern Alabama could impact this species.

Because this species is very rare, with populations restricted to extremely short stream reaches, unregulated taking for any purpose could threaten its continued existence.

Conservation and Recovery

The U. S. Fish and Wildlife Service notified federal agencies that might have had programs affecting this species. No specific proposed federal actions were identified that would likely affect the species. Federal activities that could have an impact on the species include, but are not limited to, the carrying out or the issuance of permits for reservoir construction, stream alteration, wastewater facility development, pesticide registration, and road and bridge construction.

Contacts

U. S. Fish and Wildlife Service
Regional Office, Division of Endangered Species
1875 Century Blvd., Suite 200
Atlanta, Georgia 30334
(404) 679-4000
http://southeast.fws.gov/

Ecological Services Field Office
446 Neal Street
Cookeville, TN 38501
Telephone: (615) 528-6481
Fax: (615) 528-7075

Reference

U. S. Fish and Wildlife Service. 15 April 1994. "Endangered and Threatened Wildlife and Plants: Determination of Endangered Status for the Royal Snail and Anthony's Riversnail." *Federal Register*, pp. 17994-17998.

Armored Snail

Pyrgulopsis pachyta

Status	Endangered
Listed	February 25, 2000
Family	Hydrobiidae
Description	Small snail with an ovate-conical shell of pronounced thickness.
Habitat	Submerged vegetation along streambanks.
Food	Detritus.
Reproduction	Unknown.
Threats	Siltation and pollution from waste discharges.
Range	Alabama

Description

The armored snail is a small annual, usually less than 0.16 in (4 mm) in length. The shell is ovate-conical with a pronounced thickness. The edge of the shell opening, or peristome, is complete. The male reproductive organ, called the verge, has a small raised gland on the ventral surface and two small glands along the left margin of the lobe on the tip.

It can be distinguished from other closely related species by the verge, and also shell characteristics. Shells of other species in the *Pyrgulopsis* have much thinner, almost transparent shells, and do not have complete peristome along the opening.

Behavior

Little is known about the armored snail. It is a freshwater snail that spends much of its time submerged under water amongst the vegetation.

Members of the genus prefer to be near a spring or a stream that emerges from the ground, natural pools, and marsh-like springs. They also concentrate in areas where there is stable temperature and chemistry, and a flow regime that characterizes headsprings.

Habitat

The armored snail is generally found among submerged tree roots and bryophytes along stream margins in areas of slow to moderate flow. Sometimes they are found in submerged detritus along pool edges.

Distribution

There are two populations of armored snail, one in Piney Creek and the other in Limestone Creek, in Limestone County, Alabama. Populations seem very concentrated and only cover a very small area.

Historically, these two populations may have been part of one larger population. Piney Creek was once a tributary of Limestone Creek before the creation of the Wheeler Reservoir.

Threats

Due to small population sizes, limited occupied habitat, and annual life cycle, the armored snail is extremely vulnerable. Threats include direct loss of habitat, siltation, altered water chemistry and chemical pollution.

The placement of Wheeler Reservoir has greatly impacted this snail's habitat. Dams and their impounded water can form barriers to snail movement, promote siltation and encourage changes in the flow of water and water chemistry. This reduces food and oxygen availability, affecting reproductive success and altering habitat.

In addition, when local water and habitat quality change, many isolated snail populations become more vulnerable to run-off and discharges into the watershed.

Additional sources of siltation include channel modification, agriculture, cattle grazing, logging, chip mills, unpaved road drainage, rock quarries, bridges and road expansion projects and industrial and residential development.

Discharges from polluting sources increase eutrophication, decrease dissolved oxygen concentration, increase acidity and conductivity, and create other changes in water chemistry. Some sources include leach from agricultural fields (especially cotton), residential lawns, livestock operations and leaking septic tanks which also contribute to changes in water quality.

Conservation and Recovery

Current conservation measures include the certain designation of critical habitat and a review of all projects affecting habitat. After projects are reviewed appropriate conservation measures will be taken.

The U. S. Fish and Wildlife Service has determined that dams and their impoundments prevent the natural recolonization of surviving snail populations. Even if watershed impacts improve or even disappear, the damage will continue as long as the dams are present.

Contacts

U. S. Fish and Wildlife Service
Regional Office, Division of Endangered Species
1875 Century Blvd., Suite 200
Atlanta, Georgia 30345
http://southeast.fws.gov/

Asheville Field Office
U. S. Fish and Wildlife Service
160 Zillicoa Street
Asheville, North Carolina 28801-1082
Telephone: (828) 258-3939
Fax: (828) 258-5330

References

United States Department of the Interior. 25 February 2000. "Endangered and Threatened Wildlife and Plants: Endangered Status for the Armored Snail and Slender Campeloma." *Federal Register* 65 (38).

Hershler, R. 2 January 1998. "A Systematic Review of the Hydrobiid Snails (Gastropoda: Rissooidea) of the Great Basin, Western United States. Part I. Genus *Pyrgulopsis*." *The Veliger*. 41 (1): 1-132.

Bliss Rapids Snail

Taylorconcha serpenticola

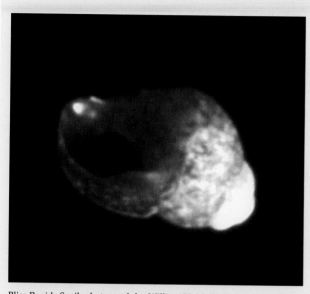

Status	Threatened
Listed	December 14, 1992
Family	Hydrobidae (Aquatic Snail)
Description	Colorless or orange-red snail with smaller rounded whorls.
Habitat	Free-flowing cool spring alcoves.
Food	Plant debris or diatoms.
Reproduction	Egg laying occurs with two months of reproduction.
Threats	Deteriorating water quality from hydro-electric development, competition with other snails.
Range	Idaho

Bliss Rapids Snail, photograph by William H. Mullins. Reproduced by permission.

Description

The Bliss Rapids snail is an example of a "living fossil." This is due to the fact that it is a relict from an ancient lake—the late Pliocene (Blancan) Lake Idaho. This snail is 0.08-0.1 in (2-2.5 mm) long with three whorls and is roughly ovoid in shape. There are two color variants, or morphs, of the Bliss River Rapids snail. One is the colorless or "pale form" and the other is the orange-red or "orange form." The pale morph is slightly smaller with rounded whorls with more melanin pigment on the body.

Behavior

Reproduction in the Bliss Rapids snail varies according to habitat. Reproduction occurs October to February in mainstem Snake River colonies and February to May in large-spring colonies. Egg laying occurs within two months of reproduction and eggs appear to hatch within one month. Adult snails exhibit a strong seasonal die-off after reproduction.

This species is known to migrate only to food sources.

Habitat

The Bliss Rapids snail is restricted to a few isolated free-flowing reaches or spring alcove habitats of the Snake River. This aquatic system is characterized by cold, well-oxygenated, unpolluted water. The Bliss Rapids snail occurs on stable, cobble-boulder substratum only in flowing waters in the Snake River and also in a few spring alcove habitats in the Hagerman Valley. The species does not burrow in sediments and normally avoids surfaces with attached plants. Known river colonies of the Bliss Rapids snail occur only in areas associated with spring influences or rapids edge environments and tend to flank shorelines. Generally, the species requires cold, clean, well-oxygenated flowing water of low turbidity. The species is found at varying depths if dissolved oxygen and temperature requirements persist and is found in shallow, (less than 0.4 in, or 1 cm) permanent cold springs. This snail is thought to be somewhat photophobic and resides on the lateral sides and undersides of rocks during daylight. The species will migrate to graze on perilithon on the uppermost surfaces of rocks nocturnally. The Bliss Rapids snail can be locally quite abundant, and is especially abundant on smooth rock surfaces with common encrusting red algae.

Distribution

Prior to 1987, the Bliss Rapids snail was known primarily from the mainstem Snake River boulder bars above King Hill and upstream in Box Canyon Springs. Prior to dam construction there was probably a single population throughout the historic range and possibly upstream as well. Based on live collections, the species currently exists as fragmented populations primarily concentrated in the Hagerman reach in tailwaters of Bliss and Lower Salmon Dams and Thousand Springs, Minnie Miller Springs, Banbury Springs, Niagara Springs, and Box Canyon Springs.

Threats

The free-flowing, cool water environments required by this species have been impacted by and are vulnerable to continued adverse habitat modification and deteriorating water quality from hydroelectric development, peak-loading effects from existing hydroelectric project operations, water withdrawal and diversions, water pollution, and inadequate regulatory mechanisms. The Bliss River Rapids snail may also be adversely affected by competition with an exotic snail (*Potamopyrgus antipodarum*). With the exception of segments of land owned by The Nature Conservancy (Thousand Springs), the aquatic habitats occupied by this species are virtually unprotected from the aforementioned threats.

Ground water mining or withdrawal may also impact spring stream habitats of the Bliss Rapids snail population above American Falls Reservoir. Biologists of the Shoshone Bannock Tribal Reservation have observed water fluctuations and seasonal declines in spring flows along this stretch of the Snake River concurrent with the irrigation season. Winter cattle grazing and recreational access may also be impacting spring habitats of the Bliss Rapids snail on the Shoshone Bannock Reservation. Al-though access is controlled, waterfowl hunters, and fishermen to some extent, utilize these spring areas throughout the fall and early winter.

Changes in the use of stored water in the Snake River basin to assist recovery efforts for other threatened and endangered species may also impact this species and its habitat. The Bonneville Power Administration, State of Idaho, and Idaho Power Company are exploring alternatives to assist outmigrating endangered Snake River Sockeye salmon and threatened Spring and Summer Chinook from utilizing water from the upper Snake River Basin. The Idaho Department of Health and Welfare, Division of Environmental Quality, under authority of the State Nutrient Management Act, is coordinating efforts to identify and implement preventative actions which will reduce nutrient loading to the middle Snake River. These efforts will address pollution control strategies.

Conservation and Recovery

The U. S. Fish and Wildlife Service published a Recovery Plan for the Bliss Rapids snail and other endangered mollusks in the Snake River Basin in 1992. Critical habitat of this species occurs on Federally owned lands (Shoshone Bannock Tribal Reservation and lands owned by the Bureau of Land Management). This publicly owned habitat must be protected from impoundment, diversion, pollution, and other threatening activities within the rivers or in their watersheds. Some of its habitat is protected in the Thousand Springs Preserve owned by The Nature Conservancy, a private conservation organization. Other habitats (including critical watershed lands) are on private land and are at risk from various human activities. These areas should be protected by acquiring the habitat and designating ecological reserves, or by negotiating conservation easements with the landowners. The populations of the Bliss Rapids snail should be monitored, and research undertaken into its biology and habitat needs.

Contacts

U. S. Fish and Wildlife Service
Eastside Federal Complex
911 N. E. 11th Avenue
Portland, Oregon 97232-4181
Phone: (503) 231-6121
http://pacific.fws.gov/

Snake River Basin Fish and Wildlife Office
1387 South Vinnell Way, Suite 368
Boise, Idaho 83709-1657
Telephone: (208) 378-5243
Fax: (208) 378-5262

References

U. S. Fish and Wildlife Service. 14 December 1992. "Endangered and Threatened Wildlife and Plants: Determination of Endangered or Threatened Status for Five Aquatic Snails in South Central Idaho." *Federal Register* 57 (240): 59244-59257.

U. S. Fish and Wildlife Service. 1995. "Snake River Aquatic Species Recovery Plan." Snake River Basin Office, Ecological Services, Boise, Idaho.

Alamosa Springsnail

Tryonia alamosae

Status	Endangered
Listed	September 30, 1991
Family	Hydrobiidae (Aquatic Snail)
Description	Minute aquatic snail with a translucent, spiral shell.
Habitat	Thermal springs.
Food	Algae and organic detritus.
Reproduction	Eggs hatch within the female's body.
Threats	Limited distribution, disruption of spring flow.
Range	New Mexico

Description

The Alamosa springsnail is a minute aquatic snail with a thin, translucent spiral shell up to 0.1 in (0.25 cm) in length. Females are about 50% larger than males. The body varies from black to gray and the tentacles are speckled with dark spots. This species breathes by means of gills rather than lungs.

Behavior

This snail feeds on algae and organic detritus. The eggs develop within the body of the female, and reproduction does not appear to be seasonal.

Habitat

This springsnail inhabits the slow-flowing currents of thermal springs. It is found on stones and submerged vegetation, but is absent from swift flowing water and muddy bottoms.

Distribution

The Alamosa springsnail was discovered in 1979, in Ojo Caliente (Socorro County), one of the largest thermal springs in New Mexico. It is currently known only from Ojo Caliente and a nearby system of smaller thermal springs. Although no population estimates have been made, the snail is considered abundant on gravel and vegetation in the shallow, slow-moving portions of the spring outflows.

Threats

The greatest threat to the Alamosa springsnail is its extremely limited distribution. Found in only a few thermal spring outflows, the species could face extinction through any change in its aquatic habitat. Impounding of the springs, pollution, the introduction of predatory species, or vandalism are ever-present threats to the species.

However, several of the smaller springs have been dug and impounded in the past. At present, the spring water flows through a canyon and then is diverted for irrigation use and to supply water to villages downstream. Future development of the springs to increase the water supply could threaten the Alamosa springsnail.

Conservation and Recovery

The thermal spring is on private land and the owners did not object to the listing of the Alamosa springsnail as Endangered.

Contact

U.S. Fish and Wildlife Service
Regional Office, Division Endangered Species
P.O. Box 1306
Albuquerque, New Mexico 87103
http://southwest.fws.gov/

References

Hershler, R. and F. G. Thompson. 1987. "North American Hydrobiidae (Gastropoda: Rissoacea): Redescription and Systematic Relationships of *Tryonia* Stimpson, 1865 and *Pyrgulopsis* Call and Pilsbry, 1886." *Nautilus* 101(1):25-32.

Mexico Department of Game and Fish. 1985. *Handbook of Species Endangered in New Mexico.* Santa Fe, New Mexico.

Taylor, D. W. 1987. *Fresh Water Mollusks from New Mexico and Vicinity.* Bulletin 116. New Mexico Bureau of Mines and Mineral Resources. Socorro, New Mexico.

Taylor, D. W. 1983. "Report to the State of New Mexico on a Status Investigation of Mollusca in New Mexico." New Mexico Department of Game and Fish, Santa Fe, New Mexico.

Anthony's Riversnail

Athearnia anthonyi

Status	Endangered
Listed	April 15, 1994
Family	Pleuroceridae
Description	Relatively large freshwater snail that is ovate and olive green to yellowish brown in color.
Habitat	Shoal areas of tributaries of big rivers.
Food	Diatoms and plant debris.
Reproduction	Annual life cycle.
Threats	Siltation contributed by coal mining, poor land use practices, and waste discharges.
Range	Alabama, Georgia, Tennessee

Description

This relatively large freshwater snail, which grows to about 1 in (2.5 cm) in length, is ovate and olive green to yellowish brown in color.

Behavior

This species eats diatoms and plant debris, which it grazes along mud surfaces, rocky surfaces and macrophytes. Anthony's riversnail has an annual life cycle.

Habitat

Anthony's riversnail is a big-river species that was historically associated with the shoal areas in the main stem of the Tennessee River and the lower reaches of some of its tributaries. Presently, only two small populations are known to survive-one in the Sequatchie River, Marion County, Tennessee; and one in Limestone Creek, Limestone County, Alabama.

Distribution

Anthony's riversnail is a big-river species that was historically associated with the shoal areas in the main stem of the Tennessee River and the lower reaches of some of its tributaries. There are histori-cal records of the species from the following rivers in Tennessee: lower French Broad, Nolichucky, Clinch, Beaver Creek, Little Tennessee, Tellico, Sequatchie, Little Sequatchie, Battle Creek; in Georgia from South Chickamauga and Tiger Creeks; and in Alabama from Limestone Creek.

Presently, only two small populations are known to survive-one in the Sequatchie River, Marion County, Tennessee; and one in Limestone Creek, Limestone County, Alabama.

Because this species has an annual life cycle, the number of individuals varies from year to year, and the precise number of individuals is unknown. The Anthony's riversnail has an extremely limited distribution and low numbers.

Threats

Many populations were lost when much of the Tennessee River and the lower reaches of its tributaries were impounded. The general water quality deterioration that has resulted from siltation and other pollutants contributed by coal mining, poor land use practices, and waste discharges was likely responsible for the species' further decline. These factors continue to impact the Sequatchie River and Limestone Creek populations. Further, timber harvesting for wood chip mills proposed for south-

Anthony's Riversnail, photograph. U. S. Fish and Wildlife Service. Reproduced by permission.

eastern Tennessee and northeastern Alabama could impact this species.

Both existing populations inhabit short river reaches; thus, they are very vulnerable to extirpation from accidental toxic chemical spills. As the Sequatchie River and Limestone Creek are isolated by impoundments from other Tennessee tributaries, recolonization of any extirpated populations would be unlikely without human intervention. Additionally, because these populations are isolated, their long-term genetic viability is questionable.

Because this species is very rare, with populations restricted to extremely short stream reaches, unregulated taking for any purpose could threaten its continued existence. Therefore, the U.S. Fish and Wildlife Service decided not to designate critical habitat since the publication of precise population locations would increase the collection threat. FWS also determined that there was little advantage to the snail to designate critical habitat.

FWS notified Federal agencies that could have a program affecting this species. No specific proposed Federal actions were identified that would likely affect the species. Federal activities that could occur and impact the species include, but are not limited to, the carrying out or the issuance of permits for reservoir construction, stream alteration, wastewater facility development, pesticide registration, and road and bridge construction.

Conservation and Recovery

The Anthony's riversnail only survives in two small, isolated populations. Its critical habitat is in short reaches of the Sequatchie River, Tennessee, and in Limestone Creek, Alabama. This habitat is in watercourses running through privately owned land. Its conservation requires the protection of its critical habitats from potential impoundment, and from pollution associated with coal mining and land-use practices in the watershed that cause erosion and inputs of nutrients and other chemicals.

The populations of the Anthony's riversnail must be monitored, and research undertaken into its basic biology and ecological requirements. If suitable habitat can be found, additional populations should be established.

Contacts

U.S. Fish and Wildlife Service
Ecological Services Field Office
446 Neal Street
Cookeville, Tennessee 38501-4027
Telephone: (931) 528-6481
Fax: (931) 528-7075

Ecological Services Field Office
P.O. Box 1190
Daphne, Alabama 36526-1190
Telephone: (334) 441-5181
Fax: (334) 441-6222

Reference

U.S. Fish and Wildlife Service. 15 April 1994 "Endangered and Threatened Wildlife and Plants: Determination of Endangered Status for the Royal Snail and Anthony's Riversnail." *Federal Register* 59: 17994-17998.

Lacy Elimia

Elimia crenatella

Status	Threatened
Listed	October 28, 1998
Family	Pleuroceridae
Description	A small, dark brown to black, aquatic snail.
Habitat	Rocky shoals and gravel bars in flowing reaches of larger rivers.
Food	Algae (periphyton) grazed from rocks.
Reproduction	Lays eggs.
Threats	Habitat destruction by impoundments and degradation by pollution.
Range	Alabama

Elimia (Snail), photograph by Art Bogan. Reproduced by permission.

Description

The *Elimia crenatella*, (lacy elimia) is a small species in the family Pleuroceridae. Growing to about 0.4 in (1 cm) in length, the shell is conic in shape, strongly striate, and often folded in the upper whorls. Shell color is dark brown to black, often purple in the aperture, and without banding. The aperture is small and ovate. The lacy elimia is easily distinguished from other elimia species by a combination of size, ornamentation, and color.

Behavior

Most elimia species graze on periphyton growing on bottom substrates. Individual snails are either male or female. Eggs are laid in early spring and hatch in about two weeks. Snails apparently become sexually mature in their first year, but in some species females may not lay until their second year. Some elimia may live as long as five years.

Habitat

The lacy elimia is usually found in tight clusters or colonies on larger rocks within a shoal. Elimia snails are gill breathing snails that typically inhabit highly oxygenated waters on rock shoals and gravel bars.

Distribution

The lacy elimia was historically abundant in the Coosa River main stem from St. Clair to Chilton County, Alabama, and was also known in several Coosa River tributaries—Big Will's Creek, DeKalb County; Kelley's Creek, St. Clair County; and Choccolocco and Tallaseehatchee Creeks, Talladega County, Alabama. The lacy elimia has not been recently located at any historic collection site. However, as a result of the recent survey efforts, previously unreported populations were discovered in three Coosa River tributaries—Cheaha, Emauhee, and Weewoka Creeks, Talladega County, Alabama. The species is locally abundant in the lower reaches of Cheaha Creek. This stream originates within the Talladega National Forest; however, no specimens of the lacy elimia have been collected on Forest Service lands. The species has also been found at single sites in Emauhee and Weewoka Creeks, where specimens are rare, and difficult to locate.

Threats

The lacy elimia has been eliminated from more than 90% of its historical habitat. This has been caused by the destruction of its shoal habitat by the construction of impoundments, and the degradation of water quality by sedimentation and pollution by nutrients. There are now only three known populations of the lacy elimia. It occurs in small stream channels in Cheaha, Emauhee, and Weewoka Creeks.

Conservation and Recovery

The habitats of the lacy elimia are on privately owned land. It is crucial that these critical habitats are protected from destruction by the construction of new dams or impoundments. Land-use in the watersheds of the aquatic habitats must be modified to reduce erosion and sedimentation, nutrient inputs,

and other potentially degrading influences. This can be done by instituting best-management practices in local forestry, agriculture, and construction activities. The populations of the lacy elimia should be monitored, and research undertaken into its biology and habitat needs.

Contacts

U.S. Fish and Wildlife Service
Wildlife and Habitat Management Office
6578 Dogwood View Parkway
Jackson, Mississippi. 39213
Telephone: (601) 965-4900
Fax: (601)965-4010

U. S. Fish and Wildlife Service
Regional Office, Division of Endangered Species
1875 Century Blvd., Suite 200
Atlanta, Georgia 30345
http://southeast.fws.gov/

Reference

U.S. Fish and Wildlife Service. 28 October 1998. "Endangered and Threatened Wildlife and Plants; Endangered Status for Three Aquatic Snails, and Threatened Status for Three Aquatic Snails in the Mobile River Basin of Alabama." *Federal Register* 63 (208): 57610-57620.

Round Rocksnail

Leptoxis ampla

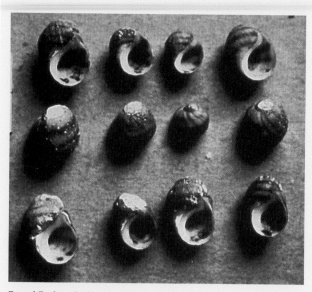

Status	Threatened
Listed	October 28, 1998
Family	Pleuroceridae
Description	A small-sized, gill-breathing, freshwater snail with a shell is spherical with an ovately rounded aperture.
Habitat	Hard substrates in strong currents of riffles and shoals of rivers and streams.
Food	Grazes on algae on rocks.
Reproduction	Lays eggs on rocks.
Threats	Habitat destruction by impoundment, and pollution by siltation, nutrients, and other chemicals.
Range	Alabama

Round Rocksnail, photograph by Art Bogan. Reproduced by permission.

Description

The *Leptoxis ampla* (round rocksnail) grows to about 0.8 in (2 cm) in length. The shell is spherical with an ovately rounded aperture. The body whorl is shouldered at the suture, and may be ornamented with folds or plicae. Color may be yellow, dark brown, or olive green, usually with four entire or broken bands. There are slight differences in DNA sequencing between the painted rocksnail and the round rocksnail, and they are considered to be sister species although they could represent isolated populations belonging to a single species.

Behavior

The round rocksnail is known to graze on algae found on rocks. In addition, the round rocksnail lays its eggs on rocks in order to reproduce.

Habitat

Round rocksnails inhabit riffles and shoals over gravel, cobble, or other rocky substrates. The round rocksnail is the only surviving rocksnail species in the Cahaba River drainage.

Distribution

The round rocksnail was historically found in the Cahaba River, and its tributary, Little Cahaba River, Bibb County, Alabama; and the Coosa River, Elmore County, and tributaries—Canoe Creek and Kelly's Creek, St. Clair County; Ohatchee Creek, Calhoun County; Yellowleaf Creek, Shelby County; and Waxahatchee Creek, Shelby/Chilton Counties, Alabama.

The round rocksnail is currently known from a shoal series in the Cahaba River, Bibb and Shelby Counties, Alabama, and from the lower reach of the Little Cahaba River, and the lower reaches of Shade and Six-mile creeks in Bibb County, Alabama.

Threats

The round rocksnail has lost more than 90% of its historical range because of habitat destruction caused by impoundment, and pollution by siltation and chemicals associated with coal mining and land-use practices. It only survives in a shoal series in the Cahaba River (in Bibb and Shelby Counties, Alabama), from the lower reach of the Little Cahaba River, and the lower reaches of Shade and Six-mile Creeks (both in Bibb County). Its few surviving populations are small, isolated, and vulnerable to impoundment, degradation of water quality, other disturbances, and random catastrophic events.

Conservation and Recovery

The round rocksnail only survives in a few, small, isolated, critical habitats. It is crucial that its few habitats are protected from any proposed impoundment, and from pollution associated with coal mining, agricultural land-use, or other sources. The surviving populations of the round rocksnail should be monitored, and research undertaken into its biology and ecological needs, including work on its propagation. If suitable habitat can be found, additional populations should be established.

Contacts

U. S. Fish and Wildlife Service
Jackson Ecological Services Field Office
6578 Dogwood View Parkway, Suite A
Jackson, Mississippi 39213-7856
Telephone: (601) 965-4900

U. S. Fish and Wildlife Service
Regional Office, Division of Endangered Species
1875 Century Blvd., Suite 200
Atlanta, Georgia 30345
http://southeast.fws.gov/

Reference

U.S. Fish and Wildlife Service. 28 October 1998. "Endangered and Threatened Wildlife and Plants; Endangered Status for Three Aquatic Snails, and Threatened Status for Three Aquatic Snails in the Mobile River Basin of Alabama." *Federal Register* 63(208):57610-57620.

Plicate Rocksnail

Leptoxis plicata

Status	Endangered
Listed	October 28, 1998
Family	Pleuroceridae
Description	A small-sized, gill-breathing, freshwater snail a with brown, or occasionally green shell.
Habitat	Hard substrates in strong currents of riffles and shoals of rivers and streams.
Food	Grazes on algae on rocks.
Reproduction	Lays eggs on rocks.
Threats	Habitat destruction by impoundment, and pollution by siltation, nutrients, and other chemicals.
Range	Alabama

Description

The *Leptoxis plicata*, (plicate rocksnail) grows to about 0.8 in (2 cm) in length. Shells are spherical with broadly rounded apertures. The body whorl may be ornamented with strong folds or plicae. Shell color is usually brown, occasionally green, and often with four equidistant color bands. The central column is smooth, rounded, and typically pigmented in the upper half. The aperture is usually bluish-white, occasionally pink or white. The operculum (plate that closes the shell when the snail is retracted) is dark red, and moderately thick. Although morphologically similar to the Basin's other three surviving rocksnail species, the plicate rocksnail is genetically distinct.

Behavior

The plicate rocksnail is known to graze on algae found on rocks. In addition, the plicate rocksnail lays its eggs on rocks in order to reproduce.

Habitat

Rocksnails are gill breathing snails found attached to cobble, gravel, or other hard substrates in the strong currents of riffles and shoals. Adult rock-

snails move very little, and females probably glue their eggs to stones in the same habitat. The related Tennessee River rocksnail has a lifespan reported to be two years. Longevity in the painted and the basin's other rocksnails is unknown.

Distribution

The plicate rocksnail historically occurred in the Black Warrior River and its tributary, the Little Warrior River, and the Tombigbee River. Status survey efforts in 1991 found populations of plicate rocksnails only in an approximately 55 mi (88 km) reach of the Locust Fork of the Black Warrior River, Jefferson and Blount Counties, Alabama. Surveys during 1996 and 1997 indicate that the snail has recently disappeared from the upstream two-third portion of that habitat and now appears restricted to an approximately 20 mi (32 km) reach in Jefferson County.

Threats

The plicate rocksnail has lost more than 90% of its historical range because of habitat destruction caused by impoundment, and pollution by siltation and chemicals associated with coal mining and land-use practices. A site on the Locust Fork River is being considered for the construction of a water supply impoundment. Plicate rocksnails occurred in riffle and shoal habitats above and below the reservoir site in 1994. In 1996, plicate rocksnails could not be relocated in the portion of the river to be flooded by the reservoir; however, their continued survival was confirmed in an approximately 20 mi (32 km) stretch of river below the potential dam site, which would be subject to impacts from construction activities and post-construction changes in water quality.

Conservation and Recovery

The plicate rocksnail only survives in three small, isolated, critical habitats. Surveys during 1996 and 1997 found that the snail only persists in a reach of about 20 mi (32 km) of the Locust Fork of the Black Warrior River, Alabama. It is crucial that its few critical habitats are protected from any proposed impoundment, and from pollution associated with coal mining, agricultural land-use, or other sources. The surviving populations of the plicate rocksnail should be monitored, and research undertaken into its biology and ecological needs, including work on its propagation. If suitable habitat can be found, additional populations should be established.

Contacts

U. S. Fish and Wildlife Service
Jackson Ecological Services Field Office
6578 Dogwood View Parkway, Suite A
Jackson, Mississippi 39213-7856
Telephone: (601) 965-4900

U. S. Fish and Wildlife Service
Regional Office, Division of Endangered Species
1875 Century Blvd., Suite 200
Atlanta, Georgia 30345
http://southeast.fws.gov/

Reference

U.S. Fish and Wildlife Service. 28 October 1998. "Endangered and Threatened Wildlife and Plants; Endangered Status for Three Aquatic Snails, and Threatened Status for Three Aquatic Snails in the Mobile River Basin of Alabama." *Federal Register* 63(208):57610-57620.

Painted Rocksnail

Leptoxis taeniata

Status	Threatened
Listed	October 28, 1998
Family	Pleuroceridae
Description	A small- to medium-sized yellowish to olive-brown, gill-breathing, freshwater snail.
Habitat	Hard substrates in strong currents of riffles and shoals of rivers and streams.
Food	Grazes on algae on rocks.
Reproduction	Lays eggs on rocks.
Threats	Habitat destruction by impoundment, and pollution by siltation, nutrients, and other chemicals.
Range	Alabama

Description

The *Leptoxis taeniata,* (painted rocksnail) is a small to medium snail about 0.8 in (2 cm) in length, and subglobose to oval in shape. The aperture is broadly ovate, and rounded anteriorly. Coloration varies from yellowish to olive-brown, and usually with four dark bands. Some shells may not have bands and some have the bands broken into squares or oblongs. All of the rocksnails that historically inhabited the Mobil River Basin had broadly rounded apertures, oval shaped shells, and variable coloration. Although the various species were distinguished by relative sizes, coloration patterns, and ornamentation, identification could be confusing. However, the painted rocksnail is the only known survivor of the 15 rocksnail species that were historically known from the Coosa River drainage.

Behavior

The painted rocksnail is known to graze on algae found on rocks. In addition, the painted rocksnail lays its eggs on rocks in order to reproduce.

Habitat

Painted snails are found attached to cobble, gravel, or other hard substrates in the strong currents of riffles and shoals of rivers and streams. Adult rocksnails move very little, and females probably glue their eggs to stones in the same habitat.

Distribution

The painted rocksnail had the largest range of any rocksnail in the Mobile River Basin. It was historically known from the Coosa River and tributaries from the northeastern corner of St. Clair County, Alabama, downstream into the mainstem of the Alabama River to Claiborne, Monroe County, Alabama, and the Cahaba River below the Fall Line in Perry and Dallas Counties, Alabama. Surveys by Service biologists and others in the Cahaba River, unimpounded portions of the Alabama River, and a number of free-flowing Coosa River tributaries have located only three localized Coosa River drainage populations.

The painted rocksnail is currently known from the lower reaches of three Coosa River tributaries— Choccolocco Creek, Talladega County; Buxahatchee Creek, Shelby County; and Ohatchee Creek, Calhoun County, Alabama.

Threats

The painted rocksnail has lost more than 90% of its historical range because of habitat destruction

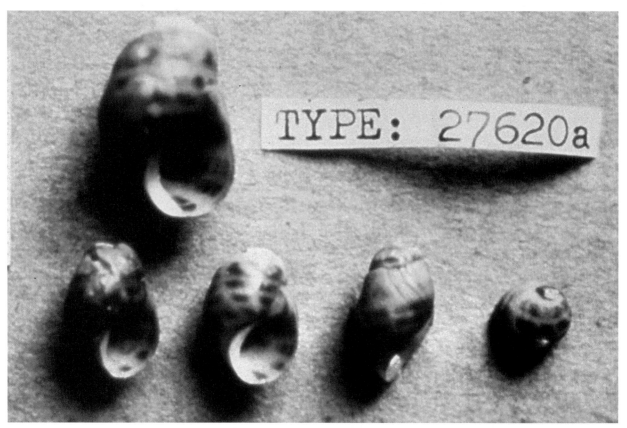

Painted Rocksnail, photograph by Art Bogan. Reproduced by permission.

caused by impoundment, and pollution by siltation and chemicals associated with coal mining and land-use practices. It is now known from only three distinct drainage localities. Extant populations and colonies of these three species are localized, isolated, and are vulnerable to water quality degradation, future human activities that would degrade their habitats, and random catastrophic events.

Conservation and Recovery

The painted rocksnail only survives in three small, isolated, critical habitats. These are tributaries of the Coosa River: Choccolocco Creek, Buxahatchee Creek, and Ohatchee Creek. It is crucial that its few critical habitats are protected from any proposed impoundment, and from pollution associated with coal mining, agricultural land-use, or other sources. The surviving populations of the painted rocksnail should be monitored, and research undertaken into its biology and ecological needs, including work on its propagation. If suitable habitat can be found, additional populations should be established.

Contacts

U. S. Fish and Wildlife Service
Jackson Ecological Services Field Office
6578 Dogwood View Parkway, Suite A
Jackson, Mississippi 39213-7856
Telephone: (601) 965-4900

U. S. Fish and Wildlife Service
Regional Office, Division of Endangered Species
1875 Century Blvd., Suite 200
Atlanta, Georgia 30345
http://southeast.fws.gov/

Reference

U.S. Fish and Wildlife Service. 28 October 1998. "Endangered and Threatened Wildlife and Plants; Endangered Status for Three Aquatic Snails, and Threatened Status for Three Aquatic Snails in the Mobile River Basin of Alabama." *Federal Register* 63(208):57610-57620.

Newcomb's Snail

Erinna newcombi

Status	Threatened
Listed	January 26, 2000
Family	Lymnaeidae
Description	A tropical, aquatic snail.
Habitat	Tropical streams.
Food	Algae and aquatic plants.
Reproduction	Lays eggs; completes its entire life cycle in its local aquatic habitat.
Threats	Habitat destruction and introduced predators.
Range	Hawaii

Description

The Newcomb's snail has a smooth, black shell formed by a single, oval whorl, about 0.25 in (6 mm) long and 0.12 in (3 mm) wide. The other three Hawaiian species in the family Lymnaeidae have a more slender, tapering shape of their shell.

Behavior

The Newcomb's snail probably feeds on algae and vegetation growing on submerged rocks. Its eggs are attached to submerged rocks or plants. Its entire life cycle occurs in local freshwater.

Habitat

The Newcomb's snail inhabits tropical, freshwater, perennial, fast-flowing streams with overhanging rocks, springs, rock seeps, and waterfalls. It occurs in small feeder streams, seeps, and waterfalls, rather than in the more erosive, main channel of larger streams.

Distribution

The Newcomb's snail is an endemic (or locally evolved) species that only occurs on the island of Kauai.

Threats

The Newcomb's snail is limited to six stream systems, each of which supports a single population.

Five of these populations were discovered before 1925. Of these, only two populations still exist, and only one (Kalalau) is relatively large (Waipahee is much smaller). Since 1990, surveys of more 46 potential habitats have located four additional populations, three of which are small (Hanalei, Makaleha, and Wailua) and one large (Lumahai; as many as about 75 snails/square foot (800 snails/square meter). The total population of the Newcomb's snail has been estimated as 6,000 to 7,000 individuals, of which about 90% occur in the two large populations at Kalalau and Lumahai. A serious ongoing threat is predation by the introduced rosy glandina snail (*Euglandina rosea*). It may also be threatened by other introduced invertebrate predators and parasites, by the non-native green swordtail (a fish; *Xyphophorus helleri*), and by two introduced frogs. Some of the known habitats of the Newcomb's snail are potentially threatened by water development and diversion projects. Because of the few populations of generally small size, the Newcomb's snail is also potentially threatened be events of severe weather, such as a hurricane or extended drought.

Conservation and Recovery

All six of the known populations of Newcomb's snail occur in streams in conservation areas managed by the State of Hawaii primarily for watershed protection, mostly to supply water for municipal, agricultural, and cultural use. However, the existing permitting process for water use lacks requirements for the protection of threatened aquatic species, although the state government is taking actions to change this circumstance. In addition, a task force advising the government has recommended that several streams be given "heritage" status, including some of the Kauai streams of Newcomb's snail. This would provide the designated streams with a higher level of protection. However, the recommendations have not yet been adopted by the government. Actions needed to conserve the Newcomb's snail include the strict protection of its known critical habitats, and research into its biology and the deleterious effects of introduced predators and parasites, and into the means of controlling those biological damages.

Contacts

U. S. Fish and Wildlife Service
Regional Office, Division of Endangered Species
Eastside Federal Complex
911 N. E. 11th Ave.
Portland, Oregon 97232-4181
(503) 231-6121
http://pacific.fws.gov/

U. S. Fish and Wildlife Service
Pacific Islands Ecoregion
300 Ala Moana Boulevard, Room 3-122
P. O. Box 50088
Honolulu, Hawaii 96850-5000
Telephone: (808) 541-3441
Fax: (808) 541-3470

Reference

U. S. Fish and Wildlife Service. 26 January 2000. "Endangered and Threatened Wildlife and Plants: Determination of Threatened Status for Newcomb's Snail From the Hawaiian Islands." *Federal Register* 65 (17): 4162-4169.

Banbury Springs Limpet

Lanx sp.

Status	Endangered
Listed	December 14, 1992
Family	Lancidae
Description	Shell with a uniform, red cinnamon color whose body length and height exceed its width.
Habitat	Free-flowing cool spring alcoves.
Food	Plant debris or diatoms.
Reproduction	Copulation after a courtship ritual during late winter or early spring.
Threats	Habitat modification and deteriorating water quality associated with hydroelectric development and operation, water withdrawals and diversions, and water pollution.
Range	Idaho

Description

The Banbury Springs lanx, or limpet, is distinguished with a shell of uniform red cinnamon color, a subcentral apex. This pulmonate snail's length and height exceed its width. Lancids lack either lungs or gills and respire through unusually heavy vascularized mantles, making them highly susceptible to water quality degradation.

Behavior

After reproduction during the late winter-early spring season, older adults will most likely expire. The hermaphroditic reproduction of this species involves the exchange of spermatophores. Courtship entails investigation using tentacles and mouths. Slowly edging closer the snails rear up at right angles to the ground with the bases of their feet in full contact. Supported by the tip of their shells and the hind part of the feet, the male and female open their orifices while caressing each other with their tentacles.

The detritivorous characteristics of this species restricts it to a diet of diatoms and plant debris. The Banbury Springs lanx grazes along mud surfaces, rocky surfaces and macrophytes.

Habitat

The Banbury Springs lanx occupies the Snake River Plains/Sagebrush ecosystem. It is restricted to a few isolated free-flowing reaches or spring alcove habitats of the Snake River. This aquatic system is characterized by cold, well-oxygenated, unpolluted water. The Banbury Springs lanx occurs on stable, cobble-boulder substratum only in flowing waters in the Snake River and also in a few spring alcove habitats in the Hagerman Valley. The species does not burrow in sediments and normally avoids surfaces with attached plants. Known river colonies of the Banbury Springs lanx occur only in areas associated with spring influences or rapids edge environments and tend to flank shorelines. Generally, the species requires cold (15-18°C or 59-64°F) clean, well-oxygenated swift flowing waters on boulder or cobble substratum. The Banbury Springs lanx is found most often on smooth basalt and avoids surfaces with large aquatic macrophytes of filamentous green algae. This species has been collected at depths from 11-30 in (30-75 cm). In a 1992 report the species was found in water as shallow as 2.5 in (5 cm) but this species is most commonly found in depths of 6 in (15 cm).

Banbury Springs Limpet, photograph by William H. Mullins. Reproduced by permission.

Distribution

This limpet was first discovered in 1988 at Banbury Springs with a second population found in nearby Box Canyon Springs in 1989. During 1991, a mollusc survey at the Thousand Springs Preserve revealed a third population in Minnie Miller Springs. This species is currently known from Banbury Springs, Box Canyon Springs and Thousand Springs.

Population density for this species was in the range of 4-48 per sq meter on the Thousand Springs Preserve. The total adult population at the Preserve was estimated at between 600-1,200 individuals. These surveys were conducted in the spring alcoves in which the species was originally located. This snail occurs in the least disturbed spring habitats at Banbury Springs, Box Canyon Springs and Thousand Springs.

Threats

The Banbury Springs limpet is only known from three little-disturbed, cool, well-oxygenated, free-flowing springs. Its habitat has been affected by habitat modification and deteriorating water quality associated with hydroelectric development and operation, water withdrawals and diversions, and water pollution. These are also ongoing threats.

Conservation and Recovery

A Recovery Plan was published in 1995 for the Banbury Springs limpet, within the context of the overall ecological recovery of the Snake River. The plan recommends actions to improve water quality and habitat conditions in the Snake River so that viable, naturally reproducing colonies of the limpet can survive. Other measures include protecting occupied habitats, preventing further diversions of water from the Snake River, addressing adequate flow conditions, improving water quality, and enhancing watershed conditions. The populations of the Banbury Springs limpet will also be monitored, and research undertaken into its biology and ecological needs.

Contacts

U. S. Fish and Wildlife Service
Snake River Compensation Plan Office
1387 South Vinnell Way, Room 368,
Boise, Idaho, 83705
Telephone: (208) 378-5321

U. S. Fish and Wildlife Service
Regional Office, Division of Endangered Species
Eastside Federal Complex
911 N. E. 11th Ave.
Portland, Oregon 97232-4181
Telephone: (503) 231-6121
http://pacific.fws.gov/

Reference

U.S. Fish and Wildlife Service. 1995. "Snake River Aquatic Species Recovery Plan." Boise, Idaho.

Snake River Physa Snail

Physa natricina

Status	Endangered
Listed	December 14, 1992
Family	Physidae (Physa)
Description	Amber to brown color snails with a thin, oval-shaped shell that spirals to the left.
Habitat	Free-flowing cool spring alcoves.
Food	Plant debris or diatoms.
Reproduction	Copulation after a courtship ritual during late winter or early spring.
Threats	Water quality degradation; the New Zealand mudsnail.
Range	Idaho

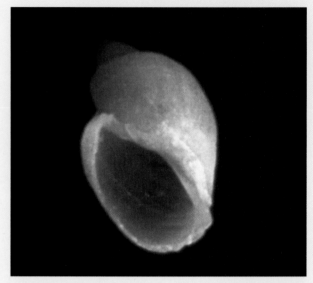

Snake River Physa Snail, photograph by William H. Mullins. Reproduced by permission.

Description

The Snake River physa snail, *Physa natricina,* is a "living fossil" in that it is a relict from Pleistocene-Holocene lakes and rivers in southeastern Idaho and northern Utah. This species possesses a 0.2 in (5-7 mm) long shell with 3-3.5 whorls. Fresh shells are amber to brown in color. Physids (bladder snails) have lungs and are quite similar to the Lancids. This family possesses a sinitral thin oval-shaped shell that spirals to the left and the body openings are on the left side. The final whorl contributes to about four-fifths of shell bulk. These snails have a broad tantaculate and the mantle margin covers the shell.

Behavior

Physids feed on algae, and delineate trails with mucus. The hermaphroditic reproduction of this species involves the exchange of spermatophores. Courtship entails investigation using tentacles and mouths. Slowly edging closer, the snails rear up at right angles to the ground with the bases of their feet in full contact. Supported by the tip of their shells and the hind part of the feet, the male and female open their orifices while caressing each other with their tentacles.

The detritivorous characteristics of this species restricts it to a diet of diatoms and plant debris. This snail grazes along mud surfaces, rocky surfaces and macrophytes.

Habitat

This snail occurs on the undersides of gravel to boulder substratum in swift current in the mainstem Snake River. Specimens have been recorded from boulders in the deepest accessible part of the river at the margins of rapids.

Distribution

Fossil records of the snail occur in deposits from Pleistocene-Holocene lakes and rivers from southeastern Idaho and northern Utah.

This species' current range is believed to be from Grandview upstream through the Hagerman Reach in Gooding, Idowyhee, and Elmore Counties, Idaho.

However, the native bottom fauna has been virtually eliminated in the Gooding County type locality and the species is believed to be extirpated from this region.

Threats

The free-flowing, cool water environments required by this species have been impacted by and are vulnerable to continued adverse habitat modification and deteriorating water quality from hydroelectric development, peak-loading effects from existing hydroelectric project operations, water withdrawal and diversions, water pollution, and inadequate regulatory mechanisms.

Water quality degradation continues from increased water use and withdrawal, aggravated by recent drought-induced low flows. The 121-mile (195-km) stretch of the Snake River is impacted by agricultural return flows; runoff from between 500 and 600 dairies and feedlots; effluent from over 140 private, state, and Federal fish culture facilities; and point source (e.g. municipal sewage) discharge. The ultimate impact of these factors are increased nutrient loads and concentrations which adversely affect the lotic fauna. Nutrient loading contributes to dense blooms of free-living and attached filamentous algae, which the species cannot utilize. This algae will often cover rock surfaces, effectively displacing suitable snail habitats and food resources.

A more recent threat is the discovery of the New Zealand mudsnail in the middle Snake River. The eurytopic mudsnail is experiencing explosive growth in the river and shows a wide range of tolerance for water fluctuations, velocity, temperature and turbidity. The mudsnail species seems to prefer warmer, polluted waters over pristine cold spring environments.

Conservation and Recovery

The U. S. Fish and Wildlife Service published a Recovery Plan for the Snake River Physa snail and other endangered mollusks in the Snake River Basin in 1992. Conservation of this endangered snail requires the protection of its surviving critical habitat in the mainstem Snake River from impoundment, diversion, pollution, and other threatening activities. Moreover, where possible, habitat quality must be improved if the Snake River Physa snail and other endangered species are to recover. The populations of the Snake River Physa snail should be monitored, and research undertaken into its biology and habitat needs.

Contacts

U. S. Fish and Wildlife Service
Regional Office, Division of Endangered Species
Eastside Federal Complex
911 N. E. 11th Ave.
Portland, Oregon 97232-4181
http://pacific.fws.gov/

Snake River Basin Fish and Wildlife Office
1387 South Vinnell Way, Suite 368
Boise, Idaho 83709-1657
Telephone: (208) 378-5243
Fax: (208) 378-5262

References

U. S. Fish and Wildlife Service. 14 December 1992. "Endangered and Threatened Wildlife and Plants: Determination of Endangered or Threatened Status for Five Aquatic Snails in South Central Idaho." *Federal Register* 57 (240): 59244-59257.

U.S. Fish and Wildlife Service. 1995. "Snake River Aquatic Species Recovery Plan." Snake River Basin Office, Ecological Services, Boise, Idaho.

Oahu Tree Snails

Achatinella spp.

Status	Endangered
Listed	January 13, 1981
Family	Achatinellidae (Hawaiian tree snails)
Description	Brightly colored spherical, conical, or egg-shaped shell.
Habitat	Undisturbed native forests.
Food	Fungi, algae.
Reproduction	Hermaphroditic; young born alive.
Threats	Deforestation, collectors, predation.
Range	Hawaii

Description

The *Achatinella* are divided into three subgenera according to shell shape, which is either spherical, conical, or egg-shaped. Adult shell length is 0.2-1 in (0.5-2.5 cm), depending on the species. The number of whorls varies between five and seven. All species are brightly colored and distinctively patterned. Most species have glossy shells, but some have a sculptured surface.

Some species of *Achatinella,* such as *A. juncea, A. buddii,* and *A. papyracea,* were rare as long ago as the 1930s. Other extremely rare species, such as *A. lehuiensis, A. thaanumi,* and *A. spaldingi,* became extinct soon after being discovered. It is believed that only 19 of 41 documented species of the snail still exist. All surviving species are federally listed as Endangered.

Those species still living, but in danger of extinction, are *A. apexfulva, A. bellula, A. bulimoides, A. byronii, A. concavospira, A. curta, A. decipiens, A. fulgens, A. fuscobasis, A. leucorraphe, A. lila, A. lorata, A. mustelina, A. pulcherrima, A. pupukanioe, A. sowerbyana, A. swiftii, A. taeniolata,* and *A. turgida.*

Behavior

Oahu tree snails live singly or in small clusters in the crevices of tree bark, on the undersides of branches and foliage, or in deep leaf litter around the base of the trunk. Most species are nocturnal, grazing on leaf and bark surfaces for microscopic algae, fungi, liverworts, and detritis, but apparently do not feed upon the leaves or bark themselves. Individual snails are sedentary and may spend their entire life on a single tree.

As a group, the *Achatinella* are hermaphroditic (with both male and female reproductive organs) but not self-fertilizing. They breed year round and usually bear one live young, born complete with shell. Studied species were found to grow at a rate of about 0.08 in (2 mm) in length per year and to reach sexual maturity in six or seven years.

Habitat

The island of Oahu encompasses some 607 sq mi (1,433 sq km). Over 35% of this land area is devoted to urban areas or agricultural crops, 45% to grazing land, and less than 20% to forest lands, mostly at high elevations. Only a small portion of this forest (2-3%) is still in relatively pristine condition.

Oahu tree snails are dependent upon the remnants of undisturbed forests and upon native trees. A single species of snail is often associated with a specific tree species. Rarely do any of these species cross over to trees that have been introduced from outside the island.

The snails occur primarily in subtropical moist or tropical wet evergreen forest land. The Oahu tree snails usually occur at elevations above 1,000 ft (305 m) where native species predominate. In mountain bogs, the snails may also inhabit forested wetlands.

Distribution

Much of the island of Oahu, Hawaii, was once heavily forested, and tree snails were dispersed throughout. It is estimated that the original extent of forested land has been reduced by about 85% by agriculture and human settlement. Native trees have declined in large numbers, losing ground to introduced, non-native trees.

Tree snails survive in scattered enclaves throughout portions of the historic range, typically at higher elevations along the crests of ridges where the forests are least disturbed. Only two such areas on Oahu remain—the Waianae Range, and the Koolau Range. Current population levels are low for all of the tree snails, perhaps only five to ten percent of 1960 levels.

The occurrence of snails on the Makua Military Reservation and Schofield Barracks Military Reservation, as well as its possible occurrence at the Mauna Kapu Communication Station, was reported in detail in the 1970s and 1980s. Snails also occur (or occurred) at the site of a now abandoned Nike Missile Facility near Peacock Flats and in the vicinity of the access road to the Air Force/Federal Aviation Administration facility on Mt. Ka'ala. The snails' occurrence on the Lualualei Naval Reservation is probably restricted. Virtually all snail populations occur on lands zoned by the State as Conservation lands and as Forest Reserves, affording the snails and their habitat considerable protection. However, their ranges are greatly reduced and observations show their numbers to be rapidly declining.

A biologist, who extensively surveyed the snails' forest habitat in the early 1980s, has suggested that the most abundant of these endangered species are *A. mustelina* and *A. sowerbyana*, numbering perhaps 400 individuals each. Estimated at about 200 individuals or less were the species *A. curta*, *A. decipiens*, and *A. lila*. The species *A. fuscobasis* and *A. pupukanioe* numbered perhaps 100 individuals each. *Achatinella concavospira* and *A. pulcherrima* numbered 50 or less individuals each. *Achatinella bellula*, *A. bulimoides*, *A. byronii*, *A. fulgens*, *A. leucorraphe*, *A. lorata*, *A. swiftii*, *A taeniolata*, and *A. turgida*, all numbered less than 20 individuals. There is no current population estimate for the species *A. apexfulva*, and population numbers for all species have probably declined from the 1980s estimates.

Threats

The ancient Hawaiians believed the tree snails sang, though later it was realized crickets were doing the "singing." But their mystique lived on, and the richly colored shells made Oahu tree snails attractive to collectors. While appreciation for tree snails helped inspire a greater awareness of the diversity and uniqueness of the Hawaiian flora and fauna, collecting also reduced certain localized populations of tree snail species.

Another obvious reason for the precipitous decline of tree snail populations is the loss of native forests on the island. Oahu's lower elevation forests were long ago converted to agriculture, pasture, or for residences. Much of the remaining forests have been degraded by the intermingling of non-native trees and plants, changing the composition of plants; this in turn affects the abundance and dispersal of the snails' chief food sources—the algae and fungi.

Hikers along forest trails often collect the brightly colored snails. But because of late sexual maturity and a slow growth rate (natural replacement of a reproducing adult takes at least six years), tree snail populations can be quickly depleted by even casual collecting. Several of these tree snails have come to the attention of more serious collectors, who seem willing to finance the depletion of these rare snails by purchasing specimens.

Another immediate threat for these tree snails is an exotic, carnivorous snail (*Euglandina rosea*), that was introduced from Florida in 1955 to control another snail pest, the giant African snail (*Achatina fulica*). This carnivorous snail had little impact on the African snail, but in areas where it has become established, Oahu tree snails are now entirely absent. Other predators, including additional alien land mollusks, a terrestrial flatworm, and ants are also thought to be a continuing threat to the tree snails. The snail's low reproductive rate and the unusually long period required for them to reach sexual maturity is another important factor rendering these snails extremely vulnerable to extinction under unnaturally high predation rates.

Conservation and Recovery

Recovery for these tree snails will depend ultimately upon saving the remaining acreage of native forests on Oahu, stopping collectors, and ridding the habitat of predators. The Fish and Wildlife Service (FWS), the state of Hawaii, and The Nature Conservancy of Hawaii cooperate in an aggressive campaign to acquire and protect forest land. The results of these efforts are slow to materialize, and it remains an open question whether many of these tree snails will survive.

The primary objective of the FWS 1992 Oahu tree snail Recovery Plan is to stabilize populations of tree snails found within essential habitats and to initiate captive propagation of all extant Oahu tree snail species. The plan notes that, before captive-reared snails are placed in the field, the snails should be individually marked so growth and migratory pattern can be followed after they are released. All introduced populations should be monitored to determine their growth or decline. The plan also outlines numerous strategies for species recovery, including surveys to assess the population status; research on population biology to understand life history parameters, reproduction, foraging behavior, etc.; habitat preservation to maintain the natural integrity of protected habitat; forest fire prevention; banning the import of noxious alien plants and animals that may prey on the tree snail or destroy its habitat, and controlling the existing populations of alien predators and parasites; coordinating recovery planning and implementation with the U.S. military (where the species occurs on military property); and enforcement against collection and poaching of the snails for their shells.

Contact

U.S. Fish and Wildlife Service
Division of Endangered Species
Eastside Federal Complex
911 N.E. 11th Avenue
Portland, Oregon 97232
http://pacific.fws.gov/

References

Hart, A. D. 1975. "Living Jewels Imperiled." *Defenders* 50:482-486.

Hart, A. D. 1978. "The Onslaught Against Hawaii's Tree Snails." *Natural History* 87:46-57.

Vander Schalie, H. 1969. "Man Meddles with Nature—Hawaiian Style." *The Biologist* 51:136-146.

Whitten, H. 1980. "Endangered Hawaiian Tree Snail." Article. *Honolulu Star Bulletin* July 14, 1980.

Young, G. 1979. "Which Way Oahu?" *National Geographic Magazine* 156(5):652-679.

U.S. Fish and Wildlife Service. 1992. "Recovery Plan for the Oahu Tree Snails of the Genus *Achatinella*." U.S. Fish and Wildlife Service, Portland.

Stock Island Tree Snail

Orthalicus reses reses

Mike Bentkin

Status	Endangered
Listed	July 3, 1978
Family	Bulimulidae (Tree snails)
Description	Large conical snail with a long, white or buff shell and narrow, flamelike purple stripes.
Habitat	Tropical hardwood forests.
Food	Minute fungi and algae.
Reproduction	Mating occurs in September, producing 8-21 eggs the following June.
Threats	Limited distribution, residential and recreational development.
Range	Florida

Description

The Stock Island tree snail is a large, conical tree snail, which attains a mature shell length of 2.2 in (5.5 cm). The translucent shell is thin and lightweight compared to most other snails of this genus. The color is white to buff with three poorly developed bands, and narrow flamelike purple stripes. The seven whorls, slightly rounded, increase regularly in size with a modestly impressed suture. The last whorl or two sometimes has two to three faint, narrow, brown spiral bands. There are also one to four dark brown bands on the shell that occur at irregular intervals. The interior of the shell is white, but distinctly shows the exterior markings through the translucent shell.

Behavior

The Stock Island tree snail lives exclusively in trees, hiding in holes, bark crevices, and leaf clusters. It feeds on lichen, fungi, and algae, and is most active between June and December after a rainfall.

Nests are constructed in soft dirt that is rich in leaf-mold directly at the base of the host tree. The nests are excavated initially with the posterior part of the snail foot to about 0.8 in (20 mm) deep. After excavation, the snail turns around and inserts the anterior head foot in the cavity, and continues to excavate the cavity to a depth of 1.6-2.4 in (40-60 mm).

The snail is hermaphroditic (with both male and female reproductive organs), although it is not self-fertilizing. It needs a mate to reproduce, and the mating process takes about 12 hours. The species begins mating at one year of age. Nest building takes place in September, shortly after mating. The eggs hatch the following June. About 8-21 eggs are laid per nest. Eggs are covered by soil as the snail crawls out of the nest. During dry weather, the snail enters a dormant state, known as aestivation. It aestivates in tree cavities that are sufficiently large for the snail to enter. A significant natural mortality occurs when tree growth decreases the size of the opening and traps aestivating specimens within.

This species is non-territorial (as many as 14 snails have been found in the same tree) but returns to the same tree cavity to aestivate. Individuals may favor certain limbs, bole, or fork in the tree to rest before foraging activities, but the species is mobile and frequently moves to new trees.

This snail is seasonally active. It aestivates during the dry season, usually December to May. In June it becomes active if the wet season has begun; otherwise it returns to aestivation on the surface of large limbs. During the wet season, it is more frequently active at night.

The Stock Island tree snail probably grazes on minute fungi and algae that grow as epiphytes on tree leaves and stems. Bacteria have also been found in the guts of some specimens but it is not know if they are a food source or a contaminant.

Habitat

The Stock Island tree snail inhabits a wide range of tropical hardwood trees and has adapted to several types of exotic ornamentals. It apparently has no host tree preference and has been found on such native trees as sweet acacia, saffron plum, gumbo-limbo, icaco-coco plum, and mahogany. Non-native trees include Jamaica caper, lead tree, and tamarind. It is most common in mature hammocks but does occur in second-growth and new-growth thickets.

Distribution

The historic range encompassed Stock Island and Key West in Monroe County, Florida. The snail has since disappeared from Key West.

When the snail was placed on the federal list in 1978, the population was estimated between 200-800 individuals, found at two sites on Stock Island. In 1986, a survey conducted by The Nature Conservancy determined that a major portion of the habitat had been lost to residential development and golf course expansion. Fewer than 100 of the snails were thought to survive on about 5 acres (2 hectares) on Stock Island adjacent to the Key West Municipal Golf Course. In 1987, Fish and Wildlife Service (FWS) biologists visited the site and determined that the snail population was confined to about 20 trees and probably numbered less than 50.

The population seems to be falling still more sharply. By the mid 1990s, surveys were unsuccessful in finding any Stock Island tree snails within its historical range. With the cooperation of the Florida Game and Fresh Water Fish Commission, Stock Island Golf Course, Key West Botanical Gardens, and U.S. Navy, the FWS is taking recovery actions, including reintroductions, to reestablish this unique mollusk into part of its historical range.

Threats

The causes of the species' decline are not certain, but fragmentation of hardwood hammocks, changes in microclimate, and increased predation have been suggested as possible reasons for its loss. The snail's remaining range is so restricted, almost any natural or man-made disaster could render the species extinct. Much of the ground area near inhabited trees has been paved to accommodate a county parking lot. County workers, in a misguided effort to protect snail-inhabited trees, surrounded the bases of the trees with gravel. This gravel deprived the snail of access to leaf litter and humus in which to lay its eggs. In 1988, the FWS successfully negotiated with the county to remove the gravel and replace the natural soil and organic litter.

Conservation and Recovery

The precipitous decline of the snail population has forced FWS personnel to consider translocating snails and eggs to a more protected location. The population has declined to such a low level, however, that translocation might actually exterminate the snail. A second problem with translocation is that no suitable habitat appears to remain in the Florida Keys. Biologists have little material to work with and no room for error. The FWS and Florida chapters of the Audubon Society and The Nature Conservancy have unsuccessfully surveyed the region for other populations of the snail. The FWS South Florida Ecosystem Office in Vero Beach was moving forward with efforts to reintroduce the Stock Island tree snail starting in 1996.

Contact

U.S. Fish and Wildlife Service
Division of Endangered Species
1875 Century Blvd, Ste 200
Atlanta, Georgia 30345
http://southeast.fws.gov/

Reference

U.S. Fish and Wildlife Service. 1982. "Stock Island Tree Snail Recovery Plan." U.S. Fish and Wildlife Service, Atlanta.

Painted Snake Coiled Forest Snail

Anguispira picta

Status	Endangered
Listed	July 3, 1978
Family	Discidae (Forest Snails)
Description	Dome-shaped snail with six whorls and off-white brown blotches.
Habitat	Limestone outcrops.
Food	Lichens.
Reproduction	Young hatch as small adults.
Threats	Logging, grazing, quarrying.
Range	Tennessee

Painted Snake Coiled Forest Snail, photograph. U. S. Fish and Wildlife Service. Reproduced by permission.

Description

The painted snake coiled forest snail, *Anguispira picta*, is a dome-shaped snail with a sharp, smooth, keel-shaped ridge along the shell called a carina. Mature shells measure up to 0.8 in (2.1 cm) long and 0.4 in (1 cm) high. Shells have six whorls and indistinct ribbing, particularly on the body whorl. The adult shell is an opaque, off-white color with chocolate brown blotches on the upper surface. The lower surface has one row of large dark blotches and a second row of narrow, flame-like markings, extending into the hole at the base of the body whorl. Juvenile shells are translucent.

This snail is similar in appearance to *Anguispira cumberlandiana* found on the Cumberland Plateau.

Behavior

Most land snails are hermaphrodites but self fertilization is rare. A courtship display generally ini-

tiates copulation and fertilization occurs internally, resulting in the production of jellylike eggs. The young hatch as small adults, their shells having fewer whorls than adults. The painted snake coiled forest snail is known to deposit clutches of small eggs with calcareous shells covered by thin membranes in the soil. Sexual maturity may come within a year after hatching. This species is not known to exhibit any parental care.

The painted snake coiled forest snail seems to have no daily periodicity even though other related species are known to be strongly diurnal. Most juveniles observed day or night were inactive and some adults were observed to forage day and night. It is likely that wet weather encourages activity while drought or cold decreases it. Individuals have been observed in the open during the height of summer and on warm days in November. They undoubtedly go under cover in the winter months.

Habitat

The coiled forest snail has been found only on damp limestone outcrops, typically in crevices or under overhanging ledges. Slopes are very steep, often terminating in sheer cliffs that drop to the creek bed below. The habitat is thickly forested and has a profuse ground cover. The forest community is composed of American beech, sugar maple, shagbark hickory, tulip poplar, white oak, and chinkapin oak. Ground cover is dominated by ironwood, dogwood, witch hazel, sycamore, and many herbaceous plants, such as walking fern, alumroot, and wild ginger. The snail does not occur in adjacent tracts that have been heavily logged or clear-cut.

Distribution

The historic range of this species is unknown, but it is probably endemic to the valleys and coves characteristic of the southwestern rim of the Cumberland Plateau in southern Tennessee west of Chattanooga.

Threats

The painted snake coiled forest snail is endangered by the restricted size of its range. Any substantial disturbance of the habitat could precipitate a sudden population decline. Logging, livestock grazing, and limestone quarrying are important sources of income to the residents of Franklin County. So far, the landowners of the cove have refused to sell timber or mineral rights to commercial interests and have cooperated with the Fish and Wildlife Service (FWS) to protect the habitat.

Conservation and Recovery

The FWS Recovery Plan for this species outlines a systematic research program that includes periodic monitoring of the population. Protection of the cove by land acquisition or by purchase of conservation easements is anticipated as funds become available. The Nature Conservancy and the Tennessee Wildlife Resources Agency have been active in securing the cooperation of local landowners.

Contact

U.S. Fish and Wildlife Service
Division of Endangered Species
1875 Century Blvd, Ste 200
Atlanta, Georgia 30345
http://southeast.fws.gov/

References

Elwell, A. S., and M. Ulmer. 1971. "Notes on the Biology of *Anguispira alternata*." *Malacologia* 11(1): 199-215.

Pilsbry, H. A. 1948. *Land Mollusca of North America (North of Mexico)*. Academy of Natural Sciences, Philadelphia.

Smith, T. 1980. "Potential Preserve Site Summary." Report. The Nature Conservancy, Tennessee Field Office.

U.S. Fish and Wildlife Service. 1982. "Painted Snake Coiled Forest Snail Recovery Plan." U.S. Fish and Wildlife Service, Atlanta.

Iowa Pleistocene Snail

Discus macclintocki

Status	Endangered
Listed	July 3, 1978
Family	Discidae (Forest Snails)
Description	Six-whorled, lightly coiled, dome-shaped snail, brown or greenish white.
Habitat	Talus slopes under logs or in leaf litter.
Food	Leaves of birch and maple trees.
Reproduction	Hermaphroditic; clutch of 2-6 eggs.
Threats	Restrictive habitat, low numbers.
Range	Iowa

Description

The Iowa Pleistocene snail is an average-sized member of its genus with an adult width of 0.5 in (8 mm). The dome-shaped shell is tightly coiled, typically with six whorls. Shell color may be brown or off-white with a greenish cast. Ribs are relatively fine and confined to the upper half of each whorl.

Behavior

This snail feeds on the leaves of white and yellow birch, hard maple, or occasionally dogwood and willow. It is active from spring through summer but becomes lethargic in August when the habitat dries. It remains near the soil surface until the first hard freeze, then burrows into the soil to hibernate.

Like most North American land snails, the Iowa snail is hermaphroditic (with both male and female reproductive organs) but not self-fertilizing. Adults can apparently lay eggs as well as fertilize the eggs of other snails. Breeding occurs from late March to August. Eggs are laid under logs and bark, in protected moist rock crevices, and in the soil. Clutch sizes vary from two to six eggs with an incubation time of 28 days. Life span is about five years.

Habitat

The Iowa Pleistocene snail is found in pockets of a very specialized microhabitat known as an algific talus slope. These cool, moist areas develop around the entrances to fissures and caves where circulating air and infiltrating water create a condition of nearly permanent underground ice. The Iowa snail lives on the surface in deep, moist leaf litter that is cooled throughout the summer by this icy substrate. The snail prefers deciduous leaf litter and typically avoids mossy ground cover or coniferous litter. Most algific talus slopes are steep and north-facing, composed of fragments of a porous carbonate rock. This cool, moist habitat reproduces conditions that were more common during previous glacial epochs. This snail is often associated with northern wild monkshood (*Aconitum noveboracense*), a federally endangered plant.

Distribution

The geologic record of the Iowa Pleistocene snail goes back over 300,000 years, when it was fairly widespread throughout the Midwest. Its maximum range during cooler glacial periods included Iowa, Nebraska, Missouri, Illinois, Indiana, and Ohio. The center of distribution apparently was once Illinois.

The snail survives at 18 known locations in a region known as the Driftless Area, which encompasses portions of Clayton and Dubuque Counties, Iowa, and Jo Davies County, Illinois. These populations are estimated to number no more than 60,000 snails.

Threats

The major long-term cause of decline is cyclic climatic change. The species has survived several such

Iowa Pleistocene Snail, photograph. U. S. Fish and Wildlife Service. Reproduced by permission.

cycles in the past and, with a return of glacial conditions, would certainly replenish itself over a large range. The most immediate threat to its survival is human disturbance. An estimated 75% of its specialized habitat has been destroyed in the last 150 years by agriculture, road construction, quarrying, and other human intrusions.

Conservation and Recovery

In 1986, The Nature Conservancy, the Iowa Conservation Commission, and the Fish and Wildlife Service implemented the Driftless Area Project in northeast Iowa to protect remaining pockets of algific talus slope habitat. Over two-thirds of all landowners that were contacted, agreed to register a commitment to conserve habitat on their properties. Registration is voluntary and is considered an interim solution, until land can be acquired and protected permanently. Public support for habitat conservation in the region is very high.

Contact

U.S. Fish and Wildlife Service
Division of Endangered Species
Federal Building, Fort Snelling
Twin Cities, Minnesota 55111
http://midwest.fws.gov/

References

Baker, F. C. 1928. "Description of New Varieties of Land and Fresh Water Mollusks from Pleistocene Deposits in Illinois." *Nautilus* 41:132-137.

Ferst, T. J. 1981. "Final Report, Project SE-1-2, Iowa Pleistocene Snail." Iowa State Conservation Commission, Des Moines.

Hulbricht, L. 1955. "*Discus macclintocki* (F.C. Baker)." *Nautilus* 69:34.

U.S. Fish and Wildlife Service. 1984. "Recovery Plan for the Iowa Pleistocene Snail (*Discus macclintocki*)." U.S. Fish and Wildlife Service, Twin Cities.

Kanab Ambersnail

Oxyloma haydeni ssp. *kanabensis*

Status	Endangered
Listed	April 17, 1992
Family	Succineidae (Land Snail)
Description	Small snail with an amber whorled shell.
Habitat	Perennially wet soils in marshes and meadows.
Food	Nothing specific is known.
Reproduction	Nothing specific is known.
Threats	Destruction of habitat.
Range	Arizona, Utah

Description

The Kanab ambersnail is a small terrestrial snail about 0.5 to 0.8 in (14 to 19 mm) long. The mottled, grayish to yellowish amber shell has three or four whorls in an elongated spire and a broad, expanded aperture. The snail's eyes are borne on the ends of long stalks; the tentacles are small protuberances at the base of the eyestalks.

This species has also been known as *Succinea hawokinsi.* Some specialists believe that the current taxonomic status of the snail should be reevaluated to determine whether it deserves classification as a full species.

Behavior

Almost nothing is known about the specific behavior of the Kanab ambersnail. Other members of the genus feed on microscopic plants and lay about a dozen jelly-like eggs at the base of plants. The eggs hatch after two or three weeks. Young snails reach full size after about two years, and die soon after.

Habitat

The Kanab ambersnail lives in marshes that are constantly watered by springs and seeps at the base of sandstone cliffs. It is found in close association with cattail *(Typha domingensis)* which it uses as vegetative cover and protection from predation by birds. It is always associated with perennially wet soils and has never been found in drier habitats, or even in places which are attractive to other land snails, such as underneath logs.

Distribution

This snail species was first collected in 1909 from an area known as The Greens, on Kanab Wash, six mi (9.6 km) above Kanab, Utah. It has only been found at two locations in Kane County in extreme southern Utah, and one in Grand Canyon, Arizona. In Arizona, surveys of 81 springs near Vaseys Paradise failed to find any Kanab ambersnails. However, in 1995, a small population of the nominate subspecies *O. h. haydeni* was found at Grand Canyon National Park's Indian Gardens Campground.

The two known Utah populations of the Kanab ambersnail are just over a mile apart on privately owned land. A colony inhabiting a marsh beneath a cliff in Kanab Creek Canyon has almost vanished. Although once common at this site, the snail population has suffered a dramatic crash. An intensive search in 1990 found only three individuals. The wetland habitat at this site was recently altered by draining much of the water to provide for domestic livestock.

The only remaining large population occurs in marshes in Three Lakes Canyon, a tributary drainage of Kanab Creek, about 6 mi (9.6 km) north-

Kanab Ambersnail, photograph. Bureau of Land Management. Reproduced by permission.

west of Kanab. In June 1990, the Kanab ambersnail population was estimated at 100,000. However, soon afterward, the landowner began modifying the marshes in preparation for development. This resulted in the destruction of a portion of the snail population.

Threats

The possible imminent destruction of the only remaining substantial Kanab ambersnail population moved the U. S. Fish and Wildlife Service (FWS) to list the snail as Endangered on an emergency basis on August 8, 1991. This emergency determination was scheduled to expire on April 3, 1992. During this eight-month period the FWS followed its normal process in proposing the species for listing. The final listing was done on April 17, 1992. A recovery plan was published in 1995.

Although private landowners had indicated a willingness to protect the snail and negotiate the sale of the property to the federal government or

The Nature Conservancy, they were still considering development of the property as a retirement home or recreational vehicle park and campground. The fact that development of the property could happen before a regular listing proposal could be finalized prompted both the emergency and final listings. Discussions are continuing between the landowners and The Nature Conservancy for sale of the property.

Conservation and Recovery

In 1995, FWS released a recovery plan for the Kanab ambersnail. The criteria for downlisting the rare mollusk are to maintain at least 10 populations large enough to ensure their long-term viability, and to establish compatible habitat management practices. These objectives are to be achieved by the following actions: control of threatening activities, such as the timing and hydrological characteristics of water releases from the Glen Canyon Dam; acquire and restore the habitat of the Three Lakes Population, as well as other suitable habitats; conduct surveys to find appropriate habitats for reestablishment attempts; conduct research into the biology and ecological needs of the Kanab ambersnail; establish new populations in suitable habitat, using stock from a captive-rearing program; and implement a program of public education, to build support for the conservation of the endangered snail. The known, privately owned habitat of the Kanab ambersnail will have to be protected. This can be achieved by acquiring the land and establishing a protected area, or by negotiating conservation easements.

Contacts

U. S. Fish and Wildlife Service
Regional Office, Division of Endangered Species
P.O. Box 1306
Albuquerque, New Mexico 87103-1306
Telephone: (505) 248-6915
Fax: (505) 248-6915
http://southwest.fws.gov/

U. S. Fish and Wildlife Service
Regional Office, Division of Endangered Species
P.O. Box 25486
Denver Federal Center
Denver, Colorado 80225
Telephone: (303) 236-7920
Fax: (303) 236-8295

Utah Ecological Services Field Office
145 East 1300 South, Suite 404
Salt Lake City, Utah 84115-6110
Telephone: (801) 524-5009
Fax: (801) 524-5021

References

Clarke, A. H. 1991. "Status Survey of Selected Land and Freshwater Gastropods in Utah." U. S. Fish and Wildlife Service, Denver, Colorado.

Pilsbry, H. A. 1948. *Land Mollusca of North America.* The Academy of Natural Science of Philadelphia Monographs, Philadelphia.

U. S. Fish and Wildlife Service. 1995. "Kanab Ambersnail (*Oxyloma haydeni kanabensis*) Recovery Plan." U. S. Fish and Wildlife Service, Denver, Colorado.

Chittenango Ovate Amber Snail

Succinea chittenangoensis

Status	Threatened
Listed	July 3, 1978
Family	Succineida (Land Snail)
Description	Slender, pale yellow to off-white egg-shaped, spiral shell with growth wrinkles and lines.
Habitat	Vegetation in waterfall spray zone.
Food	Microscopic plants.
Reproduction	Clutch of up to 15 eggs.
Threats	Extremely limited range.
Range	New York

Chittenango Ovate Amber Snail, photograph by Peter E. Nye. Reproduced by permission.

Description

The translucent shell of the Chittenango ovate amber snail is a slender egg-shape, about 0.8 in (2 cm) long, spiraling into three and one-half whorls. The color is a pale yellow to off-white. The shell surface is glossy and marked with growth wrinkles and lines. The color of the living animal is a pale, translucent yellow. The mantle (the outer covering of the soft parts) is pale yellow, tinted with olive, and often marked with black streaks and blotches.

This snail was first described as a subspecies of the more widespread ovate amber snail (*Succinea ovalis*) and is referred to in many publications as *S. o. chittenangoensis*.

Behavior

The Chittenango ovate amber snail is a terrestrial species that prefers cool, sunlit areas of lush plant growth within the spray zone of waterfalls. The snail apparently feeds on microscopic plants and in some way ingests high levels of calcium carbonate for its shell development.

Sexually mature snails deposit up to 15 transparent, jelly-like eggs at the base of plants or in loose wet soil. The young snails hatch in two to three weeks and grow to maturity during the following spring. After two years, snails reach their full size. They then die, completing their life span in about two and one-half years.

Habitat

The ovate amber snail is found among the vegetation that covers slopes adjacent to a single waterfall. It is prominent among patches of watercress at the very edges of the stream. Most of the fall's spray zone is covered with patches of mosses and liverworts. Skunk cabbages and angelica grow in the drier areas. Temperatures are mild and relatively constant, regulated by the waterfall mist. Humidity in the habitat is high.

Distribution

This species may have been widely distributed during the Pleistocene epoch throughout portions of Arkansas, Illinois, Iowa, Michigan, Missouri, Nebraska, and Ontario, as well as in New York. It was first discovered at Chittenango Falls in central New York in 1905.

One colony of this snail is known to survive at Chittenango Falls State Park (Madison County), New York. The population is divided into two groups living on either side of the falls. The total population was estimated in 1982 at less than 500 snails.

Threats

The primary reason for listing this species as threatened is its extremely limited range and its apparent decline since its discovery. Since it has been studied so little, actual causes for the decline are unknown.

Although the water quality of the stream is relatively high, these snails may be intolerant of trace amounts of chemical runoff. Most of the watershed of Chittenango Creek is used for agriculture, and fertilizers, herbicides, and pesticides enter the drainage. Winter road salt increases the salinity of the water.

Over 100,000 visitors come to the state park each year for recreation. Although the immediate falls area is fairly inaccessible, some trampling and dislodging of rocks has been observed. These disturbances can have a severe effect on the success of snail reproduction.

Conservation and Recovery

Recovery of this species will require strict protection of its habitat and reduction of pollutants entering the stream. State park personnel have developed a management plan to redirect visitors away from the habitat area and to restrict visitor access to the immediate vicinity of the falls. Further recovery actions will depend on the results of ongoing research into the snail's biology and habitat requirements. Biologists believe there is a good chance other populations of the snail may yet be found in central New York state.

Contact

U.S. Fish and Wildlife Service
Division of Endangered Species
300 Westgate Center Drive
Hadley, Massachusetts 01035
http://northeast.fws.gov/

References

Grimm, F. W. 1981. "A Review of the Chittenango Ovate Amber Snail, *Succinea chittenangoensis.*" Report. New York State Department of Environmental Conservation, Albany.

Hubricht, L. 1972. "Endangered Land Snails of the Eastern United States." *Sterkiana* 45:33-34.

Solem, A. 1976. "Status of *Succinea ovalis chittenangoensis* Pilsbry, 1908." *Nautilus* 90(3):107-114.

U .S. Fish and Wildlife Service. 1983. "Chittenango Ovate Amber Snail Recovery Plan." U.S. Fish and Wildlife Service, Newton Corner, Massachusetts.

Noonday Snail

Mesodon clarki nantahala

Status	Threatened
Listed	July 3, 1978
Family	Polygyridae (Land Snail)
Description	Rounded, glossy red shell with 5.5 whorls.
Habitat	Profuse vegetation along rocky cliffs.
Food	Probably fungi.
Reproduction	Undescribed.
Threats	Limited distribution.
Range	North Carolina

Noonday Snail, photograph. U. S. Fish and Wildlife Service. Reproduced by permission.

Description

The noonday snail, *Mesodon clarki nantahala*, has a rounded shell with five and one-half whorls and a depressed spire. It measures about 0.72 in (1.8 cm) in width and 0.44 in (1.1 cm) in height. The glossy red shell is sculptured by coarse bands.

Behavior

This snail is most active during wet weather and is presumed to feed on fungi. It is found in thick tangles of vegetation, beneath rocks, or in deep, moist leaf litter. Reproductive behavior and other aspects of its life history have not been adequately studied but it is believed that the noonday snail is hermaphroditic and prefers copulation to self-fertilization. The noonday snail appears to migrate seasonally, moving from the gorge cliffs to cavities within the cliff.

Habitat

The noonday snail is found in a damp oak-hickory woodland with a profuse, herbaceous un-dergrowth. It is particularly common along cliffs with a northern exposure. This area of rock outcroppings and rich, humus-laden soils supports a complex plant community. The habitat is kept moist year round by an abundance of springs, seepages, streams, and waterfalls. The elevation rises steeply from 1,900 to 3,100 ft (580-945 m). Dominant trees include oak, hickory, American beech, American elm, basswood, birch, and tulip poplar. Rhododendrons and many species of ferns are prominent components of the undergrowth. In recent years, non-native plants such as kudzu and honeysuckle have invaded the habitat.

Distribution

Woodland snails of the genus *Mesodon* are common throughout the eastern United States, displaying the greatest diversity in the southern Appalachians. The noonday snail was historically confined to an area of southeastern Tennessee, extreme western North Carolina, and northern Georgia. The noonday snail is found in the Nantahala

Gorge in North Carolina, along the high cliffs that line the southern banks of the Nantahala River. The portion of the gorge inhabited by the snail extends for several miles along the river near Blowing Springs from Wesser to Hewitt (Swain County). Most of the habitat falls within the boundaries of the Nantahala National Forest. No estimate of the size of the population has been attempted because of the ruggedness of the terrain.

Threats

The noonday snail is restricted to a narrow section of the Nantahala Gorge and is adapted to very specialized conditions of moisture and temperature. Any degradation of the habitat would result in the decline of this species. In recent years, the gorge has become a popular site for canoeing, kayaking, hiking, climbing, and camping. Several camping areas are located close to the habitat. This recreational traffic increased the risks of trampling, forest fires, or other disturbance.

Conservation and Recovery

Because the noonday snail is found on public land, protecting its habitat has been relatively straightforward. The Forest Service and the state of North Carolina devised a cooperative habitat management agreement and are conducting further research into the snail's biology. Recreational access to critical portions of the habitat is now closely regulated, and similar habitats along the Nantahala River are being surveyed to determine if other populations of the snail exist.

Contact

U.S. Fish and Wildlife Service
Regional Office, Division of Endangered Species
1875 Century Blvd., Suite 200
Atlanta, Georgia 30345
http://southeast.fws.gov/

References

Roe, C., and J. Moore. 1983. "Recommendations to the U.S. Forest Service Regarding the Designation of the Noonday Snail's Primary Habitat as a Protected Natural Area." Report. North Carolina Department of Natural Resources and Community Development, Raleigh.

U.S. Fish and Wildlife Service. 1984. "Recovery Plan for the Noonday Snail (*Mesodon clarki nantahala*)." U.S. Fish and Wildlife Service, Atlanta.

Magazine Mountain Shagreen

Mesodon magazinensis

Status	Threatened
Listed	April 17, 1989
Family	Polygyridae (Land Snail)
Description	Medium-sized, dusky brown or buff colored shell.
Habitat	Cool, moist, rocky crevices in rock slide rubble.
Food	Plant material.
Threats	Limited distribution, recreational development, military exercises.
Range	Arkansas

Ron Caldwell

Description

Also known as the Magazine Mountain middle-toothed snail, the Magazine Mountain shagreen, *Mesodon magazinensis*, is a dusky brown or buff-colored medium-sized land snail, 0.5 in (13 mm) wide and 0.3 in (7 mm) high. The shell surface is roughened by half-moon shaped scales. The outer lip of the aperture has a small triangular tooth, while the inner side has a single blade-like tooth. It is similar in appearance to the more common *M. infectus*.

Behavior

This mountain shagreen is active above the surface on cool, damp or wet days and retreats into the rock crevices as the weather warms. During July and August it never surfaces.

Its blade-like tooth is suitable for eating plant material.

Habitat

This snail has been collected from rock slide rubble at the base of a north-facing rocky escarpment. It prefers cool, moist conditions and burrows far back into crevices in the cliffs, during the hottest part of summer. Habitat elevation ranges from 2,000-2,600 ft (600-790 m).

Distribution

This species is known only from a single location on Magazine Mountain in Logan County, Arkansas. Magazine Mountain is relatively separate from other mountains in the region and is considered an "island" ecosystem—one that supports a diversity of endemic species within a narrowly defined range.

The shagreen's known range is included within the Ozark National Forest and is classified as a Special Interest Area. Magazine Mountain was recently proposed as a candidate for designation as a Research Natural Area.

Threats

Because of this snail's extremely limited range, it is vulnerable to any land use change or other activity that might disrupt the habitat's fragile ecological balance. In 1989 the Arkansas Department of Parks and Tourism applied for a special use permit from the Forest Service to develop a state park on Magazine Mountain. The U. S. Fish and Wildlife Service (FWS) has expressed the opinion that construction of access roads, buildings, pipelines, and trails would adversely affect the snail if these activities disrupted rock slide rubble on the north slope. The FWS, the Forest Service, and the state are currently negotiating to determine the feasibility of the proposed state park.

Conservation and Recovery

U. S. Army training exercises planned for the vicinity of Magazine Mountain will be permitted by the FWS if troop, vehicle, and artillery movements do not disturb the north slope of the mountain. Under provisions of the Endangered Species Act, the Army is required to consult with the FWS before any exercises are undertaken. Such a consultation might allow exercises to be held, so long as conditions to protect the snail's habitat are met.

Contact

U. S. Fish and Wildlife Service
Regional Office, Division of Endangered Species
1875 Century Blvd., Suite 200
Atlanta, Georgia 30345
http://southeast.fws.gov/

References

Caldwell, R. S. 1986. "Status of *Mesodon magazinensis,* the Magazine Mountain Middle-Toothed Snail." Report for Grant No. 84-1. Arkansas Nongame Species Preservation Program, Little Rock.

Hubricht, L. 1972. "The Land Snails of Arkansas." *Sterkiana* 46:15-16.

U. S. Fish and Wildlife Service. 1989. "Determination of the Magazine Mountain Shagreen, *Mesodon magazinensis,* as an Endangered Species." Federal Register 54(72): 15286-15287.

Virginia Fringed Mountain Snail

Polygyriscus virginianus

Status	Endangered
Listed	July 3, 1978
Family	Polygyridae
Description	Flat, greenish brown spiral shell with white opening.
Habitat	Damp clay soils.
Food	Unknown.
Reproduction	Clutch of two eggs per season.
Threats	Restricted range.
Range	Virginia

Description

The tiny shell of the Virginia fringed mountain snail, *Polygyriscus virginianus*, measures only 0.18 in (0.45 cm) in diameter. The shell has four to five whorls, increasing in thickness toward the rim. The shell is pale greenish brown with a white aperture. Eight to ten spiral, comb-like fringes occur inside the low spiral grooves of the shell surface. The living animal inside the shell is white with unpigmented eyestalks and is probably blind. The fringed mountain snail is the only species in it genus. It was originally described in 1947 from weathered shells found in the soil and was not known as a living species until 1971, when Leslie Hubricht found 14 living adults and seven immature specimens. This snail has been studied very little because of its rarity, limited distribution, and secretive habits. It is considered one of the rarest land snails in North America.

Behavior

Little is known about the biology of this snail. It is a burrower and almost never comes to the surface except during extremely wet weather. Its reproduction may be similar to that of *Helicodiscus parallelus*, which lays two eggs per season.

Its food sources are also unknown, but other species in this family possess radula with numerous small teeth specialized for scraping fungi, algae, and plant cells off surfaces where they graze. Rootlets of herbaceous and woody plants, as well as microscopic plants, are available in the soil layers where this species lives.

Habitat

This species has a very restricted habitat. It occurs along a steep river bank beneath the surface of permanently damp clay soils, loosened with limestone chips. The surface of the ground is relatively free of leaf litter. The site is dominated by pine and oak scrub and honeysuckle.

Distribution

The Virginia fringed mountain snail is presumed to be endemic to Pulaski County, Virginia. It has been found only at a single site on the north bank of the New River opposite the town of Radford in Pulaski County. Only about 30 of these snails have ever been found alive. The entire known range consists of a strip of bluff, embankment, and talus slope, 1.5 mi (2.5 km) long, along the river. The size of the population remains unknown because excavating to census the buried snails would severely disturb the habitat. It is considered very rare.

Threats

Any organism as rare as the Virginia fringed mountain snail can be seriously endangered by events and circumstances that would have little impact on a more plentiful species. Possible threats in-

Virginia Fringed Mountain Snail, photograph by Robert E. Batie. Reproduced by permission.

clude the application of herbicides along nearby roadsides, road construction and maintenance, and reactivation of an old quarry adjacent to the habitat. None of these activities is currently anticipated.

Conservation and Recovery

The habitat appears stable; if left strictly alone, the snail will probably continue to survive in small numbers as it has for centuries. The U.S. Fish and Wildlife Service (FWS) Recovery Plan stresses the need for additional research to aid the recovery effort. Suitable habitat within a ten- mile radius may harbor additional populations, and the FWS has negotiated conservation agreements with private landowners to protect the river bank. Eventually, the land could be acquired and managed as a snail preserve.

Contact

U.S. Fish and Wildlife Service
Regional Office, Division of Endangered Species
300 Westgate Center Dr.

Hadley, Massachusetts 01035-9589
Telephone: (413) 253-8200
Fax: (413) 253-8308
http://northeast.fws.gov/

References

Grimm, F. W. 1981. "Distribution, Habitat Requirements and Recovery Needs of the Endangered Land Snail, *Polygyriscus virginianus.*" Contract Report. U.S. Fish and Wildlife Service, Newton Corner, Massachusettes.

Hubricht, L. 1972. "Endangered Land Snails of the Eastern United States." *Sterkiana* 45: 33.

Solem, A. 1975. *"Polygyriscus virginianus:* A Helicodiscid Land Snail." *Nautilus* 89 (3): 80-86.

U.S. Fish and Wildlife Service. 1983. "Virginia Fringed Mountain Snail Recovery Plan." U.S. Fish and Wildlife Service, Atlanta.

Flat-spired Three-toothed Snail

Triodopsis platysayoides

Status	Threatened
Listed	July 3, 1978
Family	Polygyridae (Land Snail)
Description	Light or reddish-brown five whorled snail with oblique banding.
Habitat	Deciduous and mixed-pine deciduous forest.
Food	Lichens.
Reproduction	Lays a clutch of three to five eggs.
Threats	Restricted distribution, habitat disturbance.
Range	West Virginia

Description

The flat-spired three-toothed snail, *Triodopsis platysayoides*, has a thin, flattened, five-whorled shell, 1.2 in (3 cm) in diameter and up to 0.4 in (1.1 cm) thick. The shell is light brown to light reddish brown with oblique banding. The aperture is oblique with a narrow white lip. A thick, white conical tooth is present on the inner wall of the shell. This species was first classified as *Polygra platysayoides*.

Behavior

This snail feeds mainly on lichens on rock surfaces and in leaf litter and will occasionally feed on other snails. Densities must be sustained at less than four snails per square foot to prevent cannibalism. These snails breed in captivity in temperatures between 41 and 59°F (5 and 15°C). In damp, cool weather, snails venture out into the deep, shaded litter at the base of cobbles and boulders. In dry, hot weather they retreat into the crevices of exposed sandstone boulders. Predators are thought to be shrews and beetles.

Little is known about the reproductive characteristics of this species, but it is thought that individuals live for two years and breed before dying. Egg laying of clutches of three to five eggs probably occurs in May and June.

Habitat

These snails live mostly in a deep, moist layer of leaf litter among sandstone boulders along the rim of the Cheat River gorge in a mixed pine and deciduous forest. Habitat elevation ranges between 1,800 and 2,000 ft (540 and 600 m).

Distribution

This species is extremely rare and probably never ranged much outside of Monongalia County, West Virginia. The genus Triodopsis is relatively widespread in the eastern United States where 28 species are known. Closely related species are *T. complanata* in Kentucky and *T. tennesseensis* in Kentucky, Tennessee, West Virginia, Virginia, and North Carolina. The flat-spired three-toothed snail inhabits an area below the summit of Cooper's Rock adjacent to Cheat River Canyon in Monongalia County. Most of the habitat falls within the Cooper's Rock Recreational Area which is part of Cooper's Rock State Forest. Research in the early 1970s placed the population at between 300-500 individuals. More recent studies suggest that the population may number closer to 1,000.

Threats

Cooper's Rock Recreational Area and State Forest attracts more than 450,000 visitors annually. Fa-

Flat-spired Three-toothed Snail, photograph by Craig W. Stihler. Reproduced by permission.

cilities and concessions on top of Cooper's Rock draw heavy traffic to the summit. Foot traffic not only crushes the snails but also destroys the leaf litter in which they live. This project was funded by the U.S. Fish and Wildlife Service through the Ohio River Valley Ecosystem program and the West Virginia Nongame Wildlife Fund.

Conservation and Recovery

Because so little is known about this species, the recovery strategy will depend on the results of ongoing research to determine distribution, reproduction, and habitat requirements. In the meantime, state park personnel have limited access to the population site by fencing and rerouting hiking trails. If disturbance can be minimized, the snail population will probably stabilize. Construction was completed recently on a "snail fence" at Cooper's Rock State Forest in Monongalia County, West Virginia. The purpose of the fence is not to keep snails in, but to reroute human foot traffic in the area containing

the largest known population of this threatened species.

Contact

U.S. Fish and Wildlife Service
Regional Office, Division of Endangered Species
300 Westgate Center Drive
Hadley, Massachusetts 01035-9589
Telephone: (413) 253-8200
Fax: (413) 253-8308
http://northeast.fws.gov/

References

Brooks, S. T. 1933. "*Polygra platysayoides*, a New Species from West Virginia." *Nautilus* 46: 54

Hubricht, L. 1972. "Endangered Land Snails of the Eastern United States." *Sterkiana* 45: 33.

MacMillan, G. K. 1949. "Land Snails of West Virginia." *Annals of the Carnegie Museum* 31: 89-239.

U.S. Fish and Wildlife Service. 3 July 1978. "Determination that Seven Eastern U. S. Land Snails are Endangered or Threatened Species." *Federal Register* 43 (128): 28932- 28935.

U.S. Fish and Wildlife Service. 1983. "The Flat-Spired, Three-Toothed Snail Recovery Plan." U.S. Fish and Wildlife Service, Newton Corner, Massachusetts.

Morro Shoulderband Snail

Helminthoglypta walkeriana

Morro Shoulderband Snail, photograph by Barry Roth. Reproduced by permission.

Status	Endangered
Listed	December 15, 1994
Family	Helminthoglyptidae
Description	Slightly translucent snail which has five to six whorls and a globose shell.
Habitat	Coastal dune and scrub communities.
Food	Probably the fungal mycelia (webs or mats of non-reproductive fungal strands) growing on decaying plant litter.
Reproduction	Unknown.
Threats	Development, invasion of non-native plant species, senescence of dune vegetation, heavy off-highway use of recreational vehicles.
Range	California

Description

The shell of the Morro shoulderband snail (*Helminthoglypta walkeriana*), also commonly known as the banded dune snail, is slightly translucent and has five to six whorls. Its dimensions are 0.7-1.1 in (1.8-2.8 cm) in diameter and 0.6-1.0 in (1.5-2.5 cm) in height. The Morro shoulderband snail can be distinguished from another native snail in the same area, the Big Sur shoulderband snail (*H. urnbilicata*), by its more globose shell shape and presence of incised spiral grooves. The shell of the Big Sur shoulderband snail tends to be flatter and shinier. The brown garden snail (*Helix aspersa*) also occurs in Los Osos with the Morro shoulderband snail and has a marbled pattern on its shell, whereas the Morro shoulderband snail has one narrow dark brown spiral band on the shoulder. The Morro shoulderband's spire is low-domed, and half or more of the umbilicus (the cavity in the center of the base of a spiral shell that is surrounded by the whorls) is covered by the apertural lip.

Behavior

The Morro shoulderband snail. probably feeds on the fungal mycelia (webs or mats of non-reproductive fungal strands) growing on decaying plant litter. The Morro shoulderband snail, belonging in the native snail fauna of California, is not a garden pest and is essentially harmless to gardens. Sarcophagid flies have been observed to parasitize the Morro shoulderband snail. Empty puparia ("cases" left behind by adults emerging from pupae) were observed in empty snail shells. Mortality from infestations of larvae of this parasitoid fly often occurs before the snails reach reproductive maturity. The flies may have a significant impact on the population of the snail. Seasonal drought and/or heat may contribute to the snail's egg mortality. Based on shell examination, it appears that rodents may prey on the snail.

Habitat

The Morro shoulderband snail occurs in coastal dune and scrub communities. Through most of its range, the dominant shrub associated with the snail's habitat is mock heather. Other prominent shrub and succulent species are buckwheat (*Fagopyrum* sp.), eriastrum (*Eriastrum* sp.), chamisso lupine (*Lupinus chamissonis*), dudleya (*Dudleya* sp.), and in more inland locations, California sagebrush (*Artemis californica*) and black sage (*Salvia melliflora*). The Morro shoulderband snail has also been found under mats of non-native fig-marigold.

Away from the immediate coast, immature scrub in earlier successional stages may offer more favorable shelter sites than mature senescent stands of coastal dune scrub. The immature shrubs provide canopy shelter for the snail, whereas the lower limbs of larger older shrubs may be too far off the ground to offer good shelter. In addition, mature stands produce twiggy litter low in food value.

Distribution

The Morro shoulderband snail is found only in western San Luis Obispo County. At the time of listing, the Morro shoulderband snail was known to be distributed near Morro Bay. Its currently known range includes areas south of Morro Bay, west of Los Osos Creek and north of Hazard Canyon. Historically, the species has also been reported near the city of San Luis Obispo and south of Cayucos.

Threats

The Morro shoulderband snail is threatened by destruction of its habitat due to increasing development and by degradation of its habitat due to invasion of non-native plant species, especially veldt grass, structural changes to its habitat due to senescence of dune vegetation, and recreational use of heavy off-highway activity.

The Morro shoulderband snail may be experiencing competition from the brown garden snail (*Helix aspersa*). The brown garden snail, presumed to be an escapee from an adjacent golf course and housing development, has established feral populations on the spit of Morro Bay. While estivation sites and food preferences for the two snails differ, competition for shelter sites may limit the numbers of Morro shoulderband snails. The coastal dune scrub community within the survey area is mature to the point that lower limbs of the large older shrubs may be too far off the ground to offer good shelter. Both snails occasionally use the alien *M. chilense*, as well as pieces of particleboard for shelter sites. Increasing development surrounding the State Parks will increase threats from this and other exotic animals and plants that disperse from developed areas.

At least several Morro shoulderband snails have been killed as a result of controlled burning of coastal scrub that was carried out to improve habitat for the endangered Morro Bay kangaroo rat within Montana de Oro State Park. Park staff are aware of the presence of the snails, have conducted pre-burn searches for them, but have not detected any in the areas that have been burned since Roth's first reported fire-induced mortalities. Drought and/or heat may have contributed to egg mortality in the Morro shoulderband snail. Other snail taxa that occur within California's areas of Mediterranean climate copulate, oviposit, and undergo an active growth phase during the rainy season. Intact but desiccated *Helminthoglypta* eggs were found in 1985 scattered in considerable numbers within the survey area, though the species could not be determined. It was suggested that this represented several years' accumulation of egg deposits whose viability may have been lowered by drought and/or heat conditions.

The use of snail baits and non-native predatory snails to control the brown garden snail could cause mortality to the Morro shoulderband snail. Non-native predatory snails have been observed preying on other native California snails. The importation and transportation of non-native snails are prohibited in San Luis Obispo County by the California Department of Fish and Game.

Conservation and Recovery

Several habitat conservation plans are being developed to allow for the incidental take of the Morro shoulderband snail during the development of small subdivisions and single family residences. Such actions would result in the loss of habitat for the Morro shoulderband snail, but contiguous blocks of remaining habitat will likely be preserved and managed in perpetuity.

A sewer treatment facility is currently proposed for Los Osos. Construction of this facility will destroy habitat for the Morro shoulderband snail, while operation of the facility will indirectly cause destruction of habitat by allowing the lifting of a moratorium on development. The County of San Luis Obispo will acquire habitat to mitigate for the direct and indirect effects of the sewer treatment facility.

U.S. Fish and Wildlife Service is funding surveys and habitat research on the Morro shoulderband snail on state park lands. A veldt grass control project for snail habitat on state park lands began in 1998.

Contact

U. S. Fish and Wildlife Service
Regional Office, Division of Endangered Species
Eastside Federal Complex
911 N. E. 11th Ave.
Portland, Oregon 97232-4181
Telephone: (503) 231-6121
http://pacific.fws.gov/

Reference

U.S. Fish and Wildlife Service. 1998. "Recovery Plan for Morro Shoulderband Snail and Four Plants from Western San Luis Obispo County, California." U.S. Fish and Wildlife Service, Portland, Oregon. 75 pp.

Mussels
and Clams

Cumberland Elktoe

Alasmidonta atropurpurea

Cumberland Elktoe, photograph. U. S. Fish and Wildlife Service. Reproduced by permission.

Status	Endangered
Listed	January 10, 1997
Family	Unionidae
Description	A freshwater, bivalve mussel with a thin but not fragile shell, whose surface is smooth, somewhat shiny, and covered with greenish rays.
Habitat	Creeks and rivers with cool, well-oxygenated, flowing water and gravelly to rocky substrates.
Food	A filter-feeder on algae, tiny zooplankton, and organic detritus.
Reproduction	Female siphons male spawn and fertilizes eggs in her gills; the larvae are parasitic on fish, and later metamorphose into the sedentary adult stage.
Threats	Habitat destruction by dams and impoundments, and degradation by sedimentation, acid-mine drainage, oil spills, and other kinds of pollution.
Range	Kentucky, Tennessee

Description

The *Alasmidonta atropurpurea* (Cumberland elktoe), described by Rafinesque in 1831, has a thin but not fragile shell, whose surface is smooth, somewhat shiny, and covered with greenish rays. Young specimens have a yellowish-brown shell, and the shells of adults are generally black. The inside of the shell is shiny with colors ranging from white and bluish white to peach or salmon color.

This species is quite similar to *Alasmidonta marginata,* but tends to differ from the latter by its darker color, less pronounced corrugations on the posterior slope, and the less acutely angular development of the posterior ridge. In older individuals or *A. atropurpurea,* the posterior ridge may be rather high and the resulting slope may be quite steep, but the posterior ridge retains a rounded character. The two species may occur in adjacent stream systems but do not appear to be sympatric at any locality. The tendency for the shell to be compressed, highly pustulate, and have low to no knobs on the poste-

rior ridge distinguishes this morph from *Quadrula cylindrica* s.s. [i.e., *Q. c. cylindrica*]. It is not easily confused with any other sympatric species.

Behavior

This bradytictic anodontine species was found gravid from October through May, but no fish infested with its glochidia were observed until March. They found Cumberland elktoe glochidia to develop equally well on both fin and gill surfaces. Five fish species collected from the wild were parasitized by Cumberland elktoe glochidia-whitetail shiner *(Cyprinella galactura),* northern hogsucker *(Hypentelium nigricans),* rock bass *(Ambloplites rupestris),* longear sunfish *(Lepomis megalotis),* and rainbow darter *(Etheostoma caeruleum).* However, under laboratory' conditions, juvenile specimens transformed only on the northern hogsucker. The period of glochidial encystment (i.e., until transformation into free-living juveniles) took 24 days, at 66.2+°F (19+°C).

Habitat

This species inhabits medium-sized rivers and may extend into headwater streams where it is often the only mussel present. The species appears to be most abundant in fiats, shallow pool areas lacking the bottom contour development of typical pools, with sand and scattered cobble/boulder material, relatively shallow depths, and slow (almost imperceptible) currents. The species has also been observed in swifter currents and in areas with mud, sand, and gravel substratum.

Distribution

The Cumberland elktoe is endemic to very localized portions of the Cumberland River system in Tennessee and Kentucky; the latter state considers it endangered. Historic records exist from the Cumberland River and from its tributaries entering from the south between the Big South Fork Cumberland River upstream to Cumberland Falls. Specimens have also been taken from Marsh Creek above Cumberland Falls. Old records of the related species *Alasmidonta marginata* exist from other creeks above Cumberland Falls, and there is speculation that these specimens were indeed the Cumberland elktoe. Because the area above the falls has been severely damaged by coal mining, any populations of *A. atropurpurea* that might have existed there were likely lost. A record of one fresh dead specimen exists from the Collins River, Grundy County, Tennessee. However, extensive searches of the collection site, other sites in the Collins River, and adjacent rivers have failed to find another specimen. If the species did exist in the Collins River, it has likely been extirpated. Any Cumberland elktoe populations that may have existed in the main stem of the Cumberland River were likely lost when Wolf Creek Dam was completed. Other tributary populations were likely lost due to habitat degradations caused by coal mining, pollution, and spills from oil wells.

Three populations of the Cumberland elktoe have persisted, all of them associated with waters flowing through McCreary County, Kentucky. The species survives in the middle sections of Rock Creek; the upper portions of the Big South Fork Cumberland River basin in McCreary County, as well as in the Tennessee counties of Scott, Fentress, and Morgan; and in Marsh Creek, which likely contains the best surviving elktoe population.

The Cumberland elktoe has apparently been extirpated from the main stem of the Cumberland River, Laurel River, and its tributary Lynn Camp Creek. Based on post-1985 records, populations of the Cumberland lktoe persist in eight tributaries—Laurel Fork and Marsh Creek, both Whitley County, Kentucky; Big South Fork, Scott County, Tennessee, and McCreary County, Kentuclcy; Rock Creek, McCreary County, Kentucky; Clear Fork, Fentress, Morgan, and Scott Counties; Tennessee; North Prong Clear Fork, Fentress County, Tennessee; White Oak Creek, Scott County, Tennessee; and Bone Camp Creek, Morgan County, Tennessee. The latter five streams, which comprise the Big South Fork system, may represent a single metapopulation of the Cumberland elktoe; there may be suitable habitat for the species and/or its fish hosts in intervening stream reaches, potentially allowing for natural genetic interchange to occur.

Considered a "rare species" in 1981, few sites continue to harbor the Cumberland elktoe, although relatively large populations are currently known. Marsh Creek harbors the largest population known in Kentucky, although populations in Rock Creek were also sizable in 1996. In both streams the Cumberland elktoe represented the second most abundant unionid species sampled. Bakaletz. In 1991 the largest population was reported in the Big South Fork system in Tennessee located in the headwaters of Clear Fork, where several hundred specimens were secured from muskrat middens in the late 1980s. Several age classes of the Cumberland elktoe were represented in samples taken from throughout the larger tributaries of the Big South Fork system in Tennessee during a 1986 survey.

Threats

The upper Big South Fork basin population is threatened by coal mining runoff and could also be threatened by impoundments. The Marsh Creek population has been harmed by oil spills, which always remain a serious potential threat. The Rock Creek population could be threatened by logging. All three populations, especially Rock Creek and Marsh Creek, are restricted to such short stream reaches that they could be eliminated by all manner of hazardous events, toxic chemical spills being the chief among them.

Conservation and Recovery

The Cumberland elktoe only survives in three very localized portions of the Cumberland River system, in the middle sections of Rock Creek, the upper portions of the Big South Fork of the Cumberland River basin, and in Marsh Creek. Marsh Creek supports the largest population of the rare mussel. It is crucial that these critical habitats are protected against the development of new dams or impoundments, from acid drainage associated with local coal mining, and from spills of petroleum or other toxic chemicals. The surviving populations of the Cumberland elktoe should be monitored, and research undertaken into its biology and ecological needs, including work on its propagation and reintroduction techniques.

Contacts

U.S. Fish and Wildlife Service
Asheville Ecological Services Field Office
160 Zillicoa Street
Asheville, North Carolina, 28801-1082
Telephone: (828) 258-3939
Fax: (828) 258-5330

U. S. Fish and Wildlife Service
Regional Office, Division of Endangered Species
1875 Century Blvd., Suite 200
Atlanta, Georgia 30345
http://southeast.fws.gov/

Reference

U.S. Fish and Wildlife Service. 10 January 1997. "Endangered and Threatened Wildlife and Plants; Determination of Endangered Status for the Cumberland Elktoe, Oyster Mussel, Cumberlandian Combshell, Purple Bean, and Rough Rabbitsfoot." *Federal Register* 62(7): 1647-1658.

Dwarf Wedgemussel

Alasmidonta heterodon

Status	Endangered
Listed	March 14, 1990
Family	Unionidae
Description	Freshwater mussel with two lateral teeth on the right valve and one on the left.
Habitat	Creek and river areas with a slow to moderate current and a sand, gravel, or muddy bottom.
Reproduction	Eggs are fertilized in the female as sperm passes through its gills; the resulting larvae than attaches to a fish host.
Food	Filter feeder.
Threats	Water pollution and the construction of impoundments.
Range	Delaware, New York, North Carolina, Virginia

Dwarf Wedgemussel, photograph. U. S. Fish and Wildlife Service. Reproduced by permission.

Description

The dwarf wedgemussel's shell rarely exceeds 1.5 in (3.7 cm) in length. It is also the only North American freshwater mussel that has two lateral teeth on the right valve, but only one on the left. The female's shell is inflated in the back where the marsupial gills are located.

Behavior

Little is known about the species' life history and reproductive cycle. Gravid females have been observed from late August until June. Like other freshwater mussels, this species' eggs are fertilized in the female as sperm passes through its gills; the resulting larvae than attaches to a fish host. Although this host is still unknown, strong evidence suggests that it is an anadromous fish which migrates from the ocean into freshwater to spawn.

Habitat

The dwarf wedgemussel inhabits creek and river areas with a slow to moderate current and a sand, gravel, or muddy bottom. These areas must be nearly silt free.

Distribution

Once known from about 70 Atlantic Slope river systems, the dwarf wedgemussel is now known from only 12 sites. Two of these populations have recently been discovered—one in Nottoway River, Virginia, and one on Neversink Creek (Delaware River drainage), New York. Four of the existing populations are located in North Carolina one in Little River (Johnston County); another on the Tar River (Granville County); and one each in two of the Tar River Tributaries (Franklin County). The remaining populations occur in Maryland, New

Hanpshire, and Vermont. These locations are the Ashuelot River, Chesire County, New Hampshire; two Connecticut River reaches in Sullivan County, New Hampshire, and Windsor County, Vermont; McIntosh Run in St. Mary's County, Maryland; and two Tuckahoe Creek tributaries in Talbot, Queen Annes, and Caroline Counties, Maryland.

Historically, this mussel occurred in 11 States and one Canadian province. It ranged from the Petitcodiac River system in New Brunswick, Canada, south to the Neuse River System in North Carolina. The dwarf wedge mussel is extirpated from both river systems. Other former Southeastern river system sites include the Choptank River; the Rappahannock River; and the James River. In the Middle Atlantic States, the dwarf wedgemussel inhabited the Hackensack River; the Delaware River; and the Susquehanna River systems. New England habitat sites included the Taunton River, the Agawam River, the Merrimac River, the Connecticut River, and the Quinnipiac River systems. One other population from the Fort River in Hampshire County, Massachussetts, also appears extinct.

Threats

Water pollution and the construction of impoundments are the primary threats to this mussel's survival. Increased acidity, caused by the mobilization of toxic metals by acid rain, is thought to be one of the chief causes of the species' extirpation from the Fort River in Massachusetts. One of the largest remaining populations has declined dramatically in the Ashuelot River, downstream of a golf course. This population probably has been affected by fungicides, herbicides, insecticides, and fertilizers which have been applied to the golf course. Agricultural runoff from adjacent corn fields and pastures also is contributing to this population's decline. Freshwater mussels, including the dwarf wedgemussel, are sensitive to potassium, zinc, copper, cadmium, and other elements associated with industrial pollution. Industrial, agricultural, and domestic pollution is responsible for the dwarf wedge's disappearance from much of its historic range. To survive, the dwarf wedgemussel needs an almost silt free environment with a slow to moderate current. The construction of dams alters these conditions. For example, most of the Connecticut River's main stem is now a series of impoundments. Upstream from each dam, heavy silt disposition, combined with low oxygen levels, has made the area unsuitable for mussels. Downstream of the dams, water level and temperature fluctuations, caused by hypolimnetic discharges and intermit-tent power generation, have been stressful to the mussels. In some areas below the dams, the river banks have stabilized and the dwarf wedge's required substrate (sandy, gravel, or muddy) no longer exists.

Another reason the species is declining is because its anadromous fish host has been blocked from some habitat areas. For example, the Petitcodiac River system in Canada still hosts several rare mussels, but the dwarf wedge has disappeared. Apparently a downstream water causeway, constructed since the species was last seen, has denied access to the fish host. Populations in the species' remaining range are suffering a decline in reproductive capacity because of its low numbers and isolated population distribution.

Conservation and Recovery

The Maryland Natural Heritage Program has started a program to surround creeks with natural vegetated buffer strips. These strips, which are being established through voluntary landowner cooperation, will protect dwarf wedgemussel habitat by filtering out sediment, excess nutrients, and pollutants. Planned recovery efforts throughout the species' range include encouraging the development of mussel sanctuaries, and reintroducing the species into suitable historic habitats. Buffer strips, conservation easements, and other protective measures should be negotiated through management agreements with local, State and Federal government authorities and private landowners. Dwarf wedgemussel ecology and life history should be studied, and periodic population surveys conducted at historic and existing sites. It's also essential to determine the identity of the species' fish host(s).

Contacts

U.S. Fish and Wildlife Service
Division of Endangered Species
1875 Century Boulevard, Suite 200
Atlanta, Georgia 30345-3319
Telephone: (404) 679-4159
Fax: (404) 679-1111
http://southeast.fws.gov/

U.S. Fish and Wildlife Service
Office of the Regional Director
300 Westgate Center Drive
Hadley, Massachusetts 01035-9589
Telephone: (413) 253-8308
Fax: (413) 253-8308

U.S. Fish and Wildlife Service
Chesapeake Bay Ecological Services Field Office
177 Admiral Cochrane Drive
Annapolis, Maryland 21401-7307
Telephone: (410) 573-4500
Fax: (410) 263-2608
E-mail: Laurie_Hewitt@fws.gov
http://www.fws.gov/r5cbfo/index.html

U.S. Fish and Wildlife Service
1825 Virginia Street
Annapolis, Maryland 21401
301/269-5448

References

Clark, A.H. 1981. "The Tribe Alasmidontini (Union-idae, Anodontinae), Part 1 *Pegias, Alasmidonta,* and *Arcidens." Smithsonian Contributions to Zoology,* No. 326.

Fuller, S.L.H. "Freshwater and Terrestrial Mollusks." In J.E. Cooper et al, eds. *Endangered and Threatened Plants and Animals of North Carolina.* North Carolina State Museum of Natural History, Raleigh, pp. 143-194.

Havlik, M.E., and L.L. Marking. 1987. "Effects of Contaminants on Naiad Mollusks (Unionidae) A Review." Fish and Wildlife Service, Resource Publication 164. Washington, D.C.

Mcknight, Jonathan. May 1989. "The Dwarf Wedge Mussel." *Bulletin of the Maryland Natural Heritage Program* (Department of Natural Resources).

U.S. Fish and Wildlife Service. 14 March 1990. "Determination of Endangered Status for the Dwarf Wedge Mussel." *Federal Register,* 55(50):9447-9450.

Appalachian Elktoe

Alasmidonta raveneliana

Status	Endangered
Listed	November 23, 1994
Family	Unionidae
Description	A freshwater, bivalve mussel with a kidney-shaped shell.
Habitat	Creeks and rivers with cool, well-oxygenated, flowing water and gravelly to rocky substrates.
Food	A filter-feeder on algae, tiny zooplankton, and organic detritus.
Reproduction	Female siphons male spawn and fertilizes eggs in her gills; the larvae are parasitic on fish, and later metamorphose into the sedentary adult stage.
Threats	Habitat destruction by dams and impoundments, and degradation by sedimentation and other kinds of pollution.
Range	North Carolina, Tennessee

Appalachian Elktoe, photograph. U. S. Fish and Wildlife Service. Reproduced by permission.

Description

The *Alasmidonta raveneliana* (Appalachian elktoe) has a thin, but not fragile, kidney-shaped shell, reaching up to about 3.2 in (8 cm) in length, 1.4 in (3.5 cm) in height, and 1 in (2.5 cm) in width. Juveniles generally have a yellowish-brown periostracum (outer shell surface) while the periostracum of the adults is usually dark brown to greenish-black in color. Although rays are prominent on some shells, particularly in the posterior portion of the shell, many individuals have only obscure greenish rays. The shell nacre (inside shell surface) is shiny, often white to bluish-white, changing to a salmon, pinkish, or brownish color in the central and beak cavity portions of the shell; some specimens may be marked with irregular brownish blotches.

Behavior

The Appalachian elktoe is a filter-feeder of algae, tiny zooplankton, and organic detritus, which are siphoned from overlying water. The male releases sperm into the water. These are siphoned by the female, and used to fertilize eggs in the gill chamber. The mature larvae are planktonic and parasitic on species of fish. The larvae metamorphose into the sedentary, adult stage of the life-history.

Habitat

The Appalachian elktoe has been reported from relatively shallow, medium-sized creeks and rivers with cool, well-oxygenated, moderate to fast-flowing water. It has been observed in gravelly substrates often mixed with cobble and boulders, in cracks in bedrock, and occasionally in relatively silt-free, coarse, sandy substrates.

Distribution

Only two populations of the species are known to survive. The healthiest of these populations exists in the main stem of the Little Tennessee River between Emory Lake at Franklin, Macon County,

North Carolina, and Fontana Reservoir in Swain County, North Carolina. The second population occurs in the Nolichucky River system. This population appears to be restricted to scattered locations within a short reach of the Toe River and the main stem of the Nolichucky River in Yancey and Mitchell Counties, North Carolina, extending down river into the vicinity of Erwin, Unicoi County, Tennessee. A single specimen of the Appalachian elktoe has also been found in the Cane River, a major tributary to the Nolichucky River, in Yancey County, North Carolina. The complete historic range of the Appalachian elktoe is unknown, but available information suggests it was once widely distributed throughout Upper Tennessee River system in western North Carolina, including the French Broad River, Little River (French Broad River system), Pigeon River (French Broad River system), Swannanoa River (French Broad River system), and Talula Creek (Little Tennessee River system). In Tennessee, the species is known only from its present range in the main stem of the Nolichucky River.

Threats

Water quality and habitat degradation resulting from impoundments, stream channelization projects, and point and non-point sources of siltation and other pollutants appear to be major factors in reducing the species' distribution and reproductive capacity.

The most immediate threats to both remaining populations of the species currently appear to be associated with sedimentation and other pollutants (fertilizers, pesticides, heavy metals, oil, salts, organic wastes) from non-point sources. Much of the Nolichucky River in North Carolina contains heavy loads of sediments from past land disturbance activities within its watershed, and suitable habitat for the Appalachian elktoe appears to be limited in this river system. Also, the Little Tennessee River above Lake Emory (above the reach of the river supporting the Appalachian elktoe) carries a high load of unstable sediments and is without mussels. It is believed that Lake Emory has served in the past, and

continues serve to a lesser degree, as a sediment trap that has helped to protect the integrity of the river below the Town of Franklin. However, the lake is rapidly filling in with sediment and large sediment accumulations in the river below the lake are become increasing common.

Conservation and Recovery

Assuring the long-term survival of the Appalachian elktoe will require, at a minimum (1) protecting the existing water and habitat quality of the reaches of the Little Tennessee and Nolichucky River systems where the species is still surviving; and, (2) improving degraded portions of the species habitat and, reestablishing and protecting additional populations of the species within portions of its historic range. This will require compliance with existing State and Federal regulations and assistance from the public and local governments and industries in implementing recovery actions. Also, additional research on the threats to the species, the environmental requirements of the elktoe and fish host(s), and propagation and reintroduction techniques for freshwater mussels is needed.

Contacts

U.S. Fish and Wildlife Service
Asheville Ecological Services Field Office
160 Zillicoa Street
Asheville, North Carolina, 28801-1082
Telephone: (828) 258-3939
Fax: (828) 258-5330

U. S. Fish and Wildlife Service
Regional Office, Division of Endangered Species
1875 Century Blvd., Suite 200
Atlanta, Georgia 30345
http://southeast.fws.gov/

Reference

U.S. Fish and Wildlife Service. 23 November 1994. "Appalachian Elktoe Determined to be an Endangered Species." *Federal Register* 59(225): 60324-60334.

Fat Threeridge Mussel

Amblema neislerii

Status	Endangered
Listed	March 16, 1998
Family	Unionidae
Description	Medium to large heavy-shelled mussel with a dark brown to black shell which is strongly sculptured with seven to eight prominent horizontal parallel ridges.
Habitat	Stable sandy and gravelly substrates in medium-sized streams to large rivers, often in areas swept free of silt by the current.
Food	Filter-feeder of phytoplankton and organic detritus.
Reproduction	Female siphons sperm from the water to fertilize her eggs, which hatch into parasitic larvae, which metamorphose into sedentary adults.
Threats	Impoundment and water pollution.
Range	Florida, Georgia

Description

The *Amblema neislerii* (fat threeridge) is a medium-sized to large, subquadrate, inflated, solid, and heavy shelled mussel that reaches a length of 4 in (10.2 cm). Older, larger individuals are so inflated that their width approximates their height. The umbos are in the anterior quarter of the shell. The dark brown to black shell is strongly sculptured with seven to eight prominent horizontal parallel ridges. Internally, there are two subequal pseudocardinal teeth in the left valve and typically one large and one small tooth in the right valve. The nacre is bluish white to light purplish and very iridescent. The host fish for the fat threeridge is unknown at this time. Several host fish families have been identified for the threeridge, a congener of the fat threeridge, and include eight species of centrarchids (the sunfish family). Minnows (Cyprinidae) may serve as hosts for the fat three-ridge. The nineteenth-century name *Unio neislerii* Lea is now believed to be a synonym of *Amblema neislerii*. This taxon was incorrectly assigned to the genera *Quadrula* and *Crenodonta* earlier this century, but modern taxonomy correctly assigned the fat threeridge to the genus *Amblema* in 1988.

Behavior

Adult fat threeridge mussels are sedentary as adults. They siphon streamwater and filter phytoplankton and organic detritus as food. The female mussels siphon water containing sperm from the water to fertilize their eggs. The eggs hatch into larvae that are parasitic on fish. The larvae later metamorphose into sedentary adults.

Habitat

The fat threeridge inhabits relatively stable reaches of sandy and gravelly substrates in medium-sized streams to large rivers, often in areas swept free of silt by the current.

Distribution

The fat threeridge was described from the Flint River in Macon County, Georgia. This species was historically endemic in the mainstems of the Flint, Apalachicola, and lower Chipola rivers, where it was generally rare over its range but locally abundant. It has been extirpated from the Flint River, which included most of its historic range. It has disappeared from most of the historical sites where it was formerly found, and only 7% of sampled sites within the historic range still have live individuals. It is currently known from six sites on the latter two rivers.

For the status survey, 86 sites were sampled within the historical range of the fat threeridge, including eight of the 12 (67%) known historical sites. Only one of the eight (13%) historical sites still had live individuals. No live fat threeridge mussels have been found since 1981 in the Flint River; the species is apparently extirpated from Georgia. This species was apparently common in Dead Lake in 1967, but no living specimens were found there in 1974 or in the status survey. The status survey found fat threeridge at six of the 86 (7%) sampled sites, three each on the Apalachicola and lower Chipola rivers. An average of 6.4 live individuals were found per site.

A 1956 study conducted in the Chipola River system reported 17 specimens from two sites (average of 8.5 per site). The same study documented 0.9 to 1.4 mussels per sq ft (10-15 mussels per sq m) over a 656 ft (200 m) stretch of Dead Lake (Chipola River) shoreline.

The smallest live fat threeridge found during the survey was 1.7 in (4.3 cm) long. A 1956 study found evidence of juvenile fat threeridge at a site in the lower Apalachicola River thought to have the best extant population of this species, where it was the second most common mussel species encountered. Three fat threeridges under 2.0 in (5.0 cm) in length were found employing total substratum removal from six 2.7 ft (0.25 m) square quadrants. The smallest specimens had fewer than the five presumed annual growth rings that might be indicative of juveniles. A fresh dead individual measured 0.9 in (2.4 cm) in length and had two to three growth rings. In 1996, three live specimens ranging from 1.6 to 2.0 in (4.0-5.0 cm) in length were located in the same bed. These data indicate that the fat threeridge is experiencing limited recruitment at the site representing its best known population.

Threats

Impoundments have altered about 29% of mainstream riverine habitat on the Flint River. Preimpoundment records from Seminole and Blackshear reservoirs exist showing one site for the flat threeridge.

A large population of the fat threeridge has been extirpated in Dead Lake, possibly from chromium contamination from an abandoned battery salvage operation. The threeridge (a relative of the fat threeridge) and the washboard (*Megalonaias nervosa*), superficially similar to both the fat threeridge and purple bankclimber, are heavily utilized as sources of shell for nuclei in the cultured pearl industry. Although commercial shell buyers generally regard shells from the Apalachicola-Chattahoochee-Flint (ACF) River system as are of poor quality, shell material from this area may be used as "filler" for higher quality material from elsewhere. In the 1980s, the price of shell increased in the 1980s, resulting in increased competition for the harvesting of shell beds in the Apalachicolan Region. This has possibly put additional pressure on the fat threeridge. Biological supply companies have used the Flint River and possibly the Ochlockonee River as sources for large mussel specimens, including the fat threeridge, to sell to academic institutions for use in laboratory studies. The practice of dissecting mussels in introductory laboratory courses is no longer widespread, and the threat posed to large species such as the fat threeridge is probably decreasing.

Nonetheless, harvest of the fat threeridge and purple bankclimber for these purposes could decimate their remaining populations. The increasing rarity of these mussels potentially makes them more appealing to shell collectors. Revealing specific stream reaches harboring these species could pose a threat from collectors.

Conservation and Recovery

The fat threeridge mussel only survives in a few critical habitats, and its reproductive success appears to be quite limited. Its surviving areas of critical habitat must be protected from impoundment and other damages, such as pollution. The rare mussel must also be strictly protected from any collection by naturalists or for commercial purposes. Its known populations should be monitored and additional ones searched for. Research should be undertaken into its ecological needs, with a view to developing management practices to maintain and improve its habitat.

Contacts

U. S. Fish and Wildlife Service
Regional Office, Division of Endangered Species
1875 Century Blvd., Suite 200
Atlanta, Georgia 30345
http://southeast.fws.gov/

U.S. Fish and Wildlife Service
Wildlife and Habitat Management
6620 Southpoint Drive South, Suite 310
Jacksonville, Florida 32216
Telephone: (904) 232-2580
Fax: (904) 232-2404

Reference

U.S. Fish and Wildlife Service. 16 March 1998. "Endangered and Threatened Wildlife and Plants; Determination of Endangered Status for Five Freshwater Mussels and Threatened Status for Two Freshwater Mussels From the Eastern Gulf Slope Drainages of Alabama, Florida, and Georgia." *Federal Register* 63(50): 12664-12687

Ouachita Rock-pocketbook

Arkansia wheeleri

Status	Endangered
Listed	October 23, 1991
Family	Unionidae (Freshwater Mussel)
Description	Medium-sized, silky textured, chestnut brown to black shell.
Habitat	Slow-moving side channels and pools with muddy or rocky bottoms.
Food	Filter-feeder.
Reproduction	Female stores sperm in gills; glochidia are released into the stream after hatching.
Threats	Impoundments, water pollution.
Range	Arkansas, Oklahoma

Ouachita Rock-Pocketbook, photograph. A. E. Spreitzer Photography. Reproduced by permission.

Description

The Ouachita rock-pocketbook is a medium-sized freshwater mussel up to 3.9 in (10 cm) long. The shell exterior is chestnut brown to black and has a silky texture. This species is also known as *Arcidens wheeleri* and by the alternate common name Wheeler's pearly mussel.

Behavior

See the Upland Combshell (*Epioblasma metastriata*) entry.

Habitat

This mussel species is usually found on muddy or rocky bottoms in side channels and backwaters where there is little or no current. Freshwater mussels feed by filtering food particles from the water.

Distribution

The Ouachita rock-pocketbook is known from the Kiamichi River in southeastern Oklahoma and the Little River near the Oklahoma-Arkansas border. It was first described in 1912 from specimens taken from the "Old River," at Arkadelphia, Arkansas, a reference to a series of connected oxbow lakes. The Ouachita River was mentioned as another collection site. It has been recorded in the Kiamichi River near Antlers, Tuskahoma, Clayton, and Spencerville Crossing, all in Pushmataha County. The site near Spencerville Crossing has been flooded by the Hugo Reservoir. In the Little River in Arkansas, historic collections include White Cliffs, Little River County, and at the border of Little River and Sevier Counties.

This mussel survives in the Kiamichi River in Oklahoma and the Little River in Arkansas. The Kiamichi River holds an estimated 1,000 individuals in a section of the river between the southwestern corner of LeFlore County and Antlers in Pushmataha County. Fewer than 100 individuals are estimated to survive in a 5-mi (8-km) section of the Little River that flows from the Oklahoma border between Little River and Sevier Counties, Arkansas. In all, the Ouachita rock-pocketbook occurs in low densities over an estimated range of 85 mi (137 km) of river.

Threats

The main factors in the decline of the Ouachita rock-pocketbook have been water pollution and the construction of reservoirs. The Ouachita River near Arkadelphia has been altered by a number of reservoirs and is now so polluted that it is unlikely that any mussel species could exist there. In the Little River, cold water discharges from Pine Creek Dam and pollution of the Rolling Fork Creek tributary has eliminated many mussel species. East of the 5-mi (8-km) stretch of the Little River where the mussel still occurs, the water quality is too poor to allow the Ouachita rock-pocketbook to survive.

The main threat to many Kiamichi River Ouachita rock-pocketbook populations is the planned construction of the Tuskahoma Reservoir in Pushmataha County, Oklahoma. This would flood mussel populations and affect habitat downstream. In addition, the proposed addition of hydropower to the Sardis Reservoir on Jackfork Creek, a tributary of the Kiamichi River, would disturb the current water regime, most likely stressing downstream mussels.

Along with other native mussels, the Ouachita rock-pocketbook face a threat from the introduced Asiatic clam (*Corbicula fluminea*). This introduced species now occurs in Hugo Reservoir and is slowly moving upstream.

Conservation and Recovery

The Ouachita rock-pocketbook is listed as an endangered species by the U.S. FIsh and Wildlife Service and by the IUCN. Conservation of this rare mollusk requires that its only known critical habitats be protected in reaches of the Little River, the Ouachita River, and the Kiamichi River upstream from Hugo Reservoir. The most important potential threats are associated with the reservoir development, but pollution by siltation and chemicals are also factors that must be controlled. The endangered mussel must also be strictly protected from any collecting. Little is known about the life history and habitat requirements of the Ouachita rock-pocketbook, so research is needed into these areas. Field surveys should continue to be made for additional populations, and the known ones and their habitat conditions should be monitored.

Contacts

U. S. Fish and Wildlife Service
Regional Office, Division of Endangered Species
P.O. Box 1306
Albuquerque, New Mexico 87103-1306
Telephone: (505) 248-6911
Fax: (505) 248-6915
http://southwest.fws.gov/

U. S. Fish and Wildlife Service
Regional Office, Division of Endangered Species
1875 Century Blvd., Suite 200
Atlanta, Georgia 30345
http://southeast.fws.gov/

U. S. Fish and Wildlife Service
Oklahoma Ecological Services Field Office
222 South Houston, Suite A
Tulsa, Oklahoma 74127
Telephone: (918) 581-7458
Fax: (918) 581-7467
http://ifw2es.fws.gov/oklahoma/

References

Harris, J. L., and M. E. Gordon. 1987. *Distribution and Status of Rare and Endangered Mussels (Mollusca: Margaritiferidae, Unionidae) in Arkansas.* Arkansas Game and Fish Commission, Little Rock.

Mehlhop-Cifelli, P., and E. K. Miller. 1989. "Status and Distribution of *Arkansia wheeleri* Ortmann & Walker, 1912 (Syn. *Arcidens wheeleri*) in the Kiamichi River, Oklahoma." U. S. Fish and Wildlife Service, Tulsa, Okla.

Birdwing Pearlymussel

Conradilla caelata

Status	Endangered
Listed	June 14, 1976
Family	Unionidae (Freshwater Mussel)
Description	Small mussel with olive or dark green shell with irregular growth lines.
Habitat	Silt-free substrates in fast-flowing streams and rivers.
Reproduction	Female stores sperm in gills; glochidia (larvae) are released into streams after hatching.
Food	Filter-feeder.
Threats	Impoundments; siltation; pollution.
Range	Tennessee, Virginia

Birdwing Pearlymussel, photograph. U. S. Fish and Wildlife Service. Reproduced by permission.

Description

The birdwing pearlymussel (*Conradilla caelata*) is a relatively small Cumberlandian mussel, seldom over 2 in (5 cm) in width. The valves are solid, slightly inflated (especially in females), and triangular or egg shaped. The surface of the shell is marked by strong, irregular growth lines, and the outer coloring is olive green or dark green. Inside coloring of the shell is always white. Fish hosts for this mussel are thought to be the shiner (*Notropis galacturus*) and at least one darter. This species is sometimes referred to as *Lemiox rimosus*, as described in 1834 from the Cumberland River.

Behavior

The life of mussels is complex, and reproduction often depends upon a stable habitat—unaltered stream conditions, clean water, and an undisturbed stream bottom. The cycle also depends upon the abundance of suitable fish hosts to complete the mussel's larval development.

To reproduce, males discharge sperm, which are dispersed by stream currents. In the process of feeding, females nearby or downstream take in sperm, which fertilizes eggs stored in their gills. The gills serve as brood pouches (marsupia), where the glochidia hatch and begin to develop. After a time, these glochidia are released into the stream. A few mussels have inner parts that resemble a tiny minnow and can be manipulated to lure host fish. When a fish gets close to the shell, the mussel expels its glochidia.

Glochidia have tiny bean- or spoon-shaped valves that attach to the gill filaments of host fish. Glochidia can only progress to the juvenile stage while attached to the fish's gills. Those that do not fortuitously encounter a host fish do not survive when released by the female mussel. They sink to the bottom and die.

When the juvenile has developed a shell and is large enough to survive on its own, it detaches from the host fish and falls to the stream bottom, beginning a long association with a single stretch of stream. Maturing mussels bury themselves in riffles and shoals with only the shell margins and feeding siphons exposed to the water. Some mussels live as long as 50 years or more.

The family Unionidae, which includes all of the freshwater mussels in the United States, is separated into two groups based on the length of time the glochidia remain in the female's marsupia. The eggs of the short-term (tachytictic) breeders are fertilized in the spring, and glochidia are released by late summer of the same year. Long-term (bradytictic) breeders hold developing glochidia in the brood pouch over winter and release them in the spring.

Freshwater mussels feed by siphoning phytoplankton and other plant matter from the water. Indigestible particles are expelled from the shell by reverse siphoning. Silt in the water can kill mussels by clogging their feeding siphons.

There are no known interspecific differences in feeding among freshwater mussels. The glochidia are obligate parasites on the gills or fins of fish. Adult mussels are filter-feeders and consume particulate matter in the water column. Identifiable stomach contents almost invariably include desmids, diatoms, algae, protozoa, and zooplankton.

Most freshwater mussel species display seasonal variations in activity associated with water temperature and reproduction. Metabolic rate is, in part, positively correlated with temperature. Many ectothermic species have the capacity to adjust their metabolic rates in response to long-term changes in temperature. Thus, metabolic rates do not continue to rise as temperatures rise in the summer, and they do not continue to fall during the winter as temperatures decline.

Some freshwater mussels also show diurnal changes in metabolic rates that indicate a tendency toward nocturnal activity patterns. Mussels may move to the surface to feed at night and move deeper into the substrate during the day; this is one way to avoid predators that hunt by visual contact.

Freshwater mussels are nonmigratory.

Habitat

Cumberlandian freshwater mussels are found in clean, fast-flowing streams and rivers in riffles and shoals where the bottom consists of firm rubble, gravel, or sand.

Distribution

The birdwing pearlymussel once was widely dispersed in small numbers within the Tennessee River and its major tributary streams. Collectors have always considered it a rare shell. Although a few records have located the birdwing pearlymussel in other watersheds, these records are now considered in error.

The birdwing pearlymussel is presently found only in larger tributaries of the Tennessee River—the Duck, Elk, Clinch, and Powell rivers. The mussel is abundant in Duck River but limited to a 40-mi (64.4-km) reach between Lillard Mill Dam and the former location of the Columbia Dam. The population there has been estimated at 20,000-30,000 individuals

Threats

Major water control projects flood upstream valleys, reduce downstream flows, alter temperature gradients, cause extreme water level fluctuations, increase turbidity and silting, and create seasonal oxygen deficits. These factors can eliminate mussels that are fixed to a single locality. The Columbia Dam on the Duck River was at one time a threat to the species, but demolition on it began in June 1999.

Conservation and Recovery

The U.S. Fish and Wildlife Service Recovery Plan for the birdwing pearlymussel stresses 1) the need to seek agreements with landowners along the rivers to preserve streambank habitat and 2) the need to develop a public education program to discuss the uniqueness of this river system and the rarity of the resources at risk. As suitable sites are identified within the historic range, reintroduction of the species will be attempted.

The TVA is currently working on a comprehensive water management plan that would guarantee constant minimum flows in all rivers in the Tennessee and Cumberland basins by timing water discharges from its dams. Such an effort might mollify many of the negative effects of dams and reservoirs on remaining stretches of mussel habitat.

Contacts

U.S. Fish and Wildlife Service
Regional Office, Division of Endangered Species
1875 Century Blvd., Suite 200
Atlanta, Georgia 30345
Telephone: (404) 679-4000
http://southeast.fws.gov/

U. S. Fish and Wildlife Service
Regional Office, Division of Endangered Species
300 Westgate Center Dr.
Hadley, Massachusetts 01035-9589
Telephone: (413) 253-8200
Fax: (413) 253-8308
http://northeast.fws.gov/

References

Bates, J.M., and S.D. Dennis. 1978. "The Mussel Fauna of the Clinch River, Tennessee and Virginia." *Sterkiana* 69/70: 3-23.

Pardue, J.W. 1981. "A Survey of the Mussels (Unionidae) of the Upper Tennessee River, 1978." *Sterkiana* 71: 41-51.

U.S. Fish and Wildlife Service. 1983. "Birdwing Pearly Mussel Recovery Plan." U.S. Fish and Wildlife Service, Atlanta.

Fanshell

Cyprogenia stegaria

Status	Endangered
Listed	June 21, 1990
Family	Unionidae (Freshwater Mussel)
Description	Mottled yellow shell with green rays and a silvery white interior.
Habitat	Gravel riffles in streams.
Food	Filter feeder.
Reproduction	Female retains fertilized eggs in gills until larvae fully develop.
Threats	Impoundments, sand and gravel mining, water pollution.
Range	Alabama, Illinois, Indiana, Kentucky, Ohio, Pennsylvania, Tennessee, Virginia, West Virginia

Fanshell, photograph. U. S. Fish and Wildlife Service. Reproduced by permission.

Description

Cyprogenia stegaria is commonly called the fanshell var. *C. irrorata*. A member of the Unionidae family (freshwater mussels), the fanshell has a medium-sized, subcircular shell that seldom exceeds 3.2 in (8.1 cm) in length. The exterior of the shell has green rays on a light green or yellow surface ornamented with green mottling. Strong concentric ridges cover the shell's lower surface. The interior of the shell is usually silvery white, sometimes flesh-colored.

Behavior

The fanshell's specific food habits are unknown; but, it likely feeds on food items similar to those consumed by other freshwater mussels. Freshwater mussels are known to feed on detritus, diatoms, phytoplankton, and zooplankton that they filter out of the water.

Although the fanshell's reproductive biology is unknown, it probably reproduces like other fresh-

water mussels. Males release sperm into the water column. The females take in the sperm through their siphons during feeding and respiration. The fertilized eggs are retained in the gills until the larvae (glochidia) fully develop. When the glochidia are released into the water, they attach and encyst on the gills or fins of a fish host. When metamorphosis is complete, they drop to the streambed as juvenile mussels. The species of fish host utilized by the fanshell and the habitat used by the juveniles are unknown.

Habitat

The fanshell inhabits medium to large rivers. It has been reported primarily from relatively deep water in gravelly substrate with moderate current.

Distribution

Since the turn of the twentieth century, the fanshell has undergone a substantial range reduction. It was historically widely distributed in the Ohio,

Wabash, Cumberland, and Tennessee Rivers and their larger tributaries in Pennsylvania, Ohio, West Virginia, Illinois, Indiana, Kentucky, Tennessee, Alabama, and Virginia. Reproducing fanshell populations are now present in only three rivers—the Clinch River, Hancock County, Tennessee, and Scott County, Virginia; the Green River, Hart and Edmonson Counties, Kentucky; and the Licking River, Kenton, Campbell, and Pendleton Counties, Kentucky.

Additionally, small remnant, apparently nonreproducing, populations may still occur in the Muskingum River in Morgan and Washington Counties, Ohio; the Walhonding River in Coshocton County; the Wabash River in White County, Illinois, and Posey and Wabash Counties, Indiana; the East Fork White River, Martin County, Indiana; the Tippecanoe River, Tippecanoe County, Indiana; the Kanawha River, Fayette County, West Virginia; Tygart Creek, Greenup and Carter Counties, Kentucky; the Barren River, Allen and Barren Counties, Kentucky; the Cumberland River, Smith County, Tennessee; and the Tennessee River, Rhea, Meigs, and Hardin Counties, Tennessee.

The population in the Green River is likely the best of the three remaining reproducing populations. Freshly dead fanshells of various age classes from juvenile to adult were found in 1988 in muskrat middens along the Green River. The Clinch River population extends over about 86 river mi (138.4 km). However, a Tennessee Valley Authority survey reported that the fanshell comprised less than 1% of the mussels collected at 11 Clinch River quantitative sampling sites in 1979 and 1988. In the Licking River, live and fresh-dead individuals of several year classes have been collected.

Threats

The distribution and reproductive capacity of this species has been seriously impacted by the construction of impoundments and navigation facilities, dredging for channel maintenance, sand and gravel mining, and water pollution. The three reproducing populations are threatened by a variety of factors. The Green River has been degraded by runoff from oil and gas exploration and production sites and by alteration of stream flows by an upstream reservoir. Land use practices along the Clinch River have contributed to a decline in water quality and mussel populations. The Clinch River has also experienced some adverse impact

from coal mining, and the river has been subjected to two mussel kills resulting from toxic substance spills from a riverside coal-fired power plant. At least 30 collecting sites on the Clinch River once contained more than 18 different species of freshwater mussels. Now, the mussel abundance in the Clinch River has decreased from an average of 11.64 mussels per 10.8 sq ft (1 sq m) in 1979, to six mussels per 10.8 sq ft (1 sq m) by 1988.

The species probably has its highest population density in the Green River, but runoff from oil and gas exploration and production is polluting the river. Stream flows have been altered by an upstream reservoir, and this is also causing problems. At one time, 66 species of mussels inhabited this river; now, only about 40 species are known to survive. Since the fanshell's population density is extremely low and only three of the 12 known populations are reproducing, about 75% of populations could be eliminated soon.

The third reproducing population, located in the Licking River, could potentially be threatened by some of the water supply development alternatives presently under preliminary review for the Licking River watershed and by wastewater discharges.

In addition, most of the fanshell populations are small, and all the populations are geographically isolated from each other. This isolation restricts the natural interchange of genetic material between the populations, and the small population size reduces the reservoir of genetic variability within the populations.

Conservation and Recovery

The recovery criterion called for the establishment of at least 12 viable populations, which might be difficult to achieve because much of the species habitat has been destroyed. The Fanshell Technical/Agency Draft Recovery Plan identifies the following tasks as actions needed to achieve recovery: (1) utilize existing legislation and regulations to protect species; (2) search for new populations and monitor existing populations; (3) develop and utilize an information and education program; (4) determine species' life history requirements; (5) determine threats and alleviate those that threaten the species' existence; and (6) through reintroduction and protection, establish nine viable populations. Mussel propagation and some life history research were initiated by 2000.

Contacts

U.S. Fish and Wildlife Service
Regional Office, Division of Endangered Species
1875 Century Blvd., Suite 200
Atlanta, Georgia 30345
http://southeast.fws.gov

U.S. Fish and Wildlife Service
Regional Office, Division of Endangered Species
1 Federal Drive
BHW Federal Building
Fort Snelling, Minnesota 55111
Telephone: (612) 713-5360
http://midwest.fws.gov/

U.S. Fish and Wildlife Service
Regional Office, Division of Endangered Species
300 Westgate Center Dr.
Hadley, Massachusetts 01035-9589
Telephone: (413) 253-8200
Fax: (413) 253-8308
http://www.northeast.fws.gov/

U.S. Fish and Wildlife Service
330 Ridgefield Court
Asheville, North Carolina 28806
Telephone: (704) 665-1195

References

Ahlstedt, Steven A. January 1986. "Cumberland Mollusk Conservation Program. Activity 1 Mussel Distribution Surveys." Tennessee Valley Authority, Norris (TN).

Bates, J. M. and S. D. Dennis. 1985. "Mussel Resource Survey—State of Tennessee." Technical Report No. 85-4. Tennessee Wildlife Resources Agency.

Cummings, K. S., C. A. Mayer, and L. M. Page. 1988. "Survey of the Freshwater Mussels [Mollusca Unionidae] of the Wabash River Drainage, Phase 11: Upper and Middle Wabash River." Technical Report. Illinois Natural History Survey.

Gordon, M., and J. Layzer. 1989. "Mussels (BIVALVIA UNIONOIDEA) of the Cumberland River Review of Life Histories and Ecological Relationships." Biological Report 89 (15). U.S. Fish and Wildlife Service.

Starnes, L. B. and A. E. Bogan. 1988. "The Mussels (Mollusca Bivalvia Unionidae) of Tennessee." *American Malacologocal Bulletin* 6 (1): 19-37.

U.S. Fish and Wildlife Service. 21 June 1990. "Endangered and Threatened Wildlife and Plants Designation of the Fanshell as an Endangered Species." *Federal Register* 55 (120): 25591-25595.

U. S. Fish and Wildlife Service. 1990. "Fanshell Technical/Agency Draft Recovery Plan." U.S. Fish and Wildlife Service, Atlanta.

Tampico Pearlymussel

Cyrtonaias tampicoensis tecomatensis

Status	Endangered
Listed	June 14, 1976
Family	Unionidae
Description	A bivalve mollusk (mussel).
Habitat	Freshwater rivers and streams.
Food	Aquatic filter feeder of algae and detritus.
Reproduction	Releases spawn in water.
Threats	Destruction of aquatic habitat, pollution, and harvesting for its pearls.
Range	Mexico

Description

The Tampico pearlymussel is a large, bivalve (two-shelled) mussel with an oblong shell. The shell-length of the Tampico pearlymussel can be as long as 5 in (13 cm). The color of the outside of the shell ranges from a dull yellowish-brown to dark brown and black. The inside of the shell (or nacre) is lustrous, and can be colored purple, lavender, pink, salmon, or white. If the mussel contains a pearl, it is the same color as the nacre. About three to four percent of mature individuals contain a pearl in their soft tissue, and a similar percentage have a less-valuable pearl attached to the shell. Gem-quality pearls can exceed 0.4 in (10 mm) in length, but these are exceedingly rare.

Behavior

The Tampico pearlymussel lives on the bottom of slow-moving rivers and streams, partly buried in fine-sediment. It feeds by filtering fine organic detritus and algae from the water. It breeds by releasing male and female gametes (ova and sperm) into the water, where external fertilization occurs. After a short time, the larvae settle to a suitable bottom habitat, where they spend the rest of their lives.

Habitat

The Tampico pearlymussel occurs in slow-moving rivers and streams, in relatively stable, soft-bottom habitat. Although its natural habitat does not include lakes, the species does well in artificial impoundments in Texas. In fact, these reservoirs now support some of the largest populations of the Tampico pearlymussel. They typically occur in water less than about 20 ft (7 m) deep, but may occur in deeper places in reservoirs.

Distribution

The Tampico pearlymussel ranges from northeastern Mexico to the Colorado and Brazos Rivers of Central Texas, with an important center of abundance in the watershed of the Rio Grande (a binational river). The Concho River in western Texas, or the "river of shells," was named by early Spanish colonists in reference to a great historical abundance of the local population of this species. The endangered subspecies *Cyrtonaias tampicoensis tecomatensis* occurs in northeastern Mexico. Some populations in Texas are still relatively healthy, and the native Tampico Pearlymussel is not listed as an endangered species in the United States.

Threats

The habitat of the Tampico pearlymussel has been degraded by siltation and other disturbances, by pollution with nutrients, sewage, industrial chemicals, and pesticides, and by other factors associated with human activities in the watersheds of their streams and rivers (such as dewatering due to excessive water withdrawals for irrigation during times of drought). It has also been excessively harvested as a source of freshwater pearls.

Conservation and Recovery

The habitat in northeastern Mexico of the endangered subspecies, *Cyrtonaias tampicoensis tecomatensis*, is not protected. Although collecting of the endangered subspecies is illegal, as is any international trade (it is listed by the Convention on International Trade in Endangered Species—CITES), the rare Tampico pearlymussel is still being poached in its Mexican range, and its habitat is still subject to degradation. Active recovery efforts have not been undertaken.

Contact

Instituto Nacional de Ecología
Av. Revolución, 1425
Col. Campestre, C.P. 01040, Mexico, D.F.
http://www.ine.gob.mx/

Reference

Howells, Robert G. 1996. "The Tampico Pearlymussel (*Cyrtonaias tampicoensis*) Shades of the Old West." *Academy of Natural Sciences.* http://coa.acnatsci.org/conchnet/how696.html. [Date Accessed: 3 August 2000].

Dromedary Pearlymussel

Dromus dromas

Status	Endangered
Listed	June 14, 1976
Family	Unionidae (Freshwater Mussel)
Description	Medium-sized triangular to elliptical shell, yellow-green with green rays.
Habitat	Shallow riffle and shoal areas.
Reproduction	Female stores sperm in gills; glochidia are released into the stream after hatching.
Food	Filter-feeder.
Threats	Impoundments, pollution.
Range	Alabama, Kentucky, Tennessee, Virginia

Dromedary Pearlymussel, photograph. U. S. Fish and Wildlife Service. Reproduced by permission.

Description

The dromedary pearlymussel, *Dromus dromas,* is a medium-sized species, round to triangular or elliptical in outline. Valves are generally solid and inflated. The outer surface of the shell has a hump with a curved row of smaller knobs near the middle of the shell. The outer covering is yellow-green with broken green rays covering the shell. The inner shell color is generally white or pinkish in the big river mussels (*D. dromas*), while the inner shell of the headwaters mussels (*D. d. caperatus*) is whitish pink, salmon, or reddish. *D. dromas* was first described from the Harpeth and Cumberland Rivers in Tennessee. *D. d. caperatus* was first described from the Clinch River in Virginia and Tennessee.

Behavior

See the Upland Combshell (*Epioblasma metastriata*) entry.

Habitat

These mussels bury themselves in the substrate in shallow riffle and shoal areas, in relatively firm rubble, gravel, and sand swept free of silt by clean fast-flowing water.

Distribution

Cumberlandian mussels are endemic to the southern Appalachian Mountains and the Cumberland Plateau region. The dromedary pearly mussel was once widely distributed in the upper Tennessee and Cumberland river basins, from the headwaters of the Tennessee River as far south as Muscle Shoals, Alabama. It was also reported from the Caney Fork of the Cumberland River system, where it may have been more abundant than in the Tennessee River.

Both forms of this mussel are now found only in portions of the Tennessee, Cumberland, Clinch, and Powell Rivers. Since 1918 only three live specimens have been reported from the Tennessee River. In 1981, five live specimens were reported from the Cumberland River, 16 from the Clinch River, and six from the Powell River. These figures provide a measure of relative abundance but do not reflect the actual population size.

Threats

The reasons for the decline of these mussels are not well understood, but stream damming and channeling, siltation, and pollution are thought to be major factors. Dams and reservoirs flood some habitats, reduce water flows in others, alter water temperatures, and increase siltation—all of which have a negative impact on mussels. The effects of pollution are intensified for filter feeders, because large quantities of water are drawn through the mussel's feeding system to extract food.

Conservation and Recovery

Transplantation of mussels from larger, more viable populations to smaller populations will be attempted. Since the largest concentrations of dromedary pearly mussels are in the Clinch and Powell Rivers, the identification, survey, and protection of these populations will be the first priority for recovery. As abundance increases, the U. S. Fish and Wildlife Service will attempt to reestablish mussel populations in at least three additional streams.

Sections of the Clinch and Powell Rivers are probably eligible for "scenic river" status under the National Wild and Scenic Rivers Act. If so designated, the law would provide additional protection for these mussels and their habitat. The state of Tennessee has designated portions of the Tennessee and Cumberland Rivers and the Clinch and Powell Rivers as mussel sanctuaries.

Contacts

U. S. Fish and Wildlife Service
Regional Office, Division of Endangered Species
1875 Century Blvd., Suite 200
Atlanta, Georgia 30345
http://southeast.fws.gov/

U. S. Fish and Wildlife Service
Regional Office, Division of Endangered Species
300 Westgate Center Dr.
Hadley, Massachusetts 01035-9589
Telephone: (413) 253-8200
Fax: (413) 253-8308
http://northeast.fws.gov/

References

Bates, J. M., and S. D. Dennis. 1978. "The Mussel Fauna of the Clinch River, Tennessee and Virginia." *Sterkiana* 69/70: 3-23.

Dennis, S. D. 1981. "Mussel Fauna of the Powell River, Tennessee and Virginia." *Sterkiana* 71: 1-7.

French, John R. P., III. November, 1990. "The Exotic Zebra Mussel: A New Threat to Endangered Freshwater Mussels." *Endangered Species Technical Bulletin* 15 (11).

Jenkinson, J. J. 1981. "The Tennessee Valley Authority Cumberlandian Mollusk Conservation Program." *Bulletin of the American Malacological Union, 1980*: 62-63.

U. S. Fish and Wildlife Service. 1983. "Dromedary Pearly Mussel Recovery Plan." U. S. Fish and Wildlife Service, Atlanta.

Chipola Slabshell

Elliptio chipolaensis

Status	Threatened
Listed	March 16, 1998
Family	Unionidae
Description	A freshwater, bivalve mussel with a smooth, chestnut colored shell.
Habitat	Coarse- to soft-sediment habitats of rivers and streams.
Food	Larvae are parasitic on fish; adults are filter-feeders.
Reproduction	Female siphons sperm from the water to achieve fertilization of the eggs, which hatch into parasitic larvae, which metamorphose into sedentary adults.
Threats	Reservoir construction, channel dredging, and sedimentation.
Range	Alabama, Florida

Description

The *Elliptio chipolaensis* (Chipola slabshell) is a medium-sized species reaching a length of about 3.3 in (8.5 cm). The shell is ovate to subelliptical, somewhat inflated and with the posterior ridge starting out rounded, but flattening to form a prominent biangulate margin. The surface is smooth and chestnut colored. Dark brown coloration may appear in the umbonal region and the remaining surface may exhibit alternating light and dark bands. The umbos are prominent, well above the hingeline. Internally, the umbonal cavity is rather deep. The lateral teeth are long, slender, and slightly curved; two in the left and one in the right valve. The pseudocardinal teeth are compressed and crenulate; two in the left and one in the right valve. Nacre color is salmon, becoming more intense dorsally and somewhat iridescent posteriorly.

Behavior

The host fish for the Chipola slabshell is unknown at this time. Centrarchids (the sunfish family) have been determined to be fish hosts for species of *Elliptio*, and may also serve as host for the Chipola slabshell. Minnows (Cyprinidae) may serve as hosts for this species. The larvae are parasitic on fish; adults are filter-feeders. The reproduction process involves the female siphoning sperm from the water to achieve fertilization of the eggs, which hatch into parasitic larvae, which metamorphose into sedentary adults.

Habitat

The Chipola slabshell occurs in warm temperate rivers and creeks. It occurs in softer-sediment habitats.

Distribution

The Chipola slabshell is only known from sites in the Chattahoochee River system, and a small tributary of the Chattahoochee River in extreme southeast Alabama.

Threats

The Chipola slabshell occurred historically at eight sites in the Chipola River and one site in the Chattahoochee River system. However, it is now extirpated from the Chattahoochee River system, and much reduced in the Chipola River system. The most recent status survey in the mid-1990s found this species only at five of 33 sites sampled within its historic range. An average of only 3.7 live individuals were found per site, and there was no evidence of recruitment into the population.

Conservation and Recovery

The Chipola slabshell is only surviving in small populations in a fraction of its historical range. It must be strictly protected from any harvesting. Its critical habitat must be protected from damage caused by new impoundments or dredging. Its surviving populations should be monitored and research undertaken into its biology (including the host species of its larvae) and habitat needs. Consideration should be given to establishing additional populations by transplanation.

Contacts

U.S. Fish and Wildlife Service
Jacksonville Ecological Services Field Office
6620 Southpoint Drive South, Suite 310
Jacksonville, Florida 32216
Telephone: (904) 232-2580

U. S. Fish and Wildlife Service
Regional Office, Division of Endangered Species
1875 Century Blvd., Suite 200
Atlanta, Georgia 30345
http://southeast.fws.gov/

Reference

U.S. Fish and Wildlife Service. 16 March 1998. "Endangered and Threatened Wildlife and Plants; Determination of Endangered Status for Five Freshwater Mussels and Threatened Status for Two Freshwater Mussels From the Eastern Gulf Slope Drainages of Alabama, Florida, and Georgia." *Federal Register* 63(50):12664-12687.

Tar River Spinymussel

Elliptio steinstansana

Status	Endangered
Listed	June 27, 1985
Family	Unionidae (Freshwater Mussel)
Description	Medium-sized, rhomboidal shell with fine concentric rings and several short spines.
Habitat	Soft mud or sand bottoms of streams.
Reproduction	Female stores sperm in gills; glochidia are released into the stream after hatching.
Food	Filter-feeder.
Threats	Low numbers.
Range	North Carolina

Tar River Spinymussel, photograph. U. S. Fish and Wildlife Service. Reproduced by permission.

Description

The Tar River spinymussel (also known as Tar spinymussel), *Elliptio steinstansana*, reaches a mature length of 2.4 in (6 cm), and the rhomboidal shell is distinguished by having several short spines. The shell surface is smooth and shiny, marked with fine concentric rings. The inequilateral valves are regularly rounded, becoming slightly wider at the hinges and ending in a blunt point. The inner shell nacre is yellowish or pinkish, and young specimens have an orange-brown outer scale with greenish rays.

Aside from the Tar River spinymussel, only two other freshwater spinymussels are known to exist: a small-shelled and short-spined species (*Fusconaia collina*) found only in the James River in Virginia and considered Endangered, and a large-shelled and long-spined species (*Elliptio spinosa*) collected from the Altamaha River system in Georgia. The shell size and spine length of the Tar River mussel is intermediate between these two. It has been alternatively classified as *Canthyria steinstansana*.

Behavior

See the Upland Combshell (*Epioblasma metastriata*) entry.

Habitat

This spinymussel has been collected on sand and mud substrates. The mussel's spines help it maintain an upright position as it works its way through the soft streambed.

Distribution

The Tar River spinymussel was first discovered in the Tar River (Edgecombe County), North Carolina, in 1966. Records suggest that the species inhabited the mainstream Tar River from Nash County downstream through Edgecombe County to Pitt County near the town of Falkland, North Carolina.

As of 1992, when the most recent Recovery Plan revision for the species was published, there were only three known remaining populations of this spinymussel—two extremely small, apparently non-reproducing populations in the main stem of the Tar River and a third, larger population, in Swift Creek, a tributary of the Tar River. Existing population estimates have ranged from a low of fewer than 100 individuals to a high of about 500 individuals.

Threats

The Tar River spinymussel may have always been rare, but its recent reduction in range and small population size make it vulnerable to extinction from a single catastrophic event, such as a tank-truck accident involving a toxic chemical spill— a real possibility, since an Interstate highway bridge passes directly over its habitat. Water quality is also a problem. The North Carolina Department of Natural Resources and Community Development reports levels of nutrients and pesticides are above average in the river.

Wastewater treatment plants are another serious threat to the spinymussel. During surveys conducted in the mid-1980s, a decline in mussel populations was noted for approximately one mile below the Tar River Regional Wastewater Treatment Plant operated by the City of Rocky Mount. Mussels were abundant above the plant and again several miles below, but the river immediately below the outfall was devoid of mussels, although the habitat appeared suitable. The wastewater plant at Rocky Mount was constructed in 1982 and has had a continuous history of National Pollution Discharge Elimination System Permit compliance problems since it opened. Several other wastewater treatment facilities that discharge into the Tar River or its tributaries, above the existing population of spinymussels in the Tar River, have also been implicated as violating water quality standards, including the plants at Franklinton, Littleton, Louisburg, Oxford, Scotlandneck and Tarboro.

Some of these plants have been upgraded, and the North Carolina Division of Environmental Management plans to upgrade and incorportae uniform, up-to-date pollution reduction requirements at all sewage treatment facilities within the Tar and Pam-lico River basin. Although spinymussel populations may be reestablished as a result of improved water quality, recolonization will probably take many years, and the species rarity makes natural reestablishment unlikely.

As a further threat, the Tar River has become infested by the Asiatic clam, considered a pest. The Asiatic clam feeds in densities estimated at 1,000 individuals per square meter in some places, reducing the availability of phytoplankton needed as a food source for the Tar River spiny mussel.

Because this species has only recently been described and its approximate range located, notoriety for such a unique and rare mussel could increase collection pressure from shell dealers and collectors. And because the population is small, the unlawful removal of any individuals could seriously affect the species' survival. North Carolina State law prohibits collecting wildlife without a state permit.

Conservation and Recovery

State law does not protect the species' habitat from the potential impact of large-scale construction projects. Federal listing protects the Tar River spiny mussel by requiring federal agencies to consult with the Fish and Wildlife Service when projects they fund, authorize, or carry out may affect the species. Three specific projects have been identified that could affect the spiny mussel a hydroelectric project on the Tar River at Rocky Mount, a navigation and flood control project on the Tar River, and a stream obstruction removal project on Tar River tributaries. These projects may have to be redesigned to protect this mussel.

The 1992 revision of the 1987 Recovery Plan for the species notes that the species' extremely low population levels and restricted distribution may preclude full recovery; therefore, the recovery goal for the foreseeable future is dowlisting from Endangered to Threatened. Downlisting could occur when a number of recovery criteria are met, including the requirement that all three existing populations show evidence of reproduction, including at least two juvenile (ages 3 or younger) age classes; and that two new, distinct, viable populations must be discovered or reestablished within the species' historic range. Other downlisting criteria include the protection of all populations and their habitats from present and foreseeable threats, and the stabilization or increase over a 15 to 20-year period of all populations.

Contact

U.S. Fish and Wildlife Service
Division of Endangered Species
1875 Century Blvd., Suite 200
Atlanta, Georgia 30345

References

French, III, John R.P. 1990. "The Exotic Zebra Mussel: A New Threat to Endangered Freshwater Mussels." *Endangered Species Technical Bulletin* 15(11).

Johnson, R. I., and A. H. Clarke. 1983. "A New Spiny Mussel, *Elliptio (Canthyria) steinstansana* (Bivalvia: Unionidae), from the Tar River, North Carolina." *Occasional Papers on Mollusks* 4(6): 289-298.

Shelley, R. M. 1972. "In Defense of Mollusks." *Wildlife in North Carolina* 36: 4-8, 26-27.

U.S. Fish and Wildlife Service. 1987. "Recovery Plan for Tar River Spiny Mussel." U.S. Fish and Wildlife Service, Atlanta.

U.S. Fish and Wildlife Service. 1992. "Tar Spinymussel Recovery Plan First Revision." U.S. Fish and Wildlife Service, Atlanta.

Purple Bankclimber

Elliptoideus sloatianus

Status	Threatened
Listed	March 16, 1998
Family	Unionidae
Description	A freshwater, bivalve mussel.
Habitat	Rivers with moderate flow and sandy to sand-silt substrate.
Food	Larvae are parasitic on fish; adults are sedentary filter-feeders.
Reproduction	Female siphons sperm from the water to achieve fertilization of the eggs, which hatch into parasitic larvae, which metamorphose into sedentary adults.
Threats	Habitat damage caused by impoundments, and overcollecting for fresh-water pearls.
Range	Alabama, Georgia, Florida

Description

The *Elliptoideus sloatianus* (purple bankclimber) is a large, heavy-shelled, strongly sculptured mussel reaching lengths of 8 in (20 cm). A well-developed posterior ridge extends from the umbos to the posterior ventral margin of the shell. The posterior slope and the disk just anterior to the posterior ridge are sculptured by several irregular ridges that vary greatly in development. Umbos are low, extending just above the dorsal margin of the shell. Internally, there is one pseudocardinal tooth in the right valve and two in the left valve. The lateral teeth are very thick and slightly curved. Nacre color is whitish near the center of the shell becoming deep purple towards the margin, and very iridescent posteriorly. Glochidia for the purple bankclimber transformed on mosquitofish (*Gambusia holbrooki*) and black-banded darter, but these species are not considered to be the primary hosts for this mussel. Centrarchids (the sunfish family) have been determined to be fish hosts for species of *Elliptio*, and may possibly also serve as host for the purple bankclimber, which is genetically very similar to *Elliptio* spp.

Modern taxonomy recognizes the nineteenth-century names *Unio sloatianus* Lea, *Unio atromar-ginatus* Lea, *Unio aratus* Conrad, and *Unio plectophorus* Conrad, 1850 as synonyms of *Elliptoideus sloatianus*. *Elliptoideus sloatianus* was included in the genus *Elliptio* until 1927. At which time the subgenus *Elliptoideus* was erected based on the presence of glochidia in all four gills instead of two gills, a characteristic of the genus *Elliptio*. For a time in the 1950s, the species was still placed under *Elliptio*, but subsequent investigators have correctly assigned this species to the monotypic genus *Elliptoideus*.

Behavior

The purple bankclimber lives on the bottom of its riverine habitat. It filters its food of algae, tiny zooplankton, and organic detritus from water siphoned from the immediate environment. Sperm are shed into the water column, siphoned by the female, and used to fertilize her ova. The larvae are parasitic on species of fish, and later develop into the sedentary adult stage.

Habitat

The purple bankclimber inhabits small to large rivers with moderate current and a bottom substrate of sand, fine gravel, or muddy sand.

Distribution

The purple bankclimber was described from the Chattahoochee River in Georgia. The Purple bankclimber historically occurred in the Apalachicola-Chattahoochee-Flint (ACF), Chipola, and Ochlockonee River systems. The type locality was restricted in the 1950s to the Chattahoochee River at Columbus, Georgia. In the ACF River system, the purple bankclimber was historically found throughout the mainstem and in a few of the largest tributaries in the Flint River system, in the vicinity of Dead Lake on the lower Chipola River mainstem, and along the mainstems of the Apalachicola and Chattahoochee rivers. The species occurred in the lower two-thirds of the mainstem of the Ochlockonee River, and in the Little River.

During the status survey, 222 sites were sampled within the historic range of the purple bankclimber, including 14 of 27 (53%) known historic sites. Live individuals were found at 41 (18%) sites, with an average of 54 individuals per site. Having been extirpated from the Chipola and Chattahoochee rivers, no extant populations occur in Alabama. Its range in the Flint and Ochlockonee River systems also has been reduced. The Purple bankclimber currently occurs in the Apalachicola, Flint, and Ochlockonee rivers, with 41 sites known. The purple bankclimber was found at six of the 14 historical sites. The species was found at 17 mainstem sites and one tributary site on the lower two-thirds of the Flint River, at five sites in the Apalachicola River, and at 18 sites on the Ochlockonee River mainstem, mostly above Talquin Reservoir.

It is uncertain if purple bankclimber populations are successfully recruiting young. Two specimens less than 2.8 in (7.0 cm) in length were collected from the Ochlockonee River during the survey; they were 2.1 in (5.3 cm) and 2.3 in (5.9 cm) in length. Based upon the large size attained by this species, both were possibly juveniles. The smallest specimen found during the survey in the ACF River system was 3.0 in (7.6 cm) in length, a size that possibly represents a juvenile. A 1996 study took six 2.7 ft (0.25 m) square substratum quadrant samples at a site below Jim Woodruff Dam in the Apalachicola River where the purple bankclimber was the second most commonly encountered species. No specimens smaller than 5.2 in (13.3 cm) were found, indicating a lack of recruitment at this site.

Threats

Impoundments have altered about 29% of mainstem riverine habitat on the Flint River. Preimpoundment records from Seminole and Blackshear reservoirs exist for two sites for the purple bankclimber. Talquin Reservoir flooded about 12% of the riverine habitat in the middle portion of the Ochlokonee river and the lower end of its largest tributary (the Little River). Preimpoundment records exist for the purple bankclimber at the upstream end of Talquin Reservoir; only occasional populations of the purple bankclimber have been found down stream of the dam, indicating the difficulty of potential host fish movements after impoundment. Populations of the purple bankclimber have been isolated due to major impoundments on the Apalachicola, Flint, and Ochlockonee rivers.

The threeridge (a relative of the fat threeridge) and the washboard (*Megalonaias nervosa*), which is superficially similar to both the fat threeridge and purple bankclimber, are heavily utilized as sources of shell for nuclei in the cultured pearl industry. Commercial shell buyers generally regard shells from the ACF River system as poor quality; however, shell material from this area may be used as "filler" for higher quality material from elsewhere. In the 1980s, the price of shell increased, resulting in increased competition for the harvesting of shell beds in the Apalachicolan Region. This has possibly put the purple bankclimber under greater pressure.

Biological supply companies have used the Flint River and possibly the Ochlockonee River as sources for large mussel specimens, including the purple bankclimber, to sell to academic institutions for use in laboratory studies. The practice of dissecting mussels in introductory laboratory courses is no longer widespread, and the threat posed to large species such as the fat threeridge and purple bankclimber is probably decreasing. Nonetheless, harvest of the fat threeridge and purple bankclimber for these purposes could decimate their remaining populations. The increasing rarity of these mussels potentially makes them more appealing to shell collectors. Revealing specific stream reaches harboring these species could pose a threat from collectors.

Conservation and Recovery

Any further collection of the purple bankclimber must be strictly prohibited, and the ban enforced. This will include educating commercial shell and pearl collectors about how to identify the rare purple bankclimber, and of the need to avoid any harvest-related mortality. Its surviving critical habitat must be protected against damage caused by potential reservoir development or other activities causing changes to hydrology or water quality. Surveys should be undertaken to determine whether there are any unknown populations of the purple bankclimber. Its known populations should be monitored, and research undertaken to determine its specific habitat needs and management practices to increase its small, isolated populations. This could include beneficial modifications of water-release practices at existing reservoirs.

Contacts

U. S. Fish and Wildlife Service
Regional Office, Division of Endangered Species
1875 Century Blvd., Suite 200
Atlanta, Georgia 30345
http://southeast.fws.gov/

U.S. Fish and Wildlife Service
Wildlife and Habitat Management
6620 Southpoint Drive South, Suite 310
Jacksonville, Florida 32216
Telephone: (904) 232-2580
Fax: (904) 232-2404

References

U.S. Fish and Wildlife Service. 16 March 1998. "Endangered and Threatened Wildlife and Plants; Determination of Endangered Status for Five Freshwater Mussels and Threatened Status for Two Freshwater Mussels From the Eastern Gulf Slope Drainages of Alabama, Florida, and Georgia." *Federal Register* 63(50): 12664-12687.

Cumberlandian Combshell

Epioblasma brevidens

Status	Endangered
Listed	January 10, 1997
Family	Unionidae
Description	Mussel with a broad, yellowish shell with broken rays.
Habitat	Medium-sized streams to large rivers on shoals and riffles in coarse sand, gravel, cobble, and boulders.
Food	Unknown.
Reproduction	Spawns in late summer, glochidia held over winter and released in late spring.
Threats	Harmful habitat effects of coal mining, poor land use practices, and pollution, primarily from nonpoint sources.
Range	Alabama, Kentucky, Tennessee, Virginia

Cumberlandian Combshell, photograph. U. S. Fish and Wildlife Service. Reproduced by permission.

Description

The Cumberlandian combshell (*Epioblasma brevidens*), described in 1831, has a thick, solid shell with a smooth to clothlike outer surface. It is yellow to tawny brown in color with narrow green broken rays. The inside of the shell is white. The shells of females are inflated with serrated teethlike structures along a portion of the shell margin.

The broad, yellowish shell with broken rays and the distinctive marsupial expansion of the female distinguish this species from most other mussels in the range except *Pychobranchus fasciolaris* and *Epioblasma lenoir*. Male *E. brevidens* are broader than *P. fasciolaris*, and the females of the latter species do not exhibit the marsupial development of the former. Raying patterns on *P. fasciolaris* usually are not developed. *Epioblasma lenior* is a considerably smaller species, has a much lighter shell, tends to be greenish, does not have as developed a marsupial expansion, and probably is extinct.

Behavior

Spawning in the bradytictic lampsiline Cumberlandian combshell probably occurs in late summer with the glochidia being held over winter and released in late spring. Gravid individuals have been observed in May and June. Gravid females were reported from early May (but probably occurred earlier) to early June at a temperature of 59.0-64.0°F (15.0-17.8°C). Estimated age of gravid females was eight to 13 years. Six host fish species have been identified: wounded darter, redline darter. Tennessee snubnose darter (*E. simoterum*), greenside darter (*E. blennioides*), logperch (*Percina caprodes*), and banded sculpin. Transformation took from 16-48 days, at 60.4-62.4°F (15.8-16.9°C).

Habitat

This species inhabits medium-sized streams to large rivers on shoals and riffles in coarse sand, gravel, cobble, and boulders. It is not associated with small stream habitats and tends not to extend as far upstream in tributaries. In general, it occurs in larger tributaries than does its congener the oyster mussel. The species prefers depths less than 3 ft (0.9 m), but it appears to persist in the deep-water areas of Old Hickory Reservoir on the Cumberland River, where there is still fairly strong flow from the Cordell Hull and Center Hill Reservoirs.

Distribution

The Cumberlandian combshell historically existed throughout much of the Cumberlandian portion of the Tennessee and Cumberland river systems in Alabama, Kentucky, Tennessee, and Virginia. Many of the Cumberlandian combshell's historic populations were lost when impoundments were constructed on the Tennessee and Cumberland Rivers by Tennessee Valley Authority and the U.S. Army Corps of Engineers. Other populations were lost due to various forms of pollution and siltation. There are now only five remaining populations of the Cumberlandian combshell.

This species survives in the Cumberland River basin as a very rare component of the benthic community in Buck Creek in Pulaski County, Kentucky, and in a few miles of the Big South Fork Cumberland River in McCreary County, Kentucky, and Scott County, Tennessee. A few old, nonreproducing individuals may also survive in Old Hickory Reservoir on the Cumberland River in Smith County, Tennessee. Within the Tennessee River basin, the species still survives in very low numbers in the Powell and Clinch Rivers, Lee and Scott Counties in Virginia; and Claiborne and Hancock Counties in Tennessee. The Clinch and Powell River populations are very small and in decline.

Threats

The present populations are threatened by the harmful habitat effects of coal mining, poor land use practices, and pollution, primarily from nonpoint sources. All the known populations are small and could be decimated by episodic events such as toxic chemical spills.

Conservation and Recovery

The taxon is considered endangered by the states of Kentucky and Virginia, and it is deemed a species of special concern in Tennessee.

Contacts

U.S. Fish and Wildlife Service
Regional Office, Division of Endangered Species
1875 Century Blvd., Suite 200
Atlanta, Georgia 30345
http://southeast.fws.gov

U.S. Fish and Wildlife Service
Regional Office, Division of Endangered Species
300 Westgate Center Dr.
Hadley, Massachusetts 01035-9589
Telephone: (413) 253-8200
Fax: (413) 253-8308
http://www.northeast.fws.gov/

Reference

U. S. Fish and Wildlife Service. 10 January 1997. "Determination of Endangered Status for the Cumberland Elktoe, Oyster Mussel, Cumberlandian Combshell, Purple Bean, and Rough Rabbitsfoot." *Federal Register* 62 (7): 1647-1658.

Oyster Mussel

Epioblasma capsaeformis

Status	Endangered
Listed	January 10, 1997
Family	Unionidae
Description	A freshwater, bivalve mollusk with varying mantle coloration.
Habitat	Small to medium-sized rivers, in areas with coarse sand to boulder substrates and moderate to swift currents.
Food	Filter-feeds on algae, tiny zooplankton, and organic detritus.
Reproduction	Female siphons male spawn from the water; eggs are fertilized and incubated in her gill chamber; the planktonic larvae are parasitic on fish, and later settle to the sedentary adult lifestyle.
Threats	Habitat destruction through the construction of impoundments, and degradation by changes in hydrology and pollution.
Range	Alabama, Georgia, Kentucky, North Carolina, Tennessee, Virginia

Oyster Mussel, photograph. U. S. Fish and Wildlife Service. Reproduced by permission.

Description

The *Epioblasma capsaeformis* (oyster mussel) described in 1834, has a dull to sub-shiny yellowish-to green-colored shell with numerous narrow dark green rays. The shells of females are slightly inflated and quite thin towards the shell's posterior margin. The inside of the shell is whitish to bluish white in color.

The pronounced development of the posterior-ventral region in females distinguishes *Epioblasma capsaeformis* from similarly shaped species. *Epioblasma capsaeformis* is recognized by the typically dark coloration and fragility of the marsupial expansion and the lack of development of the posterior ridge (e.g., not angular, no knobs). Males in comparison to similar *Epioblasma* tend to be more elliptical, have a moderately developed posterior ridge and accompanying sulcus, and have a regularly curved ventral margin. The ventral margin in species such as *Epioblasma fiorentina* and *Epioblasma turgidula* often exhibit an emargination of the ventrum just anterior to the terminus of the posterior ridge. Yellowish specimens of *Epioblasma capsaeformis* have been mistaken for *Epioblasma walkeri*. Males of *Epioblasma walkeri* tend to be broader and have a rounded posterior, ridge; females lack the distinctive darkening of the marsupial expansion.

There are color differences in female oyster mussel mantle pads, which is presumably a host fish attractant. The mantle color appears to be bluish or greenish white in the Clinch River, greyish to blackish in the Duck River, and nearly white in Big South Fork population. Varying mantle coloration may be an indication that *Epioblasma capsaeformis* is a complex species.

Behavior

The lampsiline oyster mussel appears to be bradytictic. Spawning probably occurs in late summer, as glochidia have been observed in the marsupia during May, June, and July. In the Powell River, 58% of the females were gravid, but specimens were gravid only in May at a water temperature from 59-64°F (15-18°C). The age of gravid females, using the external growth ring method, was estimated at 7-10 years. The glochidia are likely released in early summer. Four fish species have been identified as hosts-the wounded darter *(Etheostoma vulneratum)*, redline darter *(Etheostoma rufilineatum)*, dusky darter *(Percina sciera)*, and banded sculpin *(Cottus carolinae)*. Transformation took from 19-34 days, at 60.4-62.4°F (15.8-16.9°C).

Habitat

This species inhabits small to medium-sized rivers, and sometimes large rivers, in areas with coarse sand to boulder substrata (rarely in mud) and moderate to swift currents. It is sometimes found associated with water-willow *(Justicia americana)* beds and in pockets of gravel between bedrock ledges in areas of swift current. This species, like other freshwater mussels, can bury itself below the substratum surface, but females have been observed to lie on top of the substratum while displaying and releasing glochidia.

Distribution

This species historically occurred throughout much of the Cumberlandian region of the Tennessee and Cumberland river drainages in Alabama, Kentucky, Tennessee, and Virginia; in 1918, Ortmann considered the species to be very abundant in the upper Tennessee River drainage. Much of the oyster mussel's historic range has been impounded by the Tennessee Valley Authority and the U.S. Army Corps of Engineers. Other populations were lost due to various forms of pollution and siltation.

Only five populations of the oyster mussel remain. The oyster mussel still survives within the Cumberland River as a very rare component of the benthic community in Buck Creek, Pulaski County, Kentucky; and it still occurs in a few miles of the Big South Fork Cumberland River in McCreary County, Kentucky and Scott County, Tennessee. The Tennessee River system populations are also small in size and few in number, occurring at sites in the Powell River, Lee County, Virginia and Hancock and Claiborne counties, Tennessee; in the Clinch River system, Scott County, Virginia, and Hancock County, Tennessee; Copper Creek (a Clinch River tributary), Scott County, Virginia; and Duck River, Marshall County, Tennessee. Although not seen in recent years, the species may still persist at extremely low numbers in the lower Nolichucky river, Cocke and Hamblem counties, Tennessee and in the Little Pigeon River, Sevier County, Tennessee.

Threats

The present populations are threatened by the adverse impacts of coal mining, poor land-use practices, and pollution, primarily from nonpoint sources. The Duck River population could be lost if the proposed Columbia Dam on the Duck River at Columbia, Tennessee is completed as presently planned. All the known populations are small and could be decimated by episodic events such as toxic chemical spills.

Conservation and Recovery

The oyster mussel is considered endangered by the States of Kentucky and Virginia, and by the Fish and Wildlife Service. It conservation requires the protection of the five stream reaches where it persists in small, isolated populations. These critical habitats must be protected from proposed impoundments, and from pollution associated with coal mining (including acid-mine drainage) and poor land-use practices in the watershed that cause erosion and inputs of pesticides and other chemicals. The populations of the rare mussel must be monitored, and research undertaken into its basic biology and ecological requirements.

Contacts

U. S. Fish and Wildlife Service
Asheville Ecological Services Field Office
160 Zillicoa Street
Asheville, North Carolina 28801-1082
Telephone: (828) 258-3939 Fax: (828) 258-5330

U. S. Fish and Wildlife Service
Regional Office, Division of Endangered Species
1875 Century Blvd., Suite 200
Atlanta, Georgia 30345
http://southeast.fws.gov/

U. S. Fish and Wildlife Service
Regional Office, Division of Endangered Species
300 Westgate Canter Dr.
Hadley, Massachusetts 01035-9589
Telephone: (413) 253-8200
Fax: (413) 253-8200
http://www.northeast.fws.gov/

Reference

U.S. Fish and Wildlife Service. 10 Jan 1997. "Endangered and Threatened Wildlife and Plants; Determination of Endangered Status for the Cumberland Elktoe, Oyster Mussel, Cumberlandian Combshell, Purple Bean, and Rough Rabbitsfoot." *Federal Register* 62 (7): 1647-1658

Curtis' Pearlymussel

Epioblasma florentina curtisii

Curtis Pearlymussel, photograph. A. E. Spreitzer Photography. Reproduced by permission.

Status	Endangered
Listed	June 14, 1976
Family	Unionidae (Freshwater Mussel)
Description	Small, yellow-brown shell with fine, evenly spaced rays.
Habitat	Sand and gravel substrates in shallow water.
Reproduction	Eggs are fertilized in the fall and released in the spring.
Food	Filter feeder.
Threats	Impoundments, siltation, pollution.
Range	Arkansas, Missouri

Description

The oval shell of Curtis' pearlymussel, *Epioblasma florentina curtisii*, is usually less than 1.5 in (3.8 cm) in length, with males being slightly larger than females. The valve end of the shell is bluntly pointed and biangular, the front smoothly rounded. In both sexes, the shell color is yellow-brown to light brown, sometimes with fine, evenly spaced rays over most of its length. The interior shell surface (nacre) is white to whitish blue.

First described as *Truncilla curtisii* in 1915 from White River specimens, this species has also been classified as *Dysnomia florentina curtisii*. Thirteen other species of genus *Epioblasma* have been federally listed as endangered: southern acornshell *(E. othcaloogensis)*, green blossom *(E. torulosa gubernaculum)*, tubercled blossom *(E. torulosa torulosa)*, turgid blossom *(E. turgidula)*, yellow blossom *(E. florentina florentina)*, catspaw *(Epioblasma obliquata obliquata)*, white catspaw *(E. obliquata perobliqua)*, Cumberlandian combshell *(E. brevidens)*, southern combshell *(E. penita)*, upland combshell *(E. metastriata)*, oyster mussel *(E. capsaeformis)*, northern riffleshell *(E. torulosa rangiana)* tan riffleshell *(E. florentina walkeri)*.

Behavior

Curtis' pearlymussel is bradytictic—eggs are fertilized in the fall and glochidia (larvae) are released in the spring. For more information about the reproduction and diet of the freshwater mussel, see the Upland Combshell (*Epioblasma metastriata*) entry.

Habitat

This pearlymussel is found in transitional zones between swift-flowing stream headwaters and the more leisurely currents of lowland meanders. It buries itself in stable substrates of sand and gravel, or among cobbles or boulders, particularly in shallow water at depths of up to 30 in (76 cm). Populations require clear, unsilted water.

Distribution

Curtis' pearlymussel was identified from scattered locations in the White and St. Francis River basins in southern Missouri and northern Arkansas. A record from 1916 indicates that Curtis' pearly mussel also occurred in the South Fork of the Spring River, a tributary of the Black River in Arkansas.

In 1993, the U. S. Fish and Wildlife Service's Columbia, Missouri Field Office assisted the Missouri Department of Conservation in a search for the Curtis' pearlymussel. After several hours of work, the searchers finally found one live male. Extensive searching in the same pool where the male was discovered, and at other sites on the Little Black River where the species was common about eight years before, resulted in no additional finds.

Since the mid-1970s, Curtis' pearlymussel has been found in southeastern Missouri, in the Castor River, Cane Creek (a Black River tributary), and Little Black River. Only about 6 mi (9.5 km) of the upper Little Black River and 7 mi (11 km) of the Castor River upstream from the Headwater Diversion Channel still support minimal numbers. From 1981-1983 more than 140 probable locations on 26 streams were sampled, but this mussel was found at only six sites. In spite of more than two decades on the federal list of endangered species, Curtis' pearlymussel is still extremely uncommon and is thought to remain near extinction.

Threats

Much of Curtis' pearlymussel's historic range has been inundated by reservoir construction. Lake Taneycomo, completed in 1913, flooded a long stretch of its habitat. The White River has been dammed repeatedly—in 1952 to create Bull Shoals Reservoir, in 1959 to fill Table Rock Lake, and again in 1966 to create Beaver Reservoir. These impoundments drastically reduced water flows on the river, resulting in stagnant bottom waters and accumulations of silt. Stream channelization and gravel dredging have reduced substrate stability, and poor land management practices have further exacerbated problems of siltation and chemical runoff.

Conservation and Recovery

The Missouri Department of Conservation has conducted low intensity research into the biology of this species, but there are still many unanswered questions. The immediate goal of recovery is to stave off extinction by preventing further loss or damage to the habitat. When the state of research permits, biologists will attempt to transfer mussels from viable reproducing populations to depleted areas to stimulate reproduction. An effort will be made to produce juveniles by artificial culture to assist restocking of suitable habitat within the historic range.

Contacts

U. S. Fish and Wildlife Service
Regional Office, Division of Endangered Species
1 Federal Drive
BHW Federal Building
Fort Snelling, Minnesota 55111
Telephone: (612) 713-5360
http://midwest.fws.gov/

U. S. Fish and Wildlife Service
Regional Office, Division of Endangered Species
1875 Century Blvd., Suite 200
Atlanta, Georgia 30345
http://southeast.fws.gov/

References

French, John R. P., III. November, 1990. "The Exotic Zebra Mussel: A New Threat to Endangered Freshwater Mussels." *Endangered Species Technical Bulletin* 15 (11).

Hudson, R. G., and B. G. Isom. 1984. "Rearing Juveniles of the Freshwater Mussels (Unionidae) in a Laboratory Setting." *Nautilus* 98 (4): 129-135.

Johnson, R. I. 1978. "Systematics and Zoogeography of *Plagiola* (=*Sysnomia*, = *Epioblasma*), an Almost Extinct Genus of Freshwater Mussels (Bivalvia: Unionidae) from Middle North America." *Bulletin of the Museum of Comparative Zoology* 148 (6): 239-321.

U. S. Fish and Wildlife Service. 1986. "Curtis' Pearly Mussel Recovery Plan." U. S. Fish and Wildlife Service, Twin Cities, Minn.

Yellow Blossom Pearlymussel

Epioblasma florentina florentina

Status	Endangered
Listed	June 14, 1976
Family	Unionidae (Freshwater Mussel)
Description	Medium-sized elliptical honey-yellow shell with numerous green rays.
Habitat	Sand or gravel substrate in clear, flowing water.
Reproduction	Female stores sperm in gills; glochidia (larvae) are released into streams after hatching.
Food	Filter-feeder.
Threats	Impoundments; siltation; pollution.
Range	Alabama, Tennessee

Yellow Blossom Pearlymussel, photograph. A. E. Spreitzer Photography. Reproduced by permission.

Description

The yellow blossom pearlymussel (*Epioblasma florentina florentina*) is a Cumberlandian species with an elliptical shell seldom exceeding 2.4 in (6.1 cm) in length. The slightly inflated valves are of unequal length, and the shell surface is marked by uneven growth lines. The shell is a shiny honey-yellow or tan with numerous green rays uniformly distributed over the surface. The inner shell surface is bluish-white.

E. f. florentina represents the big-river form of this species, which may grade into the smaller head-waters form *E. f. walkeri*. This species has also been classified as *Dysnomia florentina florentina*.

Behavior

The life of mussels is complex, and reproduction often depends upon a stable habitat—unaltered stream conditions, clean water, and an undisturbed stream bottom. The cycle also depends upon the abundance of suitable fish hosts to complete the mussel's larval development.

To reproduce, males discharge sperm, which are dispersed by stream currents. In the process of feeding, females nearby or downstream take in sperm, which fertilizes eggs stored in their gills. The gills serve as brood pouches (marsupia), where the glochidia hatch and begin to develop. After a time, these glochidia are released into the stream. A few mussels have inner parts that resemble a tiny minnow and can be manipulated to lure host fish. When a fish gets close to the shell, the mussel expels its glochidia.

Glochidia have tiny bean- or spoon-shaped valves that attach to the gill filaments of host fish. Glochidia can only progress to the juvenile stage while attached to the fish's gills. Those that do not fortuitously encounter a host fish do not survive when released by the female mussel. They sink to the bottom and die.

When the juvenile has developed a shell and is large enough to survive on its own, it detaches from the host fish and falls to the stream bottom, beginning a long association with a single stretch of stream. Maturing mussels bury themselves in riffles and shoals with only the shell margins and feeding siphons exposed to the water. Some mussels live as long as 50 years or more.

The family Unionidae, which includes all of the freshwater mussels in the United States, is separated into two groups based on the length of time the glochidia remain in the female's marsupia. The eggs of the short-term (tachytictic) breeders are fertilized in the spring, and glochidia are released by late summer of the same year. Long-term (bradytictic) breeders hold developing glochidia in the brood pouch over winter and release them in the spring.

Freshwater mussels feed by siphoning phytoplankton and other plant matter from the water. Indigestible particles are expelled from the shell by reverse siphoning. Silt in the water can kill mussels by clogging their feeding siphons.

There are no known interspecific differences in feeding among freshwater mussels. The glochidia are obligate parasites on the gills or fins of fish. Adult mussels are filter-feeders and consume particulate matter in the water column. Identifiable stomach contents almost invariably include desmids, diatoms, algae, protozoa, and zooplankton.

Most freshwater mussel species display seasonal variations in activity associated with water temperature and reproduction. Metabolic rate is, in part, positively correlated with temperature. Many ectothermic species have the capacity to adjust their metabolic rates in response to long-term changes in temperature. Thus, metabolic rates do not continue to rise as temperatures rise in the summer, and they do not continue to fall during the winter as temperatures decline.

Some freshwater mussels also show diurnal changes in metabolic rates that indicate a tendency toward nocturnal activity patterns. Mussels may move to the surface to feed at night and move deeper into the substrate during the day; this is one way to avoid predators that hunt by visual contact.

Freshwater mussels are nonmigratory.

Habitat

The yellow blossom pearlymussel's natural habitat is in the sand and gravel substrates of shallow, fast-flowing streams and rivers.

Distribution

Cumberlandian mussels are endemic to the southern Appalachian Mountains and the Cumberland Plateau region. Historically, the yellow blossom pearlymussel was widespread in the drainages of the Cumberland and Tennessee rivers. It has been documented from the Flint, Elk, Duck, Holston, Clinch, and Little Tennessee rivers and from other Tennessee River tributaries, including Hurricane, Limestone, Bear, and Cypress creeks (in northern Alabama) and Citico Creek (in Tennessee).

Because this subspecies has not been reliably documented since the first half of the twentieth century, noted malacologist D.H. Stansbery considers it extinct. A report from the General Accounting Office issued in December 1988 also considered the mussel "probably extinct," but specimens that may represent the yellow blossom pearlymussel were collected from Citico Creek in 1957 and from the Little Tennessee River in the mid-1960s. Therefore, the U.S. Fish and Wildlife Service agreed to maintain the current status of endangered until further research can settle the question.

Threats

The single greatest factor in the decline or extinction of this species has been the construction of large dams on its habitat rivers. Since the 1930s the Tennessee Valley Authority (TVA), the Aluminum Company of America, and the Army Corps of Engineers have constructed 51 dams on the Tennessee and Cumberland rivers for flood control, generation of hydroelectric power, and recreation. Many segments of the rivers that once supported large populations of mussels have been permanently flooded. In addition, altered downstream flows have changed water temperatures and increased turbidity. Strip mining, coal washing, farming, and logging have all added loads of silt and pollutants to the streams and rivers of the region. Turbid water clogs the feeding apparatus of mussels, and siltation smothers mussel beds.

Fish species of all kinds, including those that play host to mussel glochidia, have declined, making mussel reproduction problematic. At the beginning of the twentieth century, nearly 80 species of freshwater mussels were documented from the waters of Alabama and Tennessee, but by 1964 the count had declined to only 59. Many of these surviving species are now rare or threatened with extinction.

Conservation and Recovery

Recovery strategies for this subspecies cannot be developed until a viable breeding population is discovered. The Tennessee Wildlife Resources Agency, the Tennessee Heritage Program, and the TVA continue to support research into the status of this and other freshwater mussels in the state. Mussel research in Alabama is promoted by the Al-abama Department of Conservation and Natural Resources.

Contact

U. S. Fish and Wildlife Service
Regional Office, Division of Endangered Species
1875 Century Blvd., Suite 200
Atlanta, Georgia 30345
Telephone: (404) 679-4000
http://southeast.fws.gov/

References

Bogan, A., and P. Parmalee. 1983. "Tennessee's Rare Mollusks." In *Tennessee's Rare Wildlife, Final Report*. Tennessee Department of Conservation and Tennessee Heritage Program, University of Tennessee, Knoxville.

General Accounting Office. 1988. "Endangered Species: Management Improvements Could Enhance Recovery Program." GAO/RCED- 89-5. U.S. General Accounting Office, Washington, D.C.

U.S. Fish and Wildlife Service. 1985. "Recovery Plan for the Tubercled-Blossom Pearly Mussel, Turgid-Blossom Pearly Mussel, and Yellow-Blossom Pearly Mussel." U.S. Fish and Wildlife Service, Atlanta.

Tan Riffleshell

Epioblasma florentina walkeri

Status	Endangered
Listed	August 23, 1977
Family	Unionidae (Freshwater Mussel)
Description	Dull brownish green or yellowish green shell with numerous faint green rays.
Habitat	Mid-sized streams and rivers in sand or gravel shoals.
Reproduction	Female stores sperm in gills; glochidia are released into the stream after hatching.
Food	Filter-feeder.
Threats	Restricted range, siltation, degraded water quality.
Range	Virginia

Tan Riffleshell, photograph. U. S. Fish and Wildlife Service. Reproduced by permission.

Description

The tan riffleshell, *Epioblasma florentina walkeri*, is a medium-sized freshwater mussel (2.8 in; 7 cm) characterized by a dull brownish green or yellowish green shell surface with numerous, evenly distributed, faint green rays. The subinflated valves are of unequal length and are marked with uneven growth rings. The inner shell surface is bluish white. The thin, posterior swelling of the female has one or more constrictions which give the shell a lobed appearance.

Behavior

See the Upland Combshell (*Epioblasma metastriata*) entry.

Habitat

This mussel inhabits shallow riffles and shoals of mid-sized tributaries and the mainstream of larger rivers. It buries itself in a sand or gravel bottom.

Distribution

This mussel was first collected in the East Fork Stones River in Rutherford County, Tennessee, but appears to have disappeared from this locality. It was found in the headwaters of the Cumberland River downstream to Neeley's Ford in Cumberland County, Kentucky. In the 1970s it was found in the lower Red River (a Cumberland River tributary) in Montgomery County, Tennessee, and in the Duck and Buffalo Rivers.

In the upper Tennessee River drainage, this mussel was documented from the Middle Fork Holston River (Smyth County, Virginia), the South Fork Holston River (Washington County, Virginia, and Sullivan County, Tennessee), and the main stem of the Holston River (Grainger and Knox counties, Tennessee). It was also noted from the Flint River and Limestone Creek in northern Alabama.

The tan riffleshell has not been relocated in the Duck or Red Rivers, and probably survives only in the Middle Fork Holston River in Virginia. It has been collected from near Chilhowie (Smyth County) and further downstream at Craig Bridge (Washington County).

A new population was discovered in the upper Clinch River and a tributary, Indian Creek, in southwestern Virginia. Both are part of the greater Tennessee River system.

Threats

The drastic decline in range of the tan riffleshell is probably in response to the extensive alteration of the Cumberland and Tennessee River basins by the construction of more than 50 dams and reservoirs. The South Fork Holston River was impounded by the Ruthton Dam to create the South Holston Lake, inundating miles of former mussel habitat along the river. The cold tailwaters of the reservoir have proven inimical to endemic mussels and many species of fishes that serve as hosts for mussel larvae.

The general effects of impoundments on mussel habitat have been widely documented. In addition, water quality in most watersheds within the tan riffleshell's has deteriorated significantly. Distribution has also deteriorated because of heavy siltation caused by logging, strip-mining, dredging, and poor agricultural practices.

Conservation and Recovery

The Tennessee Valley Authority is currently developing a comprehensive water management plan for the region that would establish minimum, year-round flows in all rivers in the Tennessee and Cumberland basins by carefully timing water discharges from its many dams. The recovery of the tan riffleshell will depend on the success of this and other regional efforts to improve water quality and rehabilitate freshwater mussel habitat.

The newest population, located in the upper Clinch River drainage, included evidence of reproduction, which indicates the species' fish hosts are present . The U. S. Fish and Wildlife Service (FWS) is providing funds to determine which fish species host this mussel during its parasitic larval stage. If successful, this research could lead to additional efforts to culture the tan riffleshell and return young individuals to suitable habitat.

The FWS has also initiated actions to inform residents along the upper Clinch River of the importance and uniqueness of this species, and to enlist their support for its recovery. Early efforts to work with local citizens, county officials, and other individuals and agencies have been well-received.

Contact

U. S. Fish and Wildlife Service
Regional Office, Division of Endangered Species
1875 Century Blvd., Suite 200
Atlanta, Georgia 30345
http://southeast.fws.gov/

References

Tennessee Valley Authority. 1978. "Water Quality Progress in the Holston River Basin." Report No. TVA/EP-78/08. Tennessee Valley Authority, Knoxville.

U. S. Fish and Wildlife Service. 1984. "Tan Riffleshell Mussel Recovery Plan." U. S. Fish and Wildlife Service, Atlanta.

Virginia State Water Control Board. 1982. "Water Quality Inventory: Report to EPA and Congress." Bulletin No. 546. Virginia State Water Control Board, Richmond, Virginia.

Upland Combshell

Epioblasma metastriata

Status	Endangered
Listed	March 17, 1993
Family	Unionidae (Freshwater Mussel)
Description	Small to medium mussel with a yellowish-brown or tawny shell, sometimes containing small green dots or broken green rays.
Habitat	Gravel riffles in streams.
Reproduction	Female stores sperm in gills; glochidia (larvae) are released into streams after hatching.
Food	Filter-feeder.
Threats	Impoundments; gravel mining; water pollution.
Range	Alabama, Georgia, Tennessee

Description

The upland combshell (*Epioblasma metastriata*) is a mussel that rarely exceeds 2.4 in (6.1 cm) in length. The shell is rhomboidal to quadrate in shape. The species is dimorphic. Males are moderately inflated with a broadly curved posterior ridge; females are considerably inflated, with a sharply elevated posterior ridge that swells broadly post-ventrally, forming a well-developed sulcus (the groove anterior to the posterior ridge). The periostracum (epidermis) color varies from yellowish-brown to tawny and may or may not have broken green rays or small green spots. Hinged teeth are well developed and heavy.

Behavior

The life of mussels is complex, and reproduction often depends upon a stable habitat—unaltered stream conditions, clean water, and an undisturbed stream bottom. The cycle also depends upon the abundance of suitable fish hosts to complete the mussel's larval development.

To reproduce, males discharge sperm, which are dispersed by stream currents. In the process of feeding, females nearby or downstream take in sperm, which fertilizes eggs stored in their gills. The gills serve as brood pouches (marsupia), where the glochidia hatch and begin to develop. After a time, these glochidia are released into the stream. A few mussels have inner parts that resemble a tiny minnow and can be manipulated to lure host fish. When a fish gets close to the shell, the mussel expels its glochidia.

Glochidia have tiny bean- or spoon-shaped valves that attach to the gill filaments of host fish. Glochidia can only progress to the juvenile stage while attached to the fish's gills. Those that do not fortuitously encounter a host fish do not survive when released by the female mussel. They sink to the bottom and die.

When the juvenile has developed a shell and is large enough to survive on its own, it detaches from the host fish and falls to the stream bottom, beginning a long association with a single stretch of stream. Maturing mussels bury themselves in riffles and shoals with only the shell margins and feeding siphons exposed to the water. Some mussels live as long as 50 years or more.

The family Unionidae, which includes all of the freshwater mussels in the United States, is separated into two groups based on the length of time the

Upland Combshell, photograph. A. E. Spreitzer Photography. Reproduced by permission.

glochidia remain in the female's marsupia. The eggs of the short-term (tachytictic) breeders are fertilized in the spring, and glochidia are released by late summer of the same year. Long-term (bradytictic) breeders hold developing glochidia in the brood pouch over winter and release them in the spring.

Freshwater mussels feed by siphoning phytoplankton and other plant matter from the water. Indigestible particles are expelled from the shell by reverse siphoning. Silt in the water can kill mussels by clogging their feeding siphons.

There are no known interspecific differences in feeding among freshwater mussels. The glochidia are obligate parasites on the gills or fins of fish. Adult mussels are filter-feeders and consume particulate matter in the water column. Identifiable stomach contents almost invariably include desmids, diatoms, algae, protozoa, and zooplankton.

Most freshwater mussel species display seasonal variations in activity associated with water temperature and reproduction. Metabolic rate is, in part, positively correlated with temperature. Many ectothermic species have the capacity to adjust their metabolic rates in response to long-term changes in temperature. Thus, metabolic rates do not continue to rise as temperatures rise in the summer, and they do not continue to fall during the winter as temperatures decline.

Some freshwater mussels also show diurnal changes in metabolic rates that indicate a tendency toward nocturnal activity patterns. Mussels may move to the surface to feed at night and move deeper into the substrate during the day; this is one way to avoid predators that hunt by visual contact.

Freshwater mussels are nonmigratory.

Habitat

The upland combshell has been successfully collected from the Mobile River drainage within the past 20 years and is believed to currently exist in the drainage. This species inhabits high quality lotic (living in actively moving water) habitats with stable gravel and sandy-gravel substrates. Little else is known about its habitat requirements. The habitat of the glochidia is initially in the gills of the female, then in the water column, and finally attached to a suitable host fish. Habitat associations or requirements for the juvenile stage are unknown.

Distribution

The upland combshell has been found historically in the following river systems in Alabama, Georgia, and Tennessee: the Black Warrior River and tributaries (Mulberry Fork and Valley Creek); the Cahaba River and tributaries (Little Cahaba River, Buck Creek); and the Coosa River and tributaries (Choccolocco Creek, Etowah, Conasauga, and Chatooga Rivers). All of these river systems are considered part of the Mobile River basin.

This species' population size is extremely small. The most recent record from the Coosa River drainage is a Conasauga River collection of a single specimen in 1988. The upland combshell was last recorded in the Cahaba River system in 1973, at which time the population size was said to be greatly reduced. And, finally, the last record for the Black Warrior River system was in the early 1900s. The species was not found in a 1990 survey of all three river systems.

The upland combshell is limited by an extremely low population size/low gene pool, population isolation, and possibly by competition from exotic species, primarily the Asiatic clam (*Corbicula fluminea*). Other limiting factors for this species are unknown, as are specific estimates of populations.

Threats

Habitat modification, sedimentation, and water quality degradation represent the major threats to this species. These freshwater mussels do not tolerate impoundments. More than 1,000 mi (1,609 km) of large and small river habitat in the Mobile River drainage has been impounded for navigation, flood control, water supply, and/or hydroelectric production purposes. Impoundments adversely affect riverine mussels by: 1) killing them during construction and dredging, 2) suffocating them with accumulated sediments, 3) lowering food and oxygen availability by reducing water flow, and 4) locally extirpating host fish. Other forms of habitat modification such as channelization, channel clearing and de-snagging, and gravel mining result in streambed

scour and erosion, increased turbidity, reduction of groundwater levels, sedimentation, and changes in the aquatic community structure. Sedimentation may cause direct mortality by deposition and suffocation and eliminate or reduce recruitment of juvenile mussels. Suspended sediments can also interfere with feeding. Activities that historically caused sedimentation of streams and rivers in the drainages where this mussel occurs include channel modification, agriculture, forestry, mining, and industrial and residential development. In addition, stream discharge may result in decreased dissolved oxygen concentration, increased acidity and conductivity, and other changes in water chemistry that may impact the mussels and/or fish hosts. About 230 river mi (370.1 km) of the Coosa River have been impounded for hydropower by a series of six dams. Water quality degradation caused by textile and carpet mill wastes led to the loss of several known mussel communities in some streams of this river system. Water quality degradation is a major problem in the Cahaba River system. There are 10 municipal wastewater treatment plants, 35 surface mining areas, a coalbed methane operation, and 67 other permitted discharges in this river system. Siltation from surface mining, road construction, and oil and gas development is also a problem.

Conservation and Recovery

Actions needed for the recovery of freshwater mussels include 1) conducting population and habitat surveys to determine the status and range of the species, 2) determining specific threats to the species and minimizing or eliminating these threats, 3) identifying essential habitat areas in need of protection, and 4) controlling the incidental or illegal take of mussels by commercial and noncommercial collectors. It is unlikely that the species will recover unless new populations are established by introducing individuals back into the historic range. Methods to accomplish this might include introduction of adult/juvenile mussels, glochidia-infected host fish, and artificially cultured individuals.

Contacts

U.S. Fish and Wildlife Service
Regional Office, Division of Endangered Species
1875 Century Blvd., Suite 200
Atlanta, Georgia 30345
Telephone: (404) 679-4000
http://southeast.fws.gov/

Ecological Services Field Office
P.O. Box 1190
Daphne, Alabama 36526-1190
Telephone: (334) 441-5181
Fax: (334) 441-6222

Ecological Services Field Office
446 Neal Street
Cookeville, Tennessee 38501-4027
Telephone: (931) 528-6481
Fax: (931) 528-7075

Reference

U.S. Fish and Wildlife Service. 17 March 1993. "Endangered and Threatened Wildlife and Plants; Endangered Status for Eight Freshwater Mussels and Threatened Status for Three Freshwater Mussels in the Mobile River Drainage." *Federal Register* 58 (50): 14330-14340.

Catspaw

Epioblasma obliquata obliquata

Status	Endangered
Listed	July 10, 1990
Family	Unionidae
Description	A freshwater mussel.
Habitat	Large rivers.
Food	Filter-feeds organic detritus, phytoplankton, and tiny zooplankton.
Reproduction	Lays externally fertilized eggs, and has planktonic larvae that are parasitic on fish.
Threats	Habitat destruction by impoundments, pollution, and gravel mining.
Range	Alabama, Illinois, Indiana, Kentucky, Ohio, Tennessee

Catspaw, photograph. A. E. Spreitzer Photography. Reproduced by permission.

Description

The catspaw, also known as the purple cat's paw pearlymussel, has a medium-sized shell that is subquadrate (roughly rectangular) in outline. The outside surface has numerous distinct growth lines, fine wavy green rays, a smooth and shiny surface, and is yellowish-green, yellow, or brownish in color. The inside of the shell is a lustrous purplish to deep purple.

Behavior

The specific food habits of the catspaw are unknown. Like other freshwater mussels, however, it probably filter-feeds on detritus, diatoms, phytoplankton, and zooplankton. As with other unionid bivalves, the larvae (or veligers) have a planktonic stage during which they are parasitic on species of fish. Afterwards, they settle to the bottom and adopt the sedentary, filter-feeding lifestyle of the adults.

Habitat

The catspaw inhabits large rivers with a sand/gravel substrate. It occurs in water of shallow to moderate depth, with a moderate to swift current. It inhabits boulder to sand substrates.

Distribution

The catspaw was once known from the Ohio, Cumberland, and Tennessee River Systems in Ohio, Illinois, Indiana, Kentucky, Tennessee, and Alabama.

Threats

The range and abundance of the catspaw are greatly reduced from former times. Most of its historical populations were lost through the conversion of extensive sections of its riverine habitat into a series of large impoundments (i.e., through the construction of dams). This greatly reduced the availability of riverine habitat, and also affected the distribution and availability of the fish hosts of the parasitic mussel larvae. The degradation of water quality is also a problem, including runoff from oil and gas exploration and production, the dredging of gravel, channel maintenance, and commercial fishing for other species of mussels. The rare catspaw is also threatened by the invasion of its habitat by an introduced alien species, the zebra mussel (*Dreissena polymorpha*), which out-competes many native species of unionid bivalves. Only three populations of the catspaw survive. These are located in the middle Cumberland River in Smith County, Tennessee, and in the Green River in Warren and Butler Counties, Kentucky. However, two of these populations only have old animals, and appear to be non-reproducing.

Conservation and Recovery

Surveys are needed to determine whether any additional populations of the catspaw survive, and to monitor the known populations. The known populations must be protected from obvious threats, such as gravel mining. Unless additional reproduc-ing populations can be found, or methods developed to maintain the three known populations or create new ones, the species will remain at great risk of extinction. Research is needed to better understand the life-history requirements of the rare catspaw, and to determine the threats to its existence so they can be alleviated.

Contact

U. S. Fish and Wildlife Service
Regional Office, Division of Endangered Species
1 Federal Drive
BHW Federal Building
Fort Snelling, Minnesota 55111
Telephone: (612) 713-5360
http://midwest.fws.gov/

U. S. Fish and Wildlife Service
Regional Office, Division of Endangered Species
1875 Century Blvd., Suite 200
Atlanta, Georgia 30345
http://southeast.fws.gov/

U. S. Fish and Wildlife Service
330 Ridgefield Court Telephone:
Asheville, North Carolina 28806
(704) 665-1195

References

U. S. Fish and Wildlife Service. 2000. Cat's Paw Pearlymussel (*Epioblasma [= Dysnomia] obliquata obliquata*). http://endangered.fws.gov/i/f/saf15.html

U.S. Fish and Wildlife Service. 10 July 1990. "Endangered and Threatened Wildlife and Plants: Purple Cat's Paw Pearlymussel Determined To Be An Endangered Species." *Federal Register* 55:132.

White Catspaw Pearlymussel

Epioblasma obliquata perobliqua

Status	Endangered
Listed	June 14, 1976
Family	Unionidae (Freshwater Mussel)
Description	Greenish-yellow shell with numerous green rays; females have tiny teeth along the shell margin.
Habitat	Shoals and riffles of streams and rivers.
Reproduction	Female stores sperm in gills; glochidia (larvae) are released into streams after hatching.
Food	Filter-feeder.
Threats	Siltation; pollution.
Range	Indiana, Ohio

A. E. Spreitzer

Description

The white catspaw pearlymussel (*Epioblasma obliquata perobliqua*) rarely exceeds 1.7 in (4.3 cm) in shell length. The outer surface of the shell is greenish-yellow with numerous light green rays that radiate from posterior to anterior. The species is sexually dimorphic, meaning that males and females differ in structure and appearance. The larger female is more pointed at the valve end and bears little teeth along the shell margin. The teeth give the appearance of tiny claws, hence the name "cat's paw."

Behavior

The life of mussels is complex, and reproduction often depends upon a stable habitat—unaltered stream conditions, clean water, and an undisturbed stream bottom. The cycle also depends upon the abundance of suitable fish hosts to complete the mussel's larval development.

To reproduce, males discharge sperm, which are dispersed by stream currents. In the process of feeding, females nearby or downstream take in sperm, which fertilizes eggs stored in their gills. The gills serve as brood pouches (marsupia), where the glochidia hatch and begin to develop. After a time, these glochidia are released into the stream. A few mussels have inner parts that resemble a tiny minnow and can be manipulated to lure host fish. When a fish gets close to the shell, the mussel expels its glochidia.

Glochidia have tiny bean- or spoon-shaped valves that attach to the gill filaments of host fish. Glochidia can only progress to the juvenile stage while attached to the fish's gills. Those that do not fortuitously encounter a host fish do not survive when released by the female mussel. They sink to the bottom and die.

When the juvenile has developed a shell and is large enough to survive on its own, it detaches from the host fish and falls to the stream bottom, beginning a long association with a single stretch of stream. Maturing mussels bury themselves in riffles and shoals with only the shell margins and feeding siphons exposed to the water. Some mussels live as long as 50 years or more.

The family Unionidae, which includes all of the freshwater mussels in the United States, is separated into two groups based on the length of time the glochidia remain in the female's marsupia. The eggs of the short-term (tachytictic) breeders are fertilized in the spring, and glochidia are released by late summer of the same year. Long-term (bradytictic) breeders hold developing glochidia in the brood pouch over winter and release them in the spring.

Freshwater mussels feed by siphoning phytoplankton and other plant matter from the water. Indigestible particles are expelled from the shell by reverse siphoning. Silt in the water can kill mussels by clogging their feeding siphons.

There are no known interspecific differences in feeding among freshwater mussels. The glochidia are obligate parasites on the gills or fins of fish. Adult mussels are filter-feeders and consume particulate matter in the water column. Identifiable stomach contents almost invariably include desmids, diatoms, algae, protozoa, and zooplankton.

Most freshwater mussel species display seasonal variations in activity associated with water temperature and reproduction. Metabolic rate is, in part, positively correlated with temperature. Many ectothermic species have the capacity to adjust their metabolic rates in response to long-term changes in temperature. Thus, metabolic rates do not continue to rise as temperatures rise in the summer, and they do not continue to fall during the winter as temperatures decline.

Some freshwater mussels also show diurnal changes in metabolic rates that indicate a tendency toward nocturnal activity patterns. Mussels may move to the surface to feed at night and move deeper into the substrate during the day; this is one way to avoid predators that hunt by visual contact.

Freshwater mussels are nonmigratory.

Habitat

This mussel inhabits freshwater streams and rivers and favors stable, sandy-gravel bottoms. It prefers reaches where the water is fairly shallow and the current strong enough to keep silt scoured from the bottom.

Distribution

The white catspaw pearlymussel was carried into its current range during the warming period after the last glaciation. As the Wisconsin Glacier melted, fish carried mussel eggs north into the Maumee River and its tributaries (such as the St. Joseph and Auglaize rivers, which drain into Lake Erie). There is evidence to suggest that a population was established at the edge of Lake Erie in the vicinity of Toledo, Ohio. Other populations were found in the Wabash River, which arises close to the Maumee River but drains instead to the southwest, eventually emptying into the Ohio River west of Evansville. Populations in this drainage were probably centered near the confluence of the Eel River in Cass County, Indiana.

The current distribution of the white catspaw pearlymussel is extremely limited relative to its historic range. Since 1985 surveys have located this species in the St. Joseph River that joins the St. Marys River at Fort Wayne, Indiana, to form the Maumee. Mussels were found in both the Indiana and Ohio portions of the river. Scattered individuals were also found in Fish Creek in Indiana. The catspaw survives in a few viable beds in fairly low numbers.

Threats

The great forests that once stretched across most of Ohio and Indiana have largely been cleared to support intensive agriculture. Poor agricultural practices in many cases have clouded the rivers with topsoil runoff, raising turbidity levels and smothering once-favorable stretches of mussel habitat with silt. This is probably the primary cause of the overall decline of the white catspaw pearlymussel. Pesticide and fertilizer contamination probably played a role in degrading habitat. Filter-feeders like mussels must siphon many gallons of water to extract food; if the water is contaminated, poisonous residues concentrate in their tissues.

Along with existing threats, perhaps the greatest potential for damage to the mussel population may be a catastrophic event such as a toxic chemical spill, which could extirpate a large percentage of the species. Such an event has already taken place, although fast clean-up measures limited the damage to the habitat. On September 15, 1993, a pipeline break discharged an estimated 30,000 gal (113,562 l) of #2 diesel fuel in a crop field in DeKalb County, Indiana. Spilled fuel made its way to a small drainage ditch that discharges into Fish Creek. While response action limited potential damage, it did not prevent injury, and the catastrophe may have long-term residual effects, since fuel accumulated along the banks and in detrital organic matter and sediment.

Conservation and Recovery

The U.S. Fish and Wildlife Service encourages local landowners to follow more ecologically sound agricultural practices to reduce the amount of suspended solids in habitat waters. Known populations are being monitored at least every two years to determine trends, and potential habitat in the basin is being surveyed to locate additional populations and to identify possible sites for reintroduction. The immediate goal for the recovery of this subspecies is to protect the only remaining population. Other goals include increasing present distribution and adding to current knowledge of life history.

Contact

U.S. Fish and Wildlife Service
Regional Office, Division of Endangered Species
1 Federal Drive
BHW Federal Building
Fort Snelling, Minnesota 55111
Telephone: (612) 713-5360
http://midwest.fws.gov/

References

Johnson, R.I. 1980. "Zoogeography of North American Unioniacea (Mollusca: Bivalvia) North of the Maximum Pleistocene Glaciation." *Bulletin of the Museum of Comparative Zoology* 149 (2): 77-189.

Stansbery, D.H. 1971. "Rare and Endangered Freshwater Mollusks in Eastern North America." In S. Jorgensen and R. Sharp, eds., *Rare and Endangered Mollusks (Naiads) of the U.S.* U.S. Fish and Wildlife Service, Twin Cities, Minnesota.

U.S. Fish and Wildlife Service. 1990. "White Cat's Paw Pearly Mussel Recovery Plan." U.S. Fish and Wildlife Service, Twin Cities, Minnesota.

Southern Acornshell

Epioblasma othcaloogensis

Status	Endangered
Listed	March 17, 1993
Family	Unionidae (Freshwater Mussel)
Description	Small mussel with a round to oval shiny yellow shell.
Habitat	Gravel riffles in streams.
Reproduction	Female stores sperm in gills; glochidia (larvae) are released into streams after hatching.
Food	Filter-feeder.
Threats	Impoundments; water pollution.
Range	Alabama, Georgia, Tennessee

Description

The southern acornshell (*Epioblasma othcaloogensis*) is a small mussel about 1.2 in (3 cm) in length with a round to ovate shell. The species is sexually dimorphic, with a swollen posterior ridge in females. The periostracum (external covering of the shell) is smooth, shiny, and yellow in color.

Behavior

The life of mussels is complex, and reproduction often depends upon a stable habitat—unaltered stream conditions, clean water, and an undisturbed stream bottom. The cycle also depends upon the abundance of suitable fish hosts to complete the mussel's larval development.

To reproduce, males discharge sperm, which are dispersed by stream currents. In the process of feeding, females nearby or downstream take in sperm, which fertilizes eggs stored in their gills. The gills serve as brood pouches (marsupia), where the glochidia hatch and begin to develop. After a time, these glochidia are released into the stream. A few mussels have inner parts that resemble a tiny minnow and can be manipulated to lure host fish. When a fish gets close to the shell, the mussel expels its glochidia.

Glochidia have tiny bean- or spoon-shaped valves that attach to the gill filaments of host fish.

Glochidia can only progress to the juvenile stage while attached to the fish's gills. Those that do not fortuitously encounter a host fish do not survive when released by the female mussel. They sink to the bottom and die.

When the juvenile has developed a shell and is large enough to survive on its own, it detaches from the host fish and falls to the stream bottom, beginning a long association with a single stretch of stream. Maturing mussels bury themselves in riffles and shoals with only the shell margins and feeding siphons exposed to the water. Some mussels live as long as 50 years or more.

The family Unionidae, which includes all of the freshwater mussels in the United States, is separated into two groups based on the length of time the glochidia remain in the female's marsupia. The eggs of the short-term (tachytictic) breeders are fertilized in the spring, and glochidia are released by late summer of the same year. Long-term (bradytictic) breeders hold developing glochidia in the brood pouch over winter and release them in the spring.

Freshwater mussels feed by siphoning phytoplankton and other plant matter from the water. Indigestible particles are expelled from the shell by reverse siphoning. Silt in the water can kill mussels by clogging their feeding siphons.

Southern Acornshell, photograph. A. E. Spreitzer Photography. Reproduced by permission.

There are no known interspecific differences in feeding among freshwater mussels. The glochidia are obligate parasites on the gills or fins of fish. Adult mussels are filter-feeders and consume particulate matter in the water column. Identifiable stomach contents almost invariably include desmids, diatoms, algae, protozoa, and zooplankton.

Most freshwater mussel species display seasonal variations in activity associated with water temperature and reproduction. Metabolic rate is, in part, positively correlated with temperature. Many ectothermic species have the capacity to adjust their metabolic rates in response to long-term changes in temperature. Thus, metabolic rates do not continue to rise as temperatures rise in the summer, and they do not continue to fall during the winter as temperatures decline.

Some freshwater mussels also show diurnal changes in metabolic rates that indicate a tendency toward nocturnal activity patterns. Mussels may move to the surface to feed at night and move deeper into the substrate during the day; this is one way to avoid predators that hunt by visual contact.

Freshwater mussels are nonmigratory.

Habitat

The southern acornshell inhabits high quality lotic (living in actively moving water) habitats with stable gravel and sandy-gravel substrates. Little else is known about the habitat requirements of this species.

The habitat of the glochidia is initially in the gills of the female, then in the water column, and finally attached to a suitable host fish. Habitat associations or requirements for the juvenile stage are unknown.

Distribution

The southern acornshell was historically found in the following portions of the Mobile River basin: the upper Coosa River system (including the Conasauga River, Cowan's Creek, and Othcalooga Creek) and the Cahaba River above the fall line. The southern acornshell was last collected in the Cahaba River drainage in 1938. Surveys in 1973 and 1991 failed to locate the species there.

This species is now restricted to streams in the Coosa River drainage in Alabama and Georgia. The U. S. Fish and Wildlife Service also considers this species endangered in Tennessee. Recent records for the southern acornshell in the Coosa River drainage were from the Conasauga River above Dalton, Georgia. Specimens were last collected in this drainage from 1966 to 1968. Surveys in 1990-91 failed to locate the species there.

Threats

Habitat modification, sedimentation, and water quality degradation represent the major threats to this species. These freshwater mussels do not tolerate impoundments. More than 1,000 mi (1,609 km) of large and small river habitat in the Mobile River drainage has been impounded for navigation, flood control, water supply, and/or hydroelectric production purposes. Impoundments adversely affect riverine mussels by 1) killing them during construction and dredging, 2) suffocating them with accumulated sediments, 3) lowering food and oxygen availability by reducing water flow, and 4) locally extirpating host fish. Other forms of habitat modification such as channelization, channel clearing and de-snagging, and gravel mining result in streambed scour and erosion, increased turbidity, reduction of groundwater levels, sedimentation, and changes in the aquatic community structure. Sedimentation may cause direct mortality by deposition and suffocation and eliminate or reduce recruitment of juvenile mussels. Suspended sediments can also interfere with feeding. Activities that historically caused sedimentation of streams and rivers in the drainages where this mussel occurs include channel modification, agriculture, forestry, mining, and industrial and residential development.

In addition, stream discharge may result in decreased dissolved oxygen concentration, increased acidity and conductivity, and other changes in water chemistry that may impact the mussels and/or fish hosts.

About 230 river mi (370 km) of the Coosa River have been impounded for hydropower by a series of six dams.

Water quality degradation caused by textile and carpet mill wastes led to the loss of several known mussel communities in various streams of this river system. Water quality degradation is a major problem in the Cahaba River system. There are 10 municipal wastewater treatment plants, 35 surface mining areas, a coalbed methane operation, and 67 other permitted discharges in this river system. Siltation from surface mining, road construction, and oil and gas development is also a problem.

Conservation and Recovery

Actions needed for the recovery of freshwater mussels include 1) conducting population and habitat surveys to determine the status and range of the species, 2) determining specific threats to the species and minimizing or eliminating these threats, 3) identifying essential habitat areas in need of protection, and 4) controlling the incidental or illegal take of mussels by commercial and noncommercial collectors.

It is unlikely that this species will recover unless new populations are established by introducing individuals back into the historic range. Methods to accomplish this might include the introduction of adult/juvenile mussels, glochidia-infected host fish, and artificially cultured individuals.

Contacts

U.S. Fish and Wildlife Service
Regional Office, Division of Endangered Species
1875 Century Blvd., Suite 200
Atlanta, Georgia 30345
Telephone: (404) 679-4000
http://southeast.fws.gov/

Ecological Services Field Office
P.O. Box 1190
Daphne, Alabama 36526-1190
Telephone: (334) 441-5181
Fax: (334) 441-6222

Ecological Services Field Office
446 Neal Street
Cookeville, Tennessee 38501-4027
Telephone: (931) 528-6481
Fax: (931) 528-7075

Reference

U.S. Fish and Wildlife Service. 17 March 1993. "Endangered and Threatened Wildlife and Plants; Endangered Status for Eight Freshwater Mussels and Threatened Status for Three Freshwater Mussels in the Mobile River Drainage." *Federal Register* 58 (50): 14330-14340.

Southern Combshell

Epioblasma penita

Status	Endangered
Listed	April 7, 1987
Family	Unionidae (Freshwater Mussel)
Description	Yellowish rhomboid shell with irregular growth lines.
Habitat	Sandy gravel river bottom.
Reproduction	Female stores sperm in gills; glochidia (larvae) are released into streams after hatching.
Food	Filter-feeder.
Threats	Dams; dredging; siltation.
Range	Alabama, Mississippi

Description

The southern combshell, or penitent mussel, (*Epioblasma penita*) is a bivalve mollusk about 2.1 in (5.3 cm) long. The rhomboid shell is yellowish, greenish-yellow, or tawny, sometimes with dark spots. The surface is characterized by irregular growth lines and a radially sculptured posterior. The inner shell surface (nacre) is white or straw-colored. Females have a large, grooved swelling at the rear of the shell. First described as *Unio penitus* in 1834, this species has been variously classified since then, most commonly as *Dysnomia penita.*

Behavior

The life of mussels is complex, and reproduction often depends upon a stable habitat—unaltered stream conditions, clean water, and an undisturbed stream bottom. The cycle also depends upon the abundance of suitable fish hosts to complete the mussel's larval development.

To reproduce, males discharge sperm, which are dispersed by stream currents. In the process of feeding, females nearby or downstream take in sperm, which fertilizes eggs stored in their gills. The gills serve as brood pouches (marsupia), where the glochidia hatch and begin to develop. After a time, these glochidia are released into the stream. A few mussels have inner parts that resemble a tiny min-

now and can be manipulated to lure host fish. When a fish gets close to the shell, the mussel expels its glochidia. Glochidia have tiny bean- or spoon-shaped valves that attach to the gill filaments of host fish.

Glochidia can only progress to the juvenile stage while attached to the fish's gills. Those that do not fortuitously encounter a host fish do not survive when released by the female mussel. They sink to the bottom and die.

When the juvenile has developed a shell and is large enough to survive on its own, it detaches from the host fish and falls to the stream bottom, beginning a long association with a single stretch of stream. Maturing mussels bury themselves in riffles and shoals with only the shell margins and feeding siphons exposed to the water. Some mussels live as long as 50 years or more.

The family Unionidae, which includes all of the freshwater mussels in the United States, is separated into two groups based on the length of time the glochidia remain in the female's marsupia. The eggs of the short-term (tachytictic) breeders are fertilized in the spring, and glochidia are released by late summer of the same year. Long-term (bradytictic) breeders hold developing glochidia in the brood pouch over winter and release them in the spring.

Freshwater mussels feed by siphoning phytoplankton and other plant matter from the water. In-

Southern Combshell, photograph. A. E. Spreitzer Photography. Reproduced by permission.

digestible particles are expelled from the shell by reverse siphoning. Silt in the water can kill mussels by clogging their feeding siphons.

There are no known interspecific differences in feeding among freshwater mussels. The glochidia are obligate parasites on the gills or fins of fish. Adult mussels are filter-feeders and consume particulate matter in the water column. Identifiable stomach contents almost invariably include desmids, diatoms, algae, protozoa, and zooplankton.

Most freshwater mussel species display seasonal variations in activity associated with water temperature and reproduction. Metabolic rate is, in part, positively correlated with temperature. Many ectothermic species have the capacity to adjust their metabolic rates in response to long-term changes in temperature. Thus, metabolic rates do not continue to rise as temperatures rise in the summer, and they do not continue to fall during the winter as temperatures decline.

Some freshwater mussels also show diurnal changes in metabolic rates that indicate a tendency toward nocturnal activity patterns. Mussels may move to the surface to feed at night and move deeper into the substrate during the day; this is one way to avoid predators that hunt by visual contact.

Freshwater mussels are nonmigratory.

Habitat

The penitent mussel is found in the shallow reaches of larger streams and rivers where there is a moderately strong current. It prefers riffle runs or shoals with a stable substrate composed of sandy gravel or cobbles. Specimens have rarely been found in waters deeper than 2.3 ft (0.7 m).

Distribution

The species was known from the Tombigbee, Alabama, Buttahatchie, Cahaba, and Coosa Rivers in Alabama, Georgia, and Mississippi, all of which are part of the Mobile River basin. In the Tombigbee River, it was found from the confluence of Bull Mountain Creek above Amory, Mississippi, downstream to Epes, Alabama. The Alabama River supported populations at Claiborne and Selma. A population was known from the stretch of the Cahaba River below Centreville, Alabama.

The penitent mussel has not been collected from the Alabama and Cahaba Rivers since the 1800s. It was last collected from the mainstream Tombigbee River in 1972. It disappeared from the Coosa River after 1974, when a new dam inundated its habitat there.

The penitent mussel survives in the Gainesville Bendway of the Tombigbee River (Sumter County, Alabama). This cut-off section of the river provides only marginal habitat, which is subject to siltation, reduced water flows, and degraded water quality. The species also survives in sections of the Buttahatchie River and the East Fork Tombigbee River.

All mussel populations in the lower reaches of the Buttahatchie River have declined dramatically. More than 1,200 individual mussels in the family Unionidae, including 92 specimens of *E. penita,* were sampled from two reaches in the lower portion of the river in 1977, but in 1989 only 75 unionids (including 3 penitent mussels) were found. Fortunately, the numbers of penitent mussels collected from two reaches immediately above the gravel mines approached or exceeded the 1977 survey in 1989.

Threats

The southern combshell has declined because of loss of habitat. The once free-flowing Tombigbee River has been modified into a series of locks and channels to form a barge canal. Physical destruction of mollusks during dredging and construction and the resulting increase of siltation, reduction of water flow, and disturbance of host fish movements have all but eliminated the mollusk from this river. Further siltation in the Gainesville Bendway would probably eliminate the southern combshell there.

Bull Mountain Creek contributes nearly half of the flow of the East Fork of the Tombigbee River. During canal construction, the creek was diverted and its cool waters redirected into the warm canal, resulting in warmer water temperatures in the East Fork. Warmer waters stress the mussels and diminish their food supply. Changes in current and river flow interfere with reproduction, since this species depends on currents to carry mature gametes downstream to other mussels for fertilization. Mussel beds also suffer from degraded water quality from the runoff of fertilizers and pesticides.

Impoundment of the Tombigbee River in Mississippi and Alabama for the Tennessee-Tombigbee

Waterway has affected the lower 1.9 mi (3.1 km) of the Buttahatchie River by reducing the current and scouring capacity of the river. Abandoned kaolin (clay) mines and abandoned and active gravel mines also appear to be causing problems. Above the portion of the river affected by the impoundment of the Tombigbee River, the Buttahatchie River channel has broken into gravel mines excavated adjacent to the channel, eroding former riffle areas and creating ponds. Farther north, an estimated 17,000 tons (12,690.2 metric tons) of sediment are eroding annually from abandoned kaolin mines and moving through the Buttahatchie system.

Conservation and Recovery

Both Mississippi and Alabama require permits to take freshwater mussels. It is difficult to detect and apprehend violators, however, and regulations do not prevent habitat degradation. Recovery of the penitent mussel will require developing some means to ensure adequate water flow in remaining, unmodified sections of the river. Flood control projects and canal maintenance activities will need to consider the presence of mussel beds.

The range of the penitent mussel is threatened by two proposed channel improvement projects. If implemented, these projects would dredge and straighten 59 mi (95 km) of the Buttahatchie and 53 mi (85 km) of the East Fork.

Contact

U.S. Fish and Wildlife Service
Regional Office, Division of Endangered Species
1875 Century Blvd., Suite 200
Atlanta, Georgia 30345
Telephone: (404) 679-4000
http://southeast.fws.gov/

References

Clench, W.J., and R.D. Turner. 1956. "Freshwater Mollusks of Alabama, Georgia, and Florida from the Escambia to the Suwannee River." *Bulletin of the Florida State Museum (Biological Sciences)* 1: 97-239.

Johnson, R.I. 1978. "Systematics and Zoogeography of *Plagiola,* an Almost Extinct Genus of Freshwater Mussels." *Bulletin of the Museum of Comparative Zoology* 148: 239-320.

Stansbery, D.H. 1976. "Naiade Mollusks." In H. Boschung, ed., *Bulletin of the Alabama Museum of Natural History* no. 2.

Green-blossom Pearlymussel

Epioblasma torulosa gubernaculum

Status	Endangered
Listed	June 14, 1976
Family	Unionidae (Freshwater Mussel)
Description	Medium-sized tawny or straw-colored, irregularly elliptical shell.
Habitat	Clear, fast-flowing streams with sand or gravel substrates.
Reproduction	Female stores sperm in gills; glochidia are released into the stream after hatching.
Food	Filter-feeder.
Threats	Dams, siltation, pollution.
Range	Tennessee, Virginia

Green-blossom Pearlymussel, photograph. A. E. Spreitzer Photography. Reproduced by permission.

Description

The green-blossom pearlymussel, *Epioblasma torulosa gubernaculum*, is a medium-sized Cumberlandian mussel with an irregularly elliptical shell, which is smooth and shiny, tawny or straw-colored, and patterned with numerous fine green rays. The shell surface is marked with distinct growth lines. The nacre (inner shell) color varies from white to salmon-red. The species is sexually dimorphic—i.e., the anatomies of males and females differ noticeably. The female's shell is generally larger than the male's and the posterior margin is more broadly rounded. The female possesses a large, flattened marsupial swelling, usually green in color and marked with radial furrows.

The green-blossom pearlymussel (previously classified as *Dysnomia torulosa gubernaculum*) is smaller, has a more compressed shell, and less developed knobs than its downstream relative, the tubercled-blossom pearly mussel (*E. t. torulosa*). Also federally listed as endangered, the tubercled-blossom may well be extinct.

Behavior

See the Upland Combshell (*Epioblasma metastriata*) entry.

Habitat

This mussel is found in clean, fast-flowing streams that contain firm rubble, gravel, and sand substrates, swept free of silt by the current.

Distribution

Cumberlandian mussels are endemic to the southern Appalachian Mountains and the Cumberland Plateau region. Of 90 species of freshwater mussels found in the Tennessee River, 37 are considered Cumberlandian. Twenty-seven of 78 species found in the Cumberland River are Cumberlandian. Records indicate that the green-blossom pearly mussel has always been restricted to the headwaters of the Tennessee River above Knoxville, Tennessee.

The green-blossom pearlymussel is now found only in the free-flowing reaches of the upper Clinch River above Norris Reservoir. One of the larger tributaries of the Tennessee River, the Clinch River arises in Tazewell County, Virginia, and flows southwest through the Cumberland Gap region into Tennessee. Biologists from the Tennessee Valley Authority (TVA) have conducted extensive surveys along the Clinch River from Cedar Bluff, Virginia, to the Norris Reservoir. A single live specimen was found in 1982, the first green-blossom collected since 1965.

Threats

The green-blossom pearlymussel has always been rare but is now on the verge of extinction. The genus *Epioblasma* has generally suffered because its members are typically found only in shallow portions of major rivers with rapid currents. Water control projects have greatly diminished this type of habitat. Although the green-blossom is found in a river that supports the most abundant and diverse freshwater mussel community in the United States, it is being eliminated by factors that are not yet affecting other mussels. Dam construction, siltation, and pollution are likely causes.

The TVA has built nine major dams on the main channel of the Tennessee River and 27 smaller dams on tributary streams. The Norris Dam created one of the largest reservoirs in the state and probably flooded a crucial portion of the green-blossom's historic range. Silt runoff from strip mining and agriculture has buried many of the gravel and sand bottoms in which the pearlymussel lives. It is estimated that more than 67% of coal production in the Appalachian region is extracted by strip mining. Because mussels siphon gallons of water each day while feeding, the effects of water pollutants, such as herbicides and pesticides, are intensified. Silt clogs the mussels' feeding siphons.

Conservation and Recovery

Sections of the Clinch River appear eligible for "scenic river" status under the National Wild and Scenic Rivers Act. Such a designation would provide additional protection for this and other freshwater mussels. The State of Tennessee has designated all of the Clinch River in Tennessee as a mussel sanctuary, but the headwaters for the Clinch originate in Virginia, where coal mining is extensive.

Contacts

U. S. Fish and Wildlife Service
Regional Office, Division of Endangered Species
1875 Century Blvd., Suite 200
Atlanta, Georgia 30345
http://southeast.fws.gov/

U. S. Fish and Wildlife Service
Regional Office, Division of Endangered Species
300 Westgate Center Dr.
Hadley, Massachusetts 01035-9589
Telephone: (413) 253-8200
Fax: (413) 253-8308
http://northeast.fws.gov/

References

Bates, J. M., and S. D. Dennis. 1978. "The Mussel Fauna of the Clinch River, Tennessee and Virginia." *Sterkiana* 69/70: 3-23.

Neel, J. K., and W. Allen. 1964. "The Mussel Fauna of the Upper Cumberland Basin before Its Impoundment." *Malacologia* 1 (3): 427-459.

U. S. Fish and Wildlife Service. 1983. "Green-Blossom Pearly Mussel Recovery Plan." U. S. Fish and Wildlife Service, Atlanta.

Northern Riffleshell

Epioblasma torulosa rangiana

Status	Endangered
Listed	January 22, 1993
Family	Unionidae (Freshwater Mussel)
Description	Small to medium-sized mussel with a brownish-yellow outer shell and white inner shell.
Habitat	Large and small streams with firmly packed sand and fine to coarse gravel.
Food	Filter feeder.
Reproduction	Females take in sperm; larvae are released into the water.
Threats	Loss of habitat and degraded water quality.
Range	Indiana, Kentucky, Michigan, Ohio, Pennsylvania, West Virginia

Description

The northern riffleshell can have a shell length up to about 3 in (7.5 cm). The shells of adult females are obovate in outline and appear swollen and rounded along the postventral area of the shell. Males have an ovate shell with a wide shallow sulcus. The shell's exterior surface (pereostricum) is brownish to yellowish-green with fine green rays. The inside of the shell (nacre) is usually white, but is occasionally pink.

Behavior

Although the food habits and reproductive biology of the northern riffleshell are unknown, they are probably similar to those of other freshwater mussels. Freshwater mussels feed on organic particles, algae, and minute plants and animals that they siphon out of the water. During feeding and respiration, females also take in the sperm that has been released into the water by males. Fertilized eggs remain in the gills until the larvae develop. When the larvae are released into the water, they attach and form cysts on the gills or fins of a fish host. The species of fish host used by this mussel is unknown. After the larvae's metamorphoses are complete, they drop to the streambed as juvenile mussels.

Habitat

This freshwater mussel occurs in a wide variety of streams, large and small, preferring runs with bottoms composed of firmly packed sand and fine to coarse gravel.

Distribution

Historically, the riffleshell occurred in the states of Illinois, Indiana, Kentucky, Michigan, Ohio, Pennsylvania, and West Virginia, and the species range also extended into western Ontario, Canada. It existed in the Ohio River basin in the Ohio, Allegheny, Scioto, Kanawha, Little Kanawha, Licking, Kentucky, Wabash, White, Vermillion, Mississinewa, Tippecanoe, Green, and Salt Rivers. It was found in the Maumee River basin and tributaries of western Lake Erie. The riffleshell also inhabited rivers in southern Michigan and western Ontario, such as the St. Clair, Black, Au Sable, and Sydenham Rivers.

Northern Riffleshell, photograph by Thomas Watters, Ohio DNR. Reproduced by permission.

In the late 1990s, this species survived in the Green River in Edmondson and Hart Counties, Kentucky; French Creek in Crawford, Venango, and Mercer Counties, Pennsylvania; Allegheny River in Warren and Forest Counties, Pennsylvania; LeBoeuf Creek in Erie County, Pennsylvania; Detroit River in Wayne County, Michigan; and Big Darby Creek in Pickaway County, Ohio. This distribution represented a range reduction of greater than 95%. Reproduction was documented in the late 1990s from only French Creek and the Detroit River.

The U. S. Fish and Wildlife Service considers this species to be endangered in Indiana, Kentucky, Michigan, Ohio, Pennsylvania, West Virginia.

Threats

The reduction in the riffleshell's range can be attributed to many factors. The primary factors, however, are impoundments, channelization, loss of riparian habitat, and the impacts of silt from poor land uses. Water pollution from municipalities, chemical

discharges, coal mines, and reservoir releases have also impacted the species. The invasion of the exotic zebra mussel (*Dreissena polymorpha*) poses another potential threat to this species. Zebra mussels in the Great Lakes have been found attached in large numbers to the shells of live and freshly dead native mussels, and zebra mussels have been implicated in the loss of entire mussel beds. The zebra mussel has recently been reported from the Ohio River system, including the Green River in Kentucky, but the extent of zebra mussel impacts on the basin's freshwater mussels are unknown.

Conservation and Recovery

To save the northern riffleshell, all existing state and federal legislation and regulations must be enforced. Management is needed to restore some of the species' habitat through repair of riparian habitat and control of nonpoint source pollution. Research is needed to identify the species' habitat requirements and fish host and to develop propagation and reintroduction techniques. The number of individuals needed to maintain a viable population should be determined. Also, more surveys are needed to better assess the condition of the existing populations and search for potential reintroduction sites.

Contacts

U. S. Fish and Wildlife Service
Regional Office, Division of Endangered Species
1 Federal Drive
BHW Federal Building
Fort Snelling, Minnesota 55111
Telephone: (612) 713-5360
http://midwest.fws.gov/

U. S. Fish and Wildlife Service
Regional Office, Division of Endangered Species
1875 Century Blvd., Suite 200
Atlanta, Georgia 30345
http://southeast.fws.gov/

U. S. Fish and Wildlife Service
Asheville Ecological Services Field Office
160 Zillicoa St.
Asheville, North Carolina 28801-1082
Telephone: (828) 258-3939
Fax: (828) 258-5330

U. S. Fish and Wildlife Service
West Virginia Ecological Services Field Office
P.O. Box 1278
Elkins, West Virginia 26241-1278
Telephone: (304) 636-6586
Fax: (304) 636-7824
http://www.fws.gov/r5fws/wv/wvfo.htm

References

Stansbery, D. H., K. Borror, and K. E. Newman. 1982. "Biological Abstracts of Selected Species of Unionid Mollusks Recovered from Ohio." Unpublished. Prepared for the Ohio Heritage Foundation, Ohio Department of Natural Resources.

U. S. Fish and Wildlife Service. 22 January 1993. "Determination of Endangered Species Status for the Northern Riffleshell Mussel (*Epioblasma turulosa rangiana*) and the Clubshell Mussel (*Pleurobema clava*)." *Federal Register* 58 (13): 5638-5642.

Tubercled Blossom Pearlymussel

Epioblasma torulosa torulosa

Status	Endangered
Listed	June 14, 1976
Family	Unionidae (Freshwater Mussel)
Description	Shell of medium size, either egg shaped or elliptical, and yellow or greenish with numerous green rays.
Habitat	Sand or gravel shoals in larger rivers.
Reproduction	Female stores sperm in gills; glochidia are released into streams after hatching.
Food	Filter-feeder.
Threats	Habitat loss; pollution; siltation.
Range	Indiana, Kentucky, Tennessee, West Virginia

Tubercled Blossom Pearlymussel, photograph. A. E. Spreitzer Photography. Reproduced by permission.

Description

The tubercled blossom pearlymussel (*Epioblasma torulosa torulosa*) is a medium-sized freshwater mussel, reaching about 3.6 in (9.1 cm) in shell length. The shell is irregularly egg shaped or elliptical, slightly sculptured, and corrugated with distinct growth lines. The outer surface is smooth and shiny; tawny, yellowish-green, or straw colored; and usually has numerous green rays. The inner shell surface is white to salmon-red. Females are generally larger than males and display a large, rounded marsupial swelling, which is often a darker green than the rest of the shell.

The tubercled blossom is a more inflated big-river form of the federally endangered green blossom pearlymussel (*E. t. gubernaculum*), a subspecies found in the headwater tributaries of the Tennessee River above Knoxville. The tubercled blossom was first described from the Ohio and Kentucky rivers as *Amblema torulosa* and later as *Dysnomia torulosa torulosa*.

Behavior

The life of mussels is complex, and reproduction often depends upon a stable habitat—unaltered stream conditions, clean water, and an undisturbed stream bottom. The cycle also depends upon the abundance of suitable fish hosts to complete the mussel's larval development.

To reproduce, males discharge sperm, which are dispersed by stream currents. In the process of feeding, females nearby or downstream take in sperm, which fertilizes eggs stored in their gills. The gills serve as brood pouches (marsupia), where the glochidia hatch and begin to develop. After a time, these glochidia are released into the stream. A few mussels have inner parts that resemble a tiny minnow and can be manipulated to lure host fish. When a fish gets close to the shell, the mussel expels its glochidia.

Glochidia have tiny bean- or spoon-shaped valves that attach to the gill filaments of host fish. Glochidia can only progress to the juvenile stage while attached to the fish's gills. Those that do not fortuitously encounter a host fish do not survive when released by the female mussel. They sink to the bottom and die.

When the juvenile has developed a shell and is large enough to survive on its own, it detaches from the host fish and falls to the stream bottom, beginning a long association with a single stretch of stream. Maturing mussels bury themselves in riffles and shoals with only the shell margins and feeding siphons exposed to the water. Some mussels live as long as 50 years or more.

The family Unionidae, which includes all of the freshwater mussels in the United States, is separated into two groups based on the length of time the glochidia remain in the female's marsupia. The eggs of the short-term (tachytictic) breeders are fertilized in the spring, and glochidia are released by late summer of the same year. Long-term (bradytictic) breeders hold developing glochidia in the brood pouch over winter and release them in the spring.

Freshwater mussels feed by siphoning phytoplankton and other plant matter from the water. Indigestible particles are expelled from the shell by reverse siphoning. Silt in the water can kill mussels by clogging their feeding siphons. There are no known interspecific differences in feeding among freshwater mussels. The glochidia are obligate parasites on the gills or fins of fish. Adult mussels are filter-feeders and consume particulate matter in the water column. Identifiable stomach contents almost invariably include desmids, diatoms, algae, protozoa, and zooplankton.

Most freshwater mussel species display seasonal variations in activity associated with water temperature and reproduction. Metabolic rate is, in part, positively correlated with temperature. Many ectothermic species have the capacity to adjust their metabolic rates in response to long-term changes in temperature. Thus, metabolic rates do not continue to rise as temperatures rise in the summer, and they do not continue to fall during the winter as temperatures decline.

Some freshwater mussels also show diurnal changes in metabolic rates that indicate a tendency toward nocturnal activity patterns. Mussels may move to the surface to feed at night and move deeper into the substrate during the day; this is one way to avoid predators that hunt by visual contact.

Freshwater mussels are nonmigratory.

Habitat

The tubercled blossom pearlymussel inhabited the larger rivers within its range, preferring to bury itself into sand and gravel shoals.

Distribution

This mussel was once fairly abundant and widespread throughout all the major rivers of the eastern United States and southern Ontario, Canada. These rivers included in particular the Tennessee, Cumberland, Ohio, and St. Lawrence.

One specimen, thought to be freshly dead, was collected in 1969 from the Kanawha River below Kanawha Falls in West Virginia, but no other recent collections have been made, and this subspecies may well be extinct. A General Accounting Office report released in December 1988 included this mussel among those species "believed to be extinct but not yet officially declared so."

Studies of the Kanawha River in 1982-83 found no further evidence of the tubercled blossom pearlymussel. A detailed scuba search below the Kanawha Falls turned up nothing, and scientists concluded that the species no longer occurred in the drainage.

Threats

Mussels have declined steadily in the major rivers because of increased turbidity and siltation triggered by deforestation and the spread of intensive agriculture throughout the East. The decline of the genus *Epioblasma* may have begun in earnest when settlers crossed the Appalachians to farm the rich Ohio and Tennessee river valleys.

More recently, major rivers have suffered from extensive chemical pollution caused by both agricultural and industrial runoff. Because mussels filter many gallons of water to extract food, pollutants build up in their tissues. The health of mussel populations in major rivers can be used as a general indicator of the health of the ecosystem.

Conservation and Recovery

Understandably, this mussel has been accorded a low priority in the allocation of research funds. If a viable population can be located, further recovery strategies will be designed and implemented.

Contacts

U.S. Fish and Wildlife Service
Regional Office, Division of Endangered Species
1 Federal Drive
BHW Federal Building
Fort Snelling, Minnesota 55111
Telephone: (612) 713-5360
http://midwest.fws.gov./

U. S. Fish and Wildlife Service
Regional Office, Division of Endangered Species
1875 Century Blvd., Suite 200
Atlanta, Georgia 30345
Telephone: (404) 679-4000
http://southeast.fws.gov/

U. S. Fish and Wildlife Service
Regional Office, Division of Endangered Species
300 Westgate Center Dr.
Hadley, Massachusetts 01035-9589
Telephone: (413) 253-8200
Fax: (413) 253-8308

References

Bogan, A., and P. Parmalee. 1983. "Tennessee's Rare Mollusks." In *Tennessee's Rare Wildlife, Final Report.* Tennessee Department of Conservation and Tennessee Heritage Program, University of Tennessee, Knoxville.

General Accounting Office. 1988. "Endangered Species: Management Improvements Could Enhance Recovery Program." GAO/ RCED-89-5. General Accounting Office, Washington, D.C.

Jenkinson, J.J. 1986. "Endangered or Threatened Aquatic Mollusks of the Tennessee River System." *Bulletin of the American Malacological Union* 2: 63-65.

U.S. Fish and Wildlife Service. 1985. "Recovery Plan for the Tubercled-Blossom Pearly Mussel, Turgid-Blossom Pearly Mussel, and Yellow-Blossom Pearly Mussel." U.S. Fish and Wildlife Service, Atlanta.

Turgid Blossom Pearlymussel

Epioblasma turgidula

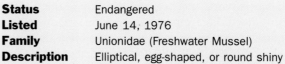

Status	Endangered
Listed	June 14, 1976
Family	Unionidae (Freshwater Mussel)
Description	Elliptical, egg-shaped, or round shiny yellow shell with irregular growth lines.
Habitat	Sand and gravel substrates in flowing water.
Reproduction	Female stores sperm in gills; glochidia (larvae) are released into streams after hatching.
Food	Filter-feeder.
Threats	Habitat loss; pollution; siltation.
Range	Alabama, Tennessee

Turgid Blossom Pearlymussel, photograph. A. E. Spreitzer Photography. Reproduced by permission.

Description

The turgid blossom pearlymussel (*Epioblasma turgidula*) is a small Cumberlandian species, seldom exceeding 1.6 in (4.1 cm) in shell length. The species is strongly dimorphic—males and females differ in shape and structure. Shells of the male tend to be more elliptical or oval, while females tend to be more rounded. Valves are inequilateral, solid, and slightly inflated. The outer shell is a shiny yellowish-green with numerous fine green rays over the entire surface. The shell surface is marked by irregular growth lines that are especially strong on females. The inner shell surface is bluish-white.

Male and female specimens were originally described as two separate species. The turgid blossom pearlymussel was previously classified as *Dysnomia turgidula*.

Behavior

The life of mussels is complex, and reproduction often depends upon a stable habitat—unaltered stream conditions, clean water, and an undisturbed stream bottom. The cycle also depends upon the abundance of suitable fish hosts to complete the mussel's larval development.

To reproduce, males discharge sperm, which are dispersed by stream currents. In the process of feeding, females nearby or downstream take in sperm, which fertilizes eggs stored in their gills. The gills serve as brood pouches (marsupia), where the glochidia hatch and begin to develop. After a time, these glochidia are released into the stream. A few mussels have inner parts that resemble a tiny minnow and can be manipulated to lure host fish. When a fish gets close to the shell, the mussel expels its glochidia.

Glochidia have tiny bean- or spoon-shaped valves that attach to the gill filaments of host fish. Glochidia can only progress to the juvenile stage while attached to the fish's gills. Those that do not fortuitously encounter a host fish do not survive when released by the female mussel. They sink to the bottom and die.

When the juvenile has developed a shell and is large enough to survive on its own, it detaches from the host fish and falls to the stream bottom, beginning a long association with a single stretch of stream. Maturing mussels bury themselves in riffles and shoals with only the shell margins and feeding siphons exposed to the water. Some mussels live as long as 50 years or more.

The family Unionidae, which includes all of the freshwater mussels in the United States, is separated into two groups based on the length of time the glochidia remain in the female's marsupia. The eggs of the short-term (tachytictic) breeders are fertilized in the spring, and glochidia are released by late summer of the same year. Long-term (bradytictic) breeders hold developing glochidia in the brood pouch over winter and release them in the spring.

Freshwater mussels feed by siphoning phytoplankton and other plant matter from the water. Indigestible particles are expelled from the shell by reverse siphoning. Silt in the water can kill mussels by clogging their feeding siphons.

There are no known interspecific differences in feeding among freshwater mussels. The glochidia are obligate parasites on the gills or fins of fish. Adult mussels are filter-feeders and consume particulate matter in the water column. Identifiable stomach contents almost invariably include desmids, diatoms, algae, protozoa, and zooplankton.

Most freshwater mussel species display seasonal variations in activity associated with water temperature and reproduction. Metabolic rate is, in part, positively correlated with temperature. Many ectothermic species have the capacity to adjust their metabolic rates in response to long-term changes in temperature. Thus, metabolic rates do not continue to rise as temperatures rise in the summer, and they do not continue to fall during the winter as temperatures decline.

Some freshwater mussels also show diurnal changes in metabolic rates that indicate a tendency toward nocturnal activity patterns. Mussels may move to the surface to feed at night and move deeper into the substrate during the day; this is one way to avoid predators that hunt by visual contact.

Freshwater mussels are nonmigratory.

Habitat

The turgid blossom pearlymussel buries itself in sand and gravel substrates of shallow, fast-flowing streams. Clear unpolluted water is required for healthy freshwater mussel populations.

Distribution

Cumberlandian mussels are endemic to the southern Appalachian Mountains and the Cumberland Plateau. This species was relatively widespread within this region and was also found in the Ozarks. It is documented from the Tennessee River and its tributaries, including Elk, Duck, Holston, Clinch, and Emory Rivers (in Tennessee) and Shoals and Bear Creeks (in Alabama). Large numbers were found in the Cumberland River and its tributaries. In the Ozark Mountains it occurred in Spring Creek, Black River, and White River (in Arkansas and Missouri).

The turgid blossom pearlymussel was last reported in the mid-1960s from the Duck River near Normandy, Tennessee. D.H. Stansbery and J.J. Jenkinson, the experts on Cumberlandian mussels, consider this species extinct. A General Accounting Office report released in December 1988 included this mussel among those species "believed to be extinct but not yet officially declared so."

Threats

The construction of dams and reservoirs by the Tennessee Valley Authority (TVA), the Aluminum Company of America, and the Army Corps of Engineers completely and abruptly changed the character of the Tennessee and Cumberland Rivers, endangering many freshwater mussels in the process. Since the 1930s, 51 dams have been constructed on the Tennessee and Cumberland Rivers for flood control, generation of hydroelectric power, and recreation.

Segments of these rivers that once supported healthy populations of mussels have been permanently inundated. In addition, altered water flows and random water releases have changed water temperatures, increased turbidity, and contributed to problems of siltation. Strip mining, coal washing, farming, and logging have all added silt and pollutants to the streams of the region. Turbid water and siltation clog the feeding apparatus of mussels and smother mussel beds.

Many fish species, including those that play host to mussel glochidia, have declined in numbers, making mussel reproduction problematic.

Conservation and Recovery

Recovery strategies for this subspecies cannot be developed until a viable breeding population is discovered. The Tennessee Wildlife Resources Agency, the Tennessee Heritage Program, and the TVA continue to support research into the status of mussels in the state. Mussel research in Alabama is promoted by the State Department of Conservation and Natural Resources.

Contact

U. S. Fish and Wildlife Service
Regional Office, Division of Endangered Species
1875 Century Blvd., Suite 200
Atlanta, Georgia 30345
Telephone: (404) 679-4000
http://southeast.fws.gov/

References

General Accounting Office. 1988. "Endangered Species: Management Improvements Could Enhance Recovery Program." GAO/ RCED-89-5. General Accounting Office, Washington, D.C.

Stansbery, D.H. 1971. "Rare and Endangered Mollusks in Eastern United States." In S.E. Jorgenson and R.E. Sharp, eds., *Proceedings of a Symposium on Rare and Endangered Mollusks (Naiades)*. U.S. Fish and Wildlife Service, Twin Cities.

U.S. Fish and Wildlife Service. 1985. "Recovery Plan for the Tubercled-Blossom Pearly Mussel, Turgid-Blossom Pearly Mussel, and Yellow-Blossom Pearly Mussel." U.S. Fish and Wildlife Service, Atlanta.

Shiny Pigtoe Pearlymussel

Fusconaia cor

Status	Endangered
Listed	June 14, 1976
Family	Unionidae (Freshwater Mussel)
Description	Smooth, shiny, dull brown shell with dark green or black rays.
Habitat	Shoals in streams and rivers.
Reproduction	Breeds in spring and releases glochidia by mid- to late summer of the same year.
Food	Parasitic on the gills of fish.
Threats	Loss of habitat, siltation, pollution
Range	Alabama, Tennessee, Virginia

Shiny Pigtoe Pearlymussel, photograph. A. E. Spreitzer Photography. Reproduced by permission.

Description

The shiny pigtoe pearlymussel—*Fusconaia cor* or *F. edgariana*—is about 2.5 in (6.4 cm) long with a very smooth and shiny outer covering (periostracum). The shell displays prominent dark green to black rays on a yellow to brown background. Young specimens generally have bold black or green ray patterns; older mussels are dull brown with indistinct rays fading toward the valve margins. Valves are triangular with concentric growth marks. The inner shell surface is white.

Behavior

The shiny pigtoe is a short-term breeder, breeding in spring and releasing glochidia (larvae) by mid- to late summer of the same year. The glochidia of the shiny pigtoe are horseshoe shaped and parasitic on the gills of fish. Some of the fish hosts are the whitetail shiner, common shiner, the warpaint shiner, and the telescope shiner.

For more on the reproduction and diet of freshwater mussels, see the Upland Combshell (*Epioblasma metastriata*) entry.

Habitat

The shiny pigtoe is found along fords and in shoals of clear, moderate- to fast-flowing streams and rivers with stable substrates. It is not found in deeper pools or reservoirs.

Distribution

The shiny pigtoe was once found in Alabama in the Elk, Flint, and Paint Rock Rivers, and in the Clinch River from Russell County, Virginia, downstream to Anderson County, Tennessee. It was found in the Powell River from Lytton Mill in Lee County, Virginia, downstream to Claiborne County, Tennessee. It was also found in the Holston River in Washington County, Virginia, downstream to Hawkins County, Tennessee, and in the Tennessee River from Knoxville downstream for 20 mi (32 km).

The shiny pigtoe is now found in the North Fork Holston River in Virginia from Broadford to Saltville. In the Clinch River, it is found in scattered locations from Nash Ford in Virginia to Kyles Ford, Tennessee, with smaller populations in the Copper Creek tributary. In the Powell River it occurs sporadically from Flanary's Ford, Virginia, downstream to Combs, Tennessee. In the Elk River it inhabits scattered localities near Fayetteville, Tennessee. A few populations occur in the Paint Rock River near Princeton, Alabama. As of 2000, no recent population figures were available.

Threats

Like other freshwater mussels the shiny pigtoe has suffered from the industrialization of its range and the massive Tennessee Valley Authority projects that have dammed and redirected all of the major rivers and streams within its historic range. In addition, runoff from strip mining, coal washing, herbicides, pesticides, and industrial pollutants—particularly heavy metals—has severely degraded water quality throughout the mussel's range.

Conservation and Recovery

It is unlikely that any major portion of the shiny pigtoe's historic habitat will ever be restored. Therefore, recovery strategies are focused on preserving habitat in the areas where the mussel can still be found. Some portions of the range, including the Paint Rock River, may be eligible for "scenic river" status under the National Wild and Scenic Rivers Act, a designation that would provide additional protection for the species.

Contacts

U. S. Fish and Wildlife Service
Regional Office, Division of Endangered Species
1875 Century Blvd., Suite 200
Atlanta, Georgia 30345
http://southeast.fws.gov/

U. S. Fish and Wildlife Service
Regional Office, Division of Endangered Species
300 Westgate Center Dr.
Hadley, Massachusetts 01035-9589
Telephone: (413) 253-8200
Fax: (413) 253-8308
http://northeast.fws.gov/

References

Bogan, A. E., and P. W. Parmalee. 1983. *Tennessee's Rare Wildlife: The Mollusks.* Tennessee Wildlife Resources Agency, University of Tennessee Press, Knoxville.

Burch, J. B. 1975. *Freshwater Unionacean Clams (Mollusca: Pelecypoda) of North America.* Malacological Publications, Hamburg, Mich.

U. S. Fish and Wildlife Service. 1983. "Recovery Plan: Shiny Pigtoe Pearly Mussel, *Fusconaia edgariana.*" U. S. Fish and Wildlife Service, Atlanta.

Fine-rayed Pigtoe Pearlymussel

Fusconaia cuneolus

Status	Endangered
Listed	June 14, 1976
Family	Unionidae (Freshwater Mussel)
Description	Medium-sized shell, yellow-green to light brown with numerous fine green rays.
Habitat	Sand and gravel shoals of streams and rivers.
Reproduction	Reproduces in the spring.
Food	Filter-feeder.
Threats	Dams, siltation, pollution.
Range	Alabama, Tennessee, Virginia

Fine-rayed Pigtoe Pearlymussel, photograph. A. E. Spreitzer Photography. Reproduced by permission.

Description

The fine-rayed pigtoe pearlymussel, *Fusconaia cuneolus*, is of medium size, up to 2.5 in (6.4 cm) in length. This Cumberlandian species is distinguished by the many fine green rays that radiate over the yellowish green to light brown background of its ovoid shell. The hinged end of the shell is rounded, while the front margin is straight. The shell surface has a smooth, satiny appearance and is indistinctly patterned with growth lines. The inner shell surface is white.

Behavior

This species is a short-term breeder, reproducing in the spring (tachytictic). For more about the reproduction and diet of freshwater mussels, see the Upland Combshell (*Epioblasma metastriata*) entry.

Habitat

The fine-rayed pigtoe occupies shallow riffles and shoals of freshwater streams and rivers. It buries itself in the stream bottom in gravel or compacted sand but is rarely found in pools. It displays a higher tolerance for muddy bottoms than most other freshwater mussels.

Distribution

Endemic to the southern Appalachian Mountains, the fine-rayed pigtoe pearly mussel was first described in 1840 from the Holston River, where it occurred in the river's North Fork in Washington County, Virginia, downstream to Grainger County, Tennessee. It was subsequently documented in Big Moccasin Creek in Scott County, Virginia; the Powell River from Lee County, Virginia, downstream to Union County, Tennessee; Clinch Creek, Emory River, and Popular Creek from Clinchport, Virginia, downstream to Roane County, Tennessee; and in the Clinch River from Tazewell County, Virginia, downstream to the Norris Reservoir in Claiborne County, Tennessee.

In the early twentieth century it was discovered in the Tennessee River and its smaller tributaries at and below Knoxville. It is believed that the mussel has been extirpated from former locations in the Little and Sequatchie Rivers.

Although this species was thought to have disappeared from its original collection site in the Holston River, four freshly dead specimens were collected along the river in 1982 at Cloud Ford, Tennessee. Industrial and chemical pollution from upstream at Saltville, Virginia, has severely degraded the water quality there. Live specimens have yet to be found but may indeed exist. Recent surveys in other upper Tennessee River tributaries, such as the Nolichucky, French Broad, Flint, and Buffalo Rivers, failed to locate specimens.

From 1975 to 1981, surveys of the Powell River located populations at Buchanan Ford and McDowell Shoal in Tennessee, and at Fletcher Ford in Virginia. Water quality in this river has also deteriorated significantly due to strip mining, coal-washing runoff, and discharge of municipal wastes.

In the late twentieth century, this mussel was found at nearly 30 sites in the Clinch River and its smaller tributaries between Cedar Bluff, Virginia, and Kelly Branch, Tennessee. Since 1970, the fine-rayed pigtoe has been collected from the Elk and Paint Rock Rivers, which are tributaries of the Tennessee River above Muscle Shols, Alabama. The mussel's former range and habitat suggests that additional populations may be located on other tributary streams of the Tennessee River in Tennessee and Alabama.

Threats

Construction of dams and multi-purpose reservoirs across the former range of the fine-rayed pigtoe have altered the free-flowing character of these rivers. Such impoundments produce siltation, fluctuating water temperatures, changes in water acidity, and lowered oxygen content. Impoundments also fragment the range of the species into isolated populations, which are then unable to interbreed.

Increased stream turbidity, caused by soil erosion and industrial runoff, reduces light penetration, which affects the growth of aquatic vegetation and decreases the population of fish hosts. Suspended solids can be fatal to mussels. Dead and dying mussels are often found with silt clogging their gills. Mussels are very susceptible to agricultural and industrial pollutants, particularly heavy metals, which become concentrated in their tissues.

Conservation and Recovery

The fairly widespread distribution of the fine-rayed pigtoe affords it some protection against early extinction, if federal, state, and local agencies act quickly to reduce habitat degradation. The U. S. Fish and Wildlife Service recovery plan for this species recommends further systematic surveys to locate new populations and a program to reestablish populations in areas of suitable habitat. Additionally, better enforcement of state and federal environmental regulations is needed to prevent further degradation of water quality. Creation of mussel sanctuaries in the Virginia headwaters, similar to those on the Clinch and Powell Rivers in Tennessee, would be highly beneficial.

Contacts

U. S. Fish and Wildlife Service
Regional Office, Division of Endangered Species
1875 Century Blvd., Suite 200
Atlanta, Georgia 30345
http://southeast.fws.gov/

U. S. Fish and Wildlife Service
Regional Office, Division of Endangered Species
300 Westgate Center Dr.
Hadley, Massachusetts 01035-9589
Telephone: (413) 253-8200
Fax: (413) 253-8308
http://northeast.fws.gov/

References

Bogan, A. E., and P. W. Parmalee. 1983. *Tennessee's Rare Wildlife: The Mollusks.* Tennessee Wildlife Resources Agency, Tennessee Department of Conservation, and Tennessee Natural Heritage Program, University of Tennessee Press, Knoxville.

Carter, L. J. 1977. "Chemical Plants Leave Unexpected Legacy in Two Virginia Rivers." *Science* 198: 1015-1020.

Dennis, S. D. 1981. "Mussel Fauna of the Powell River, Tennessee and Virginia." *Sterkiana* 71: 1-7.

French, John R. P., III. November, 1990. "The Exotic Zebra Mussel: A New Threat to Endangered Freshwater Mussels." *Endangered Species Technical Bulletin* 15 (11).

Imlay, M. J. 1982. "Use of Shells of Freshwater Mussels in Monitoring Heavy Metals and Environmental Stresses: A Review." *Malacology Review* 15: 1-14.

U. S. Fish and Wildlife Service. 1984. "Fine-Rayed Pigtoe Pearly Mussel Recovery Plan." U. S. Fish and Wildlife Service, Atlanta.

Cracking Pearlymussel

Hemistena lata

Status	Endangered
Listed	September 28, 1989
Family	Unionidae (Freshwater Mussel)
Description	Greenish brown to brown elongated shell, with dark green rays and a pale blue to purple interior.
Habitat	Riffles on medium-sized streams.
Reproduction	Female stores sperm in gills; glochidia are released into the stream after hatching.
Food	Filter-feeder.
Threats	Dam construction, water pollution.
Range	Kentucky, Tennessee, Virginia

Cracking Pearlymussel, photograph. U. S. Fish and Wildlife Service. Reproduced by permission.

Description

The cracking pearlymussel is medium-sized, with a thin, elongated shell. The outer surface is greenish brown to brown, usually with broken, dark green rays. The interior is pale blue to purple. The species has also been known as *Lastena lata*.

Behavior

See the Upland Combshell (*Epioblasma metastriata*) entry.

Habitat

The cracking pearlymussel inhabits medium-sized streams where it buries itself in gravel riffles. Freshwater mussels feed by filtering food particles from the water Their reproductive life cycle involves a stage when the mussel larvae attach to the gills of host fish species.

Distribution

The cracking pearlymussel was once widely distributed in the Ohio, Cumberland, and Tennessee River systems. In the Ohio River Basin it was found from Ohio downstream to Illinois. In Indiana and Illinois it was known from the White, Wabash, and Tippecanoe Rivers. In Kentucky the species inhabited the upper Cumberland, Big South Fork, Green, and Kentucky Rivers. In Tennessee, it was known from the Tennessee, Cumberland, Powell, Clinch, Holston, Elk, Duck, and Buffalo Rivers. It was found in Virginia in the Powell, Clinch, and Holston Rivers and in Alabama in the Tennessee River.

Only three populations of the cracking pearlymussel are known to survive: in the Clinch River, Hancock County, Tennessee, and Scott County, Virginia; in the Powell River, Hancock County, Tennessee, and Lee County, Virginia; and in the Elk River, Lincoln County, Tennessee. It is possible that small populations persist in the Green River, Hart and Edmonson counties, Kentucky, as well as in the Tennessee River below Pickwick Dam.

In 1979, the Tennessee Valley Authority (TVA) sampled 78 sites over almost 100 miles of the Powell River and found the cracking pearly mussel at only three sites. A 1980 survey of 108 sites over 172 miles of the Elk River found the species at only two sites.

The largest population of this mussel is in the Clinch River. A TVA survey of 141 sites over 174 miles in 1978 and 1983 found the species at 16 sites.

No live cracking pearlymussels have been taken from the Green or Tennessee Rivers in recent years, but there remains suitable habitat in each river and shells have been found, leading researchers to believe that small populations persist.

Threats

The cracking pearly mussel has declined over its historic range because of the alteration and pollution of its streambed habitat. The extensive series of dams constructed in the area by TVA has altered much of the original aquatic environment inhabited by freshwater mussels. The dam reservoirs convert stream environments into lakes, producing a corresponding change in the aquatic life. In addition, the water quality of the Powell River and, to a lesser extent, the Clinch River has been degraded by pollution associated with coal mining. In the past, the Clinch River has suffered large fish and mussel kills from toxic discharges from a power plant. Oil and gas production, cold water discharges from reservoirs, channel maintenance, and gravel dredging are other activities that have contributed to the decline of freshwater mussels.

Conservation and Recovery

The Fish and Wildlife Service published a Recovery Plan for the cracking pearlymussel in 1991.

The species is only known to survive at three sites, the largest of which is in the Clinch River. Conservation of this endangered mollusk requires that its critical habitat is strictly protected from potential impoundment, other disturbances (such as channel dredging), and pollution associated with coal mining, the operation of dams, and land-use practices causing siltation and inputs of nutrients and other chemicals. The known populations of the cracking pearlymussel must be monitored, additional populations searched for, and research undertaken into its basic biology and ecological requirements for breeding.

Contact

Asheville Field Office
U.S. Fish and Wildlife Service
160 Zillicoa Street
Asheville, North Carolina 28801

References

Ahlstedt, S. A. 1986. "Cumberland Mollusk Conservation Program Activity 1: Mussel Distribution Surveys." Tennessee Valley Authority, Norris, Tennessee.

Ahlstedt, S. A., and J. J. Jenkinson. 1987. "A Mussel Die-off in the Powell River, Virginia and Tennessee, in 1983." In *Proceedings of the Workshop on Die-offs of Freshwater Mussels in the United States, June 23-25, 1986*, edited by Richard Neves. Davenport, Iowa.

Bates, J. M., and S. D. Dennis. 1985. "Mussel Resource Survey—State of Tennessee." Tennessee Wildlife Resources Agency Technical Report No. 85-3.

U.S. Fish and Wildlife Service. 1991. "Cracking Pearlymussel (*Hemistena* [= *Lastena*] *lata*) Recovery Plan." Atlanta, Georgia.

Pink Mucket Pearlymussel

Lampsilis abrupta

Status	Endangered
Listed	June 14, 1976
Family	Unionidae (Freshwater Mussel)
Description	Large yellow to brown elliptical shell with wide greenish rays.
Habitat	Major rivers and tributaries.
Reproduction	Sperm released into water, taken in by female to fertilize larvae over the winter.
Food	Filter feeder.
Threats	Habitat decline, siltation.
Range	Alabama, Arkansas, Illinois, Indiana, Kentucky, Louisiana, Missouri, Ohio, Pennsylvania, Tennessee, Virginia, West Virginia

Pink Mucket Pearlymussel, photograph by Craig W. Stihler. Reproduced by permission.

Description

The pink mucket pearlymussel, *Lampsilis abrupta*, features an elliptical to quadrangular shell that attains a length of 4 in (10 cm), a width of 2.4 in (6 cm), and a thickness of 3 in (8 cm). The yellow to brown surface of the shell is smooth except for relatively dark, concentric growth marks and wide greenish rays, which are more prominent in juveniles. The shell is glossy in younger specimens and dull in older individuals. The valves are thick, heavy, and unsculptured.

Behavior

The pink mucket is a long-term breeder (bradytictic). Males release sperm into the water in late summer or autumn. Females take in the sperm then brood fertilized larvae (glochidia) over winter in gill pouches and release them the following spring.

For more on the behavior and diet of freshwater mussels, see the Upland Combshell (*Epioblasma metastriata*) entry.

Habitat

The pink mucket pearlymussel inhabits shallow riffles and shoals of major rivers and tributaries. It is found in rubble, gravel, or sand substrates that have been swept free of silt by the current.

Distribution

This pearlymussel is considered endemic to the Interior Basin and was found primarily in the Tennessee, Cumberland, and Ohio River drainages, although specimens have been collected from the Missouri, Black, and Mississippi Rivers. This mussel has been documented from 25 rivers and tributaries in 11 states—West Virginia, Pennsylvania, Ohio, Illinois, Indiana, Kentucky, Tennessee, Alabama,

Arkansas, Missouri, and Iowa. Populations appear to have been extirpated from the northern portion of the range (Ohio, Indiana, and Illinois).

As of 1991, the pink mucket pearlymussel was known from 17 rivers and tributaries, with the greatest concentrations in the Tennessee, Cumberland, Osage, and Meramec Rivers. Although it is found over a wide geographic area, this mussel was never collected in large numbers and has always been considered uncommon.

Populations occur in the Tennessee River below Pickwick, Wilson, Guntersville, and Watts Bar Dams (Tennessee and Alabama); above New Hope on Paint Rock River (Alabama); in the Clinch River below Melton Hill Dam (Tennessee); in the Cumberland River at Bartletts Bar, Cotton Bar, Rome Island, and Carters Island (Kentucky and Tennessee); in the Green River (Butler County, Kentucky); and in the Kanawha River below Kanawha Falls (West Virginia). Populations west of the Mississippi River are found in the Osage River below Bagnell Dam, in Missouri; in several other Missouri rivers: the Meramec, Big, Black, Little Black, and Gasconade; and in Current and Spring Rivers (Arkansas). In 1990 authorities identified a new population site in the Ohio River, bordering West Virginia; another new population was discovered in 1991 in a reach of the lower Elk River near Blue Creek (West Virginia), which is part of the species' historic range.

Threats

Possibly the greatest single factor in the decline of the pink mucket pearlymussel has been the construction of dams and reservoirs on the major rivers for flood control, navigation, hydroelectric power production, and recreation. Impounding the natural river flow eliminates those mussels and fishes that are unable to adapt to reduced and sporadic flows, altered water temperatures, and seasonal oxygen deficiencies. Although a few dams have actually created downstream habitat for the pink mucket, in most cases this has come at the expense of inundating large stretches of upstream habitat.

Heavy loads of silt have been introduced into most watersheds from strip mining and coal washing, dredging, and intensive logging. Deforestation and poor agricultural practices are probably responsible for the loss of many native mussel populations, particularly in the midwestern states.

Siltation smothers mussel beds or decreases the abundance of fish hosts, which are necessary to complete the mussel's life cycle.

Conservation and Recovery

The states of Tennessee and Alabama have designated portions of the Tennessee and Cumberland Rivers as mussel sanctuaries. Because of these protections the pink mucket pearly mussel is again reproducing well in localized areas. In the late twentieth century, live specimens were discovered in the upper Ohio River, where this species had not been collected for 75 years. Scientists took this discovery as evidence of improving water quality in this region.

Contacts

U. S. Fish and Wildlife Service
Regional Office, Division of Endangered Species
1 Federal Drive
BHW Federal Building
Fort Snelling, Minnesota 55111
Telephone: (612) 713-5360
http://midwest.fws.gov/

U. S. Fish and Wildlife Service
Regional Office, Division of Endangered Species
1875 Century Blvd., Suite 200
Atlanta, Georgia 30345
http://southeast.fws.gov/

U. S. Fish and Wildlife Service
Regional Office, Division of Endangered Species
300 Westgate Center Dr.
Hadley, Massachusetts 01035-9589
Telephone: (413) 253-8200
Fax: (413) 253-8308
http://northeast.fws.gov/

References

Fuller, S. 1974. "Clams and Mussels." In *Pollution Ecology of Freshwater Invertebrates,* edited by Hart and Fuller. Academic Press, New York.

Isom, B. G. 1969. "The Mussel Resources of the Tennessee River." *Malacologia* 7 (2-3): 397-425.

U. S. Fish and Wildlife Service. 1985. "Recovery Plan for the Pink Mucket Pearly Mussel." U. S. Fish and Wildlife Service, Atlanta.

Fine-lined Pocketbook

Lampsilis altilis

Status	Threatened
Listed	March 17, 1993
Family	Unionidae (Freshwater Mussel)
Description	Medium-size mussel with a yellow-brown to blackish shell with fine rays.
Habitat	Gravel riffles in streams.
Reproduction	Female stores sperm in gills; glochidia are released into the stream after hatching.
Food	Filter-feeder.
Threats	Impoundments, gravel and mining, water pollution.
Range	Alabama, Georgia, Tennessee

Description

The fine-lined pocketbook, *Lampsilis altilis*, is a medium-sized mussel seldom more than 4 in (10 cm) in length. The shell is subovate. The ventral margin of the shell is angled posteriorly in females, resulting in a pointed posterior margin. The periostracum is yellow-brown to blackish and has fine rays on the posterior half. The nacre (inner shell surface) is white, becoming iridescent posteriorly.

Behavior

See the Upland Combshell (*Epioblasma metastriata*) entry.

Habitat

The fine-lined pocketbook inhabits high-quality lotic habitats with stable gravel and sandy-gravel substrates. This species is generally found in small river and creek habitats. Little else is known about the habitat requirements of this species.

The habitat of the glochidia is initially in the gills of the female, then in the water column, and finally attached to a suitable host fish. Habitat associations or requirements for the juvenile stage are unknown.

Distribution

This species' historic range included the Tombigbee River (Sipsey and Buttahatchee Rivers); Black Warrior River and tributaries (Sipsey Fork, Brushy and Capsey Creeks); Cahaba River and tributaries (Little Cahaba and Buck Creeks); Alabama River and a tributary, Tatum Creek; Tallapoosa River drainage (Chewacla and Opintlocco Creeks); and the Coosa River and tributaries (Choccolocco and Talladega Creeks).

The fine-lined pocketbook is currently limited to the headwaters of the Sipsey Fork of the Black Warrior River drainage; Alabama River drainage (Tatum Creek); Cahaba River drainage (Little Cahaba River); Coosa River drainage (Conasauga River); and the Tallapoosa River drainage (Chewacla and Opintlocco Creeks). The fine-lined pocketbook was last collected from the Tombigbee River drainage in the early twentieth century. Specimens were collected in the Black Warrior River tributaries in 1985; no specimens were located in a 1990 survey but localized populations were found in Sipsey Fork tributaries and the North River in 1992. The fine-lined pocketbook was listed as abundant in the Cahaba River drainage in 1973; a specimen was collected in 1979 and two live specimens were collected in 1986 but a 1991 survey failed to locate this mus-

Fine-lined Pocketbook, photograph. A. E. Spreitzer Photography. Reproduced by permission.

sel. Collections from the Alabama River drainage were last recorded in 1981. Specimens from the Coosa and Tallapoosa River drainages were last taken in 1991. This species may have been eliminated from most river habitats throughout its range, except the Coosa and Conasauga Rivers.

Threats

Habitat modification, sedimentation, and water quality degradation represent the major threats to this species. These freshwater mussels do not tolerate impoundments. More than 1,000 mi (1,609 km) of large and small river habitat in the Mobile River drainage has been impounded for navigation, flood control, water supply, and/or hydroelectric production purposes. During the construction and dredging of impoundments, some riverine mussels are killed. Additionally, impoundments lead to the accumulation of sediments that can suffocate mussels, a reduction in food and oxygen due to the reduction in water flow, and the local extirpation of

host fish. Other forms of habitat modification such as channelization, channel clearing and desnagging, and gravel mining result in streambed scour and erosion, increased turbidity, reduction of groundwater levels, sedimentation, and changes in the aquatic community structure. Sedimentation may cause direct mortality by deposition and suffocation and eliminate or reduce recruitment of juvenile mussels. Suspended sediments can also interfere with feeding. Activities that historically caused sedimentation of streams and rivers in the drainages where this mussel occurs include channel modification, agriculture, forestry, mining, and industrial and residential development.

Other types of water quality degradation from both point and nonpoint sources affect this species. Stream discharge from these sources may result in decreased dissolved oxygen concentration, increased acidity and conductivity, and other changes in water chemistry that may impact the mussels and/or their fish hosts. Point sources of water quality degradation include municipal and industrial effluents, and coalbed methane-produced water discharge. Nonpoint sources include runoff from cultivated fields, pastures, private wastewater effluents, agricultural feedlots and poultry houses, active and abandoned coal mine sites, and highway and road drainages.

About 230 mi (370 km) of the Coosa River have been impounded for hydropower by a series of six dams. Water quality degradation caused by textile and carpet mill wastes led to the loss of several known mussel communities in several streams of this river system.

Water quality degradation is a major problem in the Cahaba River system. There are 10 municipal wastewater treatment plants, 35 surface mining areas, one coalbed methane operation, and 67 other permitted discharges in this river system. Siltation from surface mining, road construction, and oil and gas development is also a problem.

Conservation and Recovery

Actions needed for the recovery of freshwater mussels include: (1) Conduct population and habitat surveys to determine the status and range of the species. (2) Determine specific threats to the species and minimize or eliminate these threats. (3) Identify essential habitat areas in need of protection. Make use of land agreements, mussel sanctuaries, scenic river status, and land acquisition. (4) Introduce individuals back into the historic range, as it is unlikely that the species will recover unless new populations are established. Methods to accomplish

this might include introduction of adult/juvenile mussels, glochidia-infected host fish, and artificially cultured individuals. (5) Control the incidental or illegal take of mussels by commercial and noncommercial collecting.

Contacts

U. S. Fish and Wildlife Service
Regional Office, Division of Endangered Species
1875 Century Blvd., Suite 200
Atlanta, Georgia 30345
http://southeast.fws.gov/

U. S. Fi0sh and Wildlife Service
Daphne Ecological Services Field Office
P.O. Box 1190
Daphne, Alabama 36526-1190
Telephone: (334) 441-5181
Fax: (334) 441-6222

U. S. Fish and Wildlife Service
Cookeville Ecological Services Field Office
446 Neal Street
Cookeville, Tennessee 38501-4027
Telephone: (931) 528-6481
Fax: (931) 528-7075

Reference

U. S. Fish and Wildlife Service. 17 March 1993. "Determination of Endangered or Threatened Status for Eight Freshwater Mussels and Threatened Status for Three Freshwater Mussels in the Mobile River Drainage." *Federal Register* 58 (50): 14330-14340.

Higgins Eye Pearlymussel

Lampsilis higginsii

Status	Endangered
Listed	June 14, 1976
Family	Unionidae (Freshwater mussel)
Description	Tan or brown shell with fine black rays.
Habitat	Major rivers and tributaries.
Food	Filter feeder.
Reproduction	Fertilized larvae are released in the spring.
Threats	Dam construction, dredging, siltation, pollution.
Range	Illinois, Iowa, Minnesota, Missouri, Wisconsin

Description

The Higgins eye pearlymussel (*Lampsilis higginsii*) averages 2.4 in (6.1 cm) in length, with females slightly smaller than males. Fine black rays are present along the growth lines against a background shell of tan to brown.

Behavior

The Higgins eye is a long-term breeder, holding fertilized glochidia (larvae) over winter and releasing them in spring. The larval host fish is thought to be the sauger or freshwater drum. Females reach sexual maturity by their third year.

Habitat

This species inhabits major rivers and tributaries in depths of up to 15 ft (4.6 m). It has been found on mud-gravel bottoms in areas of swift current.

Distribution

The Higgins eye is endemic to the Mississippi River and its major tributaries. It was found in the mainstream of the Mississippi River from north of St. Louis, Missouri, to the Twin Cities, Minnesota. Population centers have been documented near Prescott, Minnesota; La Crosse and Prairie du Chien, Wisconsin; and Muscatine and Davenport, Iowa.

Populations were found in the Illinois River from Mason County to the confluence of the Mississippi; in the Sangamon River near Chandlerville, Illinois; in the St. Croix River near Hudson, Wisconsin; in the Wapsipinicon River near Dixon, Iowa; in the Cedar River near Cedar Bluff, Iowa; and in the Iowa River near Gladwin, Iowa.

Although widely distributed, this mussel occurred in discrete localities and was never considered numerous. In the late 1970s and early 1980s the Mississippi River was heavily surveyed for occurrences of the Higgins eye. Scattered populations were found to survive in sections of river near La Crosse, Wisconsin; from the Minnesota state line south to Prairie du Chien, Wisconsin; from Clayton downstream to Dubuque, Iowa; and from Clinton south to West Burlington, Iowa. Except for a remnant population near the confluence of the Missouri River, population centers south of West Burlington in the mainstream appear to have been largely extirpated. The St. Croix River still supports several populations upstream from Hudson (St. Croix County), Wisconsin.

Biologists estimate that the Higgins eye has been eliminated from nearly 55% of its historic range.

Higgins Eye Pearlymussel, photograph. U. S. Fish and Wildlife Service. Reproduced by permission.

Threats

Construction of major dams for flood control and electricity generation have created conditions along portions of the upper Mississippi River that are no longer conducive to the survival of the Higgins eye. River impoundments have inundated habitat upstream and contributed to erratic water flows, altered water temperatures, and increased siltation downstream. Degradation of water quality caused by municipal, industrial, and agricultural effluents has also contributed to this mussel's decline.

A major research study on the mussel, completed in 1989, found that habitat characteristics of adult Higgins eye mussels do not vary noticeably from those of many common species of mussels in the upper Mississippi River. Adult Higgins eye mussels were found in a wide range of main channel border habitats with various current velocities and sediment types. However, the mussel was most common at sites where summer currents ranged from 0.5-0.7 ft per second (15-21.3 cm per second) and where

there were medium-fine to fine sand substrates. These are common habitats in the main channel border area throughout much of the upper Mississippi River. Therefore, it appears unlikely that a lack of suitable hosts or habitat is responsible for the observed sparse distribution of this species. How host fish distribution relates to the distribution of the Higgins eye is still unknown, but it may be that there is an insufficient overlap of the range of the mussel and its needed hosts. This hypothesis remains untested and is difficult to study directly in the large Mississippi River system, but it may be supported by the abundance of the pocketbook mussel, which has similar hosts but prefers coarser substrates. It is also possible that habitat requirements for juveniles may be limiting factors for many species.

Conservation and Recovery

Seven sites have been designated as habitat essential to the survival of the Higgins eye pearlymussel. These are 1) the St. Croix River above Hudson, Wisconsin; 2-4) the Mississippi River at Whiskey Rock, Prairie du Chien, and McMillan Island, Wisconsin; 5) Harpers Slough, Iowa; and 6-7) Cordova and Arsenal Island, Illinois.

Relocation of mussels to existing mussel beds not currently populated with Higgins eye is recommended in the U. S. Fish and Wildlife Service Recovery Plan for this species. Research is ongoing to determine practical methods of propagation and reintroduction.

Contact

U.S. Fish and Wildlife Service
Regional Office, Division of Endangered Species
1 Federal Drive
BHW Federal Building,
Fort Snelling, Minnesota 55111
Telephone: (612) 713-5360
http://midwest.fws.gov/

References

Havlik, M. E. "The Historic and Present Distribution of the Endangered Mollusk *Lampsilis higginsii* (Lea, 1857)." *Bulletin of the American Malacological Union* (1980): 19-22.

"Recovery Plan for the Higgins Eye Pearly Mussel." 1982. U. S. Fish and Wildlife Service, Twin Cities, Minnesota.

"Relocation of Freshwater Mussels in Sylvan Slough of the Mississippi River near Moline, Illinois." 1981. Shappert Engineers/Ecological Analysts, Belvidere and Northbrook, Illinois.

"Survey of Freshwater Mussels at Selected Sites in Pools 11 through 24 of the Mississippi River." 1981. Ecological Analysts, Northbrook, Illinois.

Orangenacre Mucket

Lampsilis perovalis

Status	Threatened
Listed	March 17, 1993
Family	Unionidae (Freshwater Mussel)
Description	Medium-sized mussel with an oval, moderately thick, inflated, yellow to dark reddish shell that may or may not have green rays.
Habitat	Gravel riffles in streams.
Reproduction	Female stores sperm in gills; glochidia (larvae) are released into streams after hatching.
Food	Filter-feeder.
Threats	Impoundments; gravel mining; water pollution.
Range	Alabama, Mississippi

Orangenacre Mucket, photograph. A. E. Spreitzer Photography. Reproduced by permission.

Description

The orangenacre mucket (*Lampsilis perovalis*) is a medium-sized mussel 2-3.6 in (5.1-9.1 cm) in length. Its shell is oval, moderately thick, and inflated. The posterior margin of the shell of mature females is obliquely truncate. The nacre (inner shell) is usually rose-colored, pink, or occasionally white. The periostracum (outer shell) varies from yellow to dark reddish-brown and may or may not have green rays.

Behavior

The life of mussels is complex, and reproduction often depends upon a stable habitat—unaltered stream conditions, clean water, and an undisturbed stream bottom. The cycle also depends upon the abundance of suitable fish hosts to complete the mussel's larval development. To reproduce, males discharge sperm, which are dispersed by stream currents. In the process of feeding, females nearby or downstream take in sperm, which fertilizes eggs stored in their gills. The gills serve as brood pouches (marsupia), where the glochidia hatch and begin to develop. After a time, these glochidia are released into the stream. A few mussels have inner parts that resemble a tiny minnow and can be manipulated to lure host fish. When a fish gets close to the shell, the mussel expels its glochidia.

Glochidia have tiny bean- or spoon-shaped valves that attach to the gill filaments of host fish. Glochidia can only progress to the juvenile stage while attached to the fish's gills. Those that do not fortuitously encounter a host fish do not survive when released by the female mussel. They sink to the bottom and die.

When the juvenile has developed a shell and is large enough to survive on its own, it detaches from the host fish and falls to the stream bottom, beginning a long association with a single stretch of stream. Maturing mussels bury themselves in riffles and shoals with only the shell margins and feeding siphons exposed to the water. Some mussels live as long as 50 years or more.

The family Unionidae, which includes all of the freshwater mussels in the United States, is separated into two groups based on the length of time the glochidia remain in the female's marsupia. The eggs of the short-term (tachytictic) breeders are fertilized in the spring, and glochidia are released by late summer of the same year. Long-term (bradytictic) breeders hold developing glochidia in the brood pouch over winter and release them in the spring.

Freshwater mussels feed by siphoning phytoplankton and other plant matter from the water. Indigestible particles are expelled from the shell by reverse siphoning. Silt in the water can kill mussels by clogging their feeding siphons.

There are no known interspecific differences in feeding among freshwater mussels. The glochidia are obligate parasites on the gills or fins of fish. Adult mussels are filter-feeders and consume particulate matter in the water column. Identifiable stomach contents almost invariably include desmids, diatoms, algae, protozoa, and zooplankton.

Most freshwater mussel species display seasonal variations in activity associated with water temperature and reproduction. Metabolic rate is, in part, positively correlated with temperature. Many ectothermic species have the capacity to adjust their metabolic rates in response to long-term changes in temperature. Thus, metabolic rates do not continue to rise as temperatures rise in the summer, and they do not continue to fall during the winter as temperatures decline.

Some freshwater mussels also show diurnal changes in metabolic rates that indicate a tendency toward nocturnal activity patterns. Mussels may move to the surface to feed at night and move deeper into the substrate during the day; this is one way to avoid predators that hunt by visual contact.

Freshwater mussels are nonmigratory.

Habitat

The orangenacre mucket inhabits high quality lotic (living in actively moving water) habitats with stable gravel and sandy-gravel substrates. Little else is known about the habitat requirements of this species.

The habitat of the glochidia is initially in the gills of the female, then in the water column, and finally attached to a suitable host fish. Habitat associations or requirements for the juvenile stage are unknown.

Distribution

This species was historically found in the following portions of the Mobile River basin: the Tombigbee River drainage (Lubbub Creek; Buttahatchee, Sipsey, and East Fork Tombigbee Rivers); the Black Warrior River drainage (Brushy Creek; Mulberry and Sipsey forks); the Alabama River; and the Cahaba River drainage (Little Cahaba River).

The orangenacre mucket is currently limited to the Buttahatchee River and a short reach of the East Fork Tombigbee River; the headwaters of the Sipsey Fork; and the Sipsey and Little Cahaba Rivers. Specimens have not been collected in the Alabama River since 1834. This mussel may have been eliminated from the Mulberry Fork of the Black Warrior River.

Threats

Habitat modification, sedimentation, and water quality degradation represent the major threats to this species. These freshwater mussels do not tolerate impoundments. More than 1,000 mi (1,609 km) of large and small river habitat in the Mobile River drainage has been impounded for navigation, flood control, water supply, and/or hydroelectric production purposes. Impoundments adversely affect riverine mussels by 1) killing them during construction and dredging, 2) suffocating them with accumulated sediments, 3) lowering food and oxygen availability by reducing water flow, and 4) locally extirpating host fish. Other forms of habitat modification such as channelization, channel clearing and de-snagging, and gravel mining result in streambed scour and erosion, increased turbidity, reduction of groundwater levels, sedimentation, and changes in the aquatic community structure. Sedimentation may cause direct mortality by deposition and suffocation and eliminate or reduce recruitment of juvenile mussels. Suspended sediments can also interfere with feeding. Activities that historically caused sedimentation of streams and rivers in the drainages where this mussel occurs include channel modification, agriculture, forestry, mining, and industrial and residential development. In addition, stream discharge may result in decreased dissolved oxygen concentration, increased acidity and conductivity, and other changes in water chemistry that may impact the mussels and/or fish hosts.

Water quality degradation is a major problem in the Cahaba River system. There are 10 municipal wastewater treatment plants, 35 surface mining areas, a coalbed methane operation, and 67 other permitted discharges in this river system. Siltation from surface mining, road construction, and oil and gas development is also a problem.

Conservation and Recovery

Actions needed for the recovery of freshwater mussels include 1) conducting population and habitat surveys to determine the status and range of the species, 2) determining specific threats to the species and minimizing or eliminating these threats, 3)

identifying essential habitat areas in need of protection, and 4) controlling the incidental or illegal take of mussels by commercial and noncommercial collectors.

It is unlikely that this species will recover unless new populations are established by introducing individuals back into the historic range. Methods to accomplish this might include the introduction of adult/juvenile mussels, glochidia-infected host fish, and artificially cultured individuals.

Contacts

U.S. Fish and Wildlife Service
Regional Office, Division of Endangered Species
1875 Century Blvd., Suite 200
Atlanta, Georgia 30345
Telephone: (404) 679-4000
http://southeast.fws.gov/

Ecological Services Field Office
P.O. Box 1190
Daphne, Alabama 36526-1190
Telephone: (334) 441-5181
Fax: (334) 441-6222

Ecological Services Field Office
6578 Dogwood View Parkway, Suite A
Jackson, Mississippi 39213-7856
Telephone: (601) 965-4900
Fax: (601) 965-4340

Reference

U.S. Fish and Wildlife Service. 17 March 1993. "Endangered and Threatened Wildlife and Plants; Determination of Endangered Status for Eight Freshwater Mussels and Threatened Status for Three Freshwater Mussels in the Mobile River Drainage." *Federal Register* 58 (50): 14330-14340.

Arkansas Fatmucket

Lampsilis powelli

Status	Threatened
Listed	April 5, 1990
Family	Unionidae (Freshwater Mussel)
Description	Medium-sized, olive brown, elliptical shell with a pearly bluish-white interior.
Habitat	Deep pools and backwaters with sand or gravel bottoms.
Food	Filter-feeder.
Reproduction	Female stores sperm in gills; glochidia (larvae) are released into streams after hatching.
Threats	Impoundments; channel alteration; water pollution.
Range	Arkansas

Arkansas Fatmucket, photograph. A. E. Spreitzer Photography. Reproduced by permission.

Description

The Arkansas fatmucket (*Lampsilis powelli*) has an elliptical to long ovate shell with subinflated valves. The umbos (prominences) are moderately full and project slightly above the hinge line. Although usually of medium size, the shell can be as long as 3.9 in (10 cm). The shell's surface is generally smooth; its thin outer layer is shiny olive brown to tawny, with no rays. The inside of the shell is an iridescent bluish-white. There is sexual dimorphism.

Behavior

The life of mussels is complex, and reproduction often depends upon a stable habitat—unaltered stream conditions, clean water, and an undisturbed stream bottom. The cycle also depends upon the abundance of suitable fish hosts to complete the mussel's larval development.

To reproduce, males discharge sperm, which are dispersed by stream currents. In the process of feeding, females nearby or downstream take in sperm, which fertilize eggs stored in their gills. The gills serve as brood pouches (marsupia), where the glochidia hatch and begin to develop. After a time, these glochidia are released into the stream. A few mussels have inner parts that resemble a tiny minnow and can be manipulated to lure host fish. When a fish gets close to the shell, the mussel expels its glochidia.

Glochidia have tiny bean- or spoon-shaped valves that attach to the gill filaments of host fish. Glochidia can only progress to the juvenile stage while attached to the fish's gills. Those that do not fortuitously encounter a host fish do not survive when released by the female mussel. They sink to the bottom and die.

When the juvenile has developed a shell and is large enough to survive on its own, it detaches from the host fish and falls to the stream bottom, beginning a long association with a single stretch of stream. Maturing mussels bury themselves in riffles and shoals with only the shell margins and feeding siphons exposed to the water. Some mussels live as long as 50 years or more.

The family Unionidae, which includes all of the freshwater mussels in the United States, is separated into two groups based on the length of time the glochidia remain in the female's marsupia. The eggs of the short-term (tachytictic) breeders are fertilized in the spring, and glochidia are released by late summer of the same year. Long-term (bradytictic) breeders hold developing glochidia in the brood pouch over winter and release them in the spring.

Freshwater mussels feed by siphoning phytoplankton and other plant matter from the water. Indigestible particles are expelled from the shell by reverse siphoning. Silt in the water can kill mussels by clogging their feeding siphons.

There are no known interspecific differences in feeding among freshwater mussels. The glochidia are obligate parasites on the gills or fins of fish. Adult mussels are filter-feeders and consume particulate matter in the water column. Identifiable stomach contents almost invariably include desmids, diatoms, algae, protozoa, and zooplankton.

Most freshwater mussel species display seasonal variations in activity associated with water temperature and reproduction. Metabolic rate is, in part, positively correlated with temperature. Many ectothermic species have the capacity to adjust their metabolic rates in response to long-term changes in temperature. Thus, metabolic rates do not continue to rise as temperatures rise in the summer, and they do not continue to fall during the winter as temperatures decline.

Some freshwater mussels also show diurnal changes in metabolic rates that indicate a tendency toward nocturnal activity patterns. Mussels may move to the surface to feed at night and move deeper into the substrate during the day; this is one way to avoid predators that hunt by visual contact.

Freshwater mussels are nonmigratory.

Habitat

The Arkansas fatmucket prefers deep pools and backwater areas that possess sand, sand-gravel, sand-cobble, or sand-rock with sufficient flow to periodically remove organic detritus, leaves, and other debris. It is not generally found in riffles, nor does it occur in impoundments. It is frequently found with islands of *Justicia americana*, where substrate is typically depositional and water depth is about 3.3 ft (1 m).

Distribution

A 1988 survey of the species' habitat area found 151 individuals. The mussel's range as of the late 1990s was limited to the Quachita, Saline, and Caddo River systems in the state of Arkansas. Specifically, the Arkansas fatmucket occurs in the Quachita River upstream of Lake Quachita in Montgomery and Polk Counties and in the South Fork Quachita River upstream of Lake Quachita in Montgomery County. In the Saline River basin, the species occurs in Alum Fork, the Middle Fork, and the North Fork above their confluence with the Saline River, and in the Saline River from its formation downstream to about the Fall Line. In the Caddo River, Arkansas fatmucket populations are all located in the main stem. The species' probable historic range may have included the Caddo River from Norman downstream to the Quachita River, including at least the lower reach of the South Fork Caddo River. In the Quachita River, the species might have occurred from Malvern upstream to the species' currently known range and throughout the South Fork Quachita River. The species also probably occurred in all four forks in the Saline River drainage and in the main stem from the Fall Line upstream to the extent of permanent flowing water, as well as in Hurricane Creek upstream of the Fall Line.

Threats

The construction and operation of impoundments are the primary reasons for the reduction of the species' historic range. Within the historic range there are 16 existing impoundments, one under construction, and plans for constructing another. While these latter two impoundments will not inundate known populations of the Arkansas fatmucket, there are impacts occurring during the building process that may be adverse. During construction, there is increased threat from silt and sediment. After completion, the control of water flows during low flow periods could expose the mussel and result in lowered dissolved oxygen. Channel alterations (for highway construction and maintenance) and gravel operations are adversely altering the substrate.

Water quality degradation continues to threaten this species. A large majority of the watershed for the current range of this species is in timber and agricultural production. There is some conflicting data on the extent of impacts from sedimentation caused by silviculture; however, at least some of the sedimentation is caused by timber production and harvest. In addition, specific portions of the range are adversely affected by runoff from a barite mining operation, improperly treated municipal waste, and acidic runoff from bauxite mines.

Inundation aside, impoundments have also had a negative impact on this species, isolating various populations. The two populations in the Quachita River System are isolated from all other populations and each other by Lake Quachita. The Caddo River population is separated from the Saline River populations by about 200 river mi (321.9 km) and is adversely affected by hypolimnetic (stagnant water) discharges from DeGray Reservoir. If populations still exist in the Caddo River upstream of DeGray Reservoir, they are isolated by that impoundment. The Saline River system populations are not isolated from each other by any apparent barrier. However, if the fish host is not migratory, the exchange of genetic material between these populations would be an uncommon event.

Conservation and Recovery

The U.S. Forest Service (USFS) has funded status surveys of Arkansas fatmucket populations in streams under their jurisdiction. USFS officials have expressed a desire to conduct life-history studies on this species. The U.S. Fish and Wildlife Service is working with the Soil Conservation Service (SCS) to eliminate adverse impacts to the species from the construction and operation of SCS impoundments.

Contact

U.S. Fish and Wildlife Service
Regional Office, Division of Endangered Species
1875 Century Blvd., Suite 200
Atlanta, Georgia 30345
Telephone: (404) 679-4000
http://southeast.fws.gov/

References

Harris, J.L., and M.E. Gordon. 1988. "Status Survey of *Lampsilis powelli*." A Report to the U.S. Fish and Wildlife Service. 43 pp. + field notes.

U.S. Fish and Wildlife Service. 5 April 1990. "Threatened Status Determined for the Arkansas Fatmucket (*Lampsilis powelli*)." *Federal Register* 55 (66): 12797-801.

Speckled Pocketbook

Lampsilis streckeri

Status	Endangered
Listed	February 28, 1989
Family	Unionidae
Description	A freshwater mussel.
Habitat	Freshwater streams and rivers.
Food	A filter-feeder on algae, tiny zooplankton, and organic detritus.
Reproduction	Lays eggs; the larvae are parasitic on fish, and then settle to the bottom to develop into the sedentary adults.
Threats	Habitat destruction and pollution.
Range	Arkansas

Description

The speckled pocketbook is a thin mussel, with a dark-yellow or brown shell with chevron-like spots and chain-like rays. The shape of its shell is elliptical, about 3.1 in (80 mm) long. Female mussels have a broader shell that is more evenly rounded in the back. There is a minnow-shaped mantle flap with a small pigment spot and five triangular markings.

Behavior

The life history and reproductive cycle of the speckled pocketbook are not known, but are presumed to be similar to those of other freshwater mussels. During spawning, the males discharge sperm into the water, and females siphon them into their gills where their eggs are fertilized. The fertilized eggs develop into larvae that are discharged into the water column, where they may attach to a fish host. The parasitic larvae encysts and develops into a juvenile mussel, after which it drops off the fish and settles to the bottom to adopt the sedentary adult lifestyle. The specific host fish for the speckled pocketbook is not known. The mussel filter-feeds on algae, tiny zooplankton, and suspended organic matter.

Habitat

The speckled pocketbook occurs in coarse to muddy sand in water depths up to 1.3 ft (0.4 m). It occurs in well-oxygenated water with a steady flow.

Distribution

The speckled pocketbook is an endemic species that is restricted in range to the Little Red River, in Stone and Van Buren Counties, Arkansas.

Threats

The speckled pocketbook originally probably occurred throughout most of the Little Red River system. However, it lost most of its original habitat when the impoundment creating the Greers Ferry Reservoir altered most of the Little Red River through flooding and changes in hydrology, water chemistry, and temperature. Some of its habitat was also damaged by channel modifications for flood control undertaken by the U.S. Army Corps of Engineers. In the early 1990s, only a few hundred specimens of the speckled pocketbook were known from a 6-mi (10-km) reach of the Middle Fork of the Little Red River, between its confluence with Tick and Meadow Creeks. The rare mussel once also occurred in Archey and South Forks of that river, but these

Speckled Pocketbook, photograph. A. E. Spreitzer Photography. Reproduced by permission.

populations have disappeared. The only surviving population of the speckled pocketbook is threatened by intermittent water pollution from an unidentified source in the Tick Creek's confluence. Recent surveys have only found dead mussel shells, and no live animals, downstream of Tick's Creek, suggesting a pollution problem in the Middle Fork.

Conservation and Recovery

The surviving habitat of the rare speckled pocketbook must be conserved and protected from pollution and other damages. Its populations should be monitored, and research undertaken to determine management practices that could be used to improve conditions for the endangered mussel. Once its population increases, additional ones should be established by transplanting animals into suitable habitat elsewhere within its natural range. The apparent source of pollution to the Tick Creek's confluence should be abated, which would allow the habitat to recover and again become suitable for

the speckled pocketbook. Archey and South Forks should also be restored as suitable habitat for this endangered mussel.

Contacts

U. S. Fish and Wildlife Service
Regional Office, Division of Endangered Species
1875 Century Blvd., Suite 200
Atlanta, Georgia 30345
http://southeast.fws.gov/

U. S. Fish and Wildlife Service
6578 Dogwood View Parkway, Suite A
Jackson, Mississippi 39213-7856
Telephone: (601) 965-4900
Fax: (601) 965-4340

References

U. S. Fish and Wildlife Service. 1990. "U. S. Fish and Wildlife Service, Division of Endangered Species, Species Accounts: Speckled Pocketbook Mussel

(Lampsilis streckeri)." U. S. Fish and Wildlife Service, Endangered Species Program. (http://endangered. fws.gov/i/f/saf0z.html). Date Accessed: July 6, 2000.

U. S. Fish and Wildlife Service. 1989. "Endangered and Threatened Wildlife and Plants: Endangered Status for the Speckled Pocketbook *(Lampsilis streckeri)." Federal Register* 54 (38): 8339-8341.

Shinyrayed Pocketbook

Lampsilis subangulata

Status	Endangered
Listed	March 16, 1998
Family	Unionidae
Description	A freshwater, bivalve mollusk with a subelliptical shell and broad, somewhat inflated umbos and a rounded posterior ridge.
Habitat	Streams and small rivers with clean, flowing water.
Food	Filter-feeds on phytoplankton, tiny zooplankton, and organic detritus.
Reproduction	The female siphons male spawn from the water; eggs are fertilized and incubated in her gill chamber; the planktonic larvae are parasitic on fish, and later settle to the sedentary adult lifestyle.
Threats	Habitat destruction by impoundment, and pollution by siltation, nutrients, and other chemicals.
Range	Alabama, Florida, Georgia

Description

The *Lampsilis subangulata* (shinyrayed pocketbook) is a medium-sized mussel that reaches approximately 3.3 in (8.5 cm) in length. The shell is subelliptical, with broad, somewhat inflated umbos and a rounded posterior ridge. The shell is fairly thin but solid. The surface is smooth and shiny, light yellowish brown with fairly wide, bright emerald green rays over the entire length of the shell. Older individuals may appear much darker brown with obscure raying. Female specimens are more inflated postbasally, whereas males appear to be more pointed posteriorly. Internally, the pseudocardinal teeth are double and fairly large and erect in the left valve, and one large tooth and one spatulate tooth are in the right valve. The nacre is white, with some individuals exhibiting a salmon tint in the vicinity of the umbonal cavity. Current taxonomy recognizes the nineteenth-century names *Unio subangulatus Lea* and *Unio kirklandianus* as synonyms of *Lampsilis subangulata*.

Behavior

The shinyrayed pocketbook siphons water for oxygen and food. It feeds on phytoplankton, tiny zooplankton, and organic detritus. Reproduction involves the female siphoning male sperm from the water, after which the eggs are fertilized and incubated in her gill chamber. The planktonic larvae are parasitic on fish, and later settle to the sedentary adult lifestyle. The shinyrayed pocketbook utilizes largemouth bass (*Micropterus salmoides*) and spotted bass (*M. punctulatus*) as primary host fishes. The latter species appears to have been introduced into the Apalachicola-Chattahoochee-Flint (ACF) River system.

Habitat

Shinyrayed pocketbook inhabits stable sandy and gravelly substrates in medium-sized streams to large rivers, often in areas swept free of silt by the current. This mussel is endemic to eastern Gulf Slope streams draining the Apalachicolan region of southeast Alabama, southwest Georgia, and north Florida. The center of distribution is the ACF River basin of southeast Alabama, southwest Georgia, and northwest Florida, and the Ochlockonee River system of southwest Georgia and northwest Florida.

Distribution

The shinyrayed pocketbook was described from the Chattahoochee River in Columbus, Georgia. This species historically occurred in mainstems and tributaries throughout the ACF, Chipola, and Ochlockonee River systems. A 1940 study found this species to be generally rare but locally abundant, documenting 94 specimens at eight Chipola River system sites (average of 11.8 per site). It now occurs at only 21% of the historical sites sampled, and is extirpated from the mainstems of the ACF rivers. Populations have declined significantly in the Chipola River. The species occurs at 29 sites in tributaries of the ACF Rivers and the Chipola and Ochlockonee Rivers. Only two sites show evidence of recruitment; however, the largest known population shows no signs of recruitment. During the status survey, 380 sites within the historical range of the shinyrayed pocketbook were sampled, including 28 of 54 (52%) known historical sites. Live individuals were located at six (21%) of the historical sites. This species has apparently been eliminated from all but one site in the Chattahoochee River system in Alabama, and from much of the Chipola River system.

Live individuals were found at 23 of the sample sites during the status survey, including one site in a Chattahoochee River tributary in Alabama, 13 sites (12 on tributaries) in the Flint River system, one locality in the Chipola River, and eight sites (seven mainstem) in the upper half of the Ochlockonee River system. An average of 2.9 live individuals were found per site. During unrelated studies subsequent to the completion of the status survey, ten additional sites for the shinyrayed pocketbook were located in the ACF River system. Eight of these new occurrences were from five Flint River tributaries; one each occurred in tributaries of the Chattahoochee and Chipola Rivers. The latter two records represent streams where the species had not been previously collected. The Flint River system records include one stream where the species had never been collected (a small tributary of a stream where live

specimens were found during the status survey), and another stream where it was found during the status survey as a single dead shell; the remaining sites are in tributaries where it was found live during the status survey. The smallest shinyrayed pocketbook specimen recorded during the status survey in the Ochlockonee River system, possibly an older juvenile, measured 1.6 in (4.1 cm) in length. In the ACF River system, the three smallest specimens, measuring 2.17-2.24 in (5.5-5.7 cm) in length, were gravid females. In 1995, four live, apparently juvenile, specimens from 1.2 to 1.6 in (3.0-4.0 cm) in length were located in a Flint River tributary.

A 1996 study sampled the largest known bed of this species for juveniles. A 59 ft (18 m) by 26 ft (8 m) area had 37 adult shinyrayed pocketbooks (average of 1.7 per sq yd [2.1 per sq m]). Whole substratum removal of 54, 2.7 ft (0.25 m) square quadrats within this bed yielded no juveniles of this species. The density of shinyrayed pocketbooks at the four other sites, where quantitative work conducted subsequent to the status survey yielded specimens, never exceeded 0.01 specimens per sq yd (0.08 specimens per sq m).

Threats

Impoundments have permanently altered significant portions of the ACF system. The lower portions of many tributaries were permanently flooded because of these reservoirs, including a known site for the shinyrayed pocketbook in Walter F. George Reservoir. Impoundments have altered about 29% of mainstem riverine habitat on the Flint River. Pre-impoundment records from Seminole and Blackshear Reservoirs exist for three sites for the shiny-rayed pocketbook. Talquin Reservoir flooded about 12% of the riverine habitat in the middle portion of the Ochlockonee River and the lower end of its largest tributary (the Little River). Pre-impoundment records exist for the shinyrayed pocketbook at sites at the upstream end of Talquin Reservoir, now also absent downstream of the dam. This indicates that potential host fish movements may have been blocked. Populations of the shinyrayed pocketbook have been isolated due to major impoundments on the Apalachicola, Flint, and Ochlockonee Rivers. Future impoundments to satisfy expanding urban and surburban demand, particularly in the metropolitan Atlanta area, could damage stream habitats where small populations of the shinyrayed pocketbook exist.

Although muskrats are not common within the range of these species, Piedmont populations of the shinyrayed pocketbook in the upper Flint River system may be subject to some degree of muskrat predation.

Conservation and Recovery

The shinyrayed pocketbook mussel survives in at least 33 sites, almost all of which are in streams running through privately owned land. Its conservation requires the protection of the stream reaches where it persists in small, isolated populations. These habitats must be protected from potential impoundment, other disturbances, and from pollution associated with poor land-use practices that cause erosion and inputs of nutrients and other chemicals. The populations of the shinyrayed pocketbook mussel must be monitored, and research undertaken into its basic biology and ecological requirements. It is particularly important to understand its requirements for breeding, as most populations are not reproducing.

Contacts

U. S. Fish and Wildlife Service
Jacksonville Ecological Services Field Office
6620 Southpoint Drive South, Suite 310
Jacksonville, Florida 32216
Telephone: (904) 232-2580

U. S. Fish and Wildlife Service
Regional Office, Division of Endangered Species
1875 Century Blvd., Suite 200
Atlanta, Georgia 30345
http://southeast.fws.gov/

Reference

U.S. Fish and Wildlife Service. 16 March 1998. "Endangered and Threatened Wildlife and Plants; Determination of Endangered Status for Five Freshwater Mussels and Threatened Status for Two Freshwater Mussels From the Eastern Gulf Slope Drainages of Alabama, Florida, and Georgia." *Federal Register* 63(50):12664-12687.

Alabama Lampmussel

Lampsilis virescens

Status	Endangered
Listed	June 14, 1976
Family	Unionidae (Freshwater Mussel)
Description	Yellowish to greenish brown, elliptical shell, sometimes with faint rays.
Habitat	Sand and gravel substrates in small to medium-sized streams.
Food	Filter-feeder.
Reproduction	Female stores sperm in gills; glochidia are released into the stream after hatching.
Threats	Dams, reservoirs, siltation, pollution.
Range	Alabama, Tennessee

Alabama Lampmussel, photograph. A. E. Spreitzer Photography. Reproduced by permission.

Description

The Alabama lampmussel, *Lampsilis virescens*, has an elliptical shell, typically about 2.5 in (6 cm) long. The smooth, shiny surface of the shell ranges in color from yellowish brown to greenish brown and is sometimes faintly rayed. Shell beaks are full and sculptured with many delicate ridges. Males are more bluntly pointed at the hinge, while females are rounder and slightly more inflated.

Behavior

See the Upland Combshell (*Epioblasma metastriata*) entry.

Habitat

The Alabama lampmussel buries in sand or gravel substrates in small to medium-sized streams. It requires clear, cool water with little sediment and moderate current.

Distribution

The Alabama lampmussel is a Cumberlandian mussel, native to the southern Appalachians and the Cumberland Plateau. It was apparently restricted to the lesser tributaries of the Tennessee River from above the confluence of the Clinch River downstream to Tuscumbia, Alabama. Within this broadly defined range, this species was found in extremely localized beds in relatively low numbers.

Populations were documented in the Emory River (Roane and Morgan Counties), and Coal Creek (Anderson County), Tennessee, and in Paint Rock River (Jackson County), Beech and Brown Creeks (Marshall County), Spring Creek (Colbert County), and Bear and Little Bear Creeks (Franklin County), Alabama.

Currently, the only populations of the Alabama lampmussel known to survive occur in the Paint Rock River and its tributaries—Hurricane Creek, Estill Fork, and Larkin Fork (Franklin and Jackson Counties, Alabama). Some evidence has been collected to suggest that the species may still survive in the Little Emory River (Roane County), Tennessee.

Threats

The natural, unimpeded flow of the Tennessee River and its tributaries has been irrevocably altered by the construction of a series of major flood control, navigation, and hydroelectric dams on the main channel. Poor agricultural practices, strip mining, logging, and road construction have contributed heavy loads of silt to the basin's rivers and streams, in many cases smothering mussel beds or potential habitat. In particular, all of the mussel beds in Coal Creek, Tennessee, have been smothered by coal wastes and runoff. Gravel dredging within the range of the Alabama lampmussel has disturbed substrates and made stretches of river uninhabitable for mussels and host fishes.

Chemical and heavy metal contaminants from industries located along the river have also degraded general water quality. Because mussels filter many gallons of water each day to feed, contaminants become concentrated in the soft tissues, weakening or killing the mussel.

Conservation and Recovery

The U. S. Fish and Wildlife Service and state biologists have cooperated to redistribute the Paint Rock River population so that a single accident, such as a toxic chemical spill, would not result in loss of the total population. Pending the results of ongoing research into the ecology of this species, populations will be reintroduced to habitable streams within its historic range.

An innovative technique, being developed by the Virginia Cooperative Fishery Research Unit, would enable reintroduction of mussels by stocking a stream with host fishes, which have been inoculated with mussel glochidia (larvae). This method provides a promising alternative to transplanting adult mussels, which are typically limited in number.

Contact

Regional Office of Endangered Species
U.S. Fish and Wildlife Service
1875 Century Blvd., Ste 200
Atlanta, Georgia 30345
http://southeast.fws.gov/

References

Ahlstedt, S. A. 1983. "The Molluscan Fauna of the Elk River in Tennessee and Alabama." *American Malacological Bulletin* 1:43-50.

Isom, B. G. 1968. "The Naiad Fauna of Indian Creek, Madison County, Alabama." *American Midland Naturalist* 79(2):514-516.

Isom, B. G. 1969. "The Mussel Resources of the Tennessee River." *Malacologia* 7(2/3):397-425.

Isom, B. G., and P. Yokley, Jr. 1968. "Mussels of Bear Creek Watershed, Alabama and Mississippi, with a discussion of the Area Geology." *American Midland Naturalist* 79(1):189-196.

Carolina Heelsplitter

Lasmigona decorata

Status	Endangered
Listed	June 30, 1993
Family	Unionidae (Freshwater Mussel)
Description	Ovate, trapezoid-shaped, unsculptured greenish-brown to dark brown shell.
Habitat	Mud, muddy sand, or muddy gravel substrates along stable, well-shaped stream banks.
Food	Filter-feeder.
Reproduction	Female broods fertilized eggs in gills; glochidia are released into streams after hatching.
Threats	Habitat degradation.
Range	North Carolina

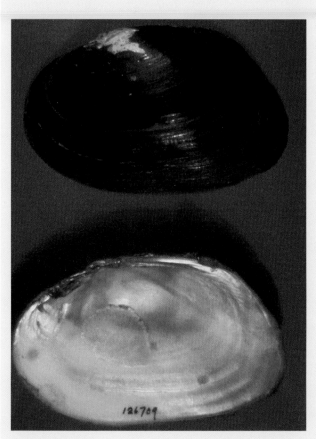

Carolina Heelsplitter, photograph. U. S. Fish and Wildlife Service. Reproduced by permission.

Description

The Carolina heelsplitter has an ovate, trapezoid-shaped, unsculptured shell. The shell of the largest specimen ever collected measured 4.6 in (118 mm) in length, 1.6 in (40 mm) in width, and 2.5 in (63.5 mm) in height. The shell's outer surface varies from greenish-brown to dark brown in color, and shells from younger specimens have faint greenish-brown or black rays. The nacre (inside surface) is often pearly-white to bluish white, grading to orange in the area of the umbo (knob at the hinge). However, in older specimens the entire nacre may be a mottled pale orange.

Behavior

Reproductive characteristics for this species are probably similar to other freshwater mussels. Males release sperm into the water column. Females then take in the sperm through their siphons during feeding and respiration. The fertilized eggs are retained in the gills until the larvae fully develop. Gravid females have been observed during mid-May. Glochidia (larvae) attach themselves to the gills or fins of their fish hosts following their release from the females' gills. Fish host species are unknown.

Habitat

The Carolina heelsplitter has been recorded from small to large streams and rivers, as well as ponds. The ponds referred to in historic records are believed to have been mill ponds on some of the smaller streams. The species is now known to occur in only three small streams and one small river and is usually found in mud, muddy sand, or muddy gravel substrates along stable, well-shaped stream banks. The stability of the streambanks appears to be very important to this species.

Distribution

The historical distribution of this species included the Catawba River, Mecklenburg County, North Carolina; several streams and ponds in the Catawba River system around the Charlotte areas of Mecklenburg County, North Carolina; one small stream in the Pee Dee River system in Cabarrus County, North Carolina; and an area in South Carolina referred to as the Abbeville District (possibly the Saluda River system). An additional record in the Oconee River in Georgia is believed to be a misidentification.

Between 1987 and 1990, surveys funded by the U.S. Fish and Wildlife Service were conducted. A total of 687 sites in 356 different streams, rivers, and impoundments within the historic range and potential habitat of the Carolina heelsplitter were surveyed including the Saluda, Catawba, Pee Dee, Broad, Rocky, and Lynches River systems. Only three populations were located: one in a Catawba River tributary in Union County, North Carolina; the second in a tributary of the Rocky River (Pee Dee River system), Union County, North Carolina; and the third in the Lynches River drainage (Pee Dee River system) in Chesterfield, Lancaster, and Kershaw Counties, South Carolina (this was the largest population).

Threats

Habitat loss/degradation and increases in water pollution caused by impoundments, stream channelization, dredging, sand mining, sewage effluents, and poorly implemented agricultural, forestry, and commercial/residential development practices are believed to be the primary factors leading to the decline and extirpation of this species from large sections of its historic range.

All three known populations are bordered by private lands except for small sections of road rights-of-ways and a state bridge.

The Lynches River sites receive heavy nutrient and pollutant loads from wastewater treatment plants and other point and nonpoint sources.

In some areas, vegetation has been cleared right up to the stream banks which increases the siltation of the streams, eliminates shading, and destabilizes the streambanks (a key habitat component for this species).

Conservation and Recovery

Actions needed to protect the Carolina heelsplitter include: (1) pursuing legal protection for the species and its habitat; (2) conducting population and habitat surveys to determine the status and range of the species, if feasible; (3) testing the potential for reintroducing the species into its historic range; and (4) determining life history and ecological requirements for *Lasmigona decorata.*

Population sizes may be too low to allow intensive research and population manipulation.

Contacts

U.S. Fish and Wildlife Service
Regional Office of Endangered Species
1875 Century Blvd., Suite 200
Atlanta, Georgia 30345
http://southeast.fws.gov/

Asheville Ecological Services Field Office
160 Zillicoa St.
Asheville, North Carolina 28801-1082
Telephone: (828) 258-3939
Fax: (828) 258-5330

References

Thorp, J. H., and A. P. Covich. 1991. *Ecology and Classification of North American Freshwater Invertebrates.* Academic Press, San Diego. 911 pp.

U.S. Fish and Wildlife Service. 1993. "Endangered and Threatened Wildlife and Plants; *Lasmigona decorata* (Carolina Heelsplitter) Determined to be Endangered." *Federal Register* 58(124): 34926-34931.

Louisiana Pearlshell

Margaritifera hembeli

Status	Threatened
Listed	Endangered—February 5, 1988
Reclassified	Threatened—September 24, 1993
Family	Unionidae (Freshwater Mussel)
Description	Dark brown to black elliptical shell with white nacre.
Habitat	Shallow flowing streams with sand or gravel substrate.
Food	Filter-feeder.
Reproduction	Female stores sperm in gills; glochidia (larvae) are released into streams after hatching.
Threats	Stream diversion; reservoir construction; pollution.
Range	Louisiana

Louisiana Pearlshell, photograph. A. E. Spreitzer Photography. Reproduced by permission.

Description

The Louisiana pearlshell (*Margaritifera hembeli*) is a freshwater mussel with a generally elliptical shell that measures about 4 in (10.2 cm) long, 2 in (5 cm) high, and 1.2 in (3 cm) wide. The outer shell surface (periostracum) is dark brown to black, and the inner shell surface (nacre) is white.

Like members of the family Unionidae, the pearlshell is a filter-feeder. It takes nourishment by siphoning water, drawing it in through the inhalant siphon, and passing it over specialized gills that filter out suspended food particles. Common food ma-

terials of freshwater mussels are desmids, diatoms, filamentous algae, detritus, bacteria, and plankton.

This species was reclassified in 1993 from "endangered" to "threatened" because of improvements in habitat management, a new population discovery, and other successful recovery efforts.

Behavior

The life of mussels is complex, and reproduction often depends upon a stable habitat—unaltered stream conditions, clean water, and an undisturbed stream bottom. The cycle also depends upon the abundance of suitable fish hosts to complete the mussel's larval development.

To reproduce, males discharge sperm, which are dispersed by stream currents. In the process of feeding, females nearby or downstream take in sperm, which fertilizes eggs stored in their gills. The gills serve as brood pouches (marsupia), where the glochidia hatch and begin to develop. After a time, these glochidia are released into the stream. A few mussels have inner parts that resemble a tiny minnow and can be manipulated to lure host fish. When a fish gets close to the shell, the mussel expels its glochidia.

Glochidia have tiny bean- or spoon-shaped valves that attach to the gill filaments of host fish. Glochidia can only progress to the juvenile stage while attached to the fish's gills. Those that do not fortuitously encounter a host fish do not survive when released by the female mussel. They sink to the bottom and die.

When the juvenile has developed a shell and is large enough to survive on its own, it detaches from the host fish and falls to the stream bottom, beginning a long association with a single stretch of stream. Maturing mussels bury themselves in riffles and shoals with only the shell margins and feeding siphons exposed to the water. Some mussels live as long as 50 years or more.

The family Unionidae, which includes all of the freshwater mussels in the United States, is separated into two groups based on the length of time the glochidia remain in the female's marsupia. The eggs of the short-term (tachytictic) breeders are fertilized in the spring, and glochidia are released by late summer of the same year. Long-term (bradytictic) breeders hold developing glochidia in the brood pouch over winter and release them in the spring.

Freshwater mussels feed by siphoning phytoplankton and other plant matter from the water. Indigestible particles are expelled from the shell by reverse siphoning. Silt in the water can kill mussels by clogging their feeding siphons.

There are no known interspecific differences in feeding among freshwater mussels. The glochidia are obligate parasites on the gills or fins of fish. Adult mussels are filter-feeders and consume particulate matter in the water column. Identifiable stomach contents almost invariably include desmids, diatoms, algae, protozoa, and zooplankton.

Most freshwater mussel species display seasonal variations in activity associated with water temperature and reproduction. Metabolic rate is, in part, positively correlated with temperature. Many ectothermic species have the capacity to adjust their metabolic rates in response to long-term changes in temperature. Thus, metabolic rates do not continue to rise as temperatures rise in the summer, and they do not continue to fall during the winter as temperatures decline.

Some freshwater mussels also show diurnal changes in metabolic rates that indicate a tendency toward nocturnal activity patterns. Mussels may move to the surface to feed at night and move deeper into the substrate during the day; this is one way to avoid predators that hunt by visual contact.

Freshwater mussels are nonmigratory.

Habitat

Louisiana pearlshells can be found in very shallow flowing streams with gravel and sand substrate. Water depths range from 12-20 in (30.5-50.8 cm). Vegetation in the surrounding watershed is mostly mixed hardwood-loblolly pine forest.

Distribution

This species is thought to have ranged throughout most of the headwater streams of Bayou Boeuf in Rapides Parish, Louisiana.

In 1983, after an extensive search, biologists from the Louisiana Natural Heritage Program found the pearlshell in 11 streams. Two years later the total population was estimated at 10,000 individuals, about 90% of which inhabited four streams: Long Branch, Bayou Clear, Loving Creek, and Little Loving Creek. Much of the pearlshell's range is within the Kisatchie National Forest, administered by the Forest Service.

Since its listing in 1988, the mussel's prospects have improved so much that the species was reclassified from "endangered" to "threatened" in 1993. One reason for the reclassification was the discovery of new populations and an expansion of the known range for the species into the Red River drainage. In the fall of 1991, based upon a report of the Louisiana pearlshell from Moccasin Branch in the Red River drainage, biologists from the U.S. Fish and Wildlife Service (FWS) and Kisatchie National Forest conducted a field survey of streams in and adjacent to the Catahoula District of the National Forest. Twelve populations of the Louisiana pearlshell were found in three different small drainages that eventually flow into the Red River. One drainage is isolated from the others by the impoundment of Lake Iatt. All of the populations were found in small, shallow, clear streams with gravel or firm sand substrate.

Threats

The pearlshell's range has been reduced by dam construction, stream diversion, and generally degraded water quality. Logging operations in Rapides Parish have included clear-cutting up to stream banks, which has increased erosion and runoff. Freshwater mussels are especially vulnerable to siltation because their feeding siphons are easily clogged. A large population was lost in the early 1980s to natural processes, when beavers constructed a dam that flooded a section of stream habitat.

The Louisiana pearlshell, one of the rarest members of its family, has been avidly sought by both amateur and scientific collectors. As this mussel is already very limited in numbers, any collection can have an adverse affect.

Conservation and Recovery

On September 24, 1993, the FWS determined that the Louisiana pearlshell warranted reclassification from "endangered" to "threatened."

In addition to documenting a larger range than known at the time of its initial listing, surveys found evidence of successful reproduction in most, if not all, populations. Management initiatives at Kisatchie National Forest to benefit the pearlshell have included the control of beavers (whose dams had fragmented the mussel's range and flooded its free-flowing habitat) and the establishment of streamside zones to minimize sedimentation during logging operations.

According to a 1990 FWS draft recovery plan, the main objective for recovery of this species is increasing population numbers in each of Long Branch, Bayou Clear, Loving Creek, and Little Loving Creek to greater than 2,000 individuals and increasing population numbers in the Mack Branch, Castor Creek, and Brown Creek to over 1,000 individuals. These minimal levels are to be maintained

for a period of at least 10 years with evidence of successful reproduction and recruitment. In the future, all streams will be surveyed to determine population status.

Because this mussel occurs within a national forest and on land administered by the U.S. Air Force, the Forest Service and the air force are required to formally consult with the FWS concerning any proposed actions that would potentially harm the pearlshell or its habitat.

Other recommended recovery efforts include the reduction of off-road vehicle activity. Better timber management could reduce siltation in the streams. In addition, public education and information on the hazards of siltation and waste runoff (such as motor oil, sewage, and agricultural pesticides) are necessary. The reclassification to "threatened" status is a clear sign that recovery efforts are on the right track.

Contact

U.S. Fish and Wildlife Service
Regional Office, Division of Endangered Species
1875 Century Blvd., Suite 200
Atlanta, Georgia 30345
Telephone: (404) 679-4000
http://southeast.fws.gov/

References

Athearn, H.D. 1970. "Discussion of Dr. Heard's Paper (Eastern Freshwater Mollusks, the South Atlantic and Gulf Drainages)." *Malacologia* 20 (1): 1-56.

French, III, John R.P. November 1990. "The Exotic Zebra Mussel: A New Threat to Endangered Freshwater Mussels." *Endangered Species Technical Bulletin* 15 (11).

Johnson, R.E. 1983. "*Margaritifera marrianae*, A New Species of Unionacea (Bivalvia: Margaritiferidae) from Mobile-Alabama-Coosa and Escambia River Systems, Alabama." *Occasional Papers on Mollusks, Museum of Comparative Zoology, Harvard University* 4 (62): 299-304.

U.S. Fish and Wildlife Service. 1990. "Endangered and Threatened Species Recovery Program, Report to Congress." U.S. Fish and Wildlife Service.

Alabama Moccasinshell

Medionidus acutissimus

Status	Threatened
Listed	March 17, 1993
Family	Unionidae (Freshwater Mussel)
Description	Small delicate mussel with a narrow, elliptical yellow to brown shell.
Habitat	Gravel riffles in streams.
Food	Filter-feeder.
Reproduction	Female stores sperm in gills; glochidia (larvae) are released into streams after hatching.
Threats	Impoundments; water pollution.
Range	Alabama, Georgia, Mississippi, Tennessee

Alabama Moccasinshell, photograph. A. E. Spreitzer Photography. Reproduced by permission.

Description

The Alabama moccasinshell (*Medionidus acutissimus*) is a small and delicate mussel that grows to 1.2 in (3.1 cm) in length. The shell is narrowly elliptical, thin, and has a well-developed acute posterior ridge terminating in an acute point on the posterior ventral margin. The posterior slope is finely corrugated. The periostracum (outer shell) is yellow to brownish-yellow, with broken green rays across the entire surface of the shell. The thin nacre (inner shell) is translucent along the margins and salmon-colored in the umbos (beak cavity).

Behavior

The life of mussels is complex, and reproduction often depends upon a stable habitat—unaltered stream conditions, clean water, and an undisturbed stream bottom. The cycle also depends upon the abundance of suitable fish hosts to complete the mussel's larval development.

To reproduce, males discharge sperm, which are dispersed by stream currents. In the process of feeding, females nearby or downstream take in sperm, which fertilize eggs stored in their gills. The gills serve as brood pouches (marsupia), where the glochidia hatch and begin to develop. After a time, these glochidia are released into the stream. A few mussels have inner parts that resemble a tiny minnow and can be manipulated to lure host fish. When a fish gets close to the shell, the mussel expels its glochidia.

Glochidia have tiny bean- or spoon-shaped valves that attach to the gill filaments of host fish. Glochidia can only progress to the juvenile stage while attached to the fish's gills. Those that do not fortuitously encounter a host fish do not survive when released by the female mussel. They sink to the bottom and die.

When the juvenile has developed a shell and is large enough to survive on its own, it detaches from the host fish and falls to the stream bottom, beginning a long association with a single stretch of stream. Maturing mussels bury themselves in riffles and shoals with only the shell margins and feeding siphons exposed to the water. Some mussels live as long as 50 years or more.

The family Unionidae, which includes all of the freshwater mussels in the United States, is separated into two groups based on the length of time the glochidia remain in the female's marsupia. The eggs of the short-term (tachytictic) breeders are fertilized in the spring, and glochidia are released by late summer of the same year. Long-term (bradytictic) breeders hold developing glochidia in the brood pouch over winter and release them in the spring.

Freshwater mussels feed by siphoning phytoplankton and other plant matter from the water. Indigestible particles are expelled from the shell by reverse siphoning. Silt in the water can kill mussels by clogging their feeding siphons.

There are no known interspecific differences in feeding among freshwater mussels. The glochidia are obligate parasites on the gills or fins of fish. Adult mussels are filter-feeders and consume particulate matter in the water column. Identifiable stomach contents almost invariably include desmids, diatoms, algae, protozoa, and zooplankton.

Most freshwater mussel species display seasonal variations in activity associated with water temperature and reproduction. Metabolic rate is, in part, positively correlated with temperature. Many ectothermic species have the capacity to adjust their metabolic rates in response to long-term changes in temperature. Thus, metabolic rates do not continue to rise as temperatures rise in the summer, and they do not continue to fall during the winter as temperatures decline.

Some freshwater mussels also show diurnal changes in metabolic rates that indicate a tendency toward nocturnal activity patterns. Mussels may move to the surface to feed at night and move deeper into the substrate during the day; this is one way to avoid predators that hunt by visual contact.

Freshwater mussels are nonmigratory.

Habitat

The Alabama moccasinshell inhabits high quality lotic (living in actively moving water) habitats with stable gravel and sandy-gravel substrates. Little else is known about the habitat requirements of this species.

The habitat of the glochidia is initially in the gills of the female, then in the water column, and finally attached to a suitable host fish. Habitat associations or requirements for the juvenile stage are unknown.

Distribution

This species' historic range included the following portions of the Mobile River basin: the Alabama River; the Tombigbee River and its tributaries (Luxapalila Creek, Buttahatchee and Sipsey Rivers); the Black Warrior River and its tributaries (Mulberry Fork, Brushy Creek); the Cahaba River; and the Coosa River and its tributaries (Talladega and Choccolocco Creeks, Chatooga River).

The Alabama moccasinshell is currently found in Luxapalila Creek and in Buttahatchee and Sipsey Rivers in the Tombigbee River drainage; in the headwaters of the Sipsey Fork of the Black Warrior River drainage; and in the Conasauga River. This species was last collected in the Cahaba River drainage in 1973. A 1990 survey discovered one specimen in the Conasauga River; a 1991 survey failed to find the species in the Coosa River drainage. The U. S. Fish and Wildlife Service list this species as also occurring in Tennessee.

Threats

Habitat modification, sedimentation, and water quality degradation represent the major threats to this species. These freshwater mussels do not tolerate impoundments. More than 1,000 mi (1,609 km) of large and small river habitat in the Mobile River drainage has been impounded for navigation, flood control, water supply, and/or hydroelectric production purposes. Impoundments adversely affect riverine mussels by (1) killing them during construction and dredging, (2) suffocating them with accumulated sediments, (3) lowering food and oxygen availability by reducing water flow, and (4) locally extirpating host fish. Other forms of habitat modification such as channelization, channel clearing and de-snagging, and gravel mining result in streambed scour and erosion, increased turbidity, reduction of groundwater levels, sedimentation, and changes in the aquatic community structure. Sedimentation may cause direct mortality by deposition and suffocation and eliminate or reduce recruitment of juvenile mussels. Suspended sediments can also interfere with feeding. Activities that historically caused sedimentation of streams and rivers in the drainages where this mussel occurs include channel modification, agriculture, forestry, mining, and industrial and residential development. In addition, stream discharge may result in decreased dissolved oxygen concentration, increased acidity and conductivity, and other changes in water chemistry that may impact the mussels and/or fish hosts.

About 230 river mi (370 km) of the Coosa River have been impounded for hydropower by a series of six dams. Water quality degradation caused by textile and carpet mill wastes led to the loss of several known mussel communities in various streams of this river system.

Water quality degradation is a major problem in the Cahaba River system. There are 10 municipal wastewater treatment plants, 35 surface mining areas, a coalbed methane operation, and 67 other permitted discharges in this river system. Siltation from surface mining, road construction, and oil and gas development is also a problem.

Conservation and Recovery

Actions needed for the recovery of freshwater mussels include (1) conducting population and habitat surveys to determine the status and range of the species, (2) determining specific threats to the species and minimizing or eliminating these threats, (3) identifying essential habitat areas in need of protection, and (4) controlling the incidental or illegal take of mussels by commercial and noncommercial collectors.

It is unlikely that this species will recover unless new populations are established by introducing individuals back into the historic range. Methods to accomplish this might include the introduction of adult/juvenile mussels, glochidia-infected host fish, and artificially cultured individuals.

Contacts

U.S. Fish and Wildlife Service
Regional Office, Division of Endangered Species
1875 Century Blvd., Suite 200
Atlanta, Georgia 30345
Telephone: (404) 679-4000
http://southeast.fws.gov/

Ecological Services Field Office
P.O. Box 1190
Daphne, Alabama 36526-1190
Telephone: (334) 441-5181
Fax: (334) 441-6222

Reference

U.S. Fish and Wildlife Service. 17 March 1993. "Endangered and Threatened Wildlife and Plants; Determination of Endangered or Threatened Status for Eight Freshwater Mussels and Threatened Status for Three Freshwater Mussels in the Mobile River Drainage." *Federal Register* 58 (50): 14330-14340.

Coosa Moccasinshell

Medionidus parvulus

Status	Endangered
Listed	March 17, 1993
Family	Unionidae (Freshwater Mussel)
Description	Small to medium mussel with yellow to dark brown shell that has fine green rays.
Habitat	Gravel riffles in streams.
Food	Filter-feeder.
Reproduction	Female stores sperm in gills; glochidia (larvae) are released into streams after hatching.
Threats	Impoundments; gravel mining; water pollution.
Range	Alabama, Georgia, Tennessee

Coosa Moccasinshell, photograph. A. E. Spreitzer Photography. Reproduced by permission.

Description

The Coosa moccasinshell (*Medionidus parvulus*) is a small mussel that rarely exceeds 1.6 in (4.1 cm) in shell length. The shell is thin and fragile, elongate, and elliptical to rhomboidal in shape. The posterior ridge is inflated and smoothly rounded, terminating in a broadly rounded point; the posterior slope is finely corrugated. The periostracum (outer shell) is yellow-brown to dark brown and has fine green rays. The nacre (inner shell) is blue and occasionally has salmon-colored spots.

Behavior

The life of mussels is complex, and reproduction often depends upon a stable habitat—unaltered stream conditions, clean water, and an undisturbed stream bottom. The cycle also depends upon the abundance of suitable fish hosts to complete the mussel's larval development.

To reproduce, males discharge sperm, which are dispersed by stream currents. In the process of feed-ing, females nearby or downstream take in sperm, which fertilize eggs stored in their gills. The gills serve as brood pouches (marsupia), where the glochidia hatch and begin to develop. After a time, these glochidia are released into the stream. A few mussels have inner parts that resemble a tiny minnow and can be manipulated to lure host fish. When a fish gets close to the shell, the mussel expels its glochidia.

Glochidia have tiny bean- or spoon-shaped valves that attach to the gill filaments of host fish. Glochidia can only progress to the juvenile stage while attached to the fish's gills. Those that do not fortuitously encounter a host fish do not survive when released by the female mussel. They sink to the bottom and die.

When the juvenile has developed a shell and is large enough to survive on its own, it detaches from the host fish and falls to the stream bottom, beginning a long association with a single stretch of stream. Maturing mussels bury themselves in riffles and shoals with only the shell margins and feeding siphons exposed to the water. Some mussels live as long as 50 years or more.

The family Unionidae, which includes all of the freshwater mussels in the United States, is separated into two groups based on the length of time the glochidia remain in the female's marsupia. The eggs of the short-term (tachytictic) breeders are fertilized in the spring, and glochidia are released by late summer of the same year. Long-term (bradytictic) breeders hold developing glochidia in the brood pouch over winter and release them in the spring.

Freshwater mussels feed by siphoning phytoplankton and other plant matter from the water. Indigestible particles are expelled from the shell by reverse siphoning. Silt in the water can kill mussels by clogging their feeding siphons.

There are no known interspecific differences in feeding among freshwater mussels. The glochidia are obligate parasites on the gills or fins of fish. Adult mussels are filter-feeders and consume particulate matter in the water column. Identifiable stomach contents almost invariably include desmids, diatoms, algae, protozoa, and zooplankton.

Most freshwater mussel species display seasonal variations in activity associated with water temperature and reproduction. Metabolic rate is, in part, positively correlated with temperature. Many ectothermic species have the capacity to adjust their metabolic rates in response to long-term changes in temperature. Thus, metabolic rates do not continue to rise as temperatures rise in the summer, and they do not continue to fall during the winter as temperatures decline.

Some freshwater mussels also show diurnal changes in metabolic rates that indicate a tendency toward nocturnal activity patterns. Mussels may move to the surface to feed at night and move deeper into the substrate during the day; this is one way to avoid predators that hunt by visual contact.

Freshwater mussels are nonmigratory.

Habitat

Coosa moccasinshell inhabits high quality lotic (living in actively moving water) habitats with stable gravel and sandy-gravel substrates. Little else is known about the habitat requirements of this species.

The habitat of the glochidia is initially in the gills of the female, then in the water column, and finally attached to a suitable host fish. Habitat associations or requirements for the juvenile stage are unknown.

Distribution

Coosa moccasinshell has been found in the following portions of the Mobile River basin: the Cahaba River; the Black Warrior River and its tributaries (Sipsey Fork); and the Coosa River and its tributaries (Choccolocco Creek; Chatooga, Conasauga, and Little Rivers). Recent surveys have found this species in the Sipsey Fork of the Black Warrior River system and in the Little and Conasauga rivers of the Coosa River system. Surveys of the Cahaba River system in 1938, 1973, and 1991 failed to locate the species.

Threats

Habitat modification, sedimentation, and water quality degradation represent the major threats to this species. These freshwater mussels do not tolerate impoundments. More than 1,000 mi (1,609 km) of large and small river habitat in the Mobile River drainage has been impounded for navigation, flood control, water supply, and/or hydroelectric production purposes. Impoundments adversely affect riverine mussels by (1) killing them during construction and dredging, (2) suffocating them with accumulated sediments, (3) lowering food and oxygen availability by reducing water flow, and (4) locally extirpating host fish. Other forms of habitat modification such as channelization, channel clearing and de-snagging, and gravel mining result in streambed scour and erosion, increased turbidity, reduction of groundwater levels, sedimentation, and changes in the aquatic community structure. Sedimentation may cause direct mortality by deposition and suffocation and eliminate or reduce recruitment of juvenile mussels. Suspended sediments can also interfere with feeding. Activities that historically caused sedimentation of streams and rivers in the drainages where this mussel occurs include channel modification, agriculture, forestry, mining, and industrial and residential development. In addition, stream discharge may result in decreased dissolved oxygen concentration, increased acidity and conductivity, and other changes in water chemistry that may impact the mussels and/or fish hosts.

About 230 river mi (370 km) of the Coosa River have been impounded for hydropower by a series of six dams. Water quality degradation caused by textile and carpet mill wastes led to the loss of several known mussel communities in various streams of this river system.

Water quality degradation is a major problem in the Cahaba River system. There are 10 municipal wastewater treatment plants, 35 surface mining areas, a coalbed methane operation, and 67 other permitted discharges in this river system. Siltation from surface mining, road construction, and oil and gas development is also a problem.

Conservation and Recovery

Actions needed for the recovery of freshwater mussels include (1) conducting population and habitat surveys to determine the status and range of the species, (2) determining specific threats to the species and minimizing or eliminating these threats, (3) identifying essential habitat areas in need of protection, and (4) controlling the incidental or illegal take of mussels by commercial and noncommercial collectors. It is unlikely that this species will recover unless new populations are established by introducing individuals back into the historic range. Methods to accomplish this might include the introduction of adult/juvenile mussels, glochidia-infected host fish, and artificially cultured individuals.

Contacts

U.S. Fish and Wildlife Service
Regional Office, Division of Endangered Species
1875 Century Blvd., Suite 200
Atlanta, Georgia 30345
Telephone: (404) 679-4000
http://southeast.fws.gov/

Ecological Services Field Office
P.O. Box 1190
Daphne, Alabama 36526-1190
Telephone: (334) 441-5181
Fax: (334) 441-6222

Ecological Services Field Office
446 Neal Street
Cookeville, Tennessee 38501-4027
Telephone: (931) 528-6481
Fax: (931) 528-7075

References

Thorp, J.H., and A.P. Covich. 1991. *Ecology and Classification of North American Freshwater Invertebrates.* Academic Press, San Diego.

U.S. Fish and Wildlife Service. 17 March 1993. "Endangered and Threatened Wildlife and Plants; Endangered Status for Eight Freshwater Mussels and Threatened Status for Three Freshwater Mussels in the Mobile River Drainage." *Federal Register* 58 (50): 14330-14340.

Gulf Moccasinshell

Medionidus penicillatus

Status	Endangered
Listed	March 16, 1998
Family	Unionidae
Description	Small mussel with yellowish to greenish-brown shell.
Habitat	Stable sandy and gravelly substrates in medium-sized streams to large rivers, often in areas swept free of silt by the current
Food	Filter-feeder of phytoplankton and organic detritus
Reproduction	Female siphons sperm from the water to fertilize her eggs, which hatch into parasitic larvae, which metamorphose into sedentary adults.
Threats	Impoundments, water pollution, possibly predation by muskrats.
Range	Alabama, Florida, Georgia

Description

The *Medionidus penicillatus* (Gulf moccasinshell) is a small mussel that reaches a length of about 2.2 in (55 mm), is elongate-elliptical or rhomboidal and fairly inflated, and has relatively thin valves. The ventral margin is nearly straight or slightly rounded. The posterior ridge is rounded to slightly angled and intersects the end of the shell at the base line. Females tend to have the posterior point above the ventral margin and are somewhat more inflated. Sculpturing consists of a series of thin, radially-oriented plications (folds) along the length of the posterior slope. The remainder of the surface is smooth and yellowish to greenish brown with fine, typically interrupted green rays. The left valve has two stubby pseudocardinal and two arcuate lateral teeth. The right valve has one pseudocardinal and one lateral tooth. Nacre color is smokey purple or greenish and slightly iridescent at the posterior end. The Gulf moccasinshell utilizes the brown darter (*Etheostoma edwini*) and black-banded darter (*E. nigrofasciata*) as host fishes.

Modern taxonomy recognizes the nineteenth-century names *Unio penicillatus* and *Unio kingi* as synonyms of *Medionidus penicillatus*. The recent taxonomic history of *Medionidus* species in the Apalachicolan Region is complex. Two species of *Medionidus*—*M. kingi* and *M. penicillatus*—were recorded in the Chipola river system in 1940. In 1956, two scientists synonymized *M. kingi* and two other nominal species, the Ochlockonee moccasinshell and Suwannee moccasinshell (*M. walkeri*) under the Gulf moccasinshell, an arrangement also followed by another scientist in 1975.

It was erroneously reported in 1970 that the Gulf moccasinshell and Suwannee moccasinshell from the Apalachicola-Chattahoochee-Flint (ACF) River system and the Suwannee moccasinshell from the Ochlockonee and Suwannee Rivers fit as well. It was not until 1977 that the Gulf moccasinshell, Ochlockonee moccasinshell, and Suwannee moccasinshell from Apalachicolan Region streams were recognized as valid and distinct based on their shell characteristics. The validity of the three allopatrically distributed Apalachicolan Region *Medionidus* species is now generally accepted.

Behavior

Adult Gulf moccasinshell mussels are sedentary as adults. They siphon streamwater and filter phytoplankton and organic detritus as food. The female mussels siphon water containing sperm from the water to fertilize their eggs. The eggs hatch into larvae that are parasitic on fish. The larvae later metamorphose into sedentary adults.

Habitat

The Gulf moccasinshell mussel inhabits relatively stable reaches of sandy and gravelly substrates in medium-sized streams to large rivers, often in areas swept free of silt by the current.

Distribution

The Gulf moccasinshell was described from three sites in the ACF River system in Georgia—the Chattahoochee River near Columbus and near Atlanta, and the Flint River near Albany. This species historically occurred in the mainstems and larger tributaries of the ACF, Chipola, Choctawhatchee, and Yellow River systems, as well as in the more westerly confines of Econfina Creek (Bay County, northwest Florida). The species was considered rare over its range but locally abundant. A 1940 study reported 166 specimens from 11 sites, including 130 from two sites in the Chipola River system, an average of 15.1 per site. It is no longer present at most of the historical sites sampled, and is apparently extirpated from the Apalachicola, Choctawhatchee, and Yellow Rivers. There are 13 known sites, none showing evidence of recruitment. During the status survey, 330 sites within the historic range of the Gulf moccasinshell were sampled, including 13 of 31 (42%) known historical sites. This species was found at eight sites (2%), including only one of the historical sites. All Alabama populations of the Gulf moccasinshell appear to be extirpated, and no specimens were found in the Chipola River system during the status survey. The species has not been collected in the Choctawhatchee River system since the early 1930s and in the Yellow River since 1963. The status survey found the species at seven sites (including one mainstem site) in the middle Flint River system, and at one Econfina Creek site. An average of 1.4 live individuals was found per site. Six new sites for the Gulf moccasinshell from tributaries of the ACF River system were found subsequent to the status survey. Three sites were streams in which this species had never been found (one tributary each in the Chattahoochee, Flint, and Chipola Rivers), two were streams (both Flint River system) where this species was found live during the status survey, and one site was a stream in the Chattahoochee River system where a single dead shell had been located during the status survey. Densities of Gulf moccasinshells at two sites where quantitative work was conducted were under 0.04 specimens per sq ft (0.4 specimens per sq m). All specimens located during and subsequent to the status survey were adults; no specimens less than 2.2 in (50 mm) were located.

Threats

Impoundments have altered about 29% of mainstem riverine habitat on the Flint River. Preimpoundment records from Seminole and Blackshear Reservoirs exist for two sites for the Gulf moccasinshell.

Populations of the Gulf moccasinshell have been isolated due to major impoundments on the Apalachicola, Flint, and Ochlockonee Rivers. Future impoundments to satisfy expanding urban and suburban demand, particularly in the metropolitan Atlanta area, could damage stream habitats where small populations of the Gulf moccasinshell exist. Although muskrats are not common within the range of these species, Piedmont populations of the Gulf moccasinshell in the upper Flint River system may be subject to some degree of muskrat predation.

Conservation and Recovery

The Gulf moccasinshell only survives in a few critical habitats, and its reproductive success appears to be quite limited. Its surviving areas of critical habitat must be protected from impoundment and other damages, such as pollution. Its known populations should be monitored and additional ones searched for. Research should be undertaken into its ecological needs, with a view to developing management practices to maintain and improve its habitat.

Contacts

U.S. Fish and Wildlife Service
Jacksonville Ecological Services Field Office
6620 Southpoint Drive South, Suite 310
Jacksonville, Florida 32216-0958
Telephone: (904) 232-2580
Fax: (904) 232-2404

U. S. Fish and Wildlife Service
Regional Office, Division of Endangered Species
1875 Century Blvd., Suite 200
Atlanta, Georgia 30345
http://southeast.fws.gov/

Reference

U.S. Fish and Wildlife Service. 16 March 1998. "Endangered and Threatened Wildlife and Plants; Determination of Endangered Status for Five Freshwater Mussels and Threatened Status for Two Freshwater Mussels From the Eastern Gulf Slope Drainages of Alabama, Florida, and Georgia." *Federal Register* 63(50): 12664-12687.

Ochlockonee Moccasinshell

Medionidus simpsonianus

Status	Endangered
Listed	March 16, 1998
Family	Unionidae
Description	Small mussel; shell is light brown to yellowish green, with dark green rays.
Habitat	Stable sandy and gravelly substrates in medium-sized streams to large rivers, often in areas swept free of silt by the current.
Food	Filter-feeder of phytoplankton and organic detritus.
Reproduction	Female siphons sperm from the water to fertilize her eggs, which hatch into parasitic larvae, which metamorphose into sedentary adults.
Threats	Impoundments.
Range	Florida, Georgia

Description

The *Medionidus simpsonianus* (Ochlockonee moccasinshell) is a small species, generally under 2.2 in (5.5 cm) in length. It is slightly elongate-elliptical in outline, the posterior end obtusely rounded at the shell's median line and the ventral margin broadly curved. The posterior ridge is moderately angular and covered in its entire length with well developed, irregular ridges. Sculpture may also extend onto the disk below the ridge. Surface texture is smooth. The color is light brown to yellowish green, with dark green rays formed by a series of connected chevrons or undulating lines across the length of the shell. Internal characteristics include thin straight lateral teeth and compressed pseudocardinal teeth. There are two laterals and two pseudocardinals in the left valve and one lateral and one pseudocardinal in the right valve. The nacre is bluish white. The host fish for the Ochlockonee moccasinshell is unknown at this time. The lampsiline Ochlockonee moccasinshell probably uses darters as host fish, as do its congeners, the Alabama moccasinshell (*Medionidus acutissimus*), Cumber-

land moccasinshell (*M. conradicus*), and Gulf moccasinshell (*M. penicillatus*).

Behavior

Adult Ochlockonee moccasinshells are sedentary as adults. They siphon streamwater and filter phytoplankton and organic detritus as food. The female moccasinshells siphon water containing sperm to fertilize their eggs. The eggs hatch into larvae that are parasitic on fish. The larvae later metamorphose into sedentary adults.

Habitat

The Ochlockonee moccasinshell inhabits stable sandy and gravelly substrates in medium-sized streams to large rivers, often in areas swept free of silt by the current.

Distribution

The Ochlockonee moccasinshell was described from the Ochlockonee River, Calvary, Grady

County, Georgia. This Ochlockonee River system endemic was known historically from the mainstem and the Little River. Museum records for this species sometimes numbered in the dozens of individuals at sites above Talquin Reservoir.

It was formerly known from eight sites. It is now known only from two sites, where there is no evidence of recruitment.

During the status survey, eight sites were sampled within the historic range of the Ochlockonee moccasinshell, including three of six (50%) known historical sites. Live individuals were found at two sites (one specimen at each site); one of these was a historic site. Another specimen was located in 1995 at a site previously sampled during the status survey. Only three live individuals are known to have been collected since 1974 despite concerted efforts by numerous investigators; none were juveniles.

Threats

Talquin Reservoir flooded about 12% of the riverine habitat in the middle portion of the Ochlokonee river and the lower end of its largest tributary (the Little River). Preimpoundment records exist for the Ochlockonee moccasinshell at the upstream end of Talquin Reservoir, now absent downstream of the dam. This indicates that potential host fish movements may have been blocked.

Conservation and Recovery

The Ochlockonee moccasinshell is a critically endangered species, with only three specimens be-

ing observed since 1974 in spite of a significant search effort. The most pressing conservation need of this rare mollusk is the protection of its surviving areas of critical habitat from impoundment. The habitat must also be protected from other damages, such as pollution. The populations of the Ochlockonee moccasinshell should be monitored and additional ones searched for. Research should be undertaken into its ecological needs, with a view to developing management practices to maintain and improve its habitat.

Contacts

U.S. Fish and Wildlife Service
Jacksonville Ecological Services Field Office
6620 Southpoint Drive South, Suite 310
Jacksonville, Florida 32216-0958
Telephone: (904) 232-2580
Fax: (904) 232-2404

U. S. Fish and Wildlife Service
Regional Office, Division of Endangered Species
1875 Century Blvd., Suite 200
Atlanta, Georgia 30345
http://southeast.fws.gov/

Reference

U.S. Fish and Wildlife Service. 16 March 1998. "Endangered and Threatened Wildlife and Plants; Determination of Endangered Status for Five Freshwater Mussels and Threatened Status for Two Freshwater Mussels From the Eastern Gulf Slope Drainages of Alabama, Florida, and Georgia." *Federal Register* 63(50): 12664-12687.

Nicklin's Pearlymussel

Megalonaias nicklineana

Status	Endangered
Listed	June 14, 1976
Family	Unionidae
Description	A freshwater mussel.
Habitat	Subtropical rivers.
Food	A filter-feeder of phytoplankton and organic detritus.
Reproduction	Releases spawn into the water, where external fertilization occurs.
Threats	Habitat degradation by pollution and siltation.
Range	Guatemala, Honduras, Mexico

Description

The Nicklin's pearlymussel is an extremely rare, little-known, freshwater, bivalve mollusk. Its shell length is about 6 in (15 cm), and the width 2 in (5 cm). The overall shape is roughly triangular, and the shell is thickest near the back (close to the hinge). The shell surface is decorated with zig-zag creases and concentric furrows. The color of the outer shell is dark brown, while the inner is a lustrous, pearly white.

Behavior

The Nicklin's pearlymussel lives on the bottom of slow-moving rivers, where it feeds on phytoplankton (single-celled algae) and particles of organic detritus, which it filters from the water. The spawn is released into the water column, where fertilization occurs. The larvae are pelagic for some time, and are likely parasites of fish. The mature larvae settle to the bottom of their river, where they adopt the sedentary adult lifestyle.

Habitat

The Nicklin's pearlymussel occurs in slow-moving, subtropical rivers.

Distribution

The Nicklin's pearlymussel is only known from a few specimens collected from rivers in Guatemala, Honduras, and southern Mexico.

Threats

Much of the known riverine habitat of the Nicklin's pearlymussel has been severely degraded by pollution with nutrients and pesticides, and by siltation (i.e., the settling of soil particles eroded from nearby agricultural land). These mussels have also been collected for their freshwater pearls, which are of some value in making jewelry. Several of its known populations are now extirpated.

Conservation and Recovery

Little is known about the surviving populations or distribution of the Nicklin's pearlymussel. There is an urgent need for surveys of its known or potential habitat, to determine the degree of risk to its remaining populations. Its best habitats should be conserved, and the local agricultural practices modified to reduce the risk to this rare mollusk.

Contact

Instituto Nacional de Ecología
Av. Revolución, 1425
Col. Campestre, C.P. 01040, Mexico, D.F.
http://www.ine.gob.mx/

Reference

Fuller, S. L. H. 1974. "Clams and Mussels (Mollusca: Bivalvia)." In: C. W. Hart and S. L. H. Fuller (eds.). *Pollution Ecology of Freshwater Invertebrates.* Academic Press. New York. pp. 215-273.

Ring Pink Mussel

Obovaria retusa

Status	Endangered
Listed	September 29, 1989
Family	Unionidae
Description	Medium-sized mussel with yellow-green to brown shell outside and dark purple with a white border inside.
Habitat	Sandy but silt-free bottoms of large rivers.
Food	Plankton and other plant matter.
Reproduction	Breeds in spring; females take in sperm and fertilize eggs in their gills.
Threats	Age of population, limited range, damming, water pollution, dredging, channel maintenance.
Range	Alabama, Indiana, Kentucky, Pennsylvania, Tennessee

Ring Pink Mussel, photograph. A. E. Spreitzer Photography. Reproduced by permission.

Description

This medium-sized mussel, also known as the golf stick pearly mussel, is one of the most endangered of all North American freshwater mussels. Its shell is yellow-green to brown on the outside and dark purple with a white border on the inside.

Behavior

Like other freshwater mussels, the ring pink mussel breeds in the spring. Males release sperm, which are carried by currents downstream to females. As they feed, the females take in the sperm, which fertilize the eggs stored in their gills. Glochidia (larvae) hatch soon after and develop in the female's gills, now modified as brood pouches. After a certain time, the glochidia are released and attach themselves to the gill filaments of host fish (glochidia that do not find host fish sink to the river's bottom and die). When they have grown and developed a shell, the now juvenile mussels detach from the fish and sink to the riverbed. Here, they bury themselves in shoals and riffles, leaving only their shell margins and siphons exposed. Through their siphons, the mussels feed on plankton and other plant matter and expel indigestible particles.

Habitat

This mussel inhabits the sandy but silt-free bottoms of large rivers.

Distribution

Its current distribution includes stretches of three rivers in Tennessee and Kentucky: the Tennessee, Cumberland, and Green Rivers. Total population figures are unavailable.

Threats

The ring pink mussel is in grave danger of extinction, because all of the known populations of the species are apparently too old to reproduce. This mussel was once found in several major tributaries of the Ohio River, including those that stretched into Alabama, Illinois, Indiana, Ohio, Pennsylvania, and West Virginia, so its current limited range signals a major decline in the species. As with many other freshwater mussels, the ring pink mussel's decline can be blamed on human manipulation of its habitat. Damming has historically been the most significant factor, but now the main threats to the surviving populations are water pollution, dredging, and channel maintenance.

Conservation and Recovery

Unless undiscovered, viable populations of the ring pink mussel exist, the future of this species in the wild is uncertain.

Contact

U. S. Fish and Wildlife Service
Regional Office, Division of Endangered Species
1875 Century Blvd., Suite 200
Atlanta, Georgia 30345
http://southeast.fws.gov/

Reference

U. S. Fish and Wildlife Service. 1991. "Ring Pink Mussel Recovery Plan." U. S. Fish and Wildlife Service, Atlanta, Georgia.

Littlewing Pearlymussel

Pegias fabula

Status	Endangered
Listed	November 14, 1988
Family	Unionidae (Freshwater Mussel)
Description	Light green or dark yellowish-brown shell with dark rays and a chalky, eroded patine (surface appearance).
Habitat	Cool, swift-flowing streams; transitional zones between rifles and pools.
Food	Filter-feeder.
Reproduction	Female stores sperm in gills; glochidia (larvae) are released into streams after hatching.
Threats	Degradation of water quality; siltation; coal exploration.
Range	Kentucky, North Carolina, Tennessee, Virginia

Littlewing Pearlymussel, photograph. U. S. Fish and Wildlife Service. Reproduced by permission.

Description

The littlewing pearlymussel (*Pegias fabula*) is a small mussel measuring 1.5 in (3.8 cm) in length and 0.5 in (1.3 cm) in width. The shell is light green or dark yellowish-brown with variable dark rays along the anterior portion. The shell surface often has an eroded chalky or ashy white patina.

Behavior

The life of mussels is complex, and reproduction often depends upon a stable habitat—unaltered stream conditions, clean water, and an undisturbed stream bottom. The cycle also depends upon the abundance of suitable fish hosts to complete the mussel's larval development.

To reproduce, males discharge sperm, which are dispersed by stream currents. In the process of feeding, females nearby or downstream take in sperm, which fertilizes eggs stored in their gills. The gills serve as brood pouches (marsupia), where the

glochidia hatch and begin to develop. After a time, these glochidia are released into the stream. A few mussels have inner parts that resemble a tiny minnow and can be manipulated to lure host fish. When a fish gets close to the shell, the mussel expels its glochidia.

Glochidia have tiny bean- or spoon-shaped valves that attach to the gill filaments of host fish. Glochidia can only progress to the juvenile stage while attached to the fish's gills. Those that do not fortuitously encounter a host fish do not survive when released by the female mussel. They sink to the bottom and die.

When the juvenile has developed a shell and is large enough to survive on its own, it detaches from the host fish and falls to the stream bottom, beginning a long association with a single stretch of stream. Maturing mussels bury themselves in riffles and shoals with only the shell margins and feeding siphons exposed to the water. Some mussels live as long as 50 years or more.

The family Unionidae, which includes all of the freshwater mussels in the United States, is separated into two groups based on the length of time the glochidia remain in the female's marsupia. The eggs of the short-term (tachytictic) breeders are fertilized in the spring, and glochidia are released by late summer of the same year. Long-term (bradytictic) breeders hold developing glochidia in the brood pouch over winter and release them in the spring.

Freshwater mussels feed by siphoning phytoplankton and other plant matter from the water. Indigestible particles are expelled from the shell by reverse siphoning. Silt in the water can kill mussels by clogging their feeding siphons.

There are no known interspecific differences in feeding among freshwater mussels. The glochidia are obligate parasites on the gills or fins of fish. Adult mussels are filter-feeders and consume particulate matter in the water column. Identifiable stomach contents almost invariably include desmids, diatoms, algae, protozoa, and zooplankton.

Most freshwater mussel species display seasonal variations in activity associated with water temperature and reproduction. Metabolic rate is, in part, positively correlated with temperature. Many ectothermic species have the capacity to adjust their metabolic rates in response to long-term changes in temperature. Thus, metabolic rates do not continue to rise with temperatures in the summer, and they do not continue to fall during the winter as temperatures decline.

Some freshwater mussels also show diurnal changes in metabolic rates that indicate a tendency toward nocturnal activity patterns. Mussels may move to the surface to feed at night and move deeper into the substrate during the day; this is one way to avoid predators that hunt by visual contact.

Freshwater mussels are nonmigratory.

Habitat

This species is restricted to cool, high-to-moderate gradient streams and is usually found only in the narrow zone where riffle flow deepens into pools. It is highly sensitive to alterations of current.

Distribution

At one time, this Cumberlandian mussel was widely distributed in at least 27 of the smaller, cool-water tributaries of the Tennessee and Cumberland Rivers. The species apparently has been extirpated from Alabama. Three populations in Kentucky, nine in Tennessee, and six in Virginia are believed to have died out.

This species is currently found in Kentucky, Tennessee, North Carolina, and Virginia. A 1986 survey of 55 potential and historic habitats located only 17 live specimens. Four of six known populations are threatened by activities associated with exploration for coal.

In the summer of 1990 biologists from the U.S. Fish and Wildlife Service's Asheville (North Carolina) Field Office and the Tennessee Cooperative Fishery Research Unit discovered a new population of the littlewing pearlymussel in a short reach of the Little Tennessee River in North Carolina. At the time of this discovery, the only known littlewing pearlymussel population in North Carolina had been lost. The discovery of this new population in the Little Tennessee River will assist in the species' recovery.

Only seven other populations of this mussel are known, including what is probably the healthiest surviving population: the one in Horse Lick Creek (Jackson and Rockcastle Counties), Kentucky. Smaller populations have been located in the Big South Fork Cumberland River (McCreary County), Kentucky; the Little South Fork Cumberland River (McCreary and Wayne Counties), Kentucky; Cane Creek above Great Falls Lake (Van Buren County), Tennessee (where suitable habitat is limited by downstream siltation); and at two locations in the North Fork Holston River (Smyth County), Virginia—one near Saltville, the others at Nebo.

Threats

Always relatively uncommon because of its more specialized habitat requirements, the littlewing pearlymussel has declined throughout its range because of degradation of water quality. Wastes from coal mining and industrial sites have made many former population sites uninhabitable. Runoff from strip mining, coal washing, and agriculture has clouded waters that were once crystal clear and smothered mussel beds beneath layers of sediment. Toxic chemical releases were apparently responsible for the demise of several mussel populations.

Conservation and Recovery

Part of the mussel's Kentucky watershed lies within the Daniel Boone National Forest, and Horse Lick Creek has been identified as one of Kentucky's Outstanding Resource Waters. State and federal biologists are cooperating to rejuvenate populations at these protected sites.

Ongoing exploration for new coal reserves in the region threatens to degrade the water quality of the remaining habitat.

State laws in Kentucky, Tennessee, and Virginia prohibit the collection of freshwater mussels without a permit. The recovery objectives for this species are to establish 13 viable populations through the protection of existing populations and through the discovery and/or creation of additional populations.

Contacts

U.S. Fish and Wildlife Service
Regional Office, Division of Endangered Species
1875 Century Blvd., Suite 200
Atlanta, Georgia 30345
Telephone: (404) 679-4000
http://southeast.fws.gov/

U. S. Fish and Wildlife Service
Regional Office, Division of Endangered Species
300 Westgate Center Dr.
Hadley, Massachusetts 01035-9589
Telephone: (413) 253-8200
Fax: (413) 253-8308
http://northeast.fws.gov/

References

Ahlstedt, S.A. 1986. "A Status Survey of the Littlewing Pearly Mussel." Report, Contract No. 14-16-0004-84-927. U.S. Fish and Wildlife Service, Atlanta.

Biggins, R.G. 1989. "Draft Recovery Plan for Littlewing Pearly Mussel." U.S. Fish and Wildlife Service, Asheville, North Carolina.

Soule, M.E. 1980. "Thresholds for Survival: Maintaining Fitness and Evolutionary Potential." In M.E. Soul and B.A. Wilcox, eds., *Conservation Biology*. Sinauer Associates, Sunderland, Massachusetts.

Stansbery, D.H. 1976. "Status of Endangered Fluviatile Mollusks in Central North America: *Pegias fabula*." Report, Contract No. 14-166-0008-755. U.S. Fish and Wildlife Service, Asheville.

U.S. Fish and Wildlife Service. 1988. "Determination of Endangered Species Status for the Littlewing Pearly Mussel." *Federal Register* 53 (219): 45861-65.

White Wartyback Pearlymussel

Plethobasus cicatricosus

Status	Endangered
Listed	June 14, 1976
Family	Unionidae (Freshwater Mussel)
Description	Thick, egg-shaped, greenish yellow or yellow-brown shell.
Habitat	Sand or gravel substrate in flowing water.
Food	Filter-feeder.
Reproduction	Female stores sperm in gills; glochidia are released into the stream after hatching.
Threats	Habitat loss, pollution, siltation.
Range	Alabama, Tennessee, Indiana

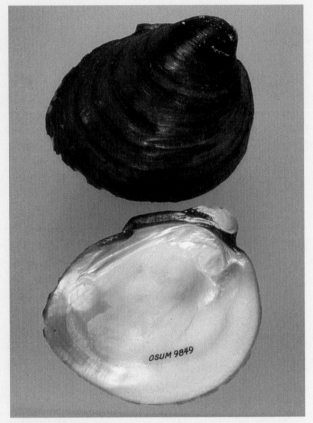

White Wartyback Pearlymussel, photograph. A. E. Spreitzer Photography. Reproduced by permission.

Description

The shell of the white wartyback pearlymussel, *Plethobasus cicatricosus*, is somewhat egg-shaped, thick, solid, and inflated. The greenish yellow or yellow-brown shell surface is marked by uneven, concentric growth lines and a row of knobs (tubercles) in the middle portion of the shell. The iridescent inner shell surface is white. Individuals can live as long as 50 years. The white wartyback has sometimes been confused with a closely related species, *Plethobasus cyphyus*.

Behavior

See the Upland Combshell (*Epioblasma metastriata*) entry.

Habitat

The white wartyback pearlymussel buries itself in sand and gravel substrates in shallow stretches of large rivers with slow to moderate currents.

Distribution

This pearlymussel was first collected in 1829 from the Wabash River in Indiana, and is thought to have enjoyed a widespread distribution in the Ohioan or Interior Basin. It was documented from the Kanawha River (West Virginia), the Ohio River (Ohio and Indiana), the Cumberland and Holston Rivers (Tennessee), and the Tennessee River below Wilson Dam (Alabama).

Since the mid-1960s, only two Tennessee River specimens have been discovered, both near Savannah, Tennessee, below the Pickwick Dam. The species may be extinct or near extinction in the Tennessee River. No live specimens have been taken from the Cumberland River since 1885. In spite of extensive surveys, there is no recent evidence of this species in the Ohio, Wabash, or Kanawha Rivers.

Threats

The white wartyback pearlymussel was historically found only in large rivers and was never very common. Possibly the single greatest factor in this mussel's decline has been the alteration of the Tennessee and Cumberland river basins by the construction of major dams for flood control, hydroelectric power production, and navigation. Dam reservoirs have inundated large stretches of river that once supported mussel populations, while sections of former habitat below the dams have been rendered uninhabitable by erratic water levels, altered water temperatures, and seasonal oxygen deficits.

In addition to numerous locks and dams, the historic conditions of the Wabash and Ohio Rivers have been significantly altered by deforestation and poor agricultural practices that have increased water turbidity and siltation. Water quality has been further degraded by chemical runoff, industrial effluents, and sewage.

Conservation and Recovery

Unless a viable reproducing population is found, little in the way of recovery can be considered. The white wartyback pearlymussel may benefit from more general efforts aimed at improving the environmental quality of the Interior Basin's major rivers. The Tennessee Valley Authority is currently working on a comprehensive water management plan, which would guarantee constant minimum flows in all rivers in the Tennessee and Cumberland basins by timing water discharges from its dams. Such an effort might mollify many of the negative effects of dams and reservoirs on remaining stretches of mussel habitat.

Although unfortunate from the standpoint of local residents, economic slowdown (the closing of steel mills and other major industrial polluters in the region of the Ohio River's headwaters) has resulted in almost immediate water quality improvement in the upper river. Recently, freshwater mussels have been rediscovered in stretches of the river where they have been absent for more than 70 years.

Contact

Regional Office of Endangered Species
U.S. Fish and Wildlife Service
1875 Century Blvd., Suite 200
Atlanta, Georgia 30345
http://southeast.fws.gov/

References

Bogan, A., and P. Parmalee. 1983. "Tennessee's Rare Mollusks." In *Tennessee's Rare Wildlife, Final Report*. Tennessee Heritage Program of the Department of Conservation and the University of Tennessee, Knoxville.

Isom, B. G. 1969. "The Mussel Resources of the Tennessee River." *Malacologia* 7(2-3):397-425.

Jenkinson, J.J. 1981."The Tennessee Valley Authority Cumberlandian Mollusk Conservation Program." *Bulletin of the American Malacological Union* 1980:662-63.

U.S. Fish and Wildlife Service. 1984. "Recovery Plan for the White Wartyback Pearly Mussel (*Plethobasus cicatricosus*)." U.S. Fish and Wildlife Service, Atlanta.

Orangefoot Pimpleback

Plethobasus cooperianus

Status	Endangered
Listed	June 14, 1976
Family	Unionidae (Freshwater Mussel)
Description	Large, nearly circular, yellowish to chestnut brown shell.
Habitat	Medium to large rivers in gravel and rubble substrates.
Food	Filter feeder.
Reproduction	Breeds in the spring and releases glochidia in the spring.
Threats	Dam construction, siltation, pollution.
Range	Alabama, Illinois, Indiana, Kentucky, Pennsylvania, Tennessee

Orangefoot Pimpleback, photograph. A. E. Spreitzer Photography. Reproduced by permission.

Description

The orangefoot pimpleback, *Plethobasus cooperianus*, is nearly circular, attains a mature shell length of up to 3.7 in (9.5 cm), and a thickness of 1.8 in (4.6 cm). Valves are solid and moderately swollen. The shell surface is yellowish brown to chestnut brown and is marked by dark, concentric, irregular growth lines. The posterior two-thirds of the shell is covered with numerous raised knobs (turbercles). Greenish rays are found only in younger specimens. The inner shell surface (nacre) varies in color from white to pink.

Behavior

The orangefoot pimpleback is probably a "tachytictic bivalve," or short-term breeder—one that breeds in spring and releases glochidia (larvae) by late summer. Individuals can live as long as 50 years. For more on the reproduction and diet of freshwater mussels, see the Upland Combshell (*Epioblasma metastriata*) entry.

Habitat

The orangefoot pimpleback is found in medium to large rivers in depths of 12-29 ft (3.6-8.8 m). It buries itself into sand and gravel with only the margin of the shell and feeding siphons exposed to the water.

Distribution

The orangefoot pimpleback is an Interior Basin species with distribution in the drainages of the Ohio, Cumberland, and Tennessee Rivers. This species was locally abundant in the Ohio River between St. Marys, West Virginia, and Marietta, Ohio, and around the confluence of the Wabash River in Indiana. In the lower Ohio River, it was found between the Cumberland and Tennessee Rivers and the Mississippi River in Illinois. It was locally abundant in the Wabash River in Indiana and common to rare in the mainstream of the Cumberland River in Tennessee. It has been documented in the Rough River of Kentucky; the Duck, French Broad, Holston, and Clinch Rivers of Tennessee; and the Kanawha River of West Virginia. The orangefoot pimpleback has been extirpated from the Kanawha, upper Ohio, and Wabash Rivers, and its range elsewhere has been greatly reduced. In the Tennessee River, orangefoot pimplebacks have been found below the Fort Loudoun Dam (Loudon County, Tennessee), Guntersville Dam (Marshall County, Alabama), and several clustered sites below Pickwick Dam (Hardin County, Tennessee).

The mussel survives in the Cumberland River only below Cordell Hull Dam (Smith County, Tennessee). Other populations survive in the lower Ohio River between Metropolis and Mound City (Massac and Pulaski counties, Illinois). The U. S. Fish and Wildlife Service lists the species as endangered in Alabama, Illinois, Indiana, Kentucky, Pennsylvania, and Tennessee.

Threats

Because it occurred in small numbers in localized beds, the orangefoot pimpleback has always been somewhat rare. Possibly the single greatest factor in this mussel's decline has been the alteration of the Tennessee and Cumberland river basins by the construction of dams for flood control, hydroelectric power production, navigation, and recreation. Dam reservoirs have inundated stretches of river that once supported mussel populations, while sections of former habitat below the dams have been rendered uninhabitable by erratic water levels. In addition to numerous locks and dams, the historic conditions of the Wabash and Ohio Rivers have been altered by deforestation and poor agricultural practices, which increased water turbidity and siltation. Water quality has been further degraded by chemical runoff, industrial effluents, and sewage.

Conservation and Recovery

The recovery of this species will depend upon the success of larger efforts to reclaim river habitat throughout the Interior Basin. The Tennessee Valley Authority is working on water management to guarantee constant minimum flows in all rivers in the Tennessee and Cumberland basins by timing water discharges from its dams. Such an effort may mollify many of the negative effects of dams and reservoirs on remaining stretches of mussel habitat. In recent years, the water quality of the upper Ohio River has improved. If this improvement continues the orangefoot pimpleback may be reintroduced to its historic range above Marietta, Ohio.

Contacts

U. S. Fish and Wildlife Service
Regional Office, Division of Endangered Species
1 Federal Drive
BHW Federal Building
Fort Snelling, Minnesota 55111
Telephone: (612) 713-5360
http://midwest.fws.gov/

U. S. Fish and Wildlife Service
Regional Office, Division of Endangered Species
1875 Century Blvd., Suite 200
Atlanta, Georgia 30345
http://southeast.fws.gov/

U. S. Fish and Wildlife Service
Regional Office, Division of Endangered Species
300 Westgate Center Dr.
Hadley, Massachusetts 01035-9589
Telephone: (413) 253-8200
Fax: (413) 253-8308
http://northeast.fws.gov/

References

Clark, C. F. 1976. "The Freshwater Naiads of the Lower End of the Wabash River, Mt. Carmal, Illinois, to the South." *Sterkiana* 61: 1-14.

U. S. Fish and Wildlife Service. 1984. "Recovery Plan for the Orange-Footed Pearly Mussel." U. S. Fish and Wildlife Service, Asheville, N. C.

Clubshell

Pleurobema clava

Status	Endangered
Listed	January 22, 1993
Family	Unionidae
Description	A freshwater bivalve mollusk.
Habitat	Rivers and streams.
Food	Adults are filter-feeders on organic particles, algae, and tiny zooplankton; larvae are parasites of fish.
Reproduction	Eggs are internally fertilized, hatching within the female to release planktonic larvae, which eventually metamorphose into sedentary adults.
Threats	Habitat destruction and degradation by siltation and pollution; risks of catastrophic loss of small population; effects of invasive zebra mussels.
Range	Alabama, Illinois, Indiana, Kentucky, Michigan, Ohio, Pennsylvania, Tennessee, West Virginia

Description

The clubshell has a shell length of up to about 3 in (7.6 cm). The shell is wedge- or triangular-shaped, solid, and its peak (or umbo) is rather pointed and fairly high. The exterior surface is colored bright-yellow to brown, with bright-green, blotchy rays. The inside of the shell (nacre) is pearly white.

Behavior

The specific food habits and reproductive biology of the clubshell are not known, but are likely similar to those of other freshwater mussels. As such, they probably filter-feed on organic particles, algae, and minute animals, which are siphoned out of the water column. During reproduction, the females take in sperm released into the water by males, so that fertilization occurs internally. Fertilized eggs remain in the gills until they hatch into tiny larvae, which are released into the water. The larvae are parasites that attach and form cysts on the gills or fins of a fish host. The larvae metamor-

phosize and settle to the riverbed, and thereafter lead a sedentary lifestyle.

Habitat

The clubshell inhabits small rivers and streams, where it lives in clean sand and gravel. It typically occurs buried in clean, loose sand to a depth of 2-4 in (5-10 cm).

Distribution

The historical range of the clubshell included Alabama, Illinois, Indiana, Kentucky, Michigan, Ohio, Pennslyvania, Tennessee, and West Virginia.

Threats

The clubshell was once a widespread and abundant bivalve in most of its range. It existed through much of the Ohio River basin in the Allegheny, Green, Kanawha, Kentucky, Licking, Lit-

Clubshell, photograph by Thomas Watters, Ohio DNR. Reproduced by permission.

tle Kanawha, Mississinewa, Ohio, Salt, Scioto, Tennessee, Tippecanoe, Vermillion, Wabash, and White Rivers. It was also found in the Maumee River basin and tributaries in western Lake Erie (Huron River and River Raison). The clubshell is now enormously reduced in range and abundance, and is only known from 12 streams in Indiana, Michigan, Ohio, Pennsylvania, and West Virginia. Its recent distribution represents a range reduction of more than 95%. The decline of the clubshell has been caused mostly by habitat destruction and damage due to the construction of dams and impoundments, channelization, loss of riparian habitat, and siltation with soil eroded by from poor land uses. Water pollution with organic matter, nutrients, and toxic chemicals from discharges of cities and towns, industries, coal mines, and reservoirs also have impacted the rare clubshell. The invasion of the non-native, very com-

petitive zebra mussel (*Dreissena polymorpha*) is another potential threat to the clubshell and other native bivalves.

Conservation and Recovery

Conservation and enhancement of the clubshell requires management to restore some of its critical areas through the repair of riparian habitat and the control of non-point and point-source pollution. Research is needed to identify the habitat needs of the clubshell and its fish hosts, and to develop methods of captive-breeding and reintroduction to wild habitats. Additional field surveys are needed to assess and monitor the condition of existing populations, and to search for suitable habitats for potential reintroduction attempts. It is crucial that the existing habitats are protected from locally incompatible land-uses and aqueous discharges.

Contacts

U. S. Fish and Wildlife Service
Regional Office, Division of Endangered Species
1 Federal Drive
BHW Federal Building
Fort Snelling, Minnesota 55111
Telephone: (612) 713-5360
http://midwest.fws.gov/

U. S. Fish and Wildlife Service
Regional Office, Division of Endangered Species
1875 Century Blvd., Suite 200
Atlanta, Georgia 30345
http://southeast.fws.gov/

U. S. Fish and Wildlife Service
Regional Office, Division of Endangered Species
300 Westgate Center Dr.
Hadley, Massachusetts 01035-9589
Telephone: (413) 253-8200
Fax: (413) 253-8308
http://www.northeast.fws.gov/

U. S. Fish and Wildlife Service
330 Ridgefield Court
Asheville, North Carolina 28806
(704) 665-1195

Reference

U. S. Fish and Wildlife Service. 1993. "Endangered and Threatened Wildlife and Plants; Determination of Endangered Status for the Northern Riffleshell Mussel (*Epioblasma torulosa rangiana*) and the Clubshell Mussel (*Pleurobema clava*)." http://endangered.fws.gov/r/fr93488.html

James River Spinymussel

Pleurobema collina

Status	Endangered
Listed	July 22, 1988
Family	Unionidae (Freshwater Mussel)
Description	Medium-sized, reddish brown shell with dark brown to blackish margins.
Habitat	Slow-flowing stretches of head-water streams.
Food	Filter-feeder.
Reproduction	Female stores sperm in gills; glochidia are released into the stream after hatching.
Threats	Habitat modification; competition with the Asiatic clam.
Range	Virginia, West Virginia

A. E. Spreitzer

Description

Also known as the Virginia spinymussel or James spinymussel, *Pleurobema collina*, the James River spinymussel is described as having an intermediate shell size (2-3.5 in; 5-9 cm) and spine length. Shells of juvenile mussels usually bear one to three short but prominent spines on each valve. Adult shells are reddish brown with dark brown to blackish margins, and typically lack spines. The foot and mantle of the adult are vivid orange; the mantle is darkened in a narrow band around the edges of the branchial and anal openings. Scientists have vari-

ously classified this species as *Fusconaia collina*, *Elliptio collina*, and *Cantheria collina*.

Only two other freshwater spinymussels are known—*Elliptio spinosa* from the Altamaha River in Georgia, and the Tar River spinymussel (*Elliptio steinstansana*) from the Tar River in North Carolina. The Tar River spinymussel was listed as Endangered in 1985.

Behavior

Spawning occurs in May, and the period of gravity in females is late May through early August.

Densities of glochidia peak in late June to mid-July as stream discharge drops to summer levels and water temperature reaches 75°F (24°C.). The host fish species required for glochidial development include bluehead chub, rosyside dace, satinfin shiner, rosefin shiner, central stoneroller, blacknose dace, and mountain redbelly dace.

For more on the reproduction and diet of freshwater mussels, see the Upland Combshell (*Epioblasma metastriata*) entry.

Habitat

The James River spinymussel requires freshwater streams with high water quality and a fairly high mineral content. It has been collected from sand and gravel substrates, generally in slow-moving water.

Distribution

The James River spinymussel was first discovered in the Calfpasture River (Rockbridge County), Virginia, in 1836. It was once widely distributed in the James River drainage, which includes the Rivanna River, Mill Creek, the Calfpasture River, Johns Creek, and numerous headwater creeks. The range of this species has been reduced to less than 10% of its historic size.

Currently, the James River spinymussel survives in a few headwater streams of the James River—Craig, Catawba, and Johns Creeks (Craig and Botetourt Counties, Virginia), and Potts Creek (Monroe County, West Virginia).

Threats

Habitat modification has been a major factor in the decline of this spinymussel. The few drainages still supporting the species are threatened by harmful agricultural runoff of silt, fertilizers, and herbicides. It is hoped that federal control over issuance of permits for mineral exploration, timber sales, recreational development, stream channelization, and bridge construction and maintenance can be used to prevent further disturbance of the watershed.

The Asiatic clam (*Corbicula fluminea*) has invaded many formerly inhabited streams. This clam establishes very dense populations which filter most of the phytoplankton from the water—in essence, starving the spiny and other native mussels.

Muskrats apparently prey on this mussel. A sample of shells collected in muskrat middens revealed that the mussels consumed by the muskrats ranged in age from three to 19 years, averaging about eight years. It is thought that the natural annual mortality rate is about 10% of the population.

Conservation and Recovery

Survival of the James River spinymussel will probably require a program to control Asiatic clam populations. However, as water quality improves in the James River, it is feasible that remnant populations could expand and recolonize some historical habitat.

Contact

U.S. Fish and Wildlife Service
Regional Office, Division of Endangered Species
300 Westgate Center Drive
Hadley, Massachusetts 01035
http://northeast.fws.gov/

References

Burch, J. B. 1975. *Freshwater Unionacean Clams of North America*. Malacological Publications, Hamburg, Michigan.

Diaz, R. J. 1974. "Asiatic Clam *Corbicula manilensis* in the Tidal James River, Virginia." *Chesapeake Science* 15(2):118-120.

U.S. Fish and Wildlife Service. 1988. "Determination of Endangered Status for the James River Spinymussel." *Federal Register* 53 (141): 27689-27693.

Zeto, M. A., and J. E. Schmidt. 1984. "Freshwater Mussels of Monroe County, West Virginia." *Nautilus* 96(4):147-151.

Black Clubshell

Pleurobema curtum

Status	Endangered
Listed	April 7, 1987
Family	Unionidae (Freshwater Mussel)
Description	Greenish-brown subtriangular shell.
Habitat	Sand and gravel substrate in flowing rivers.
Food	Filter-feeder.
Reproduction	Female stores sperm in gills; glochidia (larvae) are released into streams after hatching.
Threats	Low numbers; restricted range; dredging; siltation.
Range	Alabama, Mississippi

Black Clubshell, photograph. A. E. Spreitzer Photography. Reproduced by permission.

Description

The shell of the black clubshell (*Pleurobema curtum*) is about 2 in (5.1 cm) long and varies in color from light green in young mussels to a dark greenish-brown in older ones. The shell is subtriangular and inflated in front. The thin inner shell surface is an iridescent bluish-white. This species was first classified as *Unio curtus*.

The identity of species within the genus *Pleurobema* is currently the focus of debate among malacologists. The U.S. Fish and Wildlife Service (FWS) has adopted the majority view but acknowledges that further research may warrant reclassification of the black clubshell and other mussels of the genus.

Behavior

The life of mussels is complex, and reproduction often depends upon a stable habitat—unaltered stream conditions, clean water, and an undisturbed stream bottom. The cycle also depends upon the abundance of suitable fish hosts to complete the mussel's larval development.

To reproduce, males discharge sperm, which are dispersed by stream currents. In the process of feeding, females nearby or downstream take in sperm, which fertilizes eggs stored in their gills. The gills serve as brood pouches (marsupia), where the glochidia hatch and begin to develop. After a time, these glochidia are released into the stream. A few mussels have inner parts that resemble a tiny minnow and can be manipulated to lure host fish. When a fish gets close to the shell, the mussel expels its glochidia.

Glochidia have tiny bean- or spoon-shaped valves that attach to the gill filaments of host fish. Glochidia can only progress to the juvenile stage while attached to the fish's gills. Those that do not fortuitously encounter a host fish do not survive when released by the female mussel. They sink to the bottom and die.

When the juvenile has developed a shell and is large enough to survive on its own, it detaches from the host fish and falls to the stream bottom, beginning a long association with a single stretch of stream. Maturing mussels bury themselves in riffles and shoals with only the shell margins and feeding siphons exposed to the water. Some mussels live as long as 50 years or more.

The family Unionidae, which includes all of the freshwater mussels in the United States, is separated into two groups based on the length of time the glochidia remain in the female's marsupia. The eggs of the short-term (tachytictic) breeders are fertilized in the spring, and glochidia are released by late summer of the same year. Long-term (bradytictic) breeders hold developing glochidia in the brood pouch over winter and release them in the spring.

Freshwater mussels feed by siphoning phytoplankton and other plant matter from the water. Indigestible particles are expelled from the shell by reverse siphoning. Silt in the water can kill mussels by clogging their feeding siphons.

There are no known interspecific differences in feeding among freshwater mussels. The glochidia are obligate parasites on the gills or fins of fish. Adult mussels are filter-feeders and consume particulate matter in the water column. Identifiable stomach contents almost invariably include desmids, diatoms, algae, protozoa, and zooplankton.

Most freshwater mussel species display seasonal variations in activity associated with water temperature and reproduction. Metabolic rate is, in part, positively correlated with temperature. Many ec-

tothermic species have the capacity to adjust their metabolic rates in response to long-term changes in temperature. Thus, metabolic rates do not continue to rise as temperatures rise in the summer, and they do not continue to fall during the winter as temperatures decline.

Some freshwater mussels also show diurnal changes in metabolic rates that indicate a tendency toward nocturnal activity patterns. Mussels may move to the surface to feed at night and move deeper into the substrate during the day; this is one way to avoid predators that hunt by visual contact.

Freshwater mussels are nonmigratory.

Habitat

The black clubshell is found in clean, swift-flowing rivers where the bottom is formed of firm rubble, gravel, or sand. This mussel prefers shallow riffles and shoals, where the current is strong enough to keep the bottom scoured of silt.

Distribution

The black clubshell has been found in the East Fork and mainstream of the Tombigbee River and has been collected from only five locations. Reports of this species from the Big Black River in Mississippi are probably erroneous.

The species is thought to survive in an unmodified segment of the East Fork Tombigbee River (Itwamba and Monroe Counties, Mississippi). Only two living specimens have been found since 1974. An extensive survey of the river conducted in 1987 failed to turn up any living or recently dead specimens. The FWS believes that the black clubshell mussel survives but that its population is critically low.

Threats

When the Tennessee-Tombigbee Waterway was constructed to allow barge traffic between the Tennessee and Tombigbee Rivers, most of the East Fork Tombigbee River was modified into a series of channels, locks, and impoundments. The dams and locks inundated mussel shoals and slowed the flow of water, increasing siltation, which smothers mussel beds.

Dredging to create a navigable channel physically destroyed many mussel beds, and periodic maintenance dredging continues to disturb the river bottom. Bull Mountain Creek, which provided nearly half the water supply of the East Fork, was diverted to feed the new waterway. The creek's cooler waters are warmed when routed through the canal, making this part of the river inimical to both mussels and host fishes.

The last free-flowing stretch of the East Fork Tombigbee River is threatened by plans to dredge 53 mi (85 km) to improve navigability. Siltation in this portion of the river has become more severe since the mid-1990s and may already be smothering the surviving mussel beds. The riverbeds are also exposed to continuing runoff of fertilizers and pesticides, which can produce stream eutrophication. Filter-feeders such as mussels ingest these chemicals, which alters their siphoning period and metabolic rate.

The black clubshell may also be adversely affected by the loss of its fish host as a result of habitat alteration.

Conservation and Recovery

Under provisions of the Endangered Species Act, federal agencies are required to consult with the FWS to ensure that any actions they authorize or fund do not jeopardize an endangered species. This rule affects current and proposed flood control and navigation projects sponsored by the Army Corps of Engineers and watershed projects proposed by the Soil Conservation Service of the Department of Agriculture. In the past, similar consultations have resulted in the redesign of projects to preserve significant portions of habitat.

Recovery of the black clubshell would require construction of sediment basins and selective dredging to limit siltation.

Contact

U. S. Fish and Wildlife Service
Regional Office, Division of Endangered Species
1875 Century Blvd., Suite 200
Atlanta, Georgia 30345
Telephone: (404) 679-4000
http://southeast.fws.gov/

Reference

Stansbery, D.H. 1983. "The Status of *Pleurobema curtum.*" Unpublished Report. U.S. Fish and Wildlife Service, Atlanta.

Southern Clubshell

Pleurobema decisum

Status	Endangered
Listed	March 17, 1993
Family	Unionidae (Freshwater Mussel)
Description	Medium-sized mussel with a thick shell and a heavy hinge plate.
Habitat	Gravel riffles in streams.
Food	Filter-feeder.
Reproduction	Female stores sperm in gills; glochidia (larvae) are released into streams after hatching.
Threats	Impoundments; gravel mining; water pollution.
Range	Alabama, Georgia, Mississippi, Tennessee

Description

The southern clubshell (*Pleurobema decisum*) is a medium-sized mussel about 2.8 in (7.1 cm) in length with a thick shell and a heavy hinge plate and teeth. The shell outline is roughly rectangular, produced posteriorly with the umbos (prominences) terminal with the anterior margin or nearly so. The posterior ridge is moderately inflated and ends abruptly with little development of the posterior slope at the dorsum of the shell. The periostracum (epidermis) is yellow to yellow-brown with occasional green rays or spots on the umbo in young specimens.

The southern clubshell is distinguished from a closely related species, the black clubshell, by its elongated shape, lighter color, and the presence of a well-defined sulcus (groove) in the latter species.

Behavior

The life of mussels is complex, and reproduction often depends upon a stable habitat—unaltered stream conditions, clean water, and an undisturbed stream bottom. The cycle also depends upon the abundance of suitable fish hosts to complete the mussel's larval development.

To reproduce, males discharge sperm, which are dispersed by stream currents. In the process of feed-ing, females nearby or downstream take in sperm, which fertilizes eggs stored in their gills. The gills serve as brood pouches (marsupia), where the glochidia hatch and begin to develop. After a time, these glochidia are released into the stream. A few mussels have inner parts that resemble a tiny minnow and can be manipulated to lure host fish. When a fish gets close to the shell, the mussel expels its glochidia.

Glochidia have tiny bean- or spoon-shaped valves that attach to the gill filaments of host fish. Glochidia can only progress to the juvenile stage while attached to the fish's gills. Those that do not fortuitously encounter a host fish do not survive when released by the female mussel. They sink to the bottom and die.

When the juvenile has developed a shell and is large enough to survive on its own, it detaches from the host fish and falls to the stream bottom, beginning a long association with a single stretch of stream. Maturing mussels bury themselves in riffles and shoals with only the shell margins and feeding siphons exposed to the water. Some mussels live as long as 50 years or more.

The family Unionidae, which includes all of the freshwater mussels in the United States, is separated into two groups based on the length of time the

Southern Clubshell, photograph by Dave Dieter, Huntsville Times. Reproduced by permission.

glochidia remain in the female's marsupia. The eggs of the short-term (tachytictic) breeders are fertilized in the spring, and glochidia are released by late summer of the same year. Long-term (bradytictic) breeders hold developing glochidia in the brood pouch over winter and release them in the spring.

Freshwater mussels feed by siphoning phytoplankton and other plant matter from the water. Indigestible particles are expelled from the shell by reverse siphoning. Silt in the water can kill mussels by clogging their feeding siphons.

There are no known interspecific differences in feeding among freshwater mussels. The glochidia are obligate parasites on the gills or fins of fish. Adult mussels are filter-feeders and consume particulate matter in the water column. Identifiable stomach contents almost invariably include desmids, diatoms, algae, protozoa, and zooplankton.

Most freshwater mussel species display seasonal variations in activity associated with water temper-ature and reproduction. Metabolic rate is, in part, positively correlated with temperature. Many ectothermic species have the capacity to adjust their metabolic rates in response to long-term changes in temperature. Thus, metabolic rates do not continue to rise as temperatures rise in the summer, and they do not continue to fall during the winter as temperatures decline.

Some freshwater mussels also show diurnal changes in metabolic rates that indicate a tendency toward nocturnal activity patterns. Mussels may move to the surface to feed at night and move deeper into the substrate during the day; this is one way to avoid predators that hunt by visual contact.

Freshwater mussels are nonmigratory.

Habitat

The southern clubshell inhabits high-quality lotic (living in actively moving water) habitats with stable gravel and sandy-gravel substrates. Little else is known about its habitat requirements.

The habitat of the glochidia is initially in the gills of the female, then in the water column, and finally attached to a suitable host fish. Habitat associations or requirements for the juvenile stage are unknown.

Distribution

The Southern clubshell was historically known from every major stream system in the Mobile River basin including the Alabama River (Bogue Chitto Creek), the Tombigbee River (Buttahatchie, East Fork Tombigbee, and Sipsey Rivers and Bull Mountain, Luxapalila, and Lubbub Creeks), the Black Warrior River, the Cahaba and Little Cahaba Rivers, the Tallapossa River (Uphapee and Chewacla Creeks), and the Coosa River (Oostanaula, Conasauga, Etowah, Chatooga, and Coosawattee Rivers and Kelly, Talladega, and Shoal Creeks).

This species' current distribution is limited to the Alabama River (Bogue Chitto Creek), the Tombigbee River (Buttahatchie, East Fork Tombigbee, and Sipsey Rivers), and the Tallapossa River (Chewacla Creek).

Threats

Habitat modification, sedimentation, and water quality degradation represent the major threats to this species. These freshwater mussels do not tolerate impoundments. More than 1,000 mi (1,609 km) of large and small river habitat in the Mobile River drainage has been impounded for navigation, flood control, water supply, and/or hydroelectric production purposes. Impoundments adversely affect riverine mussels by (1) killing them during construction and dredging, (2) suffocating them with accumulated sediments, (3) lowering food and oxygen availability by reducing water flow, and (4) locally extirpating host fish. Other forms of habitat modification such as channelization, channel clearing and de-snagging, and gravel mining result in streambed scour and erosion, increased turbidity, reduction of groundwater levels, sedimentation, and changes in the aquatic community structure. Sedimentation may cause direct mortality by deposition and suffocation and eliminate or reduce recruitment of juvenile mussels. Suspended sediments can also interfere with feeding. Activities that historically caused sedimentation of streams and rivers in the drainages where this mussel occurs include channel modification, agriculture, forestry, mining, and industrial and residential development. In addition, stream discharge may result in decreased dissolved oxygen concentration, increased acidity and conductivity, and other changes in water chemistry that may impact the mussels and/or fish hosts.

About 230 river mi (370 km) of the Coosa River have been impounded for hydropower by a series of six dams. Water quality degradation caused by textile and carpet mill wastes led to the loss of several known mussel communities in some streams of this river system.

Water quality degradation is a major problem in the Cahaba River system. There are 10 municipal wastewater treatment plants, 35 surface mining areas, a coalbed methane operation, and 67 other permitted discharges in this river system. Siltation from surface mining, road construction, and oil and gas development is also a problem.

Conservation and Recovery

Actions needed for the recovery of freshwater mussels include (1) conducting population and habitat surveys to determine the status and range of the species, (2) determining specific threats to the species and minimizing or eliminating these threats, (3) identifying essential habitat areas in need of protection, and (4) controlling the incidental or illegal take of mussels by commercial and noncommercial collectors.

It is unlikely that the species will recover unless new populations are established by introducing individuals back into the historic range. Methods to accomplish this might include introduction of adult/juvenile mussels, glochidia-infected host fish, and artificially cultured individuals.

Contacts

U.S. Fish and Wildlife Service
Regional Office, Division of Endangered Species
1875 Century Blvd., Suite 200
Atlanta, Georgia 30345
Telephone: (404) 679-4000
http://southeast.fws.gov/

Ecological Services Field Office
P.O. Box 1190
Daphne, Alabama 36526-1190
Telephone: (334) 441-5181
Fax: (334) 441-6222

Ecological Services Field Office
446 Neal Street
Cookeville, Tennessee 38501-4027
Telephone: (931) 528-6481
Fax: (931) 528-7075

Reference

U.S. Fish and Wildlife Service. 17 March 1993. "Endangered and Threatened Wildlife and Plants; Endangered Status for Eight Freshwater Mussels and Threatened Status for Three Freshwater Mussels in the Mobile River Drainage." *Federal Register* 58 (50): 14330-14340.

Dark Pigtoe

Pleurobema furvum

Status	Endangered
Listed	March 17, 1993
Family	Unionidae (Freshwater Mussel)
Description	Small to medium mussel with an oval, moderately inflated dark reddish-brown shell with closely spaced, dark growth lines.
Habitat	Gravel riffles in streams.
Food	Filter-feeder.
Reproduction	Female stores sperm in gills; glochidia are released into the stream after hatching.
Threats	Impoundments, gravel and mining, water pollution.
Range	Alabama

Dark Pigtoe, photograph by Dave Dieter, Huntsville Times. Reproduced by permission.

Description

The dark pigtoe, *Pleurobema furvum*, is a small to medium-sized mussel, growing to lengths of 2.4 in (6 cm). The shell is oval and moderately inflated. Beaks are located in the anterior portion of the shell. The posterior ridge is abruptly rounded and terminates in a broadly rounded, subcentral, posterior point. The periostracum is dark reddish-brown with numerous and closely spaced, dark growth lines. The hinge plate is wide and the teeth are heavy and large, especially in older specimens. The nacre (inner shell surface) approaches white in the umbos, and is highly iridescent on the posterior margin.

Behavior

See the Upland Combshell (*Epioblasma metastriata*) entry.

Habitat

The dark pigtoe inhabits high-quality lotic habitats with stable gravel and sandy-gravel substrates. Little else is known about the habitat requirements of this species.

The habitat of the glochidia is initially in the gills of the female, then in the water column, and finally attached to a suitable host fish. Habitat associations or requirements for the juvenile stage are unknown.

Distribution

The historic distribution of this species was probably limited to the Black Warrior River system, Alabama, above the fall line.

Specimens were found in tributaries of the Black Warrior (Sipsey Fork, North River) in 1986, 1991, and 1992.

Threats

Habitat modification, sedimentation, and water quality degradation represent the major threats to this species. These freshwater mussels do not tolerate impoundments. More than 1,000 mi (1,609 km) of large and small river habitat in the Mobile River drainage has been impounded for navigation, flood control, water supply, and/or hydroelectric production purposes. During the construction and dredging of impoundments, some riverine mussels are killed. Additionally, impoundments lead to the accumulation of sediments that can suffocate mussels, a reduction in food and oxygen due to the reduction in water flow, and the local extirpation of host fish. Other forms of habitat modification such as channelization, channel clearing and desnagging, and gravel mining result in streambed scour and erosion, increased turbidity, reduction of groundwater levels, sedimentation, and changes in the aquatic community structure. Sedimentation may cause direct mortality by deposition and suffocation and eliminate or reduce recruitment of juvenile mussels. Suspended sediments can also interfere with feeding. Activities that historically caused sedimentation of streams and rivers in the drainages where this mussel occurs include channel modification, agriculture, forestry, mining, and industrial and residential development.

Other types of water quality degradation from both point and nonpoint sources affect this species. Stream discharge from these sources may result in decreased dissolved oxygen concentration, increased acidity and conductivity, and other changes in water chemistry that may affect the mussels and/or their fish hosts. Point sources of water quality degradation include municipal and industrial effluents, and coalbed methane-produced water discharge. Nonpoint sources include runoff from cultivated fields, pastures, private wastewater effluents, agricultural feedlots and poultry houses, active and abandoned coal mine sites, and highway and road drainages.

Conservation and Recovery

Actions needed for the recovery of freshwater mussels include: (1) Conduct population and habitat surveys to determine the status and range of the species. (2) Determine specific threats to the species and minimize or eliminate these threats. (3) Identify essential habitat areas in need of protection. Make use of land agreements, mussel sanctuaries, scenic river status, and land acquisition. (4) Introduce individuals back into the historic range, as it is unlikely that the species will recover unless new populations are established. Methods to accomplish this might include introduction of adult/juvenile mussels, glochidia-infected host fish, and artificially cultured individuals. (5) Control the incidental or illegal take of mussels by commercial and noncommercial collecting.

Contacts

U. S. Fish and Wildlife Service
Regional Office, Division of Endangered Species
1875 Century Blvd., Suite 200
Atlanta, Georgia 30345
http://southeast.fws.gov/

U. S. Fish and Wildlife Service
Daphne Ecological Services Field Office
P.O. Box 1190
Daphne, Alabama 36526-1190
Telephone: (334) 441-5181
Fax: (334) 441-6222

References

Thorp, J. H., and A. P. Covich. 1991. *Ecology and Classification of North American Freshwater Invertebrates.* Academic Press, San Diego.

U. S. Fish and Wildlife Service. 17 March 1993. "Determination of Endangered or Threatened Status for Eight Freshwater Mussels and Threatened Status for Three Freshwater Mussels in the Mobile River Drainage." *Federal Register* 58 (50): 14330-14340.

Southern Pigtoe

Pleurobema georgianum

Status	Endangered
Listed	March 17, 1993
Family	Unionidae (Freshwater Mussel)
Description	Small to medium mussel with a somewhat compressed yellow to yellow-brown shell, and numerous dark brown growth lines.
Habitat	Gravel riffles in streams.
Food	Filter-feeder.
Reproduction	Female stores sperm in gills; glochidia are released into the stream after hatching.
Threats	Impoundments, gravel and mining, water pollution.
Range	Alabama, Georgia, Tennessee

Description

The southern pigtoe, *Pleurobema georgianum,* is a small to medium-sized mussel that is generally less than 2.4 in (6 cm) in length. The shell is elliptical to ovate and somewhat compressed. The posterior slope is smoothly rounded. The pseudocardinal teeth are small but well-developed, and the nacre (inner shell surface) is white. The periostracum is yellow to yellow-brown. Growth lines are numerous and may be dark brown. Small specimens may have green spots at the growth lines along the posterior ridge and near the umbo.

Behavior

See the Upland Combshell (*Epioblasma metastriata*) entry.

Habitat

The southern pigtoe inhabits high-quality lotic habitats with stable gravel and sandy-gravel substrates. Little else is known about the habitat requirements of this species.

Distribution

The southern pigtoe's historic range apparently was restricted to the Coosa River system. Museum specimens of this species were collected from Coosa River, Shoal Creek, and the Chatooga and Conasauga Rivers.

Live specimens were collected from this river system in 1974, 1987, and 1990. One fresh dead specimen was collected from the Conasauga River in 1991. A 1991 survey did not find any live specimens in the Coosa River drainage.

Threats

Habitat modification, sedimentation, and water quality degradation represent the major threats to this species. These freshwater mussels do not tolerate impoundments. More than 1,000 mi (1,609 km) of large and small river habitat in the Mobile River drainage has been impounded for navigation, flood control, water supply, and/or hydroelectric production purposes. During the construction and dredging of impoundments, some riverine mussels are killed. Additionally, impoundments lead to the accumulation of sediments that can suffocate mussels, a reduction in food and oxygen due to the reduction in water flow, and the local extirpation of host fish. Other forms of habitat modification such as channelization, channel clearing and desnagging, and gravel mining result in streambed scour and erosion, increased turbidity, reduction of groundwater levels, sedimentation, and changes in the aquatic community structure. Sedimentation may cause direct mortality by deposition and suffocation and eliminate or reduce recruitment of juvenile mussels. Suspended sediments can also interfere with feeding. Activities that historically caused sedimentation of streams and rivers in the drainages where this mussel occurs include channel modification, agriculture, forestry, mining, and industrial and residential development.

Other types of water quality degradation from both point and nonpoint sources affect this species. Stream discharge from these sources may result in decreased dissolved oxygen concentration, increased acidity and conductivity, and other changes in water chemistry that may affect the mussels and/or their fish hosts. Point sources of water quality degradation include municipal and industrial effluents, and coalbed methane-produced water discharge. Nonpoint sources include runoff from cultivated fields, pastures, private wastewater effluents, agricultural feedlots and poultry houses, active and abandoned coal mine sites, and highway and road drainages.

About 230 mi (370 km) of the Coosa River have been impounded for hydropower by a series of six dams. Water quality degradation caused by textile and carpet mill wastes led to the loss of several known mussel communities in several streams of this river system.

Conservation and Recovery

Actions needed for the recovery of freshwater mussels include: (1) Conduct population and habitat surveys to determine the status and range of the species. (2) Determine specific threats to the species and minimize or eliminate these threats. (3) Identify essential habitat areas in need of protection. Make use of land agreements, mussel sanctuaries, scenic river status, and land acquisition. (4) Introduce individuals back into the historic range, as it is unlikely that the species will recover unless new populations are established. Methods to accomplish this might include introduction of adult/juvenile mussels, glochidia-infected host fish, and artificially cultured individuals. (5) Control the incidental or illegal take of mussels by commercial and noncommercial collecting.

Contacts

U. S. Fish and Wildlife Service
Regional Office, Division of Endangered Species
1875 Century Blvd., Suite 200
Atlanta, Georgia 30345
http://southeast.fws.gov/

U. S. Fish and Wildlife Service
Daphne Ecological Services Field Office
P.O. Box 1190
Daphne, Alabama 36526-1190
Telephone: (334) 441-5181
Fax: (334) 441-6222

U. S. Fish and Wildlife Service
Cookeville Ecological Services Field Office
446 Neal St.
Cookeville, Tennessee 38501-4027
Telephone: (931) 528-6481
Fax: (931) 528-7075

Reference

U. S. Fish and Wildlife Service. 17 March 1993. "Endangered Status for Eight Freshwater Mussels and Threatened Status for Three Freshwater Mussels in the Mobile River Drainage." *Federal Register* 58 (50): 14330-14340.

Cumberland Pigtoe

Pleurobema gibberum

Status	Endangered
Listed	May 7, 1991
Family	Unionidae (Freshwater Mussel)
Description	Small, triangular, yellowish brown to mahogany shell with a peach to orange interior.
Habitat	Gravel or sand stream bottoms.
Food	Filter-feeds on phytoplankton, tiny zooplankton, and organic detritus.
Reproduction	The female siphons male sperm from the water; eggs are fertilized and incubated in her gill chamber; the planktonic larvae are parasitic on fish, and later settle to the sedentary adult lifestyle.
Threats	Habitat destruction by dams and impoundments and water pollution.
Range	Tennessee

Cumberland Pigtoe, photograph. A. E. Spreitzer Photography. Reproduced by permission.

Description

The *Pleurobema gibberum* (Cumberland pigtoe) is a small freshwater mussel, rarely exceeding 2.3 in (6 cm) in length. The heavy triangular shell is yellowish brown on young mussels, turning dark mahogany with age. The shell interior is peach to orange.

Behavior

The Cumberland pigtoe draws in water using its siphon, and filter-feeds on phytoplankton, tiny zooplankton, and organic detritus. Like other Unionid mussel, the female siphons male sperm from the water, and the eggs are fertilized and incubated in her gill chamber. The larvae are planktonic and parasitic on fish. They later settle to the sedentary adult lifestyle.

Habitat

Like many other freshwater mussels, the Cumberland pigtoe prefers stream riffle areas of gravel or sand (occasionally mud or cobble). Freshwater mussels feed by filtering food particles from the water.

Distribution

The Cumberland pigtoe is known only from the Caney Fork River system in Tennessee. Historical records indicate that the mussel has been collected from five Caney Fork tributaries, all above the Great Falls Reservoir, which was constructed in the 1910s. Historic mussel collection records are very limited and given the amount of suitable habitat that was flooded by the impoundment, it is very likely that the Cumberland pigtoe was more widely distributed.

At present there are four known populations of the Cumberland pigtoe on Caney Fork tributaries: Barren Fork (Warren County), Calfkiller River (White County), Cane Creek (Van Buren County), and Collins River (Warren and Grundy counties). A 1990 survery of the river system failed to find Cumberland pigtoe mussels in the main stem of Caney Fork or any other tributaries.

Threats

Decline of the Cumberland pigtoe mussel most likely began with the construction of the Great Falls Reservoir in the 1910s, which flooded a large portion of the mussel's preferred habitat. The species' distribution has declined over the years as a result of water pollution associated with coal mining, poor land use practices, and waster discharge.

Conservation and Recovery

Although no projects with federal involvement that would affect surviving Cumberland pigtoe populations are currently being planned, federal listing of the species ensures that any actions that might affect the species would face close examina-tion. Such actions would include the construction of reservoirs, or hydroelectric and wastewater facilities, channel maintenance or stream alterations. The U. S. Fish and Wildlife Service published a Recovery Plan for the Cumberland pigtoe mussel in 1992. The aim of the Recovery Plan is to establish six viable, self- maintaining populations of the rare mussel so that it can be de-listed. This requires monitoring of its known populations, searching for new ones, and conducting research into its ecological needs and ways of improving its habitat (including reintroduction efforts).

Contacts

U.S. Fish and Wildlife Service
Asheville Ecological Services Field Office
160 Zillicoa Street
Asheville, North Carolina 28801-1082
Telephone: (828) 258-3939
Fax: (828) 258-5330

U. S. Fish and Wildlife Service
Regional Office, Division of Endangered Species
1875 Century Blvd., Suite 200
Atlanta, Georgia 30345
http://southeast.fws.gov/

References

Anderson, R. M. 1990. "Status Survey of the Cumberland Pigtoe Pearly Mussel, *Pleurobema gibberum.*" Tennessee Cooperative Fishery Research Unit, Tennessee Technological University, Cookeville, Tennessee.

U.S. Fish and Wildlife Service. 1992. "Cumberland Pigtoe Mussel (*Pleurobema gibberum*) Recovery Plan." Atlanta, Georgia.

Flat Pigtoe

Pleurobema marshalli

Status	Endangered
Listed	April 7, 1987
Family	Unionidae (Freshwater Mussel)
Description	Oval or elliptical, dark brown shell with a shallow cavity.
Habitat	Gravel and sand substrates in clean, fast-flowing water.
Food	Filter-feeder.
Reproduction	Female stores sperm in gills; glochidia are released into the stream after hatching.
Threats	Restricted distribution, dam construction, siltation.
Range	Alabama, Mississippi

Flat Pigtoe, photograph. A. E. Spreitzer Photography. Reproduced by permission.

Description

The oval or obliquely elliptical shell of the flat pigtoe mussel, *Pleurobema marshalli,* is about 2.4 in (6 cm) long, 2 in (5 cm) high, and 1.2 in (3 cm) thick. It has a shallow cavity and very low pustules or welts on the post-ventral surface. Older shells are a dark brown with irregular concentric black growth lines. The thin, inner shell surface (nacre) is bluish-white. The flat pigtoe is also known as Marshall's mussel.

In the late twentieth century, the identity of species within the genus *Pleurobema* was the focus of debate among malacologists. The U. S. Fish and Wildlife Service (FWS) adopted the majority view but acknowledged that further research could warrant reclassification of the flat pigtoe and other mussels of the genus.

Behavior

See the Upland Combshell (*Epioblasma metastriata*) entry.

Habitat

The flat pigtoe is found in clean, fast-flowing water in relatively shallow stretches where the bottom is composed of firm rubble, gravel, or sand, swept free of silt.

Distribution

This mussel was known from the main stem of the Tombigbee River from Tibbee Creek near Columbus (Lowndes County), Mississippi, downstream to Epes (Sumter County), Alabama, above the confluence of Noxubee River. The absence of specimens from anywhere except the Tombigbee River suggests that this species was historically restricted to this single stretch of river.

This mussel was collected alive in Sumter and Pickens Counties, Alabama, in 1972. The Pickens County site and former sites in Mississippi have suffered from heavy sedimentation since that time and are no longer considered viable habitat. The only remaining viable habitat for this species in the Tombigbee River is a gravel bar in the Gainesville Bendway in Sumter County, Alabama. The bendway is a remnant of the old riverbed that was bypassed when a navigable channel was constructed.

Threats

Low numbers and very restricted occurrence make the flat pigtoe one of the most immediately endangered of the freshwater mussels. Completion of the Gainesville Dam and other structures of the Tennessee-Tombigbee Waterway (a navigable canal built to connect the Tennessee and Tombigbee Rivers) effectively eliminated much of the historic habitat of the flat pigtoe except for the gravel bars in the Gainesville Bendway. A 1987 survey conducted in the bendway documented extensive siltation and found only a few common mussel species. Few of the more uncommon varieties were

found. A recently completed dam on Bull Mountain Creek, the source of most of the water for the East Fork Tombigbee River, slowed currents and reduced water flow throughout the system, causing the sedimentation. The condition of the river also caused a decline of common fish hosts.

Conservation and Recovery

Because the condition of the Gainesville Bendway has deteriorated so abruptly, the FWS may be forced to attempt an emergency relocation of mussel populations, if other suitable habitat can be found. There is some question whether enough of the mussels survive to justify such a drastic measure or whether the relocation attempt would, in itself, result in extinction for the flat pigtoe.

Contact

U. S. Fish and Wildlife Service
Regional Office, Division of Endangered Species
1875 Century Blvd., Suite 200
Atlanta, Georgia 30345
http://southeast.fws.gov/

References

Stansbery, D. H. 1983. "The Status of *Pleurobema marshalli*." Unpublished report. U. S. Fish and Wildlife Service, Atlanta.

U. S. Army Corps of Engineers. 1981. "Water Resources Development in Alabama." Report. Mobile District Office, Mobile, Ala.

U. S. Department of Agriculture. 1983. "Soil Conservation Service Watershed Progress Report Mississippi." U. S. Department of Agriculture, Washington, D.C.

Ovate Clubshell

Pleurobema perovatum

Status	Endangered
Listed	March 17, 1993
Family	Unionidae (Freshwater Mussel)
Description	Small to medium mussel with an oval to elliptical yellow to dark brown shell and a well-developed, broadly rounded, often concave posterior ridge.
Habitat	Gravel riffles in streams.
Food	Filter-feeder.
Reproduction	Female stores sperm in gills; glochidia (larvae) are released into streams after hatching.
Threats	Impoundments; gravel mining; water pollution.
Range	Alabama, Georgia, Mississippi, Tennessee

Description

The ovate clubshell is a small- to medium-sized mussel that rarely exceeds 2 in (5.1 cm) in length. The shell is ovate to elliptical and has nearly terminal inflated umbos (prominences). The posterior ridge is well-developed, broadly rounded, and often concave. The posterior slope is produced well beyond the posterior ridge. Periostracum (shell) color varies from yellow to dark brown and occasionally has broad green rays that may cover most of the umbo and posterior ridge. The inner layer of the shell is white. Due to the nearly terminal umbos in some specimens, *P. perovatum* may be mistaken for young southern clubshells (*P. decisum*). They may be distinguished from the latter by their thinner shells and a gently sloping, well-developed posterior slope.

Behavior

The life of mussels is complex, and reproduction often depends upon a stable habitat—unaltered stream conditions, clean water, and an undisturbed stream bottom. The cycle also depends upon the abundance of suitable fish hosts to complete the mussel's larval development.

To reproduce, males discharge sperm, which are dispersed by stream currents. In the process of feeding, females nearby or downstream take in sperm, which fertilizes eggs stored in their gills. The gills serve as brood pouches (marsupia), where the glochidia hatch and begin to develop. After a time, these glochidia are released into the stream. A few mussels have inner parts that resemble a tiny minnow and can be manipulated to lure host fish. When a fish gets close to the shell, the mussel expels its glochidia.

Glochidia have tiny bean- or spoon-shaped valves that attach to the gill filaments of host fish. Glochidia can only progress to the juvenile stage while attached to the fish's gills. Those that do not fortuitously encounter a host fish do not survive when released by the female mussel. They sink to the bottom and die.

When the juvenile has developed a shell and is large enough to survive on its own, it detaches from the host fish and falls to the stream bottom, beginning a long association with a single stretch of stream. Maturing mussels bury themselves in riffles and shoals with only the shell margins and feeding

Ovate Clubshell, photograph. A. E. Spreitzer Photography. Reproduced by permission.

siphons exposed to the water. Some mussels live as long as 50 years or more.

The family Unionidae, which includes all of the freshwater mussels in the United States, is separated into two groups based on the length of time the glochidia remain in the female's marsupia. The eggs of the short-term (tachytictic) breeders are fertilized in the spring, and glochidia are released by late summer of the same year. Long-term (bradytictic) breeders hold developing glochidia in the brood pouch over winter and release them in the spring. Freshwater mussels feed by siphoning phytoplankton and other plant matter from the water. Indigestible particles are expelled from the shell by reverse siphoning. Silt in the water can kill mussels by clogging their feeding siphons.

There are no known interspecific differences in feeding among freshwater mussels. The glochidia are obligate parasites on the gills or fins of fish. Adult mussels are filter-feeders and consume particulate

matter in the water column. Identifiable stomach contents almost invariably include desmids, diatoms, algae, protozoa, and zooplankton.

Most freshwater mussel species display seasonal variations in activity associated with water temperature and reproduction. Metabolic rate is, in part, positively correlated with temperature. Many ectothermic species have the capacity to adjust their metabolic rates in response to long-term changes in temperature. Thus, metabolic rates do not continue to rise as temperatures rise in the summer, and they do not continue to fall during the winter as temperatures decline.

Some freshwater mussels also show diurnal changes in metabolic rates that indicate a tendency toward nocturnal activity patterns. Mussels may move to the surface to feed at night and move deeper into the substrate during the day; this is one way to avoid predators that hunt by visual contact.

Freshwater mussels are nonmigratory.

Habitat

The ovate clubshell inhabits high-quality lotic habitats (living in actively moving water) with stable gravel and sandy-gravel substrates. Little else is known about the habitat requirements of this species.

The habitat of the glochidia is initially in the gills of the female, then in the water column, and finally attached to a suitable host fish. Habitat associations or requirements for the juvenile stage are unknown.

Distribution

This species' historic distribution included the following portions of the Mobile River basin: the Tombigbee River and its tributaries (Buttahatchie and Sipsey Rivers; Luxapalila, Coalfire, and Lubbub Creeks); the Black Warrior River and its tributaries (Locust Fork; Village, Prairie, Big Prairie, Brushy, and Blackwater Creeks); the Alabama River; the Cahaba River and the tributary Buck Creek; Chewacla, Uphapee, and Opintlocco Creeks in the Tallapoosa drainage; and the Coosa River and its tributaries (Conasauga and Etowah Rivers; Holy Creek).

The ovate clubshell is now limited to (1) the Buttahatchie and Sipsey Rivers in the Tombigbee River drainage, (2) Blackwater Creek and Locust Fork in the Black Warrior drainage, and (3) Chewacla Creek in the Tallapoosa drainage. Specimens were last collected in the Coosa drainage in 1974 and in the Cahaba River in 1978. The species was not found in the Coosa River or Cahaba River drainages in a 1991 survey.

Threats

Habitat modification, sedimentation, and water quality degradation represent the major threats to this species. These freshwater mussels do not tolerate impoundments. More than 1,000 mi (1,609 km) of large and small river habitat in the Mobile River drainage has been impounded for navigation, flood control, water supply, and/or hydroelectric production purposes.

Impoundments adversely affect riverine mussels by (1) killing them during construction and dredging, (2) suffocating them with accumulated sediments, (3) lowering food and oxygen availability by reducing water flow, and (4) locally extirpating host fish. Other forms of habitat modification such as channelization, channel clearing and de-snagging, and gravel mining result in streambed scour and erosion, increased turbidity, reduction of groundwater levels, sedimentation, and changes in the aquatic community structure. Sedimentation may cause direct mortality by deposition and suffocation and eliminate or reduce recruitment of juvenile mussels. Suspended sediments can also interfere with feeding. Activities that historically caused sedimentation of streams and rivers in the drainages where this mussel occurs include channel modification, agriculture, forestry, mining, and industrial and residential development. In addition, stream discharge may result in decreased dissolved oxygen concentration, increased acidity and conductivity, and other changes in water chemistry that may impact the mussels and/or fish hosts.

About 230 river mi (370 km) of the Coosa River have been impounded for hydropower by a series of six dams. Water quality degradation caused by textile and carpet mill wastes led to the loss of several known mussel communities in several streams of this river system.

Water quality degradation is a major problem in the Cahaba River system. There are 10 municipal wastewater treatment plants, 35 surface mining areas, a coalbed methane operation, and 67 other permitted discharges in this river system. Siltation from surface mining, road construction, and oil and gas development is also a problem.

Conservation and Recovery

Actions needed for the recovery of freshwater mussels include (1) conducting population and habitat surveys to determine the status and range of the species, (2) determining specific threats to the species and minimizing or eliminating these threats, (3) identifying essential habitat areas in need of protection, and (4) controlling the incidental or illegal take of mussels by commercial and noncommercial collectors.

It is unlikely that the species will recover unless new populations are established by introducing individuals back into the historic range. Methods to accomplish this might include introduction of adult/juvenile mussels, glochidia-infected host fish, and artificially cultured individuals.

Contacts

U.S. Fish and Wildlife Service
Regional Office, Division of Endangered Species
1875 Century Blvd., Suite 200
Atlanta, Georgia 30345
Telephone: (404) 679-4000
http://southeast.fws.gov/

Ecological Services Field Office
P.O. Box 1190
Daphne, Alabama 36526-1190
Telephone: (334) 441-5181
Fax: (334) 441-6222

Ecological Services Field Office
446 Neal Street
Cookeville, Tennessee 38501-4027
Telephone: (931) 528-6481
Fax: (931) 528-7075

Reference

U.S. Fish and Wildlife Service. 17 March 1993. "Endangered and Threatened Wildlife and Plants; Endangered Status for Eight Freshwater Mussels and Threatened Status for Three Freshwater Mussels in the Mobile River Drainage." *Federal Register* 58 (50): 14330-14340.

Rough Pigtoe

Pleurobema plenum

Status	Endangered
Listed	June 14, 1976
Family	Unionidae (Freshwater Mussel)
Description	Triangular, yellowish to reddish brown shell with heavy, inflated valves.
Habitat	Gravel or sandy bottoms in deeper waters of streams.
Food	Filter feeder.
Reproduction	Either releases glochidia by late summer or holds developing glochidia over the winter to release in the spring.
Threats	Habitat reduction, siltation, pollution.
Range	Alabama, Indiana, Kentucky, Pennsylvania, Tennessee, Virginia

Rough Pigtoe, photograph. A. E. Spreitzer Photography. Reproduced by permission.

Description

The shell of the rough pigtoe, *Pleurobema plenum*, is somewhat triangular in outline with mature dimensions of 2.5 in (6.5 cm) long, 2.8 in (7.1 cm) high, and 1.7 in (4.3 cm) wide. The inflated valves are solid and heavy. The shell surface is marked by irregular, concentric growth marks and has a clothlike texture. It is a slightly glossy, yellowish to reddish brown. The inner shell surface (nacre) varies in color from white to pinkish, reddish, or orange.

Behavior

The family Unionidae is separated into two groups based on the length of time glochidia (larvae) remain in the female. The rough pigtoe pearly mussel is probably "tachytictic," a short-term breeder—one that breeds in spring and releases glochidia by late summer of the same year. Long-term breeders hold developing glochidia in a brood pouch over winter and release them in spring. The fish hosts for this species are thought to include the rosefin shiner and possibly the bluegill.

For more on the reproduction and diet of freshwater mussels, see See the Upland Combshell (*Epioblasma metastriata*) entry.

Habitat

The rough pigtoe is a big-river shoal species, and is found in deeper waters of streams 66 ft (20 m) wide or wider. It buries itself in the gravel or sandy bottom with only the posterior margin of the shell and siphons exposed to the water.

Distribution

First discovered in the Ohio River near Cincinnati in 1840, this mussel was subsequently documented from four major regions—the basins of the Cumberland and Tennessee Rivers (Virginia, Tennessee, Alabama, and Kentucky), the Ohio River drainage (Ohio, Indiana, and Illinois), the Ozarks (Kansas, Missouri, and Arkansas), and the mainstream Mississippi River (Arkansas).

As of the late twentieth century, the rough pigtoe was known from near the confluence of the Green and Barren Rivers (Warren County, Kentucky), a river system that empties into the Ohio River near Evansville, Indiana. It survived in the Clinch River near Kyles Ford (Hancock County), Tennessee, and in the Tennessee River below Guntersville Dam (Marshall County, Alabama), Wilson Dam (Lauderdale County, Alabama), and Pickwick Dam (Hardin County, Tennessee). No population estimates were available. The U. S. Fish and Wildlife Service lists the species as endangered in Alabama, Indiana, Kentucky, Pennsylvania, Tennessee, and Virginia.

Threats

The reasons for the decline of the rough pigtoe are not fully understood, but the longevity of most mussel species—up to 50 years—and their sedentary nature make them especially vulnerable to habitat alterations caused by dam construction, dredging, siltation, and pollution.

Since the early 1930s and 1940s, the Tennessee Valley Authority (TVA), the U. S. Army Corps of Engineers, Aluminum Company of America, and other water authorities have constructed more than 50 dams in the Tennessee and Cumberland watersheds alone. The Ohio River has been extensively modified by a series of dams and locks along its

length. Heavy siltation, caused by poor agricultural practices, has rendered large portions of this mussel's historic habitat unsuitable.

Agricultural chemicals and industrial wastes have generally degraded the water quality of major rivers, such as the Ohio, Missouri, and Mississippi.

Conservation and Recovery

The states of Tennessee and Alabama have designated portions of the Tennessee and Cumberland Rivers as freshwater mussel sanctuaries; the headwaters, however, originate in Virginia, where pollutants introduced by strip mining and coal washing have affected these rivers throughout the drainage. The recovery of this species will depend upon the success of regional efforts to improve water quality. The TVA, which administers the operation of dams on the Tennessee and Cumberland Rivers, is currently developing a comprehensive water management plan. This plan would guarantee constant minimum flows in all rivers in the region by timing water discharges from TVA dams. Such an effort might mollify many of the negative effects of dams and reservoirs on remaining stretches of mussel habitat.

Contacts

U. S. Fish and Wildlife Service
Regional Office, Division of Endangered Species
1 Federal Drive
BHW Federal Building
Fort Snelling, Minnesota 55111
Telephone: (612) 713-5360
http://midwest.fws.gov/

U. S. Fish and Wildlife Service
Regional Office, Division of Endangered Species
1875 Century Blvd., Suite 200
Atlanta, Georgia 30345
http://southeast.fws.gov/

U. S. Fish and Wildlife Service
Regional Office, Division of Endangered Species
300 Westgate Center Dr.
Hadley, Massachusetts 01035-9589
Telephone: (413) 253-8200
Fax: (413) 253-8308
http://northeast.fws.gov/

References

Bates, J. M., and S. D. Dennis. 1978. "The Mussel Fauna of the Clinch River, Tennessee and Virginia." *Sterkiana* 69-70: 3-23.

Isom, B. G. 1974. "Mussels of the Green River, Kentucky." *Proceedings of the Kentucky Academy of Science* 35 (1-2): 55-7.

U. S. Fish and Wildlife Service. 1984. "Rough Pigtoe Pearly Mussel Recovery Plan." U. S. Fish and Wildlife Service, Atlanta.

Oval Pigtoe

Pleurobema pyriforme

Status	Endangered
Listed	March 16, 1998
Family	Unionidae
Description	A freshwater, bivalve mollusk with a suboviform compressed shell and shiny smooth epidermis.
Habitat	Streams and small rivers with clean, flowing water.
Food	Filter-feeds on phytoplankton, tiny zooplankton, and organic detritus.
Reproduction	The female siphons male spawn from the water; eggs are fertilized and incubated in her gill chamber; the planktonic larvae are parasitic on fish, and later settle to the sedentary adult lifestyle.
Threats	Habitat destruction by impoundment, and pollution by siltation, nutrients, and other chemicals.
Range	Alabama, Florida, Georgia

Description

The *Pleurobema pyriforme* (oval pigtoe) is a small to medium-sized species that attains a length of about 2.4 in (6.0 cm). The shell is suboviform compressed, with a shiny smooth epidermis. The periostracum is yellowish, chestnut, or dark brown, rayless, and with distinct growth lines. The posterior slope is biangulate and forms a blunt point on the posterior margin. The umbos are slightly elevated above the hingeline. As is typical of the genus, no sexual dimorphism is displayed in shell characters. Internally, the pseudocardinal teeth are fairly large, crenulate, and double in both valves. The lateral teeth are somewhat shortened, arcuate, and double in each valve. Nacre color varies from salmon to bluish white and is iridescent posteriorly. The sailfin shiner (*Pteronotropis hypselopterus*) serves as the host fish for the oval pigtoe.

Variation in this species has led to the description of various nominal species. Modern taxonomy currently recognizes the nineteenth-century names

Unio pyriformis Lea, *Unio modicus* Lea, *Unio bulbosus* Lea, *Unio amabilis* Lea, *Unio reclusum* Wright, and *Unio harperi* Wright, as well as the twentieth-century name *Pleurobema simpsoni* Vanatta as synonyms of *Pleurobema pyriforme*.

Behavior

See the Upland Combshell (*Epioblasma metastriata*) entry.

Habitat

The oval pigtoe inhabits streams and small rivers with clean, flowing water.

Distribution

The oval pigtoe was described from the Chattahoochee River, near Columbus, Georgia. This species was historically one of the most widely distributed and common mussels endemic to the Apalachicolan Region. It occurred throughout the mainstems and several tributaries of both the Flint and Chipola River systems, in the lower Chattahoochee River mainstem and several of its tributaries, in the Apalachicola River mainstem, and in the upper portion of the Ochlockonee River system. The oval pigtoe was also known from a single Suwannee River mainstem site and the confluent Santa Fe River system, and in Econfina Creek. Once a species of localized abundance, oval pigtoe populations sometimes numbered in the hundreds, as reported by a study in the 1940s. This study reported 470 specimens from nine sites (an average of 52.2 per site) in the Chopola River system. It has been extirpated from the mainstem of the Chattahoochee River, representing a significant portion of its historical range; occurrences in the Flint and Suwannee River systems have decreased from 32 to 12.

During the status survey, 410 sites were sampled within the historic range of this species, including 20 of 50 (40%) known historical sites. The oval pigtoe was found at 24 (6%) of the sample sites, including seven of the historic sites, with an average of 5.2 live individuals per site. The oval pigtoe has apparently been extirpated from the Chattahoochee River system in Alabama and much of the Chipola River system.

The oval pigtoe is currently known to occur at 26 sites, with no evidence of recruitment. The species was found at one mainstem site and seven tributary sites in the Flint River system, six mainstem Chipola River sites, six mainstem sites and one tributary site in the upper Ochlockonee River system, one site in the New River (upper Santa Fe River system), and two sites in Econfina Creek.

Five new occurrences of the oval pigtoe were subsequently located in three Apalachicola-Chattahoochee-Flint (ACF) River system tributaries. One occurrence was from a stream in the Chipola River system not previously known to have harbored this species. The other four occurrences were in two streams (two sites in each stream), that are tributaries to the Chattahoochee and Flint Rivers where the species had been recorded during the status survey.

Oval pigtoe density at the five new sites never exceeded 0.04 specimens per sq ft (0.4 specimens per sq m). The smallest individual collected during or subsequent to the status survey was 1.0 in (2.5 cm) in length, indicating that juveniles were not present in these collections.

Threats

Impoundments have altered about 29% of mainstem riverine habitat on the Flint River. Preimpoundment records from Seminole and Blackshear Reservoirs exist for one site for the oval pigtoe. Talquin Reservoir flooded about 12% of the riverine habitat in the middle portion of the Ochlokonee river and the lower end of its largest tributary (the Little River). Preimpoundment records exist for the oval pigtoe, now also absent downstream of the dam. This indicates that potential host fish movements may havebeen blocked. Future impoundments to satisfy expanding urban and surburban demand, particularly in the metropolitan Atlanta area, could damage stream habitats where small populations of the oval pigtoe exist.

Although muskrats are not common within the range of these species, Piedmont populations of the oval pigtoe in the upper Flint River system may be subject to some degree of muskrat predation.

Conservation and Recovery

The oval pigtoe survives at about 26 sites, almost all of which are in streams running through privately owned land. Its conservation requires the protection of the stream reaches where it persists in small, isolated populations. These habitats must be protected from proposed impoundment, and from pollution associated with poor land-use practices in the watershed that cause erosion and inputs of nutrients and other chemicals. The populations of the oval pigtoe must be monitored, and research undertaken into its basic biology and ecological requirements.

Contacts

U. S. Fish and Wildlife Service
Regional Office, Division of Endangered Species
1875 Century Blvd., Suite 200
Atlanta, Georgia 30345
http://southeast.fws.gov/

U.S. Fish and Wildlife Service
Wildlife and Habitat Management
6620 Southpoint Drive South, Suite 310
Jacksonville, Florida 32216
Telephone: (904) 232-2580
Fax: (904) 232-2404

Reference

U.S. Fish and Wildlife Service. 16 March 1998. "Endangered and Threatened Wildlife and Plants; Determination of Endangered Status for Five Freshwater Mussels and Threatened Status for Two Freshwater Mussels From the Eastern Gulf Slope Drainages of Alabama, Florida, and Georgia." *Federal Register* 63(50): 12664-12687.

Heavy Pigtoe

Pleurobema taitianum

Status	Endangered
Listed	April 7, 1987
Family	Unionidae (Freshwater Mussel)
Description	Brownish-black triangular shell with beaks that are narrowly pointed forward.
Habitat	River shoals.
Food	Filter-feeder.
Reproduction	Female stores sperm in gills; glochidia are released into the stream after hatching.
Threats	Navigation and flood control projects, siltation, water diversion.
Range	Alabama, Mississippi

Heavy Pigtoe, photograph. A. E. Spreitzer Photography. Reproduced by permission.

Description

The heavy pigtoe, *Pleurobema taitianum*, is a bivalve mollusk about 2 in (5 cm) long, 1.8 in (4.5 cm) high, and 1.2 in (3 cm) wide. The obliquely triangular shell is brown to brownish-black. The shell beaks are narrowly pointed forward with shallow cavities. The nacre (inner shell surface) is pinkish-white. The heavy pigtoe is also known as Judge Tait's mussel. In the late twentieth century, the identity of species within the genus *Pleurobema* was the focus of debate among malacologists. The U. S. Fish and Wildlife Service (FWS) adopted the majority view but acknowledged that further research could warrant reclassification of the heavy pigtoe and other mussels of the genus.

Behavior

See the Upland Combshell (*Epioblasma metastriata*) entry.

Habitat

This mussel prefers clear, fast-flowing water in shallow reaches where the bottom is composed of relatively firm rubble, gravel, or sand. The current must be strong enough to scour the bottom of silt.

Free-flowing, shallow riffles and shoals are increasingly rare due to extensive modification of the river channels.

Distribution

The heavy pigtoe mussel has been found in the Tombigbee River from the mouth of Tibbee Creek near Columbus, Mississippi, downstream to Demopolis, Alabama. Other populations were found far downstream in the Alabama River at Claiborne and Selma, in the lower Cahaba River, and possibly the Coosa River. In the early 1980s, several shells were found at one site on the Buttahatchie River, a Mississippi tributary of the Tombigbee River. This species has also been reported from the East Fork Tombigbee and Sipsey Rivers in Alabama.

Only four portions of suitable habitat remain for the heavy pigtoe mussel: the Gainesville Bendway of the Tombigbee River (Sumter County, Alabama); the Sipsey River (Pickens and Greene Counties, Alabama); and the East Fork Tombigbee and Buttahatchie rivers (Mississippi). A 1987 survey of the Gainesville Bendway documented extensive siltation caused by decreased water flows. No specimens of heavy pigtoe were found during this survey. This mussel was last collected from the East Fork Tombigbee River in 1972, but much of the habitat along the Tombigbee River has since been altered by the construction of the Tennessee-Tombigbee Waterway, a navigable canal built to connect the Tennessee and Tombigbee Rivers.

Threats

Habitat for the heavy pigtoe mussel on segments of the Buttahatchie and Sipsey Rivers is considered marginal, and remaining mussels must cope with siltation, reduced water flows, degraded water quality, and reduced populations of the fish hosts needed for larval development. These habitat alterations were induced by large-scale flood control and navigation projects.

Several ongoing and proposed water control projects threaten to eliminate this mussel's habitat altogether—a 59-mi (95-km) channel improvement project in the Buttahatchie, a 53-mi (85-km) clearing and snagging project in the East Fork Tombigbee, and a 84-mi (135-km) channel improvement project in the Sipsey River. These projects are directed by the U. S. Army Corps of Engineers or by the Soil Conservation Service of the U. S. Department of Agriculture.

Conservation and Recovery

The endangered status of the heavy pigtoe mussel provides the FWS with some control over these and other proposed projects that would damage or destroy remaining habitat. Under provisions of the Endangered Species Act, federal agencies are required to consult with the FWS to ensure that any actions they authorize or fund do not jeopardize federally protected wildlife. In the past, similar consultations have resulted in the redesign of projects to preserve significant portions of habitat.

Contact

U. S. Fish and Wildlife Service
Regional Office, Division of Endangered Species
1875 Century Blvd., Suite 200
Atlanta, Georgia 30345
http://southeast.fws.gov/

References

Fuller, S. L. H. 1974. "Clams and Mussels (Mollusca: Bivalvia)." In *Pollution Ecology of Freshwater Invertebrates,* edited by C. Hart Jr. and S. Fuller. Academic Press, New York.

Stansbery, D. H. 1983. "Status of *Pleurobema taitianum.*" Unpublished report. U. S. Fish and Wildlife Service, Atlanta.

Fat Pocketbook

Potamilus capax

Status	Endangered
Listed	June 14, 1976
Family	Unionidae (Freshwater mussel)
Description	Shiny yellow to brown shell with a strong S-curve hinge line.
Habitat	Flowing water in sand, mud, and gravel substrates.
Food	Filter-feeder.
Reproduction	Female stores sperm in gills; glochidia are released into the stream after hatching.
Threats	Dams, siltation, pollution.
Range	Arkansas, Illinois, Indiana, Kentucky, Mississippi, Missouri

Fat Pocketbook, photograph. A. E. Spreitzer Photography. Reproduced by permission.

Description

The fat pocketbook pearlymussel, *Potamilus capax*, has a smooth, shiny yellow to brown shell that lacks rays or other distinctive markings. The nearly spherical shell averages 4 in (10 cm) in length. The strong S-curve of its hinge differentiates fat pocketbook from similar bivalves. The beautifully iridescent inner shell surface (nacre) is bluish white. This species has also been classified as *Proptera capax*.

Behavior

See the Upland Combshell (*Epioblasma metastriata*) entry.

Habitat

The fat pocketbook has been found in the sand, mud, or gravel bottoms of flowing streams and rivers in stretches less than 8 ft (2.5 m) deep.

Distribution

This species has been documented in the Wabash River in Indiana and the Ohio River in Illinois. It was reported from the upper and lower Illinois River in Illinois, and from discrete populations in the mainstream of the Mississippi River between Wabasha, Minnesota, and Grafton, Illinois. The fat pocketbook appears to have been eliminated from most of its historic range by dam construction, artificial channeling, dredging, siltation, and agricultural chemical contamination.

The fat pocketbook was subsequently discovered in a Mississippi River tributary in Arkansas. Although geographically widespread, the fat pocketbook never occurred in large concentrations.

Surveys of the St. Francis River, conducted in 1979 and 1980, discovered a population of the fat pocketbook near the town of Madison, Arkansas (in St. Francis County). The stretch above Madison, which consists of a series of shoals and islands, is the only section of the St. Francis River that has not been dredged. A 1986 survey confirmed that the fat pocketbook was the most common mussel in the St. Francis River, numbering more than 11,000 post-juveniles.

In 1975 several specimens were found in the Wabash River near New Harmony, Indiana (in Posey County). In 1976 one live and three dead specimens were found in the White River (a tributary of the Wabash) near Bowman, Indiana (in Pike County). It is uncertain whether the fat pocketbook survives in this watershed as a viable, reproducing population.

Threats

Major rivers within the fat pocketbook's historic range have been dammed, artificially channeled, and repeatedly dredged for flood control and navigation. Sediment loosened by dredging and topsoil runoff from poor agricultural practices smother mussel beds. Agricultural pesticides, herbicides, and fertilizers are carried into streams in rain runoff, generally degrading water quality.

Conservation and Recovery

Seasonal flooding is an acknowledged problem along the St. Francis River, and there is heavy public pressure for continued dredging. The U. S. Fish and Wildlife Service recovery plan for this species recommends that dredging be prohibited in the stretch of river above Madison, and biologists hope to establish at least two other populations in suitable habitat within the St. Francis watershed. The U. S. Army Corps of Engineers has recommended that transplant attempts be made on the White River in Indiana, at two sites on the upper Mississippi River, or in the Hatchie River in Tennessee. Although the Hatchie River is not part of the historic

range of this mussel, it supports similar species and is currently protected under the Wild and Scenic Rivers Act. Transplantation outside the fat pocketbook's historic range would require special dispensation under the Endangered Species Act, but it is considered a possible recovery strategy.

Contacts

U. S. Fish and Wildlife Service
Regional Office, Division of Endangered Species
1 Federal Drive
BHW Federal Building
Fort Snelling, Minnesota 55111
Telephone: (612) 713-5360
http://midwest.fws.gov/

U. S. Fish and Wildlife Service
Regional Office, Division of Endangered Species
1875 Century Blvd., Suite 200
Atlanta, Georgia 30345
http://southeast.fws.gov/

References

Bates, J. M., and S. D. Dennis. 1983. "Mussel (Naiad) Survey—St. Francis, White, and Cache Rivers, Arkansas and Missouri." Report no. DACW66-78-C-0147. U. S. Army Corps of Engineers, Memphis.

Clark, A. H. 1984. "Draft Report Mussel (Naiad) Study; St. Francis and White Rivers; Cross, St. Francis, and Monroe Counties, Arkansas." Report no. 84M 1666R. U. S. Army Corps of Engineers, Memphis.

U. S. Fish and Wildlife Service. 1985. "Fat Pocketbook Pearly Mussel Recovery Plan." U. S. Fish and Wildlife Service, Atlanta.

Alabama Heelsplitter

Potamilus inflatus

Status	Threatened
Listed	September 28, 1990
Family	Unionidae (Freshwater Mussel)
Description	Large, thin, oval brown-to-black shell with a pink-to-purple interior.
Habitat	Soft, stable stream bottoms with slow to moderate currents.
Food	Filter-feeder.
Reproduction	Female stores sperm in gills; glochidia are released into the stream after hatching.
Threats	Impoundments, gravel dredging, channel maintenance.
Range	Alabama, Louisiana, Mississippi

Alabama Heelsplitter, photograph. A. E. Spreitzer Photography. Reproduced by permission.

Description

The Alabama heelsplitter (*Potamilus inflatus*) has a compressed to moderately inflated, thin, oval shell. The valves may gape anteriorly, the umbos are low, and there is a prominent posterior wing that may extend anteriorly to the beaks in young individuals. The shell is brown to black and may have green rays in young individuals. The umbonal cavity is very shallow and the inside of the shell is pink to purple. Shell length reaches 5.5 in (14 cm) in adults.

The heelsplitter closely resembles the pink papershell (*P. ohioensis*), yet it is easily distinguished by shell morphology. The teeth and shell of the heel-splitter are more delicate, and the shell is darker and has a pointed posterior, while the pink papershell has a rounded posterior. The heelsplitter appears more inflated due to a more developed and rounded posterior ridge. The posterior wing of the heelsplitter is more pronounced and abruptly rounded over the dorsum. The pink papershell may lack much of a wing, and when pronounced, it may be only slightly rounded and extend scarcely above the dorsum.

Behavior

See the Upland Combshell (*Epioblasma metastriata*) entry.

Habitat

The preferred habitat of this species is soft, stable substrate in slow to moderate currents. It has been found in sand, mud, silt, and sandy-gravel, but not in large gravel or armored gravel. It is usually collected on the protected side of bars and may occur in depths over 20 ft (6 m). The occurrence of this species in silt may not indicate that the life cycle can be successful in that substrate. Adult mussels may survive limited amounts of time in silt where juveniles would suffocate. The occurrence of this species in silt may be because it was established prior to deposition of the silt.

Distribution

The Alabama heelsplitter was known historically from the Amite and Tangipahoa Rivers, Louisiana; the Pearl River, Mississippi; and the Tombigbee, Black Warrior, Alabama, and Coosa Rivers, Alabama. The presently known distribution is limited to the Amite River, Louisiana, and the Tombigbee and Black Warrior Rivers, Alabama. A single specimen was collected from the Tangipahoa River, Louisiana, in 1964 but could not be found there in 1989. The species has not been reported from the Coosa or Alabama rivers since the 1970s.

This species is not abundant within any known habitat. Exact population numbers are unknown.

Threats

The species is currently known from only the Amite, Tombigbee, and Black Warrior Rivers. Other historic habitat has been affected by channel modification for navigation and flood control, impoundment (the collection and confining of water, as in a reservoir), pollution, and gravel dredging. Impoundment for navigation and sedimentation from surface mining have affected the Black Warrior River. And most of the Tombigbee River was modified by construction of the Tennessee-Tombigbee Waterway, resulting in the loss of river habitat by impoundment, channelization, and flow diversion. Habitats that otherwise would have supported mussel populations have been destroyed by heavy accumulations of sediment. Navigation dredging threatens this species by the deposition of spoil on bars along the sides of the river channel. This material washes onto mussel habitat below the bars and may suffocate mussels and make conditions unfavorable for recruitment. The major threats in the Amite River are gravel dredging and channel modification for flood control.

Thirty percent of the range of this species in the Amite River has been lost since 1976, due primarily to gravel mining. The impact of the proposed Darlington Reservoir as a flood control measure will likely be determined by the type and method of water releases incorporated. An alternative flood control measure under consideration is the widening and channelization of the Amite River. This potential action would likely eliminate the Alabama heelsplitter from the Amite River, leaving the only population in the Tombigbee and Black Warrior system.

The known populations are isolated from each other and apparently are limited in extent. This could result in low genetic variation and make these populations more susceptible to environmental disturbance due to loss of adaptability.

Conservation and Recovery

Enforcement of existing regulations will protect the known populations from channel modification. The restoration of habitat and reestablishment of this species to historic habitat may be possible.

Contacts

U. S. Fish and Wildlife Service
Regional Office, Division of Endangered Species
1875 Century Blvd., Suite 200
Atlanta, Georgia 30345
(404) 679-4000
http://southeast.fws.gov/

Jackson Ecological Services Field Office
6578 Dogwood View Parkway, Suite A
Jackson, Mississippi 39213-7856
Telephone: (601) 965-4900
Fax: (601) 965-4340

References

Hartfield, Paul. 1989. "Status Survey for the Alabama Heelsplitter Mussel *Potamilus inflatus* (Lea 1831)." A Report to the U. S. Fish and Wildlife Service.

U. S. Fish and Wildlife Service. 28 September 1990. "Determination of Threatened Status for the Inflated Heelsplitter, *Potamilus inflatus*." *Federal Register* 55 (189): 39868-39872.

Triangular Kidneyshell

Ptychobranchus greeni

Status	Endangered
Listed	March 17, 1993
Family	Unionidae (Freshwater Mussel)
Description	Medium to large mussel with an oval to elliptical yellow-brown shell and fine and wavy—or wide and broken—green rays.
Habitat	Gravel riffles in streams.
Food	Filter-feeder.
Reproduction	Female stores sperm in gills; glochidia (larvae) are released into streams after hatching.
Threats	Impoundments; gravel mining; water pollution.
Range	Alabama, Georgia, Tennessee

Triangular Kidneyshell, photograph. A. E. Spreitzer Photography. Reproduced by permission.

Description

The triangular kidneyshell (*Ptychobranchus greeni*) is a medium to large mussel that grows up to 4 in (10.2 cm) in length. The shell is ovate to elliptical, strongly compressed, and may be flattened ventral to the umbos. The posterior ridge is broadly rounded and terminates in a broad round point post-ventrally. The pseudocardinal teeth are heavy, and the laterals are heavy, gently curved, and short. The periostracum (outer shell) is straw-yellow in young mussels but becomes yellow-brown with age. It may have fine and wavy— or wide and broken—green rays anterior to the posterior ridge.

Behavior

The life of mussels is complex, and reproduction often depends upon a stable habitat—unaltered stream conditions, clean water, and an undisturbed stream bottom. The cycle also depends upon the abundance of suitable fish hosts to complete the mussel's larval development.

To reproduce, males discharge sperm, which are dispersed by stream currents. In the process of feeding, females nearby or downstream take in sperm, which fertilizes eggs stored in their gills. The gills serve as brood pouches (marsupia), where the glochidia hatch and begin to develop. After a time, these glochidia are released into the stream. A few mussels have inner parts that resemble a tiny minnow and can be manipulated to lure host fish. When a fish gets close to the shell, the mussel expels its glochidia.

Glochidia have tiny bean- or spoon-shaped valves that attach to the gill filaments of host fish. Glochidia can only progress to the juvenile stage while attached to the fish's gills. Those that do not fortuitously encounter a host fish do not survive when released by the female mussel. They sink to the bottom and die.

When the juvenile has developed a shell and is large enough to survive on its own, it detaches from the host fish and falls to the stream bottom, beginning a long association with a single stretch of stream. Maturing mussels bury themselves in riffles and shoals with only the shell margins and feeding siphons exposed to the water. Some mussels live as long as 50 years or more.

The family Unionidae, which includes all of the freshwater mussels in the United States, is separated into two groups based on the length of time the glochidia remain in the female's marsupia. The eggs of the short-term (tachytictic) breeders are fertilized in the spring, and glochidia are released by late summer of the same year. Long-term (bradytictic) breeders hold developing glochidia in the brood pouch over winter and release them in the spring.

Freshwater mussels feed by siphoning phytoplankton and other plant matter from the water. Indigestible particles are expelled from the shell by reverse siphoning. Silt in the water can kill mussels by clogging their feeding siphons.

There are no known interspecific differences in feeding among freshwater mussels. The glochidia are obligate parasites on the gills or fins of fish. Adult mussels are filter-feeders and consume particulate matter in the water column. Identifiable stomach contents almost invariably include desmids, diatoms, algae, protozoa, and zooplankton.

Most freshwater mussel species display seasonal variations in activity associated with water temperature and reproduction. Metabolic rate is, in part, positively correlated with temperature. Many ectothermic species have the capacity to adjust their metabolic rates in response to long-term changes in temperature. Thus, metabolic rates do not continue to rise as temperatures rise in the summer, and they

do not continue to fall during the winter as temperatures decline.

Some freshwater mussels also show diurnal changes in metabolic rates that indicate a tendency toward nocturnal activity patterns. Mussels may move to the surface to feed at night and move deeper into the substrate during the day; this is one way to avoid predators that hunt by visual contact.

Freshwater mussels are nonmigratory.

Habitat

The triangular kidneyshell inhabits high quality lotic habitats (living in actively moving water) with stable gravel and sandy-gravel substrates. Little else is known about the habitat requirements of this species.

The habitat of the glochidia is initially in the gills of the female, then in the water column, and finally attached to a suitable host fish. Habitat associations or requirements for the juvenile stage are unknown.

Distribution

This species' historic range included the Black Warrior River and tributaries (Mulberry Fork, Locust Fork, North and Little Warrior Rivers, Brushy Creek, Sipsey Fork); Cahaba River; and the Coosa River and tributaries (Choccolocco Creek; Chatooga, Conasauga, and Etowah Rivers), all of which are part of the Mobil River basin.

The triangular kidneyshell is currently limited to (1) the headwaters of the Sipsey Fork and Little Warrior River in the Black Warrior River drainage and (2) the Conasauga River in the Coosa drainage. Specimens were lasted collected in the Cahaba River in 1979. Surveys in 1991 failed to find other historically known populations.

Threats

Habitat modification, sedimentation, and water quality degradation represent the major threats to this species. These freshwater mussels do not tolerate impoundments. More than 1,000 mi (1,609 km) of large and small river habitat in the Mobile River drainage has been impounded for navigation, flood control, water supply, and/or hydroelectric production purposes. Impoundments adversely affect riverine mussels by (1) killing them during construction and dredging, (2) suffocating them with accumulated sediments, (3) lowering food and oxygen availability by reducing water flow, and (4) locally extirpating host fish. Other forms of habitat modification such as channelization, channel clearing and de-snagging, and gravel mining result in streambed scour and erosion, increased turbidity, reduction of groundwater levels, sedimentation, and changes in the aquatic community structure. Sedimentation may cause direct mortality by deposition and suffocation and eliminate or reduce recruitment of juvenile mussels. Suspended sediments can also interfere with feeding. Activities that historically caused sedimentation of streams and rivers in the drainages where this mussel occurs include channel modification, agriculture, forestry, mining, and industrial and residential development. In addition, stream discharge may result in decreased dissolved oxygen concentration, increased acidity and conductivity, and other changes in water chemistry that may impact the mussels and/or fish hosts.

About 230 river mi (370 km) of the Coosa River have been impounded for hydropower by a series of six dams. Water quality degradation caused by textile and carpet mill wastes led to the loss of several known mussel communities in various streams of this river system.

Water quality degradation is a major problem in the Cahaba River system. There are 10 municipal wastewater treatment plants, 35 surface mining areas, a coalbed methane operation, and 67 other permitted discharges in this river system. Siltation from surface mining, road construction, and oil and gas development is also a problem.

Conservation and Recovery

Actions needed for the recovery of freshwater mussels include (1) conducting population and habitat surveys to determine the status and range of the species, (2) determining specific threats to the species and minimizing or eliminating these threats, (3) identifying essential habitat areas in need of protection, and (4) controlling the incidental or illegal take of mussels by commercial and noncommercial collectors.

It is unlikely that this species will recover unless new populations are established by introducing individuals back into the historic range. Methods to accomplish this might include the introduction of adult/juvenile mussels, glochidia-infected host fish, and artificially cultured individuals.

Contacts

U.S. Fish and Wildlife Service
Regional Office, Division of Endangered Species
1875 Century Blvd., Suite 200
Atlanta, Georgia 30345
Telephone: (404) 679-4000
http://southeast.fws.gov/

Ecological Services Field Office
P.O. Box 1190
Daphne, Alabama 36526-1190
Telephone: (334) 441-5181
Fax: (334) 441-6222

Ecological Services Field Office
446 Neal Street
Cookeville, Tennessee 38501-4027
Telephone: (931) 528-6481
Fax: (931) 528-7075

Reference

U.S. Fish and Wildlife Service. 17 March 1993. "Endangered and Threatened Wildlife and Plants; Endangered Status for Eight Freshwater Mussels and Threatened Status for Three Freshwater Mussels in the Mobile River Drainage." *Federal Register* 58 (50): 14330-14340.

Rough Rabbitsfoot

Quadrula cylindrica strigillata

Status	Endangered
Listed	January 10, 1997
Family	Unionidae
Description	A freshwater, bivalve mollusk.
Habitat	Medium- to large-sized rivers with clean, flowing water.
Food	Filter-feeds on phytoplankton, tiny zooplankton, and organic detritus.
Reproduction	Female siphons male spawn and fertilizes eggs in her gills; the larvae are parasitic on fish, and later metamorphose into the sedentary adult stage.
Threats	Habitat destruction by impoundment, and pollution by siltation, nutrients, and other chemicals originating with coal mining, agriculture, and other sources.
Range	Tennessee, Virginia

Rough Rabbitsfoot, photograph. U. S. Fish and Wildlife Service. Reproduced by permission.

Description

The rough rabbitsfoot mussel (*Quadrula cylindrica strigillata*), described in 1898, has an elongated, heavy, rough textured, and yellow-to-greenish-colored shell. The shell's surface is covered with green rays, blotches, and chevron patterns. The inside of the shell is silvery to white with an iridescence in the posterior area of the shell. This mussel is considered threatened by the State of Virginia, and it is deemed a species of special concern in Tennessee.

Behavior

This tachytictic species has been observed spawning from May (when water temperature reached 68 to 71.6°F (20 to 22°C) through June. Fertilization success was high (95%) through late June, but by July only unfertilized ova were found. Unlike most amblemines, 65% of 82 gravid females examined utilized only the outer demibranchs as marsupia. Gra-

vidity rates of from 30-60%, peaking in late May, then gradually declining have been documented. Females release lanceolate-shaped whitish to reddish brown conglutinates (0.4 in [10 mm] long) that contain 375-505 semicircular-shaped glochidia. Fecundity has been estimated at 115,000 embryos per female. Estimated age of the females studied was 10-22 years. Three cyprinid host fish species have been identified—the whitetail shiner, spot fin shiner (*C. spiloptera*), and bigeye chub (*Hybopsis amblops*). Infestation rates ranged from as few as five to 10 glochidia on individual fishes. Transformation took from 13-23 days, at 68.9-71.4°F (20.5 to 22°C).

Habitat

This species inhabits medium-sized to large rivers m moderate to swift current but often exists in areas close to, but not in, the swiftest current. It is reported to live in silt, sand, gavel, or cobble in eddies at the edge of midstream currents and may be associated with macrophyte beds.

Distribution

Historically, this mussel was restricted to the upper Tennessee River basin in the Clinch, Powell, and Holston river systems. Only three populations of limited distributions and scant numbers still persist in these three systems. These occurrences are in the Powell River, Lee County, Virginia and the Tennessee counties of Claiborne and Hancock counties; in the Clinch River, Scott County, Virginia and Hancock County, Tennessee; the Clinch River tributary Copper Creek, Scott County, Virginia; and North Fork Holston River, Washington County, Virginia.

Threats

The rough rabbitsfoot populations in the lower Clinch, Powell, and Holston river systems were extirpated by reservoirs. The decline of the species throughout the rest of its range was likely due to the adverse impacts of coal mining, poor land-use practices, and pollution, primarily from nonpoint sources. The population centers that remain are so limited that they are vulnerable to extirpation from random episodes such as toxic chemical spills.

Conservation and Recovery

The rough rabbitsfoot only survives in localized portions of the Powell River, Clinch River, Copper Creek (a Clinch River tributary), and North Fork Holston River. It is crucial that its few critical habitats are protected against the development of new dams or impoundments, from acid drainage associated with coal mining, from sedimentation and nutrient inputs associated with agricultural land-use, and from spills of petroleum or other toxic chemicals. The surviving populations of the rough rabbitsfoot should be monitored, and research undertaken into its biology and ecological needs, including work on its propagation and reintroduction techniques.

Contact

U.S. Fish and Wildlife Service
Asheville Ecological Services
Field Office
160 Zillicoa Street
Asheville, North Carolina, 28801-1082
Telephone: (828) 258-3939
Fax: (828) 258-5330

Reference

U.S. Fish and Wildlife Service. 10 January 1997. "Endangered and Threatened Wildlife and Plants; Determination of Endangered Status for the Cumberland Elktoe, Oyster Mussel, Cumberlandian Combshell, Purple Bean, and Rough Rabbitsfoot." *Federal Register* 62 (7): 1647-1658.

Winged Mapleleaf

Quadrula fragosa

Status	Endangered
Listed	June 20, 1991
Family	Unionidae (Freshwater Mussel)
Description	Similar to the common mapleleaf, but with a more inflated shell.
Habitat	Riffle areas of large clearwater streams.
Food	Filter-feeder.
Reproduction	Female stores sperm in gills; glochidia are released into the stream after hatching.
Threats	Low numbers, reproductive failure.
Range	Kentucky, Minnesota, Tennessee, Wisconsin

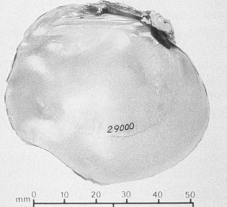

29000

mm 0   10   20   30   40   50
in

Winged Mapleleaf, photograph. A. E. Spreitzer Photography. Reproduced by permission.

Description

The winged mapleleaf (*Quadrula fragosa*) is a freshwater mussel closely related to the mapleleaf, a common mussel species in eastern North America. It can be distinguished by its more inflated shell, which is more quadrate in outline, and the beaks on the shell, which are turned forward and more elevated.

Behavior

See the Upland Combshell (*Epioblasma metastriata*) entry.

Habitat

This species occupies gravel bars in the shallow, clear waters of large rivers.

Distribution

The winged mapleleaf has been found in four river systems in eleven states: the Mississippi, Tennessee, Ohio, and Cumberland systems in Ohio, Indiana, Missouri, Tennessee, Kansas, Nebraska, Iowa, Illinois, Wisconsin, Oklahoma, and Kentucky. Collections of the winged mapleleaf were not unusual until about 1920, after which they became rare and many experts considered the species extinct.

At the dawn of the twenty-first century, a single, small population of the winged mapleleaf survived in the St. Croix River along the border of Minnesota and Wisconsin. This population was restricted to less than 5 mi (8 km) of river within a national scenic riverway administered by the National Park Service.

The population density at this one remaining site was one individual per 560 sq ft (52 sq m), constituting less than 0.02% of the mussel community. This community consists of 32 species of mussels, including rare species such as the federally endangered Higgins' eye (*Lampsilis higginsi*) and the spectacle case (*Cumberlandia monodonta*) and salamander mussel (*Simpsonaias ambigua*), which are candidates for federal listing.

Threats

The preferred habitat of the winged mapleleaf—riffles or gravel bars in large clearwater streams—has been largely eliminated by impoundment, channelization, and sedimentation.

Conservation and Recovery

The sole surviving population is at extreme risk because of an apparent reproductive failure. During surveys in 1988 and 1989 researchers failed to find any individuals less than four years old or to find females carrying eggs. Related species that were collected during the survey included individuals of all age classes. If this population is truly failing to reproduce, its extinction is certain.

Contacts

U. S. Fish and Wildlife Service
Regional Office, Division of Endangered Species
1 Federal Dr.
BHW Federal Building
Fort Snelling, Minnesota 55111
(612) 713-5360
http://midwest.fws.gov/

U. S. Fish and Wildlife Service
Regional Office, Division of Endangered Species
1875 Century Blvd., Suite 200
Atlanta, Georgia 30345
(404) 679-4000
http://southeast.fws.gov/

References

Doolittle, Thomas C. J. 1988. "Distribution and Relative Abundance of Freshwater Mussels in the Saint Croix National Scenic Riverway." Cable Natural History Museum, Sigurd Olson Environmental Institute, Ashland, Wisconsin.

Havlik, M. E., and L. L. Marking. 1980. "A Quantitative Analysis of Naiad Mollusks from the Prairie du Chien, Wisconsin, Wisconsin Dredge Material Site on the Mississippi River." *Bulletin of the American Malacological Union* 1977: 9-12.

Cumberland Monkeyface

Quadrula intermedia

Status	Endangered
Listed	June 14, 1976
Family	Unionidae (Freshwater Mussel)
Description	Medium-sized, triangular to quadrangular, greenish-yellow shell with numerous markings.
Habitat	Shallow, fast-flowing water with substrate.
Food	Filter-feeder.
Reproduction	Female stores sperm in gills; glochidia (larvae) are released into streams after hatching.
Threats	Impoundments; siltation; pollution.
Range	Alabama, Tennessee, Virginia

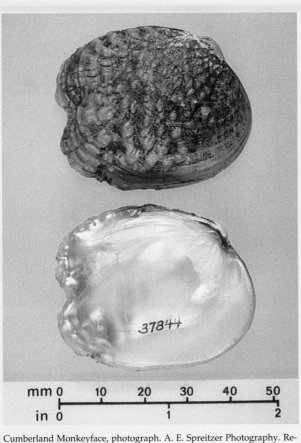

Cumberland Monkeyface, photograph. A. E. Spreitzer Photography. Reproduced by permission.

Description

The shell of the Cumberland monkeyface pearlymussel (*Quadrula intermedia*) is medium in size (2.8 in [7.1 cm]), triangular to quadrangular in outline, and marked with numerous tubercles or knobs. The valves are flat and display a deep beak cavity. The outer shell surface is greenish-yellow with green spots, chevrons, zigzags, and sometimes broken green rays. The inner shell surface is white, straw-colored, or salmon.

Behavior

The life of mussels is complex, and reproduction often depends upon a stable habitat—unaltered stream conditions, clean water, and an undisturbed stream bottom. The cycle also depends upon the abundance of suitable fish hosts to complete the mussel's larval development.

To reproduce, males discharge sperm, which are dispersed by stream currents. In the process of feeding, females nearby or downstream take in sperm, which fertilizes eggs stored in their gills. The gills serve as brood pouches (marsupia), where the glochidia hatch and begin to develop. After a time, these glochidia are released into the stream. A few mussels have inner parts that resemble a tiny minnow and can be manipulated to lure host fish. When a fish gets close to the shell, the mussel expels its glochidia. The fish hosts for this particular pearlymussel are unknown.

Glochidia have tiny bean- or spoon-shaped valves that attach to the gill filaments of host fish. Glochidia can only progress to the juvenile stage while attached to the fish's gills. Those that do not fortuitously encounter a host fish do not survive when released by the female mussel. They sink to the bottom and die.

When the juvenile has developed a shell and is large enough to survive on its own, it detaches from the host fish and falls to the stream bottom, beginning a long association with a single stretch of stream. Maturing mussels bury themselves in riffles and shoals with only the shell margins and feeding siphons exposed to the water. Some mussels live as long as 50 years or more.

A short-term (or tachytictic) breeder, this mussel produces glochidia in the spring and releases them by mid- to late summer of the same year.

Freshwater mussels feed by siphoning phytoplankton and other plant matter from the water. Indigestible particles are expelled from the shell by reverse siphoning. Silt in the water can kill mussels by clogging their feeding siphons.

There are no known interspecific differences in feeding among freshwater mussels. The glochidia are obligate parasites on the gills or fins of fish. Adult mussels are filter-feeders and consume particulate matter in the water column. Identifiable stomach contents almost invariably include desmids, diatoms, algae, protozoa, and zooplankton.

Most freshwater mussel species display seasonal variations in activity associated with water temperature and reproduction. Metabolic rate is, in part, positively correlated with temperature. Many ectothermic species have the capacity to adjust their metabolic rates in response to long-term changes in temperature. Thus, metabolic rates do not continue to rise as temperatures rise in the summer, and they do not continue to fall during the winter as temperatures decline.

Some freshwater mussels also show diurnal changes in metabolic rates that indicate a tendency toward nocturnal activity patterns. Mussels may move to the surface to feed at night and move deeper into the substrate during the day; this is one way to avoid predators that hunt by visual contact.

Freshwater mussels are nonmigratory.

Habitat

This mussel is typically found in shallow, fast-flowing water with a stable, clean substrate of sand or coarse gravel. It requires highly oxygenated water and, therefore, does not survive in still pools.

Distribution

The monkeyface pearlymussel was historically restricted to the headwaters of the Tennessee River and probably the upper Cumberland River. It is a Cumberlandian species—endemic to the southern Appalachian Mountains and the Cumberland Plateau. Of the 90 species of freshwater mussels found in the Tennessee River, 37 are Cumberlandian; of 78 species found in the Cumberland River, 27 are considered Cumberlandian. Together, these mussels represent the largest number of freshwater mussel species found in any of the world's rivers.

Threats

This pearlymussel was apparently never abundant, and the reasons for its decline are not fully understood. Impoundments, siltation, and pollution are presumed to be the major causes. The Tennessee Valley Authority (TVA) has constructed 36 dams in the Tennessee River basin. These dams and reservoirs have inundated mussel shoals upstream, disrupted stream flow, and altered downstream habitat with sporadic cold-water discharges. Siltation caused by strip-mining and poor agricultural practices often covers the substrates of gravel and sand and smothers mussel beds. Because mussels must siphon gallons of water each day to feed, the effects of water pollutants such as herbicides and pesticides are intensified.

Conservation and Recovery

Surveys conducted by the TVA in 1988 and 1989 revealed that mussel populations in the Duck River (which flows into the Tennessee River) had stabilized. The status of mussel populations in the Elk and Powell Rivers (which flow into the Tennessee and Clinch Rivers, respectively) has not yet been determined. Sections of the Powell River appear eligible for "scenic river" status under the National Wild and Scenic Rivers Act. Such a designation would provide additional protection for the Cumberland monkeyface and its habitat.

If the Columbia Dam was completed, most of the Cumberland monkeyface's habitat in the Duck River would have been lost. The dam project was stalled by controversy. Whenever the TVA has expressed an opinion that the Columbia Dam should be abandoned, powerful local interests have continued to push for its completion. The dam was never completed. Demolition started in June 1999.

Contacts

U. S. Fish and Wildlife Service
Regional Office, Division of Endangered Species
1875 Century Blvd., Suite 200
Atlanta, Georgia 30345
Telephone: (404) 679-4000
http://southeast.fws.gov/

U. S. Fish and Wildlife Service
Regional Office, Division of Endangered Species
300 Westgate Center Dr.
Hadley, Massachusetts 01035-9589
Telephone: (413) 253-8200
Fax: (413) 253-8308
http://northeast.fws.gov/

References

Dennis, S.D. 1981. "Mussel Fauna of the Powell River, Tennessee and Virginia." *Sterkiana* 71: 1-7.

Isom, B.G., and P. Yokley, Jr. 1968. "The Mussel Fauna of Duck River in Tennessee, 1965." *American Midland Naturalist* 80 (1): 34-42.

"Protest Won't Stop Columbia Dam's Demise." In *The Tennessean*, 3 June 1999.

U.S. Fish and Wildlife Service. 1982. "Cumberland Monkeyface Pearly Mussel Recovery Plan." U.S. Fish and Wildlife Service, Atlanta.

Appalachian Monkeyface

Quadrula sparsa

Status	Endangered
Listed	June 14, 1976
Family	Unionidae (Freshwater Mussel)
Description	Freshwater mussel with medium-sized, yellow-green or brown quadrangular shell with distinctive markings.
Habitat	Fast-flowing water in shallow shoals.
Food	Filter feeder.
Reproduction	Breeds from May to July.
Threats	Impoundments, siltation, pollution.
Range	Tennessee, Virginia

Appalachian Monkeyface, photograph. A. E. Spreitzer Photography. Reproduced by permission.

Description

The yellow-green or brown shell of the Appalachian monkeyface pearlymussel (*Quadrula sparsa*) is medium-sized (2.8 in [7 cm]) and nearly quadrangular in shape. The shell surface is marked with small green zig-zags, triangles, or chevrons and strong, concentric growth rings.

Behavior

This mussel is thought to breed from May to July. Its fish hosts are unknown. For more on the reproduction and diet of freshwater mussels, see the Upland Combshell (*Epioblasma metastriata*) entry.

Habitat

This freshwater Cumberlandian mussel is found most often in clean, shallow river stretches where the bottom is composed of relatively firm rubble, gravel, and sand. Swift currents in these shoals typically sweep the bottom free of silt.

Distribution

This species was first collected in 1841 from the Holston River in eastern Tennessee and is thought to have been widespread in tributaries of the upper Tennessee and Cumberland river systems.

Threats

The Appalachian monkeyface was apparently never abundant, and the reasons for its decline are not fully understood, but impoundments, siltation, and pollution are presumed to be the major causes. The Norris Dam, in particular, probably inundated this mussel's habitat shoals in both the Powell and Clinch Rivers. The cold tailwaters have made long upstream portions of the rivers uninhabitable for both mussels and host fishes.

Siltation caused by strip mining, coal washing, and poor agricultural practices have buried gravel and sand shoals and smothered mussel beds. Because mussels must siphon gallons of water each day to feed, the effects of water pollutants such as herbicides and pesticides are intensified.

Surveys conducted by the Tennessee Valley Authority (TVA) in 1988 and 1989 suggest that mussel populations in the Clinch River continue to decline. The status of populations in the Powell River has not yet been determined. Recovery for this mussel will require rehabilitation of at least part of its historic habitat to allow populations to be reestablished.

Conservation and Recovery

The TVA, which administers the operation of dams on the Tennessee and Cumberland Rivers, is working on water management to guarantee constant minimum flows in all rivers in the Tennessee and Cumberland basins by timing water discharges from its dams. Such an effort may lessen many of the negative effects of dams and reservoirs on remaining stretches of mussel habitat.

Contact

U.S. Fish and Wildlife Service
Regional Office, Division of Endangered Species
1875 Century Blvd., Suite 200
Atlanta, Georgia 30345
(404) 679-4000
http://southeast.fws.gov/

References

Bogan, A., and P. Parmalee. 1983. "Tennessee's Rare Mollusks." In *Tennessee's Rare Wildlife, Final Report*. Department of Conservation and Tennessee Heritage Project, University of Tennessee, Knoxville.

Branson, B. A. 1974. "Stripping the Appalachians." *Natural History* 83, (9): 53-60.

French, John R. P., III. November 1990. "The Exotic Zebra Mussel: A New Threat to Endangered Freshwater Mussels." *Endangered Species Technical Bulletin* 15 (11).

Fuller, S. 1974. "Clams and Mussels (Mollusca: Bivalvia)." In *Pollution Ecology of Freshwater Invertebrates*. Academic Press, New York.

Neel, J. K., and W. R. Allen. 1964. "The Mussel Fauna of the Upper Cumberland Basin before Its Impoundment." *Malacologia* 1 (3): 427-459.

Pardue, J. W. 1981. "A Survey of the Mussels (Unionidae) of the Upper Tennessee River, 1978." *Sterkiana* 71: 41-51.

U. S. Fish and Wildlife Service. 1983. "Appalachian Monkeyface Recovery Plan." U. S. Fish and Wildlife Service, Atlanta.

Stirrupshell

Quadrula stapes

Status	Endangered
Listed	April 7, 1987
Family	Unionidae (Freshwater Mussel)
Description	Quadrangular, yellowish green shell with zig-zag markings.
Habitat	Sand and gravel substrates in flowing water.
Food	Filter-feeder.
Reproduction	Female stores sperm in gills; glochidia are released into the stream after hatching.
Threats	Loss of habitat, sedimentation, dredging.
Range	Alabama, Mississippi

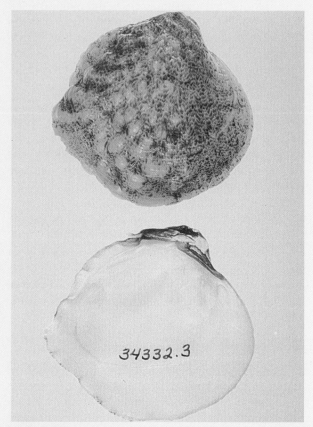

Stirrupshell, photograph. A. E. Spreitzer Photography. Reproduced by permission.

Description

The stirrupshell, *Quadrula stapes*, is a bivalve mollusk, 2.2 in (5.6 cm) long, with a quadrangular shell. The yellowish green shell is marked with zig-zag lines, which are light green on young shells and dark brown on older shells. Its truncated posterior has a sharp ridge and tubercles. The inner shell surface is silvery white.

Behavior

See the Upland Combshell (*Epioblasma metastriata*) entry.

Habitat

This mussel is found in the shoals and riffles of fast-flowing rivers, buried in relatively firm, silt-free rubble, gravel, and sand substrates.

Distribution

The stirrupshell was found historically in the Tombigbee River from near Columbus, Mississippi, downstream to Epes, Alabama, and in the Black Warrior, Sipsey, and Alabama Rivers.

The stirrupshell has not been found in the Alabama or Black Warrior Rivers for several decades.

It is presently known from only two sites in Alabama-the Sipsey River (Pickens and Green Counties), and the Gainesville Bendway (Pickens County), a meander of the East Fork Tombigbee River that was cut off by construction of the Tennessee-Tombigbee Waterway. A survey and habitat assessment of the Tombigbee River at Gainesville Bendway, Alabama, was conducted in 1988, but no specimens of this species were located.

Threats

When the Tennessee-Tombigbee Waterway was completed to allow barge traffic between the Tennessee and Tombigbee rivers, most of the East Fork Tombigbee River was modified into a series of channels, locks, and impoundments. The dams and locks inundated mussel shoals and slowed the flow of water, increasing siltation, which smothers mussel beds. Dredging to create a navigable channel physically destroyed many mussel beds, and periodic maintenance dredging continues to disturb the river bottom. Bull Mountain Creek, which provided nearly half the water supply of the East Fork, was diverted to feed the waterway. The creek's cooler waters are warmed when routed through the canal, making this part of the river inimical to both mussels and host fishes.

Mussels native to the Tombigbee and Sipsey rivers are threatened by continued flood control and navigation improvement projects. Such activities add silt to waters and increases turbidity, clogging the mussel's feeding apparatus and smothering mussel beds. A currently proposed 84 mi (136 km) channel improvement project would degrade or destroy mussel habitat on the Sipsey River.

The last free-flowing stretch of the East Fork Tombigbee River is threatened by plans to dredge 53 mi (85 km) to improve navigability. Siltation in the Bendway has become more severe in the last few years and may already be smothering surviving mussel beds.

Conservation and Recovery

Under provisions of the Endangered Species Act, federal agencies are required to consult with the U.S. Fish and Wildlife Service (FWS) to ensure that any actions they authorize or fund do not jeopardize Threatened or Endangered species. This rule affects all watershed projects proposed by the Army Corps of Engineers and the Soil Conservation Service of the Department of Agriculture. In the past, similar consultations have resulted in the redesign of projects to preserve significant portions of habitat.

The Recovery Plan calls for maintaining good water flow through the areas the stirrupshell inhabits; creating artificial habitats from gravel bars; prohibiting sand and gravel dredging; and creating land easements to protect remaining habitats.

Contact

U.S. Fish and Wildlife Service
Regional Office, Division of Endangered Species
1875 Century Blvd., Suite 200
Atlanta, Georgia 30345
http://southeast.fws.gov/

References

Fuller, S.L.H. 1974. "Clams and Mussels (Mollusca: Bivalvia)." In Hart and Fuller, eds. *Pollution Ecology of Freshwater Invertebrates.* Academic Press, New York.

Stansbery, D.H. 1976. "Naiad Mollusks." In H. Boschung, ed. "Endangered and Threatened Plants and Animals in Alabama." *Bulletin of the Alabama Museum of Natural History* 2: 42-55.

Pale Lilliput Pearlymussel

Toxolasma cylindrellus

Status	Endangered
Listed	June 14, 1976
Family	Unionidae (Freshwater Mussel)
Description	Yellowish-green, nearly cylindrical shell.
Habitat	Gravel and rubble substrates.
Food	Filter-feeder.
Reproduction	Female stores sperm in gills; glochidia (larvae) are released into streams after hatching.
Threats	Loss of habitat; pollution.
Range	Alabama, Tennessee

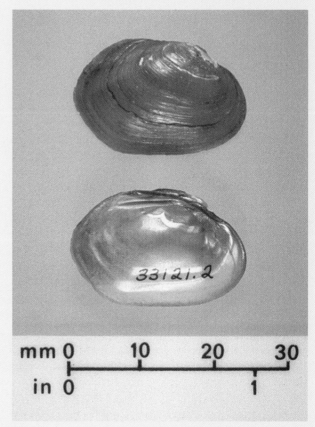

Pale Lilliput, photograph. A. E. Spreitzer Photography. Reproduced by permission.

Description

The shell of the pale lilliput pearlymussel (*Toxolasma cylindrellus*) measures 1.8 in (4.6 cm) in length, 1 in (2.5 cm) in height, and 0.64 in (1.6 cm) in width. The valves are solid, elongated, and appear nearly cylindrical. The smooth shell surface is yellowish-green. The inner shell surface (nacre) varies from white to light yellow with metallic tints of blue and purple. This Cumberlandian species was formerly classified as *Carunculina cylindrellus*.

Behavior

The life of mussels is complex, and reproduction often depends upon a stable habitat—unaltered stream conditions, clean water, and an undisturbed stream bottom. The cycle also depends upon the abundance of suitable fish hosts to complete the mussel's larval development.

To reproduce, males discharge sperm, which are dispersed by stream currents. In the process of feeding, females nearby or downstream take in sperm, which fertilizes eggs stored in their gills. The gills serve as brood pouches (marsupia), where the glochidia hatch and begin to develop. After a time, these glochidia are released into the stream. A few mussels have inner parts that resemble a tiny minnow and can be manipulated to lure host fish. When a fish gets close to the shell, the mussel expels its glochidia.

Glochidia have tiny bean- or spoon-shaped valves that attach to the gill filaments of host fish. Glochidia can only progress to the juvenile stage while attached to the fish's gills. Those that do not fortuitously encounter a host fish do not survive when released by the female mussel. They sink to the bottom and die.

When the juvenile has developed a shell and is large enough to survive on its own, it detaches from the host fish and falls to the stream bottom, beginning a long association with a single stretch of stream. Maturing mussels bury themselves in riffles and shoals with only the shell margins and feeding siphons exposed to the water. Some mussels live as long as 50 years or more.

The family Unionidae, which includes all of the freshwater mussels in the United States, is separated into two groups based on the length of time the glochidia remain in the female's marsupia. The eggs of the short-term (tachytictic) breeders are fertilized in the spring, and glochidia are released by late summer of the same year. Long-term (bradytictic) breeders hold developing glochidia in the brood pouch over winter and release them in the spring.

Freshwater mussels feed by siphoning phytoplankton and other plant matter from the water. Indigestible particles are expelled from the shell by reverse siphoning. Silt in the water can kill mussels by clogging their feeding siphons.

There are no known interspecific differences in feeding among freshwater mussels. The glochidia are obligate parasites on the gills or fins of fish. Adult mussels are filter-feeders and consume particulate matter in the water column. Identifiable stomach contents almost invariably include desmids, diatoms, algae, protozoa, and zooplankton.

Most freshwater mussel species display seasonal variations in activity associated with water temperature and reproduction. Metabolic rate is, in part, positively correlated with temperature. Many ectothermic species have the capacity to adjust their metabolic rates in response to long-term changes in temperature. Thus, metabolic rates do not continue to rise as temperatures rise in the summer, and they do not continue to fall during the winter as temperatures decline.

Some freshwater mussels also show diurnal changes in metabolic rates that indicate a tendency toward nocturnal activity patterns. Mussels may move to the surface to feed at night and move deeper into the substrate during the day; this is one way to avoid predators that hunt by visual contact.

Freshwater mussels are nonmigratory.

Habitat

This mussel inhabits narrow streams and prefers clean, shallow, fast-flowing water with a firm, silt-free rubble, gravel, or sandy bottom.

Distribution

The pale lilliput pearlymussel probably ranged in the narrower tributaries of the Tennessee River in Tennessee and Alabama. It was documented from the Flint and Elk Rivers in the 1920s, from the Sequatchie and Little Sequatchie Rivers in the 1950s, from the Buffalo River in 1973, and from the Duck River as recently as 1976. Of its reported occurrences, it continues to survive only in the Paint Rock River watershed in northern Alabama.

Threats

The pale lilliput pearlymussel has been rare at least since its discovery but has disappeared from much of its former range because of dam construction, stream siltation, and pollution. Siltation caused by strip-mining, coal washing, dredging, clear-cutting, and poor agricultural practices have buried gravel and sand shoals and smothered mussel beds in many watersheds. Because mussels must siphon gallons of water each day to feed, the effects of water pollutants such as herbicides and pesticides are intensified. All these factors have resulted in the reduction in range and numbers of most Cumberlandian pearlymussels, including the pale lilliput.

Conservation and Recovery

Recovery of this species will depend on the larger effort of rehabilitating pearlymussel habitat in the Tennessee Valley.

The Tennessee Valley Authority is currently developing a comprehensive water management plan for the region that would establish minimum year-round flows in all rivers by carefully timing water discharges from its many dams. In addition, the Paint Rock River may be eligible for "scenic river" status under the National Wild and Scenic Rivers Act, a designation that would provide additional protection for this species and its remaining habitat. Pending the results of ongoing research, the U.S. Fish and Wildlife Service may attempt to reintroduce the pale lilliput to suitable stretches of habitat within its historic range.

Contacts

U.S. Fish and Wildlife Service
Regional Office, Division of Endangered Species
1875 Century Blvd., Suite 200
Atlanta, Georgia 30345
Telephone: (404) 679-4000
http://southeast.fws.gov/

Ecological Services Field Office
446 Neal Street
Cookeville, Tennessee 38501-4027
Telephone: (931) 528-6481
Fax: (931) 528-7075

References

Bogan, A., and P. Parmalee. 1983. "Tennessee's Rare Mollusks." In *Tennessee's Rare Wildlife, Final Report.* Tennessee Heritage Program, Department of Conservation, University of Tennessee Press, Knoxville.

Isom, B.G. 1969. "The Mussel Resources of the Tennessee River." *Malacologia* 7 (2-4): 397-425.

U.S. Fish and Wildlife Service. 1984. "Pale Lilliput Pearly Mussel Recovery Plan." U.S. Fish and Wildlife Service, Atlanta.

Purple Bean

Villosa perpurpurea

Status	Endangered
Listed	January 10, 1997
Family	Unionidae
Description	A freshwater, bivalve mussel.
Habitat	Headwater streams to medium-sized rivers, in riffles with sand, gravel, and cobble substrata.
Food	Larvae are parasitic on fish; adults are filter-feeders.
Reproduction	Female siphons sperm from the water to achieve fertilization of the eggs, which hatch into parasitic larvae, which metamorphose into sedentary adults.
Threats	Reservoir construction, water pollution by acid-mine drainage, sedimentation, and agricultural runoff.
Range	Virginia

Description

The purple bean mussel (*Villosa perpurpurea*), described by Lea 1861, has a small- to medium-sized shell. The shell's outer surface is usually dark brown to black with numerous closely spaced fine green rays. The inside of the shell is purple, but the purple may fade to white in dead specimens. *Villosa perpurpurea* most closely resembles *V. trabalis*. The most obvious difference is the purple nacre of the former in comparison to the white nacre of the latter. However, this character is somewhat variable and the purple color may fade rapidly in dead specimens. With regards to other shell characters, *V. perpurpurea* tends to be more compressed, thinner, slightly broader, the beak is less developed, and the emargination of the ventral margin in female shells is not as pronounced. The base color of the periostracum in *V. trabalis* is greenish. The *perpurpurea* is less exaggerated in its particular characters than *V. trabalis*. The glochidia of the two species are also shaped differently. *V. vanuxemii* (*V. v. vanuxemensis*) may be sympatric with *perpurpurea* but it tends to be a bit larger. In *V. vanuxemii*, the nacre is shiny purple but tends to be reddish or brownish in the area of the

beak cavity and may be lighter around the periphery of the shell, the base color of the periostracum is brown, and raying is rather obscure. Female shells are strongly truncated, often with a distinct notch just ventral to the terminus of the posterior ridge which runs approximately parallel to the dorsal margin.

Behavior

The purple bean, another lampsiline species, appears to be bradytictic, as gravid females have been observed in January. Three host fish species have been identified—the fantail darter (*Etheostoma flabellare*), greenside darter, and mottled sculpin (*Cottus bairdi*) and/or banded sculpin. Transformation took from 11 to 25 days, at 70.7 to 76.1 F.

Habitat

This species inhabits small headwater streams to medium-sized rivers. It is found in moderate to fast-flowing riffles with sand, gavel, and cobble substrata and rarely occurs in pools or slack water. It

Purple Bean (Mussel), photograph. U. S. Fish and Wildlife Service. Reproduced by permission.

is sometimes found out of the main current adjacent to water-willow beds and under flat rocks.

Distribution

The purple bean historically occupied the upper Tennessee River basin in Tennessee and Virginia upstream of the confluence of the Clinch River. In 1918 it was considered "not rare" in Virginia. The purple bean populations in the lower Clinch, Powell, and Holston Rivers were extirpated by reservoirs; now only three populations remain.

The purple bean now survives in limited numbers at a few locations. In Virginia, it occurs in the upper Clinch River basin in Scott, Tazewell, and Russell Counties; as well as in the Clinch River tributaries of Copper Creek in Scott County and Indian Creek in Tazewell County. This last location is the same reach of river where the federally listed tan riffleshell mussel has also been found. In Tennessee, the purple bean occurs in the Obed River in Cumberland and Morgan Counties, in the Emory River just below its confluence with the Obed River in Morgan County, and Beech Creek in Hawkins County.

Threats

This taxon likely declined throughout its range until its current meager numbers due to the deleterious effects of reservoir construction, coal mining, poor land-use practices, and non-point pollution. These are still the primary threats to its survival. The population centers that remain are so limited that they are very vulnerable to random events such as toxic chemical spills.

Conservation and Recovery

The purple bean is considered endangered by the States of Tennessee and Virginia, as well as at the federal level. Its most pressing conservation need is the prevention of further deterioration of its limited areas of critical habitat, and the mitigation of existing stresses where possible. Specific actions include the prevention of: harvesting of specimens for commercial sale; destruction or alteration of the known habitat by dredging, channelization, or the discharge of fill material; significant habitat dewatering by water withdrawal; threatening discharges of toxic chemicals, organic matter, or other pollutants; or reservoir construction. The known populations of the purple bean should be monitored for size and the occurrence of reproduction, and research should be undertaken into its ecological needs, with a view of designing management practices to maintain and improve its habitat.

Contacts

U. S. Fish and Wildlife Service
Regional Office, Division of Endangered Species
1875 Century Blvd., Suite 200
Atlanta, Georgia 30345
http://southeast.fws.gov/

U. S. Fish and Wildlife Service
Regional Office, Division of Endangered Species
300 Westgate Center Dr.
Hadley, Massachusetts 01035-9589
Telephone: (413) 253-8200
Fax: (413) 253-8308
http://www.northeast.fws.gov/

U. S. Fish and Wildlife Service
Asheville Field Office
160 Zillicoa Street
Asheville, North Carolina, 28801
Telephone: 828-258-3939
Fax: 828-258-5330

Reference

U. S. Fish and Wildlife Service. 10 January 1997. "Endangered and Threatened Wildlife and Plants: Determination of Endangered Status for the Cumberland Elktoe, Oyster Mussel, Cumberlandian Combshell, Purple Bean, and Rough Rabbitsfoot." *Federal Register* 62 (7): 1647-1658.

Cumberland Bean Pearlymussel

Villosa trabalis

Status	Endangered
Listed	June 14, 1976
Family	Unionidae (Freshwater Mussel)
Description	Small- to medium-sized elongated shell.
Habitat	Fast-flowing water in sandy substrate.
Food	Filter-feeder.
Reproduction	Female stores sperm in gills; glochidia (larvae) are released into streams after hatching.
Threats	Impoundments; siltation; pollution.
Range	Kentucky, Tennessee

Description

The Cumberland bean pearlymussel (*Villosa trabalis*) is a small- to medium-sized Cumberlandian freshwater species with solid, elongated oval valves. The shell is unsculptured except for concentric growth marks and ridges on the beak. The surface is somewhat glossy; olive-green, yellowish-brown, or blackish; and covered with many narrow, wavy, dark green or blackish rays. The inner shell surface is white except for an iridescent blue-green posterior. This species was formerly classified as *Micromya trabalis.*

Behavior

The life of mussels is complex, and reproduction often depends upon a stable habitat—unaltered stream conditions, clean water, and an undisturbed stream bottom. The cycle also depends upon the abundance of suitable fish hosts to complete the mussel's larval development.

To reproduce, males discharge sperm, which are dispersed by stream currents. In the process of feeding, females nearby or downstream take in sperm, which fertilizes eggs stored in their gills. The gills serve as brood pouches (marsupia), where the glochidia hatch and begin to develop. After a time, these glochidia are released into the stream. A few mussels have inner parts that resemble a tiny minnow and can be manipulated to lure host fish. When

a fish gets close to the shell, the mussel expels its glochidia.

Glochidia have tiny bean- or spoon-shaped valves that attach to the gill filaments of host fish. Glochidia can only progress to the juvenile stage while attached to the fish's gills. Those that do not fortuitously encounter a host fish do not survive when released by the female mussel. They sink to the bottom and die.

When the juvenile has developed a shell and is large enough to survive on its own, it detaches from the host fish and falls to the stream bottom, beginning a long association with a single stretch of stream. Maturing mussels bury themselves in riffles and shoals with only the shell margins and feeding siphons exposed to the water. Some mussels live as long as 50 years or more.

The family Unionidae, which includes all of the freshwater mussels in the United States, is separated into two groups based on the length of time the glochidia remain in the female's marsupia. The eggs of the short-term (tachytictic) breeders are fertilized in the spring, and glochidia are released by late summer of the same year. Long-term (bradytictic) breeders hold developing glochidia in the brood pouch over winter and release them in the spring.

Freshwater mussels feed by siphoning phytoplankton and other plant matter from the water. In-

Cumberland Bean, photograph. U. S. Fish and Wildlife Service. Reproduced by permission.

digestible particles are expelled from the shell by reverse siphoning. Silt in the water can kill mussels by clogging their feeding siphons.

There are no known interspecific differences in feeding among freshwater mussels. The glochidia are obligate parasites on the gills or fins of fish. Adult mussels are filter-feeders and consume particulate matter in the water column. Identifiable stomach contents almost invariably include desmids, diatoms, algae, protozoa, and zooplankton.

Most freshwater mussel species display seasonal variations in activity associated with water temperature and reproduction. Metabolic rate is, in part, positively correlated with temperature. Many ectothermic species have the capacity to adjust their metabolic rates in response to long-term changes in temperature. Thus, metabolic rates do not continue to rise as temperatures rise in the summer, and they do not continue to fall during the winter as temperatures decline.

Some freshwater mussels also show diurnal changes in metabolic rates that indicate a tendency toward nocturnal activity patterns. Mussels may move to the surface to feed at night and move deeper into the substrate during the day; this is one way to avoid predators that hunt by visual contact.

Freshwater mussels are nonmigratory.

Habitat

The Cumberland bean pearlymussel is found in clean, fast-flowing water in gravel and sand shoals that have been swept free of silt by the action of the current.

Distribution

This species was widely distributed in many of the larger tributary streams of the upper Cumberland River and was considered rare in the Tennessee River drainage. In the 1920s it was reported in the

Tennessee River and its tributaries—South Chicamauga Creek (northern Georgia), Paint Rock and Flint Rivers (northern Alabama), and the Hiwassee and Clinch Rivers (Tennessee). It has been reported more recently from the Cumberland River and its tributaries—Buck and Beaver Creeks and the Obey and Rockcastle Rivers (Kentucky).

The U. S. Fish and Wildlife Service has declared this species endangered in Alabama and Virginia.

Threats

The Cumberland bean pearlymussel was probably eradicated from the Tennessee River watershed by the construction of major dams on the river for flood control and hydroelectric power production. Since the 1930s the Tennessee Valley Authority (TVA) has erected 36 dams in the Tennessee River basin. Five major dams have been located on the Cumberland River and six others on its tributaries. The cold tailwaters from these dams have made long upstream portions of these rivers uninhabitable for both mussels and host fishes. Siltation caused by strip mining, coal washing, logging, and poor agricultural practices within the watersheds have buried gravel and sand shoals and smothered mussel beds. Because mussels must siphon gallons of water each day to feed, the effects of water pollutants such as herbicides and pesticides are intensified.

Conservation and Recovery

Buck Creek and the Little South Fork Cumberland River are eligible for Scenic River status under the National Wild and Scenic Rivers Act. Such a designation would provide additional protection for the species and its habitat. The TVA is working on a water management plan to guarantee constant minimum flows in all rivers in the Tennessee and Cumberland basins by timing water discharges from its dams. Such an effort may ease many of the negative effects of dams and reservoirs on remaining stretches of mussel habitat.

Contact

U. S. Fish and Wildlife Service
Regional Office, Division of Endangered Species
1875 Century Blvd., Suite 200
Atlanta, Georgia 30345
Telephone: (404) 679-4000
http://southeast.fws.gov/

References

Branson, B.A. 1974. "Stripping the Appalachians." *Natural History* 38 (9): 53-60.

Jenkinson, J.J. 1986."The Tennessee Valley Authority Cumberlandian Mollusk Conservation Program." *Bulletin of the American Malacological Union* 2: 62-63.

U.S. Fish and Wildlife Service. 1984. "Cumberland Bean Pearly Mussel Recovery Plan." U.S. Fish and Wildlife Service, Atlanta.

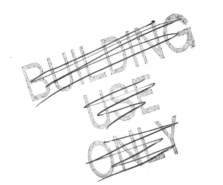

hoice Outstanding Titles